Spontaneous Order, Organization and the Law

Liber Amicorum Ernst-Joachim Mestmäcker

E. J. Mestmäcker

T.M.C. ASSER INSTITUUT

SPONTANEOUS ORDER, ORGANIZATION AND THE LAW

Roads to a European Civil Society

Liber Amicorum Ernst-Joachim Mestmäcker

Edited by

Talia Einhorn

Tel-Aviv University

T·M·C·ASSER PRESS

T·M·C·ASSER PRESS
P.O.Box 16163, 2500 BD The Hague, The Netherlands
www.asserpress.nl

Exclusive sales rights for Germany
NOMOS Verlagsgesellschaft

The contributions in the main part of this book first appeared in
European Business Organization Law Review (EBOR), ISSN 1566-7520,
Volume 2 (2001), issues 3 and 4.

ISBN 978-90-6704-163-8

www.asserpress.nl/cata/mestmaecker/fra.htm

T.M.C. Asser Instituut - Institute for Private and Public International Law, International Commercial Arbitration and European Law
Institute Address: R.J. Schimmelpennincklaan 20-22, 2517 JN The Hague, The Netherlands; P.O.Box 30461, 2500 GL The Hague, The Netherlands; Tel.: (31-70)3420300; Fax: (31-70)3420359; URL: www.asser.nl.
Over thirty years, the T.M.C. Asser Institute has developed into a leading scientific research institute in the field of international law. It covers private international law, public international law, including international humanitarian law, the law of the European Union, the law of international commercial arbitration and increasingly, also, international economic law, the law of international commerce and international sports law. Conducting scientific research either fundamental or applied, in the aforementioned domains, is the main activity of the Institute. In addition, the Institute organizes congresses and postgraduate courses, undertakes contract-research and operates its own publishing house. Because of its inter-university background, the Institute often cooperates with Dutch law faculties as well as with various national and foreign institutions. The Institute organizes Asser College Europe, a project in cooperation with East and Central European countries whereby research and educational projects are organized and implemented.

For *Ernst-Joachim Mestmäcker* on his 75th birthday

Prof. Dr. iur. Dr. rer. pol. h.c. Ernst-Joachim Mestmäcker, one of our time's most significant private law teachers, celebrates his 75th birthday on September 25, 2001. His generation had to survive the last year of the war 1944/45 as soldiers, and then begin their academic studies under most trying conditions. *Gerhard Lüke* described those early years in the Festschrift for *Mestmäcker*'s 70th birthday. During those early years, *Franz Böhm* – one of the Federal Republic's ordoliberal founding fathers – became *Mestmäcker*'s mentor, giving shape and direction to his scientific interests. Economic methods and insights thereby found access to questions of law. Further, on study visits to the USA – in 1951 for the writing of his thesis, and in 1956/57 for the completion of his postdoctoral thesis for admission as a university lecturer – *Mestmäcker* mastered comparative law methods. Thus, he was familiar with economic analysis, on the one hand, and precise differentiation of facts – as is typical of common law countries – on the other. Those were the roots of the outstanding comparative advantage of *Mestmäcker*'s work: an exact knowledge of the facts. Such knowledge is often indispensable for posing sensible questions in the first place, and then finding their answers.

It was in 1958 that *Mestmäcker* began an illustrious academic career. In its course, he held appointments in Saarbrücken, Münster and finally Bielefeld. At a difficult time – the years after 1967 – he was chairman of that university's founding committee, and later its founding rector. In 1978 he became Director of the Max Planck Institute for Foreign Private and Private International Law in Hamburg. Since 1994 he has been Professor Emeritus.

Mestmäcker's scientific work is centered on all facets of commercial law. One constant in his work has been the law relating to anti-competitive behaviour, including its European form. In the European Economic Community's first decade, he acted as special adviser to the EEC Commission in Brussels. Important decisions of that time can be traced to his influence. When the German parliament decided to set up its Monopolies Commission in 1973, it was a matter of course that *Mestmäcker* was to be its first chairman. Another facet of his work is found in his postdoctoral thesis written to qualify as a university lecturer. In it, he examined administration, the power of groups of companies and shareholders' rights under comparative law aspects. His thesis was subsequently the starting point for many studies on the law of groups. In this context reference should also be made to his works on employee participation. *Mestmäcker* was a member of the Biedenkopf-Commission in the 1960s.

His concern with press and radio issues can be traced to a similar root. Between 1964 and 1970 he was a member of the Michel-Commission, which had been set up by the German Bundestag. Since 1997 he has been a member, and is currently chairman, of the newly established Commission on the Investigation of Concentration in the Media. Ever since his move to the Max Planck Institute in Hamburg, *Mestmäcker*'s focus has been on a large research project on the commercial law of transborder telecommunications. In Germany, he laid the scientific groundwork for the – by now largely implemented – liberalisation of the telecommunications market. Beyond all these areas of law, *Mestmäcker* is also well-known in the field of legal theory. Here, *Kant* has been his largest influence.

Looking at *Mestmäcker*'s scientific work as a whole, one can recognize a theory of the private law society. It is distinct from the predominant, slightly non-historical constitutional thinking of our time. However, it also transcends the mere apolitical, technical understanding of private law. In it, private law with its value-bound institutions is seen as the guarantor of both individual self-determination and social partnership. Or, as he himself once put it, commercial law is an extension of private law, using different means. With his private law theory, *Mestmäcker* raises a legacy of the Enlightenment into a present-day context. It can be summarized with the title of a presentation he gave in 1991, just after the historic political change: The return of civil society and its law.

Both the academic and political world bestowed their honours upon him: the Ludwig-Erhard-Prize for business publications, an honorary doctorate of the University of Cologne Faculty for Economics and Business Administration, the Order of Merit of the Federal Republic, honorary senator of Bielefeld University, Münster University's Ernst Hellmut Vits-Prize, the Erasmus-Medal, honorary senator of the Max Planck Society, since 1994 a member of the Order Pour le Mérite for Arts and Sciences, and the Hanns Martin Schleyer-Prize in 1997.

Ernst-Joachim Mestmäcker is the founder of a widespread scientific school. The number of those whose postdoctoral thesis he supervised, and who now are professors of commercial law, runs into two digits. The number of his scientific "grandchildren" is heading in the same direction. What is the fascination this influential academic teacher holds? It certainly is the quality of his academic work. All of his major publications were pioneering works. In addition, there are, of course, those personality traits he shares with his unforgotten teacher, *Franz Böhm*: engagement, even passion in everything he recognised as right, and credibility lived.

Ad centum vera!

Professor Dr. Wernhard Möschel, Tübingen

Foreword

It is told of Rabbi Professor Solomon Schechter, President of the Jewish Theological Seminary, a great Jewish scholar, who gained international fame by discovering and bringing to Cambridge more than 100,000 pages of the Cairo Genizah, that he asked Louis Finkelstein, then a first year student at JTS, later to become a great scholar, as well as President and Chancellor of that university, why he came to JTS. Louis Finkelstein answered that he came to study there. "Study? That you can do better at home!", came the answer, to which Professor Shechter added: "You are here to be in the presence of greatness".

And it is the greatness of *Professor Mestmäcker* that I wish to address, for *Professor Mestmäcker* is a role model as a scholar, a teacher and a person.

As a scholar *Professor Mestmäcker* is unique. His research subjects embrace both private and public law. His publications treat the most difficult theoretical questions, yet, as Professor Möschel has so aptly written in his foreword to this Liber Amicorum, the work of our Jubilar is characterized by paying close attention to the facts. The exact knowledge of those is indispensable for posing sensible questions and for providing plausible answers. No theory will hold water if it disregards reality. This book which we have prepared to honor our Jubilar contains 29 contributions, each very different from the other, covering very different subjects, some very theoretical, others very mundane, yet each contributor has considered his contribution to be a focal point of *Professor Mestmäcker*'s research. And the beauty of it is that all authors were right!

Armed with a keen eye, an inquisitive mind and a pen mightier than a sword, *Professor Mestmäcker* has always been able to foresee problems even before they became topical. And then, long after everyone has become aware of their importance, he keeps developing them creatively and diligently, constantly adding bright ideas and fresh insights.

As a teacher *Professor Mestmäcker* is again unique. He has created for his students not one galaxy but several. Within those galaxies *Professor Mestmäcker* has given his students the opportunity to create their own heavenly, shining stars. The series on telecommunications, on economic law, the books and commentaries on competition, have all provided *Professor Mestmäcker*'s students with ample opportunity to become stars in their own right. But the creation of the galaxies is just one part of the story. *Professor Mestmäcker* is a true liberal not only in theory but also in practice, perhaps one of the most important traits of any true teacher. Since the destruction of the Tower of Babel humanity has never again tried to make the whole earth be of one language and of one speech. By destroying that tower God saved humanity from tyranny [cf. Yeshayahu Leibowitz, *Notes to the Weekly Tora Readings* (Jerusalem: Academon 1988) (in Hebrew) 14 ff.]. Therefore, human history is not only the

Talia Einhorn, ed., Spontaneous Order, Organization and the Law – Liber Amicorum Ernst-Joachim Mestmäcker © 2003 T.M.C.ASSER PRESS, *The Hague, The Netherlands*

story of crime, madness and disasters, but also the chronicles of human fights against crime, against madness and against disasters. And it is through this enduring fight, pervading all generations and all societies, that human history has developed the values which endow it with significance. *Professor Mestmäcker* has never hesitated to stand up for his ideas and values and explain his views, not only in scholarly writings but also in articles published in FAZ. As a teacher he has encouraged his students to do the same: express their opinions freely and have the courage to stand firm and be true to their values. Indeed, *Professor Mestmäcker* has always been not only an excellent lecturer but also a wonderful listener.

As a person *Professor Mestmäcker* is, once again, a role model. As a true liberal he treats his fellow men with Gerechtigkeit and Fairness, to borrow on the expressions used by Professor Zacher in his Grusswort to the Festschrift published to celebrate our Jubilar's 70th Anniversary. *Professor Mestmäcker*'s sense of justice, generosity, values, empathy for our troubles and mishaps, unwavering support upon which we can always count, are inspiring in a very special way. Sure enough, they help us see injustice done by others. But they also compel us to look into the mirror, examine ourselves closely, and assume the final responsibility for our lives and deeds rather than blame the state, the authorities, our colleagues, friends and foes. The free, open society in which *Professor Mestmäcker* wishes us to live is predicated upon the assumption of such responsibility.

This brings me to the star with which *Professor Mestmäcker* has provided me. In 1999 Dr. Gerard Tanja, then Director of the Asser Instituut in The Hague, invited me to propose a new law journal that the Institute and its newly established Asser Press would launch. Dr. Tanja invited me because his idea was to launch a new journal on international trade law to which much of my research until then was devoted. I told him that there were enough journals covering these matters already, and there would be little point in launching yet another. Dr. Tanja promised me that he would be open to other suggestions. I arrived in The Hague on 15 June 1999. On 17 June I was already in Hamburg. I knew I wanted a journal devoted to business law, but the journal had to have its special angle. Walking up and down the Zeitschriftenraum of the Max Planck Institute's library I could not see what that angle might be. A couple of days later *Professor Mestmäcker* invited me to lunch. He immediately inquired what I had on my mind. Before the end of this unforgettable lunch, *Professor Mestmäcker*, halfway through the discussion, looked at me and said: Here it is – the European Business Organization Law Review. On our way back to the MPI I was beaming. Little did I know how much work and sleepless nights would follow, how many difficulties I would face. It just occurred to me how much joy it would be to see this journal published. Of course, *Professor Mestmäcker* became the first member of EBOR's Advisory Board, constantly giving us excellent advice as well as a very beautiful contribution published in the first volume.

In the book of Psalms King David exclaims: "When I consider thy heavens, the work of thy fingers, the moon and the stars, which thou hast ordained; what is man, that thou art mindful of him? and the son of man, that thou visitest him? For thou hast made him but slightly less than divine, and hast crowned him with glory and honor." All people are but slightly less than divine, but for some, very few, this little difference is tiny indeed. Which provides us all with good reason for optimism for humanity in general.

Therefore, dear *Professor Mestmäcker*, it is here in the presence of greatness that I have the privilege and honor to present, with deep appreciation and gratitude, this modest Liber Amicorum to you.

Professor Talia Einhorn, The Hague/Tel-Aviv

Summary Table of Contents

Annex

Principles for European Integration – Roads to a European Civil Society

Table of Contents

Annex

Principles for European Integration – Roads to a European Civil Society

"Unpublished" Judicial Opinions in the United States: Law Or Not?

Stephen R. Barnett[*]

I am honored to participate in this celebration of my friend and colleague Professor ERNST-JOACHIM MESTMÄCKER. Although the topic of my contribution may jar this Law Review by being purely American, and what's more by having nothing to do with business organizations, the American part, at least, may be justified by Professor MESTMÄCKER's expertise in American law and by all he has done to promote legal and academic cross-fertilization between the European and American gardens. I myself have benefited enormously from the welcome and encouragement that Professor MESTMÄCKER has provided to me, as to so many other American scholars, at the Max Planck Institute in Hamburg. I salute him, and I trust that he will continue his own scholarly contributions for many years to come.

* * *

Europeans who think of the common law as a system of court-made law, based on precedent, may be surprised to hear that many if not most appellate court decisions in the United States today are not considered precedents. This is the phenomenon of the "unpublished" judicial opinion, a long-smoldering issue that has recently flared into wide-ranging controversy. At issue are rules of court which bring it about that most appellate court opinions in a jurisdiction will not be published and, as a result, may not be cited to other courts. In the federal Ninth Circuit Court of Appeals, for example – the huge court that covers California and seven other Western states – some 85 percent of the Court's opinions are unpublished and uncitable.[1] In California's court of appeal, the

---

[*] Elizabeth J. Boalt Professor of Law, University of California, Berkeley.
[1] Judicial Business of the United States Courts 2000, Table S-3.

Talia Einhorn, ed., Spontaneous Order, Organization and the Law –
Liber Amicorum Ernst-Joachim Mestmäcker © *2003 T.M.C.ASSER PRESS, The Hague, The Netherlands*

state's intermediate appellate court, fully 93 percent of decisions are unpublished and uncitable.[2]

Controversy over these rules has been focused by recent developments. Most notable was the decision last year of the Eighth Circuit Federal Court of Appeals in *Anastasoff* v. *United States*.[3] In an opinion by Judge Richard S. Arnold, the court held that its own court rule denying precedential effect to unpublished opinions exceeded the constitutional power of the federal courts. Although *Anastasoff* has been vacated as moot,[4] Judge Arnold's opinion has catalyzed a growing controversy and fueled a burgeoning literature about unpublished opinions.[5] Several federal appeals judges have addressed the issue in out-of-court writings;[6] a California appeals court recently has upheld California's publication and no-citation rules;[7] a California court committee recently has recommended fuller distribution of unpublished opinions, but still no

---

[2] Judicial Council of California, Administrative Office of the Courts, Court Statistics Report 2000, Court of Appeal, Table 9.

[3] 223 F.3d 898 (8th Cir.), vacated as moot, 235 F.3d 1054 (8th Cir. 2000) (*en banc*).

[4] The case involved the filing deadline for a refund of federal income taxes. The Eighth Circuit followed an unpublished case accepting the position of the Internal Revenue Service. Meanwhile the Second Circuit Court of Appeals came out the other way. *Weisbart* v. *United States Dep't of Treasury*, 2000 WL 1041231 (2d Cir. July 28, 2000). With a petition for rehearing *en banc* pending in *Anastasoff*, the Internal Revenue Service acceded to the Second Circuit's position, thus conceding Ms. Anastasoff's claim and mooting her case – and leaving the constitutionality of the rule banning citation of unpublished opinions an "open question" in the Eighth Circuit. 235 F.3d 1054.

[5] E.g., Jerome I. Braun, "Eighth Circuit decision intensifies debate over publication and citation of appellate opinions", *Judicature*, Sept.-Oct. 2000, p. 90; Deborah Jones Merritt and James J. Brudney, "Stalking Secret Law: What Predicts Publication in the United States Courts of Appeals", 54 *Vand. L.Rev.* (2001) 71; Brian Endter, "Death, Taxes and Unpublished Opinions", 33 *Ariz. State L.J.* (2001) 613; Charles E. Carpenter, Jr., "The No-Citation Rule for Unpublished Opinions", 50 *South Carolina L.Rev.* (1998) 235; Martha J. Dragich, "Will the Federal Courts of Appeals Perish If They Publish?", 44 *Am. U.L.Rev.* (1995) 757; Richard S. Arnold, "Unpublished Opinions: A Comment", 1 *J. App. Prac. & Proc.* (1999) 219; Case Note, 114 *Harv. L. Rev.* (2001) 940; K. Shuldberg, "Digital Influence: Technology and Unpublished Opinions in the Federal Courts of Appeal", 85 *Calif. L. Rev.* (1997) 541; Stephen R. Barnett, "Silent Stare Decisis", *L.A. Daily J.*, April 13, 2000, p. 4. See also, e.g., Richard H. Fallon, Jr., "Stare Decisis and the Constitution: An Essay on Constitutional Methodology", 76 *N.Y.U.L.Rev.* (2001) 570, 596 n. 115.

[6] E.g., Danny J. Boggs and Brian P. Brooks, "Unpublished Opinions & the Nature of Precedent", 4 *Green Bag* 2d 17 (2000); Alex Kozinski and Stephen Reinhardt, "Please Don't Cite This!", *California Lawyer*, June 2000, p. 44; Boyce F. Martin, Jr., "In Defense of Unpublished Opinions", 60 *Ohio St.L.J.* (1999) 177.

[7] *Schmier* v. *Supreme Court of California*, 78 Cal. App. 4th 703 (2000).

citation of them;[8] and the issue is gaining attention even beyond the legal profession.[9] It is surely the hottest procedural issue in American law today.

1. Background

In the English courts of the 18th century, the opinions rendered by the judges to explain their decisions were reported, if at all, by private court reporters, not the courts themselves. The same was true across the water; before the ratification of the United States Constitution in 1791, "there was almost no private reporting and no official reporting at all in the American states".[10] Nevertheless, in America as in England, even such spottily-reported judicial opinions were recognized as possessing precedential authority, as were decisions entered on court records without being otherwise reported at all.[11] As time passed, reporting systems for appellate court decisions became more systematic and comprehensive; by the mid-20th century, virtually all opinions of appellate courts in the United States were published.

This "publication" was accomplished either by the courts themselves in "official" reports, like the United States Reports for the United States Supreme Court, or by private publishers to whom the job was contracted by the courts, or who assumed it themselves, like the West Publishing Company in its quasi-official Federal Reporter System for the federal circuit courts of appeals. "Published" meant published in the traditional sense: printed on paper, in books, which books could be found on shelves in law libraries, lawyers' offices, and judges' chambers.

Starting in the late 1960s and early 1970s, however, the practice of universal publication began to collide with a new reality. As appellate caseloads skyrocketed, publishing every opinion in every case involved costs in paper, books, shelf space, lawyers' and judges' time, and clients' money that increasingly seemed prohibitive. At the same time, many of the countless opinions issued by the courts appeared to be routine applications of established doctrine, decisions

---

[8] Appellate Process Task Force, A White Paper on Unpublished Opinions of the Court of Appeal, March 2001 (recommending that unpublished opinions be posted on the judicial Web site "for a reasonable period of time (e.g., 60 days)", but that the rule prohibiting citation of unpublished opinions be retained without change).

[9] E.g., William Glaberson, "Legal Shortcuts Run Into Some Dead Ends", *N.Y.Times*, Oct. 8, 2000, p.4.

[10] *Anastasoff, supra* n. 3, 233 F.3d at 903.

[11] Id. ("judges and lawyers of the day recognized the authority of unpublished decisions even when they were established only by memory or by a lawyer's unpublished memorandum").

that made no "new law" and hence arguably did not deserve publication (this being especially true, many thought, of criminal appeals, for which attorneys were provided free to indigent defendants regardless of the merit of their appeals).

Hence the courts began to make rules, in the late 1960s and early 1970s, providing that opinions would not be published unless they were somehow important. (We are talking only about the opinions of intermediate appellate courts, not courts of last resort. Hardly anyone suggests that all opinions of a jurisdiction's highest court, such as the United States Supreme Court or the supreme courts of the states, should not be published; and they all are.) In California, for example, the publication rule provides that no opinion of the court of appeal may be published unless a majority of the court rendering the opinion certifies that it:

(1) establishes a new rule of law, applies an existing rule to a set of facts significantly different from those stated in published opinions, or modifies, or criticizes with reasons given, an existing rule;
(2) resolves or creates an apparent conflict in the law;
(3) involves a legal issue of continuing public interest; or
(4) makes a significant contribution to legal literature by reviewing either the development of a common law rule or the legislative or judicial history of a provision of a constitution, statute, or other written law.[12]

Inasmuch as the decision on publication is committed to the same judges who render the opinion, one might have expected that authorial pride would produce high publication rates. But contrary considerations (whatever they may be perhaps authorial modesty!) have prevailed; the statewide publication rate for the California court of appeal has declined steadily and now stands at seven percent.[13] For the federal circuit courts of appeals, nationwide, the percent of cases published is about 20 percent;[14] for the Ninth Circuit Court of Appeals, as mentioned, it is about 15 percent.[15] Many other states have similar non-publication rules and comparable non-publication rates, though others still publish all their appellate opinions; the other federal circuits differ widely in their non-publication rules, as will be seen.

That opinions are "unpublished" does not mean that they are secret. All opinions of all courts in the United States, at least of all appellate courts, are public documents, available at the court that issued them. "Unpublished" is a term of art meaning that the opinion is not printed on paper, book-bound, in the court's

---

[12] California Rules of Court, Rule 976 (b).
[13] See n. 2 *supra*.
[14] Judicial Business of the United States Courts 2000, Table S-3.
[15] Sec n. 1 *supra*.

"official" (or in some cases unofficial) case reports. Because the "unpublished" opinions are in fact available, the non-publication system rests not only on the rule limiting publication, but also on a companion rule prohibiting citation of unpublished opinions. As the California rule states, an unpublished opinion "shall not be cited or relied on by a court or a party" in any other case.[16]

When these rules were first issued, non-publication and non-citation were, for practical purposes, closely linked. If a case wasn't published in the official reports, it might be tracked down at the court house, but it wasn't generally available, so naturally it wouldn't be cited. Today, technology has changed much of that. "Unpublished" now is largely a misnomer, because unpublished opinions often are freely available on line. Some courts themselves make all their unpublished opinions available on line.[17] For other courts – including the federal Ninth Circuit – private entrepreneurs such as LEXIS and Westlaw pick up all the unpublished opinions for inclusion in their legal data bases.

On-line availability, however, is by no means universal; simple access to unpublished opinions can still be a problem[18] – an unjustified problem, one would think, given the status of court opinions as public documents. But on-line availability is plainly the way of the future, and the prospect draws little opposition (at least overtly). Thus, the chief issue today is not whether all appellate opinions should be available online; most agree that they should be. Nor, on the other hand, is the issue whether all appellate opinions should be "published" in the traditional sence; few claim that they should be, and few challenge allowing the courts to apply their publication criteria to decide which cases are significant enough to take up pages in a printed report. Courts could make all their opinions available online and still publish in printed form only those they considered important enough under the specified criteria. The key issue today is the ban on citing the unpublished opinions. Opponents of the rule ask: If a

---

[16] California Rules of Court, Rule 977 (a). As in every other jurisdiction, this is subject to exceptions for citations that refer to the case as a fact, not a precedent – such as "when the opinion is relevant under the doctrines of law of the case, *res judicata*, or collateral estoppel". See ibid., Rule 977 (b). For a case rebuffing an attorney's attempt to cite an unpublished case to show the "fact" that her opponent's position lacked legal precedent, see *Sorchini* v. *City of Covina*, 9th Circuit, May 4, 2001, 2001 DJDAR 4343.

[17] See *Anastasoff, supra* n. 3, 223 F.3d at 904. A committee has recently recommended that the California court of appeal do this. See note 8 *supra*.

[18] See "'Pinocchio' Grudge Match Continues", *L.A.Daily J.*, April 13, 2001 (reporting that advocates of movie director Francis Ford Coppola, whose $80 million jury verdict against Warner Bros. in a dispute over the movie "Pinocchio" was set aside by the court of appeal in an unpublished opinion, "are trying to have the court officially publish its March 20 decision. Official publication would make the decision easily available over the Internet, and therefore more open to criticism. Copies of the unpublished opinion can be obtained only by going to the Court or by knowing somebody who has a copy").

lawyer thinks an unpublished opinion in a prior case will aid his or her client, should the lawyer be prohibited from citing that case to the court?[19] Supporters of the rule reply that it is simply compelled by concerns of efficiency, and that courts have power to determine that certain of their opinions are not precedents for future cases.

In what follows, I will note first some of the arguments against a rule prohibiting citation of unpublished opinions, and then some of the arguments in favor of such a rule. I will close with a few comments.

2. Arguments against a no-citation rule

- First, it is argued that a no-citation rule lends itself to unequal, inconsistent application of the law. Especially in view of the common law's reliance on precedent and *stare decisis*, fairness is said to compel that a rule of law applied to one case be applicable to another case involving similar facts. At the least, it is said, an attorney ought to be able to tell the court about the prior decision. As Judge Arnold has written, courts enforcing the no-publication rule are saying to the bar: "We may have decided this question the opposite way yesterday, but this does not bind us today, and, what's more, you cannot even tell us what we did yesterday."[20]
- Second, even if unpublished opinions are available to the public, the ban on citing them to other courts allegedly makes them into a body of "secret law" that breeds public suspicion and distrust.[21] Judges may be tempted to decide cases on grounds that would not withstand judicial scrutiny,[22] to sweep

---

[19] *Anastasoff, supra* n. 3, 223 F.3d at 904.

[20] Ibid. As an example, consider *In re Kamiyama*, California Court of Appeal, 4th App. Dist., Division 3, May 29, 1998. Petitioner Michiko Kamiyama was convicted by a jury of misdemeanor child abuse for leaving her eight-year-old daughter home alone one evening, at a private residence in a gated community, while petitioner, who had been unable to find a baby-sitter, went out to audition for a job. The court, in an unpublished opinion, threw out the conviction, finding the evidence insufficient as a matter of law. A dissenter accused the majority of substituting its judgment for the jury's and departing from established precedent: "[t]he temptation to decide a case based on our own agendas or public opinion can be intoxicating . . . " The dissenter also criticized the majority for not publishing the opinions in the case. Under California's no-citation rule, a mother (or father) accused of child abuse on similar facts may not tell the court about the *Kamiyama* decision.

[21] See, e.g., Editorial, "Secret Law", *New Jersey Lawyer*, Sept. 25, 2000; Merritt & Brudney, "Stalking Secret Law. . . .", *supra* n. 5.

[22] Unpublished opinions may be reviewed on appeal; but an opinion's unpublished status is considered a substantial handicap in seeking supreme court review.

judicial embarrassments under the rug,[23] or to indulge considerations that are flatly improper. And, it is said, even if the court does no such thing, the public may suspect the worst. Like the much-ridiculed statement of the United States Supreme Court in *Bush* v. *Gore*,[24] a judicial decision that is declared not to apply to any other case is said to invite suspicion and distrust, compromising the court's credibility, legitimacy, and public respect.

- Third, this "vast underground body of law"[25] assertedly gives an advantage to institutional, repeat litigants – such as government agencies and insurance companies – who have the interest and resources to compile their own data bases of unpublished opinions. It is true that this advantage may be reduced now that unpublished opinions are broadly accessible online, and no-citation rules indeed are often defended as *leveling* the playing field by preventing either party from citing unpublished cases. When unpublished opinions are citable, however, they bring no surprises, since a copy of the cited opinion must always be provided to the opposing attorney. When those opinions may not be cited, litigants aware of them, it is said, may nonetheless refer to them in an Aesopian language comprehensible to the court (which may have issued the opinion in question) but possibly not to opposing counsel.[26]
- Fourth, a ban on citing unpublished opinions is claimed to flout the common law's doctrine of precedent and *stare decisis*, the principle that the law *is* what the courts have decided. (One of the first things students are taught in American law schools is to distinguish between what a court says ("dictum") and what it decides ("holding"), because the latter is law and the former is not.) The obligation to follow precedent has been called an inherent limit on judicial power, in contrast to the politically-legitimated legislative power, and hence a requirement of the Federal Constitution.

That is what the Eighth Circuit held in *Anastasoff*. Where an unpublished

---

[23] See Stanley I. Greenberg, "Prosecutor's Pal", *L.A. Daily J.*, Aug. 30, 1994, p. 4 (complaining that recent decision by the Ninth Circuit affirming convictions (of writers' clients) "not only mischaracterized, but completely whitewashed, substantial misconduct and bias" by the trial judge, and that "it was done in an unpublished decision that hides the judge's conduct from the public, preventing the legal community from subjecting the decision to a healthy scrutiny I don't believe the opinion could withstand").

[24] "Our consideration is limited to the present circumstances, for the problem of equal protection in election processes generally presents many complexities". 121 S.Ct. 525, 532 (2000).

[25] Arnold, *supra* n. 5, 1 *J.App. Prac. & Process*, at 225.

[26] "The litigant who garners ideas and arguments from unpublished opinions but does not cite to them... need never reveal the paper trail. This is a weakness in the use of unpublished opinions that no-citation rules will not eradicate." Martin, *supra* n. 6, 60 *Ohio St.L.J.*, at 197 (concluding, however, that this problem "is [not] sufficient to warrant the elimination of unpublished opinions").

opinion of that court was directly in point, the court deemed itself required to follow that opinion; it held that the court rule declaring unpublished opinions not to be precedents was unconstitutional because "it purports to confer on the federal courts a power that goes beyond the 'judicial'".[27] Judge Arnold wrote that the doctrine of precedent was well established when the United States was founded and, further, that "the duty of courts to follow their prior decisions was understood to derive from the nature of the judicial power itself and to separate it from a dangerous union with the legislative power".[28]

Judge Arnold's historical analysis has been criticized as giving too much weight both to the courts' asserted obligation to follow precedent and to precedent's place (if any) in the US Federal Constitution.[29] But whatever the force of the obligation to follow precedent – and even if there is no such obligation – a rule that bars courts from even being told about a large class of prior judicial decisions (as many as 80 or 90 percent of a court's annual output), and that consequently prevents courts from deciding for themselves what weight to give to those decisions, may suppress the role of precedent to the point of exceeding the limits of judicial power.

- Fifth, along with the rejection of precedent, the no-citation rule allegedly involves another questionable assertion of judicial power. Judicial power is the power to decide cases; it derives its legitimacy from that function. Here, the courts are exercising the power to decide which of their decided cases will be law and which will not.[30] Although this power is defended as a matter of judicial housekeeping, ancillary to the decision-making function, arguably it is fundamentally different from the decision of cases and is a legislative power, not a judicial one.
- Sixth, although this may be the same wine in different bottles, the non-citation rule raises other issues of American constitutional law. If the doctrine of precedent is an integral part of the judicial power, a rule that prohibits a litigant from telling the court about a precedent may deny due process of law. And such a rule obviously censors the attorney's speech, which may implicate the First Amendment. True, the same can be said of many other court rules, such as rules of evidence; it is argued, however, that

---

[27] *Anastasoff*, 223 F.3d at 899.

[28] Ibid., at 903.

[29] See Case Note, *supra* n. 5, 114 *Harv. L. Rev.*, at 943-944; Fallon, *supra* n. 5, 76 *N.Y.U.L.Rev.*, at 596 n. 115.

[30] As Judge Arnold put it in *Anastasoff*, courts are asserting that they have the power "to choose for themselves, from among all the cases they decide, those that they will follow in the future, and those that they need not". *Anastasoff*, 233 F.3d at 904.

the ban on citing unpublished opinions is content-based and not justified by a sufficient governmental interest to pass muster under the First Amendment.[31]

3. ARGUMENTS SUPPORTING A NO-CITATION RULE

- Among arguments in defense of a no-citation rule, one holds that none of the rule's asserted evils will come to pass because any opinions that "make new law" or otherwise deserve to be published will be published, and hence will be citable. As a California court of appeal declared recently, California's publication rules "specify [...] that an opinion announcing a new rule of law or modifying an existing rule be published".[32]

  This argument is easily dismissed. That the publication rules in California do not assure the publication of all opinions meeting one or more of the listed criteria is suggested by the substantial disparities in publication rates between divisions of the court of appeal – most recently ranging from 4% to 19% in civil cases[33] – and by the substantial number of unpublished opinions, in both the California and federal systems, that prove important enough to warrant supreme court review. It is also suggested by the common issuance of unpublished opinions that on their face seem significant.[34]

  Moreover, the argument seems to refute itself; if attorneys did not believe that the unpublished opinions had some precedential or persuasive value that might aid their clients, the attorneys would not be clamoring to cite those opinions. Why not let the attorneys decide? Judges deciding a case are scarcely in a good position to determine whether their decision may have legal significance in some future case. They cannot predict the facts of future cases (any more than market planners in a socialist economy can predict future consumer demand),[35] and they lack the interest and incentive of the attorneys who will look at the case from their clients' point of view (like myriad consumers making purchase decisions in the market).

---

[31] See Salem M. Katsch and Alex V.Chachkes, "Examining the Constitutionality of No-Citation Rules", *N.Y.L.J.*, April 2, 2001, p. 1.

[32] *Schmier* v. *Supreme Court of California*, *supra* n. 7, 78 Cal.App. 4th 703. Actually, the rule provides only that an opinion may not be published "unless" it meets one of the listed criteria. California Rule of Court, Rule 976 (b). The court appears to have strengthened the rule in order to defend it.

[33] See California Court Statistics Report 2000, Court of Appeal, Table 9.

[34] See, e.g., "3d Circuit Gives Lessons on Attorneys' Fees", June 8, 2001, <http://www.law.com> (reporting two opinions of Third Circuit Court of Appeals that are "chock-full of important holdings on a variety of thorny issues that often arise during fee disputes"; "[n]onetheless, both decisions are labeled: 'Unreported – Not Precedential'").

[35] See Boggs and Brooks, *supra* n. 6, 4 *Green Bag* 2d at 21.

- Other defenses of non-citation rules are based frankly on expedience, and are harder to reject. One argument stresses the time, effort, and money that would be involved in researching the unpublished cases. In California, for example, the courts of appeal decide some 13,000 cases per year, of which about 1,000 are published. Judges of those courts, together with other defenders of the no-citation rule, stress that allowing citation of the unpublished opinions would produce a 13-fold increase in citable cases annually – and hence, they say, a substantially increased burden of research and analysis for both lawyers and judges.

  These numbers may be unduly scary. More than half of those 13,000 cases are criminal cases, which need not burden lawyers working on civil cases, and *vice versa*. After eliminating criminal and juvenile cases, the number of unpublished civil cases made citable each year would be about 4,000, or a four-fold increase.

  Is that not still a heavy new burden? The answer may depend on the realities of modern legal research. It is not as if the researcher must pile the 4,000 cases on her desk and go through them one by one. We are talking about electronic database searches, in which the researcher enters a key word or a question and the computer produces responsive cases – perhaps the top 10, 20, or 50 cases. In this system, increasing 13-fold the size of the database certainly does not increase 13-fold the researcher's time.[36] But there undoubtedly would be some additional research time required.[37] How much is difficult to say. It is especially difficult because lawyers to some extent already "research" unpublished opinions, many of which are in the LEXIS and Westlaw data bases and thus are brought up automatically if responsive to a search. This is true now of some opinions, and soon may be true of all opinions, of the California court of appeal.[38]

- A second pragmatic defense stresses the additional burden that citation of unpublished opinions would impose, not on the lawyers and judges who must research the opinions after they are issued, but on the judges and courts that issue them. In a much-noted article, Judges Alex Kozinski and Stephen Reinhardt of the Ninth Circuit have pointed out that their court annually decides about 4,500 cases, approximately 700 by published opinions and

---

[36] One might suggest that it does not necessarily increase that time at all, but only makes the "top ten" cases more relevant than they would have been if drawn from a smaller data base. Unpublished opinions, however, even if not catalogued separately by the computer for search purposes (as, in the future, they should be), surely would be treated separately by researchers – as "second class" precedents that might add to, but would not displace, published opinions that otherwise were worth the researcher's consideration.

[37] See n. 36 *supra*.

[38] See n. 8 *supra*.

3,800 by unpublished ones (called memorandum dispositions, or "memdispos", and claimed not to be opinions at all). This works out to a yearly average of 150 opinions per judge, 20 published and 130 unpublished, the authors note. The memdispos "get written a lot faster than opinions", largely by staff; and "[n]ot worrying about making law in 3,800 memdispos frees us to concentrate" on the published opinions. "If memdispos could be cited as precedent, conscientious judges would have to pay much closer attention to their precise wording", and, the authors say, something would have to give: The court might have to reduce even further the number of cases in which it writes opinions, or rely even more heavily on staff, or write opinions that were less carefully reasoned, or reduce the memdispos to one-word dispositions.

Why not "just keep doing what we're doing but let the memdispos be cited as precedent"? Because, Judges Kozinski and Reinhardt insist, the memdispos are not precedents: "[W]hat does *precedent* mean? Surely, it suggests that the three judges on a panel subscribe not merely to the result but also to the phrasing of the disposition. With memdispos, this is simply not true" (apparently because the staff does the writing, "with relatively few edits from the judges"). Lawyers therefore should stop "[t]rying to extract from memdispos a precedential value that we didn't put into them", the judges assert.

This argument seems dubious in principle. "Precedent" means a decided case, not fancy writing by a judge. As another federal circuit judge, Danny Boggs of the Sixth Circuit Court of Appeals, has pointed out, Judges Kozinski and Reinhardt are claiming for judges a legislative-like power "to define the law prospectively through the use of particular authoritative language".[39]

As a practical matter, however, it is not so easy to dismiss the claim that making the memdispos citable will unacceptably reduce the quality of the judges' published opinions or of their total judicial output.[40] Will that happen? No one knows, but the best existing evidence may lie in the other federal circuits. Of the 12 territorial federal circuits, a majority of seven now *allow* the citation of unpublished opinions. They discourage such citation, as by calling it "disfavored", but, as a last resort, they allow it. Two circuits allow citation of unpublished opinions if counsel believes that the opinion

---

[39] Boggs and Brooks, *supra* n. 6, at 22.

[40] Judge Boggs stresses the claims of efficiency: "The practical need to dispose of a certain percentage of cases on an expedited basis, as a simple docket management matter, flows from the stark reality of a relatively small federal appellate bench and an ever-increasing caseload. There is no strictly legal – let alone philosophical – justification for the practice." Ibid., at 19.

has "precedential value" and that "no published opinion . . . would serve as well".[41] Four other circuits, in contrast, provide that unpublished opinions are "not precedent", but allow them to be cited if they have "persuasive" value and no published opinion would serve as well.[42] A seventh circuit, the Third, states that *the court* does not cite its unpublished opinions,[43] but has no rule preventing lawyers from doing so (as they reportedly do). Informal reports from court personnel in all seven of these circuits indicate that the rules allowing citation are working well; and the trend seems to be running in their direction.[44]

Defenders of no-citation rules argue, however, that the number of unpublished cases made citable in the Ninth Circuit, or in the California court of appeal, would be markedly greater than the numbers involved in the seven "permissive" circuits. We are talking about some 4,000 unpublished cases a year in the Ninth Circuit (some 2,800 of them civil) and, as mentioned earlier, some 4,000 civil cases per year in the California court of appeal. These numbers are indeed higher, but not very much higher, than the numbers of unpublished cases now made citable in some of the seven federal circuits: approximately 3,000 or 2,000 annually.[45] Further, it should be considered that those 4,000 unpublished cases in the Ninth Circuit are online, via LEXIS and Westlaw, so that practitioners already have to deal with them. Thus, both the burden of researching the unpublished opinions and the burden to the courts of making such opinions presentable to other courts may in fact be bearable. It would be rash, however, to claim to know.

4. Conclusion

In the end, the determining considerations, I believe, will be a convergence of three factors: attorneys' strategy, technology, and principle. As far as attorneys' strategy is concerned, the argument is made that rules allowing citation as a

---

41 Fourth Circuit Court of Appeals, Rule 36(c); Sixth Circuit Court of Appeals, Rule 28 (g).

42 Fifth Circuit, Rule 47.5.4; Eighth Circuit, Rule 28(a)(i) ; Tenth Circuit, Rule 36.3; Eleventh Circuit, Rule 36-2.

43 Third Circuit, IOP 5.8.

44 As of 1994, only two circuits allowed citation of unpublished opinions. See Barnett, *supra* n. 5, *L.A. Daily J.*, April 13, 2000. The Ninth Circuit, under pressure to relax its no-citation rule, last year adopted a compromise experiment (for two and a half years) that allows citation of unpublished opinions, but only in petitions for rehearing and requests for publication – not in ordinary appeals – and only for the purpose of showing a conflict between opinions or orders of the court. Ninth Circuit Court of Appeals, Rule 36-3.

45 About 3,000 in the Fifth and Eleventh Circuits, about 2,000 in the Fourth

"last resort", such as now exist in seven federal circuits, will not work because attorneys will abuse them, citing unpublished cases when they really are not "precedential" or "persuasive", or when published cases really would serve as well, and thus embroiling the court in distracting disputes about the propriety of the citation. But I think it more likely – as the reports from the seven circuits suggest – that attorneys' self-interest will prevent these problems. Attorneys will want to cite the *most* persuasive or *most* precedential cases they can find; they will not want to cite an unpublished opinion if there really is a published opinion that will serve as well. Given only limited time and space in which to make their arguments, attorneys – at least good attorneys! – will not want to waste time or space on citations that are unlikely to make a difference. So the problem should be self-limiting, with unpublished opinions treated as "second class precedents" the citation of which really is disfavored and used only as a last resort.

Technology, meanwhile, should have an increasing impact. As unpublished opinions become more and more readily available on line, demands by attorneys to be able to cite those opinions – to tell the courts about what everyone knows – become more insistent and harder to reject. This technological compulsion is seen both in the pro-citation trend among the federal circuits and in the recent proposal to put all the California court of appeal decisions on line.[46]

Arguments of principle remain. The concepts of precedent, equal application of the law, judicial visibility, and limited judicial power, as expressed in the *Anastasoff* opinion and in much of the writing on the subject, all militate against no-citation rules. As the issue reaches the nonprofessional public, moreover, the case for banning citation of unpublished opinions – for barring lawyers from telling the court about a prior court decision – encounters increasing resistance. Fervently as the judges try to hold the line, and plausible as their fears may be, the case for suppressing what technology now makes widely available seems fated to fail.

---

[46] See n. 8 *supra*.

Who will Protect Competition in Europe? From Central Enforcement to Authority Networks and Private Litigation

Jürgen Basedow[*]

1. Introduction

When the European Commission published its "White Paper on modernisation of the rules implementing Articles 85 and 86 of the EC Treaty" in spring 1999[1] it triggered a broad discussion on the future legal framework of the enforcement of competition law in the European Union. The most important change, which the Commission suggested, consists in the decentralisation of the application of Article 81 section 3 EC. While anti-competitive agreements and concerted

---

[*] Director, Max-Planck-Institute of Foreign Private and Private International Law, Hamburg; Professor of Law, University of Hamburg; Member, German Monopolies Commission.

[1] Commission Programme No. 99/027, *COM* (1999) 101 fin.

Talia Einhorn, ed., Spontaneous Order, Organization and the Law – Liber Amicorum Ernst-Joachim Mestmäcker © 2003 T.M.C.ASSER PRESS, *The Hague, The Netherlands*

practices, which are prohibited by Article 81 section 1 can only be exempted, for the time being, by a Commission decision taken under Article 81 section 3 and Regulation 17/62[2] the Commission wants to give up that monopoly. According to the White Paper both national competition authorities and national courts of law will be in a position to directly apply Article 81 section 3. Among the first reactions to that proposal was that of ERNST JOACHIM MESTMÄCKER to whom this paper is dedicated in longstanding respect and gratitude to celebrate his 75th Anniversary. He published an extensive, severe and outspoken critique as early as September 1999.[3] His analysis has had a strong impact on academic discussions and public opinion in Germany,[4] although it has not persuaded the European Commission which drafted a proposal for a regulation along the lines of the White Paper in late 2000.[5] Again, ERNST-JOACHIM MESTMÄCKER has reacted by a striking and even more elaborate critique which resumes and extends the discussion.[6]

The criticism advanced by MESTMÄCKER and others can be summarised as follows:

- The effective implementation of Community competition law is said to be threatened by the abolition of the notification system; since the exemption under Article 81 section 3 will no longer depend upon a previous notification

---

[2] First Regulation Implementing Articles 85 and 86 of the Treaty Issued by the Council on 6.2.1962, *OJ(EC)* [English Special Edition 1959-1962] No. 204/62, p. 87.

[3] Ernst-Joachim Mestmäcker, "Versuch einer kartellpolitischen Wende in der EU", *EuZW* [1999] 523 – 529; id., "Begrenzt abschreckend", *WuW* [2000] 683.

[4] See the critical evaluations by Monopolkommission, *Kartellpolitische Wende in der Europäischen Union?* (Baden-Baden: Nomos 1999); also published in English translation: *Cartel Policy Change in the European Union?* (Baden-Baden: Nomos 2000); Wissenschaftlicher Beirat beim Bundesministerium für Wirtschaft und Technologie, *Reform der europäischen Kartellpolitik, Gutachten vom 1.7.2000*; Wernhard Möschel, "Effizienter Wettbewerbsschutz in einer erweiterten Gemeinschaft durch Einbeziehung der nationalen Wettbewerbsbehörden und nationalen Gerichte?", *WuW* [2001] 147–148; Fritz Rittner, "Kartellpolitik und Gewaltenteilung in der EG", *EuZW* [2000] 129; Jochen Gröning, "Die dezentrale Anwendung des EG-Kartellrechts gemäß dem Vorschlag der Kommission zur Ersetzung der VO 17/62", *WRP* [2001] 83-89; Wolfgang Fikentscher, "Das Unrecht einer Wettbewerbsbeschränkung: Kritik an Weißbuch und VO-Entwurf zu Art. 81, 82 EG-Vertrag", *WuW* [2001] 446-458; Hartmut Weyer, "Nach der Reform: Gestaltung der Wettbewerbspolitik durch die Kommission?" *ZHR* 164 (2000) 611-637, 634 et seq.; see also Florian Bien, "Systemwechsel im europäischen Kartellrecht", *DB* [2000] 2309-2312; Rainer Bechtold, "Modernisierung des EG-Wettbewerbsrechts", *BB* [2000] 2425-2431.

[5] Proposal for a Council Regulation on the implementation of the rules on competition laid down in Articles 81 and 82 of the Treaty and amending Regulations (EEC) No. 1017/68, (EEC) No. 2988/74, (EEC) No. 4056/86 and (EEC) No. 3975/87 ("Regulation implementing Articles 81 and 82 of the Treaty"), *COM* (2000) 582 fin.

[6] Ernst-Joachim Mestmäcker, "The EC Commission's Modernisation of Competition Policy: a Challenge to the Community's Constitutional Order", 1 *EBOR* (2000) 401-444.

of an agreement by the parties, the practice of notifications will cease and all interested authorities and market actors including competitors, suppliers and clients, will have less knowledge about anti-competitive agreements which produce their effect upon the market and even on their own actions.

- In a system of direct applicability of Article 81 section 3 it would be up to the undertakings themselves to assess prevailing economic advantages for the purposes of that provision. It would appear doubtful whether an arrangement which assigns to the sinners the task of evaluating the benefit resulting from their own acts can promise an effective implementation of law.
- The Court of Justice has repeatedly stated that the Commission disposes of a certain discretion in the application of Article 81 section 3.[7] This case law would give evidence of the non-legal and therefore unjusticiable character of certain decisions required by that provision. How can the competence to apply Article 81 section 3 be transferred to any national judge if not even the Court of Justice considers itself fit to make such a decision?
- The legal basis of the draft regulation is put into question. Some critics take the view that the wording of Article 81 section 3 suggests that exemptions have to be taken as constitutive decisions and that they are not merely declaratory of an existent legal exception. The change in policy is therefore said to raise constitutional problems of the European Community. It would require an amendment of the Treaty.
- While the Commission points out alternative ways of enforcement, in particular private litigation, there are serious doubts about the efficient implementation of competition law in such lawsuits. Under the principles governing civil procedure the judge depends upon the factual information provided by the parties and is not allowed to investigate the case by his own initiative. At the same time an intervention of the Commission or a national authority, which may have the relevant information, could easily be regarded as a violation of judicial independence.
- The decentralised application of Article 81 section 3 by the national competition authorities of different Member States creates the risk of contradictory decisions and of an incoherent application of Community competition laws. For the time being there are no procedural rules which cope with this problem.

---

[7] Ever since Cases 56 and 58/64 *Consten & Grundig v. Commission*, [1966] *ECR* 299, at 347; a revision of that case law is recommended by Claus D. Ehlermann, "The Modernisation of EC Antitrust Policy: A Legal and Cultural Revolution", 37 *C.M.L.Rev.* (2000) 537, 559.

These and other objections have been discussed at great length in Germany,[8] and more recently also in the literature of some other Member States.[9] ERNST-JOACHIM MESTMÄCKER and other authors have elaborated on these arguments to get support for an overall rejection of the Commission proposals. The publication of the draft regulation as well as numerous appearances of Commissioner *Monti*[10] and of Director General *Schaub*[11] give however evidence of the political resolve of the Commission to have its way. At the same time the national governments of Member States appear to be charmed by the idea of getting back some of the competences they lost forty years ago; the Council is therefore rather likely to approve the reform. The third political institution of the Community, the European Parliament, only has a right to be consulted in these matters, cf. Article 83. Therefore the political odds are rather in favour of an eventual adoption of the draft regulation.

While the legality of the future regulation may still be challenged in the Court of Justice, it would appear to be equally important that a legal analysis points out the follow-up problems of the draft which will arise once the regulation comes into force. This is the purpose of the following article. If the struggle against the modernisation project turns out to be successful, the following lines will remain without significance. But it appears in all probability that the reform will be implemented and at least two consequential problems will have to be tackled: the coherent application of European competition law by national

---

[8] See *supra* n. 4.

[9] Claude Fourgoux, "La proposition de Règlement d'application des articles 81 et 82 du Traité CE – Réflexions provisoires pour un texte incomplet", *JCP* éd. E 2000, 1973-1975; David Gerber, "Modernising European Competition Law: A Developmental Perspective", *Eur.Compet.L.Rev.* [2001] 122-130; *Katherine Holmes*, "The EC White Paper on Modernisation", 23 *World Compet.* (2000) 51-79; Laurence Idot, "Le futur «règlement d'application des articles 81 et 82 CE»: chronique d'une révolution annoncée", *Dalloz* [2001] Chr. 1370-1376; M.R. Mok, "De toekomst van het Europees Kartelrecht", *Ondernemingsrecht* [2000] 448-453; Luca Nivarra, "Il «Libro Bianco sulla modernizzazione delle norme per l'applicazione degli articoli 85 e 86 del Trattato CE»: Quale futuro per il diritto europeo della concorrenza?" *Europa e diritto privato* [2000] 1001-1016; Michael Paulweber, "The End of a Success Story? The European Commission's White Paper on the Modernisation of the European Competition Law", 23 *World Compet.* (2000) 3-48.

[10] See e.g. Mario Monti, "Perspectives of European Competition Law", in: *Zukunft der Wettbewerbsordnung und des Kartellrechts – Referate des XXXIII. FIW-Symposiums* (Köln: Heymanns 2001) 9-13; id., "The application of Community competition law by the national courts in a directly applicable exception system", in: *ERA-Forum (scripta iuris europaei)* [I-2001] 3-6; see also "Monti beharrt auf grundlegender Reform des europäischen Kartellrechts", *Handelsblatt* 10/11.11.2000.

[11] Alexander Schaub, *Die Zunkunft des europäischen Kartellrechts. Zentrum für europäisches Wirtschaftsrecht der Rheinischen Friedrich-Wilhelms-Universität Bonn, Vorträge und Berichte No. 112* (Bonn 2000); id., "EC Competition System – Proposals for Reform", *[1999] Fordham Int'l L. J.* (2000) 853.

competition authorities (*infra* 2) and its efficient enforcement in civil litigation (*infra* 3). As the Commission is becoming aware of such follow-up problems it may realise that the overall level of enforcement of EC competition law might rather decrease as a consequence of the reform unless appropriate measures are enacted as part of the reform package to cope with those problems.

2. The coherent application of Articles 81 and 82 EC by national competition authorities

The risk of an incoherent practice is intrinsically linked to the existence of parallel competences and to the application of different substantive and procedural rules by the various competent bodies. Article 5 of the draft regulation, which invests the competition authorities of the Member States with the power to apply Articles 81 and 82 including Article 81 section 3, thus creates a double risk of incoherence. First, the national authorities of different Member States may arrive at contradictory results when applying Articles 81 and 82. As pointed out before, this risk is inevitably linked to the co-existence of several competent bodies and can only be reduced by rules of procedure (*infra* 2.2). Second, one or more of the authorities can refrain from applying Articles 81 and 82 altogether and instead rely on national competition law. Here, the risk of incoherence is rooted in the choice of law decision of a competent body (*infra* 2.1).

2.1 **The exclusion of national competition law**

Under the present regime enshrined in Regulation 17/62 national competition authorities may apply the substantive competition rules of the respective Member States or Articles 81 and 82, cf. Article 9 section 3 Regulation 17. However, national authorities lose their competence to apply Articles 81 and 82 as soon as the Commission opens proceedings of its own. In view of the Commission's monopoly on the granting of exemptions, such proceedings are at least inevitable when the validity of the agreement is in dispute in a national court and an application for an exemption is lodged with the Commission. Thus, under the present regime, the parties to a restrictive agreement always have access to the Commission which, by necessity, applies Articles 81 and 82.

This could change if Article 81 section 3 is turned into a directly applicable legal exception. If the Commission, as a consequence, acquires the right to reject a case in favour of a national authority (Art. 13 section 1, 2nd sentence of the draft regulation), and that national authority maintains the right to choose between national competition law and Article 81, European competition law might end up as not being applied at all. The character of legal exception and the envisaged decentralisation therefore imply the obligation of national competition authorities to apply European competition rules if a high degree of uniformity of decentralised enforcement of Articles 81 and 82 is to be maintained. Once they are put under such an obligation national authorities would still be allowed to give cumulative effect to their national rules, but, under the well-established case law of the Court of Justice, they would be bound to give priority to Community law in case of conflict.[12]

Article 3 of the draft regulation goes a step further by excluding the application of national law whenever a restrictive agreement or practice may affect trade between Member States, i.e. whenever Articles 81 and 82 may be applicable. The move from the priority to the exclusivity of Community law is questionable under the principles of subsidiarity[13] and proportionality.[14] As a consequence of such objections the Commission appears to be inclined to maintain Article 3 of the draft regulation only with regard to Article 81, whereas cumulative application and the priority principle shall remain in force with regard to Article 82.[15] But, with regard to article 81, too, it is difficult to understand the need for the exclusion of national law. An obligation to apply Article 81 in connection with the priority principle established by the Court of Justice would suffice. The exclusion of national law appears even less appropriate if we take into account that it only relates to substantive rules whereas national law is explicitly referred to with regard to procedure in Article 21 of the draft regulation. Differences between national rules of procedure may obstruct the target of a coherent application of Article 81 even more than differences in substantive rules.

2.2 Procedural tools of coherence

2.2.1 *General principles of international administrative law*

In its draft regulation, the Commission pursues the objective to create a network of national competition authorities and thereby to promote consistency and a level playing field throughout the Single Market.[16] While international cooperation basically appears to be an appropriate substitute to centralised proceedings, it should be borne in mind that in international administrative law – as opposed to international civil procedure – there is little experience in this field. Although the increasing interdependence of national economies and societies requires an interaction of national administrations, the basic principles

---

[12] Case 14/68 *Walt Wilhelm* v. *Bundeskartellamt*, [1969] *ECR* 1, paras. 4-5.

[13] Mestmäcker, *supra* n. 6, 1 *EBOR* (2000) 427 et seq.

[14] Gröning, *supra* n. 4, *WRP* [2001] 87 et seq.

[15] Cf. "EU-Kommission kommt Kartellamt entgegen", *Handelsblatt* 22.12.2000.

[16] See the Explanatory Memorandum of the draft Regulation, *supra* n. 5, section 2 C 2 (b).

in this area are still the territorial sovereignty which deprives foreign administrative acts of their effects outside their country of origin, and the exclusive application, by each state, of its own national law (*lex fori*).[17]

As a consequence, Member States take notice of administrative proceedings conducted in other Member States only insofar as international treaties or Community law so provide. International treaties on administrative co-operation are usually bilateral and very specific; with regard to competition matters a Franco-German agreement can be cited which provides for some basic rules of co-operation.[18] The European Commission has published a (non-binding) communication on the development of administrative co-operation in the application and enforcement of Community law for the Single Market, which tackles some general issues without reference to particular areas of administration.[19] With regard to specific areas of Community law various duties to co-operate have been enacted,[20] which however do not appear to be inspired by basic principles encompassing the whole area of administrative law. Outside the area of specific acts there is a general duty of co-operation among Member States which flows from Article 10 EC,[21] but for the time being it is so vague as to be almost meaningless.

Given the lack of co-operation principles in international administrative law the following analysis will borrow from the law of international civil procedure which started from a similar outset; it has not only produced coherent structures of the law in this field but also developed some helpful rules and principles. Those relate to issues of territorial competence (jurisdiction), to various matters of procedural co-operation, and to the mutual recognition of foreign proceedings.

2.2.2 *Territorial competence (jurisdiction)*

The easiest way to avoid contradictory decisions is to attribute the competence for each case to one decision-making body only. In judicial proceedings this

---

[17] See Reiner Schmidt, *Öffentliches Wirtschaftsrecht – Allgemeiner Teil* (Heidelberg: Springer 1990) 214-216, with further references; Klaus Vogel, "Administrative Law, International Aspects", in: Rudolf Bernhardt (ed.), *Encyclopedia of Public International Law*, vol. I (Amsterdam: North Holland 1992) 22, 24.

[18] Abkommen zwischen der Regierung der Bundesrepublik Deutschland und der Regierung der Französischen Republik über die Zusammenarbeit in bezug auf wettbewerbsbeschränkende Praktiken, *BGBl.* 1984-II, 758-762; see Peter Mozet, *Internationale Zusammenarbeit der Kartellbehörden* (Heidelberg: Müller 1991) 64-70.

[19] *COM* (94) 29 fin.

[20] For an excellent survey see Eberhard Schmidt-Aßmann, "Verwaltungskooperation und Verwaltungskooperationsrecht in der Europäischen Gemeinschaft", *EuR* [1996] 270-301.

[21] Case C-251/89 *Athanasopoulou*, [1991] *ECR* I-2848, para. 75.

way of case allocation is called exclusive jurisdiction; in administrative matters one could call it exclusive competence by analogy. It is however limited to cases which, by their very nature, have a very strong or even the sole link with the territory of one single state: *in rem* proceedings relating to immovables or proceedings dealing with entries in public registers or with patents, trademarks or other rights of a territorial scope.[22] Exclusive jurisdiction or competence is not appropriate for matters, which often or even typically, are connected to several or a multitude of states. In such matters the need for state action may arise at different places at the same time; moreover, the evidence required for the proceedings and the assets needed for enforcement may also be situated in different states.

In open markets, economic competition is intrinsically transnational, and anti-competitive practices very often produce their effects on several markets. Since the effects doctrine is inherent in competition law, and by now almost generally acknowledged,[23] exclusive jurisdiction of a single authority could only be envisaged if vested in a supranational body such as the European Commission. Decentralisation therefore by necessity produces a system of parallel competences of the national competition authorities of various Member States, which in turn implies the danger of conflicting decisions.

Below the level of an exclusive competence one might however think of some kind of limitation of national competences for the application of Articles 81 and 82. In a case involving the markets of ten or twelve Member States the clarity of the procedural arrangement would increase if the number of competent national authorities could be reduced to three or four. In this respect, the law of civil procedure might provide guidance. The admitted bases of jurisdiction are effectively limited with regard to judicial proceedings by the Brussels convention and its successor Regulation 44/2001.[24] Quite to the contrary, there is not the slightest restriction on the administrative competence of national competition authorities.

As far as Community law is concerned, both Article 9 section 3 Regulation 17 and Article 5 of the draft regulation only deal with the powers of "the authorities of the Member States", not with the powers of the authority of a single Member State. The basic thrust of Article 9 section 3 Regulation 17 is the demarcation of national competences and Community competences. While this will remain a relevant issue under the draft regulation, decentralisation gives

---

[22] See art. 16 of the Brussels Convention on jurisdiction and the enforcement of judgments in civil and commercial matters of 27.9.1968, as amended, *OJ(EC)* [1998] C 27/1, recently transformed into Regulation 44/2001 of 22.12.2000, *OJ(EC)* [2001] L 12/1, see Art. 22.

[23] For a comprehensive explanation and survey see Ivo Schwartz/Jürgen Basedow, "Restraints on Competition", in: *Int. Encycl. Comp. L.* vol. III, ch. 35 (1995) sec. 10 and 60 et seq.

[24] See Art. 3 of the Brussels Convention and of Regulation 44/2001, *supra* n. 22.

greater weight to the additional issue relating to the demarcation of national spheres of competence. For the national authorities will apply their respective national laws of administrative procedure which may have a great impact on the final outcome of cases.

Neither do national competition laws draw a clear dividing line between the respective national spheres of competence. In the past, such rules would have been regarded as redundant since an administrative authority established for the implementation of a certain statute, would be regarded as competent under general principles of administrative law insofar as the substantive provisions of that statute claim application. Thus, the German law against restraints of competition[25] extends its scope of application to all restrictions of competition which produce effect in Germany, § 130 section 2, and it does not further spell out the competence of German competition authorities in relation to foreign authorities. The only provision that explicitly deals with competence concerns the intra-German demarcation of competences between the Federal Cartel Office and the cartel offices of the single states, § 48.

The above-mentioned basic principle of administrative competence does not help any further when disputes on the competence of national competition authorities are to be decided in a post-decentralisation era. First, that basic principle is unilateral; it only takes into account the self-interests of a country to implement its laws, and not the concurring or competing interests of other Member States. Second, the scope of EC competition law which determines the competence of administrative authorities depends upon the implementation of an anti-competitive practice within the Common Market[26] and not within a single Member State. If an anti-competitive practice is implemented within the Community, the general principle on the competence of administrative bodies would therefore confer competence on any of the 15 national competition authorities even if the specific Member State is hardly or not at all involved. Although it is not likely that the Spanish competition authority will open proceedings in a case which affects only some northern countries it is clear that a system which allows for such unlimited powers cannot be said to be well-conceived.

The draft regulation tries to solve the problem by the Commission's right to evoke the case,[27] by consultation and by allowing national authorities to stay proceedings in favour of a competition authority in a foreign Member State

---

[25] Gesetz gegen Wettbewerbsbeschränkungen in der Fassung der Bekanntmachung vom 26.8.1998, *BGBl.* I, p. 2546.

[26] Joined cases 89/85 *Ahlström – Wood pulp*, [1988] *ECR* 5193, paras. 16-18.

[27] See art. 11 (6) of the draft regulation, *supra* n. 5.

which may be better placed to decide the case.[28] But the evocation of a case would annul the relief which decentralisation purports to achieve, and the discretionary suspension of proceedings cannot make up for some clear-cut rules on administrative competence. The criteria to be used for such allocation of cases are however far from clear and will require intensive discussion.[29]

2.2.3 *Procedural co-operation*

The co-existence, in a single market, of several competent competition authorities vested with purely national powers requires close and frequent interaction of the various bodies. Otherwise, they would not only risk making contradictory decisions, but they will also increasingly often lack the relevant information which is situated in foreign Member States. The draft regulation gives ample evidence of the Commission's awareness of this need, providing for the traditional instruments of notification, information and consultation, well-known from some bilateral co-operation agreements.[30]

In particular Article 11 section 3 puts the national competition authorities of the Member States under an obligation to inform the Commission when they start to deal with a case; the Commission will make the information accessible to the national authorities of other Member States by putting it on the intranet of the network which it plans to establish.[31] In substance this is a *notification* duty. At first sight, it goes beyond the corresponding obligations of bilateral agreements such as that between the European Community and the United States of America, since it does not require that the enforcement activities affect important interests of the addressee.[32] But, since the addressee of the notification is the European Commission which bears the final responsibility for the implementation of Articles 81 and 82, its "important interests" are always affected by enforcement activities carried out in one of the Member States. As opposed to the EC-US Co-operation Agreement the provisions dealing with the details of the notification duty, and, in particular, with the point in time when it

[28] See *infra* 2.2.3 and 2.2.4.

[29] It emerges from an internal staff paper that the Commission is not unaware of the problem; it suggests to proceed on a case by case basis, but has no clear criteria for the decision.

[30] For a closer analysis and further references see Mozet, *supra* n. 18, in particular pp. 82 et seq.; Schwartz/Basedow, *supra* n. 23, sec. 91; Jürgen Basedow, *Weltkartellrecht* (Tübingen: Mohr Siebeck 1998) 33 et seq.

[31] See the Explanatory Memorandum of the draft regulation, *supra* n. 5, comment on Art. 11 para. 3.

[32] See art. II (1) of the Agreement between the Government of the United States of America and the Commission of the European Communities regarding the application of their competition laws of 23.9.1991, *OJ(EC)* [1995] L 95/45, corr. in *OJ(EC)* [1995] L 131/38.

arises are so vague that a uniform application in a Community of 15 Member States is very unlikely.

Under Article 12 of the draft regulation, the Commission and the competition authorities of the Member States "may" provide one another with all kinds of *information*, and the recipient body may use that information in evidence. According to the explanatory memorandum, this rule not only concerns the vertical relationship between the Commission and national authorities, but also the horizontal relation between national bodies; it is also comprehensive with regard to the type of information to be conveyed and even includes the transfer of entire case files and confidential documents.[33] While Article 12 surpasses the EC-US Agreement in this respect (cf. Article VIII) it lags behind in its optional character (cf. Article III section 3). Article 12 merely deprives national provisions, which prohibit the transfer of information to foreign authorities, of their effect, but it does not put national authorities under an obligation to grant that assistance.[34]

Given the discretionary character of such administrative assistance under national law and the vagueness of the obligation of mutual assistance under Article 10 EC,[35] Article 12 of the draft regulation in its present form cannot satisfy the need for a reliable flow of information within the planned network. There can hardly be any doubt that the objectives of industrial policy which some national competition authorities (and governments) pursue in certain sectors will be in conflict with the idea of mutual information and assistance enshrined in Article 12. This conflict has to be overcome by clear-cut obligations. They should be susceptible to the approval by the Council for two reasons: in the first place, the national competition authorities can be said to exercise powers which before decentralisation were exclusively vested in the Commission; mutual exchange of information therefore is not more than a substitute to the pre-existing investigatory powers of the Commission. In the second place, the Council should accept obligations within the Community which it already has approved *vis-à-vis* a none-Member State when adopting the EC-US Agreement.

A duty of *consultation* is established by Article 11 section 4 of the draft regulation. Under that provision, a national competition authority shall consult the Commission before it issues a decision which prohibits certain anti-competitive practices, accepts commitments or withdraws the benefit of a block exemption regulation. This duty is limited to the vertical relation, but again the Commission intends to post the relevant information – a summary of the case and copies

---

33 Explanatory Memorandum of the draft regulation, *supra* n. 5, comment on Art. 12.
34 Ibid.
35 See *supra* n. 21.

of the most important documents – on the intranet allowing the national authorities of other Member States to express their views on the case. In case of substantial disagreement within the network, the Commission retains the power to withdraw a case from a national competition authority by initiating its own proceedings in the case, Article 11 section 6.[36]

The duty to consult does not arise if the national authority does not see a reason to interfere with the investigated practice. Consequently, a more lenient national authority will have to consult less often than an authority which pursues a rigid policy in competition matters. It equally follows that the Commission and the authorities of other Member States will be in a position to correct national decisions which somehow interfere with anti-competitive behaviour, but they will not even become aware of commercial practices which a national competition authority does not hold to be sufficiently anti-competitive to justify administrative interference. It should be borne in mind in this context that the information conveyed to the Commission under Article 11 section 3 of the draft regulation is given "at the outset" of the proceedings and therefore does not contain the results of the investigation. The overall effect of these provisions is such as to mitigate a very strict application of Articles 81 and 82 by national competition authorities while an overly lenient application will go unnoticed. Put in other words, it is fair to predict that the overall level of competition law enforcement in the whole network will rather decrease as compared with the present situation.

The draft regulation goes beyond the traditional co-operation agreements in allowing the national competition authorities of Member States to carry out *investigations* in their respective territories on behalf and for the account of the competition authority of another Member State, Article 21. This is a considerable progress, since the exchange of information envisaged by Article 12 of the draft regulation would otherwise be limited to information which is already available to the various national authorities. But, again, it must be pointed out that the draft regulation does not establish a duty of the national authorities to carry out an investigation in favour of another authority of the same network. Such activity is optional, Article 21 merely deprives limitations of investigations imposed by national law of their effect, but does not overcome the inherent risk that a national authority may use its discretion in a protectionist way.

2.2.4 *Mutual recognition of proceedings*

In a system of parallel competences a coherent application of Articles 81 and 82 can only be achieved if and insofar as the proceedings initiated by one authority

---

[36] See the Explanatory Memorandum of the draft regulation, *supra* n. 5, sec. 2 C 2 (b).

produce their effects in the territories of the whole network. These effects would include the recognition and enforcement of formal decisions such as negative clearances, termination orders or impositions of fines. It would be even better if the risk of contradictory decisions could be excluded from the very beginning of the proceedings by a rule which provides for the allocation of the case to one authority only. Since it is not possible to attribute exclusive competence to one authority in competition matters,[37] the second best solution would appear to be a rule which concentrates proceedings in one authority by the suspension of parallel proceedings.

The draft regulation purports to implement the latter solution. It makes a distinction between vertical relations involving national competition authorities and the Commission, and horizontal relations between the authorities of different Member States. With regard to vertical relations it is up to the Commission to determine where proceedings are conducted. It may either reject a complaint on the ground that the competition authority of a Member State is dealing with the case,[38] or evoke a case from the national authorities by opening its own proceedings under Article 11 section 6 of the draft regulation. The latter provision is of greater importance in the new system than it has been before. It now serves to ensure effective case allocation and consistent application of Community competition law.[39] The Commission may use this tool also to resolve conflicts between the national competition authorities of different Member States on the proper allocation of a case. But the price to be paid is high: it is the re-centralisation of proceedings which would withdraw the relief expected from the draft regulation.

With regard to horizontal conflicts between competition authorities of different Member States the Commission rather trusts in Article 13 of the draft regulation. Under that provision, "the fact that one authority is dealing with the case shall be sufficient ground for the others to suspend the proceedings before them or to reject the complaint". This provision supersedes conflicting national rules, which may require the national authority to terminate all proceedings opened after a complaint by a formal decision.[40] In substance, it deals with a situation called *lis alibi pendens* in private international law. Rules dealing with that situation pursue the same objectives irrespective of the parallel proceedings being judicial or administrative in nature: they are meant to increase procedural efficiency and to avoid contradictory decisions. When the Brussels Convention came into effect, the law relating to *lis alibi pendens* was still rather obscure in

---

[37] See *supra* section 2.2.2.
[38] See Art. 13 sec. 1, second sentence.
[39] Explanatory Memorandum of the draft regulation, *supra* n. 5, comment on Art. 11 para. 6.
[40] Explanatory Memorandum of the draft regulation, *supra* n. 5, comment on Art. 13.

many countries,[41] and it is still far from being settled outside the scope of Article 21 of the Brussels Convention and Article 27 of the successor Regulation 44/2001. Both provisions put the judge who is seized second, under an obligation to stay proceedings and eventually to decline jurisdiction in favour of the court first seized. Outside their scope, the following national rules can be discerned: in some countries, such as Germany,[42] or Italy,[43] the judge is bound to suspend domestic proceedings if litigation on the same matter has started in the foreign court previously and if the decision which will result from those proceedings is susceptible of producing effects at home. Under the same condition the stay of proceedings is optional under French law.[44] In England it appears to be in the unlimited discretion of the court whether it declines jurisdiction as a *forum non conveniens*.[45] But there are other legal orders such as Spain,[46] or the Netherlands,[47] which are not at all inclined to give priority to foreign proceedings.

Which lessons can be learnt from that diversity of the law for our context, i.e. for the regulation of parallel administrative proceedings in competition matters? First, we should not expect a Member State which is not prepared to suspend civil proceedings in favour of a *foreign court* to stay administrative proceedings in favour of a *foreign authority* since the political implications in the latter case are much greater than in the context of private judicial litigation. Second, even a national competition authority which would be willing to do so may ask: why? In civil litigation the answer is clear: it is the expectation of the future recognition of the foreign decision; one and the same foreign judgement would decide the case and be effective in two (or more) countries. The inherent link between the stay of proceedings and the expectation of future recognition is clearly established by the Brussels Convention which deals with both situations. But it is also spelled out by the aforementioned rules of domestic law which presuppose that the resulting foreign decision is susceptible of being

---

[41] Lennart Pålsson, "The Institute of *lis pendens* in International Civil Procedure", 14 *Scandinavian Studies in Law* (1970) 59-108, e.g., p. 77 with regard to the Scandinavian legal systems.

[42] BGH 10.10.1985, *NJW* [1986] 2195 = *IPRspr.* [1985] Nr. 167 sub I 1; Haimo Schack, *Internationales Zivilprozeßrecht*, 2nd ed. (München: Beck 1996) no. 754, p. 295.

[43] See art. 7 Legge 31.5.1995 n. 218 – Riforma del sistema italiano di diritto internazionale privato, *Gazz. Uff.* 3.6.1995 n. 128, Supplemento ordinario n. 68.

[44] Cass. 26.11.1974. *Rev. crit. dr. int. pr.* [1975] 491 (note: Dominique Holleaux); see also Hélène Gaudemet-Tallon, *Les conventions de Bruxelles et de Lugano*, 2nd ed. (Paris: Montchrestien 1996) 204 et seq., no. 281.

[45] Lawrence Collins in *Dicey and Morris on the Conflict of Laws*, vol. 1, 11th ed. (London: Sweet &Maxwell 1987) pp. 395 et seq.

[46] STS 19.12.1985 *Aranzadi* [1986] 6600; critical Miguel Virgós Soriano/Francisco Garcimartín Alferez, *Derecho procesal civil internacional* (Madrid: Civitas 2000) p. 255 no. 385.

[47] H.R. 22.12.1989 *Ned. Jur.* [1990] No. 689 p. 2783 approved by J.C.S(chultsz) in his annotation which refers to Dutch writers who take a different view.

recognised at home. If the condition is not fulfilled there is no reason to grant priority to the foreign proceedings because there will be two lawsuits anyhow in order to solve the conflict.[48]

The draft regulation proposed by the Commission does not deal with the recognition and enforcement of decisions made by a national competition authority in another Member State. Neither is there a basis for mutual recognition of decisions of national competition authorities in other Member States outside the draft regulation. Not only is there no evidence in international law that a duty to recognise foreign acts of State exists. According to the almost general practice, States still do not enforce foreign public law within their boundaries and this includes the recognition of foreign decisions based upon such foreign public law.[49] Against this background, the Community must establish clear duties of recognition and enforcement if it wants that kind of co-operation to take place. It has effectively done so, although not very often, in some other contexts,[50] for example in the recent Directive 2001/40 which obliges the national authorities to implement decisions of other Member States relating to the expulsion of third country nationals.[51] Unless the Community establishes a similar duty of mutual recognition and enforcement within the proposed network of competition authorities there is no need and no justification for the suspension of administrative proceedings allowed in Article 13 of the draft directive; the national authorities would by necessity disregard the discretion granted to them by that provision.

On the other hand, if national authorities could be under an obligation to implement the decisions of other Member States relating to EC competition law, one might consider to change Article 13 of the draft regulation from a provision conferring discretion, to a binding rule, similar to Article 21 of the Brussels Convention or Article 27 of Regulation 44/2001. Such a change would meet a different objection, however. Both provisions give strict priority to the court first seized and thereby grant a right to select the court to the plaintiff of the first lawsuit. If this method of case allocation were transposed to administrative proceedings it would consequently be up to private undertakings to select

---

[48] This context is very ably elaborated by Virgós Soriano/Garcimartín Alferez, *supra* n. 46, p. 255 no. 386.

[49] See Werner Meng, "Recognition of Foreign Legislative and Administrative Acts", in: Rudolf Bernhardt (ed.), *Encyclopedia of Public International Law*, vol. IV (Amsterdam: North Holland 2000) pp. 50, 51 et seq.

[50] See Schmidt-Aßmann, *supra* n. 20, *EuR* [1996] 293, who refers to Art. 250 of the Community customs code and to the licenses granted, under the relevant Community regulation, for the export of cultural goods.

[51] Council Directive 2001/40/EC of 28.5.2001 on the mutual recognition of decisions on the expulsion of third country nationals, *OJ(EC)* [2001] L 149/34.

the competent authority by either applying for a negative clearance or by lodging a complaint. Even if we assume that appropriate rules on competence restrict the number of accessible national authorities such private autonomy would be difficult to reconcile with the predominant public interest in competition law. The final decision on the competent authority within the network cannot be left to private undertakings, it must be taken by a public body. While a consultation between the national authorities of the Member States involved and the Commission may promote consensus on the authority which is best placed to deal with the case, a final decision must be possible which would be binding upon all authorities concerned. It follows from these considerations that the Commission should reserve the right to decide on the allocation of those plurinational cases which it does not want to investigate itself.

2.3 **Summary**

The proposed network composed of national competition authorities and the Commission could in fact replace the present system of a centralised application of Article 81 section 3. But in the form of the present draft the network does not appear to be workable. It simply has too many holes. The authors of the draft regulation rely on the good intentions of national authorities to co-operate which may exist in many cases but experience tells us that national interests to promote certain industries equally continue to exist. It is by no means unlikely that national competition authorities will use the ample discretion conferred upon them by the draft regulation in a way such as to achieve targets of national industrial policy instead of fostering competition. At present the draft regulation does not contain sufficient safeguards against such attempts to degenerate competition law. In order to knit the network tighter, binding rules would be required which limit the number of competent authorities; provide for a duty to exchange information and to investigate cases for other national competition authorities; provide for the intra-EC recognition and enforcement of foreign administrative decisions in matters relating to EC competition law; and grant the Commission the right to eventually decide upon the allocation of cases.

The Commission should also become aware of the change of relevant principles involved in its decentralisation project. Substituting a network of national administrative authorities for the centralised decisions of a single supranational body boils down to a replacement of the whole legal framework. As a consequence, the principles of supra-national law, in particular that of supremacy of Community law,[52] will give way to the traditional principles of international law, in particular that of the

[52] Case 6/64 *Costa* v. *Enel*, [1964] *ECR* 585, 594.

sovereign equality of the Member States.[53] The Commission should equally take note of the underdeveloped state of international administrative law, which is due to the principle of sovereign equality and to the strong political implications of that area of the law. It would appear irresponsible to give up the advantages of supranational law without establishing a network worthy of this name. Since the Commission in substance intends to transfer certain powers vested in itself to the Member States it should be in a position to ask for a consideration consisting in perceptible restrictions on national sovereignty in competition law.

3. Private enforcement of Article 81 EC

According to the conception of the Commission, its own partial withdrawal which is implied in decentralisation, shall be compensated by a shift of responsibility for the enforcement of EC competition law to civil courts. As pointed out in the explanatory memorandum preceding the proposal for a council regulation, the "proposal aims at promoting private enforcement through national courts".[54] It thereby refers to a framework of civil litigation which is almost exclusively provided by national law, both with regard to substantive and procedural provisions. It appears however, that the Commission has not investigated this framework. The following survey is meant to shed some light on the legal regime existing under German law and to point out deficiencies that may hinder an efficient private enforcement. As the Commission becomes aware of such flaws it may realise that the decentralisation proposal entails some further follow-up problems which have to be solved lest the overall level of enforcement of EC competition law should decrease. In this context, two types of cases should be separated: the first relates to litigation between the parties of a restrictive agreement (*infra* 3.1) and the second to third-party claims (*infra* 3.2). While proceedings of the latter type are particularly important they meet serious obstacles consisting in the proof of the relevant facts (*infra* 3.3), in the lack of legal certainty (*infra* 3.4) and in the lack of litigation incentives on the side of potential plaintiffs (*infra* 3.5).

3.1 Contractual enforcement claims

Litigation conducted between the parties to a contract containing restrictive clauses is a very common occurrence. While in those cases the plaintiff will

---

[53] On that principle see Helmut Steinberger, "Sovereignty", in: Rudolf Bernhardt (ed.), *Encyclopedia of Public International Law*, vol. IV (Amsterdam: North Holland 2000) pp. 500, 511, 515.

[54] Explanatory Memorandum of the draft regulation, *supra* n. 5, sec. 2 C 1 (a).

usually claim specific performance of a contract, payment of the agreed remuneration, or damages for breach, the defendant will invariably argue that the whole contract, or relevant parts of it, are void under Article 81 section 2 EC because of their anti-competitive content or effects. In turn, the plaintiff will plead the prevailing competitive advantages of the agreement which make it lawful under Article 81 section 3. Under Article 9 section 1 Regulation 17 the latter point falls within the exclusive competence of the European Commission, and the national court should suspend proceedings until the Commission has decided on an exemption.[55] It is certainly true that the time needed for this type of private proceedings could be reduced considerably if the courts were able to decide themselves whether the restrictive effects of the agreement are outweighed by rationalising effects and advantages for the consumer within the meaning of Article 81 section 3.

It should however be borne in mind that Article 81 section 3 also requires an assessment of the remaining competition in the market, which is difficult to assess for anyone who does not dispose of sufficient market information. While competition authorities such as the European Commission may get hold of that information by appropriate investigations, civil courts rely on the information provided by the parties.[56] If the party claiming the benefit of Article 81 section 3 cannot produce sufficient market data, it will have to bear the consequences under Article 2 of the draft regulation. It cannot expect the court to provide any information whatsoever on the relevant market. The gap could, of course, be filled by the Commission, and Article 15 of the draft regulation allows the national courts to ask the Commission for information in its possession or for its opinion. It is significant, however, that no corresponding duty of the Commission to respond is established. While such a duty flows from Article 10 EC in very general terms[57] the co-operation between the courts and the Commission could and should be based on a more reliable ground.

This defect of the draft regulation may of course be cured. But irrespective of possible modifications the contractual disputes of the aforementioned type can hardly account for private enforcement of competition law and they certainly do not increase in number once private courts are in a position to directly apply Article 81 section 3. The unlawfulness of the restrictive agreement is a point which every defendant raises effectively regardless of how long the proceedings will last, i.e. irrespective of the decentralisation of the application of

---

[55] Case C-234/89 *Delimitis* v. *Henninger Bräu AG*, [1991] *ECR* I-935, paras. 51-54.

[56] See Leo Rosenberg/Karl-Heinz Schwab/Peter Gottwald, *Zivilprozeßrecht*, 15th ed. (München: Beck 1993) pp. 424 seq.

[57] See *Delimitis*, *supra* n. 55, para. 53; Case C-2/88 *Imm.* (*Zwartveld*), [1990] *ECR* I-4405, para. 10.

Article 81 section 3. It follows that this type of proceedings need not be encouraged as a kind of compensation for the partial withdrawal of the Commission.

3.2 Third-party claims

This is different with regard to the other type of proceedings, i.e. claims made by parties who are not involved in the anti-competitive agreement and who have suffered loss as a consequence of that scheme. They will apply for an injunction or for an award of damages which compensate their losses. The Commission has explicitly pointed out that "the rôle of the national courts here complements that of the competition authorities",[58] and that the civil courts must therefore be allowed to apply Article 81 section 3 directly. But what is the reality of such claims? They appear to be virtually non-existent. Commentators have characterised their practical significance as marginal,[59] and do not cite a single reported case which ended in a damage award in favour of a cartel victim.[60]

In Germany, the reasons can hardly be ascribed to deficits of the substantive law as such. § 823 (2) of the German Civil Code (*Bürgerliches Gesetzbuch, BGB*) provides a cause of action which does not give rise to many doubts. Under that provision a person who has infringed a statute which purports the protection of another is liable to compensate the damages arising therefrom if the infringement has been committed either intentionally or by negligence. It is generally acknowledged that Article 81 section 1 is a protective statute for the purposes of § 823 (2) BGB insofar as the restriction directly affects actors on the other market side, i.e. suppliers or clients.[61] Competitors, too, may be protected depending upon the type of restrictive agreement.[62] The protective effect would appear to extend to consumers who are clients of a cartel member, but not to those who purchase the goods or services after further intermediary transactions at the end of the chain of distribution.

While the requirement of fault, explicitly set out in § 823 (2) BGB, has been criticised by the European Court of Justice in other contexts because of its

---

[58] Preliminary consideration no. 7 of the draft regulation, *supra* n. 5.

[59] See e.g. Karsten Schmidt in: Immenga/ Mestmäcker (ed.), *EG-Wettbewerbsrecht*, vol. I (München: Beck 1997) p. 318 no. 71 with further references.

[60] See Stephen Kon, "The Commission's White Paper on Modernisation: The Need for Procedural Harmonization", in: Barry Hawk (ed.), *1999 Fordham Corp. L. Inst.* (2000) 233, 247 citing in turn a Commission paper prepared by A. J. Braakman, cf. Kon at p. 240 n. 30.

[61] BGH 10.11.1987, *NJW* [1988] 2175, 2177; BGH 23.10.1979, *NJW* [1980] 1224, 1225; see Hartmut Weyer, "Gemeinschaftsrechtliches Verbot und nationale Zivilrechtsfolgen – Eine Untersuchung am Beispiel der Artikel 81, 82 EG-Vertrag", *ZEuP* [1999] 424, 439 and 447 with further references.

[62] Karsten Schmidt, *supra* n. 59, pp. 320 et seq. at no. 79.

subjective character,[63] it does not appear to be the decisive obstacle which hinders the effective enforcement of EC competition law here. The infringement of Article 81 section 1 presupposes an intentional behaviour of the participating undertakings anyway.[64] § 823 (2) BGB allows for the award of damages, but it is generally accepted that a claim for the termination of the infringement is well-founded under the same conditions on the basis of § 1004 BGB applied by analogy.[65]

Thus, the absence of third-party claims is not due to deficiencies of the substantive rules which provide for the cause of action. A need for an independent claim flowing from Community law, suggested by the Advocate General van Gerven,[66] can hardly be assessed from a German point of view, although such a cause of action may facilitate the enforcement of claims subject to the national laws of other Member States. From a German perspective, the only perceptible advantage of a cause of action provided by Community law could consist in the extension of standing to consumers and perhaps consumer associations.[67] Whoever wants to understand the present lack of third-party claims, however, should not speculate on substantive law, but rather look to the economic and procedural circumstances which determine its application and which apparently deter the victims of cartels from bringing suit. If the Commission wants to boost the rôle of civil courts in this area it will have to create conditions which encourage possible plaintiffs to enforce their rights under § 823 (2) BGB.

3.3 **Problems of proof**

Under the general rules governing civil proceedings it is up to the plaintiff to allege and to prove facts which give rise to the claim and in particular to the liability of the defendant.[68] This means that the plaintiff must prove the conclusion of the cartel or the concertation of anti-competitive practices and the active

---

[63] Case C-177/88 *Dekker*, [1990] *ECR* I-3941, paras. 23-25; Case C-180/95 *Draehmpaehl* v. *Urania*, [1997] *ECR* I-2195, para. 21; see also Joint Cases C-46/93 and C-48/93 *Brasserie du Pêcheur and Factortame*, [1996] *ECR* I-1029, paras. 76, 78.

[64] See Volker Emmerich in: Immenga/Mestmäcker, *supra* n. 59, vol. I, p. 152 no. 103, who describes both agreements and concerted practices as two forms of an "intentional coordination of behaviour".

[65] BGH 23.10.1979, *NJW* [1980] 1224, 1225; Karsten Schmidt, *supra* n. 59, p. 322 no. 85.

[66] See the opinion of Advocate General van Gerven in case C-128/92 *Banks*, [1994] *ECR* I-1209, paras. 36 et seq.; contra Weyer, *supra* n. 61, *ZEuP* [1999] 437-439.

[67] Under section 33 of the German Statute against Restrictions of Competition, industry associations have standing to apply for injunctions, but not for damages; consumer associations are not mentioned.

[68] Rosenberg/Schwab/Gottwald, *supra* n. 56, pp. 670 et seq.

involvement of the defendant in that scheme. It goes without saying that this is particularly difficult for someone who, although affected, did not actually participate in those agreements and has no access to the documents which give evidence of their conclusion. A radical solution would, of course, consist in a system of pre-trial discovery in line with the US example.[69] But there are good reasons to reject such a proposal. In the first place civil proceedings in most continental countries do not terminate in one trial which has to be prepared by a pre-trial discovery; contrary to the United States, the latter instrument is not required by the desire for procedural expediency and efficiency. Second, it would not be possible to implement the rules on pre-trial discovery limited to the small sector of antitrust litigation and to maintain the traditional methods of fact finding in all other areas of the law. In order to be effectively implemented the law of procedure must be as uniform as possible. However, a comprehensive harmonisation of the fact-finding rules of civil procedure appears to be out of reach for the Community at present.[70] Third and finally, the rules on pre-trial discovery are tailored to the structures of a court system and a legal services industry which are essentially non-existent in most European countries and which generate tremendous and deterring costs.

One might think, however, of a less radical solution which would consist in a procedural obligation of the defendant to clear up certain facts which have occurred in his sphere of influence. It is not uncommon indeed that the courts ease a party's burden of proof with regard to facts and circumstances allocated in the sphere of the other party. An example is provided by the case law dealing with the breaking of liability limits in the carriage of goods. Under Article 29 of the Convention for the international carriage of goods by road (CMR) the carrier loses the right to limit its liability in case of gross fault. It is widely acknowledged that the organisation of the carrier's transport business may have such defects as to be grossly negligent for the purposes of Article 29. While it is up to the sender or the consignee of the goods to prove gross negligence, he will usually not know the details of the carrier's internal business organisation. Therefore, he would be deprived of the benefit of full compensation for procedural reasons, which the courts do not accept. The Federal Court therefore has imposed upon the carrier a procedural duty to inform the court about its internal organisation. This duty arises as soon as the sender or consignee has made a *prima facie* case of the carrier's gross negligence relating to the internal

[69] See Rule 26 of the Federal Rules of Civil Procedure, 28 *USCA* 26.
[70] A limited legislative competence is laid down in Art. 65 (c) EC.

organisation of its business.[71] By analogy, one might envisage a corresponding duty of the defendant in case the plaintiff provides information which justifies the *prima facie* assumption of a concerted practice. In that case it would be up to the defendant to inform the court about the precise background of that business practice. A Community measure adopted under Article 83 EC could provide for such a corresponding duty of the defendant. That act would have to take precautions against the disclosure of business secrets.

Similar difficulties exist with regard to the proof of the loss sustained by the plaintiff as a consequence of the anti-competitive practice. While it may be possible for him to show a drop in his sales that may have several causes, the plaintiff will often be unable to identify the restrictive agreement or concerted practice as the relevant cause. Here again, the plaintiff's burden of proof should be eased. In the similar context of a patent or trademark infringement, the courts have allowed the plaintiff to calculate its damage in a threefold way: either by showing its precise losses, or by charging an average licence fee or by stripping the defendant of the profit derived from the infringement.[72] One might think of generalising rules of a similar kind. Thus a drop in the plaintiff's turnover that is somehow related to the market affected by the restrictive practice should be conclusive evidence of his losses and their causation by the restrictive practice if at the same time the defendant's turnover related to that market has been rising. Here again it would be indispensable that the defendant discloses the relevant information.

Community action in this field appears all the more important given the differences in the standards of proof applied in the various Member States. While in common law jurisdictions a fact is established in the light of the balance of probabilities, German and other continental laws require a "probability next to certainty", i.e. beyond reasonable doubt.[73] It goes without saying that the higher standard of proof is more difficult to match. Consequently, fact finding by the courts more often depends upon rules relating to situations of uncertainty, i.e. upon the onus of proof.

---

[71] BGH 19.6.1986, *VersR* [1986] 1019, 1020 et seq.; OLG Nürnberg 10.12.1992, *TranspR* [1993] 138, 139; see also Jürgen Basedow in: *Münchener Kommentar zum Handelsgesetzbuch*, vol. VII (München: Beck 1997) p. 1189; Art. 29 CMR no. 38.

[72] RG 8.6.1895, RGZ 35, 63 (67 ff.); RG 31.12.1898, *RGZ* 43, 56 (58 f.); BGH 6.3.1980, *NJW* [1980] 2522, 2524; Wolfgang Bernhardt/Rudolf Kraßer, *Lehrbuch des Patentrechts*, 4th ed. (München: Beck 1986) 629; Heinrich Hubmann/Heinz-Peter Götting, *Gewerblicher Rechtsschutz*, 6th ed. (München: Beck 1998) p. 213.

[73] Dagmar Coester-Waltjen, *Internationales Beweisrecht* (Ebelsbach: Gremer 1983) pp. 276 et seq.

3.4 Legal certainty

A second condition precedent to the initiation of civil litigation would be a high degree of legal certainty. While the Commission points out that "in the new enforcement system, undertakings' legal certainty will remain at a globally satisfactory level",[74] this appears to be rather meaningless. Legal certainty should not be assessed globally, but only individually with regard to a specific situation. Before making the decision to sue the defendant, the plaintiff must be reasonably sure to win.[75] Otherwise, he will either try to come to an arrangement with the members of the cartel, or will leave the relevant market altogether. He will not tie his resources to an endeavour with a very uncertain outcome.

It would appear however that the Commission is going to reduce the level of legal certainty rather than to raise it. The draft guidelines on horizontal co-operation[76] purport to lay greater weight on economic factors which are to be taken into account in the application of Article 81. Thereby, the Commission does not only increase the significance, for the outcome of a case, of economic information, which in many cases is outside the reach of civil courts. It also requires the court to make decisions which are not inherently legal, e.g. to weigh the short-term interests of consumers against their long-term interests, to weigh the interests of one consumer group against the interests of other consumer groups etc. The rising significance of economic factors, as envisaged by the Commission, will by necessity reduce the foreseeability of decisions and thereby discourage some plaintiffs from bringing suit in civil courts.[77]

3.5 Litigation incentives

The victim of a cartel or concerted practice has suffered losses from the conspiracy of his competitors or business partners and knows about the power of their combination. He is also aware of the investment in time and money that legal proceedings mean to him. He will make that investment only if he can be reasonably sure that the advantages to be expected from the litigation exceed possible losses. In this perspective, the hope for a compensation of the losses already suffered is not a very efficient incentive to bring suit. Many plaintiffs will prefer to invest in other and more lucrative activities than in conducting litigation for the mere compensation of sustained losses. If the Commission wants

---

[74] See the White Paper, *supra* n. 1, p. 29 no. 78.

[75] Cf. Jürgen Basedow, "Rechtssicherheit im europäischen Wirtschaftsrecht. Ein allgemeiner Rechtsgrundsatz im Lichte der wettbewerbsrechtlichen Rechtsprechung", *ZEuP* [1996] 570, 571-574.

[76] *OJ(EC)* [2000] C 118/3.

[77] Mestmäcker, *supra* n. 6, 1 *EBOR* (2000) 425.

to use private initiative for enforcing competition laws in the public interest, it should consider the US model of a private attorney general who is spurred to enforce the law by the expectation of treble damages.[78]

It is certainly true that a punitive element and a steering purpose are inherent in treble damages and that most legal systems in Europe reject the idea of damages exceeding pure compensation. On the other hand, this would not preclude the Community from introducing similar rules in its own legal order. To a certain extent this has already been done in the framework of Directive 2000/35 on combating late payment in commercial transactions.[79] This directive establishes a legal interest rate due for late payments, which is seven points above the refinancing rate applied by the European Central Bank. There is no question that the resulting interest rate surpasses by far the rate which the creditor would have to pay on the financial market in order to procure the sum owed by the debtor. Thus, the payment prescribed by the Directive exceeds the pure compensation of the creditor's loss. The reason is indicated in the preliminary considerations of the Directive which describe the harmful effects of late payment and which therefore conclude that the consequences of the delay in payment must be such as to "discourage" this practice.[80] It clearly emerges from the use of this word and the content of the Directive that Community law has already abandoned the limitation of damages to pure compensation and has instead espoused the idea of providing incentives to market actors by means of private law sanctions. The Commission is well advised to elaborate on that idea in order to foster private enforcement of competition law.

4. Conclusion

The preceding analysis deals with two types of proceedings which the Commission considers as substitutes for the traditional central enforcement of European competition law, in particular of Article 81 section 3: the administrative enforcement by a network of national competition authorities and the private enforcement by civil courts. On the basis of the draft regulation in its present form and in the framework provided by the present national law and by Community law it would appear however that neither type of proceedings is a workable substitute for the traditional centralised enforcement proceedings. If

---

78 Section 4 Clayton Act, 38 Stat. 730 (1914), codified as amended, 15 *USCA* § 15, grants the plaintiff treble damages for violation of the "antitrust statutes" which include the Sherman Act, see the definition in section 1 Clayton Act.

79 Directive of 29.6.2000, *OJ(EC)* [2000] L 200/35.

80 Ibid., preliminary consideration no. 16.

the main objective of the reform is to be achieved, i.e. to maintain the overall level of competition law enforcement in Europe and to provide for a coherent application throughout the Community, substantial legal reforms have to be carried out. In particular, the planned network of national competition authorities requires the following changes:

- While the competence of national authorities is already triggered by some substantial effects of an anti-competitive practice within the respective country, the Community should limit the number of potentially competent authorities in a plurinational setting by appropriate rules.
- The exchange of information must be obligatory and not optional; Member States should be prepared to accept this and other procedural obligations (see below), since the powers which they make use of when applying Article 81 section 3 EC are now vested in the Commission. Thus Member States may be said to exercise Community powers in a future decentralised enforcement system, and it should be up to the Community to fix the legal framework of that exercise of powers.
- The duty to consult the Commission should be extended to cases where the national competition authority, after investigation, does not see a reason to interfere.
- Fact-finding measures undertaken by the national competition authority on behalf of the competition authority of another Member State should not be optional, but obligatory.
- The draft regulation has to be supplemented by a rule which provides for the recognition and enforcement, by national authorities, of the decisions taken by the competition authority of a Member State.
- Such a rule on recognition would make the rule on the suspension of proceedings meaningful. While the duty to stay proceedings in favour of a foreign competition authority which was seized first, should be accepted in principle, exceptions must be granted if the authority of the Member State which was seized second is better placed to investigate the case, if the first state does not undertake any serious investigation activities or if essential national interests of the second state so require. In case of conflict it should be up to the Commission to either evoke the case or to make a binding decision on the competent national authority.

As far as private litigation is concerned, Community action should above all pursue the objective of making third-party claims filed by victims of a restrictive agreement or a concerted practice against the participating undertakings more efficient. If that type of litigation is meant to make up for the partial withdrawal of the Commission the following changes in the law are required:

- The Commission should not only allow national courts to submit requests for co-operation; it should be under a precisely framed obligation to grant that co-operation.
- The plaintiffs' burden of proof relating to the existence of a restrictive agreement or a concerted practice must be eased by presumptions and obligations of the defendants to disclose information on their business practices.
- Similarly, the plaintiff's burden of proof relating to its own loss and its causation by the restrictive practices should be eased.
- Instead of stressing the weight of economic elements in the application of Article 81 by adopting the envisaged guidelines on horizontal restrictions, the Commission should rather increase legal certainty by drafting a restatement of European competition law containing clear-cut legal rules.
- Even if those amendments are carried out it would appear highly doubtful whether private plaintiffs will take the risk of private action without a promising incentive such as the expectation of treble damages.

Public Services and the Internal Market – An Analysis of the Commission's Communication on Services of General Interest in Europe –

Peter Behrens[*]

1. Introduction

The idea that the State is, in a very general sense, responsible for the welfare of the people in terms of availability of goods and services, is probably as old as the State itself. How the State should organise the production and distribution of goods and services, however, is subject to time and ideological approach. Adam

---

[*] Professor of Law, Hamburg University, Dr.iur (Hamburg), M.C.J. (New York). The author gratefully acknowledges the support by Katharina Stasch in preparing this contribution.

Smith has shown that the "welfare of the nations" does not presuppose a State that would itself produce and distribute all goods and services. Such a State would reduce rather than enhance the welfare of the people. The balance between economic activities of the State, on the one hand, and of private actors in the market, on the other, has been a matter of theoretical as well as political debate for centuries. The central question concerns the appropriate "economic constitution". This question is the Leitmotiv of ERNST-JOACHIM MESTMÄCKER in whose honour I am pleased to submit the following contribution.

It is quite obvious, that the "economic constitution" is not only an economic question. It also has political implications and repercussions on society at large. Hence it is not surprising, that divergent answers have been given to this fundamental question – depending on the State and its political system. Since States are basically free to determine their national "economic constitution", almost every country draws the line between the State and the Market differently.

The Member States of the European Community, however, are legally bound by the EC Treaty. It follows from this Treaty that national markets shall generally be open and competitive. According to Article 3 (1) EC, activities of the Community include "an internal market characterised by the abolition, as between Member States, of obstacles to the free movement of goods, persons, services and capital" (lit. c) as well as "a system ensuring that competition in the internal market is not distorted" (lit. g). However, the Treaty expressly provides for a caveat: the Community shall pursue these objectives "as provided in this Treaty" in more detail. Certain provisions of the Treaty do indeed authorise Member States to engage in economic activities without limiting them to their supervisory or regulatory role. This applies especially to the provision by Member States of certain services which are of fundamental importance to the people. Nevertheless, Member States must pursue such activities "as provided in this Treaty", i.e. they must pay due attention to the principles of open markets and undistorted competition. Restrictions of the internal market freedoms cannot be justified unless they are "necessary in order to satisfy mandatory requirements"[1] relating to general, non-economic interests and are consistent with the principle of proportionality. Restrictions of competition may be justified, if they are necessary to guarantee the effective performance of "services of general economic interest" as stipulated in Article 86 (2) EC. From the onset the drafters of the Treaty sought to balance the principles of competition and open markets with the interest of the Member States to provide services which are in the general interest. The new Article 16 EC has not really altered this balance despite its emphasis on "services of general economic interest".

---

[1] Case 120/78 *Rewe* v. *Bundesmonopolverwaltung für Branntwein* ("*Cassis de Dijon*") [1979] *ECR* 649, 662, para. 8.

Article 16 merely confirms the prominent role of such services among the shared values of the Community, however "without prejudice to Articles 73, 86 and 87". Therefore, Article 16 does not introduce additional exemptions from the internal market freedoms or the competition rules. This was expressly recognised by a declaration, adopted at the conference on the Treaty of Amsterdam, which stated that Article 16 shall be implemented "with full respect for the jurisprudence of the Court of Justice".[2]

The Treaty's balance between services of general economic interest and the internal market was not called into question for a long time. Article 295 guarantees the Treaty's neutrality as regards the public or private ownership of means of production. Hardly any legal doubts were raised, when Member States assigned to public or private undertakings monopoly rights that were held to be necessary for the production and distribution of services of general economic interest. Economically, such monopoly rights were justified by the concept of natural monopoly. However, technological changes and new theoretical insights in the theory of market failure as well as State failure challenged these traditional justifications. The reasons put forward in favour of exempting services of general economic interest from the rules of the internal market have lost much of their persuasiveness.

To the extent that arguments in favour of a market-oriented approach to the production and distribution of services of general interest gained an upper hand, the political reasoning behind the distribution of economic activities between States and Markets became apparent. Public services are clearly sources of political power. And it is not surprising that Member States do not want to lose their political influence. Those who adhere to the corporatist Zeitgeist and turn against the so-called "neo-liberal" approach are not always motivated by the welfare of the people but rather by vested interests in the status quo. Be that as it may, from the perspective of Community law Member States are less and less able to avoid due regard to the market freedoms and competition rules to the extent that exemptions from these freedoms and rules are decreasingly plausible.

Another development has also contributed to a certain shift of the responsibility for services of general economic interest away from Member States to the Community: The EC Treaty confers upon the Community the competence to ensure the compatibility of State monopolies with Community law. For this reason it may be necessary to remove national laws that are contrary to Community law. To this extent Community law leads to de-regulation. At the same time it may be necessary for the Community to introduce, by legislative

---

[2] See Declaration No. 13 on Art. 16 [ex Art. 7d] of the Treaty establishing the European Community.

means, Community standards in order to abolish barriers to interstate trade resulting from the divergence of national regulations. Harmonisation of laws then leads to re-regulation on the Community level. To this extent it is the Commission itself that develops criteria for the production and distribution of services which are in the general interest.

In light of these developments it is of special interest that the Commission has made an effort to define its position on the legal, economic and socio-political aspects of the organisation of public services in the Community. After a first Communication of 26 September 1996,[3] the Commission has launched a new Communication on "Services of General Interest in Europe" in September 2000.[4] It is to be welcomed that the Commission discusses all relevant aspects of services of general interest in a very comprehensive framework. Yet, even this Communication lacks systematic structure, suffers from incoherence and is partly incomplete. The following discussion is meant as an attempt to overcome these deficiencies.

The objective of this paper is to systematically analyse the complex issue of services of general interest in the light of the Commission's Communication and against the background of Community law as stipulated in the EC Treaty and developed by the case law of the European Court of Justice. To begin with, the concept of services of general interest as developed by the Commission will be assessed (2); then the relevant rules of Community law will be discussed within the framework of which the production and distribution of such services must be organised (3).

2. The concept of services of general interest

In order to determine the Commission's concept of "services of general interest", it is useful to first understand the Commission's notion of "public service". This term is ambiguous. It refers to the "public" body providing the service, on the one hand, and to the general interest role assigned to the body, on the other.[5] Hence, the Commission distinguishes between public and private services according to their content as well as according to the way they are provided.[6] This distinction is most relevant, since the Commission intends to demonstrate that the difference between services which, on the one hand, are in

---

[3] *OJ* [1996] C 281/3.

[4] Communication from the Commission of 20 September 2000, *COM* (2000) 580 final, *OJ* [2001] C 17/4.

[5] See Annex II of the Communication, *supra* n. 4.

[6] This distinction is drawn from the French concept of *service public*, which has a functional (substantial) as well as an operational dimension.

the general interest, and services which, on the other hand, are in the private interest, is not determined by the way they are provided, but rather by their substance. It is precisely the Commission's objective to find out to what extent services which are in the general interest may and should be provided by private entities. A service, therefore, does not lose its general interest character merely because it is not the State that is providing it and vice versa.

2.1 Substantive characteristics of services of general interest

There is still considerable uncertainty as to what are the substantive characteristics of services of general interest. The Commission itself employs a variety of terms like "services of general economic interest"; "services of general interest" and "universal service". The differences and interdependencies of these terms are far from obvious. A thorough analysis of the Communication reveals the following:

The most general term employed by the Commission to cover all varieties of services rendered in the general interest is the term "*services of general interest*".[7] There is no legal definition of this term in the EC Treaty.[8] Article 16 and Article 86 (2) EC use the term "services of general *economic* interest" which refers to economic goods and services satisfying certain basic needs such as transportation, energy and telecommunication. Yet, there are also services that do not serve economic, but rather *non-economic* interests, linked, e.g., to cultural, social, or environmental objectives. According to the jurisprudence of the ECJ, it is precisely this non-economic nature of a general interest that is relevant in the context of Member States' justification of derogations from the internal market freedoms. Similarly, non-economic activities may be excluded from the application of the competition rules, because the entity which renders such services may then not be regarded as an undertaking within the meaning of Articles 81, 82 and 86 EC.

In sum, the term "services of general interest" as used in the Commission's Communication includes services of an economic as well as non-economic character. The distinction between the economic and non-economic character of services of general interest becomes relevant at a later stage of the analysis as will be considered below.

---

7 See Annex II of the Communication, *supra* n. 3.

8 The term is equivalent neither to the German notion of *Daseinsvorsorge* nor to the French concept of *service public*.

2.2 Organisation of services of general interest

The operational aspect of services of general interest turns on the question whether their production and distribution should be within the responsibility of the State or left to the Market.

The Commission's concept in this regard is based on the assumption that the satisfaction of certain basic needs, undoubtedly of fundamental importance to the people such as the need for food, clothing and housing, may nevertheless well be left to the market.[9] On the other hand, some services are intrinsically prerogatives of the State, notably the provision of internal and external security, the administration of justice, the conduct of foreign relations and other exercise of official authority.[10] The methods employed for the provision of other services of general interest must then be placed somewhere between the "Market" and the "State". Closer scrutiny of the Communication reveals that the Commission has developed three models according to which the production and distribution of such services may be organised:

Model 1
Firstly, public services may be organised in such a way that they are provided by one or several operators offering their services on competitive markets. The role of the State is limited to defining certain qualitative criteria which must be met by the service providers. These criteria reflect the general interest in such services. They are translated into so-called "public (universal) service obligations".[11]

Model 2
Secondly, certain services of general interest do not lend themselves to be provided by a plurality of operators, for instance where only one single provider or a small group of providers would be able to survive economically. To ensure the provision of services of general interest in these circumstances, the State may grant exclusive and special rights to the provider or providers of the service of general interest. These monopoly rights are granted by awarding concessions for limited periods of time. In order not to eliminate competition more than necessary, States should use competitive tendering procedures for the allocation of such monopoly rights.[12]

---

[9] Communication, para. 14.
[10] Communication, para. 28.
[11] Communication, para. 15.
[12] Communication, para. 17.

Model 3
Thirdly, where neither of the first two options allows for the satisfactory safeguard of the general interest in a specific service, it may be necessary for the State to assign the provision of such service to one single operator or a limited number of operators and at the same time grant or maintain special or exclusive rights in favour of the single operator or the group of operators.[13] In this case it may be necessary, therefore, to even waive competitive tender procedures and thus eliminate competition altogether.

The Commission identifies two reasons for applying these specific methods of organising services of general interest. Firstly, some markets have an inherent tendency to allow only one single competitor to survive (market failure in the form of a natural monopoly).[14] Secondly, the very existence of public (universal) service obligations imposed by the State implies that certain services should be provided regardless of whether or not the Market gives sufficient incentives to do so. In this case there is, strictly speaking, no endogenous market failure. Yet, from a non-economical point of view the Market produces sub-optimal results. By imposing upon service providers public (universal) service obligations, the State is forcing these operators to produce positive external effects. This does necessarily lead to financial problems, because the costs of the external effects cannot be covered in a competitive environment. Appropriate funding mechanisms are therefore required in order to compensate operators whose production costs cannot be recovered on the basis of market prices.

If production costs cannot be met, there are three possible sources of finance: firstly, profits generated from other products sold by the respective operator; secondly, profits made by other operators selling other products on the market; or, thirdly, money provided by the State.

The first option leads to internal subsidisation. If a service provider engages in internal subsidisation, he must be able to charge some services with prices higher than those needed to recover the costs, in order to ensure funding of those services which are serving the general interest and are therefore sold below cost. This funding mechanism presupposes that there is no effective price competition. Otherwise, excessive prices could not be sustained. Therefore, it may even be necessary to confer monopoly rights to suppliers of services of general interest in order to enable internal subsidisation. The second option, of funding services of general interest, involves all operators active in the particular market: In favour of the operators charged with public (universal) service

---

[13] Communication, para. 18.
[14] Communication, para. 17.

obligations, the State may levy a special charge or a special contribution to a fund out of which the providers of services of general interest are compensated. The third option involves payment of subsidies out of the State's budget. Besides the granting of special and exclusive rights, the establishment of a funding mechanism is, therefore, in a way the second pillar of the organisation of services of general interest. The funding mechanism cannot be dissociated from the imposition of public (universal) service obligations.

2.3 Criteria for the institutional choice

Member States' choice between the specific methods of organising services of general interest depends on a number of criteria. In order to make this choice, several decisions have to be made:

Firstly, it must be determined whether a specific service is of general interest. In its Communication, the Commission points out that services of general interest must meet certain standards in the interest of consumers, such as:[15]

- Universal access;
- High quality;
- Affordable prices;
- Respect of specific needs of certain categories of the population, such as the handicapped and those on low incomes;
- Complete territorial coverage of essential services in remote or inaccessible areas;
- High level of environmental protection;
- High levels of public health.

It is this profile of qualitative requirements in the interest of consumers which, in substance, determines the general interest in a specific service. Which services may legitimately be subject to such requirements, remains an open question at this point, however.

Secondly, the State must determine whether or not competitive markets are able to ensure the meeting of these qualitative requirements. As outlined above, the Commission recognises that there are certain basic services which may well be provided by markets and where the State would not be justified to interfere in the organisation of the provision of such services. Only where it can be established that pure competition does not provide sufficient incentives to meet these

[15] Communication, paras. 8 et seq.

requirements and where markets would not lead to acceptable results should Member States be free to opt for one of the three models outlined above.

Thirdly, the State must then determine which model to apply. In its Communication, the Commission indicates a number of principles that should determine this choice:[16]

- Efficiency;
- Transparency, particularly regarding tariffs and financing of providers;
- Effective competition between suppliers;
- Freedom of choice of consumers;
- Independence of regulatory bodies.

Furthermore, the Commission recognises that the institutional choice may depend on the following factors:

- Technical and economic characteristics of the service in question;
- Specific requirements of users;
- Cultural and historical traditions in the Member State concerned.

Those matters mentioned above which are intrinsically prerogatives of the State do not fit into this scheme, since they are *a priori* left entirely to the State.

3. Legal framework

The objective of the following discussion is to determine the legal restrictions imposed by Community law on Member States' choices regarding the contents and the organisation of services of general interest. Firstly, it will be assessed how Community law constrains Member States' freedom to define what they regard as services of general interest (3.1). Secondly, it will be examined how Community law determines Member States' decisions as to how services of general interest should be provided (3.2). Finally, it will be analysed how Community law controls the activities of service providers (3.3).

3.1 Legal control of Member States' freedom of definition

As has already been emphasised, the term "services of general interest" is unknown to Community law. Article 86 (2) and Article 16 EC both refer to

---

[16] Communication, paras. 11, 13.

"services of general economic interest". This terminology implies two distinctions: firstly, there is a difference between services rendered in the *general interest* and those rendered in an *individual interest*; secondly, there is a distinction between *economic services* and *non-economic services*. Both distinctions will be assessed separately in the light of the constraints imposed by Community law on Member States' sovereign powers to apply these concepts.

3.1.1 *Distinction between general and individual interests*

Member States are primarily responsible for defining what they regard as services of *general interest*. This principle is consistent with Article 5 (1) EC which stipulates that the Community shall only act within the powers conferred upon it by the Treaty. It has also been emphasised by the Commission in its Communication.[17] Furthermore, Article 86 (2) EC presumes that Member States are also primarily responsible for entrusting undertakings with the task of providing services of general interest. By entrusting an undertaking with the operation of services of general interest, a Member State defines the nature and the scope of the general interest to be served. Consequently, the general interest is primarily defined according to the national public interest of Member States. Each Member State decides in accordance with its preferences whether a service is to be provided as a private matter or a matter of general interest.

However, Member States' freedom to define services of general interest is also constrained by Community law. Whereas the national public interest served by a specific service may, pursuant to Article 86 (2) EC, under certain conditions prevail over Community law, the prevalence must necessarily be determined according to the same criteria for all Member States alike. This follows from the principle of equal application of Community law in the Member States as developed in the case law of the European Court of Justice. For this reason, any reference to Member States' long standing traditions of *service public* (France) or *Daseinsvorsorge* (Germany) is beside the point. Therefore, the *general interest* cannot be defined exclusively by the Member States. Services which clearly and entirely serve *individual interests* and which may well be subject to the competitive forces of markets cannot be regarded as services of general interest. As a matter of Community law, such services cannot be excluded from the application of the internal market freedoms and the competition rules. Otherwise, the limits to the exemption provided by Article 86 (2), first sentence, of the EC Treaty could be made meaningless by the Member States.

The Commission's Communication contains at least some indication as to how Member States should determine the general interest character of a service.

[17] Communication, para. 22.

As outlined above, services of general interest have to satisfy a number of standards in order to meet the needs of users. These standards yield some guidance for the definition of the general interest character of a service. However, these criteria are far too vague to be used as yardsticks for the legality or illegality of Member States' decisions. Therefore, it is very unlikely that the European Court of Justice will be able to exercise judicial control on the basis of these criteria. Not surprisingly, the Court has never dismissed a Member State's contention as regards the general interest of a service. On the contrary: The Court held explicitly that Member States may use undertakings as "an instrument of economic or fiscal policy",[18] even to the detriment of the unity of the common market and the system of undistorted competition. This judicial self-restraint leaves Member States a wide margin for shaping their policies, in particular for deciding what constitutes a service of general interest.

Yet, at the same time the Court has made it very clear that the scope of monopoly rights conferred by Member States upon certain undertakings in order to ensure the provision of services of general interest may be considerably constrained by the rules relating to the control of abuses of dominant positions (Art. 82 EC). In *RTT/GB-Inno-BM* the Court held that the elimination or restriction of competition on the market for telephone equipment cannot be justified by simply defining the distribution of such equipment as a service of general interest. Production and distribution of telephone equipment was held to be an economic activity that should be open to any undertaking. In order to ensure that the equipment meets the essential safety requirements, the Court held it sufficient to lay down specifications which the said equipment must meet.[19] Consequently, services may not be declared to be of general interest, if it is obvious, that the Market itself is able to properly serve consumers' needs by offering them the sufficient volume of products at adequate prices and high technical quality as specified by regulation. Therefore, although Member States enjoy large discretion in defining services of general interest, they are subject to control by the Court with regard to manifest errors.

3.1.2 *Distinction between economic and non-economic services*

From the perspective of Community law, the distinction between *economic* and *non-economic* activities is also of fundamental importance. The internal market freedoms as well as the competition rules are applicable to economic activities only.

---

[18] Case C-202/88 *France* v. *Commission* [1991] *ECR* I-1223, 1263, para. 12; Case C-157/94 *Commission* v. *Netherlands* [1997] *ECR* I-5699, 5779, para. 39.

[19] Case C-18/88 *RTT* v. *SA GB-Inno-BM* [1991] *ECR* I-5941, 5980 et seq., para. 22.

Therefore, Member States are exclusively competent to decide how to organise non-economic services. They may freely opt for providing non-economic services as private or public services, and for or against using competitive markets. However, once Member States engage in economic activity and act like undertakings, they are, as a matter of Community law, subject to the same rules of the game as private undertakings. This is the whole purpose of Article 86 EC which provides for the application of the internal market freedoms as well as of the competition rules, including the rules on state aid, to public undertakings and to services of general economic interest. Member States cannot simply escape from the application of Community law by declaring economic services to be of a non-economic nature.

As far as the freedoms of the internal market are concerned, the Court often had to distinguish between economic activities and matters that are intrinsically prerogatives of the State. This distinction is of particular relevance for the free movement of persons (Art. 39 (4) and Art. 45 EC) and the free movement of services (Art. 55 in connection with Art. 45 EC). According to the Treaty, these freedoms do not apply to activities that are connected with the exercise of official authority. In theory, Member States could attempt to declare any activity to be connected with the exercise of official authority in order to circumvent the application of the provisions. Yet, the Court strongly objects to such efforts. Therefore, the Court has given the concept of "exercise of official authority" (Art. 45 EC) an autonomous interpretation, i.e. an interpretation exclusively based on Community law. The point of reference is not a Member State's own definition, but the nature of the activity. The dominant consideration is whether the activity involves "direct or indirect participation in the exercise of powers conferred by public law and duties designed to safeguard the general interests of the State".[20] As far as the traditional prerogatives of the State are concerned – such as ensuring internal and external security, the administration of justice and the conduct of foreign relations – Member States' freedom of definition is not constrained by Community law. Outside this sphere of traditional prerogatives, however, Member States have to give good reasons why an activity should to be connected with the exercise of official authority and should thus be excluded from the application of internal market freedoms.

The distinction between economic and non-economic interests is important when it comes to justify restrictions of the freedoms of movement, in particular restrictions on trade between Member States. Such restrictions may, in particular, be caused by Member States' regulation of services of general interest. They can normally be justified by the protection of *non-economic* general

[20] Case 149/79 *Commission* v. *Belgium* [1980] *ECR* 3881, 3900 para. 10.

interests, provided they meet the proportionality test.[21] Such interests are, e.g., the protection of public health, the environment, national treasures possessing artistic, historic or archaeological value and consumer protection. Economic policy or any other economic objective can never justify derogations from the internal market freedoms. The unity of the internal market is not at the Member States' disposal.

In the context of the competition rules, the distinction between *economic* and *non-economic* activities is crucial for the determination of whether or not an entity is to be treated as an undertaking. This determination is especially relevant for the application of Article 86 (2) EC. It is therefore important to know how Community law controls Member States in their discretion to define the *economic* or *non-economic* nature of certain activities. The ECJ has always stressed that in this context also it will control Member States' discretion by applying objective criteria developed under Community law. The Court has held, for example, that services provided by public employment agencies (the case at hand involved head hunting activities) may constitute an economic activity, since such services may be equally well provided by private undertakings.[22] On the other hand, the Court held that compulsory social security schemes, which are based on the principle of solidarity and where the benefits paid are not proportional to the amount of the compulsory contributions, fulfil an exclusively social function and do not involve the exercise of an economic activity.[23] Similarly, national education may be excluded from the application of Community law to the extent that it is organised as a not-for-profit activity.[24] At first sight this criterion could have been equally applied to the services provided by employment agencies. However, it may be argued that in the case of national education schemes social and cultural objectives prevail: its services are often provided freely to guarantee equal access, i.e. access regardless of the financial ability of the users. This reasoning does not apply to employment agencies. One generally applicable criterion for the distinction between *economic* and *non-economic* services may be derived from the Court's case law: it is crucial whether or not the objective of the service may be equally well achieved by transactions for remuneration.

---

[21] Case 120/78 *Rewe* v. *Bundesmonopolverwaltung für Branntwein* ("*Cassis de Dijon*") [1979] *ECR* 649, 662, para. 8.

[22] Case C-41/90 *Höfner and Elser* v. *Macrotron GmbH* [1991] *ECR* I-1979, 2016, para. 22.

[23] Joined Cases C-159/91 and C-160/91 *Poucet and Pistre* v. *AGF and Cancava* [1993] *ECR* I-637, 670, paras. 18 et seq.

[24] This conclusion may be drawn form Case C-263/86 *Belgian State* v. *Humbel* [1988] *ECR* 5365, 5388, para. 18. Even though this case dealt with the concept of "services" according to Art. 50 EC, it also has implications for the concept of "undertaking" in Art. 86 EC, which is generally defined in terms of *economic* activities.

3.1.3 *Summary*

The Community institutions tightly supervise Member States as regards the distinction between economic and non-economic activities. Member States cannot easily escape from the application of Community law by formally declaring economic activities to be of a non-economic nature. At the same time Member States enjoy broad discretion to define what they regard as services of general interest. These decisions are only subject to limited control by the Court. In the language of the Commission's Communication: Member States' definition "can only be subject to control for manifest error".[25] Consequently, Member States do not have to prove any market failure. Criteria derived from the economic theory of markets and competition are hardly relevant. In sum, Member States' definition of services of general interest, as well as their imposition of public service obligations, are subject to a relatively superficial control of apparent mistakes only. It can be doubted whether this interpretation of the first sentence of Article 86 (2) EC is really doing justice to the Treaty provision. The consequence of the ECJ's rather lenient approach is that the Member States themselves may, to a large degree, strike a political balance between market oriented and corporatist structures in the Community and that the Community's economic constitution is based on legal rules to a lesser degree than it should be.

Nevertheless, Member States' discretion and the prevalence of national interests are not unlimited. According to the second sentence of Article 86 (2) EC, "the development of trade must not be affected to such an extent as would be contrary to the interests of the Community." Hence, national economic interests, on the one hand, have to be balanced against the Community's interest in open markets and undistorted competition, on the other. This balance is supervised by the Court. Yet, it was the Court that imposed the burden of proof on the Commission.[26] It is therefore the Commission's responsibility to prove whether the interests of the Community are violated or not. This is not an easy task. Whereas it may be relatively simple to demonstrate discrimination on grounds of nationality, the high standards of proof set by the Court cannot easily be satisfied in other cases. The Court held the Commission responsible for defining the interests of the Community in more detail in directives and decisions. To the extent the Commission would do so, the Court seems prepared to exercise a more stringent control over Member States. Therefore, the Commission has considerable impact on determining to which extent

[25] Communication, para. 22.

[26] Case C-157/94 *Commission* v. *Netherlands* [1997] *ECR* I-5699, 5786, paras. 66 et seq.; Case C-159/94 *Commission* v. *France* [1997] *ECR* I-5815, 5847 et seq., paras. 109 et seq.

Community law limits Member States' freedom to define what constitutes a service of general interest.

3.2 Legal control of the operation of services of general interest

The following discussion is aimed at an assessment of legal controls imposed by Community law on Member States' decisions as to how services of general interest should be operated.

3.2.1 *Principle of Member States' discretion*

It follows from the foregoing that Member States enjoy discretion in several respects:

- As far as non-economic services are concerned, Member States are generally unconstrained in their institutional choice regarding the operation of such services; however, any negative effects on the internal market freedoms must meet the proportionality test;
- As far as economic services are concerned, Member States enjoy large discretion regarding the determination of the general interest character of specific services by subjecting their providers to "public (universal) service obligations". This discretion is subject to control for manifest errors only;
- Once Member States have determined a specific service to be of general interest, they are free to decide whether the bodies responsible for providing the general interest services should be public or private undertakings. This principle is referred to by the Commission in its Communication as the principle of "neutrality" enshrined in Article 86 (2) EC. It should be noticed that this provision does not require privatisation of public undertakings. Neutrality of Community law as regards the public or private ownership of undertakings is also guaranteed by Article 295 EC.

3.2.2 *Limits to Member States' discretion*

Article 86 (2) EC constrains Member States in two ways: Firstly, it affects the way "special or exclusive rights" are assigned to suppliers of economic services of general interest (3.2.2.1). Secondly, the principle of proportionality enshrined in Article 86 (2) EC constrains Member States' choice of how services of general interest should be operated. Hence, it affects the choice between the three models developed, as outlined above, by the Commission in its Communication (3.2.2.2).

3.2.2.1 "Particular tasks " assigned by the State

According to the case law of the Court, "particular tasks" must be explicitly assigned to an undertaking through an act of public authority. According to the Commission's Communication, this requirement is necessary to ensure legal certainty as well as transparency.[27] Moreover, this requirement has been imposed for more fundamental reasons and it is crucial for the understanding of the entire system of exemptions enshrined in Article 86 (2) EC: Since all undertakings to which "particular tasks" are assigned equally benefit from these exemptions, the exemptions are reserved to activities which are not based on purely commercial decisions taken by the undertakings, i.e. to activities for which the undertakings themselves cannot be held responsible. On the other hand, in order to justify an exemption from market freedoms and competition rules it is not sufficient that the relevant general interest is merely expressed in general laws (e.g. environmental protection laws), which all undertakings have to follow and must therefore be regarded as the general legal framework within which undertakings have to compete anyway. The fact that a specific act of public authority is required for assigning a "particular task" is, therefore, justified by the consideration that the behaviour of the undertakings exempted by Article 86 (2) EC must be forced upon them by specific State interference with the production and distribution of goods and services and must not be the result of ordinary market forces within the framework of general laws. In other words, Article 86 (2) EC applies only where the State uses undertakings as instruments to achieve outcomes which would not be achieved under normal market conditions within the general legal framework.

The criteria outlined above, which determine, according to the Commission, the general interest character of a service, may, therefore, be understood in the present context as defining the "public (universal) interest obligations" necessary for the fulfilment of the "particular tasks" assigned to undertakings by an act of public authority. Accordingly, the Court held in one of the *Electricity* cases that, "for obligations imposed on an undertaking entrusted with the operation of services of general economic interest to be regarded as falling within the particular tasks entrusted to it, they must be linked to the subject-matter of the service of general interest in question and designed to make a direct contribution to satisfying that interest."[28] The Court added that this could not apply to general obligations regarding the environment and regional policy. Consequently, Article 86 (2) EC is not meant to exempt entire sectors of the economy, in particular regulated industries, from the application of Community

[27] Communication, para. 22.
[28] Case C- 159/94 *Commission* v *France* [1997] *ECR* I-5815, 5837, para. 68.

law. Rather an exemption depends on a specific act of public authority which expresses the State's specific preference for public interests to the detriment of the interests of the undertaking.[29]

3.2.2.2 Proportionality of market restriction and fulfilment of "particular tasks"

Article 86 (2) EC ensures that exemptions from Community law do not exceed what is necessary to guarantee effective fulfilment, in law or in fact, of the "particular tasks" assigned to an undertaking. It also stipulates that the means used to fulfil the general interest mission must not affect the development of trade to an extent that would be contrary to the interests of the Community. Thus, Article 86 (2) of the Treaty demands a double control of proportionality. This section will first outline some general aspects of the proportionality test (a). Subsequently and based on this analysis, the models of organisation as envisaged by the Commission in its Communication will be assessed (b).

(a) General considerations

According to the Commission's Communication, Member States have the choice between three models to operate their (economic) services of general interest. Each model restricts competition and limits the freedoms of the internal market to a different extent. It is thus necessary to assess the proportionality of the respective model on a case by case basis. As a general rule, Member States have to chose the model which interferes to the smallest extent possible with the freedoms of the internal market and the competition rules.

The most important elements of all three models are the public (universal) service obligations, eventually exclusive and special rights granted to one or several suppliers, and certain funding mechanisms. If services are to be rendered in the general interest, public (universal) interest obligations are crucial. The determination of such obligations implies the definition of those externalities and collective goods which a Member State considers desirable and necessary for the users but which cannot be provided by market forces. Public (universal) service obligations have to be consistent with the principle of proportionality enshrined in Article 86 (2) EC. Therefore, the specific public service obligation has to be an appropriate means of achieving the envisaged objective. In addition, the public service obligation should not exceed what is

---

[29] See for a more detailed discussion Mestmäcker, in: Immenga/Mestmäcker (Hrsg.), *EG-Wettbewerbsrecht – Kommentar* [*EC Competition Law – Commentary*], Vol. II (1997), Art. 90 (2), paras. 31 et seq.

necessary to guarantee effective fulfilment of the mission. Here again reference may be made to one of the *Electricity* cases where the Court held that "for obligations imposed on an undertaking entrusted with the operation of services of general economic interest to be regarded as falling within the particular tasks entrusted to it, they must be linked to the subject-matter of the service of general interest in question and designed to make a direct contribution to satisfying that interest."[30]

A good example to demonstrate the impact of the legal control of Member States is the directive on telecommunications terminal equipment.[31] This directive was issued by the Commission on the basis of Article 86 (3) EC. The directive recognises that the Market is a better mechanism for providing telecommunications terminal equipment than any operation as a service of general interest. Similarly, the Commission has qualified other public (universal) service obligations to be contrary to Community law – for example the obligation to provide for a complete territorial coverage of voice telephony services.[32] The Commission's efforts to liberalise and deregulate certain sectors of the economy by means of directives reflect in a way a general application of the proportionality test to Member States' imposition of public (universal) service obligations.

This contention is consistent with the aforementioned conclusion that Member States enjoy large discretion to define services of general interest, only subject to control by the Court for manifest error. The Court has charged the Commission with finding more specific definitions by means of directives and decisions. Until now the Commission has mainly liberalised alleged "natural monopolies" whose economic justification could not be upheld any more because of technical developments. In these cases proportionality can be applied along the line of clear economic standards. General service obligations are, however, imposed also for political reasons. In these cases, application of the proportionality test by the Court and the Commission is much more difficult as was illustrated in the *Electricity* cases decided by the Court in 1997.[33] According to the Commission, the "particular tasks" could have also been fulfilled, if they were subject to market forces. However, the ECJ refrained from examining whether the anti-competitive methods employed in the cases before the Court did not exceed what was necessary to satisfy the users' needs for

---

[30] Case C- 159/94 *Commission* v. *France* [1997] *ECR* I-5815, 5837, para. 68.

[31] Commission Directive 88/301/EEC of 16 May 1988 on Competition in the Markets in Telecommunications Terminal Equipment (*OJ* [1988] L 131/73).

[32] Commission Directive 96/19/EC of 13 March 1996 amending Directive 90/388/EEC with regard to the implementation of full competition in telecommunications markets (*OJ* [1996] L 74/13).

[33] See *supra* n. 30.

electricity. Instead, the Court limited itself to examining whether the application of Community law would jeopardise the specific method of providing services of general interest chosen by the Member States in question.[34] In addition, the Court charged the Commission with the burden of proof.

(b) The three models

In order to provide services of general interest, the State may chose between the three models. When doing so, the Member States have to take into consideration whether the chosen model satisfies the standards of proportionality. Unfortunately, the Commission's Communication is not as specific on this account as one would wish, but limits itself to rather general and broad guidelines. Nevertheless, the following may be said:

Model 1

If public authorities decide, according to the first model, to apply general interest obligations on all, or on a limited number of operators on a market without granting special or exclusive rights, the issue of funding mechanisms, installed or supported by the State may give rise to particular concerns with regard to proportionality. According to the Court in *Corbeau*[35], suppliers charged with public service obligations must be able to fulfil their obligations under "economically acceptable conditions". In principle, this is only possible, if suppliers are allowed to pass on their additional costs to consumers by increasing prices. Yet, charging higher prices may not be possible, either because the Market does not support higher prices than those necessary to cover production costs, or because the State has fixed price ceilings to make the products or services affordable to low income consumers. If this is the case, suppliers have to be compensated. In order to finance the net extra costs of the service of general interest, the State may install a public service fund or subsidise the supplier.

A public service fund solution involves all operators active in a certain relevant market in the financing of the net extra costs of the service of general interest. Those competitors who are not charged with public (universal) service obligations have to contribute to the public service fund out of which the

---

[34] Case C-157/94 *Commission* v. *Netherlands* [1997] *ECR* I-5699, 5780 and 5782 et seq., paras. 43 and 51-65; Case C-159/94 *Commission* v. *France* [1997] *ECR* I-5815, 5832 and 5843 et seq., paras. 45 and 94-108; critical Mestmäcker, "Grenzen staatlicher Monopole im EG-Vertrag" [*Limits to State Monopolies in the EC Treaty*], in: FIW, "Erfahrungen mit der Privatisierung von Monopolunternehmen" [*Experiences with the Privatization of Monoplistic Undertakings*], *Referate des XXXII. FIW-Symposiums, FIW-Schriftenreihe*, Heft 179 (1999) 71, 82.

[35] Case C-320/91 *Corbeau* [1993] *ECR* I-2533, 2569, para. 16.

providers of the service are compensated. If competitors from other Member States are asked to contribute to the fund, the obligation to do so may violate the internal market freedoms. On the other hand, if a State opts for subsidising providers of services of general interest with taxpayer's money, such subsidies may be contrary to the rules on State aid.

Within the framework of Article 86 (2) EC, limitations of the internal market freedoms as well as derogations from the prohibition of subsidies are subject to review for proportionality. The Member States' choice of an adequate funding mechanism is therefore constrained, because compensation of service providers must not exceed what is necessary to guarantee effective fulfilment of the general interest mission. Points of reference are the net extra costs. Suppliers charged with public (universal) service obligations may attempt to artificially boost their net extra costs. Yet, competitive markets may not leave the suppliers much leeway for doing so. In any case, subsidies and contributions levied on competitors in excess of net extra costs, cannot be justified in light of the proportionality test and are therefore unlawful. If competitors are asked to contribute to public service funds, the share borne by each undertaking should be proportionate to its activity on the market and be clearly separated from other charges that it may bear in the normal exercise of its activities.[36]

Model 2

If Member States decide to grant exclusive and special rights to suppliers of services of general interest, they should, according to the second model, do so through tendering procedures or auctions. By conferring monopoly rights to service suppliers, Member States prevent actual or potential competitors from entering the market. According to the principle of proportionality, such market foreclosure must be necessary and appropriate for the fulfilment of the general interest obligations.

Exclusion of competitors from the market may be necessary for two reasons: firstly, the relevant market for the respective service of general interest may display an inherent tendency towards a monopolistic structure (natural monopoly); secondly, the effective provision of the service of general interest may require an adequate funding of the additional costs involved in the fulfilment of the general interest obligations.

In case of natural monopolies – which are, for instance, typical for certain infrastructure networks – the legal exclusion of competition is normally justified by the assumption that it would be a waste of scarce resources, if competition were allowed. If there really is a natural tendency towards monopoly in the market, actual and potential suppliers would engage in fierce

[36] Communication, para. 15.

competition which would anyway lead to the survival of only one of them. However, this reasoning is only persuasive where market entry barriers are low and potential competitors are able to offer better prices because of cheaper production costs. If this is the case, competition for the monopoly may indeed enhance general welfare, because one would expect the most efficient supplier to survive. If, however, market entry barriers are high because of large sunk costs, natural monopolies are difficult to attack anyway. In that case, a legal monopoly may not be necessary to protect the natural monopoly. Consequently, purely economic reasons based on natural monopoly considerations are barely capable of justifying the granting of monopoly rights to suppliers of services of general interest.

Yet, States may have other non-economic reasons to prevent suppliers' competition for the monopolistic position in the market: This may be justified, for instance, where such competition would lead to the depletion of resources that cannot be recovered, like the natural environment in case of roads or telecommunication networks. However, even where this is so, competition for the monopolistic position in the market needs not to be eliminated altogether; it is normally at least possible to auction away monopoly rights for a limited period of time. Such tendering procedures are explicitly referred to in the Commission's Communication.

Besides natural monopoly considerations, there may be other justifications for the granting of monopoly rights which are related to the financing of suppliers' additional costs resulting from the fulfilment of general interest obligations. In order to put the supplier of a service of general interest in the position to be able to internally subsidise the non-profitable services out of the revenues derived from profitable activities, the State may have to prevent competitors from concentrating exclusively on the profitable activities (cream skimming). This issue is of particular relevance with regard to public (universal) service obligations aimed at complete accessibility of the service everywhere in the whole national territory (including remote areas) and/or for the whole population (including people with low income).

As mentioned above, restrictions of the internal market freedoms triggered by monopoly rights are subject to the proportionality test. This test may either be exercised along the lines of the general exemptions from the freedoms of the internal market developed by the ECJ, or along the standards set by Article 86 (2) EC. According to the first alternative, restrictions can only be justified, if they satisfy mandatory requirements of non-economic nature, whereas the standards set in Article 86 (2) EC refer to the general economic interests served by the "special tasks" in question. According to the case law of the Court, the review for proportionality is to be exercised along the lines of Article 86 (2) EC. In the *Electricity* Cases the Court concluded that the wording of Article 86 (2) EC showed, that "exemptions to the Treaty rules are permitted provided that they are necessary for the performance of the particular task assigned to an undertaking entrusted with the operation of a service of general economic interest."[37] The Court therefore concluded, that it was sufficient if "the application of those rules obstruct the performance, in law or in fact, of the special obligations incumbent upon that undertaking."[38] It was not necessary to prove that the survival of the undertaking itself was threatened. Subsequently, the Court charged the Commission with issuing appropriate directives and decisions to define the Community interest in relation to which the development of trade must be assessed and which marks the bottom line of the proportionality test.

In theory, the justification of monopoly rights according to the principle of proportionality enshrined in Article 86 (2) EC requires proof that there is no appropriate solution available which would interfere less with the internal market freedoms and the competition rules. Therefore, it should be examined whether the "particular task" assigned to the supplier could also be funded without granting monopoly rights but rather by some kind of a public service fund according to the first model. Although the Commission had argued that proportionality should be assessed in such a way, the Court has explicitly refused to do so in the *Electricity* cases. The Court expressly stated that it was not in a position to consider whether the specific solution chosen by the Member State interfered more or less with Community law than an alternative hypothetical solution.[39] Instead, the Court reduced its control to examining whether the application of Community law would jeopardise the operation of the regulatory system set up by the Member State. This judicial self-restraint clearly implies a considerable shift of emphasis in the Court's control of Members States at the expense of the internal market freedoms and the competition rules. In this situation, the Commission's task to constrain Member States by issuing directives and decisions according to Article 86 (3) EC becomes extremely important.

Model 3

If Member States decide to apply the third model, competition is eliminated not only by the granting of monopoly rights but also because potential suppliers don't even have to compete for these rights in an auction or tendering procedure. Again, whether or not this additional elimination of competition may satisfy the standards of proportionality according to Article 86 (2) EC, must be examined in light of the specific general interest mission. Yet, the Court

---

[37] Case C-157/94 *Commission* v. *Netherlands* [1997] *ECR* I-5699, 5779, para. 38; Case C-159/94 *Commission* v. *France* [1997] *ECR* I-5815, 5834, para. 54.

[38] Case C-157/94 *Commission* v. *Netherlands* [1997] *ECR* I-5769, 5780, para. 43; see also Case C- 159/94 *Commission* v. *France* [1997] *ECR* I-5815, 5832, para. 45.

[39] Case C-157/94 *Commission* v. *Netherlands* [1997] *ECR* I-5699, 5785, paras. 63 et seq.; Case C-159/94 *Commission* v. *France* [1997] *ECR* I-5815, 5846 et seq., paras. 106 et seq.

is likely to exercise judicial self-restraint in these matters as well. Likewise, it would be the Commission's responsibility to use its power to issue directives and decisions conferred to it by Article 86 (3) EC.

3.3 Legal control of undertakings' market behaviour

Even if Member States are justified in conferring public (universal) service obligations and in granting suppliers specific and exclusive rights, the respective undertakings themselves are not allowed to operate in the markets as they like. The competition rules (Arts. 81 and 82 EC) continue to control market behaviour which is not justified by the fulfilment of the general interest obligations. This assessment may be subject to change with time and technological development, and thus needs to be made continuously.

Article 81 (1) EC prohibits horizontal and vertical restrictions of competition as regards price, quality, quantity etc. It is hardly imaginable that the exemption in Article 86 (2) EC exceeds the exemption in Article 81 (3) EC. Suppliers charged with public (universal) service obligations are therefore also bound to avoid horizontal and vertical restraints of competition which are prohibited and not exempted. Therefore, suppliers of services of general interest will not be able, for instance, to fund their net extra costs by price cartels. Neither price cartels nor any other type of anti-competitive agreement may be justified by public (universal) service obligations.

Article 82 prohibits the abuse of a dominant position. This applies also to monopoly undertakings subject to public (universal) service obligations. To the extent that the State excludes competitors from the market by conferring monopoly rights, suppliers enjoying such legal monopolies cannot possibly abuse their dominance by obstructing competitors. Yet, the scope of the monopoly rights is subject to control by the Court. According to the case law of the Court, an undertaking is abusing its dominant position, if it extends its right to exclude competitors to markets on which the undertaking is in fact not active.[40] Likewise, Member States are not allowed to force monopoly undertakings to engage in abusive behaviour or to create a situation where such undertakings cannot avoid abuses of their market dominance.[41] It is from this perspective that the Court already controls the very act of granting exclusive and special rights to undertakings. This is of particular interest for suppliers who produce and distribute products which are dependent upon a certain infrastructure also covered by the monopoly. Where production and distribution of goods and

---

[40] Case C-41/90 *Höfner and Elser* v. *Macrotron GmbH* [1991] *ECR* I-1979, 2018, para. 31; Case C-18/88 *RTT* v. *SA GB-Inno-BM* [1991] *ECR* I-5941, 5979 et seq., paras. 17 et seq.

[41] Case C-41/90 *Höfner and Elser* v. *Macrotron GmbH* [1991] *ECR* I-1979, 2017, para. 27; Case C-18/88 *RTT* v. *SA GB-Inno-BM* [1991] *ECR* I-5941, 5980, para. 21.

services may well be left to the market mechanism, the scope of the monopoly must be reduced to the infrastructure in order to avoid an abusive extension of the monopoly. In addition, the supplier himself may not exercise control over the market entry of his competitors. Market entry rights have to be supervised by entities independent of the supplier in question.

Monopoly undertakings are prone to all types of abuses by exploiting their customers, in particular by charging excessive prices. The Court held that Member States must not oblige undertakings to demand unfair or excessive prices.[42] Also, monopolists may not restrict competition in neighbouring markets by predatory pricing or by internal cross-subsidisation of products or services out of revenues derived from the monopoly.

4. Conclusion

The recent Communication of the Commission on "Services of General Interest in Europe"[43] discusses the critical relationship between public services and open and competitive markets in the Community in a very broad context. Also, the Commission takes a very fundamental view regarding the relationship between States and Markets in the Community. An in-depth analysis of the Communication reveals that the Commission recognises the fundamental importance of a proper balance between the internal market freedoms and the competition rules, on the one hand, and the politically determined structure of Member States' economic systems, especially their national public services, on the other. Where the line between the two should be drawn is an extremely difficult question. Nevertheless, it cannot be resolved on purely political considerations. It must be treated as a question of Community law to be resolved on the basis of Article 86 (2) EC. Therefore, the criteria to be used for the determination of the relationship between national public services and the internal market are basically legal criteria subject to review by the Court of Justice. As regards these criteria, the Commission is unfortunately vague in its Communication. Admittedly, this is partly the responsibility of the Court that has increasingly practised a considerable degree of judicial self-restraint. Further discussion is clearly needed and should be directed towards clarifying the different legal approaches available for controlling Member States in their desire to organise public services (services of general interest) on the national level. This would be in the interest of equal chances for all economic actors in the Community.

---

[42] Case C-30/87 *Bodson* v. *Pompes funèbres des régions libérées* [1988] *ECR* 2479, 2516, para. 33.

[43] *Supra* n. 4.

Federalism and Corporate Litigation

Richard Buxbaum*

1. Introduction

It is moving on towards half a century now since Mestmäcker's *Verwaltung, Konzerngewalt und Rechte der Aktionäre* appeared.[1] It was among the first significant postwar studies of modern corporation law in a comparative context[2] and one that productively used his comparative mastery of American law in

---

* Professor of Law, School of Law (Boalt Hall), University of California, Berkeley.

[1] (Karlsruhe 1958).

[2] I include Ballerstedt, *Kapital, Gewinn und Ausschüttung bei Kapitalgesellschaften* (Tübingen 1949) and Wiethölter, *Interessen und Organisation der Aktiengesellschaft im amerikanischen und deutschen Recht* (Karlsruhe 1961) in this first cohort. A somewhat later but fully comparative work to add here is Großfeld, *Aktiengesellschaft, Unternehmenskonzentration und Kleinaktionär* (Tübingen 1968).

Talia Einhorn, ed., Spontaneous Order, Organization and the Law – Liber Amicorum Ernst-Joachim Mestmäcker © 2003 T.M.C.Asser press, The Hague, The Netherlands

ways that in turn were influential in shaping the terms of reference for the 1965 reform of the *Aktiengesetz*. Two topics dominated his study: the treatment of conflict-of-interests transactions by managers and controlling shareholders, and the application of appropriate principles of corporation law to the affiliated-enterprise system, the *Konzern*. On both counts the book repays reading today; at the same time, because of the clarity of its conception and organization, it encourages the reader to reflect on what a *Habilitand* of today might bring back from a similar intellectual voyage.[3]

The subject that soon thereafter began and still continues to engage MESTMÄCKER; namely, the relationship of state to federal legal regimes, was less apparent in 1958, even if the coincidental timing of the book's publication with the coming into effect of the Treaty of Rome might be worth noting. There is one exception to this comment, however, and it is the subject of this short presentation.

2. THE DIVISION OF POWERS IN COMPANY AND CAPITAL-MARKET LAW

The difficult relationship of a federal capital-market regime and a state company-law one was already identified by MESTMÄCKER in that early work; in particular, in his treatment of the interplay in US law between federal securities regulation and state norms regarding the duties of directors and controlling shareholders. What might in simplified terms have been regarded as a clean separation – that state norms bear on the misuse of power, federal ones on the misuse of information – never was a clear borderline. It became irretrievably blurred when friendly mergers and hostile takeovers challenged both the state and the federal strands of the American legal regime. In a variety of ways this situation now is developing within the European Community and its member states as well, in both substantive- and private-international-law terms.[4] Now,

---

[3] There is no shortage of good studies of current vintage. Major explanatory texts such as Merkt, *US-amerikanisches Gesellschaftsrecht* (Heidelberg 1991) and, despite its narrow title, Bungert, *Das Recht ausländischer Kapitalgesellschaften auf Gleichbehandlung im deutschen und US-Amerikanischen Recht* (Munich 1994) have kept the German reader abreast of US corporation-law developments across the board. There also have been any number of sectoral studies of fields such as mergers and takeovers.

[4] See, e.g., Ebke, "Company Law and the European Union: Centralized Versus Decentralized Lawmaking", 31 *International Lawyer* (1997) 961.

with the (perhaps only temporary) failure of the Community to enact its version of the Williams Act into law, the politics of company and capital-market law reform have moved into public view. Indeed, some of the responses of national governments to the new salience of corporate governance in this era of corporate consolidation, such as the very creation let alone the statement of mission of the *Regierungskommission* of the Federal Republic, openly reflect this political fact of life.

One element of this political substratum of the federal-state division of powers is featured in the following discussion. It is presented as a cautionary tale, not as a prediction of European developments let alone a model for them.

2.1 **Federal-state division of powers in the litigation context**

The particular facet that is the focus of this paper is not corporate governance norms as such, but their enforcement by means of private litigation. Obviously, there are limits to the value of such a review. The US practice of contingent-fee litigation, the predominance of the class action, the pretrial and trial processes themselves – these systemic particularities are not found on the German or even the European side, yet they are the principal reasons for the recent US developments discussed below. Nevertheless, while both the nature of the causes of action and the methods of their implementation differ, some convergence is occurring, and with that partial convergence some value to their comparative evaluation. The Report of the *Regierungskommission* entertains the possibility of increasing the opportunities for litigation by dissident shareholders over a variety of issues, ranging from the quality of the information provided to the Shareholders' Meeting as the basis for its decisions to the misuse of information in the context of merger decisions to the issue of providing for the exclusive venue of one specialized court of first instance over intra-corporate disputes. Furthermore, the recent if perhaps temporary failure to achieve a European Community-wide legal framework for takeover battles on the one hand, and the implications of *Centros* on the other, suggest a new concern with federal-state relations, a concern that revives the salience of some look at the recent US experiences with these matters. In short, the common thread between these two systems is not the nature of the underlying civil actions which are to be encouraged or discouraged, but the implications of the division of powers in a federal system in the search for the means to the desired ends.

Starting over a decade ago, and fueled largely by the new capital flows into the new firms of the new information society, a rise in litigation brought with it a rise in complaints about the misuse of that form of monitoring. It is not my brief to evaluate the pros and cons of those complaints; and, indeed, the many studies of greater or lesser rigor on this subject do not allow for a straightforward evaluation.[5] What is relevant for present purposes is the turn of the new economy to the federal Congress for relief from what its protagonists characterized as the abuse of class actions based on the loose contours of federal law, in particular of the famous Rule 10b-5.

2.1.1 *Substantive law developments*

The substantive law developed under that general clause was not the main issue. In a series of decisions dating from the 1970s the United States Supreme Court already had trimmed the sails of that cause of action and its sibling, the private action challenging corporate actions taken by shareholder vote in the shadow of misleading proxy solicitations. These decisions had redefined Section 10b – and where relevant Section 14a – to require a showing of fraud and deceit and not only negligent misstatements or omissions;[6] required the plaintiff to have been a transacting party (a buyer or seller) at the relevant time;[7] rebuffed an effort to extend the Rule to cases of overreaching;[8] created more rigorous standards of causation that connected the wrong to the plaintiffs' action;[9] substantially shortened the limitations period and thus hastened the arrival of prescription of litigation;[10] and most recently ended the extension of liability to secondary defendants – the auditors and accountants – who aided and abetted

---

[5] The single most significant study in this new era probably was Alexander, "Do the Merits Matter? A Study of Settlements in Securities Class Actions", 43 *Stanford L. Rev.* (1991) 497; see also Romano, "The Shareholder Suit: Litigation Without Foundation?", 7 *J. Law Econ. Org.* (1991) 55.

[6] *Ernst & Ernst* v. *Hochfelder*, 425 US 185 (1976) so held as to Rule 10b-5. That issue still is open as to proxy-fraud litigation under Section 14a and Rule 14a-9; see *Virginia Bankshares, Inc.* v. *Sandberg*, 501 US 1083, 1090, n. 5 (1991).

[7] *Blue Chip Stamps* v. *Manor Drug Stores*, 421 US 723 (1975).

[8] *Santa Fe Industries* v. *Green*, 430 US 462 (1977).

[9] *Virginia Bankshares, Inc.* v. *Sandberg*, *supra* n. 6. While this decision so held as to proxy violations and the private Section 14a-9 action, it also may have implications for litigation under Rule 10b-5, which had allowed a more generous concept of transaction causation since the ruling in *Affiliated Ute Citizens* v. *United States*, 406 US 128 (1972).

[10] *Lampf, Pleva, Lipkind, Prupis & Petigrow* v. *Gilbertson*, 501 US 350 (1991), requiring private Rule 10b-5 actions to be brought within one year after discovery of the violation and in any event no more than three years after the event.

primary defendants in achieving their wrongful goals.[11] Furthermore, the Court did so in many instances despite the plea of the Securities Exchange Commission that private litigation was a major component of the agency's regulatory arsenal.[12]

2.1.2 *Raising the bar for civil litigation in the federal courts*

The debate of the early 1990s focused on the risk of frivolous litigation brought for its nuisance and settlement value, and the attendant lack of control by the investor community at large over the decision to litigate. Another relevant factor was the argument that accountants and other professional parties, despite the assistance of the *Central Bank of Denver* case, were in risk of liability out of all proportion to their financial gain from their role in possible securities violations. In the 1994 bi-election, the Republican Party regained control of the House and Senate; shortly thereafter the Litigation Reform Act of 1995 was passed, and then, with some support from the minority party, reenacted over President Clinton's veto.[13]

The Act contained mostly procedural not substantive provisions. This is not surprising, since its avowed purpose was to control baseless securities litigation. These provisions – or rather, these alleged abuses – are so specific to the

---

[11] *Central Bank of Denver* v. *First Interstate Bank of Denver*, 511 US 164 (1994).
Only two major cases went against the grain: *Herman & MacLean* v. *Huddleston*, 459 US 375 (1983) authorized Rule 10b-5 private actions even if the transaction might have been challenged under an express private remedy of the 1933 Securities Act; and *Basic, Inc.* v. *Levinson*, 485 US 224 (1988) relaxed the requirement of plaintiff's reliance on the misstatement or omission by accepting a "fraud on the market" theory with its rebuttable presumption of reliance. The 1995 statute discussed below may, however, weaken this presumption.
While I do not discuss the problems concerning the definition of insiders herein, it is important also to mention the Supreme Court's struggle with the conceptual dilemma that the duty to speak requires a preexisting relationship with the issuing company. This still has not been unambiguously resolved; see *United States* v. *O'Hagan*, 521 US 642 (1997).

[12] This has been the standard position of the SEC since its articulation in the original case finding an implied private right of action under the proxy regulations of Section 14a of the Securities Exchange Act, *J. I. Case Co.* v. *Borak*, 377 US 426 (1964). See the early study of Mestmäcker, "Das Verhältnis des Rechts der Wettbewerbsbeschränkungen zum Privatrecht I", *DB* [1968] 787; see also Buxbaum, *Die private Klage als Mittel zur Durchsetzung wirtschaftspolitischer Rechtsnormen* (Karlsruhe 1972) 56 et seq.

[13] Public Law 104-67, December 22, 1995, 109 Stat. 737, adding Section 27 to the Securities Act of 1933, and codified in 15 U.S.C. Section 77z-1, -2; and adding Section 21D to the Securities Exchange Act of 1934, and codified in 15 U.S.C. Section 78u-4. References hereafter are to the codified version.
The essentially political story of the Act's passage is told in Avery, "Securities Litigation Reform: The Long and Winding Road to the Private Securities Litigation Reform Act of 1995", 51 *Business Lawyer* (1996) 335.

American litigation scene that it would serve little purpose to describe them in detail here. They relate to peculiarities of the class action, with its multiple filings, competing sets of plaintiffs' attorneys, and the like. Only one abuse, and its remedy, may have some value in comparative terms: the effort to "empower investors so that they, not their lawyers, control private securities litigation". The remedy expected to address this underlying problem was to encourage the courts to appoint the representatives of the investors with the most at stake – sc. institutional investors – to become "lead plaintiffs" and thus take control of litigation and negotiation away from the attorneys with their merely nominal lead plaintiffs.[14] That approach has essentially failed for a variety of reasons, most having to do with the delicate relationships of both private-sector and public-sector institutional investors with their portfolio companies and the financial markets generally.[15] And as is usual with this kind of ad-hoc legislation, it is coarsely meshed and open to different interpretations, leaving many issues unresolved and perhaps even leading to the opposite results from those which were hoped for by its private-sector proponents.[16]

2.1.2.1 The new pleading requirements

The closest thing to a substantive provision in the Act[17] is the apparent (though contested) requirement of an unusually high standard of pleading of the alleged violations. The Federal Rules of Civil Procedure already required that allegations of fraud – the essential issue in these cases – be pleaded with particularity so far as the falsity of the statements was concerned, though the additionally required pleading of the defendants' state of mind – *Vorsatz* – might be pleaded more generally, for example, by suggesting the motivation for the behavior.[18] The new Act requires the pleadings to "specify each statement alleged to have

---

[14] See Weiss, "The Impact of the Lead Plaintiff Provisions of the Private Securities Litigation Reform Act", 39 *Ariz. L. Rev.* (1997) 561.

[15] See Fisch, "Class Action Reform: Lessons from Securities Litigation", 39 *Arizona L.Rev.* (1997) 533, 542 et seq.; Levine & Pritchard, "The Securities Litigation Uniform Standards Act of 1998: The Sun Sets on California's Blue Sky Laws", 54 *Business Lawyer* (1998) 1.

[16] To these more general issues see especially Coffee, "The Future of the Private Securities Litigation Reform Act: Or, Why the Fat Lady Has Not Yet Sung", 51 *Business Lawyer* (1996) 975.

[17] I leave aside one other reform; namely, the introduction of a new regime of proportionate joint and several liability, a matter of particular importance to peripheral participants in the alleged violations, especially professionals such as accountants. For a discussion, see Langevoort, "The Reform of Joint and Several Liability Under the Private Securities Litigation Reform Act of 1995: Proportionate Liability, Contribution Rights, and Settlement Effects", 51 *Business Lawyer* (1996) 1157.

[18] Rule 9(b), Federal Rules of Civil Procedure.

been misleading, the reason or reasons why the statement is misleading, and, if an allegation regarding the statement or omission is made on information and belief, the complaint shall state with particularity all facts on which that belief is formed".[19] This provision was one of the most controversial of the statutory draft, was highlighted in the Presidential veto,[20] and has led to significant differences of opinion as to its implementation that may well require an authoritative opinion of the Supreme Court in due course.[21]

2.1.2.2 The stay of pre-trial discovery proceedings

Finally, and of even greater importance so far as the litigation tactics of the plaintiffs' bar are concerned, the Act placed a moat before the now higher pleading walls of the fortress. It prohibited all discovery proceedings that might lead to facts supporting the more particularized pleading allegations.[22]

2.1.2.3 The flight to state courts and state law

This, in sum, was an attempt to limit litigation over the informational standards applicable to new issues of securities, and to a lesser degree to the secondary trading thereof. It is not this statute, however, but the reactions to it that lead us to the issues of federalism justifying this discussion. Not surprisingly, class-action plaintiffs' attorneys now looked at the possibility of state court litigation in a new light. In some cases, this was simply a matter of bringing similar cases under state statutory or decisional law that more or less replicated the typical Rule 10b-5 causes of action for fraudulent statements or omissions in connection with the issuance or secondary trading of securities. This was especially true of states like California, which had enacted "little Section 10b" causes of

---

[19] U.S.C. Section 78u-4(b)(1)(B).

[20] On the textual battle, see Olson, Mahaffey & Casey, "Pleading Reform, Plaintiff Qualification and Discovery Stays Under the Reform Act", 51 *Business Lawyer* (1996) 1101.

[21] This is reflected in the major cases in conflict; they are, respectively, *In re Silicon Graphics, Inc. Securities Litigation*, 183 F.3d 970 (9th Cir. 1999) and *Press* v. *Chemical Investors Service Corp.*, 166 F.3d 529 (2d Cir. 1999).

[22] U.S.C. Section 78u-4(b)(3)(B): "In any private action arising [hereunder], all discovery and other proceedings shall be stayed during the pendency of any motion to dismiss . . . [except if needed to preserve evidence or prevent 'undue prejudice']." In addition, a little-noted and apparently unused subsection of this provision, Section (b)(3)(D), added by the 1998 Uniform Standards Act discussed below, permits the federal court to "stay discovery proceedings in a State court, as necessary in aid of its jurisdiction, or to protect or effectuate its judgments in an action subject to a stay of discovery [in the federal action]."

action as a part of their Corporate Securities codes.[23] In the majority of cases, however, the recourse to state courts was to regain the important tactical advantage that now was no longer available in federal courts after the 1995 reform; namely, the just-mentioned pretrial discovery. This diversionary maneuver was needed to give plaintiffs access to the facts that would support the task of pleading the federal cause of action with the newly required specificity.[24] Armed with the evidence obtained through the state process, plaintiffs then could return to the federal court, plead their federal causes of action at the new, heightened level of particularity, and thus, at least at that stage, defeat any motions to dismiss their case.

2.1.3 *The federal preemption of state litigation*

The reaction was not long in coming. Up to this point, the federal Congress simply had redefined the substantive and procedural elements of the federal securities laws. Now, for the first time, Congress brought in the heavy artillery of the Constitution's Supremacy Clause. As a leading recent case put it, "Congress determined that class action attorneys were attempting to circumvent the [1995] Reform Act's requirements by filing frivolous securities lawsuits in state court and under state law."[25] However one may feel about this characterization as a factual matter,[26] it now was a reality. In response to this "attempt to circumvent", Congress enacted the Securities Litigation Uniform Standards

---

[23] California Corporations Code Section 25104. For a still useful discussion of the role of state securities regulation within a federal regime – today rapidly fading in importance – see Jennings, "The Role of the States in Corporate Regulation and Investor Protection", 23 *Law & Contemp. Problems* (1958) 193. To this day, at least, the Supreme Court has been careful not to find in the Securities Act of 1933 and Securities Exchange Act of 1934 any Congressional intention to preempt state regulation; see to this the otherwise divergent cases of *Edgar* v. *MITE Corp.*, 457 US 624 (1982) and *CTS Corp.* v. *Dynamics Corp. of America*, 481 US 69 (1987). This is an issue under the Supremacy Clause. The indirect preemptive effect of the Commerce Clause is another matter, and one which caused *Edgar* and *CTS* to reach different conclusions.

[24] See *Levine & Pritchard, supra* n. 15.

[25] *Gibson* v. *PS Group Holdings, Inc.*, 2000 U.S.Dist. LEXIS 3158 (S.D.Calif. 2000).

[26] In factual terms it is a highly disputed matter. A recent important investigative article suggests that especially in the new information- and bio-technology sectors a substantial amount of actionable misinformation was occurring. Schoenberger, "When the Numbers Just Don't Add Up", *New York Times*, 19 August 2001, Section 3 page 1. This may be a factor in the "failure" of the 1995 Act to reduce the number of class actions. Thus, in 2001 alone, 270 cases had been filed through mid-August, as compared with 211 for all of 2000. Id., citing the Stanford Law School Securities Class Action Clearinghouse, available at <http://www.securities.stanford.edu/index.html>.

Act of 1998.[27] Its approach was straightforward. It simply forbade the filing of class actions involving the mentioned types of securities-law violations in state courts, if the same cause of action could have been brought under federal law. In the context of the Constitutional division of powers, it justified this with the statutory finding that "it is appropriate to enact national standards for securities class action lawsuits involving nationally traded securities. . . "[28] The Securities Exchange Act of 1934 always had been within the exclusive jurisdiction of the federal courts; that is, state courts were not competent to exercise jurisdiction over cases involving the rights and remedies it provided.[29] Now the Congress took the further step of not permitting analogous state causes of action, whether statutory or common-law, to survive.

2.1.3.1 The difficult separation of company and capital-market rules: the derivative suit

The details of inclusion and exclusion are not of particular interest in the comparative context with two exceptions, but those two are central to the division-of-powers issue. Covered by this prohibition is litigation over investment decisions, whether made by defendants or by the shareholders of the involved corporation. Abuses of power that allegedly harm the corporation, on the other hand, whether made by corporate decision-makers in the capacity of director or of dominant shareholder, are a proper subject for a derivative action and specifically excluded from the reach of the statute.[30] These are the typical conflict-of-interests transactions. They would not, generally speaking,[31] involve "an untrue statement or omission of a material fact in connection with the

---

[27] Public Law No. 105-353, November 3, 1998, 112 Stat. 3227, codified in Section 28 of the Securities Act of 1933, 15 U.S.C. Section 77p. The references to this Act below are to the codified version.

[28] From the Congressional findings introducing Public Law 105-353, Section 2(5), 112 Stat. 3227 (1998).

[29] Section 27 of the 1934 Securities Exchange Act, 15 U.S.C. Section 78aa, has from its original enactment provided that the federal courts "shall have exclusive jurisdiction of violations of this chapter or the rules and regulations hereunder". Paradoxically, the much more technical Securities Act of 1933, governing the initial issuance of securities, is open to the jurisdiction of the state courts.

[30] U.S.C. Section 77p(f)(2)(B).

[31] Of course, self-dealing or related transactions may be accompanied by deception, and if the deception is "in connection with the purchase or sale of a security" the entire transaction may be within the reach of the federal cause of action – but these are relatively rare cases, closer to the promoters'-fraud arena. See, e.g., *Hooper* v. *Mountain States Securities Corp.*, 282 F.2d 195 (5th Cir. 1960). The possible conflicts of interests arising in the context of takeover battles and the like are another matter, though as described below, the new statutory regime speaks to that matter as well.

purchase or sale of a . . . security". This distinction between overreaching and deception roughly comports with the already mentioned common distinction between state corporation law governing the power relations between the organs of the corporation and federal securities law governing the information relations of company, investor, and market.[32] Traveling along that historic fault line, the 1998 Uniform Standards Act now removes the latter transactions from the reach of the states.

As mentioned, the Congressional finding on this issue was that "this shift [to state litigation] has prevented the. . . [1995 Act] from fully achieving its objectives"; its solution was "to enact national standards for securities class action lawsuits involving nationally traded securities. . . " The procedural device to implement that solution in the Uniform Standards Act was the grant of the right of removal to the state-suit defendants,[33] thus bringing the case back to the more stringent threshold barriers in the post-1995 federal court.

2.1.3.2 The criteria to establish the finding of identity of actions

Critical to the removal motion, however, is a finding that the complaint is cast as a class action (involving 50 or more members and a nationally traded security) and alleges a state version of a Rule 10b-5 cause of action, in particular a misstatement or omission occurring "in connection with the purchase or sale of a security".[34] Three elements turn out to be important to this preliminary characterization review needed to find identity of the causes of action: the exceptions to the states' exclusion contained in the federal statute itself; standing; and substantive standards of liability.

The statutory exceptions to what otherwise would be a finding of identity already have been mentioned, and are the least problematical.[35] The second element, however, the standing requirement, judicially created in the previously mentioned *Blue Chip* case, is critical to the threshold finding of functional identity of the state cause of action with the federal one. Not surprisingly,

---

[32] This is the same distinction that provided the Supreme Court with the rationale to support state anti-takeover legislation against the argument that this legislation conflicted with the (dormant; i.e., unexercised) Commerce Clause of the US constitution. *CTS*, *supra* n. 23.

[33] Removal is the procedural device that permits a defendant to transfer the case to the appropriate federal court. Under certain circumstances, including the present one, it is automatic when demanded. Remand is the return trip to state court; and as will be seen below, it is the remand context within which the two parties' conflict in fact plays out.

[34] U.S.C. Section 77p(f)(2)(A).

[35] Thus, *Gibson*, *supra* n. 25, rebuffed the defendant's removal effort because the complaint involved misstatements or omissions made in connection with a tender or exchange offer and the suit was brought in the state of incorporation. This so-called "Delaware carve-out" exception is discussed further below.

plaintiffs have been alleging the breach of a state fiduciary duty unconnected with that transactional element; that is, that plaintiffs were deceived into retaining their stock instead of selling it (or, as in *Blue Chip*, from purchasing it in the first place). Some federal trial-level decisions have accepted this form of complaint as sufficient to distinguish the state cause of action from the federal one, and thus to permit the remand of the removed case back to the state courts.[36] This transactional requirement indeed is an important limitation on the standard Rule 10b-5 civil action; it is essentially a prudential limitation purporting to keep both evidentiary and damage-calculation issues under control.[37] Indeed, it is one of the few reasons why the almost mandatory recourse to industry arbitration in individual investor-broker disputes may provide relief unavailable in court, since complaints that poor advice or misinformation caused an investor to hold onto the stock are arbitrable though not, under Rule 10b-5, litigable.[38]

The third component of the preemption criteria – the identity of liability and relief – may in time become more important. From the plaintiff's perspective, the argument is that the nature of the relief requested, if differing from the "compensation" relief definitional element in the Uniform Standards Act,[39]

---

[36] Two recent cases in the federal courts sitting in California illustrate differing judicial views of the new pleading strategy. *Shaev* v. *Claflin* (N.D. Calif. 2001), CCH FedSecLRep para. 91,452, granted the remand; *Bertram* v. *Terayon Communications Systems, Inc.* (C.D. Calif 2001), 2001 US Dist LEXIS 6215, denied it on the basis of pleadings that established the plaintiffs as purchasers. See also *Lasley* v. *New England Variable Life Ins Co*, 126 FSupp2 1236 (ND Cal 1999) and, elsewhere, *Wald* v. *C M Life Insurance Company* (ND Texas 2001), 2001 US Dist LEXIS 2593 and *Gordon* v. *Buntrock* (ND Ill 2000), 2000 US Dist LEXIS 5977.

[37] The Court's reasoning in *Blue Chip* is instructive in this regard:

"...[I]n the absence of the [transactional standing] rule, ... [p]laintiff's entire testimony could be dependent upon uncorroborated oral evidence of many of the crucial elements of his claim, and still be sufficient to go to the jury... The very real risk in permitting those in [plaintiff's] position to sue under Rule 10b-5 is that door will be open to recovery of substantial damages on the part of one who offers only his own testimony to prove that he ever consulted a prospectus of the issuer, that he paid any attention to it, or that the representations contained in it damaged him."

Blue Chip, *supra* n. 7, at . Of course, it should be noted that this was a case of non-purchasers, a "class" so protean as to mock all pretense that the implied civil remedy under Rule 10b-5 is based on a *Schutznorm* focused on an identifiable group of beneficiaries in the traditional doctrinal sense. The case of fraudulently induced non-sale or retention is more limited. This is a factor in the California litigation discussed further below.

[38] See Morgensen, "Why Investors May Find Arbitrators on Their Side", *New York Times*, 19 August 2001, p. C1.

[39] The Uniform Standards Act applies only when "one or more named parties seek to recover damages... " 15 USC §§ 77p(f)(2)(A)(I), (II).

justifies its escape from the statute and its preemptive effect. So far, that argument has not succeeded, but it remains an open issue.[40]

2.2 The federal referee of inter-state regulatory competition

2.2.1 *Privileging the state of incorporation*

That is where the vertical federal-state division of powers issue stands at the moment. The Uniform Standards Act, however, also contains an important provision taking a further step that has an important additional impact, in this case not on federal-state competition but on the competition among states in a federal system. The statute excludes from its preemptive coverage state litigation concerning informational deficiencies that occur in connection with shareholders' decisions "with respect to voting their securities, acting in response to a tender or exchange offer, or exercising dissenters' or appraisal rights"[41] – but only if that litigation is brought in the state of incorporation of the involved corporation. In rough, more political than doctrinal analogy to *Cassis de Dijon* and *Centros*, this privileges the state of incorporation. Since under traditional United States conflict of laws rules the law of the state of incorporation governs the internal affairs of the corporation, and since this has led to the well-known "Delaware effect", the consequence of the Congressional "Delaware exception" is a significant rearrangement of corporate litigation in the United States. This can be demonstrated by going through the prototypical scenarios that make up that litigation.

Current Delaware law, while self-consciously insistent on its fact-based narrowness,[42] and avoiding any judicial pronouncement of general doctrine,

---

[40] *Bertram, supra* n. 36, brought under the protean Section 17200 of the California Business and Professions Code that addresses unfair business practices generally, is the more troubling case in this connection. It applied a "functional equivalence" standard to the pleadings, and on the pleaded facts recharacterized the action as one similar to a Rule 10b-5 action. The court refused to characterize the requested restitutionary relief as anything other than typical damages; it thus caused it to fail, under the federal proscription. In support of this approach, it cited the California Supreme Court's opinion in *Rubin* v. *Green*, 847 Pac.2d 1044, 17 Calif.Reptr.2d 828 (1993) as creating a strict rule against "manipulative" efforts to recharacterize pleadings in order to avoid a result that the more appropriate pleading would have produced. In other words, again from the division-of-powers point of view, the court accepted the state-law characterization of the relief as determinative of the issue under the federal statute.

[41] U.S.C. Section 77p(d)(1)(A), (B).

[42] A typical example, in this case from the leading case of *Paramount Communications, Inc.* v. *QVC Network, Inc.*, 637 Atl.2d 34 (Del. 1994), at n. 13: "We express no opinion on any scenario except the actual facts before the court, and our precise holding herein. Unsolicited tender offers in other contexts may be governed by a different precedent." This approach has led to a mi-

now provides a degree of autonomy to corporate directors both in the negotiation of the terms of a friendly merger or takeover and in the resistance to a hostile one that would surprise any observer whose knowledge was based on the great debates of the 1980s.[43] In the case of friendly mergers, the uniform "gatekeeper function" of the target company directors[44] now extends, by judicial development, not only to the acceptance by target-company boards of prohibitions on shopping for better bids but even to the creation of what can only be characterized as penalty clauses.[45] Taken together, these fences around a negotiated merger proposal render the ostensible authority of the shareholder body to reject a friendly merger little more than a meaningless gesture; in addition, these penalty and related clauses in effect preclude or at least sharply inhibit rival bids. In the case of hostile takeover bids, Delaware law now permits not only the traditionally high degree of pre-battle entrenchment of defensive walls, but also a new range of countermoves during the actual battle.[46] In essence, this leaves any disfavored bidder either frozen out or obliged to negotiate with the target management instead of going over its head to the shareholders in the classic style of a takeover bid.[47]

---

nor academic debate over the motivation of the Delaware Supreme Court and the Delaware Court of Chancery to withhold appropriate guidance from its corporate and law-firm "clientele". Compare Macey & Miller, "Towards an Interest-Group Theory of Delaware Corporate Law", 65 *Texas Law Rev.* (1987) 469 with Kamar, "A Regulatory Competition Theory of Indeterminacy in Corporate Law", 98 *Colum. Law Rev.* (1998) 1908.

[43] For an overview of both issues from that time, see Buxbaum, "The Internal Division of Powers in Corporate Governance", 73 *Calif. Law Rev.* (1985) 1671.

[44] To this structure of US law, see Buxbaum, "Die feindliche Übernahme der anderen Art", in: *Festschrift Lutter* (Uwe Schneider et al. [eds.]) (Cologne 2000) 1295.

[45] For a recent and well-named example, see *Brazen* v. *Bell Atlantic Corporation*, 695 Atl.2d 43 (Del. 1997). The subject is a large one, however, and not captured solely by focusing on penalty clauses, offers to sell "crown jewels", etc. See generally Carney, *Mergers and Acquisitions – Cases and Materials* (New York 2000) 588 et seq.

[46] The evolution of this tendency is well-traced in *Unocal Corp.* v. *Mesa Petroleum Co.*, 4493 Atl.2d 946 (Del. 1985), *Paramount Communications, Inc.* v. *Time Incorporated*, 571 Atl.2d 1140 (Del. 1990), and *Unitrin, Inc.* v. *American General Corp.*, 651 Atl.2d 1361 (Del. 1995) on the one hand, and the slow descent into irrelevancy of the judicial oversight announced in *Revlon, Inc.* v. *MacAndrews & Forbes Holdings, Inc.*, 506 Atl.2d 173 (Del. 1986) and reformulated in *Mills Acquisition Co.* v. *Macmillan, Inc.*, 559 Atl.2d 1261 (Del. 1989), on the other. Some concern with the grant of inappropriate advantages to the favored bidder remains, once the target is "in play", but it no longer has the strength it once did.

[47] Only when the defense moves would even preclude a proxy battle for control does there still seem to be judicial control of some significance. *Quickturn Design Systems, Inc.* v. *Mentor Graphics*, 721 Atl.2d 1281 (Del. 1999), discussed in Buxbaum, *supra* n. 43.

2.2.2 *Privileging Delaware*

By privileging the state of incorporation in this area of shareholder voting and shareholder tendering decisions, the Uniform Standards Act privileges the de facto sovereignty of Delaware over the field of state corporation law. It is the substantive law governing the role of target-company management that mattered to the legislature, not the abstract question of division of powers. At the least, this legislative action has the effect of preserving the Delaware judiciary's monopoly on the development of the substantive law in the field. Cases involving Delaware corporations frequently are brought in the courts of other states, providing that personal jurisdiction over the necessary individual as well as corporate defendants is available.[48] In the field of class actions, seeking damages for informational breaches in the context of mergers or takeovers, this will no longer be possible. Looming behind this tactical point, finally, lurks the always sensitive question whether the Congress will choose to "constitutionalize" the internal-affairs doctrine for a wider range of subject matter.[49]

2.3 **The response of the states**

The next and in this context probably last act in this running drama is the response of state courts, in both their statutory-interpretation and common-law roles, to this question of "functional similarity" between the federal and state causes of action.[50] That response now is pending, not surprisingly in California, which has the most explicit statutory regulation and the most developed common-law version thereof in the nation.

2.3.1 *The state courts' role in the establishment of identity of actions*

The two critical factors in any ultimate determination of the non-identity with and thus non-preemption of these state causes of action by the Uniform Standards Act are the standing and substantive requirements needed to support

---

[48] Of course, if the substantive point involves the internal-affairs doctrine, these other courts typically would apply Delaware law to the matter (but as the derivative-suit field teaches, there is Delaware Delaware law and non-Delaware Delaware law).

[49] On this point generally, see Buxbaum, "Back to the Future? From 'Centros' to the 'Überlagerungstheorie'", in: *Festschrift Sandrock* (Klaus Peter Berger et al. [eds.]) (Heidelberg 2000) 149, 159ff.

[50] While it is possible that a state-court characterization of its law might be challenged or disregarded by a federal court hearing a post-removal remand motion, this would have to be based on the notion that the difference found by the state court was not a difference relevant under the federal Uniform Standards Act, not on any lack of authority of the state court to find that difference.

an action based on either common-law fraud or violations of a state's statutory treatment of securities. An authoritative analysis of both is pending at the time of this writing, in the form of an appeal from an exhaustive review of the matter by an intermediate California appellate court.[51] That intermediate decision does not once mention the Uniform Standards Act, but a review thereof makes clear that it was written in a clear effort to distinguish both strands of the California law – common-law as well as statutory – from federal law, in order to save cases brought thereunder from the preemptive reach of that Act.[52] Whatever the awaited outcome, the facts of the case and their treatment warrant a review, specifically because of the comparative lessons this division-of-powers battle may hold for the European Community. At the same time, the opinion provides some interesting insights into the common-law development of the substantive-law aspects of a cause of action based on fraud and on negligent misrepresentation in the securities field, substantive issues that also are under constant review outside of the United States.

2.3.2 *The first judicial response*

Plaintiff did not claim to have purchased or sold securities but only to have retained them as a result of defendant's misleading statements or omissions. Thus its causes of action would have fallen afoul of the threshold *Blue Chip* standing requirement. This thus created one disparity between the federal and the state causes of action, which in turn satisfied one element of the preemption exceptions. As a result, however, he faced the challenge that California law, too, required him to allege damages as a result of buying or selling shares, not merely as a result of holding them through the period of "false buoyancy" created by defendant's behavior. The decision rejects this view of California law:

> "Starting almost a century ago, virtually identical causes of action have already been recognized. . . [elsewhere]. We conclude that California should join these ranks. . .

---

[51] *Greenfield* v. *Fritz Companies, Inc.*, 98 Calif. Rptr.2d 530 (2000), (Supreme Court) review granted, November 21, 2000, 2000 Cal LEXIS 8710 (technically, the opinion now has been superseded by the grant of review; it would, e.g., not be citable at this time in other California court proceedings).
That the first State (re)actor would be California is not surprising, given its continuing unique role as a counterpart – if a steadily diminishing counterpart – to the leveling effect of Delaware and Model-Act norms in the field of corporation law.

[52] *Greenfield* does not address that federal preemption issue directly. Instead, it cites the "1934 Security [sic] Exchange Act of 1934" as "disclaim[ing] preemption of state remedies and tolerat[ing] some overlap with state authority", without mentioning either the 1995 or 1998 statutory changes. Ibid., at 541.

> There is no reason in either law or logic why the same result [as in transaction cases] should not apply to a situation where corporate stockholders are fraudulently induced to retain or refrain from selling their shares. The principle of inaction invoked by plaintiff goes by the legal rubric of forbearance. . . There is no reason why forbearance which is induced by fraud and which is the cause of damages should not be actionable."[53]

The next, and more central issue under state law was the question whether California's statutory remedies under the Corporate Securities Law occupied the field, or whether an evolving common-law doctrine continued to exist in parallel. The question is important because the relevant statutory provision does require a purchase or sale transaction in exact analogy to the federal remedy. A previous opinion of the California Supreme Court had so held, though in the context of a case involving a transaction[54] The intermediate *Greenfield* court, using exactly that distinction, ruled that in a non-transaction case the issue of statutory exclusivity has no force. Indeed, it went on to argue the prudential policy point directly. It deemed inapplicable *Mirkin's* injunction that courts "should be hesitant to impose [new tort duties] when to do so would involve complex policy decisions" that were more properly the subject of legislative resolution.[55]

The substantive basis on which *Greenfield* distinguishes *Mirkin* – and this too bears on the federal preemption issue – concerns the issue of plaintiff's reliance on fraudulent statements or omissions. As *Greenfield* points out, the *Mirkin* plaintiff tried to combine the statutory presumption of reliance with the common-law possibility of punitive damages and a longer prescriptive period. "By seeking to import the fraud-on-the-market theory and its presumption of reliance from the statutory cause of action into common law fraud, the plaintiff in *Mirkin* was seeking to have the best of both worlds."[56] In the present case there can be no such result, since the statutory remedy is limited to transacting plaintiffs. To prevail under this common-law analogue, plaintiff will have to prove reliance (as well, presumably, as the two other necessary badges of fraud,

---

[53] Ibid., at 539, citing Section 525 of the American Law Institute's Restatement 2nd of Torts.

[54] *Mirkin* v. *Wasserman*, 23 Calif.Rptr.2d 101, 858 Pac.2d 568 (1992).

[55] It did so on the ground that "judicial common law authority operates under no statutory inhibition; indeed, it enjoys positive legislative sanction". *Greenfield, supra* n. 51, at 541. The principal basis for its conclusion is the provision in Section 25510 of California's Corporate Securities Law that the statutory provisions for civil liability shall not "limit any liability which may exist by virtue of any other statute or under common law if this law were not in effect". In this, *Greenfield* follows the early decision in *Bowden* v. *Robinson*, 136 Calif.Rptr. 871 (1977), which rejected the notion that the new statute had supplanted rather than supplemented common law actions and remedies.

[56] Ibid., at 541.

materiality and causation). The fraud-on-the-market "automatic-reliance" ruling of *Basic, Inc.* v. *Levinson*[57] has not yet been deemed an inherent element in the identity equation that triggers the federal preemption. To the extent it may come to play a role in the judicial development of those identity criteria, however, *Greenfield* renders it unavailable for that purpose so far as common-law fraud claims are concerned.[58]

If affirmed, *Greenfield* thus would be more than an anti-preemption decision; it "extends" California law, as the opinion puts it, by permitting the common-law fraud remedy, admittedly with its high standard of proof, to apply to the non-transaction situation. Whether those standards, which in particular include actual knowledge of and reliance on the misrepresentation, are so particularized as to prevent class certification is another matter.[59] From the preemption point of view, however, that may not be the critical issue. The critical issue would be whether a federal court would permit the results of the state court's discovery process to be used in a concurrently filed federal action, particularly if plaintiff, to avoid the "covered class action" trap of the Uniform Standards Act, does not seek class certification of the state action. To this issue, the *Greenfield* opinion's comment on the reliance pleading may be the key:

> "Any lingering doubts [as to the reliance allegations] is dispelled by two factors. The first is that defendants have at all times possessed unquestionably greater knowledge of the corporation's financial affairs, a consideration that 'mitigate[s] the rigor of the rule requiring specific pleading of fraud.' [citation omitted] . . . The second factor relaxing the strict pleading rule is that the individual defendants who are corporate directors are fiduciaries to shareholders. . . "[60]

This reminder that even the common-law pleading of a fraud cause of action may be more generous than the pleadings now possible under federal law as circumscribed by the 1995 Litigation Reform Act of course only highlights the issue of recourse to the state litigation process.

---

57 *Supra* n. 11.

58 It should be noted that other courts have rejected the automatic reliance inherent in the fraud-on-the-market theory when interpreting state causes of action in the securities field. See in particular *Malone* v. *Brincat*, 722 Atl.2d 5 (Del. 1998).

59 *Greenfield, supra* n. 51, seems to consider that possibility as a given.

60 Ibid., at 537.

3. Conclusion

Two points may be of comparative interest at the conclusion of this narrative of recent US developments. The first is the primacy of the political – perhaps policy – issues inherent in the vertical division of powers. In consequence thereof, differential access to state and to federal legislators may generate different policy outcomes in this important field. The second is the centrality of the institutional issue inherent in the horizontal separation of powers at each level of the vertical division of powers. In consequence thereof, it may well be the judiciaries of both systems that will turn out to be the conflict-resolution institutions. Though the Council of Ministers and the Court of Justice will play their dominant roles in accordance with the constitutional architecture of the European Community, the room left for the Member States and their political and judicial branches may be large enough to lead to some version of the type of struggle currently engaging their US counterparts in this complex and charged field.

Recent Legislative Trends in The Field of Personal Security

Ulrich Drobnig[*]

1. Introductory remarks

1.1 Real and personal security

Personal and proprietary security are the two basic types of instruments for securing credit. In the more frequent and better known case of proprietary security, usually the debtor of the credit offers an asset owned by him to serve as security for the creditor by transferring a limited proprietary right to the creditor. By contrast, in the case of personal security a third person assumes a security obligation vis-à-vis the creditor; potentially he is liable for that obligation – up to its agreed limit – with all his property.

---

[*] Emeritus Professor of Law, University of Hamburg; Emeritus Director, Max Planck Institute for Foreign Private and Private International Law, Hamburg.

Talia Einhorn, ed., Spontaneous Order, Organization and the Law – Liber Amicorum Ernst-Joachim Mestmäcker © 2003 T.M.C.Asser Press, The Hague, The Netherlands

The fact that – up to the agreed maximum, sometimes even without such limit – the security giver bears unlimited liability for the security granted to the creditor is an important reason for the popularity of personal security with creditors. These obtain an additional debtor. On the other hand, it is this unlimited liability which makes personal security so dangerous for security givers and has consequently triggered the enactment of a considerable number of protective provisions in recent legislation. It is this modern protective legislation that will be emphasized in the third part of the following survey.

1.2 Types of personal security

Personal security consists in most countries of two major types of instruments. The first and historically most popular is suretyship. This is characterized by the very narrow relationship between the security obligation and the secured debt. As a rule, the security giver's liability, especially its validity, extent and terms, depends upon the validity, extent and terms of the secured obligation. The security giver may, as a rule, invoke all the exceptions and defences to which the secured debtor is entitled. Since terminology to some extent differs even within the Anglophonic orbit, for convenience sake this basic type of personal security will be called a dependent guarantee.

By contrast, in recent decennia practice has created a second basic type of personal security, the validity, extent and terms of which do not depend upon the validity, extent and terms of the secured debt. This modern variation of personal security is called an indemnity in England and a guarantee or autonomous guarantee in other countries. It will here be called an independent guarantee, thus emphasizing its distinctive feature as contrasted to the traditional dependent guarantee.

1.3 Contemporary trends

In our days, the core ideas of personal security are still embodied in the institution of the dependent guarantee, which appears to be known in most countries. Its basic rules regulate the dependency of the guarantee upon the secured debt. In spite of variations in detail, the major traits are quite similar from country to country.

However, on the fringe two important and contradictory developments have taken place. One is the commercialisation of personal security by evolving various forms of independent security. Most of this development has taken place outside any legislation, by commercial practice, and partly under new names, such as letter of credit. One may even say that due to the abstention of national legislatures, on the one hand, and the untiring efforts to achieve international coordination deployed by banks as well exporters and importers, as coordinated by the International Chamber of Commerce in Paris, on the other hand, in this field uniformity of practice and law have been achieved.[1] But even outside this special branch of commercial personal security, legislative activity in the field of independent guarantees is scarce.

By contrast, in the opposite direction, i.e. in the area of consumer protection, many countries have been active. That activity is directed essentially at protecting the consumer who has given a dependent guarantee as security for debts of close relatives, against the effects of ill-considered, exploitative terms of such personal security. In some countries, especially Germany, the brunt of this protection has been afforded by the courts.[2] By contrast, in many others the legislator has intervened in order to amend some of the general rules of the traditional provisions on dependent guarantees or to introduce new protective rules.

The following survey attempts to present the salient features of recent legislation in the two opposite fields of commercial independent guarantees, on the one hand, and the special protection for consumer guarantors, on the other hand. It goes without saying that in the limited space available, neither of these modern legislative trends can be presented in an exhaustive way; rather, exemplary presentations only can be offered.

2. Independent guarantees

As has been mentioned before (*supra* at 1.3), legislative activity in the typically commercial field of independent guaranties is a rarity. The more remarkable is a set of provisions on this topic that has been enacted by a new supranational legislator in Africa, the *Organisation pour l'Harmonisation en Afrique du Droit des Affaires* (OHADA) created in 1993.[3] On 17 April 1997, this Organisation adopted a Uniform Act on Security Rights, dealing with both personal and proprietary security.[4] The Act entered into force on 1 January 1998 and is

---

[1] This uniformity is embodied in the *Uniform Customs and Practice for Documentary Credits*, 1993 Revision (ICC Publication no. 500).

[2] For recent surveys and analyses see especially Lwowski, *Das Recht der Kreditsicherung*, 8th ed. (Berlin 2000), and Bülow, *Recht der Kreditsicherheiten*, 5th ed. (Heidelberg 1999).

[3] See generally Lohoues-Oble, "L'apparition d'un droit international des affaires en Afrique", *Rev.int.dr.comp.* (1999) 545-591; reports by Agboyibor, "OHADA: Droit des affaires en Afrique", *Rev. du droit des affaires internationales/Internat.Bus.L.Journal* (1999) 228-236. OHADA has at present 16 member states, mostly Francophonic countries in Central Africa as well as two non-Francophonic states, i.e. Equatorial Guinea and Guinea-Bissau.

[4] French text and English translation in Anoukaha, Le droit des sûretés dans l'Acte Uniforme OHADA (Yaounde 1998) 79 et seq., 119 et seq.; Text and commentary by Issa-Sayegh in Issa-Sayegh, Pougoué and Sawadogo (eds.), *OHADA. Traité et Actes uniformes commentés et annotés* (Futuroscope Cedex 1999) 615-698.

binding on all 16 member states, taking precedence over their national laws.[5]

The independent guarantee (called a Guarantee Letter, *Lettre de garantie*) is defined by Article 28 (1) as an agreement by which, at the request or upon the instruction of the principal, the guarantor undertakes to pay a fixed amount to the beneficiary upon the latter's first demand. It creates an independent obligation, distinct from any agreement, act or fact which may serve as its basis (Art. 29 (2)); in a related provision, this basis (*base*) is called the "*cause*" of the issue of the guarantee.[6] The autonomy of the independent guarantee is confirmed by the warning which must be contained in any guarantee letter, that the guarantor cannot invoke the exceptions to which a surety is entitled.[7] In sum, these three provisions clearly specify the autonomous character of the independent guarantee on first demand, in keeping with international standards.

By contrast, the requirements for the valid assumption of an independent guarantee reflect a special policy of protecting and warning of the persons involved. In the first place, guarantee letters may not be assumed upon sanction of nullity by natural persons (Art. 29 (1)). In the second place, an elaborate and strict writing is prescribed for guarantee letters. The following indications are obligatory, any disregard leading to the nullity of the letter:[8] (1) The document must be designated as letter of guarantee on first demand; (2) it must contain the names of the principal, of the beneficiary and of the guarantor; (3) it must mention the underlying agreement, act or fact; (4) the maximum amount of the guarantee; (5) its date of expiration; (6) the requirements of the demand; and (7) the guarantor's preclusion from invoking the exceptions of a surety.[9]

The effects of a valid guarantee letter essentially correspond to international standards. A beneficiary's demand for payment must be in writing and must be accompanied by the documents prescribed in the guarantee letter. The demand must state that the principal has not performed its obligations towards the beneficiary and in which respects (Art. 34 (1)).

Article 35 outlines the guarantor's rights and obligations upon receipt of a demand for performance: The guarantor has a reasonable period within which to examine whether the demand and its accompanying documents are in conformity with the guarantee letter (para. 1); before payment, the guarantor has to transmit the beneficiary's demand and accompanying documents to the principal for information (para. 2); if the guarantor decides to reject the demand, it has to advise the principal and the beneficiary as soon as possible (para. 3);

[5] Cf. art. 10 OHADA Treaty, ibid.

[6] Art. 30 second sentence fifth dash. In the Romanic legal systems, any contract requires a "*cause*" to be valid, cf. French Civil Code art. 1131.

[7] Art. 30 second sentence last dash.

[8] Art. 30 second sentence.

[9] Ibid.

and, finally, the guarantor must as soon as possible inform the principal of any reduction of the guarantee or any event terminating it (para. 4).

The widely known exception to the guarantor's obligation to pay is also recognised. The only objection to which both the guarantor and the principal are entitled against a demand for performance is a "manifestly abusive or fraudulent" demand by the beneficiary (Art. 36). It is remarkable and sensible to extend this exception, normally conceived as one to which the guarantor is entitled, to the principal who indeed is generally allowed to ward off performance by the guarantor and demand by the beneficiary.

A progressive solution has also been found for the guarantor's claims against its principal: The guarantor who has made a "useful", i.e. legitimate payment to the beneficiary is entitled to the same rights against its principal as a surety (Art. 37). According to Articles 20 and 21, a surety is upon payment to the creditor subrogated to the latter's rights against the main debtor; in addition it has a personal claim for reimbursement of all its payments to the creditor and even for damages which it has suffered due to executions by the creditor.

The OHADA provisions on independent guarantees on first demand are almost without exception a useful codification which is largely in line with international standards. The exclusion of individuals serves a legitimate interest of protection; only the formal requirements for the guarantee letter appear to be too restrictive. By contrast, extending the exception of abuse to the benefit of the guarantor's principal is a welcome clarification. And the regulation of the guarantor's recourse and reimbursement against its principal upon the model of the corresponding rights of the surety is a definite progress.

3. Guarantees by consumers

Modern legislative provisions designed to protect consumers who have granted a guarantee, are extremely diverse as to location and contents. Due to limitations of space, time and information, only a broad survey can be offered here.

3.1 **Location of protective rules**

Protective rules for consumer guarantors are spread over quite diverse kinds of legislation. In the Netherlands such provisions are contained in the new Civil Code of 1992,[10] while in France a few provisions have been inserted into the Civil Code of 1804. In non-code countries, special laws on guarantees may

[10] Arts. 7:857 to 7:863 of the new Civil Code entered into force on 1 January 1992.

contain relevant rules, as is the case in Finland[11] and Israel;[12] amazingly, the OHADA Uniform Law (discussed *supra* section 2) does not deal specifically with guarantees by consumers. A third typical source is legislation on consumer protection, generally, as in Austria[13] and France[14] or specifically in consumer credit legislation, as in Belgium.[15] Finally, Norway has chosen an atypical location, namely a law on banking.[16]

However, the *locus* does not prejudice the contents or number of relevant provisions. Quite to the contrary: the rules contained in civil codes are usually very small and of limited importance, while the recent Norwegian banking law has a surprisingly broad and dense network of relevant provisions.

3.2 Scope of application of protective rules

3.2.1 *Personal scope of application*

With respect to the creditor, almost all countries investigated here (except the Netherlands) require it to be a commercial lender.[17] This excludes application of the protective rules to guarantees granted in favour of a creditor not acting in a commercial function, i.e. a consumer.

Although central for the proper application of protective rules, there is much less unanimity in defining those *givers* of a personal security that are to enjoy special protection. Only five of the seven countries under investigation offer a definition. The simplest is the Austrian which defines a consumer as a person who is not an entrepreneur.[18] Finland, Israel, the Netherlands and Norway, while agreeing that the protected person must be a natural person, variously qualify this requirement for those persons who in one way or another are closely related to the debtor of the secured obligation. Only Israel excludes a security giver who is the spouse of the debtor from protection.[19] The thrust of the exceptions in all four countries is the security giver who as manager or major shareholder can

---

[11] Law on Guarantee of 19 March 1999 no. 361.

[12] Guarantee Law 5722-1967, as amended 1992 and re-amended 1998.

[13] Consumer Protection Law of 8 March 1979, frequently amended, ss. 25a–25d.

[14] Code de la consommation, Première partie (Législative) (Loi no. 93-949 of 26 July 1993) (frequently amended), especially art. L. 313-7 to 313-10.

[15] Consumer Credit Act of 12 June 1991, arts. 34-38 and 97.

[16] Act on Financial Contracts of 25 June 1999 no. 46.

[17] Austria § 1 (1) no. 1; Belgium art. 1 no. 2 and art. 3 no. 5; Finland § 2 no. 7; France Code consomm. art. L. 313-7 *juncto* art. L. 311-2 para. 1 and art. L. 312-2; Code monétaire et financier Art. L. 313-22 para. 1; Law 94-126 of 11 Feb. 1994 art. 47, as modified by Law 98-657; Israel s. 19 s.v. Creditor; Norway § 57 para. 1.

[18] Austria § 1 (1) no. 2.

[19] Israel s. 19 s.v. single guarantor.

exercise a strong influence on the debtor company. The Norwegian criterion is whether the security giver has a "decisive influence" on the debtor company.[20] According to Dutch law, there is no protection if the security giver acted in the capacity of manager of an incorporated company and either the security giver or the board of managers collectively holds the majority of the shares.[21] Finland uses similar criteria, but it suffices if they exist alternatively.[22] The Israeli criterion is the "stakeholder" in an incorporated entity. Moreover, Israel has two categories of protected security givers, the "single guarantor" (which includes the debtor's spouse and the stakeholder) and the "protected guarantor"; the latter is a "single guarantor" whose guarantee does not exceed NIS 60,000 (or NIS 500,000 if the secured debt concerns the residence of the debtor or his family members).[23]

By contrast, Belgium and France do not generally define and thereby limit the security giver; their protective rules therefore apply to all persons. However, these protective rules are applicable only to credits to consumers.[24] The French protective rules specify further that only natural persons are protected as security givers.[25] Security for consumer debtors will usually only be granted by persons closely related to the debtor, especially by spouses and family members. Therefore, in effect, although only indirectly, consumers will benefit from the protective rules.

3.2.2 *Scope of application by subject-matter*

The traditional core institution of personal security is the guarantee (or suretyship), in the present context designated as dependent guarantee (*supra* 1.2).

Four of the seven countries, while starting from the concept of the dependent guarantee, use a flexible formula indicating that other or even all forms of personal security are to be covered. Israel uses the formula "guarantees . . ., however that guarantee may be entitled", and mentions specifically

---

[20] Norway § 57 para. 4.

[21] Netherlands art. 7:857.

[22] Finland § 2 no. 6. If the connection with the debtor company is terminated, the security giver enjoys protection (§ 11).

[23] The two categories are defined in s. 19. The NIS amounts are indexed and today amount to approx. US $ 16,000 and 135,000, respectively (information provided by Prof. Einhorn).

[24] Belgium art. 1 no. 1 defines "consumer" as every natural person who "for the transactions governed by this Law acts for a purpose which may be regarded as alien to its commercial, professional or artisanal activities". French Code consomm. art. L. 313-7 para. 1.

[25] French Code consomm. arts. L. 313-7 to 313-10.

an "undertaking to indemnify".[26] Most of the relevant Belgian provisions are contained in a subdivision entitled "Personal securities" and the legislator uses (not very skilfully) in all relevant provisions the heavy formula "the dependent guarantee and, where applicable, any other form of personal security" or "the dependent guarantor and, where applicable, the giver of a personal security".[27] The Dutch legislator provides that the rules of the subdivision on consumer guarantees apply by analogy to contracts of a security giver as defined earlier who obliges itself to make a certain performance in case a third person does not perform a certain obligation of a different kind to the creditor.[28] Writers are agreed that this provision is meant to cover especially the giver of an independent guarantee.[29]

The Austrian approach differs from that of the other countries. Instead of a general formula extending protection beyond the dependent guarantee, the protective provisions individually extend coverage to different types of personal security, namely to independent guarantees and the cumulative assumption of an existing obligation.[30]

3.3 Precontractual phase: Creditor's duties of information and investigation

Several countries oblige the creditor before obtaining a consumer security giver's promise to inform the latter about various factors that are relevant for its decision to enter into the contract. Israel and Norway have quite extensive catalogues of relevant items, whereas Austria and Finland limit themselves to a smaller number and the statutes of the remaining three countries do not oblige the creditor at all.

The major points that must be disclosed or investigated relate to the security, the secured obligation(s), the financial situation of the debtor and that of the security giver.

Norway requires information about the general risk of a *personal security* and about other security rights with prior liability to the creditor,[31] while in

---

[26] Israel s. 18. "Indemnity" is the English name for an independent guarantee, i.e. a guarantee whose validity as well as extent and conditions of liability do not depend upon the validity or extent and conditions of an underlying obligation.

[27] Cf. especially arts. 34–36; cf. also arts. 33, 38 and 97.

[28] CC art. 7:863, referring expressly to the qualified definition of the dependent guarantor in art. 7:857, cf. *supra* 3.2, text preceding n. 21.

[29] Castermans, "Borgtocht", in: Nieuwenhuis, Stolker and Valk (eds.), *Vermogensrecht* (1999) 1045 et seq., 1057; Wessels, "Borgtocht", in: van den Berg, van der Heijden a.o. (eds.), *Compendium Bijzondere Overeenkomsten*, 8th ed. (1995) 449 ss., 459.

[30] Especially §§ 25c and 25d; cf. also §§ 25a and 25b (2).

[31] Norway § 59 para. 1 litt. a) and f), cf. also d).

Israel the nature of the personal security and the existence of other such securities and the security giver's share of liability must be disclosed.[32] A Finnish creditor must give information on the terms and conditions of the guarantee including the conditions for the guarantee becoming due and "other circumstances that are of essential importance for the position of the guarantor".[33] The Austrian provision requires written information on the special position of spouses as co-obligors and the impact of a divorce.[34] In Israel the draft of the contract must be made available to the security giver, and after signature a copy of the final contract must be given to the guarantor.[35]

With respect to the *secured obligation(s)*, Finland and Norway require the creditor to give information on the amount of its claims against the debtor.[36] By contrast, Israel has a catalogue of no fewer than seven items including, in particular, the contractual and the default rates of interest, variations of these rates and compound interest, and any indexation.[37] Belgium imposes upon the creditor the duty to transmit a copy of the (offered or final) contract of loan with the debtor to the would-be guarantor; violation of this duty discharges the guarantor![38] In Norway a copy of the loan contract must be handed over to the guarantor, in Israel this is necessary only upon the guarantor's request.[39]

The creditor's obligation to disclose the *debtor's financial situation* is regulated quite differently. A Finnish general clause merely obliges the creditor in general terms to disclose those circumstances of the debtor's financial situation that are important for the guarantor; the creditor is expressly relieved of any duty of confidentiality![40] The most elaborate provision is to be found in Austria: the creditor must inform the security giver if he recognizes or ought to recognize that the debtor probably will not, or not fully, be able to perform its obligations. However, the creditor may prove that the security giver would nevertheless have assumed, fully or at least partly, the security.[41]

The last item of precontractual investigation rather than disclosure relates to the *guarantor's financial situation*. Austria and Finland provide for this in rather similar terms: the security giver's obligation towards the creditor must be reduced (and in Austria even be completely released) if the creditor at the time

---

[32] Israel s. 22 (b).
[33] Finland § 12 para. 1.
[34] Austria § 25a.
[35] Israel s. 24 (a).
[36] Finland § 12 para. 2; Norway § 59 para. 1 litt. a) and b).
[37] Israel s. 22 (a).
[38] Belgium arts. 34 para. 1, 97.
[39] Israel s. 24 (2); Norway § 59 para. 2.
[40] Finland §§ 12 para. 2, 34.
[41] Austria § 25c; Supreme Court 25 July 2000, *Österreichische Juristenzeitung* (2001) 59 Evidenzblatt no. 10.

of assumption of the security knew or ought to have known that the security giver's obligation was obviously disproportionate to its financial capacity. In applying this rule, the security giver's age, solvency and interest in the creditor's performance must be taken into account.[42] A related provision of a general nature is to be found in France, except that it envisages a possible improvement of the guarantor's financial situation which remedies the initial defect.[43] Contrary to these incisive rules, a Norwegian creditor who in view of the would-be guarantor's financial means has serious doubts about the advisability of assuming the guarantee, shall inform so the candidate in writing.[44]

The most frequent sanction for non-performance of the various duties of information and investigation is a reduction of the guarantor's obligation.[45] In Austria in one case and in Israel in several cases, non-disclosure of specified points discharges the guarantor.[46] No sanction is provided for in Norway.

3.4 The consumer's contract of guarantee

Israel and Norway supplement their precontractual duties of disclosure by certain requirements as to the contents of the contract of guarantee. By contrast, France, Belgium and the Netherlands which refrain from imposing any precontractual duties compensate this gap by emphasizing the guarantor's protection by special rules on the contents of the guarantee contract and France imposes also special formalities.

In the four countries (except the Netherlands), the guarantee contract must indicate the amount of the guarantee,[47] in France and Norway also its duration.[48] In the Netherlands, a maximum amount regarding the principal must only be indicated where the secured credit is not fixed at the time of the assumption of the credit.[49] An Israeli "protected guarantor" incurs only subsidiary liability.[50] Norway very sensibly combines precontractual disclosure and contract by firstly demanding that all required specific precontractual information be incorporated into the contract; this is supplemented by the formula that all the creditor's precontractual information should be regarded as terms of the contract.[51] In

---

[42] Austria § 25d; Finland § 7.

[43] Code consomm. art. L. 313-10.

[44] Norway § 60 para. 2.

[45] Generally Finland §§ 7 para. 1 and 12 para. 3.

[46] Austria § 25 d; Israel s. 23 (a) no. (1) and (5). Cf. also for Belgium text *supra* at n. 38.

[47] Belgium art. 34 para. 1, CC art. 1326; France: Code consomm. art. L. 313-7, CC art. 1326; Israel s. 21; Norway § 61 para. 1.

[48] France: Code consomm. art. L. 313-7; Norway § 61 para. 2 *juncto* § 59 para. 1 lit. b).

[49] Dutch CC art. 7:858.

[50] Israel s. 27.

[51] Norway § 61 para. 2.

the Netherlands, a guarantee for future credits can at any time be limited to obligations that have already arisen, if no time limit had been agreed; and if a time limit had been agreed, it can be correspondingly limited after five years.[52]

Belgium, France and Norway demand that the consumer guarantor sign the contract by hand.[53] France goes even further by demanding a handwritten sentence which must exactly reproduce a statutory text summarizing the important points of the guarantee contract, i.e. the debtor's name, the amount and duration of the guarantee as well as the promise to pay the guarantee from the guarantor's income and assets if the debtor fails to pay the secured amount.[54] If a guarantor assumes solidary liability, an additional text has to be written and signed by hand and the guarantee be limited to a maximum amount.[55]

Any disregard of the prescribed minimum contents of the contract or its formalities is sanctioned by the discharge of the guarantor.[56]

3.5 Contractual duties of information

After conclusion of the contract of guarantee, two different kinds of a duty of information may be imposed: one of a general nature, independently of any specific occurrence, the other in the event of the debtor's default of payment.

Two countries impose for certain types of guarantees a periodical duty of information. In France, the creditor of an extended guarantee must annually inform the guarantor about the amounts of principal and accessory obligations.[57] In Finland, a corresponding semi-annual duty of information rests upon the creditor of a global guarantee, including one for a current account.[58] In addition, a guarantor can request at any time information on the amount of the debtor's obligations and facts about its financial capacity that may be relevant for the guarantor.[59] If these duties are violated, the French guarantor need not pay any accessory obligations, whereas its Finnish counterpart may obtain a reduction of its obligations.[60]

Four countries oblige the creditor to notify the guarantor about the debtor's default. In France, this duty has to be fulfilled at once, in Austria within a

---

[52] Dutch CC art. 7.861 paras. 1-2. Paras. 3-4 limit the guarantor's liability for two special situations.

[53] Belgium and France: CC art. 1326; Norway § 61 para. 1 sent. 2.

[54] Code consomm. art. L. 313-7 para. 2.

[55] French Code consomm. art. L. 313-8 para. 2 and Law 94-126 art. 47 para. 1.

[56] Belgium art. 97; France : the texts cited *supra* n. 47 and 55; Israel s. 21 (b); Norway § 61 para. 1.

[57] CC art. 2016 para. 2, as inserted in 1998; Code monétaire art. L. 313-22 para. 1.

[58] Finland § 13 para. 1.

[59] Finland § 14.

[60] France: cf. *supra* n. 57 ; Finland § 13 para. 2, § 14 para. 3.

reasonable time after the default, and in Israel within 90 days.[61] By contrast, in Belgium the guarantor need only be notified after the debtor has defaulted upon two instalments or at least one fifth of his payment obligations. The creditor must give information on delays or reductions that it may have granted.[62] Non-notification discharges the guarantor in Austria and France from payment of the accessory claims that arise during the period of non-notification.[63] In Israel the guarantor may claim damages,[64] while the Belgian statute does not provide a sanction.

3.6 Guarantor's obligation of payment

In Belgium, a consumer guarantor's obligation of payment does not fall due until the debtor has defaulted on two instalments or on one fifth of its total obligations or on the last instalment; further, the debtor must not have made payment within one month after the notice of default was sent to him by registered mail.[65] If the secured credit has been called in by the creditor because of the debtor's actual or threatening default of payment, a Finnish guarantor is entitled to make payment according to the terms that would apply if the secured credit would not have been called in. However, two additional conditions must be met: First, the guarantor must make payment within a time to be fixed by the creditor which must not be less than one month; and secondly, the guarantor must provide another guarantee or security to secure the debtor's remaining indebtedness.[66]

Very important for needy consumers is a new French rule inserted in 1998 into the Civil Code and designed to assure a minimum protection to over-indebted consumer guarantors. In no case may the obligations arising from guarantees have the effect of depriving the guarantor of the minimum resources fixed by the *Code de la consommation*.[67] Indeed, that Code, also amended in 1998, now provides that in fixing the rate of protected earnings of a debtor's salary a portion must be reserved that is necessary to cover the current expenses of the household.[68] Guarantors in Belgium may invoke a somewhat comparable

---

[61] French Code consomm. art. L. 313-9 first sentence; Austria § 25b para. 2 ; Law 94-126 art. 47 para. 3; Israel s. 26 (a) ; in Israel, the notice must describe certain special rules for "protected guarantors", s. 26 (b).

[62] Belgium art. 35.

[63] Austria § 25b second sentence; French Code consomm. art. L. 313-9 second sentence.

[64] Israel s. 26 (a).

[65] Belgium art. 36.

[66] Finland § 25 para. 1. The creditor must approve the substitute guarantee unless it is one issued by certain public authorities or by banks subject to public supervision.

[67] CC art. 2024 second sentence, as inserted by Law of 29 July 1998.

[68] Code consomm. art. L. 331-2, as revised by Law of 29 July 1998.

procedure designed to assist over-indebted consumers who have obtained consumer credits.[69]

3.7 Mandatory rules and their protection

The special rules protecting consumer guarantors which have been presented can only fulfil their protective function if they cannot be deviated from to the guarantor's disadvantage. This rule is laid down almost everywhere.[70] Only the French provision is less differentiated by proclaiming the protective rules simply as mandatory.[71]

Israel, the Netherlands and Norway go one step further by imposing mandatory character also on certain general provisions on guarantees. Dutch law extends mandatory character to virtually all general rules on guarantees.[72] Israel selects five rules, *inter alia* the provisions protecting the guarantor against unconsented alterations of the secured obligation; allowing him to invoke all the debtor's defences; and providing for his right of recourse against the debtor.[73] In Norway only the guarantor's right to invoke all the debtor's defences is made mandatory.[74]

Finland and Norway reinforce the mandatory character of the protective rules by declaring expressly that the mandatory provisions will be applied even if the parties have submitted the contract of guarantee to a foreign law.[75]

An additional means of protection for consumer guarantors is the Finnish and Norwegian rule under which arbitration clauses entered into before a dispute are not binding upon those guarantors.[76] Norway also offers the mediation of disputes by mediation boards which may be instituted by agreement between finance institutions (or an organisation of such institutions) and consumer organisations. While such proceedings are pending, the parties may not bring their dispute before the ordinary courts.[77]

---

[69] Belgium art. 38 para. 3.

[70] Austria § 2 para. 2; Belgium art. 4; Israel s. 32; Netherlands art. 7:862 lit. a); Norway § 2 para. 1.

[71] Code consomm. art. L. 313-16.

[72] Dutch CC art. 7:862 lit. a).

[73] Israel s. 32 *juncto* ss. 5, 7 and 12.

[74] Norway § 65 para. 4.

[75] Finland § 38; Norway § 2 para. 3.

[76] Finland § 37; Norway § 5 para. 2.

[77] Norway § 4.

3.8 Conclusion

First, a note of caution is necessary. The juxtaposition and comparison of the consumer-specific rules protecting guarantors suffers from one dilemma: in the narrow confines of the present article it was not possible to analyse also the general rules on the protection of guarantors. Generally it may be said, however, that this general level of protection is in most countries rather similar, except in the very recent statutes of the two Nordic countries of Finland and Norway.

Secondly, disregarding all details and concentrating on general trends, there appear to be three major approaches to protecting consumer guarantors. Under one approach which is exemplified by Finland, protection is based primarily upon precontractual duties of information with which the creditor is charged for the benefit of the would-be guarantor. Their violation is sanctioned by a reduction of the guarantor's obligation. The weak point however is the basis on which this reduction is to be determined. If it is left to the judge's discretion, this would cause uncertainty and therefore invite litigation.

The classical approach of the Continental countries is demonstrated by France and the Netherlands: special mandatory rules for the form and the terms of the contract of guarantee are established. In addition, certain general and optional protective rules for guarantors may be made mandatory for the benefit of consumer guarantors. The sanctions for violation of these rules are very clear: either the whole contract is void or at least any individual contract term which purports to deviate from a mandatory rule.

These two approaches are not mutually exclusive. Nothing speaks against, and much speaks for, combining them. The possible advantage of precontractual information on the financial status of the debtor is that careful would-be guarantors may be warned against foreseeable possible risks of an undertaking and therefore may desist from signing a guarantee. Any such refusal is to be preferred over subsequent disputes arising from the uninformed assumption of an obligation. However, the remedy for non- or misinformation on the financial status of a debtor should be clear and sharp: the consumer guarantor should be entitled, during a relatively short period of (about) 10 days, to reduce or completely avoid its guarantee. In addition, a qualified hand-written signature should be prescribed; the core protective rules of existing legislation should be made mandatory; and certainty on the amount and duration of the guarantee should be demanded.

Monitoring Directors in Public Companies under Israeli Law: Comparative Perspectives

Talia Einhorn*

---

* Dr. iur. (Hamburg). Professor of Law, Concordia International University Estonia/ Senior Research Fellow, T.M.C. Asser Institute, The Hague. I am very grateful to Mrs. Davida Lachman-Messer, Deputy Attorney General, Economic and Fiscal Legislation, Israel Ministry of Justice, and to Adv. Chaim Indig, Tel-Aviv, for providing me with insights into the special problems of the Israeli law on corporate governance.

Talia Einhorn, ed., Spontaneous Order, Organization and the Law –
Liber Amicorum Ernst-Joachim Mestmäcker © 2003 T.M.C.Asser Press, The Hague, The Netherlands

1. INTRODUCTION

Professor MESTMÄCKER opened his seminal work on *Verwaltung, Konzerngewalt und Recht der Aktionäre*[1] with the following citation: "The directors of such [i.e., public] companies . . . being the managers rather of other people's money than of their own, it cannot well be expected, that they should watch over it with the same anxious vigilance with which the partners in a private co-partnery frequently watch over their own . . . Without an exclusive privilege they have commonly mismanaged the trade. With an exclusive privilege they have both mismanaged and confined it".[2]

Directors may be tempted to act out of an egoistic compulsion. To remedy this situation, legislators are well advised to pay heed to the following corollary of Kant's categorical imperative:

> "The problem of organizing a state, however hard it may seem, can be solved even for a race of devils, if only they are intelligent. The problem is: 'Given a multitude of rational beings requiring universal laws for their preservation, but each of whom is secretly inclined to exempt himself from them, to establish a constitution in such a way that, although their private intentions conflict, they check each other, with the result that their public conduct is the same as if they had no such intentions'."[3]

Whereas ordinary people may only be inclined to misbehave, company directors are constantly in the position to make profits at the expense of others since they always deal with "other people's money".

Designing the proper legal rules that will restrain directors from exploiting others unfairly, on the one hand, yet encourage them to harness their entrepreneurial spirit and seize the opportunities that come their way for the benefit of their company, on the other, is a challenge for any legal system. It is to manifestations of this problem in Israeli law that I am devoting my article, dedicated in deep appreciation and gratitude to Professor MESTMÄCKER, a great master and teacher of liberal thinking and profound researcher of the role of law, private and public, in an open society, also a follower of Kant.

---

[1] E.-J. Mestmäcker, *Verwaltung, Konzerngewalt und Recht der Aktionäre* (Karlsruhe: Müller 1958) p. 3.

[2] Adam Smith, *Wealth of Nations* (New York: Random House 1937) p. 700.

[3] Kant, *On History* (L.W. Beck [ed.]) (Indianapolis: Bobbs-Merrill 1985) p. 112 (*Perpetual Peace*).

2. BASIC FEATURES OF ISRAELI COMPANY LAW AND CORPORATE GOVERNANCE

In 2000 the new Israeli Companies Law came into effect,[4] substituting the Company Ordinance, the original version of which dated back to the British Mandate and was based on the English Companies Act of 1929. Israeli Securities Law is governed by a separate legislative act.[5] In the beginning of the 1980s A first draft of the Companies Law was prepared by Professor Uriel Procaccia of the Hebrew University of Jerusalem. A Committee established by the Ministry of Justice in 1985, and chaired by Professor Aharon Barak, President of the Israel Supreme Court, drafted the Bill submitted to the *Knesset* (Israel's Parliament) in 1994. Its critical analysis and proper interpretation are decisive for determining the duty of loyalty imposed on directors in public companies under Israeli law.

Although it has been maintained that the Barak Committee carried out a comparative research among different legal systems, the minutes of the Committee meetings seem to indicate that the influence of English and American law prevailed.[6] This is also logical. The language barrier creates a formidable obstacle to the engagement in a serious study of Continental European legal systems. In addition, culture[7] as well as legal education and training play a significant role. The Israeli legal system is mixed.[8] Major parts of it, such as the law of torts and company law, are based on English common law imported into Palestine during the British Mandate (1918-1948). Other, no less important parts of the law of obligations and property have been reformed by the *Knesset* in a series of enactments based on Continental, essentially German

---

[4] Companies Law, 5759-1999, *sefer ha-chuqqim* (official publication of Israeli legislation) 1711, 189; the Companies Law was translated into English by Aryeh Greenfield (Haifa: A.G. Publications 1999).

[5] Securities Law, 5728-1968, *sefer ha-chuqqim* 541, 234, and all amendments published since.

[6] The Barak Committee Report, embodied in the draft Bill, mentions the legal systems it had studied: England, the US, Canada, New-Zealand, France, Germany, the EC, and others [sic]. It emphasizes that it has not given priority to any legal system. However, since English law formed the basis for Israeli commercial law and legal education is based on English Common Law, the Committee, for the sake of harmonizing the new law with the old, was inclined to adopt English law whenever appropriate. Cf. Draft Bill, 5756-1996, explanatory notes: introduction, basic principles, section 2.

[7] Cf. A. Licht, "The Mother of All Path Dependencies Toward a Cross-Cultural Theory of Corporate Governance Systems", 26 *Del. J. Corp. L.* (2001) 147.

[8] A. Barak, "The Tradition and Culture of the Israeli Legal System", in: A.M. Rabello (ed.), *European Legal Traditions and Israel* (Jerusalem: Sacher Institute 1994) 473, 483 et seq.; Zweigert/Kötz, *An Introduction to Comparative Law*, 3rd ed. (Oxford: Clarendon 1998) 235 et seq.

law. However, even when Israeli legislation is similar to Continental law in form, the style and method of legal development are in the tradition of the Common Law.[9] Even here differences must be taken into account. The American experience is varied, every state having its own company law, with securities legislation being governed by both federal and state law.[10] In addition, the duty of loyalty and the remedies for its breach have been developed extensively by the American and British courts. Israel with its 6.5 million citizens is too small for the legal system to develop on the basis of common law. Since proper conduct of business requires certainty, the behavior of directors in public companies should be governed, insofar as possible, by categorical rather than selective rules.[11] As we shall see this is not always possible, not always even advisable.[12] Many rules must be left to *ex post* interpretation and elaboration.

The legal rules adopted must fit the special features of the Israeli capital market, which is characterized by a high concentration of control in the listed companies. The majority of the shares of listed companies are held by owners of a controlling interest, whereas the Israeli public holds directly only 21% of the shares on the average. This makes it almost impossible for a hostile tender-offer to succeed in acquiring control of a company. A large proportion of companies is owned by companies controlled by public entities. The government owns directly companies in major sectors of the economy, such as transportation, aviation, defense industries, telecommunications, electricity etc. A significant percentage of the public companies is owned, or directly controlled, by families. Finally, "pyramidization" in large concerns (company groups) is widespread on the stock exchange.[13]

---

[9] D. Friedmann, "The Effect of Foreign Law on the Law of Israel", 10 *Israel L.Rev.* (1975) 192.

[10] Cf. R. Romano, *The Genius of American Corporate Law* (Washington D.C.: AEI 1993), suggesting that the US states have engaged in an inter-jurisdictional competition for corporate charters, which yielded a race more to the top than the bottom. State competition has benefited rather than harmed shareholders. Cf., however, the nuanced view provided by J. Coffee, in a symposium on the occasion of 100th Anniversary of the Delaware General Corporation Law of 1899: "The Direction of Corporate Law: The Scholars' Perspective", 25 *Del.J.Corp.L.* (2000) 79, 88 et seq., 95 et seq.

[11] Categorical rules are fairly precise and specific and apply uniformly to a broad category of situations. They do not allow much leeway for exceptions and defenses. Selective rules, in contrast, allow for differentiation in the treatment of cases within a general category of situations, due to the varying facts and circumstances of each case. Cf. R.C. Clark, *Corporate Law* (Boston: Little, Brown and Co. 1986) 234 et seq.

[12] Cf. L. Kaplow, "Rules versus Standards: An Economic Analysis", 42 *Duke L.J.* (1992) 557.

[13] Cf. *The Tel-Aviv Stock Exchange Annual Review 2000*, p. 15. The concentrated structure of Israeli public companies has been highlighted by Agmon/Lachman-Messer, "The Theory of Enforcement in the Draft Company Law", 26 *Mishpatim* (1995) 543, at pp. 547(16), 561 (in Hebrew). Regarding the development of the Stock Exchange during 1981-1990, see Saul Bronfeld,

3. THE STRUCTURE AND ROLE OF MANAGEMENT IN PUBLIC COMPANIES: OVERVIEW

Israeli Company Law foresees three organs: the shareholders' general meeting (hereinafter – the "general meeting"), the board of directors (hereinafter – the "board") and the general manager. In principle, the general meeting appoints the directors (s. 59) and the board appoints the general manager (ss. 250, 92(a)(7)). In practice, however, the general meeting usually appoints those directors that have already been selected by the general manager and the executive management of the company.[14]

The Israeli legislature opted for a one-tier management. The board has to formulate the company's policy and supervise the exercise of the general manager's office and his acts (s. 92, which also contains a non-comprehensive list of the board's powers and responsibilities).[15] The board has to elect one of its members to serve as chairman whose role it is to conduct its meetings (ss. 94, 96). The general manager (appointed, dismissed and monitored by the board – ss. 92(a)(7), 122) may not serve as chairman.

The board must include two outside directors appointed by the general meeting.[16] The majority of the votes at the meeting should include at least 1/3 of

---

Foreign Investment in Israel via the Tel-Aviv Stock Exchange (The Israeli International Institute for Applied Economic Review, Discussion Paper No. 2-11-90, November 1990); cf. also Y. Gross, *The New Companies Law* (Tel-Aviv 2000) (in Hebrew) 22 (15). Gross bases the conclusions regarding takeovers on an unpublished study by R. Harel/J. Abramovitch (January 1998), according to which almost all tender offers made in 1995-1997 were friendly rather than hostile.

[14] Gross, ibid., p. 110.

[15] I agree with Gross that it would have been better to formulate the board's duty as requiring supervision of the executive management. Cf. Gross, *supra* n. 13, p. 30.

[16] According to Procaccia, the new Companies Law was initially planned to require that every large public company would have to be directed by a board comprised of a majority of outside directors: U. Procaccia, *A New Corporate Law for Israel* (1989) (in Hebrew) 342. The Israeli final requirement of two outside directors may be compared with the English Cadbury Committee Code of Best Practice, recommending that the board of a listed company should include non-executive (defined similarly to outside directors), independent directors of sufficient caliber and number for their views to carry significant weight on the board's decisions (s. 1.3): Sir Adrian Cadbury, *Report of the Committee on the Financial Aspects of Corporate Governance* (1992). The Hampel Committee recommends that non-executive directors comprise at least one third of the membership of the board: Sir Ronald Hampel, *Committee on Corporate Governance – Final Report* (1998). The ALI *Corporate Governance Project* proposes a rule requiring a majority of outside directors on the boards of public companies. Although criticized, in general, for its assumption that "one size fits all", which has resulted with the American states paying it no heed, many public companies in the US have paid heed to this rule. For the criticism see F.H. Easterbrook/D. Fischel, *The Economic Structure of Corporate Law* (Cambridge, Mass.: Harvard University Press 1991) 14 (2). Regarding the composition of boards in US public firms see S. Bhagat/B. Black, "The Relationship Between Board Composition and Firm Performance", in:

all the votes of non-controlling shareholders, or their representatives present at the vote (s. 239(b)(1)). The total of opposing votes may not exceed 1% of all the voting rights in the company (the Minister of Justice may set a different percentage) (s. 239 (b)(2)-(c)). The outside director has to be an Israeli resident qualified to be appointed director (s. 240 (a)).

An individual may not be appointed an outside director, if at the time of the appointment or during the two years preceding it, he, his relative, partner, employer or a body corporate of which he is a controlling member, had an interest in the company, or in a person who was a controlling member of the company at the time of appointment, or in another body corporate, in which the company or a controlling member of it is a controlling member at the time of the appointment or during the two preceding years. "Interest" means an employment relationship, commercial or professional ties in general or control, as well as service as an officer.[17] This definition would exclude external attorneys, financial advisers and accountants providing services to the company. The board must convene at least once in three months (s. 97). Protocols of the proceedings at board meetings must be prepared and kept in the company's registered office during a period of seven years after the date of the meeting (s. 108).

The board must appoint an audit committee of at least three of the board members (ss. 114, 115(a)). All outside directors must be made members (s. 115(a)). In contrast, the chairman, any director employed by the company or regularly giving it services, a controlling shareholder or his relative, must not be members (s. 115 (b)-(c)). The tasks of the audit committee include (s. 117) finding defects in the business management of the company and proposing to the board ways of correcting them, as well as deciding whether to approve acts and transactions that require its approval. The latter include certain acts involving a conflict of interest of officers owing a duty of loyalty to the company (s. 254 (a)). To be competent to give such approval the audit committee must include among its members at least two outside directors, at least one of whom must be present at the meeting in which the approval is granted (s. 279).

Hopt/Kanda/Roe/Wymeersch/Prigge (eds.), *Comparative Corporate Governance – The State of the Art and Emerging Research* (Oxford: Clarendon 1998) 281.

[17] Under s. 1 of the Companies Law: "'Officer' – Director, General Manager, Chief Business Manager, Deputy General Manager, Vice General Manager, any person who holds a said position in the company, even if he has a different title, and also any other manager who is directly subject to the General Manager."

4. THE SCOPE OF THE DUTY OF LOYALTY: ANGELS, MEN OR WOLVES?

The President of the Israel Supreme Court, Professor Barak, has defined the duty of loyalty as a high standard of proper behavior, requiring that man to man be an angel,[18] going beyond the regular requirement under civil law to act *bona fide*. This latter duty Justice Barak interprets as a requirement that man to man be a man.[19] Section 254 of the Companies Law has turned the officers' duty of loyalty previously developed by the case law into an integral part of the law in the books. It reads:

> Obligation of loyalty
> 254. (a) An officer owes an obligation of loyalty to the company, shall act in good faith and shall act to its benefit, and inter alia he shall –
> (1) refrain from any act that involves a conflict of interest between the performance of his function in the company and his performances of any other function or his personal affairs;
> (2) refrain from any activity that involves competition with the company's business;
> (3) refrain from exploiting a business opportunity of the company in order to obtain a benefit for himself or another person;
> (4) disclose to the company any information and deliver to it any document that relates to its affairs, which came into his possession by virtue of his position in the company.
> (b) The provisions of subsection (a) shall not derogate from any obligation of loyalty by the officer toward any other person.

Under the new law officers must refrain from acts which place them in a conflict of interests with the company (s. 254 (a)(1)). However, in certain cases they may seek approval thereof.

The following sections will analyze the scope of the duty of loyalty and its monitoring under Israeli law, in several kinds of conflict of interest, or self-dealing, of officers, arising within a company or a group of companies. All these cases have the following features in common: they involve transactions between the company and another person who may or may not be the officer; the officer has decision-making influence over the action taken by the company;

---

[18] A. Barak, *Judicial Discretion* (Tel-Aviv: Papirus 1987) (in Hebrew) p. 495 § 546. This reference, like many others to Israeli law, its analysis and interpretation, have been omitted from the English translation bearing the same title (translated by Yadin Kaufmann, New Haven: Yale 1989).

[19] Ibid., pp. 492-493, § 524.

and, finally, the officer has a greater personal interest in the welfare of the other person involved in the transaction than in the welfare of the referent company.[20]

4.1 **Basic self-dealing**

This kind of conflict of interest is characterized by a transaction involving a bilateral exchange between the referent company and some other person, who might or might not be identical with the influential insider, in our case a director. In an early Israeli decision such basic self-dealing was prohibited.[21] The court cited and followed an English decision of the House of Lords, stating that "it is a rule of universal application that no one, having such duties to discharge, shall be allowed to enter into engagements in which he has, or can have, a personal interest conflicting, or which possible may conflict, with the interests of those whom he is bound to protect".[22] In line with that English decision, the court considered the principle prohibiting a fiduciary from putting himself in a conflict of interests so absolute that it did not allow any examination of its fairness. The prohibition of such transactions has proved to be impractical and was abandoned in the US, England and in Israel.

4.1.1 *Special approval*

A transaction between the company and its officer, as well as a transaction between the company and another person in which an officer has a personal interest, require special approval (s. 270(1)). Such approval may only be granted if the transaction does not harm the company's welfare (s. 270, first sentence). If the transaction is not exceptional approval by the board will suffice, unless the company by-laws prescribe a different manner of approval (s. 271). If the transaction is exceptional it must first be approved by the audit committee and then by the board (s. 272). An "exceptional transaction" is defined as "a transaction that is not in the ordinary course of the company's business, a transaction not on market terms, or a transaction that is liable to have

---

[20] Cf. Clark, *supra* n. 11, 147 et seq. A nuance of this paradigm is provided (ibid., 149) by the case where the insider has no particular interest in the welfare of the third person, yet he has some interest in a side effect of the transaction. For example, if the company repurchases the shares of an insurgent, resulting in the influential insider retaining control and reaping its rewards.

[21] *Tocatly* v. "*Shimshon*", Civil appeal 267/55, 11 P.D. (Law Reports of the Israel Supreme Court) 1569.

[22] *Aberdeen Railway* v. *Blaikie Bros.* (1854) 1 Macq. HL 461 (H.L.). Cf. also H. Marsh, "Are Directors Fiduciaries?", 22 *The Business Lawyer* (1966) 35, 36 et seq. In the US, too, transactions between a director and his corporation were prohibited and, as such, voidable at the instance of the corporation or its shareholders.

a substantial effect on the company's profitability, property or obligations" (s. 1). If a majority of the board members are interested in the approval of an exceptional transaction the transaction requires an approval of the general meeting as well.

The determination of which transactions are considered "exceptional" is a matter of interpretation. The question would revolve around the meaning given to the terms "not in the ordinary course of the company's business", or "not on market conditions", as well as "liable to have a substantial effect on the company". It is submitted that the better interpretation would cover any transaction which cannot be compared with others carried out regularly by the referent company and not involving any special financial calculations. An example of a transaction which is not exceptional would be the purchase or sale of fungible goods which have a fixed market price on any given day and therefore there is no fear that the transaction with the officer will be lop-sided.

4.1.2 *Disclosure*

> "If a company officer . . . in a public company knows that he has a personal interest in an existing or proposed transaction of the company, then – without delay and no later than the Board of Directors' meeting at which the transaction is first discussed – he shall disclose to the company the nature of his personal interest, including every substantive fact or document" (s. 269(a)).

It has been pointed out that more American litigation on ratified self-dealing transactions, especially in the case of public companies, concerns the adequacy of disclosure of a conflicting interest than the effect that ratification should have.[23]

According to the Securities Regulations (preparation of annual financial reports), 1993, the annual reports must include a description of transactions made between the referent company and its subsidiaries and interested parties (that is, anyone who holds at least five percent of the issued stock, or may appoint one or more of its directors or its general manager, or is himself a director or a general manager, or an incorporated entity in which such a person holds at least 25% of its share capital or of its voting rights or may appoint at least 25% of its directors). The report should mention the sums involved, the method for determining prices, terms of credit, and other terms relevant to the pertinent case (s. 64(3)).

---

[23] Clark, *supra* n. 11, p. 179.

4.1.3 *Transaction must not harm the company*

The approval of the board may only be granted if the transaction does not harm the company's welfare (s. 270, first sentence). It is submitted that this requirement should be interpreted as commanding fairness.[24]

In the US, the concept of fairness has two basic aspects: fair dealing[25] and fair price.[26] The former treats the questions of how the transaction was initiated, structured, negotiated, disclosed to the directors, approval for it sought, etc. The "fair price" aspect relates to the economic and financial considerations, account being taken of all relevant factors. A self-dealing transaction is unfair to the referent company if it is less advantageous than a similar arm's length transaction concluded by a rational, independent, well-informed board. Alternatively, the transaction could be compared, as to its fairness, with a comparable transaction made between independent parties in a competitive market. However, making use of this alternative depends on the existence of a relevant competitive market.

"The test for fairness is not a bifurcated one as between fair dealing and price. All aspects of the issue must be examined as a whole since the question is one of entire fairness."[27] The requirement that the company not be harmed should be interpreted as the equivalent of having both aspects fulfilled.

4.1.4 *The process of approval*

In a transaction which is not exceptional the interested director may take part in the board meeting (s. 278(a)). "Exceptional transactions" require the approval of the audit committee first. The board may not delegate its powers to approve such a transaction to a committee (s. 112(a)(7)). The audit committee may only grant its approval if two outside directors are members of the committee and at least one of them was present at the meeting in which the approval was granted.

It is submitted that the proper interpretation of the requirement that the approval of the board be given, requires that disclosure be made to a *meeting* of the board. This interpretation is not straightforward since, under the Companies Law, the board need not convene to take a decision if all directors entitled to be present and vote have agreed to that (s. 103). In such cases, the Chairman writes

---

[24] Cf., I. Haviv-Segal, *Corporate Law in Israel*, vol. 1 (Tel-Aviv 1999) 435 et seq.

[25] *Weinberger* v. *UOP, Inc.*, 457 A.2d 701, 711 (Del.Supr. 1983); Knepper/Bailey, *Liability of Corporate Officers and Directors*, 5th ed. (Charlottesville, Virginia: Michie 1988, 1994 suppl.) 133 et seq.; cf. also The American Law Institute (ALI), *Principles of Corporate Governance: Analysis and Recommendations* (St. Paul, Minn.: ALI 1994) § 5.01 et seq.

[26] *Weinberger* v. *UOP, Inc.*, ibid.; Knepper/Bailey, ibid., 141 et seq.

[27] *Weinberger* v. *UOP, Inc.*, ibid.

a protocol to which the signatures of the directors are then added. It may be that, as a rule, it is not a very good one. It is submitted that, where approval is needed for a transaction involving conflict of interest, a proper meeting must be held. Of course, use may be made of modern technology so the meeting would be held by telephone or video conference. Meetings are necessary for the group of directors to check the transactions from different perspectives. It is through discussion that irregularities can be detected. *Baldwin* v. *Canfield*[28] provides an excellent example. A director engaged in a self-dealing transaction which had been approved by each disinterested director separately and at different times. Had there been a proper directors' meeting the fraud would have reasonably been detected. Properly written minutes may save hours, providing the court with the necessary evidence regarding the propriety of the approval procedure.[29]

In an English case it was held that, even if all the directors knew, such knowledge does not comply with the statutory requirement that disclosure be made to "'a meeting of the directors of the company' (which is a wholly different thing from knowledge by individuals and involves the opportunity for positive consideration of the matter by the board as a body)".[30]

The interested director must not be present neither at the meeting of the audit committee nor at the meeting of board convened to approve the transaction and he may not participate in the vote (s. 278(a)). An exception is made if the majority of the directors are interested. In that case they may be present and vote at both meetings (s. 278(b)). However, such cases call for the additional approval by the general meeting (s. 278(c)). Unless the transaction involves a controlling shareholder (a situation covered by s. 275, in which at least 1/3 of the votes of shareholders without personal interest are required, or, alternatively, an opposition of no more than 1% of all voting rights), no special majority is required.[31]

---

[28] N.W. 261 (Minn. 1879), and its discussion by Clark, *supra* n. 11, pp. 110-113.

[29] Among many cases, see, for example, the careful assessment by the Delaware court of the board meetings' records in *Weinberger* v. *OUP*, *supra* n. 25; *Unocal Corp.* v. *Mesa Petroleum Co.*, Del. Supr., 493 A.2d 946 (1985); *Kahn* v. *Lynch Communication Systems*, Del. Supr., 638 A.2d 1110 (1994).

[30] *Guinness plc* v. *Saunders*, [1988] 2 All ER 940 (CA); affirmed by the House of Lords: [1990] 2 AC 663 (HL).

[31] Cf., in contrast, with Delaware where, although the Delaware Statute does not on its face mandate disinterested shareholder approval, the Delaware Supreme Court has held that shareholder approval of interested director transactions must come from a majority of disinterested, independent, fully informed stockholders: *Fliegler* v. *Lawrence*, 361 A.2d 218, 221 (Del. 1976): "The purported ratification by shareholders would not affect the burden of proof in this case because the majority of shares voted in favor of exercising the option were cast by the interested directors in their capacity as shareholders. Only about one third of the 'disinterested' shareholders voted, and we cannot assume that such nonvoting shareholders either approved or disapproved". See, however, the fine distinctions drawn in *William* v. *Geier*, 671 A. 2d 1368 (Del. 1996).

4.1.5 *Onus of proof*

Many cases involving conflict of interest are decided on the basis of onus of proof which in turn depends upon the standard of review chosen.[32] Therefore, this question is of the utmost importance.

In a landmark decision in Israeli company law, given under the Companies Ordinance, the court held (per J Barak) that where there is real danger that a director does not act in good faith and in the interest of the company he has to discharge the onus of proof.[33] It is submitted that, as soon as there is a conflict of interest, the onus of proving fairness should shift to the defendant director.

In the US, where company officers stand on both sides of the transaction the burden of proof shifts to them to demonstrate that the transaction is fair and serves the best interests of the company.[34] The rationale is that "where corporate fiduciaries, because of a conflict, are disabled from safeguarding the interests of the stockholders to whom they owe a duty, the Court will furnish compensatory procedural safeguards by imposing upon the fiduciaries an exacting burden of establishing the utmost propriety and fairness of their actions".[35]

"The requirement of fairness is unflinching in its demand that where one stands on both sides of a transaction, he has the burden of establishing its entire fairness, sufficient to pass the test of careful scrutiny by the courts."[36] Where the entire fairness standard of review is used, the self-dealing fiduciary must show that the transaction was at an entirely fair price. To have the protection of the business judgement rule, a director "can neither appear on both sides of a transaction nor expect to derive any personal financial benefit from it in the sense of self-dealing, as opposed to a benefit which devolves upon the corporation or all stockholders generally."[37]

---

[32] Block/Barton/Radon, *The Business Judgment Rule: Fiduciary Duties of Corporate Directors*, 5th ed. (New York: Aspen 1998) 33, with further references to case law.

[33] *Kosoi* v. *Bank Feuchtwanger*, Civil appeal 817/79, 38(1) PD 253.

[34] Knepper/Bailey, *supra* n. 25, 132; Block/Barton/Radon, *supra* n. 32, 29 et seq. with references therein.

[35] *Van de Walle* v. *Unimation, Inc.*, 1991 Del. Ch. LEXIS 27; Fed. Sec. L. Rep. (CCH) P95, 834.

[36] *Weinberger* v. *UOP, Inc.*, *supra* n. 25, 710.

[37] *Aronson* v. *Lewis*, 473 A.2d 805, 812 (Del. 1984); *Williams* v. *Geier*, 671 A.2d 1368, 1377 n. 19 (Del. 1996)

4.1.6 *Good faith*

Directors must act in good faith (s. 254). This is a standard of behavior expected from company officers not only in Israel.[38] The business judgement rule presumes that company directors act in the honest belief that the action taken was in the best interests of the company.[39] However, in a self-dealing transaction mere good faith should not preclude a finding of a breach of the duty of loyalty.[40] The transaction must also be fair.

4.1.7 *Effect of transaction*

A transaction of a company with its director is of no effect for the company and the director if the transaction was not approved according to the requirements of the Companies Law, or if there was a substantial defect in the process of approval or if the transaction was carried out in substantive digression from the approval (s. 280(a)). Such a transaction is also of no effect toward any other person who knew of the director's personal interest in the approval of the transaction, and also knew or should have known that the transaction had not been approved as required. (s. 280(b)).

An exceptional transaction made by a company with another person without the required approval being received is voidable, at the choice of the company, if that person knew of the personal interest of the company director in the approval of the transaction and knew or should have known that the transaction had not been approved as required. Such a person may also have to compensate the company for the damage caused to it (s. 281). It has been persuasively argued that a voidability rule makes more sense for public companies than for close ones.[41]

As aforementioned, one of the pre-conditions to approval is that the transaction does not harm the company. If the transaction is unfair to the company, the approval cannot be considered to have been properly given. It is submitted that the application of the objective, entire fairness standard of review should affect the measure of damages assessed against directors in the event of liability. If

---

[38] Cf. also American case law: Block/Barton/Radon, *supra* n. 32, 80 et seq., and cases referred to therein.

[39] Interestingly, an Israeli scholar has suggested that the good faith requirement has been inserted "due to the suspicion that the authorization procedures will not assure that beneficial transactions are approved . . . this is essentially an additional mechanism for overseeing the quality of transactions": Z. Goshen, "Controlling Corporate Agency Costs: A United States – Israeli Comparative View", 6 *Cardozo J. Int'l & Comp. L.* (1998) 99, 106.

[40] Knepper/Bailey, *supra* n. 25, 132.

[41] Clark, *supra* n. 11, pp. 164-165.

they fail to discharge their burden under the fairness test they may be liable not only to compensate the corporation or its shareholders for losses sustained, but also be required to rescind the transaction or pay restitutionary damages. This measure may certainly exceed the losses to the corporation and its shareholders and may, in analogy to trust measures of recovery, in some instances, capture their profit from the transaction.[42] It is submitted, that a *per se* rule of damages should apply if the directors failed to make proper disclosure.[43]

4.2 Directors' remuneration

Similarly to basic self-dealing, this category of transactions, too, is bilateral.[44] The directors provide services and are paid therefor. These transactions are always carried out directly between the company and its influential, self-interested insiders. But, unlike basic self-dealing, there is no way for company law to prohibit such transactions.

A contract of the company with its director regarding the conditions of his service, or his employment in other assignments, must be approved by the board, and must further fulfill the condition that the contract does not harm the company (s. 270(3)).[45] If the director also controls the company (as defined therein) the transaction is considered "exceptional" (such transactions are further governed by special regulations enacted under the law). The rules discussed in section 4.1 apply to the approval procedure.

---

[42] D. Friedmann, *The Law of Unjust Enrichment, vol. 1*, 2nd ed. (Aviram 1998) (in Hebrew) pp. 537 et seq.. Cf. also Lord Hoffmann, "Duties of Company Directors", in: Andenas/Sugarman (eds.), *Developments in European Company Law. Vol. 3: Directors' Conflicts of Interests* (London: Kluwer Law International 2000) 1, 6; Knepper/Bailey, *supra* n. 25, 178 et seq.; Block/Barton/Radon, *supra* n. 32, 33; *Cinerama, Inc.* v. *Technicolor, Inc.*, 17 Del. J. Corp. L. 551, 569 (Del. Ch. 1991), affirmed in part and revised in part in *Cede & Co.* v. *Technicolor, Inc.* (*Technicolor II*), 634 A.2d 345 (Del. 1993).

[43] Cf. Block/Barton/Radon, *supra* n. 32, 530 et seq. with further references: "[i]n Delaware existing law and policy have evolved into a virtual *per se* rule of damages for breach of the fiduciary duty of disclosure".

[44] The characterization of these transactions is further discussed by Clark, *supra* n. 11, pp. 148 et seq.

[45] Sir Richard Greenbury, *Directors' Remuneration – Report of a Study Group* (1995) requires that, to avoid potential conflicts of interest, boards of directors should set up remuneration committees of non-executive directors to determine, within agreed terms of reference, the company's policy on executive remuneration, and specific remuneration packages for each of the executive directors (art. A1). The board should determine the remuneration of the non-executive directors, including the members of the remuneration committee.

If the majority of the directors are interested, the approval of the remuneration program requires the approval of the general meeting (s. 278(c)).[46] The example of *Noerr* v. *Greenwood*[47] is instructive. In this case the Delaware Court of Chancery rejected a claim that two "nearly identical" stock option plans, one for non-employee directors and the other for employee directors, had been approved by disinterested directors. The court held that the vote approving the two plans should not be 'separated' to enable the directors to establish disinterested director approval. Otherwise, boards could grant their members any degree of benefit they desired yet escape scrutiny by creating a separate plan for each director and then having all directors other than him vote to approve each plan.

The approval of the general meeting is likewise needed if the director in question has also a controlling interest (s. 270(4)). This is especially warranted in the Israeli structure of corporate governance, where it often happens that the directors of public companies also have a controlling interest therein. However, the approval of only 1/3 of the shareholders at the general meeting may not suffice to provide the necessary monitoring.[48]

It has been suggested that, since the evaluation of directors' remuneration defies review for its reasonableness, courts give substantial weight to apparent defects in the process whereby remuneration has been decided.[49] This helps to eliminate payments for past services which the company has not contracted to pay. Such payments constitute illegal waste or a gift of corporate assets and as such are illegal. Not even a majority of the shareholders have the power to give away company property against the protest of the minority.[50] In addition, it makes directors' compensation transparent, alerting both investors and potential investors to the way the company uses its assets.

The English experience is noteworthy. In the 1990s the media produced reports on the excessive level of directors remuneration. The public outcry led to the enactment of primary and secondary legislation, to the publication of the Greenbury report,[51] and to further requirements imposed on listed companies by the London Stock Exchange. All of those have made directors compensation quite transparent. Ironically, according to the Hampel report, the practical

---

[46] See the discussion in section 4.1.1 above.

[47] Del Ch. Lexis 121, 1997 WL 419633 (Del. Ch. July 16, 1997).

[48] Cf. the decision of the Delaware court in *Fliegler* v. *Lawrence*, *supra* n. 31.

[49] Clark, *supra* n. 11, 195; cf. also E.G. Orlinsky, "Corporate Opportunity Doctrine and Interested Director Transactions: A Framework for Analysis in an Attempt to Restore Predictability", 24 *Delaware Journal Of Corporate Law* (1999) 451, 522 et seq. with further references.

[50] *Rogers* v. *Hill*, 289 US 582, 591-592 (1933); cf. also Clark, *supra* n. 11, 198.

[51] The Greenbury Report, *supra* n. 45.

consequences of the detailed disclosure was an increase in the remuneration received by directors.[52]

Finally, a word about remunerating directors, at least in part, with stock options.[53] Their potential effect on membership structures has resulted with a wide-spread requirement in the US and in Europe that such plans be approved by a general meeting resolution.[54] On the one hand, stock options seem to align the interests of the directors with those of the shareholders. However, it is not necessarily so. It has been evidenced that option plans may pose a threat of massive managerial opportunism through transfers of large equity stakes to executive insiders.[55] Option plans may create a conflict between the interest of shareholders in receiving dividends and the directors' interest to maximize the value of the shares.[56] Another difference between the interests is that shareholders are expected to diversify their investments and become risk-neutral regarding the risks assumed by companies. Therefore, they are interested in the company undertaking risky projects with the expectation of higher returns. The director who has tied his fortunes with one company will be less willing to assume risks than may be desirable for the company.[57] For that reason, he may also tend to expand the company's line of business rather than specialize. Whereas the shareholders may be interested in specialization, his own risks would clearly be higher if all eggs are put in one basket.

Furthermore, even the apparent alignment of the director's interests to the welfare of the company may not be as straightforward as it seems. Although successful executive directors profit from the increase in share price, failing directors may receive from their companies "failure rewarding" remuneration packages that ease their way out.[58] There is also the regular "free rider" problem,

---

[52] Sir Ronald Hampel, *Committee on Corporate Governance – Final Report* (1998). Cf. C. Villiers, "Disclosure and Corporate Governance", in: *UK Law for the Millenium* (London: UK National Committee of Comparative Law 1998) 148, 164 et seq. with further references; B. Cheffins, *Company Law: Theory, Structure and Operation* (Oxford: Clarendon 1997) 655 et seq. provides a sharp analysis anticipating these results.

[53] For further studies of this matter cf. S. Levmore, "Symposium Norms and Corporate Law: Puzzling Stock Options and Compensation Norms", 149 *U. Pa. L. Rev.* (2001) 1901, with further references; J. Wulff, *Aktionen für das Management* (Köln: Heymann 2000), comparing the legal systems of Germany, England, France and Austria; Monks/Minow, Corporate Governance (Malden, Mass: Blackwell 1995) 242 et seq.

[54] H. Hirte, "Convertible Bonds and Option Bonds: A Comparative Study", 1 *EBOR* 507, 515; Thomas/Martin, "The Effect of Shareholder Proposals on Executive Compensation", 67 *U. Cin. L. Rev.* (1999) 1021, 1033-1034, 1039, 1051-1053.

[55] Wenger/Kaserer, "German Banks and Corporate Governance: A Critical View", in: *Comparative Corporate Governance, supra* n. 16, 499.

[56] Wulff, *supra* n. 53, 8-9.

[57] Wulff, ibid., 9.

[58] Cheffins, *supra* n. 52, 657 et seq. with further references.

since it is difficult to give each director stock options according to his contribution to the company's success. It may also not be a good idea, since he may then engage in tactics that would increase his share at the expense of others, and, ultimately, compromise the best interests of the company. Companies have also engaged in "repricing" options when the market goes down. Finally, it is often the case that the price of shares is often dependent on the general performance of the capital market more than on the efforts of the individual directors.[59] In view of these of these conflicts of interests, an alternative rule may be more appropriate whereby monitoring be achieved by a decision of the majority of the votes of uninterested shareholders at the general meeting.

4.3 **Directors' appropriation of corporate opportunities**

Whereas sections 4.1 and 4.2 dealt with bilateral transactions made by the company *with* its directors, this section deals with one way takings by the director *from* the company.[60]

Under Israeli company law, a director must, as part of his duty of loyalty, refrain from any activity that involves competition with the company's business (s. 254(2)), and also from exploiting a business opportunity of the company in order to obtain a benefit for himself or another person (s. 254(3)). The company may nevertheless approve any of these acts provided that the director acted in good faith and the act or its approval do not cause the company harm; and that the officer disclosed the nature of his personal interest in the act, including all substantive facts and documents, to the company at a reasonable time before the approval was discussed (s. 255(a)). If the acts are "substantial" (that is, according to s. 1, acts which are liable to have a substantial effect on the company's profitability, property or obligations), they should be approved in the same procedure as "exceptional transactions". Otherwise, they require approval similar to that given to transactions which are not exceptional.[61]

Much depends on interpretation. Courts should distinguish between full-time executive directors and outside directors. The former are expected to devote all their time and efforts to enhance the best interests of the company they serve. Therefore, it has been submitted that a good rule should forbid them from taking any active business opportunities (passive opportunities do not pose similar problems).[62] According to that view, no concessions should be made even if the company does not want to pursue the opportunity itself, or the

---

[59] Wulff, *supra* n. 53, 8-9.

[60] Clark, *supra* n. 11, 149; Orlinsky, *supra* n. 49, 457.

[61] See the discussion of the procedure of approval in section 4.1.1 *supra*.

director is willing to resign before seizing the opportunity. This rule is easily enforceable, on the one hand, and the injustice and waste created by it in a very limited number of cases make its negative effects negligible, on the other. It will often not be possible to receive a shareholders' consent that would be adequately informed and impartial. In the least, the rule should require explicit consent given for a specific opportunity by a majority of disinterested shareholders.[63] However, this is not the rule chosen by the Israeli legislature. According to s. 255, the director is only required to act in good faith and receive the approvals needed according to whether or not the act is considered substantial. It has likewise been submitted that the preferable rule for outside directors should be different from that applicable to the executive director: those should not be allowed to use the company's resources, including its information, to develop or acquire business opportunities.[64] Once again, Israeli law is more permissive.

The remedy for breach of this fiduciary duty should be profit disgorgement by imposing a constructive trust on the director's new business.[65]

4.4 **The company group context**

Nowadays the public company "no longer stands in the firmament like an independent fixed star; it is rather, merely one component in a galaxy of heavenly bodies. Entrepreneurial functions need no longer be carried out by alliances of the most varied form . . . In the course of this evolution, larger companies have diversified their activities either by allowing certain functions to be performed by independent entities . . . The result has been the formation of satellite systems".[66]

---

[62] Cf. Clark, *supra* n. 11, pp. 243-247; see however the rules proposed by ALI, *supra* n. 25, § 5.05.

[63] Ibid., 248-251.

[64] Ibid., 252. On information belonging to the company see also Easterbrook/Fischel, *supra* n. 16, 254 et seq.

[65] See Friedmann, *supra* n. 42, 559 et seq.; "It is an act of disloyalty for a fiduciary to profit personally from the use of information secured in a confidential relationship, even if such profit or advantage is not gained at the expense of the fiduciary. The result is nonetheless one of unjust enrichment which will not be countenanced by a Court of Equity." (*In re Tri-Star pictures*, 634 A.2d 319, 334 (Del. 1992)); cf. R.C. Nolan, "Conflicts of Interest, Unjust Enrichment, and Wrongdoing", in: *Restitution: Past, Present and Future: Essays in Honour of Gareth Jones* (Cornish et al [eds.]) (Oxford: Hart 1998) 87; Solomon/Schwartz/Baumann/Weiss, *Corporations: Law and Policy* (St. Paul, Minn.: West 1994) 812.

[66] U. Immenga in: *International Encyclopedia of Comparative Law*, vol. XIII: Business and Private Organizations, Chapter 7: Company Systems and Affiliations (1979), at p. 3.

Despite the importance of company groups in Israeli business life, this subject-matter was not regulated by the new company law. The Bill included the following provision which was not incorporated into the law:

> 279. (a) Notwithstanding the provisions of s. 279 [s. 254 of the law], the following acts would not, in themselves, be deemed acts made in conflict of interests:
> (1) The serving of an officer in several companies belonging to the same company group;
> (2) The presence and voting in the board by an officer serving in both the parent company and a subsidiary wholly owned by the parent company;
> (b) S. 279 does not prevent an officer in a company belonging to a company group from taking into account the interests of the company group, provided that he is convinced that his decision would not harm the company in which he serves in the long run; if he so acted – he would not be deemed to have violated his duty of loyalty.

The only rule left from this section is s. 270(1) last sentence providing: "However, an officer in a parent company and also in a wholly-owned and wholly-controlled subsidiary shall not be deemed to have a personal interest in a transaction between the parent company and the subsidiary only because he is an officer in both." It is probably fortunate that s. 279 was not enacted. It would have raised many difficult questions of interpretation and it is very doubtful that it is good law. Comparative perspectives may help to see that.

A special regime for corporate groups must have the objective of providing protection to "outsiders" in a dependent company (i.e. its minority shareholders) and creditors.

The German Law on Joint Stock Companies (*Aktiengesetz*) has a special chapter on company groups. To make up for the losses resulting from diverted corporate opportunities, outside shareholders of subsidiaries of a German contractual group must be adequately compensated. They have a right to an annual dividend, calculated according to the value of their shares when the group was formed and the likelihood of such dividends had such a group not been formed.[67]

Under US law the basic operative rule is that the interests of a subsidiary must not be impaired. Shareholders and directors are prevented by fiduciary obligations from exerting detrimental influence.[68] In *Perlman* v. *Feldman*[69] the court held that a director and dominant shareholder stands in a fiduciary

---

[67] K. Hopt, "Legal Elements and Policy Decisions in Regulating Groups of Companies", in: Schmitthoff/Woolridge, *Groups of Companies* (London: Sweet & Maxwell 1991) 81, 100.

[68] Immenga, *supra* n. 67, 46 et seq.

[69] F.2d 173 (2d cir.), cert. denied, 349 US 952 (1955).

relationship to the corporation and to the minority stockholders as beneficiaries. Absolute and most scrupulous good faith are the very essence of a director's obligation to his corporation. Therefore, when the sale of a controlling block of stock necessarily resulted in a sacrifice of the element of corporate good will and in unusual profit to the fiduciary who caused the sacrifice, the latter should account for his gains. In this way a rule was imposed concerning the mandated sharing of the rewards of taking a corporate opportunity between the taking fiduciary and the minority shareholder.[70]

The rule providing that a director sitting on both sides of a transaction must discharge the burden of establishing its entire fairness applies with the same stringency to directors holding dual or multiple directorships (so-called interlocking directors), as in a parent-subsidiary context.[71] "Thus, individuals who act in a dual capacity as directors of two corporations, one of whom is parent and the other subsidiary, owe the same duty of good management to both corporations, and in the absence of an independent negotiating structure, or directors' total abstention from any participation in the matter, this duty is to be exercised in light of what is best for both companies".[72]

The existence of such duties can create difficult problems, such as the duty to disclose or not to disclose confidential information about one corporation to the other. Dual directorships may be "rife with 'catch 22' conflict situations".[73]

There is hardly a developed state in which the specific risks to minority shareholders and creditors within company groups are not seriously coped with by the legal system.[74] The solutions may differ fundamentally, yet the problem has not gone unattended. Israeli law will have to come to grips with these problems, too.

---

[70] Cf. Clark, *supra* n. 11, p. 254 with further references.

[71] *Weinberger* v. *UOP, Inc.*, *supra* n. 25, 710; cf. also *Levien* v. *Sinclair Oil Corp.*, 261 A.2d 911, 915 (Del.Ch. 1969).

[72] *Weinberger*, ibid.; cf. also *Warshaw* v. *Calhoun*, 221 A.2d 487, 492 (Del.Supr. 1966).

[73] Block/Barton/Radon, *supra* n. 32, 270; referring also to *Management Techs., Inc.* v. *Morris*, 961 F. Supp. 640, 645 (SDNY 1997) noting conflicting duties owed by director of parent corporation and two wholly-owned subsidiaries (1) to the parent corporation, and (2) to creditors of the subsidiaries in light of the perilous financial circumstances of those companies; cf. also Monks/Minow, *supra* n. 53, 198.

[74] Forum Europaeum Corporate Group Law, "Corporate Group Law for Europe", 1 *EBOR* (2000) 165-285, 172 et seq.; cf. also the articles of C. Windbichler, "'Corporate Group Law for Europe': Comments on the Forum Europaeum's Principles and Proposals for a European Corporate Group Law", 1 *EBOR* (2000) 265-285; and J. Kluver, "European and Australian Proposals for Corporate Group Law: A Comparative Analysis", 1 *EBOR* (2000) 289-315.

5. Monitoring by the company

5.1 Monitoring by management

It is clear that only the executive management can run the company's daily business. The executive managers are hired to devote their time and effort to create value from the capital provided by the shareholders. The general manager must enjoy wide discretionary powers to make decisions quickly even if those involve reasonable risk. His business judgement should not be second-guessed. At the same time, it is clear that the discretion is not given to an executive manager to maximize his own wealth. Can the board monitor the general manager and other inside directors?

The inside directors may have the information to monitor but may be constrained by considerations such as loyalty to other insiders, or fear that they may lose their office if they monitor their colleagues effectively, or have their interests ignored when the board is called to approve a transaction in which they are interested.

The effectiveness of outside directors as monitors has been questioned and studied without however conclusive results being reached. One study[75] provides an analysis of seven such studies, some finding positive correlation between outside directors and firm performance, another showing negative correlation, others – no correlation, and the last showing either positive or negative correlation according to the criteria used for carrying out the measurements. It is therefore small wonder that the Chancellor of Delaware Court of Chancery has concluded that "courts should not rely reflexively on the status of a director as an 'inside director' or an 'independent director' to inform their determination of whether that director's actions were right or wrong, proper or improper, informed or uninformed".[76] Nevertheless, the study is useful in that it distinguishes between different types of outside directors, according to their backgrounds and experience, and according to the different monitoring roles they are required to fulfill in different types of firms.

In any case, there are several factors that should alert us to the deficiencies of this monitoring device. To begin with, the persons selected are usually compromising rather than critical and challenging. The general manager or CEO will often play an important role in the selection of outside directors, who, in turn, will be careful not to disrupt their relationship with him. Even if such a director

---

[75] L. Lin, "The Effectiveness of Outside Directors as a Corporate Governance Mechanism: Theories and Evidence", 90 *Nw. U. L. Rev.* (1996) 898.

[76] William B. Chandler III, "On the Instructiveness of Insiders, Independents, and Institutional Investors", 67 *U. Cin. L. Rev.* (1999) 1083.

wishes to monitor he will be constrained by limited information. Outside directors often depend on the insiders for receiving the information necessary to make evaluations of corporate decisions.[77] Usually, they do not meet often enough to be able to supervise the board. Finally, their interests are not identical to those of the shareholders. Shareholders with diversified investments are interested in the company undertaking risky projects with the expectation of higher returns. In contrast, outside directors may be expected to adopt a more cautious and conservative approach.[78]

In Israel the law provides for only two outside directors, only one of whom is required to attend the meeting of the audit committee. Further research will be required to assess the role of outside directors and the audit committee in Israel.[79]

The above deficiencies should not make the legislature give up boards altogether. Whereas individuals can excel in tasks requiring creativity and bright ideas ("How many great novels or symphonies were written by committees?"[80]), small groups, like boards of directors, are better at revealing the flaws in these brilliant ideas. Therefore, board meetings are important formalities which should not be dispensed with.

5.2 **Monitoring by shareholders**

5.2.1 *Enhancing shareholders' participation*

The new company law has introduced several rules to enhance the capability of shareholders to monitor directors at general meetings. Among those are the following: the "one-share, one-vote" rule; the voting through a proxy (s. 83; Other rules included in the Bill concerning the proxy statement were not enacted by the *Knesset*); an obligation imposed on institutional investors to take part in general meetings (s. 77(a), Law on Mutual Funds).

To be effective, rules regarding proxy statements must still be elaborated. However, it may be that even the proxy mechanism would not help arouse the interest of individual shareholders. If they have diversified their portfolios they

---

[77] For a checklist of the necessary information see Monks/Minow, *supra* n. 53, 185 et seq.

[78] Cf. Cheffins, *supra* n. 53, 105-107; Clark, *supra* n. 11, 183 et seq.

[79] The Law Commissions' Report on Directors' Conflicts of Interest calls for further research on the role of non-executive directors in overseeing service contracts: Joint Consultation Paper by the English and Scottish Law Commissions, *Company Directors: Regulating Conflicts of Interests and Formulating a Statement of Duties* (London: The Stationary Office 1998) marginal number 3.70. Empirical studies in the UK have not been promising: Villiers, *supra* n. 52, 164-165 with further references.

[80] Clark, *supra* n. 11, 110.

may not be interested in investing the time and effort needed to monitor.[81] They may often find it easier to "exit" than to take meaningful part in general meetings. If, as is often the case in Israel, their chances of affecting the decision of the controlling majority are small (despite the improvement due to the "one-share, one-vote" rule), they would not make a special effort to try. The situation is of course different where there are controlling shareholders. Those are able to monitor the directors, unless they, or their family members, are the directors themselves. Transactions with controlling shareholders are subject, under Israeli law, to more stringent provisions and regulations regarding disclosure and approval.

The mandatory participation of institutional investors creates a different problem. To begin with, it is not clear that they will best represent the interests of individual shareholders. The problem of "agents watching agents" looms high.[82] Additionally, or alternatively,[83] they too would often find it more efficient to "exit" and shift from one investment to another.

Again, the deficiencies of the monitoring by shareholders' participation should not be a reason to give up this monitoring mechanism. First of all, the duties of disclosure to shareholders provide them with a very important tool for evaluating their investment and deciding whether they have reason to complain or exit.[84] "Sunlight is said to be the best of disinfectants; electric light the most efficient policeman".[85]

Secondly, shareholders' voting rights are necessary for tender offers to take place. This creates a market for corporate control when another person identifies a potential in a company that the current management does not. In the current Israeli capital market companies are not prone to hostile takeovers. This however may change in the future.

5.2.2 *Enhancing shareholders' remedies*

The new law includes provisions on derivative and class actions (ss. 194-206 and 207-218 respectively).[86] A derivative suit may be brought if the company

---

[81] Easterbrook/Fischel, *supra* n. 16, 81-88.

[82] B.S. Black, "Agents Watching Agents: The Promise of Institutional Investor Voice", 39 *UCLA L. Rev.* (1992) 811; E.B. Rock, "Foxes and Hen Houses? Personal Trading by Mutual Fund Managers", 73 *Wash.U.L.Q.* (1995) 1601; Chandler, *supra* n. 76.

[83] Easterbrook/Fischel, *supra* n. 16, 88 et seq.

[84] Cf. Law Commissions' Report on Directors' Conflicts of Interest, *supra* n. 80, part 3: economic considerations, § 3.64.

[85] Louis D. Brandeis, *Other People's Money* (New York: Stokes 1932) 92.

[86] Cf. U. Procaccia, "Crafting a Corporate Code from Scratch", 17 *Cardozo L. Rev.* (1996) 629, 641 et seq.; Agmon/Lachman-Messer, *supra* n. 13, 574 et seq.

sustained the injury. However, if the shareholder himself primarily sustained an injury different from that caused to the company he may bring a direct action, in which case he will also collect the proceeds. It should be possible to bring both direct suits and derivative suits as class actions.[87] Moreover, sometimes the same factual situation may give rise to both kinds of claims. If the company bought property from a majority shareholder. The transaction was approved by a majority of the shareholders, including the majority shareholder himself. One minority shareholder challenges the transaction, claiming that its terms were unfair. He may choose to bring a derivative suit claiming that the transaction was a case of unfair self-dealing. Alternatively, he may choose to bring a direct action, claiming that his voting rights were impaired. Had the majority shareholder not voted, his own vote would have had its proper influence on the result, and the approval would not have been granted.[88] Another important aspect of the derivative suit is the *pro-rata* recovery.[89] If the corporation is already in liquidation and its assets are about to be distributed, or if the wrongdoers continue to control the company and there is reason to fear that they will dissipate the corporate recovery, the court may award the proceeds *pro rata* directly to the individual plaintiff.

Enhancing shareholder remedies does not itself solve the problems of monitoring either. It is not yet clear how permissive the courts will be in allowing class actions. Especially in companies dominated by a few controlling shareholders, a shareholder will require special incentives and enhanced remedies to bring a case in court.

6. Monitoring by the Securities Authority

The American capital markets have attained the size that enables issuers to raise long-term equity capital and, at the same time, permit investors to remain highly liquid. This overall success in attracting both investors and companies wishing to be listed has many reasons. The importance of the formidable securities laws, and the high standards of accounting and disclosure, cannot be overstated.[90]

---

[87] Cf. Clark, *supra* n. 11, 663.

[88] Ibid.

[89] B. Grossfeld, in: *International Encyclopedia of Comparative Law*, vol. XIII: Business and Private Organizations, Chapter 4: Management and Control of Marketable Share Companies, 121.

[90] See e.g. R.S. Karmel, "Will Convergence of Financial Disclosure Standards Change SEC Regulation of Foreign Issuers?", 26 *Brooklyn J. Int'l L.* (2000) 485; L. Lowenstein, "Financial Transparency and Corporate Governance: You Manage What You Measure", 96 *Colum. L. Rev.* (1996) 1335.

Therefore, securities authorities need not fear to make exacting demands. This has also implications for the monitoring conundrum: "People who are forced to undress in public will presumably pay some attention to their figures."[91] It is the role of securities laws to make directors pay attention to their figures rather than resist the order to disrobe. Silence may not be gold!

However, even this mechanism is not perfect. To begin with, it is limited in manpower and cannot be expected to monitor all self-dealing directors. For the enforcement of most rules it must rely on other mechanisms. In addition, regulators may be tempted to over-deter. It has been pertinently observed that "market professionals who estimate [costs and benefits of a practice] wrongly suffer directly; academics and regulators who estimate wrongly do not pay a similar penalty. Persons who wager with their own money *may* be wrong, but they are less likely to be wrong than are academics and regulators who are wagering with other people's money".[92]

7. Monitoring by the court

"In most matters it is more important that the applicable rule of law be settled than that it be settled right".[93] It has been pointed out that this statement is especially true for business people who must make economic decisions every day based upon the rule of law.[94] This brings me to the final point. The success of Delaware in attracting almost half of the companies listed on the New York Stock Exchange and nearly 60% of Fortune 500 companies should be attributed not only to its superior legislation. This feature alone could have easily been emulated elsewhere. The role of Delaware's judge-made law is perhaps even more significant.[95] In Delaware, corporate law cases are heard in the chancery court rather than in courts of general jurisdiction as in other US states. The judges appointed to this court have expertise in business law. In addition, the judges are appointed for renewable twelve-year terms. Judges who are not responsive to the State policy on corporate law will not be re-appointed. Delaware's courts have distinguished itself for dealing expeditiously with complicated cases of law and fact in the fields of corporate and securities law.

If Israel wishes to have a thriving capital market, it must also have a

---

91 Louis Loss, *Fundamentals of Securities Regulation*, 2nd ed. (1988) 33 (cited by Lowenstein, ibid., 1344).

92 Easterbrook/Fischel, *supra* n. 16, 31

93 *Burnet* v. *Coronado Oil & Gas Co.*, 285 US 393, 406 (1932) (Brandeis J, dissenting).

94 Orlinsky, *supra* n. 49, 452.

95 Romano, *supra* n. 10, 39-40; cf. J.E. Fisch, "The Peculiar Role of the Delaware Courts in the Competition for Corporate Charters", 68 *U. Cin. L. Rev.* (2000) 1061.

specialized court that will deal with corporate law, insolvency, and securities. Israel has just enacted a new law which will require extensive interpretation. The field is dynamic. New techniques of public offerings and new financial products are constantly being developed. The judge must be able to recognize methods employed by directors' abusing their powers, yet not be unnecessarily suspicious and second guess their business judgement. Such matters cannot be settled only on the basis of general principles such as "good faith". The judge must be able to appreciate the underlying economic and business considerations, be acquainted with the practical aspects of running the business, and read the pertinent financial reports and understand the accounting methods used. Monitoring by directors and shareholders is deficient. Hence, the great importance of the "fairness" test decided by the court. But to decide this issue the judge must be highly qualified to begin with and gain further expertise through experience and learning.

In the world of today all countries are competing for investors. Security and confidence in the market attract investors. Certainty regarding the governing legal rules is a precondition to security and confidence. Certainty is also a precondition to attracting business people to make public offerings on the Israeli market. A specialized court can provide not only certainty but also qualitative decisions given in real time, that the rule decided will be both right and timely.

8. Conclusion

The new Companies Law prescribes an assortment of remedies to combat self-dealing by directors. Some are prophylactic, i.e. meant to prevent a breach of the loyalty duty in the first place. Others operate *ex post*. Not one of those promises to bring the ultimate cure. Indeed, each is substantially deficient and flawed. Yet, the combination of them all should make it possible to place the directors of Israeli public companies on the right side of the angels.

It is recommended that a court be established, with expertise in the highly specialized fields of company and securities law, to decide cases qualitatively and timely and provide the certainty so necessary to attract enterprises and investors alike.

Academic lawyers should play a very important role in the development of Israeli law. Israel is too small for the legal system to develop on the basis of judge-made law alone. In addition, it is almost impossible for a court of law to engage in serious comparative study when solving a case at hand. The academic lawyers can provide the new legislative basis with the support of legal literature that would carefully, conscientiously, and modestly, being aware of its own fallibility, analyze theories and solutions advanced in Israel and in other jurisdictions. Extensive theoretical and empirical studies, devoted to all aspects of business organization, are published as a matter of course in every developed country. One could say that the words are all there. There is only an urgent need to rearrange them with the final goal of tailoring to the Israeli measure the best legal rules that would check abuse yet enhance business and bring to bear the entrepreneurial spirit which provides the drive for success. Since this field is very dynamic every rule designed will then serve as a new starting point for further debate and refinement.

Professor MESTMÄCKER with his outstanding writings on the role of private law in an open, civil society, with the theories he has developed all based on intimate and detailed knowledge of the underlying facts, economic consequences carefully considered, is a role model for any academic wishing to engage in such an endeavor.

The Law on the National Book Price Maintenance

Volker Emmerich*

> "... It is even more surprising to see for how long a well organized trade sector succeeds, even in our media concentrated century, to hide its own particular economic interests behind arguments of a holy war for the cultural values of a nation. Clearly, an important role must be attributed to the fact that the same enterprises published books and newspapers alike. ...
> It is important ... to realize that business circles may rely on the support of the German government in enforcing their own particular interests. This is wicked. In this respect, the dispute over the book price maintenance was not an isolated phenomenon..."
> *Karel van Miert, Markt, Macht, Wettbewerb. Meine Erfahrungen als Kommissar in Brüssel [Market, Power, Competition. My Experiences as Commissioner in Brussels]*[1]

1. Introduction

The above lines were written by Karel van Miert, acting as the competent Commissioner for Competition in Brussels from 1993 to 1999. In short,

---

* Dr. iur., Ordinary professor at the University of Bayreuth. Previously Judge at the High Court (Oberlandesgericht) of Nuremberg. Dr. Katerina Elmaliah, Adv., attorney at law in Tel Aviv, Israel, translated the German original text into English.

1 Stuttgart/München: Deutsche Verlagsanstalt 2000, p. 164-165.

Talia Einhorn, ed., Spontaneous Order, Organization and the Law –
Liber Amicorum Ernst-Joachim Mestmäcker

unequivocal words, he describes the attitude of politicians, publishers and media to the dispute on the German and Austrian book price maintenance, realized in the German "Law for Safeguarding the National Book Price Maintenance" of 30 November 2000[2] and the Austrian "Federal Law on the Price Maintenance of Books".[3] Both acts were aimed at rescuing the maintenance of book prices, after the expiration of the last transitional period for the adaptation to Article 81 EC granted to the publishers by the Commission.[4]

The enactment of the laws was preceded by a campaign unique in its form. To "save the book as a cultural value", enormous pressure was exerted to force the European Commission to grant the motion of the publishers for an exemption, notwithstanding the well-founded doubts of the Commission. For once, the scandalous details of this campaign are well documented in the published report of a directly involved commissioner,[5] on the one hand, and by the rational analysis of the German Monopoly Commission,[6] on the other. We may refer the reader to both texts. However, to complete the picture, we cannot abstain from illustrating some crucial points:

Everything had started with a motion for exemption under Article 81 para. 3 EC, filed by the German and the Austrian publishers for their cross-border price maintenance system. Subsequently, the Commission issued an administrative notification of 29 July 1994 expressing the opinion that a Collective Undertaking contributed to an optimized distribution of goods and, consequently, contributed to the promotion of the book as a cultural value.[7] In view of the fact that, due to an arbitrary exchange rate, the price level in Austria was higher than the one for identical books in Germany (80% of the books sold in Austria were produced in Germany), the Commission requested an alignment of prices until 30 June 1996. However, the publishers rejected any change and started the above-mentioned campaign against the Commission which was, subsequently, urged to extend the period for the alignment by several years.[8] In 1998, after it turned out that, again, nothing had happened, the Commission formulated the

---

[2] *BGBl* 2000 I no. 52, p. 1634.

[3] *öBGBl.* 2000 I no. 40.

[4] See the reasons to the draft bill of the above law, *Bundestags-Drucksache* (*BT-Dr.*) 14 (2000)/3509, p. 4.

[5] Karel van Miert, *supra* n. 1, pp. 144-165.

[6] *Wettbewerbspolitik in Netzstrukturen* [*Competition Policies in Net Structures*], 13th Main Opinion, 1998/1999 (Baden-Baden: Nomos 2000) text numbers 687 et seq. (pp. 390 et seq.).

[7] Letter of 29/7/1994, no. 07363-IV/34.657 (printed in BUCH 1994 brochure 16, p. 2 = Th. Hoffmann, "Buchpreisbindung auf dem Prüfstand des Europarechts" ["Book Price Maintenance at the Test Bench of European Law"] *GRUR* [2000] 555, 562 fn. 75.

[8] Letter of 28/6/1996 – IV/34.657.

grounds for a complaint.[9] In response to the adherence of the publishers to their negative position, van Miert proposed that the Commission reject the exemption motion of the publishers. However, his intent was jeopardized by the resignation of the Santer Commission in 1999.[10]

Presumably, the publishers had counted on that resignation. However, to their astonishment, the new Commissioner Prodi continued the proceedings. Consequently, they suddenly accepted the changes the Commission had requested since 1994(!).

The Commission reacted with its notification of 10 June 2000,[11] in which it first specified the most important characteristics of the new Collective Undertaking, which, in particular, waived the price maintenance for the cross-border trade in books. Subsequently, the Commission held that the new Collective Undertaking was incompatible with Article 81 para. 1 EC.[12] However, in view of the fact that price maintenance had been abolished for books re-imported into Germany, the Commission specified that such a breach ceased to have any substantial impact on the trade between Member States and that, therefore, Article 81 para. 1 ECT, read literally, did not apply to it.[13] The above-mentioned laws enacted in Austria and Germany were the answer of the German and Austrian legislators to this notification.

In the following lines, we shall briefly relate the contents of the above laws, in order to understand whether the "solution" offered therein is suitable to achieve the envisaged objective of safeguarding the national book price maintenance in Germany and Austria (see 2 and 3 hereunder). Subsequently, we shall examine, whether the principle of these laws, i.e. the acceptance of the national price maintenance (subject to the exclusion of the cross-border trade by the Commission[14]), is indeed compatible with Article 81 para. 1 EC.

---

[9] K. van Miert, *supra* n. 1, pp. 152 et seq.

[10] Ibid., pp. 159 et seq.

[11] *OJ* [2000] C 162/25.

[12] Notification of 10/6/2000, *supra* n. 11, para. 12.

[13] Ibid., para. 13.

[14] Explicitly K. van Miert, *supra* n. 1; Notification of 10/6/2000, *supra* n. 11, at p. 26, paras. 13 et seq.

2. The German Law for Safeguarding the National Book Price Maintenance of 30 November 2000[15]

2.1 Overview

The EU Member States have adopted various attitudes towards the institution of book price maintenance:[16] In six Member States no book price maintenance exists (namely, Belgium, Finland, UK, Ireland, Luxembourg and Sweden). Switzerland adopted the same legal position in 1997. All other Member States decided to preserve a book price maintenance by crystallizing two different systems: Portugal, Spain and, since 2000, Austria, follow the "example" of the French *Loi Lang* of 1981 and based the price maintenance on a legal act. In Germany, Denmark, Italy and the Netherlands, the price maintenance is based on an agreement between the publishers and the book traders, which, in Germany, has been exempted from the general price maintenance prohibition of § 14 GWB (the German Law against Restricted Trade Practices) by § 15 GWB.[17]

The Law for Safeguarding the National Book Price Maintenance of 30 November 2000 added three new sentences to § 15 GWB. In the following lines, we shall discuss these sentences 2 to 4 to § 15 para. 1 GWB in detail.

2.2 The right to price maintenance

§ 15 para. 1 GWB, which has *not* been amended in 2000, states that the price maintenance prohibition of § 14 GWB does not apply in the event that an enterprise either binds the buyer of *its* publications, legally or economically, to keep to certain prices when reselling the products, or if such an enterprise binds the buyers to uphold certain product prices until the product reaches the consumer. "Publications" for the purposes of this clause are books and magazines.[18]

---

[15] *BGBl.* 2000 I, p. 1634.

[16] See the overviews in: Monopolies Commission, 13th Main Opinion, *supra* n. 6, text numbers 667 et seq. (pp. 384 et seq.); A. Obert, *Die Preisbindung im Buchhandel in Deutschland und im Vereinigten Königreich in der Sicht des europäischen Rechts* [*Price Maintenance in the Book Trade in Germany and in the UK froom the Perspective of European Law*] (Munich: Beck 2000); Id., "Die Buchpreisbindung in Deutschland und im Vereinigten Königreich" ["Book Price Maintenance in Germany and in the UK"], *GRURInt.* [1999] 1017.

[17] For details, see Emmerich, *Kartellrecht* [*Antitrust Law*], 9th ed. (Munich: Beck 2001) § 14 (pp. 108 et seq.); Id., in: Immenga/ Mesmäcker, *GWB*, 3rd ed. (Munich: Beck 2001) § 15; Obert, *Preisbindung im Buchhandel*, *supra* n. 16, pp. 49 et seq.; Id., *GRURInt.* [1999] 1017, *supra* n. 16.

[18] Emmerich, *Kartellrecht* [*Antitrust Law*], *supra* n. 17, § 14 1c (p. 110 f.); Id., in: Immenga/ Mestmäcker, *GWB*, *supra* n. 17, § 15, at n. 8 et seq.

To date, the generally accepted conclusion from the wording of the law was that the exemption privilege for publications was granted exclusively to publishers and not to other enterprises including the book importers. Only a publisher is capable of binding the buyers of "*its publications*", whereas importers deal with the publications of third parties and not with their own, which, in the common understanding, excluded the applicability of § 15 para. 1 GWB. The original wording of the GWB of 1957 emphasized this distinction by explicitly limiting the price maintenance privilege to "publishing enterprises". The new wording, enacted in 1973, was not aimed at changing the above fact.[19] Therefore, book importers were and still are entitled to conclude price maintenance arrangements only if they have explicitly been entitled thereto by the foreign publisher, or, in the event of re-importation of German books, by the domestic German publisher.[20]

In the wording of the Law for Safeguarding the National Book Price Maintenance, § 15 para. 1 sent. 2 GWB now states that the book price maintenance may be applied equally in cross-border trade. The legislators intended to clarify that price maintenance arrangements were now accessible not only to publishers but equally to all other enterprises including, in particular, the exclusive importers of German and foreign publishers.[21]

Such "clarification" leads to confusion: The new sent. 2 of § 15 para. 1 does not amend sent. 1 of the provision, stating that an enterprise may bind only the buyer of "its (own) publications" with respect to reselling prices, the generally accepted interpretation being that importers are excluded thereof. Therefore, it remains unclear, what is meant in sent. 2 of § 15 para. 1 GWB. With sent. 1 remaining unchanged, importers may conclude price maintaining agreements exclusively with a respective authorization by the publishers. However, this has already been clear even without the clarification...

---

[19] *BGHZ* 46, 74, at p. 78 = *NJW* [1967] 343 (to the original wording of the law); *BkartA Tätigkeitsbericht* 1962, p. 32; Bechtold, *GWB*, 2nd ed. (Munich 1999) § 15 n. 7; Emmerich, in: Immenga/ Mestmäcker, *GWB*, *supra* n. 17, § 15 marginal notes 11 et seq.; Klosterfelde/ Metzlafff, in: Lange/ Bunte, *Kommentar zum deuschen und europäischen Kartellrecht* [*Commentary on the German and European Antitrust Law*], vol. I, 9th ed. (Neuwied/ Berlin: Luchterhand 2001) § 15 n. 10 f.

[20] Bundeskartellamt, (BkartA) (Federal Antitrust Office), *Tätigkeitsbericht* [*Activity Report*] *1962*, p. 58; 1964, p. 27; 1970, p. 77; Bechtold, Emmerich and Klosterfelde/Metzlaff, *supra* n. 19; Obert, *Die Preisbindug im Buchhandel*, *supra* n. 16, p. 143.

[21] Reasons, *Bundestags-Drucksache* (*BT-Dr.*) 14 (2000)/3509, p. 4.

2.3 The form of the price maintaining agreement and horizontal elements

Under § 15 para. 2 sent. 1 GWB, a price fixing agreement must be in writing specifying the prices and their components. In Germany, there are approx. 3,350 book publishers and over 5,100 traders producing and selling 70 to 80,000 new publications each year,[22] not including the Austrian book traders and publishers that must be added to the above figures. In view of these quantities, it is clearly impossible that each of these many publishers will bind every single book trader in Germany and Austria with respect to every new publication in writing to maintain the stipulated consumer price. Therefore, the German and previously also the Austrian publishers developed the system of Collective Undertakings. These documents list the fixed prices of the listed German publishers and are distributed to and countersigned by every single trader, thereby binding him or her to maintain the consumer prices fixed by the publishers.[23] The distribution of this document is made by a Trustee of the publishers. Until the year 2000, the price maintenance of re-imports was included in the conditions of the Collective Undertaking.[24] Such a system of general unification of conditions and discounts clearly includes horizontal aspects which interfere with the cartel prohibitions of § 1 GWB and Article 81 EC. Nevertheless, German practice to date rejected all doubts regarding the effectiveness of the Collective Undertaking to save the book price maintenance under all circumstances.[25]

The doubts regarding the effectiveness of the German book price maintenance were clearly not eliminated by the new Law for Safeguarding the National Price Maintenance enacted in 2000. This law was neither aimed nor in

---

[22] Sources: Monopolies Commission, 13th Main Opinion, *supra* n. 6, text numbers 661 et seq. (pp. 379 et seq.); Obert, *Die Preisbindung im Buchhandel*, *supra* n. 16, pp. 18 et seq.; to the economic analysis of the book market see, *inter alia*, H. Henning, *Marktstruktur und Marktverhalten im deutschen Buchmarkt* [*Market Structures and Market Behaviour on the German Book Market*] (Baden-Baden: Nomos 1998); H. Stumpp, *Die Preisbindung für Verlagserzeugnisse: Wettbewerbsbeschränkung oder Regulierung zur Beseitigung von Marktunvollkommenheiten?* [*Price Maintenance for Publications: Restriction of Competition or a Regulation for the Correction of Market Failures?*] (Baden-Baden: Nomos 1999).

[23] For the wording of the Collective Undertaking of 1974, which has been amended in 1979 and 2000 see in Franzen, *Die Preisbindung des Buchhandels* [*Price Maintenance of the Book Trade*], 3rd[d] ed. (Munich: Beck 1987) text numbers 126 et seq. (pp. 133 et seq.).

[24] No. A 5 para. 3 of the Collective Undertaking of 1974, printed in Franzen, ibid., text numbers 161 et seq. (pp. 154 et seq.).

[25] See in particular BGH, LM no. 32 to § 1 GWB = *NJW-RR* [1986] 259 = *WuW/E* BGH 2175; LM no. 18 to § 16 GWB (Bl. 2 f.) = *NJW* [1990] 1993 = *WuW/E* BGH 2615; to the criticism see LG Düsseldorf, *WuW/E* LG/AG 589; Emmerich, in: Immenga/ Mestmäcker, *GWB*, *supra* n. 16, § 15 n. 21; Id., *Kartellrecht*, *supra* n. 16, § 14, 1d (p. 111 f.).

a position to limit the applicability of the cartel prohibitions in § 1 GWB or Article 81 EC. Therefore, considering its indisputable horizontal elements,[26] the book price maintenance cannot be reasonably expected to find the approval of the cartel authorities in the long run.

2.4 Universality, the problem of re-imports

In Germany as well as in Austria, the prevailing opinion is that the book traders may be reasonably expected to abide by the book price maintenance only as long as the price fixing system is, in fact, applied universally.[27] This means that the price fixing publishers must organize their distribution channels in such a way that will include every single re-seller, committing him or her to honor the fixed prices or, at least, to transfer the fixed prices onwards to its buyers (theoretical universality). In addition, the price maintenance must in fact be implemented by the book-traders, in order to grant equal competitive conditions to all of them (factual universality).[28]

The fulfillment of these preconditions (which are basically a corollary of § 242 and 273 BGB) is difficult enough in a closed national market. However, with the realization of the Common Market in the European Union, it has become virtually impracticable. For various reasons, it is impossible to maintain the price fixing practice universally towards both bound book traders and outsiders:[29] The most important reason is, naturally, that cross-border price maintenance systems are in direct conflict with Article 81 para. 1 part 2 lit. a EC, which also regulates the vertical price maintenance as previously practiced

---

[26] Blanke/ Kitz, "Grenzüberschreitende Buchpreisbindung und europäisches Gemeinschaftsrecht" ["Cross-Border Book Price Maintenance and European Community Law"], *JZ* [2000] 118, 121; Hoffmann, *supra* n. 7, at pp. 567 et seq.; Chr. Kirchner, "Preisbindung für Verlagserzeugnisse?" ["Price Maintenance for Publications?"], *AfP* [1999] 227; Thurnher, "Hält oder fällt die Preisbindung für Bücher?" ["Can the Price Maintenance for Books be upheld?"], *ÖBl.* [1995] 155 (however, positively to Art. 81 para. 3 EC); Differently H. Grosshardt, *Die Preisbindung für Verlagserzeugnisse nach Europäischem Gemeinschaftsrecht* [*Price Maintenance for Publications under the Law of the European Community*] (Diss. Konstanz 1995).

[27] Fundamental *BGHZ* 142, 192 = *NJW* [1999] 3043; *BGHZ* 143, 232 = *NJW* [2000] 2504; hereto Emmerich, "Unlauterer Wettbewerb" ["Unfair Competition"], in: *50 Jahre Bundesgerichtshof, Festgabe aus der Wissenschaft* [*50th Anniversary of the Federal Court, Festive Edition of Scientists*], Vol. II (Munich: Beck 2000) 627, at pp. 634 et seq.; Id., in: Immenga/ Mestmäcker, *GWB*, *supra* n. 16, § 15 marginal numbers 103 et seq.

[28] In detail see Emmerich, ibid.; Obert, *Preisbindung im Buchhandel*, *supra* n. 16, pp. 73 et seq.

[29] See already Mestmäcker, *Europäisches Wettbewerbsrecht* [*European Competition Law*] (Munich: Beck 1974) § 47 III 2/3 (pp. 586 et seq.).

in both Germany and Austria.[30] In addition, we must take into account that in many Member States price maintenance is prohibited and, therefore, price fixing for re-imports will encounter insoluble problems. Last but not least, we must keep in mind that price maintenance for re-imports has been, correctly, interpreted as a violation of domestic law, i.e. against the general price maintenance prohibition of § 14 GWB, in particular, as far as the conditions of the exemption in § 15 para. 1, sent. 1 GWB have not been met.[31]

Already in the early 1970s, all these circumstances crystallized into the fact that the price maintenance for brand products could not be upheld in Germany. Therefore, it was abolished by the legislators. With this background, it is understandable why the German and Austrian publishers were so much opposed to every loosening of the book price maintenance. It is clear that, if cross-border trade is excluded, national price maintenance cannot be reasonably upheld. This is so in Germany due to the fact that re-imports of German literature are very common. In Austria this is due to the fact that the Austrian Market is almost entirely dominated by German publishers and their "imported" books, which, we have seen, cannot in principle be submitted to price maintenance (Art. 81 para. 1 part 2 lit. a EC).

In Germany, the Law for Safeguarding the National Book Price Maintenance of 30 November 2000 was designed to solve the above difficulties.[32] As a natural consequence of the given facts, the law was aimed at incorporating imports and re-imports of German literature into the price maintenance system. It should have thereby removed the deadly danger of the lacking universality and maintained the price fixing practices in all circumstances. The first step towards the above objective is § 15 para. 1 sent. 2 GWB stating that price maintenance may be applied indiscriminately in international trade, thereby extending the possibility of price fixing arrangements to importers (see thereto section 2 above). Sent. 3 of the same provision – a linguistic accident – adds that the competence to apply price fixing mechanisms to importers does not apply to price fixing systems which substantially influence cross-border trade within the EU in relation to buyers within the EU, **unless** such price fixing arrangements are made exclusively in order to prevent the circumvention of an admitted national price maintenance system. Sent. 4 of § 15 para. 1 GWB further specifies that the duties emanating from the EC do not hinder the validity and enforceability of the book price maintenance.

---

[30] Fundamental joined cases 43/82 and 63/82 *VBVB/VBBB*, [1984] *ECR* 19, at 65 et seq., paras. 44 et seq.; case 229/83 *Leclerc*, [1985] *ECR* 1, at 33, para. 19; case 243/83 *Binon*, [1985] *ECR* 2015, 2046 para. 44; *Novalliance*, Commission Decision of 4/12/1996, *OJ* [1997] L 47/11, 18.

[31] BkartA, *Tätigkeitsbericht 1978*, p. 84; Emmerich, in: Immenga/ Mestmäcker, *GWB*, *supra* n. 16, p. 143.

[32] *BGBl.* 2000 I, p. 1634; to the legal situation in Austria see section 3 *infra*.

With these complicated wordings, the legislators meant to express that, firstly, (only) re-imports intended to circumvent the German price maintenance are forbidden. Secondly, re-imports made lawfully and free of price fixing arrangements did not affect the required universality of the system. Consequently, they did not constitute an abuse in the sense of § 15 para. 3 sent. 1 GWB.[33] However, whether the objective has been reached, or rather, whether such an objective could have been reached at all, remains very doubtful.

The most important conclusion of the new provision is that importers and re-importers of German literature may principally not be subject to national price maintenance in view of Article 81 para. 1 sent. 2 lit. a EC. This has remained unchanged under both the old and the new law. The legislators, in their explanations to the draft bill, explicitly referred to the notification of the Commission published on 10 June 2000, repeatedly emphasizing that German publications re-imported into Germany from another Member State must, in principal, be excluded from the price maintenance. In the same notification, the Commission further maintained that this principle is valid in Germany as well as in other Member States. It includes, *inter alia*, cross-border sales of publications to *consumers* and, with respect to re-imports by book traders, the book price maintenance may be upheld only if the respective publication has been exported with the exclusive purpose of being re-imported in an attempt to circumvent the price maintenance.[34] § 15 para. 1, sent. 3 GWB is a direct consequence of the above statements. We may, therefore, summarize the legal situation as follows:

Direct sales of publications to consumers in Germany and in other EU Member States are excluded from the price maintenance. Therefore, German consumers, including libraries, may purchase German Literature from abroad, i.e. from Austria or France, without being subjected to any price maintenance arrangements or laws. An important field of application will naturally be the trade over the internet. The same will apply to the sale of German books to *traders* in other EU Member States, in particular in Austria. Therefore, such traders cannot be bound by price fixing arrangements, neither with respect to their sales to consumers in their state of domicile, nor with respect to re-imports into Germany, either directly or through exclusive importers appointed by the respective publishers. All these publications may, therefore, be sold in Germany without price fixing limitations at any price.

In contradiction to the legal practice applied by the courts to date, the legislators maintained that even substantial re-imports of German literature (which is not subject to price fixing arrangements), will not affect the enforceability of the price maintenance (see § 15 para. 1 sent. 4) under arguments of lacking

---

[33] See the reasoning to the draft law, *BT-Dr.* 14 (2000)/3509, pp. 4 et seq.

[34] Notification of 10/6/2000, *supra* n. 11, paras. 8, 10, 13.

universality. In other words, the traders will be bound to price fixing arrangements, even though other traders are in the position to sell imported or re-imported books at competitive prices. However, we may doubt whether the courts will indeed agree to cooperate.

With a view to the prevailing legal practice, which required the universality of the price maintenance as a precondition to its enforceability, the law added (§ 15 para. 1 sent. 3) that, as an exception, price maintenance practices may be extended to the re-import of German publications, if such an extension is aimed at protecting lawful national price fixing arrangements against circumvention. Therefore, the revised Collective Undertaking had to limit the binding force of price fixing arrangements on re-importers to cases of circumvention. In case of dispute, the publisher would have to discharge the burden of proof regarding the importer's intent of circumvention.[35]

In such case, the crucial question will be what is, or what should be meant, by "circumvention" of the German price maintenance under § 15 para. 1 sent. 3 GWB. Under Austrian Law, a circumvention is defined as a situation in which the re-imported goods were exported "with the exclusive objective of being re-imported to circumvent this Federal Law" (i.e. the Law on the Price Maintenance of Books).[36] This wording indicates that a circumvention may be assumed only if the re-importing trader had the intention of re-importing the respective publications and selling them on the domestic market already at the time of the export, i.e. the sale to a foreign trader within the European Union. In such cases, the export is only a fictitious transaction. However, such narrow understanding would deprive the exception for re-imports (§ 15 para. 1 sent. 3) of any practical importance, and, therefore, could not have been intended by the legislators.[37]

The circumvention exception for re-imports has been developed by the ECJ in its practice to the French *Loi Lang* of 1981, which committed publishers as well as re-importers to fix the consumer prices for their publications. The ECJ repeatedly accepted such legal book price maintenance. However, it maintained that, with respect to imported books, the law was incompatible with Article 28 EC [ex Art. 30 ECT]. (Only) in the first decision concerning the *Loi Lang*, the Court stated that such incompatibility will not be maintained if, in the circumstances of the case, it must be assumed that the respective books were exported

---

[35] With the argument, that as an exception from the rule that re-importers are generally not bound to price fixing arrangements: Jungermann, "Neues zur Preisbindung" ["What is new in price maintenance"], *NJW* [2000] 2172; Id., "Auch re-importierte Bücher sind der Preisbindung zugänglich" ["Re-imported Books may be equally subject to the price maintenance"], *NJW* [2000] 3189.

[36] § 3 para. 4 of the Austrian Federal Law on the Price Maintenance for Books, *ÖBGBl.* 2000 I no. 45.

[37] As a rule, intention cannot be proven.

with the exclusive purpose of re-importing them and thereby circumventing a national legal provision (i.e. the *Loi Lang*).[38] As we know, this cautious practice of the ECJ was the reason why the Commission has to date refrained from attacking purely national price maintenance systems under Article 81 para. 1 EC, thereby limiting itself to eliminating cross-border price maintenance systems, again with the exception of re-imports which fulfill the conditions formulated in the *Leclerc* ruling.[39]

We have some doubts whether the above practice is justified. Even the ECJ specified explicitly that the exceptions of Article 28 EC [ex Art. 30] must be "interpreted strictly".[40] This explains also why the Commission, in its notification of 10 June 2000, examined the legality of price maintenance with respect to re-imports exclusively under the aspect whether the German price maintenance could substantially impair the trade between Member States.[41] This means that re-imports, as a rule, are *not* bound by the price fixing arrangements and that their liability to price maintenance is an exception of the rule. This has been explicitly confirmed by the Commission, in contradiction to the interpretation insinuated by the German media and the German publishers. It is easy to understand what this means for the Austrian market, where 80% of the publications are imported from Germany. Even in Germany, the price maintenance may, most probably, not be upheld if re-imports become more frequent, for the simple reason that German traders will cease to abide by the price fixing arrangements in order to save their businesses.

However, the German publishers, and, apparently, along with them also the German legislators, took a fundamentally different view, interpreting, in principle, every re-import as a circumvention of the German price maintenance, enabling the importers to apply the price fixing arrangements. Yet, in view of the undeniable, substantial impact of such a restrictive practice on the trade between the Member States, this view can hardly be compatible with Article 81 para. 1 EC. It follows from the above that the Law for Safeguarding the National Price Maintenance is unsuitable as a shelter for the national price fixing arrangements, as soon as it becomes public knowledge that re-imports are generally not bound by the century old, anti-competitive practices of the German book trade, and as soon as traders as well as consumers will increasingly take advantage of the free market, making use of new distribution methods such as the e-commerce.

---

[38] *Leclerc, supra* n. 30, para. 17; case 355/85 *Cognet,* [1986] *ECR* 3231, 3240, para. 5, 3241, paras. 8 et seq.; Case C-9/99, *Französische Buchpreisbinding* [French Book Price Maintenance], 3/10/2000, WuW/E EuR 375, pp. 377 et seq. paras. 22 et seq.

[39] For references, see *supra* n. 14

[40] *Leclerc, supra* n. 30, at p. 35, para. 30.

[41] Notification of 10/6/2000, *supra* n. 11, para. 13.

3. The Austrian Federal Law on Price Maintenance for Books

Similar to Germany, the Austrian price maintenance was formerly based on a Collective Undertaking of the German and Austrian publishers. However, in 2000, under the pressure of the European Commission, the Austrian legislator decided to enact the Federal Law on the Price Maintenance for Books modeled on the French *Loi Lang*.[42] Under § 3 para. 3 to the Law, publishers of German language books and music are *committed* to fix consumer prices for their publications and imports. However, imports and re-imports of books and music from EEA Member States (§ 3 para. 3 of the Law) as well as cross-border electronic trade (§ 1 of the Law) are exempted from the above legal duty.

As will be remembered, the principle that imports and re-imports are not bound by the national price maintenance does not apply to books and music exported with the exclusive aim of their re-import, thereby circumventing the Law on the Price Maintenance for Books (§ 3 para. 4). Regarding the question what is meant by circumvention of the Law and what impact the respective answer will have on international trade, we may refer to our considerations on the German price maintenance (*supra* section 2.4).

4. Are national price maintenance systems compatible with Article 81 EC?

For many years, a widespread discussion has been conducted on the question of whether and to what extent national price maintenance systems for publications are compatible with Article 81 EC. Lately, Article 151 EC [ex Art. 128] started to play an increasing role in the discussion.[43] It is impossible to elaborate the entire, varied discussion in this article. Therefore, we shall limit our considerations to one single aspect, namely, the circumstances under which national contractual price fixing arrangements are capable of substantially affecting the trade between Member States, thereby conflicting with Article 81 para. 1 EC (without taking into consideration Art. 151 EC)?

---

[42] *ÖBGBl.* 2000 I no. 45.

[43] Recently, the Monopolies Commission, 13th Main Opinion, *supra* n. 6, text numbers 677 et seq. (pp. 388 et seq.); Blanke/ Kitz, *supra* n. 26; Eilmannsberger, "Zur EG-rechtlichen Zulässigkeit der Buchpreisbindung" ["Regarding the Compatibility of the Book Price Maintenance with EC Law"], *ÖWBl.* [1995] 105; H. Grosshardt, *supra* n. 26; Hoffmann, *supra* n. 7; Kirchner, *supra* n. 26; Obert, *Die Preisbindung im Buchhandel, supra* n. 16; Id., "Die Buchpreisbindung in Deutschland und im Vereinigten Königreich", supra n. 16; Thurnher, *supra* n. 26.

In numerous decisions, the Community Organs have applied Article 81 para. 1 EC to purely national anti-competitive contractual arrangements made in Member States. The decisive aspect, under which these restrictive practices were reviewed, varied from one decision to another. Usually, the judges examined whether the contractual arrangement directly or indirectly impeded foreign suppliers from entering the market. Article 81 para. 1 EC was applied, in particular, in those cases where the respective arrangement referred equally to imports and exports.[44] Such was the case with respect to the book price maintenance in the Net Book ruling. The European Court of the First Instance examined the permissibility of the British book price maintenance.[45] The ruling was confirmed by the ECJ. However, the ECJ, in its interpretation of Article 81 para. 3 EC, held it possible to consider the consequences resulting from the fact that one and the same language is spoken in several Member States.[46]

Nevertheless, the doctrine attempts repeatedly to demonstrate that, due to the fact that Germany and Austria are both German speaking countries, the price maintenance for re-imports fails to be capable of affecting the trade between these Member States.[47] However, this view is incompatible with the wording of Article 81 para. 1 EC and may be refuted on the simple grounds that price fixing for re-imports would apply equally to Member States the population of which is not German speaking.[48]

The condition of inter-state trade is considered to be fulfilled as soon as the restrictive practice could influence the development of trade between Member States, i.e. if it is possible that the trade between Member States will develop differently than it would have without the restrictive practice in question (Art. 3 para. 1 lit. g EC). It can hardly be questioned that the German and Austrian

---

[44] In detail see Emmerich, "Art. 81 and 82 ECT", in: Dauses, *Handbuch des EU-Wirtschaftsrechts* [*Handbook of the EC Economic Law*] (Munich: Beck 2000) H I § 1 marginal note 34; Rehbinder, in: Immenga/ Mestmäcker, *EG-Wettbewerbsrecht* [*EC Competition Law*], Vol. I (Munich: Beck 1997) Introduction I, marginal notes 31 et seq. (pp. 62 et seq.); Schüter, in: v.d. Groeben/ Thiesing/ Ehlermann, *EU/EG-Vertrag* [*EU/EC Treaty*], Vol. II/1, 5th ed. (Baden-Baden: Nomos 1999) Art. 85 para. 1, marginal notes 163, 172 et seq. (pp. 229, 237 et seq.).

[45] Case T-66/89 *Publishers Association* (*Net Book Agreements*), [1992] *ECR* II-1995, at pp. 2016 et seq., paras. 55 et seq.

[46] Case C-360/92 P *Publishers Association* [1995] *ECR* I-23, at pp. 67 et seq., paras. 25 et seq. = *EuZW* [1995] 180.

[47] So especially Everling, "Die Buchpreisbindung im deutschsprachigen Raum und europäisches Gemeinschaftsrecht", in: *Die Buchpreisbindung in europarechtlicher, ökonomischer und kulturhisrischer Sicht*, Buchhändler-Vereinigung (Frankfurt a.M. 1997) 1, 38 et seq.; ebenso offenbar: Eilmannsberger, "Zur EG-rechtlicher Zulässigkeit der Buchpreisbindung", *ÖWBl.* [1995] 105.

[48] Of the same opinion: Blanke/ Kitz, *supra* n. 26, at p. 122; Hoffmann, *supra* n. 7, at pp. 559, 561 et seq.; Obert, GRURInt. [1999], *supra* n. 16, at p. 1032; Id., *Die Preisbindung im Buchhandel*, *supra* n. 16, at pp. 148 et seq.; Thurnher, *supra* n. 26.

books and magazines market would be different under free competition, without national price maintenance systems. Otherwise, the parties involved would never be so outspoken in defending the price maintenance. Under the rules of free competition, cross-border trade of books and magazines would be dealt with as a matter of course and the prices, which today vary considerably from State to State, would, with time, be adjusted.[49]

As we have seen, the maintenance of the national price fixing arrangement in Germany has an increasingly thin legal basis. This is true in particular if the collective elements of the entire system are taken into account. It is clear that the complex order of the Collective Undertaking with its unified prices, discounts and conditions, may work out exclusively if we have a widespread common understanding among the publishers.[50] Therefore, in fact, the Commission should disallow also national price fixing systems even if those exempt imports and re-imports.

We shall abstain from the discussion whether there is recourse to an exemption under Article 81 para. 3 EC,[51] and limit ourselves to the consideration that it is hardly understandable how consumers could adequately participate in the advantages of a price maintenance in the sense of Article 81 para. 3 EC. It is precisely the opposite in this case. The book price maintenance is aimed at granting a "sufficient margin" to the book traders, i.e. at robbing the consumer by fixing exorbitant prices. In addition, the universal price maintenance system, by entirely eliminating price competition, is clearly incompatible with Article 81 para. 3 lit. b EC.

5. Final remarks

We have referred to the frightening circumstances under which the "compromise" between the German publishers and the Commission has been reached. Many aspects of this procedure as well as the details of other, similar proceedings, raise doubts regarding the character of Germany as a state governed by the rule of law. In the book written by *Karel van Mierts*, we may find many other, shocking examples.

A second irrational characteristic of the book price maintenance is that the consumers' interests, which should have been considered as paramount, are entirely ignored. Further, the perspective is narrowed to the so-called "cultural

---

[49] Of the same opinion: Mestmäcker, *Europäisches Wettbewerbsrecht*, *supra* n. 29, § 47 III 2 (pp. 586 et seq.).

[50] Of the same opinion: Thurnher, *supra* n. 26.

[51] Thereto in detail Obert, *Die Preisbindung im Buchhandel*, *supra* n. 16, pp. 153 et seq.

value of the book", therewith neglecting the entire market of magazines which is also counted among the publications in the sense of § 15 GWB. Therefore, it is no exaggeration to argue that magazines "hitch-hiked" the "cultural value of the book" and, as such, have come to profit from privileges designed for books. No one has endeavored to examine whether the particularities of the book market apply equally to magazines.

In fact, in particular the German readers of scientific magazines have to abide every year with exorbitant, unfounded price raises under the reference to § 15 GWB which leaves them the choice between canceling the subscription (which is often impossible) and accepting unjustified price raises. The consequences, *inter alia* for the scientific budgets of libraries, are self explanatory. The time has come to erase the entire unjustified book price privilege from our legal system.

Hybrid Governance Across National Jurisdictions as a Challenge to Constitutional Law

Christoph Engel*

1. INTRODUCTION

A technology often reaches perfection when its successor is already in place. Miraculously speedy and reliable punch card readers were finally available on the market when demand shifted to personal computers, to cite only one example. Do constitutions follow the same evolutionary pattern? Constitutional law, in general, and the doctrine of fundamental freedoms, in particular, are in admirable shape. Their dogmatics have been amply tested; they are elegant and rich. But they have been developed for the nation state. Yet governance reality is increasingly different. The state is competing with foreign, international and private governing authorities, or it is joining them in hybrid efforts. Will de-constitutionalisation ensue? Or will the existing constitutions be able to face, or even alter, the new reality?

---

* Director, Max Planck Project Group "Common Goods: Law, Politics and Economics", Bonn.
Helpful comments by Florian Becker, Adrienne Héritier, Dirk Lehmkuhl and the audience of a workshop at the European University Institute in Florence, research assistance by Christian Schmies and the linguistic trimming of the paper by Darrell Arnold are gratefully acknowledged.

Talia Einhorn, ed., Spontaneous Order, Organization and the Law – Liber Amicorum Ernst-Joachim Mestmäcker © 2003 T.M.C.ASSER PRESS, *The Hague, The Netherlands*

This is a paper about governance. Hardly any term is more disputed in the social sciences.[1] This paper looks at (potentially) global, not national or European governance. It therefore cannot avoid using the broadest of all possible definitions of governance. Since on the global scale there is no such thing as a widely undisputed higher order system, the term governance must comprise all modes of social ordering, by whatever actor or actor configuration.[2]

The focus of this paper is on divergent governance bodies, not governance tools. It does not want to explore whether the pertinent body uses (quasi-)legal rules, incentives, moral suasion or any other tool for governing the behaviour of its addressees. It simply looks at who purports to change the behaviour of a class of addressees, in the alleged interest of some protectees.

Moreover, when it speaks of governance, the paper exclusively looks at intentional attempts to change the behaviour of addressees. The limitation inherent in this becomes clear when looking at a constitutional court. To the extent that it has jurisdiction one can interpret such a court as the supreme legal authority. At the limit, the court can even overrule the legislator. But, strictly exceptional instances notwithstanding, a constitutional court does not itself write the law. At most, it invalidates existing rules, or gives them a different meaning. In both cases, parliament remains the governing body.

Finally, this is an interdisciplinary paper in that it draws on insights from the social sciences, and from political sciences in particular. But it does so exclusively in the interest of better understanding a dogmatic problem of constitutional law: how can and how should a national constitution react when governance activities cannot (exclusively) be attributed to the governance bodies created by the constitution? More specifically even, the paper does not intend to design the appropriate reaction for a concrete instance of not exclusively public national governance. Its goal is much more modest. It wants to provide constitutional lawyers with a conceptual framework for addressing such concrete design problems. This explains why the paper does not by far exploit the richness of the discussion on hybrid international governance in the political sciences.[3]

---

[1] A coherent overview of competing definitions, and how they have evolved, is to be found in R. Mayntz, *New Challenges to Governance Theory* (Florence: European University Institute 1998, The Robert Schuman Centre, Jean Monnet Chair Papers 50).

[2] Ibid., 18 et seq., see also 16.

[3] Out of the rich literature on the public/ private divide see in particular W. Streeck/ Ph.C. Schmitter (eds.), *Private Interest Government. Beyond Market and State* (London: Sage 1985); W. Streeck (ed.), *Staat und Verbände*, special issue 25 of *Politische Vierteljahresschrift* 35 (1994) 1-401. On the international dimension see in particular A. Hasenclever/ P. Mayer/ V.

The following sketch purports to address these questions from the angle of the German constitution. It starts with a taxonomy of governance authorities (2). It briefly summarises the normative arguments for and against international, private and hybrid governance (3). It points to the option of privatising, internationalising and hybridising the constitution itself (4), but focuses on strategies for the existing national constitutions in the face of an altered reality (5). The concluding dogmatic treatment is confined to fundamental freedoms. It starts by isolating the international (6) and the private dimension (7), then goes on to address the more complex private international (8) and hybrid forms of governance (9).

2. A TAXONOMY OF GOVERNANCE BODIES

The basic forms of governance bodies are contained in the following figure:

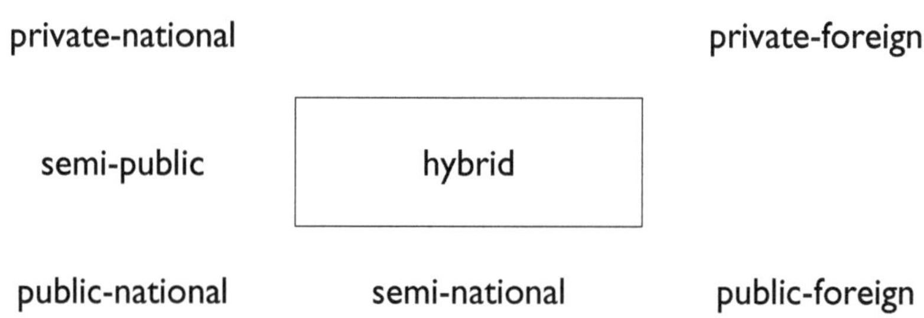

Public-national governance is the classic form of state governance. An example of public-foreign governance is the extraterritorial application of US antitrust law to a merger of two German firms (because they do business on the US market, for instance).[4] Private national governance is exercised by the German Green Dot organisation. Its primary business is price regulation for the disposal

Rittberger, *Theories of International Regimes* (Cambridge Studies in International Relations 55, Cambridge: Cambridge University Press 1997); M. Hewson/ T.J. Sinclair (eds.), *Approaches to Global Governance Theory* (New York: State University of New York Press 1999).

[4] For more on the extraterritorial application of national public law see A.K. Schnyder, *Wirtschaftskollisionsrecht. Sonderanknüpfung und extraterritoriale Anwendung wirtschaftsrechtlicher Normen unter besonderer Berücksichtigung von Marktrecht* (Zürich: Schulthess 1990); W. Meng, *Extraterritoriale Jurisdiktion im öffentlichen Wirtschaftsrecht* (Berlin: Springer 1994).

of packaging waste.[5] The electronic tools used by AOL are one example of private foreign governance. They are meant to prevent children from accessing all websites that it does not deem "family-friendly",[6] and to prevent spammers from reaching the AOL audience.[7]

Each of these dimensions is a scale. In semi-national cases, the German government has at least some influence on a transnational governing body. In semi-public cases, government has at least some influence on a not-fully-public governing body. In both cases, the influence can stem from the delegation of governance powers, from membership, from legal supervisory authority, from legal or factual threat power, or from the governing body's interest in incorporating its output into state law. The private and the foreign dimensions can be combined. The two dimensions thus open up a space for hybrid governance authorities.

3. Normative arguments

National constitutions are basic charters for public-national governance. This simplifies the constitutional discourse. The normative problem is not an open choice among alternative governance authorities. The constitutionalist needs a justification for moving away from the normal public-national governance. The constitution assumes that this governance authority has struck the right balance between competing constitutional concerns.

The basic reason for accepting, fostering or demanding an alternative governance authority is the expectation that it will exhibit a greater problem-solving capacity, due to the nature of the policy problem, the power structure beyond the reach of the national constitution, diminished regulatory cost, or overriding normative concerns about the available public regulatory options.

International governance is natural if the policy problem has transnational reach. Nation states are not helpless then. In particular, they can apply their own rules beyond the boundaries of their own territory. But transnational bodies may be more effective, more elegant or cheaper. Globalisation is transnationalising many policy problems that have previously been purely national. Likewise, governance that is not purely public is natural if the policy problem has to

---

5 This is not obvious at first sight. For the details see Lehmann, "Private Institutions in Waste Management Policy and Their Antitrust Implications. The Case of Germany's Dual Management System", *Preprints aus der Max-Planck-Projektgruppe Recht der Gemeinschaftsgüter Bonn*: 1999/13.

6 http://www.aol.com/info/onlinesafety.html (04-23-2001).

7 http://www.aol.com/info/bulkemail.html (04-23-2001).

address the self-referentiality of social sub-systems.[8] Again, the constitution is not helpless. It can strive to bring private governance "under the shadow of hierarchy".[9] In the more theoretical terms of systems theory, it can increase the resonance of the sub-system for public governance attempts, or even destroy its autonomy.[10] But the constitution may not want either of these strategies, or these strategies may seem too costly. Moreover, in both dimensions there may be a value in openness. It triggers regulatory competition, which can be an evolutionary advantage and can help control interested policy makers.[11] Finally, hybrid governance can help overcome conflict among nations, or between the governance body and the social actors that hold veto positions.[12]

Hybridisation engenders constitutionally relevant costs.[13] It weakens the democratic legitimation of governance and judicial control. It loosens the protection of minorities and individuals. It circumvents organisational and procedural checks and balances. It results in a less clear separation between law and politics, which in turn leads to partial de-differentiation.[14] Hybrid bodies usually have narrowly limited authority. They can become single-issue constituencies.[15] It becomes difficult to link issues. Veto-positions are harder to overcome.[16] Social conflict is more likely. Disintegration is possible.[17] There is also a risk of over-fitting,[18] which is an evolutionary drawback. Once hybrid

---

[8] Basic (and sceptical) N. Luhmann, *Ökologische Kommunikation* (Opladen: Westdeutscher 1986); (mildly optimistic) Teubner, "Privatregimes: Neo-Spontanes Recht und duale Sozialverfassungen in der Weltgesellschaft?", in: *Zur Autonomie des Individuums, Liber Amicorum Spiros Simitis* (Simon/ Weiss [eds.]) (Baden-Baden: Nomos 2000) 437-453.

[9] Using the famous term dubbed by F. Scharpf, *Games Real Actors Play. Actor-Centred Institutionalism in Policy Research* (Boulder: Westview 1997) 22 and 138 et seq.

[10] More by Teubner, *supra* n. 8.

[11] Out of the rich literature see only L. Gerken (ed.), *Competition Among Institutions* (Houndmills: Macmillan 1995); Monopolkommission, Sondergutachten 27, *Systemwettbewerb* (Baden-Baden: Nomos 1998); Markus Müller, *Systemwettbewerb, Harmonisierung und Wettbewerbsverzerrung* (Baden-Baden: Nomos 2000).

[12] Cf. Der Wissenschaftliche Beirat beim Bundesministerium für Wirtschaft, "Aktuelle Formen des Korporatismus", in: *Gutachten vom Februar 1998 bis Juli 2000* (Stuttgart: Lucius 2000) 2077-2103.

[13] For more on the following see Engel, "Institutionen zwischen Staat und Markt", 34 *Die Verwaltung* (2001) 1, at pp. 18-24.

[14] Luhmann, *supra* n. 8, at pp. 218-226 and passim.

[15] Cf. Roemer, "A Theory of Policy Differentiation in Single Issue Electoral Politics", 11 *Social Choice and Welfare* (1994) 355-380.

[16] The concept has been developed by E. Immergut, *Health Politics. Interests and Institutions in Western Europe* (Cambridge: Cambridge University Press 1992).

[17] The classic legal text on integration theory is R. Smend, *Verfassung und Verfassungsrecht* (Munich: Duncker & Humblot 1928).

[18] On over-fitting, see e.g. Geman, Bienenstock and Doursat, "Neural Networks and the Bias/ Variance Dilemma", 4 *Neural Computation* (1992) 1-58.

governance is accepted in principle, interested actors can strategically increase the degree of such governance. All this can be addressed as partial de-constitutionalisation. The constitution loses control over governance activities. The distinction between the ordinary and the constitutional level of law gets partially blurred. In the extreme case, governance boils down to what the governance body can do without running the risk of being overthrown.

4. Hybridising the Constitution, or Constitutionalising Hybrid Governance?

A radical reaction to the diffusion of hybrid governance bodies would be to hybridise the constitution itself, or to constitutionalise international, private and hybrid governance. Constitutionalisation of a governance body means that its actual governance activities are bound by rules on organisation, procedure and substance that are not at the disposition of the body itself, at least not on an *ad hoc* basis, and using its ordinary procedure.

The idea of constitutionalising private, international or hybrid governance is becoming increasingly popular. Public international lawyers have called for the constitutionalisation of their field,[19] as have European Community lawyers.[20] Human rights and other humanitarian rules of public international law go even further and claim authority over national action that has no international element. *A fortiori*, they do apply to semi-national governance. Constitutionalising (semi-)private governance is not discussed in these terms. But in essence this is the solution to the US-EU conflict over data protection. Under European pressure, the FTC is being turned into a supervisory authority for private self-governance.[21]

The contrasting concept rests on legally incorporating (semi-)private or (semi-)foreign bodies into the national constitution. Theoretically, this could be done without hybridising the constitution. The private or foreign body would then become an exceptional organ of the constitutionalised order of a country. The technical legal term characterises the idea: the constitutional order would "borrow" an institution from another legal entity. But this is hardly ever a practical option. For it would fully bring the borrowed institution under the

---

[19] Programmatic Frowein, "Konstitutionalisierung des Völkerrechts", 39 *Berichte der Deutschen Gesellschaft für Völkerrecht* (1999) 427-448.

[20] Comprehensive 60 *Veröffentlichungen der Vereinigung der Deutschen Staatsrechtslehrer* (2001) 148-415.

[21] Farrell, "Negotiating Privacy in the Age of the Internet – Analysing the EU-US 'Safe Harbor' Negotiations", in: *Common Goods and Governance Across Multiple Arenas* (A. Héritier [ed.]) (forthcoming).

jurisdiction of the borrowing legal order and its constitution. The institution would have to fully play by these constitutional rules. The legal entity of origin will normally not be willing to accept such alienation. If, however, the legal order of destination foregoes full legal control over the inserted governance body, hybridisation of the constitution ensues. The constitution legalises governance activities, although they are legally not fully under its control.

But hybridising the constitution and constitutionalising hybrid governance are, at best, incubating concepts. It will take a long time before they can give adequate guidance and satisfactory legal certainty. Due to the hybrid element, they will never be able to address some of the constitutional concerns, like disintegration. In all likeliness, national constitutions will not disappear in the process. They will still want to have an impact on private, international and hybrid governance bodies. At the very least, the threat of unilateral constitutional action will spur the process of constitutional hybridisation.[22]

5. Strategies for the national constitutions

Vis-à-vis private, international and hybrid governance bodies, national constitutions basically have three strategic options: forbearance, mitigation and adaptation.

Forbearance is a passive strategy. The constitution allows governance even where it has no, or limited, influence. If it opts for this strategy, the constitution must make sure that its own normativity is not eroded. Two lines of argument can help: compensation and encapsulation. Compensation stresses the fact that the outside regulator has indeed constitutionalised itself. It demonstrates that the level of protection is similar to that offered by the national constitution, or at least adequate, given the type of action. The German Constitutional Court has basically relied on this strategy with respect to the European Union.[23]

Encapsulation presupposes that constitutional standards are only deviated from in exceptional cases, which are, for obvious reasons, beyond the reach of the constitution. The German Constitutional Court has used this strategy twice: in the Saar,[24] and in the Second Register for Vessels case.[25] In the first case, it

---

[22] A graphic example of the strategy is the Maastricht judgement of the German Constitutional Court (*Bundesverfassungsgericht*). It in essence means that the German Court threatens the European Court of Justice, i.e. that it will apply German fundamental rights to European legislation, should the autonomous European fundamental rights appear grossly unsatisfactory, *BVerfGE* 89, 155.

[23] See again *BVerfGE* 89, 155.

[24] *BVerfGE* 4, 157.

[25] *BVerfGE* 92, 26.

referred to post-war conditions, in the second to the fully global character of sea transportation. The problem with encapsulation is constructivist: will the public accept the exceptional character (or just overlook the cases)?

Mitigation is a defence strategy. The constitution strives to immunise national public regulation from the effects of regulatory competition, or to attenuate its effects.[26] Occasionally mitigation is nearly impossible. This was the central argument of the Constitutional Court in the Second Register for Vessels case. Vessels travelling over the oceans can be registered everywhere in the world. A single regulatory haven is enough to make futile all co-operative efforts to keep the standards up. Mitigation is often costly, especially in terms of opportunity costs, i.e. foregone benefits. And not all effective defence techniques are normatively acceptable for the constitution. Putting foreigners into jail because their country of origin engages in unfair regulatory competition is an obvious example.

Adaptation can be either conceptual or real. Conceptual adaptation closes the gap between the constitutional standard and regulatory reality by lowering the standard. Occasionally, the private or international challenge teaches the constitution that it had overlooked or not properly balanced a true concern. European administrative law might have had such an effect in that it helped the German constitution find a proper dogmatic place for administrative efficacy.[27] More often, constitutional standards can, and should, be differentiated. If a person voluntarily goes abroad or engages in international trade, he deserves less constitutional protection.[28] If a case lies partly or even fully outside the reach of German sovereignty, the constitution has less responsibility for it.[29] If the individuals, or at least the group to which they belong, have viable tools to protect themselves,[30] the constitution might accept less public protection.

Real adaptation means partly redesigning the constitution. This is what hybridising the constitution is about. But it can come in small steps. One example is the Maastricht decision of the Constitutional Court. The Court claims jurisdiction for the testing of secondary Community law against German

---

[26] For an overview of dogmatic avenues to be used for the purpose see Engel, "Legal Experiences of Competition among Institutions", in: *Competition among Institutions* (L. Gerken [ed.]) (Houndmills: Macmillan 1995) 89-118.

[27] Comprehensive Rengeling, "Deutsches und Europäisches Verwaltungsrecht – Wechselseitige Einwirkungen", 53 *Veröffentlichungen der Vereinigung der Deutschen Staatsrechtslehrer* (1994) 202-239.

[28] Although the dogmatic consequences derived from the idea are too strong in Elbing, the idea is to be found in G. Elbing, *Zur Anwendbarkeit der Grundrechte bei Sachverhalten mit Auslandsberührung* (Berlin: Duncker & Humblot 1992) 317.

[29] Cf. ibid., 190.

[30] The idea is offered by K.W. Dam, *Self-Help in the Digital Jungle* (Chicago: John M. Olin Law & Economics Working Paper 59, 1998).

fundamental freedoms. But it claims to do so "in co-operation" with the European Court of Justice.[31] In practical terms, this makes constitutional complaints a fall-back position for German nationals who feel that the European Court of Justice has not given them adequate protection.

Forbearance and conceptual adaptation do not involve redesigning rules. Mitigation and real adaptation do. The constitution has basically four options. It can control the formation of private, international or hybrid regulatory bodies. It can control their output. It can influence the outcomes of their regulatory activities by controlling their effects within the German territory or on German nationals.[32] And it can compensate the victims for deviations from the German constitutional standards, be that in money or in kind.

6. Fundamental freedoms and international governance

The constitutional dogmatics of international governance have a formal as well as a substantive dimension. The formal dimension addresses regulatory organisation and procedure.[33] The substantive dimension addresses regulatory content. The following observations are confined to the core of the substantive dimension, fundamental freedoms.

Adapting fundamental freedoms to international governance is an old problem.[34] The dogmatics for addressing it are relatively well-developed. They start by asking whether the respective governance act can be attributed to an entity that is passively legitimated by the fundamental freedoms of the German constitution.[35] Passive legitimation means that the fundamental freedoms directly bind the entity.[36] This is obvious for the government and any autonomous public entity, such as the *Länder* or the municipalities. Traditional wisdom was that social actors were not directly bound by fundamental

---

[31] *BVerfGE* 89, 155, Leitsatz 7.

[32] The distinction between outputs and outcomes is basic in implementation research of political scientists, see A. Windhoff-Héritier, *Politikimplementation* (Königstein: Hain 1980) 5 and passim.

[33] On attempts to reach substantive regulatory aims by affecting the organisation or procedure see Engel, "Regulierung durch Organisation und Verfahren", in: *Festschrift für Ernst-Joachim Mestmäcker* (Immenga/ Möschel/ Reuter [eds.]) (Baden-Baden: Nomos 1996) 119-138.

[34] Besides Elbing, *supra* n. 28, see R. Hofmann, *Grundrechte und grenzüberschreitende Sachverhalte* (Berlin: Springer 1993); Kronke, "Die Wirkungskraft der Grundrechte bei Fällen mit Auslandsbezug", 38 *Berichte der Deutschen Gesellschaft für Völkerrecht* (1998) 33-67.

[35] Elbing, *supra* n. 28, 190.

[36] Cf. Kronke, *supra* n. 34, 42 (using the category of active legitimation for a related question).

freedoms; the freedoms had no third-party effects, to use the common jargon.[37] At most, government was constitutionally obliged to protect one individual against the intrusions of other individuals into his constitutionally protected sphere.[38] The Maastricht decision of the Constitutional Court might have broken with this tradition, however. For the German fundamental freedoms are now directly applied to secondary Community law, because it applies legally within the domain of the German constitution.[39] Along the same lines, one could argue that private governance comes under direct constitutional scrutiny, once the legal order acknowledges in principle its legal validity.

Governance can be attributed to the German government if it has legally delegated regulatory authority to an international body;[40] if the government has participated in the rule-making activity;[41] probably also, if it had membership rights without using them; and if it has autonomously incorporated the foreign regulatory output into the German legal order.[42]

The dogmatic technique for encapsulation is known as "closer to" jurisprudence. Open deviations from substantive constitutional standards are accepted if the constitution would otherwise have to accept an outcome that is even

[37] Comprehensive K. Stern/ M. Sachs, *Staatsrecht III/1* (München: Beck 1988) 1511 et seq.

[38] J. Dietlein, *Die Lehre von den grundrechtlichen Schutzpflichten* (Berlin: Duncker & Humblot 1992).

[39] *BVerfGE* 89, 155, Leitsatz 7: "Auch Akte einer besonderen, von der Staatsgewalt der Mitgliedstaaten geschiedenen öffentlichen Gewalt einer supranationalen Organisation betreffen die Grundrechtsberechtigten in Deutschland. Sie berühren damit die Gewährleistungen des Grundgesetzes und die Aufgaben des Bundesverfassungsgerichts, die den Grundrechtsschutz in Deutschland und insoweit nicht nur gegenüber deutschen Staatsorganen zum Gegenstand haben (Abweichung von *BVerfGE* 58, 1 (27)). Allerdings übt das Bundesverfassungsgericht seine Rechtsprechung über die Anwendbarkeit von abgeleitetem Gemeinschaftsrecht in Deutschland in einem ‚Kooperationsverhältnis' zum Europäischen Gerichtshof aus"; literally the same sentences are to be found in *BVerfGE* 89, 155, 175; there the passage ends with "[...] ‚Kooperationsverhältnis' zum Europäischen Gerichthshof aus, in dem der Europäische Gerichtshof den Grundrechtsschutz in jedem Einzelfall für das gesamte Gebiet der Europäischen Gemeinschaften garantiert, das Bundesverfassungsgericht sich deshalb auf eine generelle Gewährleistung der unabdingbaren Grundrechtsstandards [...] beschränken kann."

[40] Classic on the conceptual structure of delegation H. Triepel, *Delegation und Mandat im öffentlichen Recht* (Stuttgart: Kohlhammer 1942).

[41] This is why the European Court of Human Rights has recently held that the fundamental rights of the European Convention on Human Rights apply to secondary law of the European Union *qua* the participation of Member States governments in the Council of Ministers, *ECtHR* 18.2.1999, Case 24833/94, R 32 – *Matthews*.

[42] This is how the German Constitutional Court brought foreign private law under constitutional control, if autonomous German rules of conflict of laws oblige German courts to apply such rules, *BVerfGE* 31, 58 – *Spanier*.

worse.[43] The Saar would otherwise have remained under French occupation;[44] almost all vessels would otherwise have registered under foreign flag.[45] The outside pressure, which Germany alone would not be able to quash or parry, is decisive here.

Conceptual adaptation fully uses the dogmatics of fundamental freedoms. Foreign nationals are not protected at all by some freedoms (like freedom of commerce), and not fully by others.[46] Transnational cases are not protected by some freedoms (like freedom of movement), and not fully by others.[47] If the German government only had an indirect impact on international regulatory activities, this might not be enough to justify interference with the respective fundamental freedom.

Respecting the properties of international relations may count as a legitimate aim for the interference. An illustrative example is provided by the decentralised mechanism for generating rules in public international law. States are not only addressed by public international law, they also generate it. If one state dislikes the contents of a rule, it will pretend that the actual contents of public international law are different. If the opponents do not protest, the mere contention can set in motion a process aimed at changing the rule. The German Constitutional Court has held that the German government should not be constitutionally prevented from playing this game.[48]

An act of interference with a fundamental freedom must be conducive to the legitimate aim, it must be the least intrusive measure, and it may not be overly onerous.[49] Given the imponderables of international relations, under the first test, the Constitutional Court finds for conduciveness as soon as there is at least some chance of success.[50] In international cases, it accords the government an

---

[43] Comprehensive Chr. Engel, *Völkerrecht als Tatbestandsmerkmal deutscher Normen* (Berlin: Duncker & Humblot 1989) 166-171; see also Puttfarken, "Grundrechte im internationalen Rechtsraum", 41 *Recht der Internationalen Wirtschaft* (1995) 617-627; Geefken, "Soziale Grundrechte unter Vorbehalt?", 12 *Neue Zeitschrift für Arbeitsrecht* (1995) 504-508.

[44] *BVerfGE* 4, 157, 168 and 170.

[45] *BVerfGE* 92, 26, 26 and 41 et seq.

[46] *BVerfGE* 31, 58, 77.

[47] *BVerfGE* 6, 32, 44 (restricted right to leave the country); *BVerfGE* 6, 290, 299 (limited protection of property lying abroad); *BVerfGE* 77, 1, 47 (only the conditional right of foreign spouses to immigrate).

[48] *BVerfGE* 55, 349, 366 et seq. – *Hess*; see also *BVerfGE* 58, 1, 41 – *Eurocontrol I*; Engel, *Völkerrecht als Tatbestandsmerkmal, supra* n. 43, 101-130 (on consensus over the interpretation of public international law rules).

[49] These are the basic elements of the dogmatics of fundamental freedoms under German constitutional law. In German they read "geeignet, erforderlich, angemessen". For an overview see e.g. J. Ipsen, *Staatsrecht II (Grundrechte)*, 3rd ed. (Neuwied: Luchterhand 2000), R 169-182; B. Pieroth/ B. Schlink, *Grundrechte (Staatsrecht II)*, 16th ed. (Heidelberg: Müller 2000) R 279-297.

[50] *BVerfGE* 92, 26, 43 et seq.

exceptionally large margin of appreciation when comparing the actual interference with alternative means for reaching the same end, and when weighing the interference with the legitimate aim.[51] In other words, the level of protection is particularly low in international cases.[52] Judicial self-restraint is exceptionally strong.[53]

If the international governance is not attributed to the German government, or to another entity passively legitimated by German fundamental freedoms, government may nonetheless have a constitutional duty to protect individuals from the ensuing interference with their fundamental freedoms. Government is in principle obliged to exercise its legal and factual powers in favour of individuals who are under the spell of foreign or international regulators. The classic case is diplomatic protection.[54] By this, public international law means the right of a country to intervene on behalf of its nationals and to ask another country to respect their internationally protected rights, such as property. But the German government is under no strict constitutional obligation to diplomatically protect its nationals abroad. They only have a justiciable right that government exercises its discretion in a proper way.[55]

Foreign or international governance bodies are not themselves protected by the German Basic Law. They have no subjective, justiciable rights. But the constitution explicitly acknowledges international openness as an objective constitutional value.[56] And it gives some international governance bodies special treatment. These provisions can be interpreted as early adaptations of the constitutional order to international governance. These provisions cover the European Union and other supranational public regulators.[57] In a broader sense, one may also interpret the provisions on international treaties,[58] and on customary public international law,[59] as constitutional adaptations to a governance reality that partly escapes its control.

The constitutional provisions in favour of international governance have limits. International governance must respect the essence of fundamental freedoms, and may not overstep the explicit boundaries for constitutional

---

[51] Ibid., 44.

[52] *BVerfGE* 59, 63, 90 et seq. – *Eurocontrol II.*

[53] *BVerfGE* 55, 349, 364 et seq.

[54] Leading case *BVerfGE* 55, 349 – *Hess*; more by Hofmann, *supra* n. 34, 108-111; E. Klein, "Anspruch auf diplomatischen Schutz?", in: *Der diplomatische Schutz im Völker- und Europarecht* (G. Ress/ T. Stein [eds.]) (Baden-Baden: Nomos 1996) 125-136.

[55] *BVerfGE* 55, 349, 364 et seq.

[56] See in particular the preamble, Art. 1 II, Art. 23-26, Art. 59 Basic Law; classic K. Vogel, *Die Verfassungsentscheidung für die offene Staatlichkeit* (Tübingen: Mohr 1964).

[57] Art. 23 and 24 Basic Law.

[58] Art. 59 Basic Law.

[59] Art. 25 Basic Law.

change.[60] These limits can be interpreted as a constitutional obligation to mitigate the effects of international governance so that they remain within these confines. Occasionally, the Constitutional Court itself engages in mitigation. The above-mentioned Maastricht decision is the most prominent instance.[61] It means that the court claims subsidiary authority to control European secondary legislation.

7. Fundamental freedoms and private governance

Bringing private governance under the control of fundamental freedoms would make sense. Governance is more than a mere exercise of individual freedom; it is also more than a simple exercise of economic or social power. A private governing body, at least purportedly, does not have an impact on the freedoms of others in its own interest, but in the interest of some protectees. This may justify intervention that would be unacceptable for individual purposes. But the addressees deserve no less protection from such allegedly benevolent intervention than vis-à-vis public regulators. Private governance bodies are no less likely to get the balance between the freedom of addressees and the legitimate interests of protectees wrong.[62] Consequently, the Federal Court of Labour Law has directly controlled the collective agreements between the unions and the employers' associations against fundamental freedoms.[63] The Constitutional Court has objected, however, that fundamental freedoms have no third-party effects.[64] It remains to be seen whether the doctrine will shift back in light of the Court decision in the Maastricht case.

If not, the entire constitutional control of private governance must be couched in terms of a governmental duty to protect the addressees from excessive intrusions into their freedom. This is particularly unsatisfactory, because some elements that help justify international governance are not present in private governance. If the international governance is not entirely foreign, it can rely on the will of the democratically elected legislator. Public international governance bodies can themselves seek some form of electoral control, and they can protect their addressees by a bill of rights.

There is, however, one difference that points in the opposite direction. Private governance bodies are themselves constitutionally protected. They have

---

[60] *BVerfGE* 4, 157, 170.

[61] *BVerfGE* 89, 155.

[62] See in greater detail Engel, "A Constitutional Framework for Private Governance", *Preprints aus der Max-Planck-Projektgruppe Recht der Gemeinschaftsgüter Bonn*: 2001/4.

[63] *BAGE* 1, 185, 193.

[64] Consequently, the Federal Court for Labour Law gave in, *BAGE* 52, 88, 97 s.

a justiciable right, which they can direct against governmental intrusions into their autonomy. The distinction between individual freedom and regulatory autonomy is not yet established doctrine, however. It is a way of adapting the German constitution to the reality of systems autonomy.[65]

The other two constitutional strategies are even less explicit with respect to private governance. There is great reluctance to intervene in the governing activities of the unions and the employers' associations. One may interpret this as an instance of encapsulation. So far constitutional jurisprudence has not combated private governance, but rather ignored it; or the parties have managed to deprive the court of the opportunity to sound its voice on the issue.

8. Fundamental freedoms and private transnational governance

The international and the private elements are combined in private transnational governance. This is not hybrid governance, *nota bene*. The international element is purely private. There does not seem to be constitutional jurisprudence on this type of governance. The treatment should start with the principles developed for private national governance. At each step it should ask whether the international element makes a decisive difference.

Suppose private national governance can be directly controlled by the German fundamental freedoms: does that still hold true if the governing body has only some German members; if it only exercises governance activities within Germany, or toward German nationals; if it is only the functional equivalent for earlier German regulation? Is the duty to protect Germans or inhabitants of the country from private governance weaker if it is international in one of these senses? Can the German government invoke the exceptionally large margin of discretion for diplomatic protection? Does the justiciable right to autonomy, or at least the underlying objective constitutional value, extend to private international governance? Is protection even stronger than in domestic cases, because the general constitutional value judgement in favour of international openness applies to purely private governance as well?

---

[65] More by Engel, "Constitutional Framework", *supra* n. 62.

9. Fundamental freedoms and hybrid governance

Hybrid governance mixes the public and the private element. Hybrid international governance also mixes the national and the international element. The constitutional effects of these mixtures are still largely unclear. The foregoing offers a blueprint for dealing with them in the constitution. The treatment is again confined to fundamental freedoms.

It is easier to justify the direct application of fundamental freedoms to hybrid governance than to pure private governance. In principle, there is no problem with third-party effects, since the government is formally involved. But the problem re-enters the scene through the backdoor. Is one small public element enough to attribute the whole regulatory activity to government? Or, can this element alone be directly constitutionally controlled? If one decides in principle for the latter, one is again faced with the problem of third-party effects. It is, however, easier to opt for this solution in hybrid cases. They are closer to the logic of the Maastricht case.

The "closer to" principle can have two effects. One is straightforward. The other less so. One may ask whether the hybrid activity can profit from this principle as an exceptional justification of results that would otherwise be unconstitutional. But one may also ask whether the formation of a hybrid (international) governance body could not itself be interpreted as a tool for reserving as much influence as possible for the German constitution.

The hybrid character makes the ordinary treatment of governance under the fundamental freedoms ambivalent. Does the public (national) element mean that the governance activities can profit from the direct democratic legitimacy of the German government? Does the private element mean that they can profit from the constitutional protection of autonomy? Do the limitations to the fundamental freedoms of the addressees thus accumulate? Or, on the contrary, is the constitutional standard particularly strict, since autonomy is tainted by the public element, and democratic legitimacy by the private element? Is the constitution thus biased in favour of adaptation or in favour of mitigation?

Venture Capital Funding for Biotech Pharmaceutical Companies in an Integrated Financial Services Market: Regulatory Diversity within the EC

Brigitte Haar*

1. The need for capital in European biotechnology

Opening up markets has been one of Ernst-Joachim Mestmäcker's key endeavors.[1] But what to do if markets have yet to emerge? Biotechnology is one of the key emerging technologies and exemplifies the major problems of innovative industrial activity in Europe. Broadly defined, biotechnology includes "...any technique that uses living organisms (or parts of organisms) to make or modify products, to improve plants or animals, or to develop microorganisms for specific uses".[2] In light of its approach on a genetic and molecular level

* Dr. iur., LL.M. (Univ. Chicago), Research Associate, Max Planck Institute.

[1] A prominent example being the market of telecommunications: Mestmäcker (ed.), *Kommunikation ohne Monopole* (Baden-Baden: Nomos 1980); Mestmäcker (ed.), *Kommunikation ohne Monopole II* (Baden-Baden: Nomos 1995).

[2] Office of Tech. Assessment, US Congress, *Commercial Biotechnology: an International Analysis* (1984) p. 3.

Talia Einhorn, ed., Spontaneous Order, Organization and the Law – Liber Amicorum Ernst-Joachim Mestmäcker © 2003 T.M.C.Asser Press, *The Hague, The Netherlands*

biotechnology is research-intensive and driven by innovation.[3] The Commission's Green Paper on Innovation identified the biotechnology sector as one of dynamic growth and importance for Europe.[4] However, a study by *Ernst & Young* shows that as of 1997 the United States outperforms all other countries in the biotech sector in terms of its number of companies and employees as well as in terms of sales and research and development expenditures.[5] In addition, all top ten products were developed in the US, and most of them sold by US companies.[6] Thus, Europe lags behind the US in most indicators of economic performance in biotechnology and therefore biotechnology has been identified as an area of prime importance to the future economic development and competitiveness in Europe.[7] For example, in Germany quite successful basic research has been conducted over the years at universities and research institutes.[8] However, these innovative advances in research could not be translated into success on the German pharmaceutical market.[9] What then are the ingredients of the American success in biotechnology?

---

[3] Summing up this molecular approach Burk, "Introduction: A biotechnology primer", 55 *U. Pitt. L. Rev.* (1994) 611, 612-621.

[4] *COM* (95) 688 final, December 1995, p. 15, 24, Annex 1: p. 16/14; hint at "biotechnology . . . as one of the most promising and crucial technologies for sustainable development in the next century" in European Commission, White Paper on growth, competitiveness, and employment: The challenges and ways forward into the 21st century, *COM* (93) 700 final, Brussels, 5 December 1993; for the latest official statement on the status of biotechnology in Europe and the legal protection of biotechnological inventions, see the opinion of the Advocate-General of 14 June 2001 in Case C-377/98 *Kingdom of the Netherlands* v. *European Parliament and Council of the European Union.*

[5] Ernst & Young, *Aufbruchstimmung 1998. Erster Deutscher Biotechnologie Report* (Stuttgart: Schitag Ernst & Young 1998); this is not changed by the recent growth of the European biotech industry, which leaves the top fifty European biotech firms at a quarter of the size in annual turnover and in stock value in comparison with US firms: Hofmann, "Europäische Industrie noch im Rückstand" ["European Industry still behind"], *Handelsblatt* (27 May 2001).

[6] Giesecke, "The contrasting roles of government in the development of biotechnology industry in the US and Germany", 29 *Research Policy* (2000) 205, 207 and 208, with reference to Ernst & Young, *Biotech 97, Alignment: a new economy* (The Ernst & Young Annual Report on the Biotechnology Industry) (Palo Alto 1996).

[7] European Commission, *A User's Guide for SMEs in the Biotechnology Field* (May 1999) p. 2.

[8] Identifying the early government support for biotechnology development in Germany Giesecke, *supra* n. 6, at 206-207.

[9] Dolata, *Internationales Innovationsmanagement; Die deutsche Pharmaindustrie und die Gentechnik* (Diskussionspapier 3-94, Hamburger Institut für Sozialforschung 1994) 66-70; Streck, "Deutsche Biotechnologieforschung mit großem Nachholbedarf", *Ifo-Schnelldienst* (1994/18) 10-17.

Certainly, quite a few variables make up the supportive institutional arrangement for the US biotech industry. One important factor has been the smooth technology transfer from academic research labs to industry nurtured by legislative and institutional measures, such as supportive patent rules and public technology transfer offices.[10] Another major undisputed factor in the different developments in European and US biotechnology, becoming ever more important with the advent of the European Monetary Union and the ensuing deep and liquid capital market in the EU, has been the role of venture capital funds in financing biotech enterprises.[11] According to Stanley Erck, CEO of Procept, Inc, a biopharmaceutical company, it has been the "availability of venture capital, combined with the willingness of Wall street to support companies with initial public offerings that has put the United States as much as five to ten years ahead of Europe and Japan in developing a biotechnology industry. Either venture capital was not available in those areas, or the ability to cash out as a venture capitalist into a public market was much more difficult".[12]

The specific problems of finance and the importance of venture capital in the biotech industry become clear only after a closer look at the industry structure. Especially transaction cost economics has provided useful insights into the basic reasons for the particular strategies and structure in the biotechnology pharmaceutical industry.[13] The biotechnology-based approach to the innovation

---

[10] In detail Abramson/ Encarnacao/ Reid/ Schmoch, *Technologietransfer-Systeme in den USA und Deutschland* (Karlsruhe/ Washington D.C.: Fraunhofer IRB 1997).

[11] Ashworth, "Development of the European Biotechnology Industry", 33 *Cal. W. L. Rev.* (1996) 83, 93; Ernst & Young, *Biotech 97: Alignment: a new economy*, *supra* n. 6, pp. 42-45; European Commission, *A User's Guide for SMEs in the Biotechnology Field*, *supra* n. 7; Giesecke, *supra* n. 6, at 216-218.

[12] Erck, "Symposium: Financing the Biotech Industry: Can the Risks be Reduced?" 4 *B.U.J. Sci. & Tech.* (1998) 1, 21; for the link between venture capital and IPOs in liquid capital markets, see Black/ Gilson, "Venture Capital and the Structure of Capital Markets: Banks versus Stock Markets", 47 *J. Fin. Econ.* (1998) 243-277; for the latest attention to the global capital markets as an exit option, see Rock, *Greenhorns, Yankees and Cosmopolitans: Venture Capital, IPOs, Foreign Firms and US Markets* (U. Penn., Inst. For Law & Econ. Res. Paper 01-07 (forthcoming in *Theoretical Inquiries in Law*) (available in Social Science Research Network Electronic Library). From the German perspective: Hopt, "Stärkung des Kapitalmarktes Deutschland, Förderung des Aktiensparens und Verbesserung der Risikokapitalversorgung", in: The Institute of Comparative Law in Japan (ed.), *Toward Comparative Law in the 21st Century* (Tokyo: Chuo Univ. Press 1998) 67-70.

[13] By way of example: Pisano, *Innovation through markets, hierarchies, and joint ventures: Technology strategy and collaborative arrangements in the biotechnology industry* (Ph.D. thesis, UMI 1989); Shan, *Technological Change and Strategic Cooperation; Evidence from Commercialization of Biotechnology* (Ph.D. thesis, UMI 1987); more general with respect to technological innovation Teece, "Firm Organization, Industrial Structure, and Technological Innovation", 31 *J. Econ. Behavior & Org.* (1996) 193-224.

in pharmaceuticals is marked by a fundamental departure from traditional pharmaceutical research and development. It represents a new set of techniques based on different scientific disciplines for discovering and synthesizing therapeutic molecules. This is why supportive patent rules have been so important in the US and much of the early research and development in biotechnology was undertaken by start-up companies, instead of relying on established pharmaceutical companies.[14] However, the importance of downstream competencies in clinical development, regulatory affairs, and marketing for these new competencies for drug discovery brought about specific forms of integration and collaborative agreements in the biotech industry.[15] In the beginning of the development of the biotech industry (1976-1981) every new biotechnology firm formed relationships with one or more larger corporate enterprises despite getting finance from venture capitalists.[16] Its further development has been marked by a trend toward vertical integration, new biotechnology firms integrating into manufacturing and distribution, established firms integrating into biotechnology research and development, so that transaction costs would be reduced.[17] In addition, literature in the property rights field suggests that it is optimal for ownership of a project to be assigned to the party with the greatest ability to affect the outcome.[18] An adaptation of this general model to a research and development alliance between two firms in the finance literature shows that an inefficient allocation of the property rights occurs, with the financier retaining the rights to the invention, if the research unit is without financial resources of its own, cannot borrow any funds, and has no ability to

---

[14] Pisano/ Mang, "Collaborative Product Development and the Market for Know-how: Strategies and Structures in the Biotechnology Industry", in: Burgelman/ Rosenbloom (eds.), *Research on Technological Innovation, Management and Policy* (Greenwich: JAI Press 1993) 109, 120; for differences in the development of the European biotechnology, see Acharya/ Arundel/ Orsenigo, "The evolution of European biotechnology and its future competitiveness," in: Senker/v. Vliet (eds.), *Biotechnology and Competitive Advantage* (Cheltenham: Elgar 1998) 89, 95-104.

[15] Empirical study on choice between internal vs. external research and development: Pisano, *supra* n. 13, pp. 137-206; Pisano/ Mang, ibid., pp. 120-121; Pisano, "The governance of innovation: Vertical integration and collaborative arrangements in the biotechnology industry", 20 *Research Policy* (1991) 237, 241-247.

[16] Pisano, 20 *Research Policy*, ibid., at 239.

[17] Pisano, *supra* n. 13, pp. 137-206.

[18] Grossman/ Hart, "The Costs and Benefits of Ownership: A Theory of Lateral and Vertical Integration", 94 *J. Pol. Econ.* (1986) 691-719; Hart/ Moore, "Incomplete Contracts and Renegotiation", 56 *Econometrica* (1988) 755-785; Hart, *Firms, Contracts, and Financial Structure* (New York: Oxford University Press 1995) 29-55.

commercialize the innovation itself.[19] Thus, access to finance is crucial for an optimal economic performance of biotech firms. Only recently has this claim been confirmed by an empirical study.[20] Therefore, finance does matter in biotechnology and its improved availability could be a first step in a European catch-up strategy in this field.

With the changes in the European Union's financial structures, European biotechnology has begun to grow thanks to an increased access to capital from European financial markets.[21] Improved private finance of European biotech enterprises could be the key for catch-up strategies in Europe to overcome blockages of the European innovation system. Therefore, this study undertakes to examine the specific problems of finance in biotechnology (2), the role of venture capital funds to overcome those (3), the regulatory measures in support of venture capital in Europe so far (4), and the remaining demands to be met by European capital markets and their regulation in order to create a functioning market for risk capital (5).

2. INFORMATION ASYMMETRIES AS THE MAJOR PROBLEM OF FINANCING BIOTECH PHARMACEUTICALS

What is it that makes access to finance for small start-up biotech companies so difficult? Other industries also have large capital needs. Biotechnology, however, combines this need for large sums with the possibility of no return on this investment for years. It can easily take seven or eight years, or longer, to develop a drug, run clinical trials, and obtain the necessary administrative approval to market the drug.[22] What is more, the assets from which new biotech firms want to extract rent streams present additional difficulty. The know-how necessary to develop new drugs is difficult to evaluate and therefore raises specific transactional problems. Those problems relate to the costs and risks associated with making specialized investments in the face of uncertainty, potential appropriability problems in case of inadequate protection by

---

[19] Aghion/Tirole, "On the Management of Innovation", 109 *Quarterly J. Econ.* (1994) 1185-1209; empirical corroboration in Lerner/ Merges, *The Control of Strategic Alliances: an Empirical Analysis of Biotechnology Collaborations* (NBER Working Paper No. W6014, April 1997).

[20] Lerner/ Tsai, *Do Equity Financing Cycles Matter?: Evidence from Biotechnology Alliances* (Harvard Business School Working Paper No. 00-038; NBER Working Paper No. 7464).

[21] Burrill, "The European Biotech Industry: Gathering Momentum", *Biopharm* (1 May 1995) (1995 WL 13882566); Ernst & Young, *Biotech 97: Alignment: a new economy*, *supra* n. 6, 42-45.

[22] With respect to these peculiarities of the biotech industry Gevurtz, "Biotechnology: Business Organization Issues", 32 *McGeorge L. Rev.* (2000) 237, 238; on the length of the development process DiMasi/Seibring/Lasagna, "New Drug Development in the United States from 1963-1992", *Clinical Pharmacology Therapeutics* 55 (1994) 609-622.

intellectual property, and tremendous information asymmetries between the developing firm and potential financiers.[23] These information asymmetries create problems similar to the lemons hypothesis developed by *Akerlof*.[24] *Akerlof* showed how asymmetric information about quality can lead to a situation where only poor quality products ("lemons") become available in the market. Likewise, there is an incentive for some licensors in the market for know-how to overstate the favorable aspect of the project, while downplaying the negatives. Since the licensee cannot discern which licensors are open and which ones are not, all licensors say that they have a high quality project. As a consequence, licensees discount the price they are willing to pay for projects. Thus, asymmetric information in the market for know-how can drive out projects with good prospects for success and leave only "lemons" available for licensing. This process provides an economic rationale for vertical integration in biotechnology.[25]

However, even in the case of vertical integration, the problems resulting from information asymmetries with respect to project quality are also reflected by the scarce availability of capital on capital markets for those projects. Since the management is better informed about the investment opportunities of the firm, managers acting in the interest of current shareholders only issue new shares when the company's stock is overvalued. Thus, the lemons problem repeats itself with equity offerings[26] and makes raising capital more expensive. Similar informational problems exist in debt markets. They form the basis of the dominant model of credit rationing.[27] According to this model, credit rationing results from the inability of the lender to determine how risky the proposed project is. Under these circumstances, raising interest rates can have perverse selection effects because it attracts high-risk projects. In light of the ensuing decline in quality of the loan pool, a bank will therefore ration the credit it extends at a lower rate. Therefore, credit rationing is an equilibrium result.

---

[23] Pisano, "The R & D Boundaries of the Firm: An Empirical Analysis", 35 *Adm. Science Quarterly* (1990) 153, 157-162; Teece, *supra* n. 13, at 194-197.

[24] Akerlof, "The Market for 'Lemons': Qualitative Uncertainty and the Market Mechanism", 84 *Quarterly J. Econ.* (1970) 488-500; application of the 'lemons' hypothesis to biotechnology, see Pisano, *R & D Performance, Collaborative Arrangements, and the Market-for-Know-How: A Test of the "Lemons" Hypothesis in Biotechnology* (Harvard Business School Working Paper No. 97-105).

[25] Pisano, ibid.

[26] Greenwald/ Stiglitz/ Weiss, "Informational Imperfections in the Capital Market and Macroeconomic Fluctuations", 74 *Am. Econ. Rev., Papers and Proceedings* (1984) 194-199; Myers/ Majluf, "Corporate Financing and Investment Decisions when Firms Have Information that Investors do not Have", 13 *J. Fin. Econ.* (1984) 187-221.

[27] Stiglitz/ Weiss, "Credit Rationing in Markets with Imperfect Information", 71 *Am. Econ. Rev.* (1981) 393-410; Stiglitz/ Weiss, "Asymmetric Information in Credit Markets and Its Implications for Macro-Economics", 44 *Oxford Econ. Papers* (1992) 694-724.

3. The intermediary function of venture capital funds

The information asymmetries between new biotech firms and potential investors lead, as shown, to financing constraints in debt and equity markets.[28] Overcoming these constraints therefore presupposes a solution to the information problems. This is why the financing firm has to perform the function of a financial intermediary attenuating the information obstacles to the financing of new technology-based firms. As such it can exploit economies of specialization, scale, and scope in the processing of information. By evaluating sensitive information about the new firm without spilling it to other contracting partners and to competitors, intermediaries bridge the information gap between these new firms and capital markets.[29] Banks and venture capitalists are two types of financial intermediaries between investors and start-up firms. The crucial difference between these two is the regulation of banking activities that obviates the need for private negotiation of terms.[30] However, the privately negotiated mechanisms that venture capitalists use to reduce information problems illustrate how organizations can overcome problems that markets fail to solve.

The two types of information asymmetries that venture capitalists have to master are that of hidden information exemplified by the adverse selection problem of *Akerlof*s "lemons" hypothesis and that of hidden action resulting from the inobservability of the new firm's effort by the investor and the bringing about of the risk of moral hazard.[31] In order to reduce adverse selection problems venture capital funds require the submission of extensive business

---

[28] For empirical work on such capital constraints of new firms, see Hall, *Investment and Research and Development at the Firm Level: Does the Source of Financing Matter?* (NBER Working paper No. W4096 June 1992); Himmelberg/ Petersen, "R & D and internal finance: A panel study of small firms in high-tech industries", 76 *Rev. Econ. & Statistics* (1994) 38-51; for review of literature, see Hubbard, "Capital-market imperfections and investment", 36 *J. Econ. Lit.* (1998) 193-225.

[29] Leland/ Pyle, "Informational Asymmetries, Financial Structure, and Financial Intermediation", 32 *J. Fin.* (1977) 371-387.

[30] For similar comparison, see Triantis, "Financial Contract Design in the World of Venture Capital", 68 *U. Chi. L. Rev.* (2001) 305, 306.

[31] For a formal model that uses asymmetric information to explain the existence of venture capitalists and a corresponding study of evidence in Canada, see Amit/ Brander/ Zott, "Why do Venture Capital Firms Exist? Theory and Canadian Evidence", 13 *J. Bus. Venturing* (1998) 441-466; for early influential work on moral hazard, see Arrow, *The Limits of Organization* (New York: Norton 1974) 33-79; Pauly, "Overinsurance and Public Provision of Insurance: the Roles of Moral Hazard and Adverse Selection", 88 *Quarterly J. Econ.* (1974) 44-62; pointing out adverse selection and moral hazard as the essential obstacles to strong public securities markets and therefore also to the availability of finance Black, "The Legal and Institutional Preconditions for Strong Securities Markets", 48 *UCLA L. Rev.* (2001) 781-855.

plans and tie their investment decision to the entrepreneur's skill level.[32] In addition, before agreeing to invest, venture capitalists often insist on the identification of a syndication partner who confirms that this is an attractive investment.[33] For a reduction of moral hazard problems, staged investment works as a monitoring device.[34] In effect, the venture capitalist performs a dual role, providing financing and sending project quality signals to the capital market.[35] Control by way of staging is supplemented by intensive monitoring on the part of the venture capitalists who demand preferred stock with numerous restrictive covenants and representation on the board of directors.[36] Thus, all in all venture capitalists replace capital market incentives that fail to work because of information asymmetries with contractual agreements. The contractual framework in fact compensates for capital market imperfections.

4. Mimicking allocative effects of capital markets in support of venture capital in Europe

What has been done in Europe to overcome these informational obstacles and the resulting lack of risk capital especially for small and medium-sized enterprises in the biotechnology field? The failures of European firms to bring high technology and innovative products to the market as speedily as competitor nations has long been noted.[37] The Commission's Green Paper on Innovation

---

32 For empirical work, see Amit/ Glosten/ Muller, "Entrepreneurial ability, venture investments, and risk sharing", 36 *Management Science* (1990) 1232-1245.

33 Lerner, "The Syndication of Venture Capital Investments", 23 *Fin. Management* (1994) 16-27.

34 Sahlman, "The structure and governance of venture-capital organizations", 27 *J. Fin. Econ.* (1990) 473, 506-507; Gompers, "Optional investment, monitoring and the staging of venture capital", 50 *J. Fin.* (1995) 1461-1489; for a formal model, see Hellmann, *Essays in Financial Market Imperfections and Institutional Responses* (Ph.D. thesis, Department of Econ. of Stanford Univ. 1994) pp. 36-105; for a model showing that staging of commitment of capital is used as a key to resolve informational asymmetries, see Admati/ Pfleiderer, "Robust Financial Contracting and the Role of Venture Capitalists", 49 *J. Fin.* (1994) 371-402.

35 Admati/ Pfleiderer, ibid.

36 For documentation of oversight role, see Gompers, "Optional Investment, Monitoring and the Staging of Venture Capital", 50 *J. Fin.* (1995) 1461-1489; Lerner, "Venture Capital and the Oversight of Private Firms", 50 *J. Fin.* (1995) 301-318; for new forms of off-balance sheet R&D financing in biotechnology to raise large sums of equity without losing independence of flexibility, see Schoemaker/ Shapiro, "Innovative Financial Strategies for Biotechnology Ventures", in: Day/ Schoemaker/ Gunther (eds.), *Wharton on Managing Emerging Technologies* (New York: Wiley 2000) 307-332.

37 European Commission, *European industrial policy for the 1990s* (Brussels 1991) 31, 33; European Commission, "Green Paper on Innovation", *COM* (1995) 688 final (December 1995) p. 6.

finally recognized the importance of innovative small and medium-sized enterprises in the biotech sector as well as their difficulties in obtaining venture capital.[38] The ensuing discussion process led to the First Action Plan for Innovation in Europe.[39] In its framework the Innovation and Technology Equity Capital (I-Tec) scheme was launched.[40] This program is a pilot scheme open to venture capitalists in the EC and the Associated States aiming to make early stage high-tech investment. Recognizing the additional costs in making early stage venture capital investment in new technology-based firms, the Innovation and Technology Equity Capital scheme contributes up to 50% of the costs related to initial appraisal and hands-on management, but not exceeding 5% of the investments effectively made, with a maximum of 500,000 Euro. In a similar way, the European Investment Fund created new financial schemes, such as the European Technology Facility Start-up and the Joint European Venture program both of which have also been an attempt to solve the issue of the cost of managerial governance in early-stage funds.[41]

In addition, Member States also pursue policies to encourage the supply of venture capital from established capital markets. In order to implement some down-side protection especially for smaller funds from full or partial loss of the investment, insurance schemes have been instituted (SOFARIS in France) or measures have been taken to share in the cost of investment (BTU [*Beteiligungskapital für Technologieunternehmen*] scheme in Germany).[42] The disadvantage of such protection is its potential consequence of reducing investors' incentives.[43] Therefore, additional strategies of upside leverage have been implemented, allowing each dollar of a venture capitalist's fund to be matched with one or more dollars of the government's money (BTU scheme in Germany). In essence, such government participation amounts to a loan that is less costly than one provided by capital markets.

---

[38] *COM* (95) 688 final (December 1995) pp. 6, 10.

[39] European Commission, *First action plan for innovation in Europe* (Brussels 1997); for download visit <http://www.cordis.lu/innovation/src/action.htm>

[40] For details on the program and its participants visit <http://www.cordis.lu/finance/home.html> from a German perspective towards these and similar German programs, see Hopt, "Verbesserter Zugang zu Risikokapital für Existenzgründer sowie kleine und mittlere Unternehmen", in: Pfeiffer/ Kummer/ Scheuch (eds.), *Festschrift für Hans Erich Brandner* (Köln: Schmidt 1996) 541, 543-545.

[41] European Commission, "Creating an entrepreneurial Europe; The activities of the European Union for small and medium-sized enterprises" (Brussels 1.3.2001), *COM* (2001) 98 final, p. 72-76; Murray/ Marriott, "Why has the investment performance of technology-specialist, European venture capital funds been so poor?", 27 *Research Policy* (1998) 947, 958.

[42] European Commission, *Commission Staff Working Paper, Report on the implementation of the Action Plan to promote Entrepreneurship and Competitiveness*, Annexes (Brussels 27.10.2000) pp. 18, 33.

[43] Murray/ Marriot, *supra* n. 41, at 957.

Over the last years, the EC risk capital market has been growing. In 1999 venture capital investment increased 70% to about 12 billion Euro (0.14% of GDP) from about 7 billion Euro (0.09% of GDP) in 1998.[44] However, despite this progress, the EC risk capital market remains small in comparison to that of the United States, especially as far as early-stage investment is concerned.[45] Ultimately, the strategies of down-side protection, upside leverage, and support for the fund's operating costs cannot replace the functioning of capital market mechanisms.[46] Instead of implementing such market mechanisms, these strategies replace the allocative effects of capital markets by lowering the cost of capital.

5. Integrated financial services markets as a requirement for risk capital

With a view to the promotion of entrepreneurship and innovation for the creation of a knowledge-based economy the special Lisbon European Council (March 2000) identified the development of a pan-European market for risk capital as a high priority and called for the implementation of the Risk Capital Action Plan by 2003. This Risk Capital Action Plan was part of the Communication of the European Commission on "Risk Capital: A Key to Job Creation in the European Union" in 1998.[47] In this communication the Commission recognizes that, in order to offer to investors a suitable alternative to the US market, a sufficient pool of companies being available for investment can only be achieved on a Europe-wide basis.[48] Thus, the point of departure to encourage the formation of risk capital in Europe shifts from mimicking the allocative effects of functioning capital markets by way of regulation (such as down-side protection, upside leverage, and financial support for operating costs) to the creation of Europe-wide integrated capital markets. The introduction of the Euro offers the opportunity to transform financial markets, to complete the single market for financial services and thereby to accelerate the emergence of liquid capital markets.[49]

---

[44] European Commission, "Progress Report on the Risk Capital Allocation Plan", *COM* (2000) 658 final (Brussels 18.10.2000) p. 4.

[45] European Commission, "Progress Report on the Risk Capital Allocation Plan", *COM* (2000) 658 final (Brussels 18.10.2000) p. 7; Murray/ Marriott, *supra* n. 41, at 948.

[46] Empirically with respect to small fund size Murray/ Marriott, *supra* n. 41, at 974.

[47] European Commission, *Risk Capital: A Key to Job Creation in the European Union* (Brussels 1998).

[48] European Commission, ibid., p. 10.

[49] European Commission, *Progress report on the risk capital action plan*, Supplement A, Economic trends, No. 8/9 (August/ September 2000) p. 4.

5.1 The internal market as a system ensuring undistorted competition

By aiming at the accomplishment of a Europe-wide market for risk capital the EC pursues a strategy well-known from the realization of the internal market and the free movement of goods. At the heart of the internal market lies the concept of a system ensuring that competition between firms is not distorted (Art. 3g of the EC Treaty). The freedom of movement of goods has been an essential step towards realizing this goal. In particular, the judgments of the European Court of Justice regarding Art. 28 of the Treaty in the famous *Cassis de Dijon* decision helped remove obstacles to the free movement of goods by requiring mandatory reasons of public policy as a justification of restrictions to the free movement of goods, thus scrutinizing economic policies of Member States.[50] This broad anti-discriminatory impact of Art. 28 of the Treaty has been limited later in that selling arrangements do not fall under this rule unless they are shown to be discriminatory.[51] Similarly, the creation of a level playing field becomes crucial to the creation of a Europe-wide market for risk capital. Only recently did the Commission point out the absence of a harmonized regulatory framework, preventing effective cross-border competition in the financial services market.[52] However, this area does not fall under the provisions dealing with the free movement of goods (Art. 28 of the Treaty), but under those of the free movement of capital (Art. 56 of the Treaty). In principle, the anti-discriminatory concept of the fundamental freedoms of movement of the Treaty applies to the free movement of capital as well, thus allowing only restrictions justified

---

[50] Case 120/78 *Rewe* v. *Bundesmonopolverwaltung für Branntwein*, [1979] *ECR* 649; see for analysis of the developments Barents, "New Developments in Measures having Equivalent Effect", 18 *C.M.L. Rev.* (1981) 271-308; Baron van Voorst tot Voorst/ van Dam, "Europe 1992: Free Movement of Goods in the Wider Context of a Changing Europe", 25 *C.M.L. Rev.* (1988) 693-709; Mortelsman, "The Common Market, the Internal Market and the Single Market, What's in a Market?" 35 *C.M.L. Rev.* (1998) 101-136; Weatherill, "After Keck: Some Thoughts on How to Clarify the Clarification", 33 *C.M.L. Rev.* (1996) 885-906.

[51] Cases C-267 & 268/91 *Keck & Mithouard*, [1993] *ECR* I-6097 and the case law which followed; in light of the focus of this article on the cross-border activity of financial service providers it does not matter whether these restrictions equally apply to the freedom of movement of capital (applicability favored by Eilmansberger, "Zur Reichweite der Kapitalverkehrsfreiheit" ["The Scope of the Freedom of Movement of Capital"], *ÖBA* [2001] 377, 380-381; disfavored with respect to the freedom to provide services Kulms, "Rentenversicherung, private Zusatzvorsorge und Europäischer Binnenmarkt für Versicherungsleistungen", in: Basedow/ Drobnig/ Ellger/ Hopt/ Kötz/ Kulms/ Mestmäcker [eds.], *Aufbruch nach Europa* (Tübingen: Mohr 2001) 183, 187.

[52] European Commission, "Commission Recommendation for the 2001 Broad Guidelines of the Economic policies of the Member States and the Community", *COM* (2001) 224 final (Brussels 25.4.2001) p. 15; for the applicability of the competition rules to financial services, see Usher, *The Law of Money and Financial Services in the EC*, 2nd Ed. (New York: Oxford University Press 2000) 59-88.

on grounds of the general interest not disproportionate in relation to the objective pursued.[53] With respect to institutional and regulatory barriers to risk capital set up by Member States, special emphasis is given to the adoption of prudential rules applicable to traditional institutional investors, to the upgrading of directives on prospectuses and to the legislative follow-up to the EC accounting strategy by the Commission.[54] Therefore, in view of the realization of an internal market for risk capital, it remains to be seen whether a system of undistorted competition between offerees for risk capital has been implemented and in how far reasons of the general interest can be put forward by the Member States in defense of their national economic policies.

5.2 A "single passport" for issuers to facilitate companies raising cross-border capital as a means to implement a system of undistorted competition

A first step towards integrating European capital markets has already been undertaken on the basis of Directive 85/611/EEC of 20 December 1985 on the coordination of laws, regulations and administrative provisions relating to undertakings for collective investment in transferable securities (UCITS).[55] This directive introduced the principle of mutual recognition for UCITS (Art. 4 para. 1).[56] The focus on the investment product offered was later replaced by the focus on the institution of the offeror, i.e. regulation has been tied to supervision of the financial institution by the Member States. Thus, the "single passport" for issuers has been granted to credit institutions,[57] investment firms[58] and insurance undertakings.[59] The fragmentation of European capital markets has long been recognized as a major barrier to the development of large pan-European risk-capital markets.[60] In order to raise cross-border capital, an investment fund

---

[53] Case C-148/91 *Vereniging Veronica Omroep Organisatie* v. *Commissariaat voor de Media*, [1993] *ECR* I-487, I-519-I-520; Hatzopoulos, "Recent Developments of the Case Law of the ECJ in the Field of Services", 37 *C.M.L. Rev.* (2000) 43, 72 Fn. 162; Usher, ibid., pp. 105-110.

[54] European Commission, "Progress Report on the Risk Capital Action Plan" (Brussels 18.10.2000), *COM* (2000) 658 final, p. 11.

[55] *OJ* [1985] L 375/3.

[56] *OJ* [1985] L 375/3.

[57] Directive 89/646/EEC (15.12.1989), *OJ* [1989] L 386/1.

[58] Directive 93/22/EEC (10.5.1993), *OJ* [1993] L 141/27.

[59] Directive 92/49/EEC (18.6.1992), *OJ* [1992] L 228/1 (direct insurance); Directive 92/96/ EEC of 10.11.1992, *OJ* [1992] L 360/1 (direct life assurance).

[60] European Commission, Communication of the European Commission, "Risk Capital: A Key to Job Creation in the European Union", *SEC* (1998) 552, p. 11-12; European Commission, "Progress Report on the Risk Capital Action Plan" (Brussels, 18.10.2000), *COM* (2000) 658 final, p. 10; The Committee of Wise Men, *Final Report on the Regulation of European Securities Markets* (Brussels, 15.2. 2001) pp. 10-13.

needs better access to investment capital on a Europe-wide basis. That is why the necessity of a single passport for issuers is widely accepted.[61] Therefore, all measures of financial regulatory nature in the risk capital action plan have been integrated into the implementation of the Financial Services Action Plan to ensure European financial market integration.[62] In line with this framework, a political agreement has been reached on the amendment of Directive 85/611/ EEC on the coordination of laws, regulations and administrative provision relating to UCITS with a view to regulating management companies and simplified prospectuses.[63] This amendment, which was politically agreed to by the Council on 12 March 2001, facilitates the widest possible access to investment capital on an EC-wide basis by aligning the regulation for management companies, the regular business of which is the collective portfolio management of UCITS, with that existing for other operators of the financial services area.[64] For this purpose, Art. 5 – 5b of the proposal introduce an authorization procedure corresponding to that existing for other financial service providers, such as banks, investment firms, and insurance companies.[65] On the basis of such a European Passport, management companies are allowed to set up branches in other Member States (Art. 6a of the proposal) and engage in cross-border distribution (Art. 6b of the proposal).[66] In this way, the mutual recognition of the principle of home country supervision in the framework of a European Passport implements the right of establishment and the freedom to provide services in the EC for management companies. As underlined by the European Commission, these freedoms of movement prove again – just like in the case of the freedom of movement of goods – their ability to establish a

---

[61] European Commission, Communication from the Commission to the Council and the European Parliament, "Progress Report on the Risk Capital Action Plan" (Brussels, 18.10.2000), *COM* (2000) 658 final, p. 10; The Committee of Wise Men, *Final Report on the Regulation of European Securities Markets* (Brussels, 15.2.2001) p. 13.

[62] European Commission, "Financial Services Action Plan" (Brussels 11.05.1999), *COM* (1999) 232, p. 6.

[63] Council – ECOFIN, 2335th Council meeting, Press Release 6925/01, (Brussels, 12 March 2001), p. 19; European Commission, Financial services: "Commission welcomes political agreement on investment fund management Directive", 12 March 2001 <http://www.europa.eu.int/comm/internal_market/en/finances/mobil/01-345.htm> visited 27 May 2001.

[64] European Commission, Amended Proposal for a Directive of the European Parliament and Council amending Directive 85/611/EEC on the coordination of laws, regulations and administrative provisions relating to undertakings for collective investment in transferable securities (UCITS) with a view to regulating management companies and simplified prospectuses, *COM* (2000)331 final as amended by document no. [500PC0331] <http://www.europa.eu.int/eur-lex/en/com/dat/2000/en_500PC0331.html>

[65] European Commission, ibid.

[66] European Commission, ibid.

system of undistorted competition in the financial services area, "assuring in all Member States equivalent market access rules and operating conditions for such (management) companies", thus putting them on an equal footing with their competitors in the financial services area.[67] The introduction of the single passport based on mutual recognition will result in financial service providers from various Member States, whose securities conform with their country's regulations, having the right to sell in all other Member States as well, even if they do not conform with domestic regulations, just as has been exemplified by the freedom of movement of goods (Art. 28 of the Treaty) and its consequences for producers. From the investors' perspective, the Member States may issue mandatory regulations for investor protection, but have to recognize regulations and authorizations by other Member States as a result of the principle of mutual recognition.[68] Such regulations on investor protection can hence only be agreed upon on the EC level.

5.3 Regulatory diversity of EC regulators, self-regulation by market forces, and Member State regulation to accomplish a market of risk capital

This type of regulation can also be exemplified by the above-mentioned amended proposal for a European Parliament and Council Directive amending Directive 85/611/EEC on the coordination of laws, regulations and administrative provisions relating to undertakings for collective investment in transferable securities (UCITS) with a view to regulating management companies and simplified prospectuses.[69] In Article 27 para. 1, 28 para. 1 of the directive, the proposal introduces a simplified prospectus as a mandatory information document, which always has to be offered to the investor before the conclusion of the contract.[70] Thus, in the area of investor protection on the basis of information on the investment, the principle of mutual recognition in the framework of a European Passport for financial service providers tends to break up rigid national regulations by ensuring a single market, at the same time leading to

---

[67] European Commission, ibid.

[68] For this reason, calling for effective home Member State supervision Hertig, "Regulatory Competition for EU Financial Services", 3 *J. Int. Econ. L.* (2000) 349, 352-354; for parallel argument in context of freedom of movement of goods, see Kerber, "Interjurisdictional Competition within the European Union", 23 *Fordham Int'l L.J.* (2000) 217, 243; for limits of this principle of mutual recognition because of abuse and resulting dangers for the investors, see Calliess, "Heimatstaatprinzip und Europa-Paß im Finanzmarktrecht" ["Home country supervision and the European passport in the law of financial services"], *EWS* (*Europäisches Wirtschafts- & Steuerrecht*) [2000] 432, 435-439.

[69] European Commission, *supra* n. 64.

[70] European Commission, *supra* n. 64.

EC-wide harmonization of investor protection.[71] Disclosure practice, however, shows that this harmonization of disclosure standards is often pushed above minimum requirements by International-style Offerings targeted at institutional investors and governed by an evolving system of market standards that currently requires disclosure documents roughly comparable to those prepared for private placements in the US.[72] Thus, harmonization seems to be superseded by market forces and resulting non-regulated, surprisingly high standards. In sharp contrast to this attempted harmonization of investor protection ensued by the principle of mutual recognition for financial service providers, there has been wide agreement that there is no need for Community legislation covering specific closed-end funds, e.g. venture capital funds.[73]

The principle of mutual recognition seems at first sight to be at odds with the widely-spread practice in Member States to tie jurisdiction over companies to the location of their effective administration ("theory of real seat") excluding recognition of the legal personality of companies from other Member States at times. This practice, however, might be in decline after the *Centros* decision of the European Court of Justice,[74] and the concept of a jurisdictional competition for corporate charters based on the theory of incorporation might prevail.[75]

---

[71] For a similar assessment of harmonization in the field of freedom of movement of goods, see Kerber, *supra* n. 68, at 243.

[72] See for empirical evidence Jackson/ Pan, "Regulatory Competition in International Securities Markets: Evidence from Europe in 1999, Part I", 56 *Bus. Law.* (2001) 653, 655, 684-687.

[73] European Commission, Directorate General for Economic and Financial Affairs, Supplement A, Economic trends, No. 12 – December 1999, "Risk capital: a key to job creation. Implementation of the Action Plan", p. 9 Fn. 12; European Commission, Progress report on the risk capital action plan, (Brussels, 18.10.2000), *COM* (2000) 658 final, p. 24.

[74] Case C-212/97 *Centros Ltd.* v. *Erhversog Selskabsstyrelsen*, [1999] *ECR.* I-1459 (ECJ decision of 9.3.1999); on this decision, see, for example, Behrens, "International Company Law in View of *Centros* decision of the ECJ", 2 *EBOR* (2000) 125-146; but note at the same time the political agreement reached by the EU's Council of Ministers on December 20 on the Regulation to establish a European Company Statute.

[75] Fundamental in this respect is Winter, "State Law, Shareholder Protection, and the Theory of the Corporation", 6 *J. Leg. Stud.* (1977) 251-292; under the same assumption concerning the control capacity of the capital market, see Romano, *The Genius of American Corporate Law* (Washington D.C.: AEI 1993); dissenting: Cary, "Federalism and Corporate Law: Reflections upon Delaware", 83 *Yale L.J.* (1974) 663-705; skeptical with regard to Canadian corporate law recently Cumming/ MacIntosh, "The role of interjurisdictional competition in shaping Canadian corporate law", 20 *Int'L Rev. L & Econ.* (2000) 141-186; on the perspective of jurisdictional competition in this decision, see Freitag, "Der Wettbewerb der Rechtsordnungen im Internationalen Gesellschaftsrecht" ["Competing Laws in International Company Law"], *EuZW* [1999] 267-270 (269); Kieninger, "Niederlassungsfreiheit als Rechtswahlfreiheit" ["Freedom of establishment as the freedom of choice of law"], *ZGR* [1999] 724, 747-749; Merkt, "Das Centros-Urteil des Europäischen Gerichtshofs – Konsequenzen für den nationalen Gesetzgeber" ["The Centros-Decision of the ECJ – Consequences for the National Legislator"], in: Gesellschaftsrechtliche Vereinigung VGR (ed.), *Gesellschaftsrecht in der Diskussion 1999* [*Corporate Law in the Debate 1999*] (Köln: Schmidt 2000) 111, at 120 et seq.

According to this concept, the applicability of the law of the state of incorporation of a company provides the only incentive for the legislators to optimize corporate law regulations in order to succeed in the "state competition for corporate charters".[76] In light of this approach of jurisdictional competition towards the Member States' legislation covering company law and the legal framework for venture capital funds as opposed to the steps towards harmonization of investor protection and prospectus regulation, a clear distinction between these areas becomes necessary.

Looking at the standard example of modern disclosure rules in the area of investor protection, i.e. United States securities regulation, such a distinction at first seems difficult. These mandatory securities disclosure rules arose out of the disclosure obligations traditionally owed by an agent when dealing adversely with his principal as developed in mandatory disclosure rules in England.[77] The latter were to solve two basic forms of the promoter problem arising in the context of new-company promotion in the late nineteenth century. Often the promoter was also the vendor to the corporation of its principal assets and tried to hide the extent of his profit by arranging a series of sales to nominees at increasing prices, thus "loading" the purchase price.[78] Another common practice was to omit the amount of fees a professional promoter typically received for his services from the vendor which amounted to as much as 50% of the supplied capital.[79] The courts judged the promoter to be a fiduciary of the corporation and therefore to have a duty to disclose an interest

[76] Romano, *The Genius of American Corporate Law*, ibid.; on the transfer of the concept to investor protection, see Romano, "Empowering Investors: A Market Approach to Securities Regulation", in: *Comparative Corporate Governance: The State of the Art and Emerging Research*, (Hopt/ Kanda/ Roe/ Wymeersch/ Prigge [eds.]) (Oxford: Clarendon 1998) 143-217; for the German literature hereto, see Dreher, "Wettbewerb oder Vereinheitlichung der Rechtsordnungen in Europa?" ["Competition or a Unified Legal System in Europe?"], *JZ* [1999] 105-112; Kieninger, ibid., at 747-749; Kübler, "Rechtsbildung durch Gesetzgebungswettbewerb? Überlegungen zur Angleichung und Entwicklung des Gesellschaftsrechts in der Europäischen Gemeinschaft" ["Legislation by Competing Legal Systems? Thoughts on the Harmonization and Development of Corporate Law in the EC"], 77 *KritV* (1994) 79-89; Merkt, "Das Europäische Gesellschaftsrecht und die Idee des Wettbewerbs der Gesetzgeber" ["European Community Law and the Idea of a Competition of Legislators"], 59 *RabelsZ* (1995) 545-568; Müller, *Systemwettbewerb, Harmonisierung und Wettbewerbsverzerrung* [*Competition of Legal Systems, Harmonization and Distortions of Competition*] (Baden-Baden: Nomos 2000); Schön, "Mindestharmonisierung im europäischen Gesellschaftsrecht" ["Minimal Harmonization in European Community Law"]: 160 *ZHR* (1996) 221, 232-238.

[77] For an overview of this development in English and US law, see Mahoney, "Mandatory Disclosure as a Solution to Agency Problems", 62 *U. Chi. L. Rev.* (1995) 1047, 1054-1077.

[78] For examples, see *Erlanger* v. *New Sombrero Phosphate Co.*, (1878) 3 A.C. 1218, 1218-1223 (HL); *Whaley Bridge Calico Printing Co.* v. *Green*, (1879) 5 Q.B.D. 109, 109-110.

[79] See for example *Emma Silver Mining Co.* v. *Grant*, (1879) 11 Ch.D. 918, 918-925.

adverse to that of the corporation.[80] Dogmatically speaking, this was the exact same legal technique used in American corporate law to resolve conflicts of interest among shareholders. It was also the root of what the disclosure provisions of England's Companies Act of 1900[81] and the Companies Act 1929[82] arose from. Only later did the Blue Sky laws of the individual US states and the federal US securities regulation enacted as legislation separate from the companies codes.[83]

This division between harmonized mandatory disclosure rules and decentralized companies codes seems to repeat itself, to a certain extent, on the EC level. The question therefore arises whether the dividing line between these two regulatory concepts can plausibly be drawn. As shown above, the mandatory character of disclosure rules for investor protection can be ensured on the Member State level only by a rule of home country control.[84] Therefore, decentralized competences for securities regulation are abolished with the introduction of the European Passport for financial service providers and the rule of mutual recognition connected herewith. The European Passport for financial service providers is part and parcel of the completion of the internal market as a basic principle of European integration, ensuring a level playing field in a system of undistorted competition. However, the concept of the internal market only covers the EC-wide provision with private goods and services, but not an overall alignment of Member States' economic policies. The importance of an EC-wide access to capital has frequently been underlined as a constituent of the realization of the Risk Capital Action Plan.[85] It stands to reason that mandatory disclosure rules have an immediate impact on this access and therefore have to be regulated on a EC-wide basis in order to avoid competitive distortions. In contrast, the rest of company laws more or less constitute a public good providing a contractual framework for individuals to deploy economic activities in the marketplace.[86] In order to ensure that a state as a monopolist in the provision of public goods fulfills the preferences of its constituents, one is

---

[80] *Erlanger* v. *New Sombrero Phosphate Co.*, (1878) 3 A.C. 1218 (HL), 1229-1230, 1236.

[81] 63 & 64 Vict., ch. 48 (1900).

[82] 19 & 20 Geo. 5, ch. 23 (1929).

[83] For details, see Seligman, *The Transformation of Wall Street*, Rev. Edition (Boston: Northeastern University Press 1995) 44-46, 53, 57, 63.

[84] With respect to similar principles in the area of the freedom of movement of goods, see Kerber, *supra* n. 68, at 243.

[85] European Commission, *Risk Capital: A Key to Job Creation in the European Union* (April 1998) pp. 10-12.

[86] For the assessment of the character of corporate codes as public goods, see Easterbrook/Fischel, *The Economic Structure of Corporate Law* (Cambridge: Harvard University Press 1991) 34-35; for the role of interjurisdictional competition for the provision of public goods, see Kerber, *supra* n. 68, at 224-226.

inclined to favor a policy of interjurisdictional diversity for the provision of public goods.[87] The effectiveness of such diversity presupposes mobility of firms, individuals and resources as ensured by the concept of the internal market in the EC. It necessarily results in heterogeneity among economic policies in EC jurisdictions, thereby strengthening decentralization and fighting the dangers of monopolized economic policies on the EC level. Therefore, harmonization in the area of financial services should only go as far as the economic policy agreed upon by the Member States to constitute an internal market reaches. With the emergence of International-style Offerings in European capital markets, the evidence of disclosure practice indeed shows how market forces might correct this economic policy by drawing upon more stringent disclosure standards, thus replacing the harmonized disclosure regime.[88] With respect to European risk capital, an internal market has yet to be accomplished on the basis of EC-wide access to capital markets to ensure undistorted competition among financial service providers. This access can be usefully complemented by interjurisdictional diversity in the provision of company laws and the emergence of market standards of securities regulation. In sum, the interplay between interjurisdictional diversity in the provision of the company laws and the internal market for the provision of financial services proves to be key to the development of the market of risk capital in the EU. Only on this basis can innovation as exemplified by biotech pharmaceutical companies take hold.

[87] Going even further and calling for effective competition Vanberg/ Kerber, "Institutional Competition among Jurisdictions: An Evolutionary Approach", 5 *Const. Pol. Econ.* (1994) 193-219.

[88] See for evidence of International-style Offerings in Europe, Jackson/ Pan, *supra* n. 72, at 684-686.

The Changing Role of the State

Attila Harmathy*

The present short paper is written in honour of Professor MESTMÄCKER on the occasion of his birthday. How can one pay tribute to his activity? Perhaps by choosing a topic that has been the centre of his interest for several years: the role of the state and the change in this role. The role of the state and its changes have been the subject of books and articles by Professor MESTMÄCKER and many other authors. It was one of the main issues at the meetings that German and Hungarian lawyers held every second or third year, organised by the Max-Planck Institut für ausländisches und internationales Privatrecht, Hamburg, and these meetings have assisted in the transformation of law in Hungary. I remember that in the 1980s, during one of these colloquies, some questions of a new Hungarian legal regulation, based on elements of market economy, were being discussed and Professor MESTMÄCKER remarked that the new rules were important but they still seemed to belong very much to a planned economy. After having thought it over one had to come to the conclusion that the remark was correct.

The aim of this paper is no more than to express respect and gratitude by recalling some aspects of this vast subject.

1. PRIVATISATION

Privatisation has different meanings, different reasons in countries with a market economy and in countries with a planned economy.

The idea of privatisation is not new in countries with a market economy. According to some political scientists, it goes back at least to Adam Smith.[1] The state has long been involved in the economy, though the size and scope of the involvement has been different in accordance with the political and economic circumstances of the different countries. After World War II the proportion of state ownership increased in the European countries but some privatisation had

* Professor of the Faculty of Law, Eötvös University, Budapest, Judge of the Hungarian Constitutional Court.

Talia Einhorn, ed., Spontaneous Order, Organization and the Law – Liber Amicorum Ernst-Joachim Mestmäcker © 2003 T.M.C.ASSER PRESS, *The Hague, The Netherlands*

taken place already at the end of the 1950s in Germany and Austria. However, privatisation was limited and sporadic until the 1970s. It was in the 1980s that privatisation assumed wide-ranging and political forms.

In Germany questions of privatisation have been discussed since the second part of the XIXth century. Immediately after World War II, the important political parties were in favour of an increase in the role of state enterprises but later opinion changed due, to a great extent, to the reaction to the political system established in the Eastern part of Germany. It means that privatisation was strongly influenced by political attitudes, although financial aspects also gained importance in the 1970s.[2]

In Great Britain economic aims received a special emphasis. In a paper, first published in 1983, which had a considerable influence, Michael Beesley and Stephen Littlechild stressed that the main idea of privatisation is to improve industry performance by increasing the role of market forces. The authors hinted at the political reasons, too, mentioning that political freedom depends on private property and that government intervention should be minimised. Nevertheless, they did not consider privatisation to be desirable in itself. The interest of consumers was of decisive importance and in this connection privatisation of certain industries was ruled out as not beneficial to consumers.[3]

In France the process of privatisation started after the first oil shock, in the 1970s, in a form which was qualified as illegal and, therefore, the process continued by the Acts of 1986.[4] The main reason for the privatisation seems to have been economic.

A particularly important consequence of privatisation was the increased interpenetration of the public and private economy in all these countries.[5] Privatisation has not meant, however, the transfer of shares or the transformation of public enterprises. The great variety of privatisation techniques includes also, among others, contracting out of public services, deregulation, and the changes in the financing of publicly-funded bodies.[6] The interpenetration of private and public law elements has caused many subsequent problems as the process of privatisation involved ever greater public administration.

---

[1] J. Vickers, "The Politics of Industrial Privatisation in Western Europe: An Overview", *West European Politics* (1988) 4.

[2] G. Püttner, *Die öffentlichen Unternehmen* (Stuttgart, München 1985) 9-15.

[3] M. Beesley/ S. Littlechild, "Privatization: 'Principles, Problems, and Priorities'", in: M. Bishop/ J. Kay/ C. Mayer (eds.), *Privatization & Economic Performance* (Oxford, New York 1994) at pp. 15-16.

[4] L. Rapp, "Les lois de privatisation et la 'respiration' du secteur public", *Revue française de droit administratif* (1987) 154-157.

[5] Vickers/ Wright, *supra* n. 1, at pp. 27-28.

[6] T. C. Daintith, "Legal Forms and Techniques of Privatisation", in: *Legal Aspects of Privatisation*, (Strasbourg: Council of Europe 1993) 50-51.

Privatisation has had a different meaning and importance in countries with a planned economy in which a fundamental change of the political and economic system took place in the years starting from 1990. The situation in these countries was properly characterised by Jean Rivero at a conference held in 1988 in Aix-en-Provence who stated, summarising the reports on privatisation of different countries, that the group of socialist countries would be happy if privatisation were possible but it would mean revolution for them.[7] Privatisation has been really a fundamental transformation of the whole economy connected with the establishment of a new political system. After the changes problems associated with the former political system, problems in the structure of the economy, the inadequacy of the earlier growth strategy, the slow change in the artificial price system, the lack of a capital market and several other factors caused serious difficulties for several years.[8]

The process of transformation was particularly complicated because of the fact that no one was prepared for the transformation of the whole political and economic system, no theoretical basis existed, nobody knew the effects of the changes on public attitudes nor the political consequences of the measures to be taken. Among the other far-reaching consequences of privatisation in countries with a planned economy was the inevitable wide range of wealth transfers and it has been characterised, with good reason, as explosive because the result is clashing with social perceptions about what is fair.[9] The great changes which took place require new ways of thinking and the population has needed a long learning period to understand what has been happening in the economy and in political life.[10]

The process of privatisation in countries which had a system of planned economy is, consequently, different in many respects from that of those countries with a market economy. Beside the special features, there are, however, many similarities too. A general evaluation of the privatisation, that has not yet finished in most of the former socialist countries, is not the aim of the present paper. It is worth mentioning, nevertheless, that there have been considerable differences in the forms of privatisation in the countries concerned. In the following, reference will be made only to some recent problems of privatisation

---

[7] J. Rivero, "Rapport de synthèse", in: Ch. Debbasch (ed.) *Les privatisations en Europe*, Actes du colloque tenu à Aix en octobre 1988 (Paris 1989) 229.

[8] There are many publications on this topic, here only an early analysis is referred to: H. J. Blommestein/ M. Marrese/ S. Zecchini, "Centrally planned Economies in Transition: an Introductory Overview of Selected Issues and Strategies", in: H. Blommestein/ M. Marrese (eds.), *Transformation of Planned Economies* (Paris 1991) 12-14.

[9] Blommestein/ Marrese/ Zecchini, *supra* n. 8, at p. 13.

[10] Ch. J. Anderson/ K. M. O'Connor, "System Change, Learning and Public Opinion about the Economy", 30 *British Journal of Political Science* (2000) 151-153.

as discussed by the legal literature and a few examples will be mentioned from the special Hungarian experience.

Privatisation is at the centre of the political debates in every country. Sceptical opinion about privatisation is not an exception. According to this view it is difficult to assess the truth of many of the claims made for and against privatisation.[11] In countries with a planned economy the political question was, however, not simply more or less state involvement but system transformation. Western observers have paid attention from the very beginning to what extent the former ruling stratum could preserve positions[12] and how far political constraints have influenced the position of former managers and of trade unions in the process of privatisation.[13]

In Hungary, privatisation did not mean restitution of the property taken by the state to the former owners, i.e. there was no re-privatisation. The meaning was broader than "selling the state". It covered different ways of changing the property structure in which the state was the owner of the majority of the means of production and creating a property structure in conformity with a market economy. Although the two phenomena, the change of property structure and privatisation, cannot be identified, delimitation is not easy because of the unclear property situation during the previous system. Reference is made here only to three points:

- the regulation of property rights concerning land;
- the position and property rights of the so-called social organisations;
- the position of local administration.

Each of the three points would require separate analysis. For the present purpose we shall restrict their treatment to very brief and simplified statements.

In Hungary, agricultural land was in principle in the ownership of small holders but in practice the land was used by agricultural co-operatives and in the land registry it was not specified who owned what. A great part of immovable land, not qualified as agricultural land, became state property after 1949 and some of the immovable land was alienated by the state in the period between 1950 and 1989. Therefore, there were different categories of people who were

---

[11] Cento Veljanovski, *Selling the State* (London 1988) 17.

[12] G. Ajani/ B. Dallago/ B. Grancelli, "Introduction", in: B. Dallago/ G. Ajani/ B. Grancelli (eds.), *Privatization and Entrepreneurship in Post-Socialist Countries* (London 1992) 10.

[13] M. K. Young, "Privatization in Eatern Europe: Experience and Expectations", in: H. Smit/ V. Pechota (eds.), *Privatization in Eastern Europe: Legal, Economic and Social Aspects* (New York, Dordrecht 1993) 16-17.

owners of immovable land prior to 1949 and in only one category the immovable land was in an unchanged condition, in the ownership of the state. It was a hot political issue whether people belonging to this category can claim the land back. According to the decision of the Constitutional Court made in 1990 no regulation, ordering restitution of land in one category while denying re-privatisation in all other categories, could be considered to be in harmony with the constitutional principle of non-discrimination.[14] This was the starting point of regulating privatisation. Later on several other questions were also submitted to the Constitutional Court.

Prior to the changes local governments were part of the monolithic structure of the state. An important part of the changes was to ensure the independence of local governments and to bring about a property basis for that independence. The state transferred a considerable volume of property to local governments. It was a special part of the privatisation process. In order to state clearly the principle that local governments are independent the Constitution was amended in 1990 and several new rules formulated the rights (including property rights) of local governments. Under the new rules local governments are entitled to submit complaints to the Constitutional Court in case of violation of their rights. There have been many problems in connection with the transfer of state property to local governments (the Constitutional Court made three decisions on this issue already in 1991) and in connection with other questions of the independence of local governments.

Before the political changes the legal position of the so-called social organisations was not clearly regulated and this was particularly so as far as their property was concerned. They received financial subsidies from the state and property too without clearly stipulating what was in state ownership. Trade unions belonged to the category of social organisations. The trade unions, functioning as part of the monolithic structure of an association, fulfilled special tasks in managing the economy. In the process of the political transformation several new trade unions were organised independently of the former ones and, consequently, without any subsidy and without any property. After the elections of 1990 the question of different trade unions and their property situation was much debated and the Parliament passed an Act in 1991 prohibiting in part the alienation of the property of the trade unions' association until the whole issue was regulated by an Act to be worked out. The Association submitted a complaint against the Act to the Constitutional Court. Although the Court has not stated that the question concerned privatisation, the decision has referred to the unclear property situation and the involvement of state property (it stated

---

[14] 21/1990. (X. 4) AB határozat, ABH 1990, 73.

that the Act was not contrary to the Constitution).[15] A similar issue was decided by the Supreme Court: the association of the trade unions had made a contract transferring the ownership of 16 buildings a few days before the Parliament voted on the bill concerning prohibition of alienation. According to the Supreme Court decision the contract was not valid.[16]

Although the questions mentioned above do not belong strictly to privatisation they do show the circumstances under which privatisation has started in countries with a planned economy.

2. Public sector reform

In the 1980s and early 1990s privatisation was one of the favourite topics in legal literature. In the discussion the various ways and means of withdrawal of the state from the economy have been analysed. For some years it has been possible to observe a shift of emphasis. Privatisation is no longer new, public opinion has become accustomed to it. Nevertheless, the problems of privatisation have not been resolved. Instead, they appear under new headings. It is not so much the question of how to do it that is in the forefront but the consequences of doing it. There are several new or not so new aspects of the same old problem. Only some of them are mentioned.

Several authors state with some astonishment that not only is the state still present but the current variation of the topic of privatisation is discussed intensively. The new formulation is regulation. The state cannot be uninterested in the field it left. It has to regulate and control.[17] In addition, in some cases, the state has to provide for basic services.[18] The phenomenon is a complex one for it concerns several fundamental questions. One of these questions is, what the task of the state is in the changed relationship with the economy.[19] In reality, the concept of the state was already questioned in the former privatisation debate stressing the unsettled issue of state ownership.[20]

Another formulation of the question is the reform of the public sector. Under fiscal stress the state had to reconsider its service-providing commitments and

---

[15] 20/1992. (IV. 30.) AB határozat, ABH 1992, 135, at 141.

[16] Bírósági Határozatok 1993/10. 604.

[17] T. Prosser, "Regulation, Markets and Legitimacy", in: Jeffrey Jowell/ Dawn Oliver (eds.), *The Changing Constitution*, 4th ed. (Oxford, New York 2000) 229-230.

[18] J. A. Kämmerer, "Verfassungsstaat auf Diät?", *Juristen Zeitung* (1996) 1048, 1050.

[19] M. Ronellenfitsch, "Staat und Markt: Rechtliche Grenzen einer Privatisierung kommunaler Aufgaben", *Die öffentliche Verwaltung* (1999) 705.

[20] T. Prosser, "Constitutions and Political Economy: The Privatisation of Public Enterprises in France and Great Britain", 53 *Modern Law Review* (1990) 318-319.

to look for new forms such as contracting out and regulation with all the dangers connected with them.[21] It has been well-known for many years, however, that public ownership has been used to implement specific socio-economic policies as an alternative to governmental regulation. Thus in a mixed economy, where public authorities act both as a regulator of public interest and as a participant of economic life, this double role can endanger both competition and the free movement of goods.[22]

The above remark was made on the basis of a market economy. A mixed economy, privatising public services, can give rise, however, to other concerns, too. The British legal literature has reacted to the idea of the public sector reform by expressing serious doubts from the point of view of constitutional law. It has been stressed that if a public body places some of its functions beyond the reach of public law by identifying them as purely commercial ones, the danger is that the Rule of Law will not be fully implemented.[23] It has also been stated that the more explicit rules the constitution of a country has the greater the difficulty will be when the government intends to go ahead with a privatisation programme.[24] This statement seems to be reflected by the fact that since some years in the German legal literature, well-known for its strong constitutional law basis, the importance of constitutional law aspects has increased in the analysis of privatisation problems. Thus, the limits of privatisation deriving from constitutional law have been stressed,[25] the consequences of privatisation concerning the protection of fundamental rights, the observance of the principles of democratic legitimisation and *Rechtsstaat*,[26] and the question has been raised to what extent public bodies are free to choose civil (commercial) law forms for pursuing their activity.[27] Although the Hungarian constitutional law is not so developed as the German one, nevertheless, there

---

[21] C. Scott, "Services of General Interest in EC Law: Matching Values to Regulatory Technique in the Public and Privatised Sectors", 6 *European Law Journal* (2000) 310-312.

[22] A. Verhoeven, "Privatisation and EC Law: Is the European Commission 'neutral' with respect to public versus private ownership of companies?" 45 *International and Comparative Law Quarterly* (1996) 864-865.

[23] M. Freedland, "Government by Contract and Public Law", *Public Law* (1994) 101, 104.

[24] T. Daintith/ M. Sah, "Privatisation and the Economic Neutrality of the Constitution", *Public Law* (1993) 474.

[25] T. Mayen, "Privatisierung öffentlicher Aufgaben: Rechtliche Grenzen und rechtliche Möglichkeiten", *Die Öffentliche Verwaltung* (2001) 110, 112, 115.

[26] G. Teubner, "After Privatization? The Many Autonomies of Private Law", 57 *Current Legal Problems* (1998) 393.

[27] R. Schmidt, "Der Übergang öffentlicher Aufgaben in private Rechtsformen", *Zeitschrift für Unternehmens- und Gesellschaftsrecht* (1996) 349, 356; W. Spannowsky, "Der Einfluß öffentlich-rechtlicher Zielsetzungen auf das Statut privatrechtlicher Eigengesellschaften in öffentlicher Hand", *Zeitschrift für Unternehmens- und Gesellschaftsrecht* (1996) 404, 406-407.

are signs in cases before the Constitutional Court that a similar tendency may appear. From the beginning the privatisation process has been closely connected with constitutional law aspects and the connection has not ceased to exist. The principles stipulated in the Hungarian Constitution may cause uneasy problems because of the consequences of the special privatisation means applied during the transition from a planned economy to a market economy.

Appraisal Rights in Japanese Company Law – Can They Be Used as Modern Weapons for Minority Shareholders?

Masaru Hayakawa*

1. Preface

Our honoree, Professor MESTMÄCKER, in applying Albert O. Hirschmann's formularization of "exit" and "voice"[1] to company law, places "exit" as a compensation claim under such law (*Anspruch auf Abfindung*), and clearly points out the difference between the function of public and close companies.[2] Although Japanese company law does not expressly state as much, "exit" means the repayment of one's holdings. As such, in principle, it is impermissible from the standpoint of protecting company creditors. However, in certain circumstances, small shareholders opposing a majority decision may require the company, for their protection, to buy back its shares so they can leave that company (appraisal rights).

---

* Doshisha University, Kyoto

[1] Albert O. Hirschmann, *Exit, Voice, and Loyalty: Responses to Decline in Firms, Organizations, and States* (Cambridge, Mass: Harvard 1970).

[2] Mestmäcker, "Organisationen in spontanen Ordnungen", *Recht in der offenen Gesellschaft* (Baden-Baden: Nomos 1993) 81.

Talia Einhorn, ed., Spontaneous Order, Organization and the Law – Liber Amicorum Ernst-Joachim Mestmäcker © 2003 T.M.C.ASSER PRESS, *The Hague, The Netherlands*

Appraisal rights pose problems in three different areas. The first is the difficulty of protecting shareholders who oppose fundamental changes to the company, such as a merger. The second area concerns the company's ability to buy shares of less than one unit,[3] or fractional shares,[4] at any time,[5] as a technical means of facilitating its control of shares. Finally, as Professor MESTMÄCKER has pointed out, although in Japan appraisal rights have been considered as a way of resolving conflicts of interest among the shareholders of close companies, the discussion has only been a legal one.[6]

---

[3] Under the 1981 Company Law amendment, when establishing a new company, the minimum par value of shares and the minimum issue price of no-par-value shares is set at 50,000 yen. However, since the system was not imposed upon existing companies, the unit share system was established only temporarily. For example, in a company with 50 yen par-value shares, and with 1,000 shares forming one unit, it was planned to combine the shares for each unit in the future. Until then, the unit share system would serve as a measure. Under this system, one can exercise one's rights only with one unit of shares, placing the holder of 999 shares at a disadvantage. Therefore, a shareholder who only owns shares of less than one unit may ask the company to repurchase its shares. Recently, the number of companies reducing the unit of shares is growing, making it possible for people to invest more easily.

[4] In accordance with minority shareholder wishes, the 1990 Company Law revision gave fractional shareholders certain rights besides voting rights (a share which represents less than one share and a fraction corresponding to an integral multiple of 1 percent of one share is called a fractional share, and the fractional shareholder). The company makes a fractional share ledger corresponding to the register of shareholders. However, the company is not required to issue certificates for fractional shares nor is it required to record on the ledger share splits, consolidations or new share allotments to a third party. A company may state in its Articles of Incorporation, or comparable document, that it does not issue fractional share certificates. Therewith, a fractional shareholder may ask the company to repurchase its fractional shares against cash.

[5] For fractional shares, when the shareholder's declaration of intent to demand a stock repurchase has reached the company, the demand has the same legal implications as a sales contract. If the share is listed, the repurchase price coincides with the Stock Exchange's final share price on the day the repurchase request is made. For non-listed companies, the method used corresponds to that used for shares with transfer restrictions. If the repurchase price is not agreed upon within 20 days of the repurchase request, the courts will be asked to determine the price by calculating the company's net assets, based on the latest balance sheet, divided by the number of issued shares. Fractional share prices are determined in the same manner approximately.

[6] In 1986, the Bureau of Civil Affairs of the Ministry of Justice announced its "Tentative Plans for the Commercial Code and Limited Liability Company Law." The Bureau asked for opinions whether it should approve appraisal rights in cases where minority shareholders of non-listed companies are grossly discriminated against. Very few supported such an approval. However, according to detailed scholarly research of actual situations, an unconditional appraisal right is appropriate to resolve an internal dispute within a close company, and this is a reasonable assessment. Hamada, "A Shareholder's Unconditional Appraisal Right (parts 1, 2, and 3): A Proposal for Close Company Legislation", 982 *Commercial Law Review* (1983) 59; 983 *Commercial Law Review* (1983) 12; 984 *Commercial Law Review* (1983) 24. See also Mori, "The Maintenance of Power in a Closed Company and the Withdrawal of Invested Capital", 56 (11) *Horitsu Jihou* (1984) 26.

Indeed, appraisal rights, as a coherent legal system for protecting minority shareholders, are not very satisfactory. However, with the amendment of company law, their range of application has increased. This increase occurred not out of necessity, but rather as a means of emphasizing the legislators' concern with protecting minority shareholders.

Given the large number of legislative articles that provide for them, company law appraisal rights are not very systematic. Rather, it seems to be a patchwork system. Consequently, it is necessary to sort out many problems. A plan announced recently by the Ministry of Justice provides a good opportunity for that to occur. However, to sort out these problems, it is necessary to first examine appraisal rights under the present law.

2. DETAILS ON THE ENACTMENT OF APPRAISAL RIGHTS

2.1 The enactment of appraisal rights and its evaluation

Japanese company law dates back to the draft Commercial Code of Herman Roessler, a former Professor of Rostock University. Roessler's draft became the essence of the 1890 Commercial Code. The present Commercial Code, enacted in 1899, was also strongly influenced by German law. However, after World War II, the American system was introduced, resulting in the abandonment of the principle of the almighty stockholders' general meeting. Following the American system, the 1950 amendment of the Commercial Code saw the adoption of the Board of Directors' system. The revision of the shares system, which strengthened the directors' authority and provided for functional decision-making, allowed for more flexibility in raising capital.

At the same time, in the interest of creating a balance, the amended law gave minority shareholders the right to directly control the company's management. Examples include the right to demand the suspension of directors and the right to file a shareholder's derivative suit.[7] Additionally, following the American system, minority shareholder status was strengthened with the adoption of appraisal rights.

The appraisal rights system, adopted by various states in the US, allows a majority of the stockholders to decide extraordinary and unusual changes to a company's structure. Such changes include a merger or a change in shareholder objectives, and, as a general rule, do not require the approval of all shareholders.

---

[7] Kawamoto, "Die Praxis der Aktionärsklage im Japan", in: *Festschrift Grossfeld* (Heidelberg: Recht und Wirtschaft 1999) 525; Hayakawa, "Die Aktionärsklage im Japanischen Gesellschaftsrecht", in: *Festschrift Mesetmäcker* (Baden-Baden: Nomos 1996) 891.

However, the appraisal rights system allows dissenting shareholders to leave the company.[8]

In Japan, objections[9] to adopting this system[10] put forward the following arguments: it is against majority rule; by allowing a refund of investment it contradicts the principle of maintaining company capital; the system could be misused; withdrawal of invested capital should be done by transfer of shares; and, the trading price is hard to estimate.

For these reasons, the enactment of the 1950 amendment did not end the assertions that appraisal rights are unnecessary. Yet, the system's ability to reconcile conflicts of opinions and conflicts of interest among majority shareholders has recently drawn favorable comment. The appraisal system's ability to protect minority shareholders has also been emphasized.[11] As discussed below, following many other amendments of the Commercial Code, as well as the expansion of the scope of these rights, legislators are now relying on the system as a firm defensive wall used to protect minority shareholders.

2.2 Circumstances allowing appraisal rights

Although the concept of appraisal rights was imported into Japanese law from the United States, there is a difference between the two countries in the presence of, and in the ability, to exercise such rights. For example, unlike the situation in the US, when a company changes the objectives specified in its Articles of Incorporation, Japanese law does not grant appraisal rights.[12]

Originally, when the system was introduced in 1950, a shareholder could require a company to repurchase his shares in two cases: upon a decision to transfer all or a majority of the company's business operations (Commercial

---

[8] In Japan, the appraisal right is not the only way to get relief because in decisions regarding the changes to a company's basic structure, like merger, one can argue the decision's invalidity (Commercial Code Article 415). This is therefore a Japanese characteristic. Tatsuta, "Fairness in Corporate Mergers", 82 *Hogakuronso (Kyoto Law Review)* (1968) 262, at p. 278.

[9] Kanda, "Conflicts of Interest in Shareholder Voting", 98 *Hogaku Kyokai Zassi* (1982) 761, at p. 811.

[10] When the appraisal right was initially introduced, of equal importance was the protection of minority shareholders and the ability of companies and major shareholders to freely undertake measures such as merger. Osumi/ Omori, *Commentary on the Amended Corporate Law, Article by Article* (Tokyo: Yuhikaku 1951) 221.

[11] Hasegawa, *Annotation of Corporate Law*, Vol. 4, Commercial Code Article 245-2 (Tokyo: Yuhikaku 1968) 156; Shisido, *New Edition Annotation of Corporate Law*, Vol. 5, Commercial Code Article 245-2 (Tokyo: Yuhikaku 1986) 283 et seq.

[12] This has been criticized on the account that it upsets the balance because a change in a company's objectives is a matter of a special decision which has a strong connection with the shareholders' interests: Kitazawa, *Corporation Law*, 6th ed. (Tokyo: Seirin Shoin 2001) 332. There are other comments approving this from a legal perspective: Hasegawa, *supra* n. 11, at p. 156.

Code Articles 245-2 to 245-4; Limited Liability Company Law Article 41),[13] or upon the approval of a merger (Commercial Code Article 408-3; Limited Liability Company Law Article 63). Subsequently, the right to exercise appraisal rights was expanded to include additional circumstances: upon a decision to become a closed company by changing the company's Articles of Incorporation, or a comparable document, that restricts the transfer of shares;[14] upon a decision to change the company's organizational structure to that of a limited liability company;[15] upon a decision to approve a written contract for the trading,[16] or transfer,[17] of shares; upon a decision to approve a written plan to divide a company;[18] and, upon a decision to approve a written contract for the takeover or division of a company[19]. Therefore, today there are altogether eight circumstances in which minority shareholders can exercise their appraisal rights.

2.3 The procedure for exercising appraisal rights

The exercise of appraisal rights involves a three-step procedure. First, before the relevant meeting, a shareholder must submit a written objection to a proposed change. Second, the shareholder must object to the change at the general meeting itself. Finally, the shareholder must ask the company to repurchase its shares at a price which would have been deemed fair had the relevant decision not been made. Concerning the price, the parties first discuss the matter. If they can not come to a consensus, they may ask the court to determine it.

2.4 Appraisal rights in cases not involving shareholder decisions

Originally, appraisal rights were meant to be exercised upon a special majority decision made at a shareholders general meeting. However, pursuant to a series of recent amendments of the Commercial Code aimed at making reorganization easier, a structural change to a company no longer requires a general meeting decision because of the minor effect on shareholders' interests. For example,

---

[13] However, there are no appraisal rights if a dissolution decision is made at the same time as the decision to transfer business operations (Commercial Code Article 245-2).

[14] Commercial Code Article 349 (1966).

[15] Limited Liability Company Law Article 64-2 (1990).

[16] Commercial Code Article 355 (1999).

[17] Commercial Code Article 371 (1999).

[18] Commercial Code Article 374-3; Limited Liability Company Law Article 63-2 (2000).

[19] Commercial Code Article 374-31, Section 5; Limited Liability Company Law Article 63-9, Section 3 (2000).

since 1997, a simple merger does not require the approval of the shareholders of an existing large joint-stock company, because such a merger generates few new shares,[20] and has little effect on shareholders.[21] Although a decision by a shareholders general meeting is no more deemed necessary, dissenting shareholders have recently nevertheless been afforded appraisal rights in cases of simple share trades,[22] simple business takeovers,[23] and simple divisions of companies that succeed to businesses.[24]

---

[20] According to the 1997 amendments of the Commercial Code (Ministry of Justice [ed.] 1998) 85 et seq. this situation is metaphorically described as similar to a situation when a whale swallows a killifish: Maeda, *Introduction to Company Law*, 6th ed. (Tokyo: Yuhikaku 1999) 665. This is not allowed for limited liability companies. As for the merging and disappearing companies, an approval decision is necessary.

[21] According to Commercial Code Article 413-3, Section 1, when companies merge, the total number of new shares issued by the company devising the merger can not exceed five percent of the total number of issued shares. Regarding the merged company, the total amount of money paid to it by the surviving company can not exceed two percent of the surviving company's pre-merger net assets. In addition, a merged company is required to obtain shareholder approval. If one-sixth of the shareholders disapprove, a simple merger is not allowed.

[22] 1999 amendment. When the scale of a company, that has become a holding company merely by share exchange, is considerably larger than that of the company which has become its wholly-owned subsidiary, the effect on the interests of the holding company's stockholders is minimal. Therefore, the parent company may forego an approval decision: Commercial Code Article 358. Dissenting shareholders are entitled to appraisal rights under the same conditions and procedures of a simple merger. However, rejecting the assertion that the parent company shareholders need protection, there are some that question the necessity of the current law that provides dissenting parent company shareholders appraisal rights. Yet, the law is necessary to protect the profit of shareholders of the company that is now the subsidiary: Morimoto, *Lecture on Company Law* (Tokyo: Yushindo 2001) 255.

[23] 2000 amendment. When the *quid pro quo* of the whole takeover operation does not exceed an assets standard of 5 percent of the net assets based on the final balance sheet, an approval decision is not necessary: Commercial Code 245–5, Section 1. Shareholders opposing the action may exercise their appraisal rights under the same conditions as a simple merger: Commercial Code Article 245-5, Sections 3 and 4.

[24] Commercial Code Article 245- 5, Section 3; Article 358, Section 5; Article 374-23, Section 5; Article 413-3, Section 5. 2000 amendment. When the total number of shares issued by a company succeeding division and the amount of money that the company pays for a divided company or its shareholders is small, as in the case of simple mergers, the succeeding company is not required to have an approval decision: Commercial Code Article 374–23, Section 1). Shareholders opposing the division are entitled to exercise appraisal rights: Commercial Code Article 374–23, Section 5. Conversely, if the divided company receives a quota of shares issued by the succeeding company and the value of the taken-over property does not exceed the five percent assets standard, a divided company general meeting decision is not necessary. However, because the action does not directly influence the percentage of shares held by shareholders and also not permitted in cases involving the alienation of a part of an unimportant operation (Harda (ed.), *Legal System of Spin-offs and Split-outs* (Tokyo: Shojihomkenkyukai 2000) 98 et seq., or the value company takes over is relatively small: Kitazawa, *supra* n. 12, at p. 738, the divided company's shareholders have no appraisal rights: Commercial Code Article 374–22, Section 3.

A representative case of a simple merger may be exemplified as follows: an existing company notifies its shareholders, or announces publicly, that there will be a merger without a shareholder decision. Shareholders are informed of their rights to dissent. The dissenting shareholders may ask the company to repurchase their shares at a price deemed to be the fair market price had the merger not occurred.[25] This same procedure is followed for all proceedings that do not require a general meeting approval. This right to make a claim is different from the usual type because it is not linked with the general meeting of shareholders. Therefore, in these instances, appraisal rights may be characterized not only as a means of protecting minority shareholders, but also as a means of enabling mergers of companies desired by the majority to move ahead smoothly. In this sense, appraisal rights are part of a Japanese loosening of restrictions on company mergers.[26]

When appraisal rights were first legislated in company law, various legislative theories analyzing the American experience were asserted.[27] Regrettably, while preparing the recent Commercial Code amendments, lawmakers did not consider comparative legal research studies.

3. Regulation problems in the present law

3.1 Simplification of Appraisal Right Procedures

To exercise their appraisal rights, shareholders must give written notice of their opposition to a proposed change before the relevant general meeting. They must also oppose the decision at the general meeting itself.[28] For the latter, either the shareholders themselves, or their agents, are allowed to exercise the right to vote.[29] This complicated procedure exists because the company must confirm dissenting shareholders' intentions as well as the number of supporting

---

[25] Commercial Code Article 413-3, Sections 5 and 6.

[26] Regarding regulation of company law see Hayakawa, "Zum Gegenwärigen Stand des Konzernrechts in Japan", in: Mestmäcker/ Behrens (eds.), *Das Gesselschaftsrecht der Konzerne im internationalen Vergleich* (Baden-Baden: Nomos 1991) 391.

[27] For example, to speed up the procedure, the company is obliged to propose a purchase price: Hukami, "The System of Appraisal Rights in American Company Law", 64(5) *Hogakuronso* (*Kyoto Law Review*) (1958) 73; Waza, Valuing Shares under Appraisal Statutes in American Law, Law and Economics (Kanazawa University, No. 5 1958) 167 et seq.; Shimamoto, "Appraisal Statutes", 83 *Doshisha Law Review* (1964) 1, at pp. 15 et seq.

[28] Commercial Code Article 245-2; Article 349, Section 1; Article 408-3, Section 1.

[29] Commercial Code Article 239, Section 2.

shareholders. However, other means may be used to achieve the same objective. Shareholders of large companies[30] are already exceptionally allowed to exercise their right to vote by letter.[31] This exception has been considered the best possible method to convey shareholder intentions to the general meetings of companies that have many shareholders. This system should be extended to companies that are not large;[32] Even if participation in decision-making by letter were to be generally approved for the exercise of appraisal rights, the interests of shareholders would not be harmed. Furthermore, in the future shareholders of all companies might perhaps be allowed to use one written notice to both indicate their intent to oppose a decision and also exercise their right to vote, as is currently the case for shareholders having less than one unit and fractional shareholders when exercising their appraisal rights.[33] This would result in preserving the balance of the whole system of appraisal rights as a means of protecting minority shareholders.

3.2 Criteria for determining the Sale Price

When appraisal rights are exercised, the sale price of the shares is, in theory, dependent upon the autonomy of the adversary parties to determine the price. If the parties are unable to reach an agreement on the price, the court will decide "the fair price that these shares hold" in court proceedings for the determination of the price.[34] Although the criterion of "fair price" is not specified in the law, courts have held that they must determine the sale price having regard to all of the relevant circumstances without being bound by allegations or evidence presented by the parties.[35] However, since only a small number of cases actually end up in court, the methods used by the courts to reach their decisions are

---

[30] Stock companies with a capital amount of 500 million yen or more, or having a total liability of 20 billion yen or more, and 1,000 shareholders or more.

[31] Law for Special Exceptions to the Commercial Code Concerning Audits, etc. of Stock Companies (kabusikikaisha no kansa to ni kansuru shoho no tokureini ni kansuru horitsu) Article 21-3, Section 1.

[32] Kimita, "The Modern Significance of Appraisal Rights and the Protection of Minority Shareholders", 143 (2) *Hogakuronso* (*Kyoto Law Review*) (1989) 81, at pp. 89 et seq., claims that exercising the right to vote is needed because the protection of minority shareholders and prevention of abuse of appraisal rights can only be achieved by linking appraisal rights and a special shareholders' approval decision.

[33] These shareholders are able to demand share repurchase at any time. When the shareholder's declaration of intent to ask the company to buy back its shares has reached the company, it has the same legal implications as a sales contract.

[34] Commercial Code Article 245-2; Article 349, Section 1; Article 408-3, Section 1; Non-Contentious Procedure Law (hishojiken tetsuzuki ho) Article 126, Section 1 and Article 132-6.

[35] Supreme Court Decision, 1 March 1973, 27(2) *Law Reports of the Supreme Court* 161.

inconsistent. The most common criteria used are a comparison of stock price, dividend per share, and the profits and net assets of a company in the same type of industry.[36,37]

For listed companies, the existence of the capital market makes the assessment of stock price problematic in a different way. Since shareholders can collect invested capital by negotiating stocks on the market, the significance of granting appraisal rights may itself be called into question. However, since the price of shares is likely to be influenced by speculation, the raison d'être of such a right is maintained.[38] Consequently, the question is whether listed shares should be assessed on the basis of their market price. It is often asserted[39] that it is reasonable that the market price should serve as a criterion when making an assessment, and that it is inappropriate to make calculations of the real value of the shares.[40] The value of the company's assets is another legal criterion to be considered in making the price assessment.[41] This means that parties may rely on a court to determine the price. Courts set the price by considering the company's financial situation and all other relevant factors. When parties

---

[36] This is one of the methods of assessment provided in Fundamental Rulings of the National Tax Administration for assessment of an inheritance for imposition of inheritance tax (No. 179, 180). The Osaka District Court Sakai Branch Decision, 26 September 1986, 19 (9, 10) *Law Reports of the Inferior Court* 568; the Tokyo High Court Decision, 19 January 1972, 22 (1, 2) *Law Reports of the Inferior Court* 9; the Yokohama District Court Decision, 21 January 1969, 669 *Hanreijiho* 91; the Takamatsu High Court Decision, 31 March 1975, 787 *Hanreijiho* 109; the Tokyo District Court Decision, 30 August 1977, 533 *Kinyusyojihanrei* 22; and the Nagoya High Court Decision, 4 October 1979, 949 *Hanareijiho* 121. One problem of this assessment method is the difficulty in finding a sample company that would serve as the basis for comparison. See Egashira, *Assessment of Stocks, System of Judicial Practice*, Vol. 3: Company Action and Corporate Reorganization (Tokyo: Seirin Shoin 1986) 86 et seq.

[37] There are a few examples of cases using other ways to decide the sale price of transfer-restricted shares. For details, see Shishido, "Ways to Achieve Financial Fairness in Coping with Internal Dissension of the Closely-Held Corporation", 101(11) *Hogaku Kyokai Zasshi* (1984) 1758, at pp. 1760 et seq.

[38] The system of appraisal rights is not an elixir, as the Tatsuta essay pointed out. See *supra* n. 8, at pp. 290 et seq.

[39] Egashira, *supra* n. 36, at p. 88 et seq. In this case, the influence on the stock price caused by unusual speculation could be negated by calculating the average of the market prices of the concerned stocks during a certain period of time. The Tokyo District Court Decision, 10 February 1983, 1068 *Hanreijiho* 110.

[40] Some cases employ a comparative method to assess listed stocks. The Tokyo District Court Decision, 19 April 1971, 22 (3, 4) *Law Reports of the Inferior Court* 446; the Kobe District Court Decision, 18 June 1976, 27 (5-8) *Law Reports of the Inferior Court* 378.

[41] As an opinion emphasizing the appropriateness of a method setting a standard of net assets of a company, there is a case of transfer of transfer-restricted stock: Shisido, *supra* n.11, at pp. 1829 et seq.

forego court intervention, the price is based on the net assets per share, calculated on the basis of the most recent balance sheet.[42]

To summarize, the method of determining the sale price differs depending on matters such as whether the shares of the company are listed as well as on the basis chosen for making the assessment. The courts have not established a model method, nor have academics offered a predominant theory. However, "fair price" certainly encompasses the market price for listed stocks, and, in the case of non-listed stock, at least the net assets showing the actual value of the company, calculated in certain cases – such as those involving shares of less than one unit and fractional shares – in accordance with special provisions.[43]

---

[42] Supplementary Provisions of the 1981 Revision of the Commercial Code (kaisei shoho husoku) Article 19, Sections 4 and 5; Commercial Code Article 204-4, Section 2; Non-Contentious Procedure Law Article 132-7.

[43] I believe that the most appropriate method to decide the sale price of transfer-restricted stock is to consider the nature of the issue in cases for which appraisal rights are sought to protect minority shareholders. The Commercial Code originally permitted clauses prohibiting the transfer of shares in a company's Articles of Incorporation, but under the 1950 Amendment Law, restrictions on the transfer of shares were prohibited in principle. Due to capital liberalization, the 1966 amendment made it possible to write in the Articles a restriction on the transfer of shares that requires the approval of the Board of Directors (Commercial Code Article 204) to prevent foreign capital from taking over domestic companies. Changes in the Articles to restrict transfers have more conditions than those necessary for ordinary changes (Commercial Code Article 343). It is also possible to make such restriction changes by a vote of the majority of the total number of shareholders, or by the majority of more than two thirds of the total amount of issued shares (Commercial Code Article 348). Again, dissenting shareholders have appraisal rights (Commercial Code Article 349). In a closed company, shares transferred in this way by a shareholder may remain in the company and the price is decided as follows: first, shareholder A informs the company in writing that it would like to transfer its shares to a company-designated buyer, or to B, who can request the company's approval for such transfer (Commercial Code Article 204-3). If the company rejects B as a buyer, it must designate an alternate. In order to demonstrate its solvency, a company-designated buyer must deposit funds equivalent to the book value of the shares with a depository. The parties then discuss the price. If no agreement is reached, the sale is concluded at the deposit value (Commercial Code Article 204- 4, Section 3). If a court determines the price, the court considers the company's financial situation and all other relevant circumstances, to decide the price. If the company is unable to find a buyer within a designated period of time, the Board of Directors may nominate the company itself as the buyer. The purchase of shares is determined by a special decision of the general meeting, and funds equivalent to the book value of the shares to be transferred are deposited. A is then required to sell the shares back to the company (Commercial Code Article 204-3, Section 2). When, after failed negotiations, a court sets a price exceeding the limit of the company's financial resources and the numbers specified by law, the company can not buy shares of A (Commercial Code Article 204-3-2, Sections 5 and 7). A is then permitted to transfer his shares to B as per his initial request (Commercial Code Article 204-4, Subsections 6 and 7).

4. Interim Draft of the Ministry of Justice regarding amendments of the Commercial Code and appraisal rights

In preparation of submitting a Bill for amendment of Japanese company law, the company law section of the Legislative Council recently studied a major revision of company law.[44] The Council announced the results in an interim draft in April 2001,[45] referring to opinions regarding amendments.

Regarding appraisal rights, two amendments have been proposed. The first concerns the sale or purchase of the shares of subsidiaries. If a parent company sells all of the shares it holds in a subsidiary, or if it buys shares of its subsidiary held by another company, such transactions require the approval by a special decision of the shareholders of the parent company. Shareholders opposing such a decision would be granted appraisal rights (Draft Article 11). Under present law, when a company takes over all, or a substantial portion of another company, special shareholder approval must be obtained. The Council's proposal reasons that the subsidiary is part of the parent company's operations regarding the latter's economic condition. Considering the significant impact on the parent company shareholder profits, the scope of this proposed expansion of appraisal rights seems acceptable.

The second proposed amendment would allow shareholders to use electronic devices to make claims against the company. It would also allow voting rights to be exercised using electronic, digital or electromagnetic methods (Draft Article 25). Consequently, shareholders might also be allowed to use these same methods to exercise appraisal rights. If the technical problem of identity confirmation can be solved, the current disadvantages to small and medium-sized company shareholders stemming from the different requirements of exercising appraisal rights versus large company shareholders discussed above could be eliminated. However, imposing the use of these new technologies on small companies with few shareholders is questionable. Thus, the proposed amendment may need to stipulate that small companies are allowed to choose for themselves whether to implement the use of the new devices.

Apart from the accounting system, there is no detailed proposal concerning the regulation of company groups. This is somewhat strange in view of the

---

[44] It resulted from the necessity to respond to social economic changes including more competition among companies, the diffusion of computer networks, technological innovations or so-called IT revolution, the change from indirect to direct financing, and the increased demand for new company financing.

[45] Specifically, it examined this matter from four perspectives, i.e., how to secure effective corporate governance, how to respond to the advanced information society, how to improve enterprise fund-raising, and how to respond to the internationalization of corporate activities. Every area is under consideration in this overall reform.

actual existence of many, diffused company groups. Shareholder conceptions have changed greatly since the introduction of the consolidated accounting system in 2000. Shareholders now view themselves as members of a group of companies rather than members of just one. Moreover, when judging stock price, shareholders are more interested in the results of the group as a whole. These are explicit examples of a considerable change of attitude.

Applying these changes to appraisal rights, there is a need to respond to the emergence of this new breed of shareholders, namely, shareholders leaving individual companies yet preferring to remain within the same group of companies. Therefore, shareholders should be granted the right to move to another company within a group of affiliated companies, especially to become shareholders of the parent company. This could be considered a sort of stock-exchange system from the shareholders' point of view.[46] However, there is still a need to consider the scope for concrete changes. Appraisal rights in this instance would be worth considering as a protective measure for shareholders' profits relevant to this new era.

Regarding expanded appraisal rights, it is necessary to organize and amend the present regulations to distinguish between rules for closed and non-listed companies,[47] listed companies and corporate groups. It is also necessary to adopt regulations that would most appropriately protect minority shareholder profits in each type of company. This means considering amendments depending on company type. For closed and non-listed companies, appraisal rights should be maintained as they are, and shareholders could use such rights as a way of transferring shares the transfer of which is restricted. For listed companies, rights should be made easier to exercise and a system should be established to assess stock based on its capital value, while also continuing the present dual system with the means of collecting capital in the market[48]. Finally, for joint-stock companies, an amendment to establish appraisal rights allowing a shareholder to exchange presently held shares for shares of other companies within the same group should be enacted.

---

[46] Regarding the exchange of stock, see Hayakawa, "Erleichterung der Konzernierung durch Aktientausch und Aktienübertragung", 5 *ZjapanR* (1999) 5.

[47] According to a 1997 Ministry of Justice commercial registration survey, at that time there were 19,411 general partnerships, 78,697 limited partnerships, 1,613,886 limited liability companies and 1,225,923 joint-stock companies. Small sized closed companies comprise the majority. Only 36,798 companies held capital of more than a hundred million yen. Kawamoto/ Kishida/ Morita/ Kawaguchi, *Japanese Company Law*, 4th ed. (Tokyo: Shojihomukenkyukai 2001) 17 et seq. These statistics underscore the need for special close company regulation.

[48] The stock trading law is directly aimed at protecting investors in the stock market. Baum, "Der Markt für Unternehmen und die Regelung von öffentlichen Übernahmeangeboten im Japan, *Aktiengesellschaft* [1996] 399, correctly notes that Japanese securities law does not offer enough protection for minority shareholders, especially in takeover bids.

The announcement of the interim draft of the major amendment of company law has been described as providing a good opportunity for making appraisal rights practical while getting rid of dust and mold, as opposed to just letting them remain on display as if in a museum.[49] Hopefully, such changes will come to pass.

---

[49] There are no studies, documentary records or accurate statistics on the extent of the use of appraisal rights: Takenaka, "Claims for Purchase Upon Merger and Determining the Price", 705 *Juristo* (1979) 66; Kawamoto, *Modern Company Law*, 8th ed. (Tokyo: Shojihomukenkyukai 1999) 548, footnote 1. Although, compared to America, the system is rarely used in closed companies (Shishido, *supra* n. 11, at pp. 811 et seq.), it has been pointed out that the use of appraisal right is expected to propagate with the increase in joint enterprises: Kanda, *supra* n. 9, at pp. 811 et seq. Conversely, because appraisal rights serve as a safety valve for complaints, there is strong opinion emphasizing the need for the system to exist mainly on paper, as it is desirable that shareholders will not use it regardless of whether or not it is easy to use": Takeuchi, *Mergers and Spin-offs of Enterprises, Course for Modern Corporation Law* (Tokyo: Iwanami Shoten 1985) vol. 3, p. 432.

International Economic Relations in the 21st Century

John H. Jackson*

1. THE WORLD TRADE SYSTEM AFTER SEATTLE: FACING THE GLOBALIZATION BACKLASH

1.1 Globalization and markets

It surprises few people today to see comments about the profound and growing extent of international economic linkages and interdependence. The causes of these developments are numerous: incredible advances in efficiency of communication, extraordinary reductions in transport costs, growing prevalence of instant tele and cyber transactions, treaty and other norms causing reduction of governmental barriers to trade, an economic climate more favorable to principles of markets economics, cross border influences of competition which have

---

* University Professor of Law, Georgetown University Law Center (GULC), and Director, Institute of International Economic Law at GULC.

This article is based partly on a series of articles by this author, which may interest the reader, namely: John H. Jackson, "Global Economics and International Economic Law", 1 *Journal of International Economic Law* (1998) 1–24; "International Economic Law in Times that are Interesting", 3 *Journal of International Economic Law* (2000) 3–14; "The WTO 'Constitution' and Proposed Reforms: Seven 'Mantras' Revisited", 4 *Journal of International Economic Law* (March 2001) 67-78; and *The Jurisprudence of the GATT and the WTO: Insights on Treaty Law and Economic Relations* (New York: Cambridge University Press 2000).

Talia Einhorn, ed., Spontaneous Order, Organization and the Law – Liber Amicorum Ernst-Joachim Mestmäcker © 2003 T.M.C.ASSER PRESS, *The Hague, The Netherlands*

driven increases in production and service efficiencies, and last but not least, the blessing of relative peace in the world.

Manifestations of this "globalization" abound: stock market trends that flow quickly around the world; international impacts of monetary and fiscal decisions of national governments; effects of fraud within certain banking or other financial enterprises; worries about health and safety of products moving across borders such as foodstuffs, pharmaceuticals, machinery, appliances; effects of governmental mismanagement and sometimes corruption; worries about the power of non-governmental and private enterprises and their capacity in some cases to operate on the global economy while largely ignoring particular national governmental regulatory protections; and flows of "cultural" influences involving various media often moving swiftly with new communication techniques to transmit music or drama across borders (with substantial economic implications and other effects, even to cause a new taste in Paris for Halloween pumpkins!). A roadmap of the various links and cause-effects of a multitude of economic actions becomes an impenetrable maze of pathways, commonly without clear guidebooks to assist their understanding.

Whether economic policies based on market principles[1] are the best approach for maximizing human satisfaction is, of course, controversial. Various alternatives have been much debated, and many of those largely rejected, but substantial arguments are made in favor of some sort of mixture of policies, perhaps to temper the perceived negative effects of "too pure market approaches". Whatever mixture may appeal to certain societies, however, it seems reasonably clear that markets can be very beneficial,[2] and even when not beneficial, market forces demand respect and can cause great difficulties when not respected.[3]

Yet even when stressing the benefits of market economics, important thinkers note the importance of human institutions which guide and shape markets.[4] Human institutions embrace many structures and take many forms,

---

[1] See Richard Lipsey/ Paul Courant/ Douglas Purvis/ Peter Steiner, *Microeconomics,* 10th Edition (Harper Collins College Publishers 1993); Dixit & Nalebuff, *Thinking Strategically* (Norton Publ. Co. 1991); Corden, Max, *Trade Policy and Economic Welfare* (Oxford: Clarendon Press 1974); Peter B. Kenen, *The International Economy* (Cambridge University Press 1994); Paul Krugman, *International Economics: Theory and Policy* (Harper Collins College 2000).

[2] For an overview of the economic principles, which support policies of liberal international trade rules, see Alan Sykes, "Comparative Advantage and the Normative Economics of International Trade Policy", 1 *Journal of International Economic Law* (1998) 49.

[3] See, e.g., James Flanigan, "Turmoil is Free Market Watershed", *Los Angeles Times* (29 October 1997, Home Edition) p. 1.

[4] See, e.g., two Nobel Prize winning economists who stress this proposition: Ronald Coase, *The Firm, the Market and the Law* (University of Chicago Press 1988) ch. 5 (reprint of 1960 article); and Douglas C. North, *Institutions, Institutional Change and Economic Performance* (Cambridge Univ. Press 1990). See also C.A.E. Goodhart, "Economics and the Law: Too Much One-

but it is very clear that law and legal norms play the most important part of the institutions, which are essential to make markets work. The notion that "rule of law" (ambiguous as that phrase is) or a rule-based or rule-oriented system of human institutions is essential to a beneficial operation of markets is a constantly recurring theme in many writings.

1.2 Institutions for international economic relations and markets

With respect to international economics, the world is fortunate to have institutions such as the Bretton Woods system (including the General Agreement on Tariffs and Trade, or GATT) established through the vision of statesmen, scholars and diplomats at the end of World War II. At least some of the credit for relative peace and economic growth of the past half century goes to those institutions and their rules.[5] And now, of course, we have a major new organization in our landscape of economic institutions, namely the World Trade Organization (WTO), established January 1, 1995, that has an extraordinarily elaborate set of rules.

Despite the general praise for these institutions, there exists much cynicism about the importance or effectiveness of international law rules, "why do they matter?" The public can read news of violations of such rules by major and minor nations. In some cases such violations, even when admitted to be such (often there is bitter and inconclusive argument on this question), are rationalized or declared "just" by national leaders. Thus, cynicism about international rules cannot be surprising.

However, more careful examination of the role and effectiveness of international rules is necessary. First, it should be observed that not all domestic rules are always obeyed either. Yet there are many international rules that are remarkably well observed. Why this is so has been the subject of much speculation, which will not be repeated here.[6] Notions of reciprocity and a desire to depend on other nations' observance of rules lead many nations to observe rules even when they don't want to.

At least in the context of economic behavior, however, and particularly when that behavior is set in circumstances of decentralized decision-making, as in a market economy, rules can have important operational functions. They may provide the only predictability or stability to a potential investment or trade-

---

Way Traffic?", 60 *Modern Law Review* (1997) 1.

[5] Jackson, *World Trade and the Law of GATT* (Bobbs-Merrill Company 1969) chapter 2.

[6] See Henkin, *How Nations Behave*, 2nd ed. (Council on Foreign Relations 1979); Roger Fisher, *Improving Compliance With International Law* (Charlottesville: University Press of Virginia 1981) 12-16; Chayes, *The New Sovereignty: Compliance with International Regulatory Agreements* (Harvard University Press 1995).

development situation. Without such predictability or stability, trade or investment flows might be even more risky and therefore more inhibited than otherwise. If "liberal trade" goals contribute to world welfare, then it follows that rules that assist such goals should also contribute to world welfare. To put it another way, policies that reduce some risks lower the "risk premium" required by entrepreneurs to enter into international transactions. This should result in a general increase in the efficiency of various economic activities, contributing to greater welfare for everyone.

1.3 Regulating cross border economic activity

New or recurring problems in the regulation of cross border economic activity are suggested almost daily by the news media. The recent case of an airline merger involving Boeing and McDonnell Douglas is an example of potential problems for nation-states attempting to regulate international commercial activity.[7] Tainted foodstuff imports,[8] the international "breakthrough" in early 1997 regarding an international telecommunications agreement,[9] and the banking crisis in Asia and various response attempts (often involving IMF activity) are other examples.

In the financial services area of today, we also have to worry much more about problems of fiduciary relationships, prudential protections of consumers, and fraud. Other subjects include environmental regulation, continuing work on agricultural trade, product standards, consumer protection in its broader ramifications, and securities regulation as we move into a 24-hour market. If you begin to push the frontier of the subject, you have to think also of such things as labor regulations, labor standards, and even human rights.

Indeed, almost every conceivable area of economic activity, which, for one reason or another, attracted governmental concern and often regulation, is now impacted by actual or potential international regulation of one kind or another. Thus we need to step back and ask what are the common elements of these many specific topics and often ad hoc government responses? The fundamental question appears to be that of "regulation of economic behavior which crosses national borders". How should policy makers (and scholars) approach this broad question? Are there some general principles for government regulatory

---

[7] See, e.g., Teresa Wyszomierski & Christopher Lingle, "Lessons of the Boeing Merger", *The Journal of Commerce* (29 July 1997) at p. 8.

[8] See, e.g., Stephanie Nall, "Meat Dispute Threatens to Spoil U.S.-Europe Trade", *The Journal of Commerce* (27 March 1997) at p. 1; Stephanie Nall, "EU, U.S. Sling Charges, Threats at One Another", *The Journal of Commerce* (3 April 1997) at p. 1.

[9] See, e.g., John Zarocostas, "U.S. Urged to Back Telecom Accord", *The Journal of Commerce* (14 February 1997) at p. 1a.

activity, which could be applied in most or all situations involving cross border economic behavior? Can we develop some sort of general framework for policy analysis of this type? Here is a preliminary and tentative ("work in progress") attempt to do that.[10] These and many more questions can appropriately engage scholarly and policy makers' attention for years to come.

Look first at typical economic analysis of regulation.[11] Generally speaking, market oriented economists talk about avoiding governmental interference, except when there is something called "market failure".

As to market failure, the most familiar and the most commonly reiterated in the economics literature are the problems of monopoly (competition policy); the problems of asymmetry of information (for instance the consumer versus the expert sellers); as well as the problems of government distortions (those can get very troublesome because there are many different valid policy reasons why governments step in that do not have to do with the functioning of the market, and yet cause distortions in the market). There is also the public goods problem – where the market cannot adequately give incentive for the creation of things that the public needs, because there is the opportunity for the whole public to use it, or capture it, i.e., to "free ride". This is a subject, of course, that is very close to intellectual property. And there is a question that is related to some of the others just mentioned – the question of distributive justice, or other alternative policies of governments.

One of the interesting features of this fairly traditional economic analysis is that it is almost always developed in the context of a single domestic economy. We must now ask, "What difference does it make that we are in the internationally-linked world that we are in?" Look first at monopoly, or competition policy. In some cases, you are really talking about a world economy, not a national economy. That may change entirely your first judgment as to whether government intervention is necessary. For example, a national monopoly may not actually represent a market failure if national borders are thrown open so that the product might be forced to compete in the world market. But, you can also see the opposite conclusion possible. It may be that things that do not seem to represent market failure domestically, when you look at or hypothesize a closed economy. However, when you move to the international system, because of formal or informal linkages of various kinds, you may indeed find that there

---

[10] These thoughts are drawn partly from the author's following publications which may also interest the reader: Jackson, Hyman Soloway Lecture: *The Uruguay Round, World Trade Organization, and the Problem of Regulating International Economic Behavior* (Ottawa: Centre for Trade Policy and Law, May 1994) published in 1995; Jackson, "Reflections on Constitutional Changes to the Global Trading System", 72 *Chicago Kent Law Review* (1996) 511.

[11] See, e.g., Richard Lipsey/ Paul Courant/ Douglas Purvis/ Peter Steiner, *Microeconomics*, *supra* n. 1, especially Part 4.

is market failure. So, the international dimension creates the potential for different judgments on questions of market failure, monopoly or competition policy.

Asymmetry of information is another case ripe for difficulties enhanced by the international market. First of all, we have language differences worldwide, which makes it much harder for people to understand information. We have deep cultural differences where a "yes" means "no", a "no" means "maybe", and vice-versa. There are a whole variety of factors: distance, differences in legal systems, the ability to enforce contracts in different ways, and so on. So, the asymmetries of information can give rise to a lot of different conclusions, based on international activities.

Government distortions, of course, raise many questions. Are we beginning to face *international* government distortions? Are we beginning to face the regulations, for instance, of GATT, such as its textile system, as an illustration of how the international regulatory system begins to create distortions?

Public goods provide yet another set of market failure possibilities. There are a lot of public goods in the worldwide *international* landscape. One example is peace and security- peacekeeping in the United Nations, for instance. Another is human rights. There are certain values broader than just economic market-oriented values. Again, the international landscape would lead us to a conclusion that the market is not able to cope the way that we think that it ought to.

Distributive justice suggests a variety of policies within the scope of a domestic market—progressive taxation, welfare, safety nets, a social market economy, etc. But, internationally, of course, we have this problem also – the developing countries argue for certain preferences. They argue for an international financial safety net, almost the equivalent of international bankruptcy.

The next question is what should be the government response to market failure? In the economic literature, there are generally several kinds of responses that have been suggested –ways in which governments can intervene. The government can tax. The government can subsidize. The government can regulate, and create penalties for deviant behavior of various kinds. The government can try to alter various market incentives, such as by creating a system of permits, for instance to allow certain environmental degradation under certain systems.

However, some of the governmental responses suggested in the event of national market failure cannot easily be used in a globalized situation. How is a government going to tax foreigners? Suppose a national government tries to regulate, but a foreign government sees an opportunity to assist its own business participants by lax regulations, a so-called "race to the bottom" idea, or "regulatory competition". Thus many of the tools for government response may not work in a globalized situation the way they might work domestically. That forces us to consider the problems of regulatory competition, "race to the bottom", and downward harmonization, things that environmentalists have warned about during the last few years. When one begins to analyze these situations, sometimes with the aid of game theory (particularly the so-called "prisoner's dilemma"),[12] one is pushed towards *international* cooperation as a necessary ingredient for handling these issues.

However, there are arguments for and against such internationalization. Governments may or may not be acting in the best interests of their society because of the distortions on governmental policy that are described by public choice theories. For example, a government leader wants to get re-elected this fall and therefore won't vote for a trade treaty. There is also a reverse side. An international institution can provide an additional buffer for national policy officials to make arguments in favor of the goals of an international institution. They can say that their nation is constrained by international law and must obey these obligations.

2. The WTO and its emerging constitutional problems

2.1 The evolving World Trade Organization in its formative years

The new WTO is now just over six-years old, but it clearly is having a profound impact on these issues of cross-border economic activity or international economic relations. As one observer wrote in the *New York Times*, noting the huge protests planned for the Seattle WTO Ministerial, "The trade group has become such a target of ire in part because it has proved one of the most powerful world bodies of any kind."[13] And UN Secretary General Kofi Annan said recently "globalization should not be made a scapegoat for domestic policy failures . . . the WTO must not be distracted from its own vital task: extending the benefits of free trade fully to the developing world."[14]

The 1994 Uruguay Round treaty that created the WTO has enormous implications for almost every topic of nation-state economic regulation. Already it is being invoked in a variety of different economic situations, including some relating to recent financial crises. The development of treaty norms did not stop with the Uruguay Round either. After 1994, negotiators continued to pursue

---

[12] Dixit & Nalebuff, *supra* n. 1.

[13] Joseph Kahn, "Global Trade Forum Reflects a Burst of Conflict and Hope", *New York Times* (28 November 1999) pp. 1, 14. He added: "Unlike the trade and tariffs group, its predecessor, this trade group has the power to decide disputes on its own and impose penalties on countries that do not abide by its conclusions. To avoid pressure from lobby groups and possible adverse effects on international financial markets, three-judge panels decide cases in closed chambers without having to reveal much about the process. Most of the appointee judges are trade lawyers".

[14] Kofi Annan, *New York Times* (29 November 1999) p. A28.

agreements in various other subjects, notably financial services and telecommunications. Negotiators for both of these subjects were basically trying to catch up with the fast moving developments of globalizing markets. These agreements would truly astonish sovereigns of several decades ago, as they penetrate deep into national regulation and government. The launching of a new round of negotiation could take the WTO system further in these directions.

Probably the most significant characteristic and evolution of the WTO is the nature of its dispute settlement system. Building on the GATT and its remarkable dispute settlement procedures shaped by over 40 years of practice and experimentation, the WTO has corrected some of the GATT defects and created a stronger, more rule-oriented dispute settlement process, including automatic adoption of reports that have binding international law force, an appellate process that has increased the rigor and careful reasoning of first level panels, and appellate reports that are grappling with very sophisticated systemic "governing questions" of the international trade system. These tough questions include reconciling interests competing with international trade policies, such as national "sovereignty" and "subsidiarity", environmental considerations, and risk levels appropriate for human health impacts of food. Profoundly important and elaborately reasoned decisions such as those in the Shrimp Turtle[15] and the Beef Hormones[16] cases are clearly landmark tribunal opinions for international law generally.

With treaty clauses as profound as those mentioned above, and with dispute settlement cases facing deep philosophical questions of national versus international governance, come some important constitutional problems. Because it was negotiated with over 120 national participants and diplomatic needs, it is not surprising that the Uruguay Round treaty has many gaps and ambiguities. To reach closure in such circumstances often dictates papering over differences. A key question facing the dispute settlement system is therefore whether it is appropriate or feasible to pass to it the responsibility of filling these gaps and ambiguities. Many of these cases would dictate that the panels and appellate body undertake tasks that would appear to be law *making* rather than law

---

[15] *US – Import Prohibition of Certain Shrimp and Shrimp Products*, WT/DS58/AB/R, adopted on 6 November 1998. See Arthur E. Appleton, "Shrimp Turtle: Untangling the Nets", 2 *Journal of International Economic Law* (1999) 477.

[16] *EC – Measures Affecting Meat and Meat Products (Hormones)*, WT/DS26&48/AB/R, adopted 13 February 1998.

See Reinhard Quick/ Andreas Bluethner, "Has the Appellate Body erred? An appraisal and criticism of the ruling in the WTO Hormones case", 2 *Journal of International Economic Law* (1999) 603, and Donna Roberts, "Preliminary assessment of the effects of the WTO Agreement on Sanitary and Phytosanitary trade regulations", 1 *Journal of International Economic Law* (1998) 377.

applying. Law making is arguably more appropriate for a legislature that does not exist within the international framework, or in negotiations that substitute for legislation. Yet the WTO rules regarding decision making and negotiation were purposely designed by the Uruguay round negotiators to preserve so-called "sovereignty" for the nation-states, and thus impose a number of constraints on the exercise of power. These restraints could result in stalemate or impasse. In such cases, the temptation will be stronger to overburden the dispute settlement process, despite treaty clauses also aimed at constraining the authority of that process. The GATT/WTO history thus stimulates many generalizations. To mention only a few:

- Treaties are often an awkward, albeit necessary, method of designing institutions needed in today's interdependent world, but they do not solve certain problems. The human institutions established, like those in other contexts (including that of the U.S. constitution), have a way of evolving, and indeed surprising, the participants (including the creators). Probably no nation that accepted the Uruguay round really knew quite what it was getting into.
- Such institutions need on-going attention to help them evolve in appropriate directions because they certainly will evolve, whether intentionally or not.
- History shows a strong tendency, at least in economic matters, for international institutions to develop in the direction of rule orientation.
- These processes must be understood in the context not only of international law and practice, but also in the context of the very great influence of national constitutions and diverse legal systems. The nation-state is still very important. There is continuing tension between the role of the nation-state and the need for international institutions to facilitate cooperative mechanisms to enhance the efficient and just operation of markets, especially as these markets become more globalized.

In the light of these fundamental changes for economic diplomacy, two recent WTO events stand out, namely, the Seattle WTO Ministerial and the US–China agreement, which produces the greater probability of China's membership of the WTO in the near future.

The 1999 Seattle meeting attracted troubling attention and diplomatic divisions almost as soon as it was scheduled in mid-1998. The causes of the failure are numerous and many fingers are pointed to various problems, inside and outside the conference halls. Seattle became a lightening rod for protest, but in addition the major participating governments found it virtually impossible to achieve a consensus on the agenda. Deep divisions existed between various industrial countries, as well as between industrial and developing countries. Furthermore, the United States, approaching a major election (in November 2000), found it quite difficult to exercise much leadership. Other major participants had similar problems. Thus, the failure of the Seattle Ministerial meeting in December 1999 was not too surprising. The real issue is now the impact of the failure. Does it pose a risk of serious damage to the WTO as an institution and to the efforts and trends to cope with the forces of globalization? Or is it a temporary set back, not more serious than, say, the Uruguay round ministerial failures in 1988 and 1990, which were followed in 1993 and 1994 by a stunningly successful result to the round? Arguments can be made on both sides (and in the middle) of these possibilities. The next Ministerial scheduled for November 2001 in Qatar, will be very significant.

China's membership in the WTO will also be a major event for the WTO. Few people doubt that Chinese membership will have a deep and serious impact on the world trading system and the WTO. Such a serious impact is likely inevitable, even without formal Chinese WTO membership. Worries are expressed about the suitability of the Chinese economic structure for the disciplines and rules of the WTO.[17] However, even those with worries seem to feel that Chinese membership is better than the alternative. Indeed, perceptive journalists have commented on the significance of the potential impact of the WTO and its rules structure on the further evolution of the Chinese economic structure.[18]

2.2 Implications

The failure of the 1999 Seattle ministerial meeting and the potential impact of a future Chinese WTO membership have added considerably to the problems and challenges facing the WTO, as well as to the opportunities of that organization. These events also show us that even the world of the recent decades of the 1980s and '90s is no longer the landscape that we have to deal with today. As the countries of the world become increasingly interdependent, nation-state governments cannot regulate effectively on many subjects. As a result, they cannot meet the expectations of their constituents and cannot deliver upon promises made to their constituents. This imposes a considerable burden on governments, and makes governing much more difficult. Within this context, there is a worry that there will be a "race to the bottom" and that there will be a tendency for governments to redress their inability by using barriers of one type or another. For example, it leads to what some economists analyze as the

[17] James V. Feinerman, "Free Trade, To a Point", *New York Times* (27 November 1999) p. A31; Robert Herzstein, "Is China Ready for the WTO's Rigors?" *Wall Street Journal* (16 November 1999) p. A30.

[18] David E. Sanger, "At the Last Hour, Down to the Last Trick, and It Worked", *New York Times* (17 November 1999) p. A14; John Pomfret, "China's Bold Leap Into World Markets", *The Washington Post* (16 November 1999) p. 1; Thomas Friedman, *New York Times* (1 December 1999) p. A31.

prisoners' dilemma: when one country raises barriers, another is likely to follow, and soon all countries will be hurt.

Cooperative mechanisms at the international level may be the solution. These mechanisms should be based on rule orientation, as opposed to power orientation. These rules should be well formulated and effective. In other words, they should cause certain kinds of behavior and inhibit other kinds of behavior.

Two factors are of particular importance for the internal constitution of the WTO, and there are similar dimensions for external relations of the WTO. The two dimensions are: (1) the dispute settlement process and (2) the rest of the decision-making or negotiating process (all non-dispute settlement processes). To some extent, we could think of these dimensions as analogous to political structures at the national level, namely, the relationship of the judiciary to the legislature. One of the questions is: Do we have an effectively working legislature? Do we have an effectively working decision-making or rule-making process? These issues are of considerable importance. Currently, we have a very effective judicial process, certainly more effective than before. It has received a lot of credit, although it is not without some problems. But the effectiveness of the institutions is enhanced by the predictability and stability that the dispute settlement system adds to the implementation of the rules.

However, if the decision-making and rule-making processes fail to produce results, there is a tendency to throw their issues at the dispute settlement process. Therefore, there could be a tendency to ask the dispute settlement process to take on issues that it ought not to. As we saw, there could be temptations to put in the hands of the dispute settlement process, issues that are really rule *making* instead of rule *applying*.

There are real concerns about the current decision-making structure. This structure developed in the Uruguay Round negotiations, when negotiations focused on a World Trade Organization, particularly in the fall of 1993, when major players worked hard to alter some of the previous drafts. While alterations were appropriate in many ways, one of the things that the negotiators did was to constrain and put checks and balances on the decision-making process. They did this by requiring decision by consensus and by super-majorities and through certain other kinds of procedures. Today we realize that those constraints can lead to a lack of effectiveness of the decision-making process. This is one of the issues and one of the dilemmas that we have before us and that requires more examination.

This discussion, of course, also raises the issue of sovereignty. We are seeing that the rule-oriented measures that emerged from the Uruguay Round and earlier rounds of multilateral trade negotiations deeply affect national regulation internally, not merely at the borders. As a result, some people in the United States have argued that we should reverse course and take the WTO back to the time when it was only responsible for border measures, thereby limiting its ability to affect national regulation internally. This is folly because such a time never existed. It was always recognized that there were measures in the GATT that would have effects behind the border. In particular, Article III, paragraph 4, of the GATT, which deals with internal regulations and national treatment, has always had enormous implications for sovereignty and sovereign decisions relating to internal regulations.

2.3 The constitutional worries about the WTO: the seven "mantras" of WTO governance

To illustrate the constitutional concerns about the WTO, I will introduce here a series of what I call "mantras." These are phrases that are used commonly, particularly in Geneva and among those who are well experienced as well as some of those who are less experienced. Quite often, these phrases are used in a context in which they do not easily suggest that the content of the phrase should be examined in depth. In other words, the phrases are used to *avoid* thinking certain issues through. Some of the ideas expressed here can be attributed to ambassadors, governments, or academics. I have not tried to identify authorship for each piece of this puzzle, because usually there have been a number of parallel suggestions. I will provide a brief overview of seven of these mantras.

(1) The first mantra is that "**consensus is great or even sacred**." It is said that we must maintain the consensus system of decision-making. Often, this is in the context of thinking that there are only two approaches to decision making, that this is a binary choice—one choice is consensus, and the other is voting—and you have to choose between them. However, we do not have to choose between those two. There are a lot of things in between, and there are some pitfalls about the consensus rule that at least should make us think more about *where* in between we might focus attention.

(2) Another mantra is that the **WTO is an organization that is "government to government**." This implies that non-governmental entities have no role here. We should seriously think this through.

(3) The third mantra relates to the **preservation of national or nation-state sovereignty**. This mantra is used not only in Geneva, but also in Washington and other capitals. This "mantra" overlooks a good many things. Again, it is not a binary question; it is not a question of all or nothing. The word "sovereignty" has overtones that are totally out of date, but nevertheless the concept of sovereignty probably has some policy merit that we should consider. The policy question actually involved in the sovereignty question is: How do you want to

allocate power?[19] What decisions do you want made in Geneva, Washington, California, Berkeley, or a neighborhood in Berkeley? By viewing it as a decision about how to *allocate power,* we can disaggregate the question of sovereignty and make people think about how to correctly designate that allocation. Some of the reasons for going to a higher level of decision making are to solve such questions as the prisoner's dilemma or the race to the bottom.

(4) Another mantra often used is that **the organization is "member driven**." Member-driven means that the members want to keep the WTO Secretariat out of their hair. They do not want to give the Secretariat, the officials, or the Director-General any power whatsoever. A totally member driven organization is, in many cases, counterproductive, and certainly inefficient. Furthermore, if this mantra is used to question the independence of the dispute settlement organs, it undermines the integrity of the adjudicative process of the system.

There are three additional points, which I will call mantras just to put them in sequence, although they are more targeted to current negotiating atmospheres and ideas of structure. Yet, like the mantras mentioned above, these may not have been fully understood or examined.

(5) One further mantra is the notion of "**single undertaking**," a single package idea. I have great concerns and doubts about the single undertaking concept, although I can see its advantages. (Indeed, I can discern the advantages of all these mantras. I do not mean to suggest that they are totally useless.) But I can also perceive certain circumstances where it might be wise to experiment with an approach that would not be part of a single package. There might be different subjects that would require a different time line or a different composition of participants.

(6) Similarly, another mantra is **"MFN"** or the idea of most-favored-nation treatment. MFN has enormous strength and advantages in the system, but we should not view it as sacrosanct in its purity, because it has major problems, such as the free-rider problem and the tendency towards the lowest common denominator.

(7) Finally, there has been talk about the need for so-called **"deliverables"**. At the outset of discussions regarding a new trade negotiating round, diplomats

---

[19] See John H. Jackson, "The Great 1994 Sovereignty Debate: United States Acceptance and Implementation of the Uruguay Round Results", in: John H. Jackson, *The Jurisprudence of GATT and the WTO: Insights on Treaty Law and Economic Relations* (Cambridge University Press 2001) 367.

have worried about the length of time a round often takes (ten years or more) and have spoken of the need to conclude some parts of the round early and have those implemented so that the benefits are "delivered" early. Indeed, deliverables have advantages, as do these other items. On the other hand, deliverables tend to push policymakers towards sacrificing longer-term institutional strengths for short-term political advantages.

My suggestion is that each of these mantras could benefit from examination and should not be off limits from more careful scrutiny.

2.4 **External relations in the WTO constitution**

The Role of Non-Governmental Organizations (NGOs)

When referring to the failure in Seattle, many people talked about the "inside problem" and the "outside problem". The "inside problem" is what was really going on in the negotiations and the various half a dozen or more factors that prevented success there. The "outside problem" includes the demonstrations, the tensions involved with that, and the organization of NGO and public participation. You can look at these problems under both dispute settlement and decision-making dimensions. There are really two parts under each of those, and it may be helpful to view it as a two-by-two matrix. One is the subject of "transparency" and the other is the subject of "participation." Please note that I separate these terms rather dramatically because, quite often, the word transparency is used in an ambiguous way to cover both subjects. Transparency, as I (and others) see it, really means information for the public. But it can also mean internal flow of information. Ways of making information available to the public include available documentation, open hearings, and open meetings (open, at least, to the press). Participation, on the other hand, is somewhat more of a problem and is a more delicate issue. Participation by civil society or non-governmental entities means that they have an opportunity to be heard and present their views.

The basic question, and the one most vital here, is the role of NGOs. There are arguments both for and against NGO participation. We should thus recognize both the advantages and disadvantages of NGO participation. The governments are the authorized legitimate representatives in the WTO structure. The NGOs sometimes forget that, as we see in some of their arguments and in how they go about their business. In some cases, an NGO may have no legitimate role and no true constituency. Sometimes it is also said that some NGOs are part of the so-called "uncivil" society. They can be abusive and destructive and can cause various problems, including safety problems. Generally NGOs, even the good ones, can create resource problems. For example, it will involve some resources to open hearings and provide additional documentation, space, and time.

On the other hand, there are advantages to NGO participation. First, they can be quite useful. Sometimes they have resources for study and analysis that governments lack. They can bring to the table information that can be very helpful in the proceedings. They can also transmit information to concerned and important constituencies in the various countries. They can come to an understanding and then explain the issues to a broader constituency that has not had the time or the information to try to grasp them. In addition, they have real power, as demonstrated by the Multilateral Agreement on Investment (MAI) exercise and the impact of the Internet, and as, to some extent, demonstrated in Seattle.

So what are the solutions? It is surprising how far behind the WTO is, compared to most of the international organizations in Geneva and other cities, with respect to how it handles NGOs. Other organizations have very elaborate methodologies of accreditation of NGOs based on a variety of criteria, which vary from organization to organization. For example, the United Nations has been accrediting NGOs for forty or fifty years.[20] The International Labor Organization (ILO) also has fairly elaborate measures, as does the World Intellectual Property Organization (WIPO). WIPO integrates key NGOs that have expertise in some of the technical aspects, such as its "domain name" exercise. UNCTAD also has similar measures. Why not the WTO? At a minimum, there should be a study, which could be done by a committee reporting to the General Council chairman or a committee under the supervision of the Director-General.

3. Perspectives and Conclusions

This article examined the world trading system in its historical context and in light of recent developments. But it is useful to further consider how to move forward. By providing leadership, the trade superpowers – the United States, the European Union, and Japan – can play a major role. There are other groups of countries that could get together and try to thrash out ideas and discuss the pros and cons of some of these measures, and then see if there are some in-between measures that can maximize the advantages and minimize the disadvantages. Such measures could then be introduced for limited periods of time.

Already suggested by the European Community and the Director-General and others, is an idea of forming a group of parliamentarians to meet at the

[20] *United Nations Non-Governmental Liaison Service, The NGLS Handbook of UN Agencies, Programmes and Funds Working for Economic and Social Development*, 2nd ed. (1997).

WTO on a regular basis to exchange information, ideas, and attitudes. Other ideas that have been set forth include the formation of a steering group[21] and an NGO consultative group. There may be a parallel here in the European Community, which has an economic and social consultation committee to work with it on various subjects. Suggestions for increasing transparency include public sessions and increased access to reports and other documents. Short of amending the agreements, there are many steps that can be taken to strengthen the institution and its agreements. It is worthwhile to focus our efforts on these steps. Clearly, this brief article only touches the surface; so let us hope much further analysis and discussion on these and other WTO "constitutional issues" will occur in the near future.

[21] *See* Jeffrey J. Schott & Jayashree Watal, *Decision-making in the WTO* (Institute of International Economics Policy Brief No. 00-2, March 2000) <http://www.iie.com/NEWSLETR/news00-2.htm> (suggesting that "the WTO needs to establish a small, informal steering committee (20 or so in number) that can be delegated responsibility for developing consensus on trade issues among the member countries").

Regulatory Reform of European Telecommunications: Past Experience and Forward-Looking Perspectives

Günter Knieps*

1. From legal monopolies towards global entry deregulation

1.1 Early liberalisation initiatives on the EU level

A cornerstone for the take-off of the development towards competition in European telecommunications markets was the Commission of the European Communities' British Telecom decision in 1982 and its confirmation by the European Court of Justice in 1985. According to this decision, British Telecom should no longer be permitted to forbid the high-speed forwarding of telex messages between foreign countries by competitive agencies in Great Britain. The procedural setting of this case was most unusual because the Italian government and not British Telecom appealed against the Commission's decision. Moreover, the British government intervened, taking sides not with the Italian government, but with the Commission. The important message of the British

* Prof. Dr. Günter Knieps, Albert-Ludwigs-Universität, Freiburg.

Talia Einhorn, ed., Spontaneous Order, Organization and the Law – Liber Amicorum Ernst-Joachim Mestmäcker © 2003 T.M.C.ASSER PRESS, *The Hague, The Netherlands*

Telecom case has been that the Commission of the European Communities is able to apply the Treaty of Rome's competition rules in the European telecommunications administration based on the public law of the different member countries.[1]

Since then, the Commission has initiated a wide-ranging discussion on the possibilities of completing the common internal market for telecommunications in the European Community. Obviously, this effort was strongly related to the Commission's endeavour to complete the accomplishment of the common market by 1992. The "Green Paper on the Development of the Common Market for Telecommunications Services and Equipment" – issued by the Commission in June 1987[2] – proposed that the provision of terminal equipment as well as enhanced telecommunications services should be liberalized within and between the member countries.[3] Basic services (mainly voice telephony) as well as the largest parts of physical networks could still be monopolized by the national telecommunications administrations;[4] however, arguments concerning the public interest in such a monopoly should periodically be investigated.

1.2 The period of partial entry deregulation

Under the strong influence of the Commission's Green Paper of June 1987 partial entry deregulation was introduced in European countries. In Germany a new law was passed on 1 July 1989,[5] restructuring the traditional *Deutsche Bundespost* into three independent enterprises: Postal Services, Telecommunications Services and Postbank, which were finally privatized.[6] There have been controversial debates on the costs and benefits of global entry deregulation. The obstacles to comprehensive entry deregulation did not, however, exclude the possibility of partial entry deregulation. Partial deregulation means free entry into terminal equipment supply and into value added network services (VANS) on the basis of the physical network provided by the network monopolist. Partial entry deregulation was politically feasible for two reasons. First, partial entry deregulation was a useful measure to avoid large business users placing

---

[1] For a detailed explanation of this case see Schulte-Braucks, "Das 'British Telecom'-Urteil: Eckstein für ein europäisches Fernmelderecht?", 3 *Wirtschaft und Wettbewerb* (1986) 202-215.

[2] *COM* (87) 290 fin.

[3] In addition, the Commission pleaded for a liberalization of the procurement policy of the national telecommunications administrations as well as for an introduction of European-wide telecommunications standards.

[4] Only the margin of physical networks (mobile radio and low speed satellite communications) were opened for competition.

[5] Gesetz zur Neustrukturierung des Post- und Fernmeldewesens und der Deutschen Bundespost (Poststrukturgesetz) of 8 June 1989, *Bundesgesetzblatt* Teil I (14 June 1989) 1026-1051.

[6] For the telecommunications sector, the Deutsche Telekom AG was founded.

their telecommunications centers abroad and maintaining only enlarged terminals within the country. This danger was imminent because European countries are relatively small and therefore in a potentially competitive situation vis-à-vis each other. Second, the network monopolist had an interest in allowing partial entry deregulation and promoting VANS competition on its network. For as a public monopoly, the network monopolist was relatively inefficient and unable to exploit the whole innovation potential within the telecommunications market. By means of the exclusive provision of network facilities, however, it could always skim part of the innovation rents generated by private entrepreneurs.

1.3 **Abolishment of all legal entry barriers**

The "Green Paper on the Liberalization of Telecommunications Infrastructure and Cable Television Networks" issued by the Commission in October 1994[7] again strongly influenced the process of liberalization of European telecommunications. The "Full Competition Directive"[8] of 13 March 1996 demanded the member countries to allow free entry into all sectors of telecommunications. The new telecommunications laws allowing overall market entry were enacted by the national parliaments during 1996, coming fully into effect on 1 January 1998. In order to make free entry into all sectors of telecommunications politically acceptable it was necessary to split the silent coalition between the telecommunications administration and small users. An important solution was the implementation of the concept of a universal service fund into the new telecommunications law.[9] The purpose of the universal service fund is to keep the traditional subsidy of the small users stable and only change the way it is financed from internal to external subsidization. In order to make sure that the small users would not oppose deregulation it seemed to be important to guarantee the price-

---

[7] *COM* (94) 440 fin.

[8] Commission Directive 96/19/EC of 13 March 1996 amending Directive 90/388/EEC with regard to the implementation of full competition in the telecommunications markets, *OJ* [1996] L 74/13.

[9] See for example section 2 (§§ 17-22) of the new German telecommunications law TKG (of 25 July 1996) as well as the Telekommunikations-Universaldienstleistungsverordnung (of 30 January 1997).

level of the traditionally internally subsidized services as upper boundary ("social contract" pricing).[10]

Under a universal service fund every supplier of a subsidized service has the right to obtain an external subsidy, financed out of this fund.[11] The amount of subsidy depends on the difference between the incremental costs to provide the socially desired services and the "social-contract" prices. The competition for subsidies would also reveal the actual burden of the universal services and the minimum costs of traditionally internally subsidized services. It can not be expected that the traditional carrier will necessarily be the most cost-effective supplier, if new firms with cost-saving technologies (e.g. mobile telephone and microwave systems) enter the market.[12] Therefore, the bidding for the subsidized markets may strongly reduce the volume of required subsidies. In particular, an increase of the universal service fund to finance the traditionally internally subsidized services can be excluded as long as the scope of universal services is not extended.

One possibility of financing the required subsidies through the universal service fund would be the public budget. Nowadays, an increase of the public budget may create strong political resistance. Therefore, a more realistic approach was the concept of an entry tax, which all suppliers of lucrative telecommunications activities would have to pay. This entry tax should be designed in such a way that entrants and incumbents would have to make the same contribution to finance the required subsidies. The entry tax would have to be raised in analogy to the value added tax – depending on the net revenue – in order to avoid any tax advantage for the incumbent when it considers providing value added services on its own basic networks.[13]

---

[10] The literature on price-cap regulation, in contrast, has developed the concept of rate stability in order to restrain monopoly power (as a substitute for rate of return regulation); e.g. Brennan, "Regulation by 'Capping' Prices", US Department of Justice, *Economic Analysis Group D.P.* (1988), EAG 88, 11 September. In this context "social contract" transition methods have been outlined, for example, by Haring/ Kwerel, "Competition Policy in the Post-Equal Access Market", *Office of Plans and Policy of the Federal Communications Commission, O.P.P. Working Paper 22* (February 1987).

[11] We are aware that, from an allocative viewpoint, cost-oriented tariffs would be superior. However, the purpose was to make the efficiency aim of free entry into telecommunications politically acceptable. Therefore redistribution considerations had to be taken into account. Cf. Blankart/ Knieps, "What Can We Learn From Comparative Institutional Analysis? The Case of Telecommunications", 42/4 *Kyklos* (1989) 579-598.

[12] Kahn, "The Future of Local Telephone Service: Technology and Public Policy", *Wharton, Fishman-Davidson Center, D.P. No. 22* (1987).

[13] Blankart/ Knieps, *supra* n. 11, 592-594.

2. Market power regulation within the EU context

2.1 The concept of ONP in partially entry-deregulated markets

The establishment of the internal market for liberalized services within Europe required a harmonizing of conditions for access to and use of public telecommunications networks and services. The concept of open network provision (ONP) was introduced in the Commission's 1987 Green Paper on Telecommunications Services and given substance in the "Framework Directive"[14] 90/387/EEC of 28 June 1990. Subsequent specific Directives and Recommendations applied the principles of open network provision to leased lines, voice telephony, packet switched data services and integrated services digital networks (ISDN).[15]

The purpose of the ONP policy during the period of partial entry deregulation was to stimulate entry into the VANS market and to ensure "fair" competition between VANS suppliers and the VANS operations of the existing telecommunications organizations. Article 3 of the "Framework Directive" 90/387/EEC therefore laid down several basic principles ONP conditions must comply with. These principles are as follows:

- conditions must be based on objective criteria;
- conditions must be transparent, and published in an appropriate manner;
- conditions must guarantee equality of access, and must be non-discriminatory, in accordance with Community law.

Furthermore, it was explicitly stated that ONP conditions must not restrict access to public telecommunications networks or public telecommunications services except for reasons based on essential requirements (e.g. security of network operations, maintenance of network integrity).

Focussing on the preconditions for competition on the VANS market, only a minimally harmonized offering of those public telecommunications networks and public telecommunications services identified as being in the European interest was required.

---

[14] Council Directive 90/387/EEC of 28 June 1990 on the establishment of the internal market for telecommunications services through the implementation of open network provision, *OJ* [1990] L 192/1.

[15] For an illustrative survey of these developments the reader is referred to European Commission: ONP COMMITTEE Subject: Revision of the ONP Framework Directive ONPCOM 95-31, Brussels (17 July 1995).

The EU's ONP policy may also have been pursued as an instrument to avoid structural separation between the VANS activities of the existing telecommunications organisations and their traditional network activities.[16] Since the established carrier was (correctly) considered to be a monopolist on a large part of the market, global regulation of market power was still considered to be necessary, but left to the national regulatory authorities.

2.2 The concept of ONP in globally entry-deregulated markets

The "Full Competition Directive" 96/19/EC of 13 March 1996 amended the "Framework Directive" 90/387/EEC by abolishing all legal entry barriers, thus enabling free entry into the markets for telecommunications services as well as the set-up and provision of telecommunications infrastructure networks. Since the telecommunications infrastructure in Europe is developing towards a set of interconnected networks, owned and operated by many different organizations, the importance of interconnection is strongly increasing. Interconnection takes place among different providers of long distance networks, among providers of mobile or satellite networks and public cable-based long distance networks, and also between long-distance telecommunications service providers to local networks etc. This changing role of interconnection also led to a revision of ONP principles. The basic philosophy behind the EU ONP policy seems to be that the infrastructure should be open to all users in the EU, open to any service provider and open to any provider of elements of the overall infrastructure. The "Full Competition Directive" (sections 4a-4d) extended ONP principles to the new fully entry-deregulated environment, focussing on interconnection and public switched networks. In addition to the well-known criteria of non-discriminatory, reasonable and transparent conditions, the criterion of cost-orientation was explicitly introduced. Priority was given to commercial negotiations between the interconnecting parties involved.

During the period of legal entry barriers, sector-specific regulation of market power was unchallenged. Network industries like telecommunications were exempted from general competition law (so-called *wettbewerbliche Ausnahmebereiche*). Sector-specific regulatory instruments (e.g. price controls, tariff approvals) were applied *ex ante*. After abolishing all legal entry barriers, the question arose whether and to what extent sector-specific *ex ante* regulation would still be necessary.

---

[16] Similar ONP policies can also be observed in other network industries, e.g. railroads and airlines (e.g. Knieps, "Competition, coordination and cooperation – A disaggregated approach to transport regulation", 3/3 *Utilities Policy* (1993) 201-207).

2.3 Sector-specific market power regulation versus general competition law

The "Interconnection Directive"[17] 97/33 EC, which was adopted in June 1997 and implemented into the Member States' national laws by 31 December 1997, went further than the "Full Competition Directive" by introducing a two-tiered approach to ONP regulation. Providers of public telecommunications networks or public telecommunications services which are classified as possessing significant market power are subjected to more restrictive ONP regulation. This entails the general obligation to provide network access (section 4 (2)), the burden of proof that interconnection charges are cost-based and the possibility of *ex ante* regulation of interconnection charges (section 7 (2)), as well as principles for cost accounting systems (section 7 (5)).

According to the "Interconnection Directive", an organization with a market share of over 25% in a given telecommunications market is considered to possess significant market power (section 4 (3)). Nevertheless, the major responsibility for ONP regulation has still been left in the hands of the national regulatory authorities. National regulatory agencies have the authority to determine whether an organization has significant market power. According to section 4 (3) they are free to decide whether an organization with more or less than 25% is to be classified as possessing market power in the sense of the "Interconnection Directive". Moreover, principles for interconnection charges and cost accounting systems (section 7), including supervising whether tariffs are cost-based etc., are considered to be the responsibility of the national regulatory authorities. Thus, the "Interconnection Directive" laid down the general principles of future ONP regulation but left the responsibility for the concrete regulation of interconnection to the regulatory authorities of the individual Member States.

Meanwhile, the EU Commission tended more towards a differentiated regulatory approach. The "Access Notice" of the European Commission[18] extended the role of competition policy, pointing out the importance of the concept of "essential facilities", indispensable for reaching customers (section 68). Thus the European Commission's recommendation on leased line markets has been based on a differentiated analysis of the question of market power. According to

---

[17] Directive 97/33/EC of the European Parliament and of the Council of 30 June 1997 on interconnection in telecommunications with regard to ensuring universal service and interoperability through application of the principles of open network provision (ONP), *OJ* [1997] L 199/32.

[18] European Commission, Notice on the application of the competition rules to access agreements in the telecommunications sector (Framework, Relevant Markets and Principles (98/C265/02), *OJ* [1998] C 265/2-28).

this assessment by the Commission the remaining market power is clearly located in the area of the local leased lines, whereas long-distance telephony is considered to be a market where workable competition exists.[19]

2.4 The 1999 EU Review

The basic goal of the 1999 Review of the European Commission[20] was to consider to what extent phasing out of sector-specific market power regulation should take place. The key objectives stated at the beginning of the reviewing process were the maximization of the application of the general European competition law, the minimization of sector-specific regulation, a rigorous phasing-out of unnecessary regulation and the introduction of "sunset clauses" (ONP COM 98-42, p. 3).

On 12 July 2000 the European Commission presented its "1999 Review Package", with five proposals for Directives of the European Parliament and the Council and one proposal for a Regulation: an ONP Framework Directive,[21] an Access and Interconnection Directive,[22] a Licensing Directive,[23] a Universal Service Directive,[24] a Personal Data/Protection of Privacy Directive[25], and a Proposal for the Regulation of Unbundled Access to the Local Loop. In the

---

[19] "Major commercial investments in long-distance optical fibre infrastructure are underway in Europe, and it is expected that several thousand kilometres of optical fibre will become operational by the early part of 2000, linking all major European cities. This massive investment in alternative infrastructure is expected to create for the first time significant competition for the incumbent operators' leased line offers, in particular on their long-distance and cross-border leased line markets. However, new entrants may not be able to provide complete end-to-end leased lines to meet all their customers' needs, and will often have to rely on the incumbent to provide a short-distance leased circuit to link the customers premises to the new entrant's network (a "leased line part circuit"). This is particularly the case for new entrants wishing to serve Small and Medium Enterprises (SMEs).", Commission of the European Communities, Commission Recommendation on leased lines interconnection pricing in a liberalised telecommunications market, Brussels, C (1999) 3863, 24.11.1999, at 5.

[20] Cf. European Commission, Directorate General XIII ONP COMMITTEE, Subject: The 1999 Review of the Telecommunications Regulatory Framework, ONP COM 98-42, Brussels, 11 September 1998.

[21] Proposal for a Directive on a common regulatory framework for electronic communications networks and services (*COM* (2000) 393).

[22] Proposal for a Directive on access to, and interconnection of, electronic communications networks and associated facilities (*COM* (2000) 384).

[23] Proposal for a Directive on the authorisation of electronic communications networks and services (*COM* (2000) 386).

[24] Proposal for a Directive on universal service and users' rights relating to electronic communications networks and services (*COM* (2000) 392).

[25] Proposal for a Directive on the processing of personal data and the protection of privacy in the electronic communications sector (*COM* (2000) 385).

meantime the latter proposal has been passed by the European Parliament and the Council and was enacted in January 2001.[26]

The legal instrument of regulation has not been used before in European telecommunications policy. In contrast to a directive (*Richtlinie*), a regulation (*Verordnung*) is the most powerful legislative tool made available by the EC Treaty. It is binding in its entirety and directly applicable in all Member States. This means that regulations automatically become part of each Member State's legal system without the need for any intervention by national governments or national legislators. Unlike directives, which require national implementation measures,[27] regulations become law in all Member States as soon as they are enacted. The incumbent operator with significant market power is obliged to provide full unbundled access as well as shared access to the copper local loop under transparent, fair, and non-discriminatory conditions. The implementation of price regulation is left to the national regulatory authorities. As long as the level of competition in local access markets is insufficient to prevent excessive pricing, national regulatory authorities are required to ensure that the principle of cost orientation is applied.

Both the draft for the ONP Framework Directive and that for the Access and Interconnection Directive leave the planned extent of the future sector-specific market power regulation in long-distance networks in the dark. Compared to the Interconnection Directive, Article 13 of the draft for the ONP Framework Directive provides a new interpretation of the criterion of "significant market power", moving in the direction of establishing the criterion of dominance on a given market as a prerequisite for sector-specific market power regulation. But this is only an apparent step forward. Article 14 gives the commission discretionary power to identify a variety of markets for which the introduction of sector-specific regulatory measures should at least be considered. The draft for the Access and Interconnection Directive (Article 12) already indicates that sector-specific regulation may be extended to competitive markets (e.g. mobile telephony) as well as newly developing innovative markets (e.g. the Internet). This would be a definite step backward from the Access Notice of August 1998, which extended the role of competition policy, pointing out the importance of ensuring non-discriminatory access to essential facilities.

---

[26] Regulation on unbundled access to the local loop (European Parliament and Council 2000/0185 (COD), 5 December 2000).

[27] This does not rule out the fact that directives may have direct effect in Member States, provided that the provisions of the directive are sufficiently precise and unconditional.

3. Phasing out sector-specific regulation in competitive telecommunications

3.1 The proper identification of sector-specific market power

Criteria like relative market share, financial strength, access to input and service markets etc. can only serve as a starting point in order to evaluate the existence of market power; but the development of an *ex ante* regulatory criterion creates a need for a more clear-cut definition of market power. This is even more important, because "criteria for conjecturing a dominant position" (*Vermutungskriterien*) on the basis of market shares can lead to wrong criteria for government intervention in the telecommunications sector.

It is important to identify the regulatory basis by means of Stigler's concept of entry barriers, focussing on the long-run cost-asymmetries between incumbent and potential entrants:

> "A barrier to entry may be defined as a cost of producing (at some or every rate of output) which must be borne by a firm which seeks to enter an industry but is not borne by firms already in the industry".[28]

The sector-specific characteristics of network structures (economies of bundling) are not a sufficient reason to conclude that market power must exist. It is necessary to differentiate between those areas in which active and potential competition can work and other areas, so-called monopolistic bottleneck areas, where a natural monopoly situation (due to economies of bundling) in combination with sunk costs exists. It can be demonstrated that the regulation of network-specific market power is only justified in monopolistic bottleneck areas. In all other cases, the existence of active and potential competition will lead to efficient market results. The pressure of potential competition can be sufficient to discipline the behavior of the active supplier, even if he is the owner of a natural monopoly. Such networks are called "contestable".[29]

An essential condition for the functioning of potential competition in order to discipline a firm already providing network services is that the incumbent firm does not have asymmetric cost advantages in comparison with potential entrants. In contrast, if sunk costs are relevant, consumers, who would

---

[28] Stigler, "Barriers to Entry, Economies of Scale, and Firm Size", in: Stigler (ed.), *The Organization of Industry* (Irwin, Homewood, Ill. 1968) 67-70, at p. 67.

[29] Cf. Baumol/ Panzar/ Willig, *Contestable Markets and the Theory of Industry Structure* (Harcourt Brace Jovanovich, San Diego 1982).

intrinsically be willing to switch immediately to less costly firms, cannot do this.[30] Sunk costs are no longer decision-relevant for the incumbent monopoly, whereas the potential entrant is confronted with the decision whether or not to build network infrastructure and thus spend the irreversible costs. The incumbent firm therefore has lower decision-relevant costs than potential entrants. This creates scope for strategic behavior of the incumbent firm, so that monopoly profits (or inefficient production) will not necessarily result in market entry.

Market entry therefore cannot be expected easily, if sunk costs are sufficiently high. Therefore we can conclude that sector-specific *ex ante* regulatory intervention in order to discipline market power can only be justified in non-contestable networks (monopolistic bottleneck areas), i.e. where economies of bundling in combination with irreversible costs are relevant. The basic concept of the disaggregated identification of network-specific market power can be illustrated by the following table:

Table 1

submarket	with sunk costs	without sunk costs
Natural monopoly (bundling advantages)	(1) monopolistic bottleneck	(2) potential competition (contestable network)
no natural monopoly (bundling advantages exhausted)	(3) competition among active providers	(4) competition among active providers

An interesting question is the relation between "pure economic" analysis and real life networks (and the services that are provided via those networks). What about the reality of "contestable networks"? It seems obvious that, as soon as competition works, the behavior of markets for network services becomes more complex than is assumed in the "simple" model of the theory of contestable markets. Examples may be strategies of product differentiation, price differentiation, creation of goodwill etc. However, even strategic behavior on competitive markets for network services should not lead to the opposite conclusion to re-regulate these markets. In contrast, the very point of the disaggregated approach is the development of the *preconditions* for competition on the markets for network services. The only purpose of the theory of contestable

---

30 Cf. Knieps/ Vogelsang, "The Sustainability Concept under Alternative Behavioral Assumptions", 13/1 *Bell Journal of Economics* (1982) 234-241, at p. 239.

markets is therefore the localization of stable network specific market power, which systematically hampers the development of competition on the vertically related markets for network services. Whereas strategic behavior and informational problems do not lead to stable market power on the markets for network services, monopolistic bottlenecks – due to sunk costs – do create stable market power even if all market participants are well informed. The development of a set of rules for dealing with transactions across the boundary between contestable networks and monopolistic bottlenecks is therefore important in order to guarantee the preconditions for competition on the markets for network services.

3.2 End-to-end regulation versus disaggregated regulation

Regulatory instruments can be differentiated according to whether they are limited to the bottleneck areas (disaggregated regulation) or applied globally (end-to-end), including the competitive segment.[31] Since the application of regulatory rules is not cost-less and may also be abused strategically to disturb market forces, the advantage of the disaggregated regulatory approach is the strict limitation of the regulatory basis to bottleneck services. Its disadvantage, however, is that incentives may be created to discriminate against firms in vertically related competitive segments.[32] This should be kept in mind when designing *adequate* rules for disaggregated bottleneck regulation.

It is well known from the positive theory of regulation that regulators have strong incentives to overregulate, mix regulatory instruments in an unsuitable way, favour the application of detailed regulation and call for a heavy-handed supervision of firms.[33] This is the very reason why an *a priori* "framing" decision to limit the regulatory basis to some extent is of particular importance.

This leads to the disaggregated regulatory approach which not only identifies network-specific market power properly as monopolistic bottlenecks but also designs a combination of regulatory instruments limited to the bottleneck.[34] Price-cap regulation limited to monopolistic bottleneck services must be

---

[31] E.g. Laffont/Tirole, *Competition in Telecommunications* (Cambridge, Massachusetts, London, England: MIT Press 2000) ch. 4.

[32] E.g. Mandy,"Killing the Goose That May Have Laid the Golden Egg: Only the Data Know Whether Sabotage Pays", 17/2 *Journal of Regulatory Economics* (2000) 157-172.

[33] E.g. Stigler, "The Theory of Economic Regulation", 2 *Bell Journal of Economics* (1971) 3-21; Knieps, "Costing and Pricing of Interconnection Services in a Liberalized European Telecommunications Market", in: American Institute for Contemporary German Studies (ed.), *Telecommunications Reform in Germany: Lessons and Priorities* (Washington D.C. 1998) 51-73.

[34] E.g. Knieps, "Phasing out Sector-specific Regulation in Competitive Telecommunications", 50/3 *Kyklos* (1997) 325-339, at p. 331.

combined with additional regulatory instruments (e.g. accounting separation) and technical regulation (e.g. number portability, preselection) in order to deal with the problem of non-discriminatory access. Although the bundle of these instruments cannot be perfect, it moves regulatory attention into the right direction.

The aim of future regulatory policy should not be the global regulation of markets. Instead, only a disaggregated regulation of non-contestable networks is justified. The aim is then to localize the market power in monopolistic bottleneck areas and discipline this market power by regulatory intervention. Asymmetry of market power due to monopolistic bottleneck facilities, however, does not in itself require asymmetric regulation. Instead, the symmetry principle requires that all firms have access to local telecommunications networks on terms identical to those of the incumbent (nondiscriminatory access). The symmetry principle demands that only bottleneck facilities are regulated, irrespective of whether the owner is the incumbent or a newcomer, for example a cable television provider who upgrades his traditional local cable network.[35]

3.3 The remaining regulatory problem in the local loop

Since the comprehensive opening of the networks, massive investments in alternative long distance infrastructures have been undertaken. In the area of long distance infrastructure there is now both active and potential competition. Competition fulfills the function of mitigating market power. It can be expected that private bargaining of interconnection/access conditions between the different owners of long-distance networks will lead to economically efficient solutions. As a consequence, the European Commission would be well advised to restrain from recommending interventions within the area of long-distance telecommunications networks.

It is traditionally assumed that local networks constitute monopolistic bottlenecks, for which neither active nor potential substitutes are available. The European Commission still proceeds from this assumption and concludes that there is a remaining need for regulation of the incumbent operator's local access network, including the local components of leased lines.[36]

When applying the rules of competition in order to discipline network-specific market power, the "Access Notice" of the European Commission[37]

---

[35] See also Shankerman, "Symmetric regulation for competitive telecommunications", 8 *Information Economics and Policy* (1996) 3-23, at p. 5.

[36] Commission of the European Communities, *supra* n. 19, p. 1.

[37] European Commission, *supra* n. 18, 2-28.

strongly emphasizes the concept of the "essential facility". A facility is to be considered as essential, if it fulfills the conditions that it is indispensable for reaching customers, because there is no second or third such facility, i.e. there is no active substitute available, and if the facility cannot be practically or reasonably duplicated in order to discipline the active provider, i.e. there is no potential substitute available. Clause 69 specifically assumes that an enterprise that controls the access to an essential facility has a dominant position as defined by Article 82 [ex Art. 86 ECT].

Obviously, monopolistic bottlenecks can be characterized as essential facilities. To the extent and as long as local networks constitute monopolistic bottlenecks, *ex ante* regulation seems justified. Non-discriminatory access to essential facilities has to be guaranteed. However, it is important to view the application of the Essential Facilities Doctrine in a dynamic context. Therefore, one objective in the formulation of access conditions must be not to impede infrastructure competiton, i.e. not to destroy incentives for either research and development activities or innovations and investments on the facilities level. This is the only way to reach a balance between service and infrastructure competition.

Since unregulated tariffs would allow excessive profits to the owners of monopolistic bottlenecks, the instrument of price-cap regulation should be introduced.[38] Its major purpose is to regulate the level of prices, taking into account the inflation rate (consumer price index) minus a percentage for expected productivity increase. It seems important to restrict such price-cap regulation to the non-contestable parts of telecommunications networks, where market power due to monopolistic bottlenecks is a regulatory problem. In all other subparts of telecommunications networks price-setting should be left to the competitive market forces.

Concentrating on the regulation of the "last mile" does indeed constitute the one remaining task of a tailored sector-specific market power regulation. Non-discriminatory access to this bottleneck facility must be guaranteed for all competitors. The EU Regulation on unbundled access to the local loop contains an obligation for full unbundling as well as line-sharing. In order to guarantee competition on long distance telecommunications markets global access to local networks seems already sufficient.[39] In any case, one variant of non-discriminatory access to the local loop should be considered sufficient to overcome the monopolistic bottleneck problem.

---

[38] E.g. Beesley/ Littlechild, "The regulation of privatized monopolies in the United Kingdom", 20/3 *Rand Journal of Economics* (1989) 454-472.

[39] Engel/ Knieps, *Die Vorschriften des Telekommunikationsgesetzes über den Zugang zu wesentlichen Leistungen: Eine juristisch-ökonomische Untersuchung* (Baden-Baden: Nomos 1998).

Local network competition started with business customers in urban centres. There the preferred access technology is optical fibre.[40] However, after the granting of licences for point-to-multipoint microwave systems, the wireless local loop has also gained increasing importance.[41] Consequently, ever since the comprehensive opening of the telecommunications market, the pressure of innovation has increased in local networks, too. This has lead to considerable technological variety (e.g. optical fibre, wireless networks, CATV networks, satellite technology) and a consequent increase in product variety. Because of these rapid developments the local loop facilities in bigger cities and agglomerations in Germany are increasingly loosing their character of monopolistic bottlenecks.

Competitive conditions cannot be expected to change all of a sudden and simultaneously in all local loops. Therefore it is necessary to examine at regular intervals which subclasses of local loops still constitute monopolistic bottlenecks and in which subclasses there is already workable active and/or potential competition – for example because of wireless local loop facilities or alternative cable providers. The European Commission would indeed be well advised to exploit the increasing potential for phasing out sector-specific regulation in competitive European telecommunications.

---

[40] Cf. Distelkamp, "Möglichkeiten des Wettbewerbs im Orts- und Anschlußbereich des Telekommunikationsnetzes", *WIK Diskussionsbeitrag No. 196* (Bad Honnef 1999) 94.

[41] Regulierungsbehörde für Telekommunikation und Post, *Jahresbericht 1999*, 24.

Local network competition started with business customers in urban centres. There the preferred access technology is optical fibre. However, after the [illegible]

Money, Civil Law and European Integration

Eckart Koch*

1. THE CIVIL LEVEL

1.1 Money and the creation of money from the view of civil law

Money as something corporeal is represented in coins and banknotes, which the legislator defines to be legal payment. They are fungible goods and therefore it is necessary to have regard to the principles of the law of property for their transfer. It is impossible for there to be more coins and banknotes than the legal authorities (the government is responsible for coins, the central bank is responsible for notes) have issued into circulation; were it to be more, it would be counterfeit money.

Every national economy has many more assets at its disposal than cash in circulation. How does this money come into being? I have not found any legal essay that raises this question or even tries to answer it.[1] That is even more astonishing if one considers that money is regarded as a product of the legal system.[2] Therefore, the coming into being of money must be explainable from a

* Universitätsprofessor Dr. Eckart Koch, Leiter der Abteilung Rechtswissenschaft, Technische Universität Braunschweig.

[1] Simitis stresses the barter value and talking about the "negating of substance", presumably meaning that money is only a measure for the value of goods. S. Simitis, "Bemerkungen zur rechtlichen Sonderstellung des Geldes", *AcP* (1960) 159, 160, 406 et seq.

[2] On this Karsten Schmidt, in: Staudinger, *Kommentar zum Bürgerlichen Gesetzbuch*, 12th ed. Vorbem. A 2 bb zu § 244.

*Talia Einhorn, ed., Spontaneous Order, Organization and the Law –
Liber Amicorum Ernst-Joachim Mestmäcker © 2003 T.M.C.ASSER PRESS, The Hague, The Netherlands*

legal perspective. The political economy deals, of course, with this problem as a major question, but the discussion concerns only the subject of money as an aggregated quantity, which grows and shrinks, and not the question from which units this quantity of money derives. But this question may also be important for economic policy.

The businessman who takes his cash – coins and notes – to the bank in the evening does not become poorer. An economist would say that the businessman has deposits and that he always has access to these deposits and the opportunity to get his money back as cash. But that is not the central point from a juristic view. The businessman has signed a contract with his bank. He is no longer the owner of his cash, but in place of his ownership he has obtained a claim against the bank. This claim is expressed in ciphers and signs (Euro) – on paper or as an electronic signal – and represented in his account. The bank now has the duty to administer this account properly.

In the juristic literature this metamorphosis of money is described as the "institutional idea of money". This term characterizes money as an abstract power, which is expressed in currency units.[3] Hence, that is what makes up the legal relations between the members of a legal system: a claim (§ 241 BGB), which is the creditor's legal power to demand action or omission of action of the debtor.

The bank keeps the corporeal, ready money, the creditor has the legal claim, i.e. the money in the institutional sense. The creditor's money even increases with the interest paid by the bank. The bank offers the creditor convenient facilities of payment. With electronic communication it is possible for him to assign debts. This has the effect that the creditor does not want his cash back and the bank can keep it.

Comparable with the discussion about a corporeal and an institutional idea of money is the economic debate about the question: is corporeal money just a symbol or does it embody a claim?

If it embodies a claim, is it a claim against the central bank (see the Reichsbanknote of 1910 on the next page), or has the central bank a claim against the owner of the note?[4] All modern currencies lack a gold coverage, so the banknote's owner has no claim against the issuing institution. With regard to the central bank's counter claim, it has to be noted that in a working currency system no institution will give money away systematically. The primary issue of paper-money is made on the basis of a reciprocal contract about a loan. This

---

[3] Palandt, *Kommentar zum Bürgerlichen Gesetzbuch*, 60th ed., § 245 Rz 2.

[4] H. Riese, "Geld, das letzte Rätsel der Nationalökonomie", in: Schelkle/ Nitsch (eds.), *Rätsel Geld* (Marburg 1955) 45, 58.

contract binds the borrower to pay back the principal plus interest. In addition to this, he may be obliged to secure the loan with securities in advance.

The economics proceed from the assumption that the creation of money is based on the offering of loans and that the institution that has the primary right to offer loans is the central bank. This assumption has to be doubted, because the increase of money is not based directly on the offering of loans. The reason why money increases is the reciprocal contract with the borrower that binds him to pay back the principal plus interest. So it is the civil law contract, which effects the creation of money and not an act of public authority, i.e. the commercial banks can carry out this act, too.[5]

Back to the commercial bank doing everything to offer customers convenient facilities of payment in order that they do not withdraw their money. In this context, it has to be considered that the customer has to act within the legal system, if he wants to vest claims by signing contracts, and to equate money with the claim on money. If he acts without the legal system, i.e. in the underworld (illicit money, illegal contracts), he will need cash – corporeal money.

If the customer needs only a small amount of cash, the bank can sign a contract with a borrower, who probably will not need any cash either. As a creditor the customer can dispose of his claim of paying out the principal, while

---

[5] A possible question is: may the central bank, which has no contractual risks as a creditor, book the interest produce as profit and deliver it to the circulation of money in the state? (in Europe the battle between the Member States over the distribution of money is an additional problem).
That would be an argument against Riese's system analysis, which states that the foundation of the monetary economy is not liberal norm orientated, but mercantile.

the bank carries out bookings to his account. As a debtor he can assign claims, about which the bank keeps a record.

One can see how money is increasing: in the beginning it splits up into corporeal money and claims, then it increases with the interest on the customer's side or the side of the bank. The basis for everything are civil law contracts, precisely their effect to create a claim.

Further it has to be seen that there is no awareness of the difference between money and the claim for money. Claims for money are recorded and expressed in quantitative signs, more and more stored only electronically or magnetically. The legal system guarantees that no money arises without a contract and a debtor-creditor-relationship. No "debtor" would agree to be recorded as a debtor without an existing obligation and the courts will support his attempts. The legal system is only responsible for the fixing of the signs for communication (Deutsche Mark, Euro, GBP, Dollar), the quantity of money and the value of the signs depend on the contracts concluded between the members of this legal system.

Until now we have only discussed reciprocal credit-contracts, where the debtor pays for the loan with money. But mostly one party to the contract offers services or goods and the other party pays for this.

A young entrepreneur with a good enterprising idea gets from his commercial bank a loan credited to his account. The entrepreneur rents an office, buys the means of production, hires staff and makes profit and turnover, which he uses to pay back his debts including the loan. The entrepreneur's creditors (lessors, employees, suppliers) have, like him, accounts. Therefore, every payment can be made without cash. It is the same with the entrepreneur's customers (debtors), who have accounts, too, and can pay their debts without using cash. The result of this may be (but that is not certain) that everyone has increased his bank balance, i.e. they have acquired money claims against the bank. The cause for this development is not the loan, but the successfully realised enterprising idea. The loans have made this possible. But that is not only the bank's achievement. The lessors, employees and suppliers have offered the entrepreneur a "loan", too, because they do their job before they get paid.

1.2 Money system and competition system

In the legal theoretical discussion about money it is the common opinion that money as legal tender – no matter whether coins or notes – can only fulfil its function (as a means for exchange, to keep a value or to measure a value) if it is generally accepted. If such a general acceptance is given, it will be discernible under the conditions of a free-enterprise exchange of goods for money. Under such conditions the negotiated claim for payment characterizes the value of money and is in itself the cause of the coming into being of money. Therefore, it is correct to consider the claim for money as identical with the money itself. The claim for money is the cause of the existence of money and gives the money its value.

If there exists no voluntary exchange of goods under the conditions of the competition, this results in defects in economic growth and in the currency system. If the members of the national economy are forced somehow to achieve certain results, these results will not be equal with what they can achieve voluntarily when they are paid for it with valid money.

If the baker is forced to sell his bread for a lower price than the market price, he must be forced to bake for longer or he must get subsidies. These subsidies must be financed by taxes which would disturb the balance of the system.

If it is nearly impossible to give someone notice of termination of the lease of a flat let for rent in a densely populated area, the tenant will take advantage of the economic imbalance between rent and the right of use. He will want to get paid for his removal or else sell his contractual usufruct to the next tenant or he will profit by the advantages himself and stay in the flat. In all probability fewer flats will be built and the imbalance will increase. That will cause even stricter rules, which only seemingly can help to overcome the imbalance. § 5 sentence 4 of the German *Kreislaufwirtschafts- und Abfallgesetz* states that an entrepreneur has to utilise waste even if the utilization is more expensive than the disposal. How much bureaucracy is necessary to enforce and to control such an irrational behaviour?

1.3 Care for the civil law instead of global policy

Money comes into being with reciprocal contracts. Time is important for this development and also the connection with the service provided in return. This focuses attention on the contracts and may lead to different recommendations compared with recommendations from the perspective of the national economy which operates with aggregated quantities. The macro-economic relevance of micro-economic creation of law does not receive enough attention.

It is particularly the equation of quantity and circulation that repeatedly causes wrong ideas and economic activities. This is in keeping with the following formula:

(quantity of money) x (speed of circulation) = (average price) x (real income)

The money's speed of circulation can be imagined as the quantity of concluded contracts, which corresponds to the thesis that the conclusion of a contract creates money. But what is the stipulated quantity of money? It caused the theory of inflation based on the assumption that speed of circulation and real income are constant. If that is the case, the quantity of money determines prices.

It has never been my experience that a rich man haggling about a contract had to pay more than a poor man. This is true even if he is so rich that he would not anyway be able to spend all of his money during his lifetime. On the contrary: it is often the rich man who is in a much better position to negotiate the terms of the contract.

The assumption that the speed of circulation is constant reduces the possibilities of acquiring new insights, because the speed of circulation increases the quantity of money just like the real income does if prices are constant. Put differently: the number of contracts concluded is the basis for economic growth. Price increases happen if there is a surplus demand because of reduced competition; they do not happen because the quantity of money is too high. But the formula does not say anything about the possibilities of increasing the supply of goods and services.

1.4 Stability of the cash value: quantity of money or competition

The connection between the claim for money and the claim for services or goods in a reciprocal contract ensures that the growth of the quantity of money[6] and the growth of real income take place in a similar manner (in a well-balanced way).

But this does not mean that the quantity of money in a national economy has to correspond to the stock of goods. It does not mean either that that would have any effect on the price structure. Where the value of goods decreases, where they are no longer useful and a burden for the national economy, because one wants to get rid of them (refuse disposal), the importance of services is generally brief.[7] On the money market the quantity of money alters with the investment's changing prices. It is not possible to identify the transfer of money to the new lands in the east, or the growth and loss of money on the stock markets during the last ten years, or the enormous growth of funds in the Federal Republic of Germany, as causes for alterations of the price structure. What is crucial for the price structure is the competition situation, which has an effect on the contracts relating to the production and exchange of goods and services. The stabilization of the European currencies is not an achievement of the states or their central banks, but the effect of the intensifying of competition, specially caused from the European and global integration.

Two points have to be at the centre of attention for a policy which wants to support stability and growth: first, freedom of contract and, secondly, the

---

[6] It is a philosophical question whether it is actually ingenious to quantify the amount of money isolated or if it only gives a quantitative measure for goods and results; see *supra* n. 1.

[7] It made no sense to promote the heavy industry in the new lands with the argumentation that it produces durable goods. Investments make sense when it can be expected that a market exists for the products.

general consciousness that the only way to get money is to offer goods or services.

To make it clear: these statements are only valid for the economic sector, not for public social transfers or allowances.

But they make clear that it is not enough to support underdeveloped countries financially. It is necessary to make efforts to intensify trade, i.e. the number of contracts concluded in the underdeveloped countries. The sentence "the value of money results from its scarcity" therefore has to be interpreted as follows: the state does not give any money away. If you want to get money, you will have to earn it, i.e. you will have to offer something for it – a service in return.

1.5 **European money and European civil law**

The conclusion for the development of the European integration is obvious: the unified currency system must be complemented by a unified civil and commercial law. The basis for this conclusion are the freedom of contract and the rules for competition. The effect of already existing rules would be much more powerful in a unified legal system. The unification of the procedural rules and the rules for the judgment summons would be consistent.[8] The development of a European legal system should abolish the separation between national and border crossing state affairs.

Of course, directives have supported the growing harmony, but the European integration of civil law cannot be achieved with them. Directives always relate to subjects which happen to be politically topical. It is necessary to implement them into national law. Therefore, they do not represent European law or support a European identity. They complicate the interpretation of the law and its application to a specific case, because it is always necessary to consider them in connection with the national law. The result of this is often that it is necessary to make a submission to the European Court. Dealing with selected points of national law can easily cause difficulties elsewhere.

The European Parliament, in 1989[9] and 1994[10] has already evolved ideas for a European civil law, the effects of which are now unfolding.[11] Until now no one has emphasized their connection with the currency union. The supporters of the

---

[8] About the development of European procedural rules on the basis of Art. 65 EC see B. Heß, "Die 'Europäisierung' des internationalen Zivilprozessrechts durch den Amsterdamer Vertrag – Chancen und Gefahren", *NJW* (2000) 23.

[9] *OJ* [1989] C 158/400-401.

[10] EP-Doc A 3-329/94. See also *EuZW* (1994) 612.

[11] On this with many references to the initiatives in science and European legal policy see Grundmann, "Europäisches Schuldvertragsrecht", *NJW* (2000) 15.

culmination theory were of the opinion that a currency union was only possible when European integration would have succeeded and the instruments of economic policy would have been used in common. This kind of policy understanding aims at global-controlling and intervening public activities. Their effect on economic progress is overrated. Policy means to create law and if the understanding of money is derived from contract law, the currency union is an urgent task.

2. Money system and state system

2.1 States without a currency system in history

Economic growth, competition, market economy and division of labour can only exist on condition that there is a working money system. A working money system is necessary if a state wants to develop and extend its functions. The state participates in the money system by asking its citizens to pay taxes, charges and distributions. This money secures the state's and its representatives' existence and so fulfils its tasks.

Historically seen, states with an insufficient money system could only come into being and exist under the condition that their authorities had enough money to find followers. There was no economic growth and the necessity to preserve power decreased the funds. Therefore, wars and colonisation were the political means to preserve the state. Neither a longing for democracy nor the French Revolution could change these facts. The nation states of the 19th century tried to avoid this with a balance of powers secured by international treaties but without success.

2.2 Self-protection: restriction of quantity through guarantee of coverage

Because of the state's own interest in money it was on a long term basis impossible to create money through state legislation. No one trusted money, which quantity the state as a legislator could increase optionally and which increase would be in the state's interest. Precious metals as scarce goods filled the function of money between businessmen. Precious metals were replaced by paper written instructions (i.e. to hand over the precious metals) in a developing bank system. Public money systems followed this example. This created confidence in the national currencies because of the legal binding to scarcities. This development corresponded with an enormous economic growth characterizing the industrial revolution. The natural scientific and engineering abilities had existed a long time beforehand, but there had been no possibility to translate them into economic success.

The loss of the gold coverage in connection with reparation payments caused an enormous inflation in Germany at the beginning of the 1920s. The reactions were the first independence of the Reichsbank (later pension bank) and the restriction of the pension-mark-quantity with the construed pension coverage. The bank law from 1924 created an obligation of scarcity through the gold coverage. The recession in the USA in connection with the foreign exchange repatriation and the restriction of the credit possibilities caused the economic crisis of 1931.[12]

After World War II the Bretton Woods' system established with the IMF the link to gold, which had to be given up in 1971 because the quantity of money was not covered by the gold price. Money may grow and must grow to support the growth of production of goods and services. The stability of money is not guaranteed with a restriction of quantity, but with the certain knowledge that money is only created with reciprocal contracts, e.g. contracts where money is paid in return for goods or services or contracts where principals are paid back with interest. It is impossible to restrict the money stock permanently, but – provided that the rules of competition are observed strictly within the legal system and the state does not obtain money without the legal system – this will not cause inflation.

Many states have difficulties in avoiding using legal instruments to intervene against mis-developments. Their attitude is supported by mathematical monetary and mathematical economic theories (Keynesian liquidity trap). In Germany this happened in 1973. In the following it is shown how impossible it is to influence the conduct of economic citizens and how big the damage for the legal system is.

> 1973 was in the beginning characterized by high inflation rates. In expectation of higher taxes the number of purchases increased, which caused an even higher inflation (announcement effect). Starting on 7 June 1973 (*Bundesgesetzblatt*, p. 530), depreciation on the basis of decreasing annual rates was abrogated retrospectively to 8 May 1973, with the higher deduction for one or two family homes and freehold flats being suspended. By Statute of 26 June 1973 (*Bundesgesetzblatt*, pp. 676, 686; amendment of § 30 *Umsatzsteuergesetz*) the input tax deduction was retrospectively neutralized for economic assets which had been purchased after 9 May 1973 and had been made use of since 8 May 1973.
>
> There was much backdating of concluded contracts, and many civil law actions and criminal proceedings involving fiscal offences. Economic activity slowed down abruptly during the second half of 1973. The taxation of investments was abolished

---

[12] On this, H. J. Hahn, *Währungsrecht* (München 1990) §§ 10–12.

with effect from 30 November 1973, the depreciation on the basis of decreasing annual rates (for immovables) was admitted again from 31 December 1973. The exclusion of depreciation on the basis of decreasing annual rates relating to economic assets purchased in the meantime lasted for the following years. The confidence in a state that tried to direct economic activities was lost. The state caused the cyclical fluctuations rather than damming them up. Entrepreneurial planning is much more difficult if it is necessary to consider not only the market, but the state's conduct, too.

2.3 The state independence of the Euro and its civil law dependence

It is a major progress that the European Central Bank is state independent (Art. 108, Treaty of Amsterdam) and primarily committed to the aim of stability (Art. 105, Treaty of Amsterdam). The existence of this rule is much more important for the stability of the European monetary system than the possibilities of the European Central Bank to influence interest rates.

The state is involved in the formation of prices and monetary value but the state itself is not controlled by the market. The external value of the national currency shows the economic assessment of this political dimension. The external value of a currency shows how willing aliens are to conclude contracts within this economic area and its currency. The expectations of a higher external value with the European monetary union were disappointed. The reason for the low external value may be the fact that the differences between the Member States still exist, especially the fiscal differences. An internal market does not yet exist. It is characteristic of the lack of integration that the currencies of the Community Member States, that have not participated in the monetary union (Great Britain, Sweden) were developed in a different and better way than the Euro. If their economic area were part of a real internal market, the value of these currencies would develop similarly to the Euro.

The rules regarding the allocation of competencies in the European Community Treaty are very unclear. In part, they are functionally fixed (especially according the fundamental freedoms and the harmonization of laws). To a certain extent, they can be compared with party programmes with idealistic aims. The dogma of the limited single authorization is not apparent. It is possible to find a European responsibility for nearly everything in the European Community Treaty. These responsibilities are also discharged. On the other hand, the development of national law drifts apart in areas which are very important for integration policy (taxes, traffic, environment, commercial law). It is nearly impossible to convey the importance of the Treaty on European Union which has supplemented the European Community Treaty. Much more European bureaucracy was created instead of sharing and concentrating sovereignty. The problematic nature of directives has already been discussed above.

The result is the same, even from the view of the state. The durable establishment of the monetary union does not make it less necessary to consolidate it with a European civil and procedural law.

The Impact of Equity Markets on Business Organization: Some Comparative Observations Regarding Differences in the Evolution of Corporate Structures

Friedrich Kübler*

1. What determines the evolution of corporate structures?

After World War II it became obvious that the American way of allowing an open and highly competitive economy was superior to the traditional German system of concentrated groups of companies, cartels, and regular government interference. For the organization of large firms it was the "Berle-Means" corporation[1] which presented itself as the model for reforming German corporate law. In fact, the separation of ownership and control offered considerable advantages. Management functions were awarded on the basis of merit, abandoning the feudal rule of inheritance. Investors were able to reduce risk by diversification. The dispersion of ownership allowed managers to escape the control of banks or other financial institutions, enabling the corporation to become an autonomous player in competitive markets. Management had to serve the interests of all – and not only of big shareholders; it was held accountable by the judicial enforcement of fiduciary duties, the monitoring of

---

* Professor of Law, University of Pennsylvania, Philadelphia/Professor (emeritus), Johann Wolfgang Goethe-Universität Frankfurt am Main/Attorney (of Counsel), Clifford Chance Pünder, Frankfurt a.M. Assistance by Heath Price Tarbert is gratefully acknowledged.

[1] Berle/ Means, *The Modern Corporation and Private Property* (New York: Commerce Clearing House 1933).

independent directors and the emerging market for corporate control.[2] ERNST-JOACHIM MESTMÄCKER had been the first German author to point to this model;[3] in his path-breaking analysis he confronted the American public corporation with the corporatist German structures and suggested far-reaching changes, mostly following the American example. Other publications followed.[4] They all had some impact. The comprehensive reform of the Joint Stock Corporation Act in 1965 was inspired by the policy objective of allowing an increasing number of investors to buy equity in order to contain the concentration of ownership and provide for a broad dispersion of shares.[5] And there were clear improvements compared to the statute enacted in 1937: more disclosure, enhanced powers for shareholders' meetings, regulation of bank proxies and new avenues for shareholder litigation.[6] But in spite of these improvements the corporate system as a whole hardly changed. It did not move toward the American model of the autonomous public corporation with dispersed ownership. On the contrary, it basically preserved its traditional features. The – comparatively few – stock corporations retained their links through the mutual crossholding of shares[7] and a closeknit web of interconnected membership in managing and supervisory boards.[8] Banks continued to exercise considerable influence through extended block holdings,[9] their function as primary lenders, proxies given by – mostly small – shareholders[10] and the holding of many positions on the supervisory board of companies in other industries.

At the same time, (West) Germany's economy was quickly recovering from the distortions of the Nazi regime and the destruction inflicted by the war. Thus

---

[2] For details and references see Roe, "Some Differences in Corporate Structure in Germany, Japan, and the United States", 102 *Yale L.J.* (1927) 1933, at p. 1993. For the impact of this model on comparative corporate law analysis see Rock, "America's Fascination with German Corporate Governance", *Die Aktiengesellschaft* (*AG*) [1995] 291.

[3] *Verwaltung, Konzerngewalt und Rechte der Aktionäre. Eine rechtsvergleichende Untersuchung nach deutschem Aktienrecht und dem Recht der Corporations in den Vereinigten Staaten* (Karlsruhe: Müller 1958).

[4] See in particular Wiethölter, *Interessen und Organisation der Aktiengesellschaft im amerikanischen und deutschen Recht* (Karlsruhe: Müller 1961).

[5] This had been the official explanation of the bill; see *Bundestagsdrucksache* IV/71, 93.

[6] For details see Assmann, Einleitung, in: Hopt/ Wiedemann (eds.), *Großkommentar zum AktG*, 4th ed. (Berlin: de Gruyter 1992) notes 191-209.

[7] Adams, "Die Usurpation von Aktionärsbefugnissen mittels Ringverflechtung in der 'Deutschland AG'", *Die Aktiengesellchaft* [1994] 148; Adams, "Crossholdings in Germany", 155 *JITE* (1999) 80.

[8] Mülbert, "Empfehlen sich gesetzliche Regelungen zur Einschränkung des Einflusses der Kreditinstitute auf Aktiengesellschaften?" *Gutachten E zum 61. Deutschen Juristentag* (1996) 20 with references.

[9] Mülbert, ibid., at pp. 16 et seq.

[10] See the figures in Gottschalk, "Der Stimmrechtseinfluß der Banken in den Aktionärsversammlungen der Großunternehmen", *WSI-Mitteilungen* (1989) 294, 298.

we are faced with the question of why in fact there has been no – or at least so little – convergence towards the American model. The most elaborate answer so far points to the impact of political decisions: it is politics that determines corporate structures. In the US, on the one hand, Congress had imposed the strict segmentation of financial markets: Glass-Steagall mandated the separation of commercial from investment banking, McFadden and other provisions dealt with interstate banking, and the Bank Holding Company Act continues to restrict stock holdings of banks in non-financial industries.[11] Germany, on the other hand, had always allowed its universal banks to offer the full range of financial services as well as to control other industries by unlimited holdings of stock. In addition, it introduced the codetermination of workers on the supervisory boards of corporations. It is argued that this has had major effects on German corporate structures. In order to reduce employee influence in the firm, the powers of the supervisory board were in fact restricted: "Board meetings are infrequent, information flow to the board is poor, and the board is often too big and unwieldy to be effective";[12] governance would instead be exercised by block holders, in particular by banks, outside the board room. At the same time, codetermination weakens German securities markets. It encourages large block holdings as a counterweight to the influence of workers and their unions in the board room. "This poor fit between codetermination and diffuse ownership makes firm founders less willing to sell off their blocks of stock in initial public offerings (IPOs) and makes distant potential buyers much more wary of owning stock in the German firm than they would be otherwise".[13] This explains why there are so few IPOs as buyers are reluctant to pay the "full" price for the stock of a company which is burdened with codetermination and the owners will therefore prefer not to sell to the public.[14] For these reasons, a general incompatibility is assumed to exist between (European type) social democracy and the Berle-Means firm.[15]

These are strong and persuasive arguments. But there are several reasons why they may not be fully convincing. In the first place, it should be asked why politics shaped corporate structures in such a different way. German

---

[11] Roe, *supra* n. 2, at pp. 1930 et seq.; Roe, *Strong Managers, Weak Owners: The Political Roots of American Corporate Finance* (Princeton, N.J.: Princeton University Press 1997) pp. 94 et seq., 169 et seq.

[12] Roe, "German Codetermination and German Securities Markets", 5 *Col. J. of Eur. L.* (1999) 199, 200.

[13] Roe, ibid., at p. 201.

[14] Roe, ibid., at p. 208.

[15] Roe, *Political Preconditions to Separating Ownership from Control: The Incompatibility of the American Public Firm with Social Democracy* (Col. Law and Economics Working Paper 1999).

codetermination has a long and complex history;[16] the various statutes in the 1920s, 1950s and 1970s had been designed for more purposes than simply "to co-opt revolutionary forces after the German revolution of 1918 and to pacify the unions in the 1970s".[17] Another aspect may be still more important. Recently, there is increasing evidence that the German system has started to change. At least the big private banks that had previously emphasized their commercial business have become much more interested in investment banking. For this and probably also for other reasons, they appear to be determined to reduce their holdings in other industries. Such a strategy will be supported by the most recent tax reform. The fate of Mannesmann has shown that even very big German enterprises can no longer be sure that they will not be the target of a successful tender offer. At the same time, there have been some legal changes such as the relaxation of an enormously rigid regime of preemptive rights,[18] that has moved the German system by small steps closer to the American model. On the other hand, the US has started to move away from its political tradition of strict segmentation of its financial services industries: limitations on interstate banking have been abolished; and recently the Gramm-Leach-Bliley Act has repealed most of the Glass-Steagall separation of commercial and investment banking.[19] At the turn of the century we do see at least some convergence between corporate structures in the US and those in Germany.

The purpose of this paper is to look for a different explanation of the development of business organization in Germany in the second half of the 20th Century. The hypothesis to be tested is that German corporate structures have been shaped primarily – or at least to a large extent – by the lack of a primary market for equity, forcing industries to look for other sources of corporate finance. The evidence supporting this theory is discussed in Part 2. Part 3 raises the question if and to what extent additional support can be gained by looking more closely at some similar features of postwar Japan.[20] Part 4 is designed to further explain the common patterns as well as the significant differences between the outcomes in Japan and Germany.

---

[16] For a summary see Kübler/ Schmidt/ Simitis, *Mitbestimmung als gesetzgebungspolitische Aufgabe* (Baden-Baden: Nomos 1978) 113 et seq.

[17] Roe, *supra* n. 2, at p. 1970.

[18] § 186 par. 3 sentence 4 AktG; for the background see Kübler/ Mendelson/ Mundheim, "Die Kosten des Bezugsrechts", *Die Aktiengesellschaft* [1989] 461; Seibert/ Köster/ Kiem, *Die kleine AG*, 3rd ed. (Köln: RWS 1996) fn 182.

[19] Pub. L. No. 106-102, 113 Stat. 1338 (1999).

[20] These similarities have been observed before; see e.g. Roe, *supra* n. 2, and Buxbaum, "Institutional Owners and Corporate Managers: An International Perspective", 57 *Brooklyn L. Rev.* (1991) 1, 26 et seq.

2. GERMANY: BUSINESS ORGANIZATION OF THE RECONSTRUCTION ECONOMY

The specific features of Germany's "cooperative managerial capitalism" date back to the emergence of large enterprises in the last quarter of the 19th Century: "...Germany's capital markets were much smaller and less developed than those of the United States and Britain. Therefore financial institutions, particularly the new, all-purpose Großbanken, played a greater role in financing the first movers' initial investment in production and distribution, and hence a greater role in their subsequent governance than was the case in the other two countries".[21] With the beginning of World War I, the primary market for equity started to decline even further. And after World War II, the situation had become still more dramatic. On the one hand, West German industries were in desperate need of funds for investment. All the establishments in the territory occupied by the Soviet army were lost; wherever their input was indispensable, they had to be recreated in the West. Many of the facilities in Western Germany had been destroyed by bombs. From the remaining plants equipment had been removed for reasons of reparation. And last but not least, production had to be reorganized in order to serve peaceful rather than military purposes.

At the same time, there was no market where corporations could raise equity.[22] As already mentioned, this market had never been as strong as in the US or in Britain, and it had been further weakened by World War I. By the late 1940s and early 1950s, most private savings had been wiped out by two world wars and two disastrous inflations. People continued, or started again, to save money; but the comparatively small amounts they could spare went into real estate or bank accounts. Little was left to be invested in the stock market. Major evidence for this fact can be derived from the steady decline of the number of stock corporations, public corporations (with dispersed ownership) and listed companies.[23] This trend is primarily explained by the complete lack of any "going public" of firms by an initial public offering (IPO). And this means that there was no incentive to transform a limited company (GmbH) or limited partnership (KG) into a stock corporation, which would have increased accounting

---

[21] Chandler, Jr., *Scale and Scope. The Dynamics of Industrial Capitalism* (Cambridge: Belknap 1990) p. 588.

[22] Some evidence is referred to by Kropff, "25 Jahre AktG – was waren die Ziele und was wurde erreicht?" in: Lutter (ed.) *25 Jahre AktG* (Düsseldorf: Das Wertpapier 1991) pp. 19, 20.

[23] For figures and references see Kübler, *Gesellschaftsrecht*, 5th ed. (Heidelberg: Müller 1998) pp. 160 et seq. The lowest point was reached in the late 1970s and early 1980s. In 1979 there were only 2,139 stock corporations left; in 1983 only 442 were listed on one of the German stock exchanges.

and other burdens – including a stiffer regime of codetermination – without providing any advantages.

This lack of funds available for equity investment has profoundly shaped the practice of corporate finance for most of the second half of the 20th Century. Basically, there have been three strategies used to collect and/or retain the funds necessary for the reconstruction of industrial plants and the expansion of business operations.

a) A first source of financing had been debt, in particular, borrowing from banks. This is documented by the continuing decline of the equity ratio of German enterprises from the early 1950s throughout the 1970s.[24] At the same time, this ratio had become much lower than in nearly all other industrialized countries.[25] Only Japanese firms had still less equity. It will be shown that this analogy can be explained in similar terms.[26] Such an extreme degree of leverage increased the exposure and the risks incurred by banks. This explains, at least in part, why banks were able to obtain such an important stake in the governance of German firms: the credit risk resulting from excessive long-term lending required close monitoring of the borrowers. As some of these firms were facing liquidity and repayment problems, some debt was transformed into equity, thus increasing bank holdings in other industries.
b) A second strategy of similar importance had been self-financing. To a very large extent, earnings were not distributed but retained and reinvested within the enterprise. For the public corporation this was made possible by two structural elements. As most shareholders' proxies were given to the banks in their capacity as brokers, these financial institutions in fact controlled shareholders' meetings. Apart from the seats reserved for the representatives of employees under the codetermination statutes, most members of supervisory boards had been – and to a considerable extent still are – the top managers of other public corporations. All of them faced the same problems and therefore had a common interest to contain distributions to shareholders. Because management could not hope to attract new shareholders, it had no reason to use dividend payments as an incentive for investment in the stock of the corporation. Existing shareholders were

---

[24] Deutsche Bundesbank, "Ertragslage und Finanzierungsverhältnisse der Unternehmen im Jahr 1976", *Monatsberichte der Deutschen Bundesbank* (November 1977) pp. 31 et seq.; Kübler, "Unternehmensstrukturen und Kapitalmarktfunktion", *Die Aktiengesellschaft* [1981] 5, at pp. 6 et seq.

[25] Jacobi, "Die Bedeutung der Eigenkapitalbasis im internationalen Vergleich", in: Bruns/ Häuser (eds.), *Eigenkapital und Kapitalmarkt* (Frankfurt a.M.: Knapp 1978) 55, at pp. 58 et seq. and 73.

[26] See *infra* part 3.

benefited by the internal growth of the firm and the leverage effect of the low equity ratio. Both factors caused stock prices to rise throughout the 1950s and 1960s. In addition, corporations would distribute preemptive rights allowing the acquisition of new shares far below the current market price. This provided the company with some additional funds and the shareholders with the opportunity to sell either their preemptive rights or newly acquired shares. For tax reasons, most shareholders preferred this form of distribution.[27]

c) A third form of financing can be described as deferred compensation for labour. In the 1950s and 1960s wages and salaries stayed rather low. But the large firms had established remarkably generous programmes offering many of their white and blue collar employees pensions after retirement. They did not use pension funds or insurance programs, but committed themselves to make the later payments out of their corporate funds. In doing so, they created claims against the company which could be used as liabilities on the balance sheet. This allowed them to protect earnings against the demands of the tax authorities and shareholders as well as retain liquidity which could safely be used for investment. In fact, the firms borrowed money from their workers. This was long-term debt; maturities were foreseeable and no interest had to be paid. For companies like Siemens, Daimler-Benz or the "big three" chemical firms, who enjoyed continued profitability and growth, this proved to be a splendid device to reduce their financial problems and concurrently build huge amounts of liquid funds.

The extended weakness of the market for equity[28] and the substituting means of corporate finance appear to have had considerable impact upon the basic concepts and structures of corporate law:

a) A particularly important aspect is the emphasis on creditor protection. In the course of the 20th Century, American legislators have largely abolished mandatory rules on legal capital.[29] At the same time, Germany has extended and further refined a very rigid regime which burdens the foundation of a

---

[27] Before the 1978 tax reform, dividends had to bear the double burden of the corporate and the individual income tax; both were high. Because there was (and is) no tax on capital gains, shareholders in the higher brackets of income taxation were much better off as long as they were not paid dividends but were able to cash in the additional value of their stock. This could be achieved by the sale of preemptive rights.

[28] Roughly speaking, it lasted four decades: from the beginning of World War I to the mid 1950s.

[29] For details see Manning/ Hanks, *Legal Capital*, 3rd ed. (Westbury, NY: Foundation Press 1990); Kübler, *Aktie, Unternehmensfinanzierung und Kapitalmarkt* (Köln: Ges. für Bankwissenschaftliche Forschung 1989); Bauer, *Gläubigerschutz durch eine formelle Nennkapitalziffer – Kapitalgesellschaftliche Notwendigkeit oder überholtes Konzept?* (Frankfurt a.M.: Lang 1995).

stock corporation as well as the issue of additional shares via capital increases with a cumbersome and costly procedure, going considerably beyond the requirements imposed by the 2nd Company Law EC Directive.[30] All non-cash contributions have to be evaluated by independent experts;[31] certain contracts between the corporation and one of its shareholders have to be approved by a qualified majority of the shareholders' meeting and filed with the commercial register.[32] The courts expanded this regime by allowing creditors to derive windfall benefits to the detriment of shareholders. Even financial institutions such as leasing companies have been allowed to disregard the corporate entity of its debtor (and the contractual allocation of risk) and enforce repayment by the controlling shareholder.[33] Shareholders who have made a non-cash contribution without following the mandated procedure are obliged to make full payment in cash even if the corporation had already received partial or full consideration.[34] The preference given to the interests of creditors over those of equity investors and shareholders is also reflected in the accounting rules. They encourage the accumulation of undisclosed or "hidden" reserves by allowing firms to undervalue assets and overvalue liabilities in the balance sheet and thus distort the information given to the market.[35] This regime is again justified by the proclaimed needs of creditors: the undisclosed reserves should provide a financial cushion in order to enhance their safety. In this respect it reflects the policy considerations supporting the rules on legal capital: since debt is much more important than equity for financing business operations, corporate law gives debt investors preference over equity investors. In addition, the accounting rules support self-financing of the corporation: they allow management to transform earnings into undisclosed reserves and thus avoid corporate income taxation as well as the distribution of dividends.

b) The weakness of the market for equity means, as mentioned above, that shareholders are no longer expected to make significant financial contributions to the corporation. Since this is usually their key function, they are no

---

30 From 13 December 1976: *OJ(EC)* [1977] L 26/1.

31 § 32 paras. 2 and 3 AktG.

32 §§ 52 and 53 AktG. This requirement has been relaxed recently.

33 *Bundesgerichtshof in Zivilsachen* (*BGHZ*) 95, 330, 337 et seq. (*Autokran*). Some years later this doctrine was – at least in part – abandoned: *BGHZ* 122, 123, 129 et seq. (*TBB*).

34 *BGHZ* 110, 47, 52 et seq.; *BGHZ* 113, 335, 340 et seq.; *BGHZ* 118, 83, 91 et seq.

35 For details see Kübler, "Institutioneller Gläubigerschutz oder Kapitalmarkttransparenz?" 159 *Zeitschrift für das Gesamte Handels- und Wirtschaftsrecht* (*ZHR*) (1995) 550; Walz, "Strategien zur Überwindung des bilanzrechtlichen Anpassungsbedarfs", in: Assmann et. al. (eds.), *Wirtschafts- und Medienrecht in der offenen Demokratie* (Heidelberg: Müller 1997) 557.

longer important and can be marginalized. This is what happened in Germany. It started in the 1920s with a new theory of the corporation as an "enterprise per se",[36] proclaimed by the then CEO of Allgemeine Elektrizitäts-Gesellschaft (AEG) and later minister of foreign affairs, Walter Rathenau.[37] This concept of the firm emphasizes the contributions made by management and the workforce; they are the true "members" of the entity. Shareholders are viewed as outsiders, very much like creditors. This is one of the roots of the "stakeholder" theory which used to dominate German corporate law[38] and continues to be very influential.[39] Its political impact has been considerable. It provided the justification for corporate structures which are designed to keep shareholders from interfering with corporate governance. This is an important aspect of the two-tier-system which mandates the separation of a managing and a supervisory board. Shareholders are not allowed to interfere with management decisions;[40] the same is largely true for the supervisory board.[41] Shareholders face considerable difficulties in removing inefficient management. Members of the managing board can be dismissed by the supervisory board, but this can be done only "for good cause".[42] Members of the supervisory board representing shareholders are elected by a simple majority of the shareholders meeting;[43] but during the four-year term, their replacement requires a majority of at least three quarters of shareholders' votes.[44] In addition, the voting power of large blocks could be restricted.[45] And the large public corporations, including the major banks and insurance companies, retained

---

[36] *Unternehmen an sich.*

[37] The theory is explained and discussed by Mestmäcker, *supra* n. 3, pp. 14 et seq.; Wiethölter, *supra* n. 4, pp. 38 et seq.; Zöllner, Die Schranken mitgliedschaftlicher Stimmrechtsmacht bei den privaten Körperschaften (München: Beck 1963) pp. 70 et seq.

[38] Its most obvious expression is the claim for *Unternehmensverfassung*, a (political) "constitution of the enterprise"; see e.g. Boettcher/ Hax/ Kunz/ von Nele-Breuning/ Ortlieb/ Preller, *Unternehmensverfassung als gesellschaftspolitische Forderung* (Berlin: Duncker & Humblot 1968); Steinmann, *Das Großunternehmen im Interessenkonflikt* (Stuttgart: Poeschel 1969); Th. Raiser, *Das Unternehmen als Organisation* (Berlin: de Gruyter 1969); Ott, *Recht und Realität der Unternehmenskorporation* (Tübingen: Mohr 1977).

[39] For a recent document, see Bertelsmann-Stiftung/Hans Böckler-Stiftung (eds.), *Mitbestimmung und neue Unternehmenskulturen – Bilanz und Perspektiven. Bericht der Kommission Mitbestimmung* (Gütersloh: Berterlsmann-Stiftung 1998).

[40] §§ 76 par. 1, 119 para. 2 AktG.

[41] §§ 76 par. 1, 111 para. 4 AktG.

[42] § 84 para. 3 AktG.

[43] § 101 para. 1 AktG does not require a qualified majority.

[44] §§ 102 para. 1, 103 para. 1 AktG.

[45] § 134 para. 1 sentence 2 AktG. The restriction could be introduced by amending the articles of incorporation (*BGHZ* 70, 117, 121 et seq. (*Mannesmann*)).

a complex system of cross-holdings.[46] All of this was designed to discourage and prevent the *Überfremdung* (alienation) of German corporations by takeovers from abroad. For a long time these patterns were generally accepted. Foreign ownership of German industries was viewed as a threat to national independence and the prospects of the economy. In retrospect these fears do not appear to have been completely irrational. The highly leveraged corporations might have been an easy target for American tender offers. And the foreign acquisition of only a few of the key enterprises might have seriously jeopardized the stability of a corporate system which put managers and employees above shareholders.

c) Codetermination, finally, can be explained as another keystone of the German corporate structure. The representation of employees within the enterprise perfectly fits a stakeholder concept of the firm. Having the top union leaders on the board may have helped to keep wages at a level which allowed effective competition on foreign markets. And codetermination may have had some legitimacy even from a capitalist point of view. As a consequence of the pension commitments, many employees had made considerable financial contributions to the firm.[47] Technically, their investment had been made in the form of debt. But in fact it was long term, and it implied additional risk due to the low ratio of equity capital. Thus, it could be argued that these liabilities show considerable similarity with equity and therefore justify that their beneficiaries be allowed to have a stake in the governance of the corporation.[48]

3. The Japanese analogy

Until the end of World War II, the development of modern law in Japan followed primarily the patterns of continental Europe's codifications. France prevailed in criminal law; the Civil Code from 1898 and the Commercial Code from 1899, which included the rules on partnerships and corporations, were largely inspired by the drafts of the emerging German codification.[49] After 1945, under the impact of the US occupation, Japan shifted its attention to

---

[46] Adams, *supra* n 7.

[47] See third form of financing discussed in c) above.

[48] Steindorff, "Einzelfragen zur Reichweite des Mitbestimmungsgesetzes", 141 *ZHR* (1977) 457, 464; Kübler/ Schmidt/ Simitis, *supra* n. 16, pp. 195.

[49] Murakami, *Einführung in die Grundlagen des japanischen Rechts* (Darmstadt: Wiss. Buchges. 1974) pp. 49 et seq.; Zweigert/ Kötz, *Einführung in die Rechtsvergleichung*, 3rd ed. (Tübingen: Mohr 1996) pp. 289 et seq.

American law.[50] This was particularly true for the organization and the regulation of business: new statutes on antitrust, corporate law and securities regulation adopted the policies and the style of American legislation. This included restrictions on financial institutions. Article 65 of the Securities Exchange Law (SEL) imposed the Glass-Steagall separation of commercial from investment banking;[51] and banks were not allowed to hold more than 5% of the stock of non-financial corporations.[52] In addition, the military government had succeeded in eliminating the *zaibatsus*, the family owned business conglomerates of the pre-war era. Under these circumstances, it could have been expected that Japan's business organization would move towards the Berle-Means model of the independent public corporation. This did not happen. Instead, the *keiretsu* structure emerged.[53] The Japanese economy became dominated by groups of corporations linked by reciprocal (or cross) stock holdings, preferential business relations, and mutual monitoring; very often – but not necessarily – such a group was organized around a main bank.[54] Because a *keiretsu* may comprise more than 20 companies, control can stay within the group even if none of the participants owns more than 5% of the stock of any other.[55]

There may be several reasons why the *keiretsu* emerged. Like the *zaibatsu*, it reflects some of the traditional features of Japanese society: the emphasis on long-term relationships, group responsibility, and resolving conflicts by informal procedures. At the same time, it serves as a mechanism for vertical integration[56] as well as an anti-takeover device.[57] This feature reflects the

---

[50] Zweigert/Kötz, ibid., pp. 292 et seq.; Tanaka, *The Japanese Legal System* (Tokyo: University of Tokyo 1976) pp. 249 et seq.

[51] Roe, *supra* n. 2, p. 1955.

[52] Aoki, *Information, Incentives and Bargaining in the Japanese Economy* (Cambridge: Cambridge University Press 1988) p. 119.

[53] For a comprehensive description, see Aoki, ibid., pp. 116 et seq.; Gerlach, *Alliance Capitalism. The Social Organization of Japanese Business* (Berkeley: University of California Press 1992) pp. 3 et seq.

[54] Gilson/ Roe, "Understanding the Japanese Keiretsu: Overlaps between Corporate Governance and Industrial Organization", 102 *Yale L. J.* (1993) 871, 879; Colin Mayer, "Financial Systems and Corporate Governance: A Review of the International Evidence", 154 *JITE* (1998) 144, 154 et seq.; Milhaupt, "Creative Norm Destruction: The Evolution of Non-Legal Rules in Japanese Corporate Governance" (typoscript 2000, on file with author) 149 *U. Penn. L. Rev* (2001) (forthcoming) p. 4.

[55] Gerlach, *supra* n. 53, at p. 55, assumes that 70 – 75% of the stock of Japanese corporations had been owned by "stable investors", that it is to say: by the other members of the group.

[56] Gilson/ Roe, *supra* n. 54, pp. 885 et seq.

[57] Gilson/ Roe, *supra* n. 54, pp. 987 et seq.; Miwa, "The Economics of Corporate Governance in Japan", in: Hopt et al. (eds.), *Comparative Corporate Governance* (Oxford: Clarendon 1998) pp. 877 et seq., 881.

strategy behind "Deutschland AG",[58] and it may indicate that there are still more similarities between post-war Japan and post-war Germany. In fact, after 1945 Japan was facing very much the same problems we have seen in Germany. The industries had suffered from the war, and they had to be transformed into types of producers which would no longer serve military purposes. At the same time, there was no capital market strong enough to provide sufficient equity for financing the reconstruction.[59] There is strong evidence that in this situation Japanese firms turned to the same financing strategies used in Germany:

a) A main source of funding had been borrowing from banks.[60] The lender was primarily the bank which was a member of the same *keiretsu*. This "main bank" would even step in to bail out a failing *keiretsu* member;[61] in return this bank could rely on an implied promise that the Central Bank would provide financial support if the bank had to exhaust its liquid funds.[62] This may have been necessary since the equity ratio of Japanese corporations was very low, in fact inferior to that in Germany.[63] The commitment to lend support to failing industrial and financial companies helped to stabilize a corporate system which was largely based on debt.
b) Similar to Germany, self-financing by retained earnings had been an important instrument to fund the reconstruction and the expansion of the economy. It even appears that it became more important over time as managers were eager to reduce monitoring of their companies by the main banks.[64] Very much like in Germany, there were no incentives to distribute earnings. Shareholders were not expected to make new contributions; and shareholders' meetings were controlled by the other members of the *keiretsu* who were motivated by the common desire to reinvest their earnings.
c) We even find the third element which we have seen in Germany: deferred compensation of employees. Like in Germany, employment in Japan

---

[58] See text to n. 47 *supra*.

[59] Gerlach, *supra* n. 53, p. 116; Roe, *supra* n. 2, p. 1966 (pointing to the German analogy). There is considerable evidence that groups of companies primarily serve the function of risk sharing in order to compensate for an underdeveloped capital market; see Khanna/ Yafeh, "Business Groups and Risk Sharing around the World"; *Col. L. School Law & Economics Workshop Paper* (March 2001).

[60] Aoki, *supra* n. 52, p. 127.

[61] Gilson/ Roe, *supra* n. 54, p. 879; Mayer, *supra* n. 54, pp. 154 et seq.; Hoshi, "Japanese Corporate Governance as a System", in Hopt et al., *supra* n. 57, 847, 860.

[62] Milhaupt, *supra* n. 54, p. 4 (indicating that from the 1950s to the early 1990s there had been not a single bank failure in Japan.

[63] Jacobi, *supra* n. 25, pp. 55 et seq. and 60.

[64] Kester, *Japanese Takeovers: The Global Contest for Corporate Control* (Boston: Harvard Business School 1991) p. 197; Gilson/Roe, *supra* n. 54, p. 880; Hoshi, *supra* n. 61, p. 172.

tended to be long-term. Workers started with below market wages, but these were offset by supra-market salaries in the later stages of the employees' careers.[65] In between, the retained funds could be used to finance the expansion of operations.

There are also common features beyond corporate finance. During the reconstruction period Japanese, like German firms, were more interested in maximizing growth and market share than profits.[66] This may help to explain why Japanese and German industries were seen as following long term-strategies compared to the "short-termism" of American business. Another aspect of this strategy had been the aim to penetrate foreign markets by pushing the export of locally produced goods to other countries. There had been and still are markets where every player is exposed to stiff competition. It may well be that Japanese and German firms had been in a better position because they were facing much less competition at home. In both countries corporate management was exempt from control by the market for equity and the market for corporate control. Instead, managers were monitored by the managers of other corporations, including those of banks. The mechanisms differ to some extent. In Germany mutual monitoring was and still is primarily achieved through interlocking membership on corporate boards; in Japan the same function is exercised by the "Presidents' Council" within each *keiretsu*.[67] Finally, in both countries cross-holdings successfully served the purpose of discouraging any takeover by a foreign or domestic bidder.[68]

4. THE DECLINE OF THE RECONSTRUCTION ECONOMY

It is evident that both Japan and Germany had been extremely successful in rebuilding their economies after World War II, although their firms no longer had the opportunity to make use of an efficient capital market to broaden their equity basis. Both countries had been able to develop a corporate system which allowed them to finance the reconstruction of their industries in other ways. But it appears no less obvious that both success stories have ended. Since the sudden blow up of its "bubble economy" in the late 1980s, Japan is facing a never-ending economic crisis. And Germany continues to suffer from low growth and

---

[65] Gilson/ Roe, "Lifetime Employment: Labor Peace and the Evolution of Japanese Corporate Governance", 99 *Columbia L. Rev.* (1999) 508, 534; Milhaupt, *supra* n. 54, p. 6.

[66] Roe, *supra* n. 2, p. 1978; Gerlach, *supra* n. 53, p. 30.

[67] Aoki, *supra* n. 52, p. 120; Roe, *supra* n. 2, p. 1943.

[68] In Japan, there had been unfriendly takeovers under the *zaibatsu* system: Milhaupt, *supra* n. 54, p. 9.

high unemployment. We are thus faced with the question why these systems, which had worked so well, all of a sudden ran into increasing problems. Of course, some of the circumstances which had allowed them to emerge did not exist any more. In Japan as well as in Germany wages had gone up, thus both countries had to cope with higher production costs and stiffer price competition on domestic and foreign markets. Even if they were able to maintain a high amount of exports, their industries were facing much higher risks. At the same time, financial markets started to change. With higher incomes, equity markets came back. As a consequence less money was deposited in bank accounts, and banks had less funds for lending to their industrial customers. Perhaps still more important, barriers to the transborder movement of money disappeared. Therefore, large public corporations could raise funds on foreign capital markets but were facing increasing competition from foreign corporations on their home markets. More and more, they had to meet the expectations of foreign – mostly institutional – investors who were looking for high dividends, timely and comprehensive disclosure, and the opportunity to benefit from movements of share prices generated by unfriendly tender offers. Corporations who were unable to offer these advantages and – in addition – had still to cope with preemptive rights and complicated capital requirements, were facing the competitive disadvantages of higher costs for capital.[69] Finally, increased competition provided a much less stable environment for operations. Industries were facing higher risks and therefore had to pay higher rates for their borrowings from banks. German universal banks started to move their activities from risky corporate lending to fee-generating investment banking. Japanese banks had to learn that they were unable to meet the expectations of their *keiretsu* members once several among them were facing liquidity problems and the government was no longer willing or able to continue its bailing out commitments.

Compared with the lasting crisis in Japan, Germany appears to be somewhat better off: so far, it has enjoyed a "soft landing". This is probably due to the fact that the internal market mandated by the European Community has forced all member states to open up their frontiers and adapt at least some of their traditionally rather rigid structures to a more competitive environment. But at the same time the historical analysis suggests that even Germany will have a long way to go in order to remain an attractive place for the incorporation of business, allowing its firms to compete effectively on globalized markets. In

---

[69] This is illustrated by the empirical evidence that German corporations have reduced their costs for capital by switching from German to IAS or US GAAP accounting rules: see Christian Leuz/ Robert Verrechia, "The Economic Consequences of Increased Disclosure" (Finance & Accounting Working Paper, Univ. of Frankfurt, No. 40) *Journal of Accounting Research* (2001) (forthcoming).

many respects the legal framework continues to be shaped by the mechanics of an economy functioning without equity markets. At least some of the rules dealing with accounting,[70] legal capital,[71] preemptive rights,[72] and codetermination,[73] no longer serve the purposes for which they were enacted a long time ago; in various ways they have become a cost and burden needlessly restricting useful economic activities. This allows the conclusion that corporate law reform continues to be desirable.[74]

---

[70] Walz, *supra* n. 35, pp. 557 et seq.; Kübler, "Fragen und Wünsche des Gesellschafts- und Kapitalmarktrechts an das Recht der Rechnungslegung", *ZGR* [2000] 550.

[71] See *supra* n 29.

[72] See Heinsius, "Bezugsrechtsausschluß bei der Schaffung von genehmigtem Kapital", *Festschrift für Kellermann* (Berlin: de Gruyter 1991) 115 et seq.; Martens, "Der Ausschluß des Bezugssrechts", *ZIP* [1992] 1677 et seq.; Kübler, "Sind zwingende Bezugsrechte wirtschaftlich sinnvoll?" *ZBB* [1993] 1.

[73] See Kübler, "Aufsichtsratsmitbestimmung im Zugwind der Globalisierung", in: Freundesgabe für Wulf H. Döser (Baden-Baden: Nomos 1999) 237; Manfred Weiss, "Zur aktuellen Bedeutung des Mitbestimmungsurteils (BVerfGE 50, 290 ff.)", *KritV* [2000] 405.

[74] For a comprehensive analysis of the need for further deregulation of German corporate law see Escher-Weingart, *Reform durch Deregulierung im Kapitalgesellschaft* (Tübingen: Mohr Siebeck 2001).

A Shareholder's Freedom of Contract in Close Corporations – Shareholder Agreements in the USA and Germany

Rainer Kulms*

1. Why shareholder agreements?

"A well-drawn stockholders' agreement entered into contemporaneously with the formation of a corporation is (generally acknowledged to be) the most effective means of protecting the minority shareholder".[1] In authorizing such agreements courts have come to recognize the needs of shareholders in close corporations who want to protect themselves from each other and from hostile

---

* Dr. iur. LL.M. (Michigan), Max Planck Institute, Hamburg.
[1] *Blount* v. *Taft*, 246 S.E. 2d 763 (770) (N.C., 1978).

Talia Einhorn, ed., Spontaneous Order, Organization and the Law –
Liber Amicorum Ernst-Joachim Mestmäcker © *2003* T.M.C.ASSER PRESS, *The Hague, The Netherlands*

invaders.[2] Nowadays, shareholders experience little difficulty in enforcing voting or pooling agreements.[3] But courts feel much more uncomfortable about the implications of shareholder agreements defining the business strategy of the corporation and interfering with the core function of the directors.[4] Both, under German and US states' laws there is uncertainty about the shareholders' freedom of contract and the ground rules governing a contractual relationship between shareholders. This contribution will examine the common intellectual origins of shareholders' agreements under German and US laws. It will demonstrate where German and US corporate laws began to move apart and it will analyze to what extent one legal system might instruct the other.

2. THE SHAREHOLDERS CONTRACT AND THE COURTS REACT

2.1 Early judicial doctrine and public policy

Courts in the US did not welcome shareholders' agreements. In an age where statutes and common law rules focused on corporations with publicly traded stock judges displayed a considerable amount of hostility towards close corporations and contracting shareholders.[5] Voting and other shareholders' agreements were considered to be unenforceable as they were against public policy.[6] A closer look at early case law suggests two basic motives which guided judicial doctrine on shareholders' agreements. One aspect concerns the position of an investor with respect to "his" corporation. The other one is more

---

[2] See generally 1 O'Neal's *Close Corporations*, 3rd ed. (1997) § 4.03 et seq.; 5 *Fletcher Cyclopedia of the Law of Private Corporations*, (1996 ed.) § 2064 et seq.; Clark, *Corporate Law* (1986) 773 et seq.; Klein/ Ramseyer, *Business Associations* (1997) 564 et seq.; for the German law perspective see *infra* part 3.

[3] *Weil* v. *Beresth*, 220 A. 2d 456 (Conn., 1966); *Echols* v. *Brewer*, 524 S.W. 2d 731 (Tex.Civ.App., 1975); *Zion* v. *Kurtz*, 428 N.Y.S. 2d 199 (N.Y., 1980); *Brenner* v. *Hart Systems, Inc.*, 493 N.Y.S. 2d 881 (A.D. 2nd Dept., 1985); *Ramos* v. *Estrada*, 10 Cal Rptr. 2d 833 (Cal.App. 2nd Dist., 1992); *Harrington* v. *Batchelor*, 2001 WL 193791 (Fla.App. 3rd Dist., 2001); Bundesgerichtshof (BGH) May 29, 1967, *BGHZ* 48,163 (172 et seq.); 20 January 1983, *NJW* [1983] 1910, 1911; 27 October 1986, *ZIP* [1987] 293, 295; 7 June 1993 *BGHZ* 123,15, 19.

[4] This is notably a problem for courts in the US: *McQuade* v. *Stoneham*, 189 N.E. 234 (N.Y., 1934) *Long-Park, Inc.* v. *Trenton-New Brunswick Theatres Co. et al.*, 77 N.E. 2d 633 (N.Y., 1948); *Wells Fargo Bank* v. *Superior Court*, 811 P.2d 1025 (1033, per Kennard, J.) (Cal., 1991); 1 *Fletcher Cyclopedia*, *supra* n. 2, § 280; *McDonald* v. *Dalheim*, 683 N.E. 2d 447 (Ohio App. 11th Dist., 1996).

[5] *Gage* v. *Fisher*, 65 N.W. 809 (N.D., 1895); *Harvey* v. *Improvement Co.*, 24 S.E. 489 (N.C., 1896); *Morel* v. *Hoge*, 61 S.E. 487 (Ga., 1908).

[6] *Morel* v. *Hoge*, 61 S.E. 487, 490 (Ga., 1908); cf. 5 *Fletcher Cyclopedia*, *supra* n. 2, § 2064.

fundamental as it is directly related to the role of the state in the development of corporation law.

Early judicial doctrine does not ignore legitimate business interests of investors buying stock. But the very fact that an investor has turned into a shareholder transforms him into a different type of businessman: In pursuing his portfolio strategy he has to be mindful of the best interests of the corporation and of this co-shareholders.[7] In Harvey v. Improvement Co. the Supreme Court of North Carolina declared that "each stockholder . . . must be free to cast his vote . . , the other shareholder being entitled to the benefit of such free exercise of his judgement by each".[8] A valid shareholders' vote is required to be "untrammelled by dictation and unfettered by the obligation of any contract".[9] In this context courts relied on the principle that the right to vote stock cannot be separated from the ownership.[10] This is a regulatory argument founded on the assumption that corporations are creatures or concessions of the state.[11] As late as 1987 the US Supreme Court[12] cited with approval chief Justice Marshall's description of a corporation as "an artificial being, invisible, intangible, and existing only in the contemplation of the law".[13] Thus a corporation "possesses only those properties which the charter of its creation confers upon it".[14] In adhering to the so-called concession theory courts have severely restricted the freedom for shareholders wishing to tailor a corporation to their needs.[15] There was room for side-agreements if the statute or common law would allow for it. Historically concerns about creditor protection and the proper functioning of the capital market dictated the judicial attitude towards contracting around the statute. In Jackson v. Hooper the Court of Errors and Appeals of New Jersey emphasized that the "corporation itself (was) an entity wholly separate and

---

[7] *Cone* v. *Russell*, 21 A. 847, 849 et seq. (N.J.Ch., 1891).

[8] *Harvey* v. *Improvement Co.*, 24 S.E. 489, 490 (N.C., 1896).

[9] Ibid.

[10] *White* v. *Thomas Inflatable Tire Co.*, 28 A. 75, 79 (N.J.Ch., 1893); *Morel* v. *Hoge*, 61 S.E. 487, 490 (Ga., 1908).

[11] Cf. Ribstein, "Limited Liability and Theories of the Corporation", 50 *Md. L.Rev.* (1991) 80, 82.

[12] *CTS Corporation* v. *Dynamics Corporation of America*, 481 U.S. 69, 89 (1987).

[13] *Trustees of Dartmouth College* v. *Woodward*, 17 U.S. 518, 636 (1819)

[14] Ibid.

[15] Ribstein, *supra* n. 11, at p. 92; for a modern statement on the freedom of contract in corporation law see: Bebchuk, "Limiting Contractual Freedom in Corporate Law: The Desirable Constraints on Charter Amendments", 102 *Harv. L.Rev.* (1989) 1820; Gordon, "The Mandatory Structure of Corporate Law", 89 *Colum. L.Rev.* (1989) 1549; Coffee, "The Mandatory/Enabling Balance in Corporate Law: An Essay on the Judicial Role", 89 *Colum. L.Rev.* (1989) 1648; Easterbrook/ Fischel, *The Economic Structure of Corporate Law* (Cambridge, Mass.: Harvard University Press paperback ed. 1996) 15 et seq.

distinct from the individuals who compose and control it".[16] Moreover, the law had never contemplated an incorporated partnership. The stockholders could not be "partners inter sese and a corporation as to the rest of the world".[17]

2.2 Close corporations – shareholders may unite

As close corporations became a more frequently used type of business association the courts in the US began to re-evaluate their position on shareholders' agreements. Characteristically enough, change did come through an evolution of common law rules on corporations; the state legislatures stepped in much later.[18] The traditional capital market philosophy was perceived to be ill-equipped for accommodating the particular concerns of close corporations.[19] The courts acknowledged that shareholders continued being selfish, profit-maximizing business people even after they had bought the shares of the corporation. Shareholders' voting agreements were authorized as long as they would not work to the detriment of the corporation or other shareholders.[20] The language of the Supreme Judicial Court of Massachusetts is indicative of the new approach towards shareholder activism: "It is as legitimate for a majority of stockholders to combine as for other people. The fact that they expect gain and advantage ... to accrue to them does not make the combination unlawful . . . If stockholders want to make their power felt they must unite. There is no reason why a majority should not agree to keep together".[21]

2.2.1 *Voting agreements*

By the 1950s most courts in the US were prepared to authorize agreements in which shareholders undertook to vote their shares in a particular way or not to

---

[16] *Jackson* v. *Hooper*, 75 A. 568, 571 (N.J. Err. & App., 1910).

[17] Ibid.

[18] *Brightman* v. *Bates*, 55 N.E. 809 (Mass., 1900); *Venner* v. *Chicago City Ry.*, 101 N.E. 949 (Ill., 1913); *Manson* v. *Curtis*, 119 N.E. 559 (N.Y., 1918); *Hayden* v. *Beane*, 199 N.E. 755 (Mass., 1936); *Stott* v. *Stott*, 242 N.W. 747 (Mich., 1932); *Galler* v. *Galler*, 203 N.E. 2d 577, 581 et seq. (Ill., 1965); *Blount* v. *Taft*, 246 S.E. 2d 763, 769 et seq. (N.C., 1978); *Neuman* v. *Pike*, 591 F. 2d 191, 194 (2nd Cir., 1979) (New York law); *Lane* v. *Abel–Bey*, 430 N.Y.S. 2d 41 (N.Y., 1980); *Penley* v. *Penley*, 332 S.E. 51 (N.C., 1985); 5 *Fletcher Cyclopedia*, *supra* n. 2, §§ 2064, 2064.1.

[19] See *Blount* v. *Taft*, 246 S.E. 2d 763, 769 et seq. (N.C., 1978).

[20] O'Neals *Close Corporations*, *supra* n. 2, §§ 5.02, 5.03; Krüger, "Corporate Pooling Agreements and Restriction-of-Directors Agreements", 10 *Anglo-Am. L.J.* (1981) 73.

[21] *Brightman* v. *Bates*, 55 N.E. 809, 810 et seq. (Mass., 1900).

vote in a particular way.[22] Voting agreements would be invalidated if they contemplated fraud upon other shareholders or upon creditors of the corporation.[23] Voting agreements would also be void if they would not work to the benefit of all shareholders equally[24] or if they were to accomplish a purpose forbidden by law.[25] Delaware ceased to classify voting arrangements as an illegal device to undermine the statutory rules on voting trusts[26] which require that the voting rights be divorced from the ownership of stock.[27] Nowadays, Delaware courts advocate a "liberal approach to all contractual arrangements limiting the incidents of stock ownership".[28]

2.2.2 *Close corporations and the capital market*

The judicial acceptance of shareholder voting agreements might be read as an attempt to reconcile traditional concepts of corporate theory with the absence of a working capital market. Shareholder agreements are concluded when the decision-making process in a corporation is not scrutinized by the capital market.[29] Efficient bargaining insures the shareholders of a close corporation against a loss of their investment through an abuse of power where otherwise the market would have helped had there been a corporation with publicly traded stock:[30] The bargaining shareholders of a close corporation substitute the capital

---

[22] Klein/ Ramseyer, *supra* n. 2, 564 et seq., 578 et seq.; 5 *Fletcher Cyclopedia, supra* n. 2, § 2066 (Cumulative Supplement 2000).

[23] *Fletcher Cyclopedia, supra* n. 2, § 2066 (Cumulative Supplement 2000).

[24] *Bostwick* v. *Chapman*, 24 A. 32 (Conn.Super., 1890); *Kreissl* v. *Distilling Co. of America*, 47 A 471 (N.J.Ch., 1900); *White* v. *Snell*, 100 P. 927 (Utah, 1909); *Bowditch* v. *Jackson Co.*, 82 A. 1014 (N.H., 1912); *Luedke* v. *Oleen*, 4 N.W. 2d 201 (N.D., 1942); *Ringling* v. *Ringling Brothers – Barnum & Bailey, Comb. Shows.*, 49 A. 2d 603 (Del. Ch., 1946); *Schwartz* v. *Miner*, 146 A. 2d 801 (Del.Ch., 1958).

[25] *Hoggett* v. *Brown*, 971 S.W. 2d 472 (Tex.App., 1997).

[26] *Oceanic Exploration Company* v. *Grynberg*, 428 A. 2d 1 (5 et seq.) (Del., 1981), overruling *Abercrombie* v. *Davies*, 130 A. 2d 338, 346 et seq. (Del., 1957).

[27] Del. C § 218; cf. *Peyton* v. *William Peyton Corporation*, 194 A. 106, 111 (Del.Ch., 1937).

[28] *Schreiber* v. *Carney*, 447 A. 2d 17, 25 (Del.Ch., 1982).

[29] Hochstetter/Svejda, "Statutory Needs of Close Corporations – An Empirical Study: Special Close Corporation Legislation or Flexible Corporation Law?"10 *J.Corp.L.* (1985) 852, 904 et seq., 933 et seq.; Garza, "Rethinking Corporate Governance: The Role of Minority Shareholders – A Comparative Study", 31 *St. Mary's L.J.* (2000) 615, 649 et seq.; cf. *Blount* v. *Taft*, 246 S.E. 763, 769 et seq. (N.C., 1978); *Donahue* v. *Rodd Electrotype Company of New England, Inc.*, 328 N.E. 2d 505, 515 et seq. (Mass., 1975).

[30] See analysis in: *Nixon* v. *Blackwell*, 626 A 2d 1366, 1379 (Del., 1993); *G & N Aircraft, Inc.* v. *Boehm*, 743 N.E. 227, 244 (Ind., 2001); *Simmons* v. *Miller*, 544 S.E. 2d 666, 675 (Va., 2001) and Peeples, "The Use and Misuse of the Business Judgement in the Close Corporation", 60 *Notre Dame L.Rev.* (1985) 456, 469 et seq.

market by contractual design.[31] Nonetheless, courts in the US have had considerable difficulty in accommodating shareholder agreements which employ market standards as incentive or renegotiation mechanisms for the daily life of a close corporation.[32] The judiciary finds it equally problematic to reconstruct market mechanisms once the relationship among the shareholders of a close corporation has deteriorated.[33]

2.3 The response of state legislatures

Most states have enacted specific legislation on shareholders' agreements. As to legislative technique some states lay down the ground rules for voting trusts and provide for an exemption for shareholders' voting agreements.[34] Others have modelled their respective corporation law provisions on § 7.31 of the Model Business Corporation Act (MBCA):[35] A voting agreement between two

---

[31] In fact, corporation law serves as an incentive to negotiate: *Bagdon* v. *Bridgestone/ Firestone, Inc.*, 916 F. 2d 379, 384 (7th Cir., 1990): " . . .Corporations are *not* partnerships. Whether to incorporate entails a choice of many formalities. Commercial rules should be predictable; this objective is best served by treating corporations as what they are, allowing the investors and other participants to vary the rules by contract if they think deviations are warranted. . . " (Delaware law); but see the sceptical approach towards bargaining processes in: *Meiselman* v. *Meiselman*, 307 S.E. 2d 551, 558 (N.C., 1983).

[32] *Crowder Construction Co.* v. *Kiser*, 517 S.E. 2d 178, 190 et seq. (N.C.App., 1999) (Book value clause in Shareholder Stock Purchase Agreement); *Royals et al.* v. *Piedmont Electric Repair Co.*, 529 S.E. 2d 515, 517 et seq. (N.C.App., 2000) (Shareholder Restriction Agreement); and Delaware's refusal to develop special rules for a "closely-held corporation": *Nixon* v. *Blackwell*, 626 A. 2d 1366, 1379 et seq. (Del., 1993); Ragazzo, "Toward a Delaware Common Law of Closely Held Corporations", 77 *Wash.U.L.Q.* (1999) 1099.

[33] See the detailed analysis of the various approaches towards the fairness test in the majority-minority relationship: *Lerner* v. *Lerner Corporation*, 750 A. 2d 709, 721 et seq. (Md. App., 2000) (all fairness test); *Meiselman* v. *Meiselman*, 307 S.E. 2d 551, 563 et seq. (N.C., 1983) (Reasonable expectations); *Exadaktilos* v. *Cinnaminson Realty Co., Inc.*, 400 A. 2d 554, 559 (N.J.Super.L., 1979) (Business Judgment Rule). – Courts are reluctant to allow minority shareholders to sue under an individual or derivative action in case of breach of a fiduciary duty: *Bordelon* v. *Cochrane*, 533 So. 2d 82, 85 et seq. (La.App., 1988); *G & N Aircraft, Inc.* v. *Boehm*, 743 N.E. 2d 227, 244 et seq. (Ind., 2001); *Simmons* v. *Miller*, 544 S.E. 2d 666, 675 (Va., 2001).

[34] 8 Del.Code Ann. § 218; Hawaii Rev. Stat. § 415-34; Mich.Stat.Ann. § 21.200 (461); Minn.Stat.Ann. §§ 302A 455, 302A 457 (West); Ohio Rev.Code Ann. § 1701.49; Tenn.Code Ann. § 48-17-302; Tex.Bus.Corp.Act Ann. (Vernon) Art. 2.30B; W.Va. Code Ann. § 31-1-94.

[35] § 7.31 MBCA: "(a) Two or more shareholders may provide for the manner in which they will vote their shares by signing an agreement for that purpose. A voting agreement created under this section is not subject to the provisions of section 7.30. (b) A voting agreement created under this section is specifically enforceable."

Ala.Code § 10-2B-7.31; Ark.Code Ann. § 4-27-731; Ariz.Rev.Stat.Ann. § 10-731; Cal.Corporations Code Ann. § 706; Colo.Rev.Stat. § 7-107-302; Conn.Gen.Stat.sec. 33-716; Ga.Code Ann. § 14-2-731; Fla.Stat.Ann. § 607.0731; Idaho Code § 30-1-731; Ill.C.S.Ann. Ch. 805 § 5/

or more shareholders is invalid if it is not in writing. Utah even recognizes agreements where one of the parties is not a shareholder.[36] Many states impose a maximum initial period of ten years for a voting agreement. Georgia and Tennessee invalidate voting agreements that exceed a period of more than 20 years.[37] Most state corporation laws provide for the specific enforcement of voting agreements. The MBCA also seeks to modify common law rules on shareholder agreements on matters traditionally within the realm of the directors of a corporation: With respect to close corporations § 7.32 MBCA[38]

7.70; Ind.Stat.Ann. § 23-1-31-2; Iowa Code Ann. § 490.731; Me.Rev.Stat.Ann.tit 13A § 617; Mass.ALM.GL.c.156 § 41A; Miss.Code Ann. § 79-4-7.31; Mont.Code Ann. § 35-1-533; N.H.Rev.Stat.Ann. § 293-A: 7.31; Neb.Rev.Stat. § 21-2068; N.J.Stat.Ann. § 14A:5-21; N.Y.Bus.Corp.L.Ann. § 620; N.C.Gen.Stat § 55-7-31; 15 Pa.Cons.Stat.Ann. § 1768(b); S.C. Code Ann. § 33-7-310; Vt.Stat.Ann.tit 11A § 7.31; Va.Code Ann § 13.1.671; Wash.Rev. Code Ann. § 23.B.07.310; Wis.Stat.Ann. § 180.0731; Wyo.Stat.Ann. § 17-16-731.

[36] Utah Code Ann. § 16-10a-731

[37] Ga.Code Ann. § 14-2-731; Tenn.Code Ann. § 48-17-302

[38] § 7.32 MBCA: "(a) An agreement among the shareholders of a corporation that complies with this section is effective among the shareholders and the corporation even though it is inconsistent with one or more other provisions of this Act in that it:
(1) eliminates the board of directors or restricts the discretion or powers of the board of directors;
(2) governs the authorization or making of distributions whether or not in proportion to ownership of shares, subject to limitations in section 6.40;
(3) establishes who shall be directors of officers of the corporation, or their terms of office or manner of selection or removal;
(4) governs, in general or in regard to specific matters, the exercise or division of voting power by or between the shareholders and directors or by or among any of them, including use of weighted voting rights or director proxies;
(5) establishes the terms and conditions of any agreement for the transfer or use of property or the provision of services between the corporation and any shareholder, director, officer or employee of the corporation or among any of them;
(6) transfers to one or more shareholders or other persons all or a part of the authority to exercise the corporate powers or to manage the business and affairs of the corporation, including the resolution of any issue about which there exists a deadlock among directors or shareholders;
(7) requires dissolution of the corporation at the request of one or more of the shareholders or upon the occurrence of a specified event or contingency; or
(8) otherwise governs the exercise of the corporate powers or the management of the business and affairs of the corporation or the relationship among the shareholders, the directors and the corporation, or among any of them, and is not contrary to public policy.
(b) An agreement authorized by this section shall be:
(1) set forth (A) in the articles of incorporation or bylaws and approved by all persons who are shareholders at the time of the agreement or (B) in a written agreement that is signed by all persons who are shareholders at the time of the agreement and is made known to the corporation;
(2) subject to amendment only by all persons who are shareholders at the time of the amendment, unless the agreement provides otherwise; and
(3) valid for 10 years, unless the agreement provides otherwise.
(c) The existence of an agreement authorized by this section shall be noted conspicuously on the

proposes to authorize shareholder agreements which restrict the powers of the directors or provide for specific (weighted) voting rights for certain shareholders. Many states now allow control agreements if they are part of the articles of incorporation or if, subsequent to incorporation, all shareholders have signed a corresponding document.[39] Such control agreements become ineffective when the shares of the corporation are listed on national securities exchanges or regularly traded in a market maintained by members of a national

---

front or back each certificate for outstanding shares or on the information statement required by section 6.26 (b). If at the time of the agreement the corporation has shares outstanding represented by certificates, the corporation shall recall the outstanding certificates and issue substitute certificates that comply with this subsection. The failure to note the existence of the agreement on the certificate or information statement shall not affect the validity of the agreement or any action taken pursuant to it. Any purchaser of shares who, at the time of purchase, did not have knowledge of the existence of the agreement shall be entitled to rescission of the purchase. A purchaser shall be deemed to have knowledge of the existence of the agreement if its existence is noted on the certificate or information statement for the shares in compliance with this subsection and, if the shares are not represented by a certificate, the information statement is delivered to the purchaser at or prior to the time of purchase of the shares. An action to enforce the right of rescission authorized by this subsection must be commenced within the earlier of 90 days after discovery of the existence of the agreement or two years after the time of purchase of the shares.
(d) An agreement authorized by this section shall cease to be effective when shares of the corporation are listed on a national securities exchange or regularly traded in a market maintained by one or more members of a national or affiliated securities association. If the agreement ceases to be effective for any reason, the board of directors may, if the agreement is contained or referred to in the corporation's articles of incorporation or bylaws, adopt an amendment to the articles of incorporation or bylaws, without shareholder action, to delete the agreement and any references to it.
(e) An agreement authorized by this section that limits the discretion or powers of the board of directors shall relieve the directors of, and impose upon the person or persons in whom such discretion or powers are vested, liability for acts or omissions imposed by law on directors to the extent that the discretion or powers of the directors are limited by the agreement.
(f) The existence or performance of an agreement authorized by this section shall not be a ground for imposing personal liability on any shareholder for the acts or debts of the corporation even if it were a partnership or results in failure to observe the corporate formalities otherwise applicable to the matters governed by the agreement.
(g) Incorporators or subscribers for shares may act as shareholders with respect to an agreement authorized by this section if no shares have been issued when the agreement is made.

[39] Ala.Code § 10-2B-7.32; Alaska Stat. § 10.06.424; Ariz.Rev.Stat.Ann. § 10-732; Conn.Gen.Stat. § 33-717; Fla.Stat.Ann. § 607.0732; Ga.Code Ann. § 14-2-732; Idaho Code § 30-1-732; Ill.C.S.Ann. Ch. 805 § 5/7.71; Me.Rev.Stat.Ann. tit. 13A § 618; Mich.Stat.Ann. § 21.200 (488); MinnStat.Ann. § 302A. 457; Miss.Code Ann. § 79-4-7.32; N.C.Gen.Stat. § 55-7-31 (outsiders may be a party to the agreement); Neb.Rev.Stat. § 21-2069; N.H.§ 293 –A:7.32; Or.Rev.Stat. § 60.265; Tenn.Code Ann. § 48-17-302; Tex.Bus.CorpActAnn. (Vernon) Art. 2.30-1. Utah § 16-10a-732; Va.Code Ann. § 13.1.-671.1; Wash.Rev.Code Ann. § 23B.07.320; Wyo.Stat.Ann. § 17-15-732.

securities association.[40] In accordance with § 7.32 MBCA state law shifts liability from the directors of the corporation to the shareholders who are parties to the control agreement.[41] Partnership law may be applicable to the agreement. But the very existence of such an agreement shall not be a ground for holding a shareholder personally liable for acts or omission of the corporation.[42] It is noteworthy that neither state law nor § 7.32 MBCA attempt to lay down any further substantive rules on how to make market mechanisms work within a close corporation.

3. SHAREHOLDER AGREEMENTS UNDER GERMAN CORPORATION LAW

3.1 Early hostility

3.1.1 *The "healthy functioning" of the corporation...*

In 1884 the German government presented a reform bill on stock corporations to parliament. The official report on the preparatory works does not mince its words as to the capital market interests of shareholders: "The shareholders . . . do not entertain any personal relationship with the enterprise, (they) . . . do not intend to assume responsibility with respect to the amount of their investment. Instead they expect to receive maximum dividends without abandoning the prospect of retiring from the enterprise through a sale of stock at any given time".[43] The report cautions against extending individual shareholders' rights as this would endanger "the organization and healthy functioning of the corporation".[44] *Gierke* who had investigated the "spheres of corporative life" of co-operatives (*körperschaftliche Lebenssphäre*)[45] provided the intellectual underpinnings for stock corporations: Stock corporations were built on a social concept of organizing the individual wills of their member-shareholders

---

[40] Alabama, Alaska, Arizona, Connecticut, Florida, Georgia, Idaho, Maine, Michigan, Mississippi, North Carolina, Nebraska, New Hampshire, Oregon, Texas, Utah, Virginia (applicable to corporations with 300 shareholders or less), Washington, Wyoming; see supra N. 39.

[41] Alabama, Connecticut, Florida, Georgia, Idaho, Michigan, Minnesota, Mississippi, North Carolina, Nebraska, New Hampshire, Oregon, Tennessee, Texas, Utah, Washington, Wyoming; see supra N. 39.

[42] Alabama, Connecticut, Florida, Georgia, Idaho, Michigan, Mississippi, Nebraska, New Hampshire, Oregon, Texas, Utah, Washington, Wyoming; see supra N. 39.

[43] Entwurf eines Gesetzes betreffend die Kommanditgesellschaft auf Aktien über die Aktiengesellschaft of 7 March 1887; in: Schubert/ Hommelhoff (eds.), *Hundert Jahre modernes Aktienrecht* (1985) 386, 412 (translated by author).

[44] Ibid., 466.

[45] Gierke, *Die Genossenschaftstheorie und die Deutsche Rechtsprechung* (1887) 637.

(*Prinzip sozialrechtlicher Willensorganisation*). Shareholders could ask for the protection of the "sphere of corporative life" and challenge any attempt to wipe out their investment.[46] It is against this doctrinal background that the German parliament passed the 1892 law on close corporations (*Gesellschaft mit beschränkter Haftung (GmbH)*).[47] This new type of business organization was designed to address the needs of enterprises where a limited group of shareholders would be prepared to make an investment.[48] The official report on the 1892 law puts considerable faith in the personal ties among shareholders. Shareholders of close corporations are described as more willing to inject additional money should business necessities so dictate.[49] The stock of a *GmbH (Geschäftsanteile)* is freely tradable. But, in fact the German *GmbH* is quite remote from traditional capital market influences. The official report on the 1892 law makes it clear that "membership" (*Mitgliedschaft*) in a close corporation is expected to be of a long-term nature.[50] Today, shareholder agreements restricting the transferability of stock are quite common.[51]

3.1.2 ... *as explained by the Reichsgericht*

Although the *GmbH* was on the statutebook before the turn of the last century and the directors were subject to the instructions of the shareholders[52] German corporation law principles did not start moving ahead of their US counterparts. Instead the German Supreme Court, the *Reichsgericht*, was just as hostile to shareholder voting agreements as US courts around 1900. The *Reichsgericht* ruling of 16 March 1904 invalidates a voting agreement between the

---

[46] Gierke, ibid., 249

[47] RGBl. 477; cf. Birkenbihl, *Das Reichsgesetz betreffend die Gesellschaften mit beschränkter Haftung vom 20. April 1892* (1893) 1 et seq., on the legislative history of the 1892 law on close corporations (*GmbH-Gesetz*).

[48] Birkenbihl, ibid., 9.

[49] Quoted from Birkenbihl, *supra* n. 47, 10; on current GmbH law and on the importance of the close corporation (GmbH) as a standard type of business organization in Germany cf. Lutter/ Hommelhoff, *GmbH-Gesetz*, 15th ed. (2000) Einleitung Rn. 1 et seq.

[50] Birkenbihl, *supra* n. 47, 104.

[51] Baumann/ Reiß, "Satzungsergänzende Vereinbarungen – Nebenverträge im Gesellschaftsrecht", *ZGR* [1989] 157, 184; Zöllner, in: Henze/ Timm/ Westermann (eds.), *RWS-Forum 8, Gesellschaftsrecht* (1996) 89, 93; Noack, *Gesellschaftervereinbarungen bei Kapitalgesellschaften* (1994), 282 et seq.; cf. Lutter, "Die Rechte und Pflichten des Vorstands bei der Übertragung vinkulierter Namensaktien", *AG* [1992] 369; Reichert/ Winter, in: Lutter/ Ulmer/ Zöllner (eds.), *Festschrift 100 Jahre GmbH-Gesetz* (1992) 209, 210 et seq.; Hoffmann-Becking, "Der Einfluß schuldrechtlicher Gesellschaftervereinbarungen auf die Rechtsbeziehungen in der Kapitalgesellschaft", *ZGR* [1994] 442, 443.

[52] See § 37 GmbH-Gesetz and Hommelhoff, "Unternehmensführung in der mitbestimmten GmbH", *ZGR* [1978] 119, 121.

shareholders of a close corporation *(GmbH)*[53]. The *Reichsgericht* feels that such an agreement is incompatible with public policy and the core functions of a corporation[54]. The *Reichsgericht* recites arguments very similar to those advanced by US courts at that time: The individual shareholder is not entitled to restrict his freedom to vote stock by an act of contractual arbitrariness. With respect to a vote in a shareholders' meeting such an agreement would deprive him of the opportunity to freely exercise his judgement on what was in the best interest of the corporation[55]. The judicial hostility is motivated by the fear that voting agreements might work to the detriment of minorities[56]. Change did come in the early 1920s when the *Reichsgericht* reconsidered its classification of voting agreements.

3.2 Voting agreements in the *Reichsgericht* – 1923 and after

The ruling of 19 June 1923[57] is not marked by an outspoken awareness of capital market issues or an appreciation of shareholder investment behaviour. Instead, the *Reichsgericht* describes a voting agreement as a special obligation separate from the articles of incorporation. As to legal doctrine the *Reichsgericht* strikes a balance between a shareholder's freedom of contract and established principles of corporation law. The shareholder's position as a member of a corporation does not affect his right to enter into a voting agreement to be exclusively construed in accordance with the law of obligations.[58] In refusing specific enforcement of a voting agreement the *Reichsgericht* shows a preference for corporative procedures for ascertaining the "will" of the corporation *(Verbandswillen)*.[59] It is unclear whether this approach is motivated by corporate efficiency considerations or a somewhat diffuse notion of minority protection.[60]

The *Reichsgericht* cases on shareholder agreements do not differentiate between corporations with publicly traded stock and close corporations. The court remains faithful to *Gierke*'s idea of the "sphere of corporative life"

---

[53] Reichsgericht (RG) 16 March 1904, *RGZ* 57,205, 208.

[54] Ibid.

[55] See also: RG 7 June 1908, *RGZ* 69, 134, 137, and Müller-Erzbach, *Das private Recht der Mitgliedschaft als Prüfstein eines kausalen Rechtsdenkens* (1948) 249.

[56] R. Fischer, in: *Festschrift Kunze* (1969) 95, 99.

[57] RG 19 June 1923, *RGZ* 107, 67.

[58] RG 19 June 1923, *RGZ* 107, 67, 70; see also RG 11 June 1931, *RGZ* 133, 90, 95.

[59] RG 20 November 1925, *RGZ* 112, 273, 279; 10 January 1928, *RGZ* 119, 386, 390; 12 October 1940, *RGZ* 165, 68, 78 et seq.; see comment by Fischer, *supra* n. 56, 103.

[60] See criticism by Fischer, "Zulässigkeit und Wirkung von Abstimmungsvereinbarungen", *GmbHR* [1953] 65, 68; generally on aspects of minority protection: Zöllner, in: Henze/ Timm/ Westermann, *supra* n. 51, 89, 104.

(körperschaftliche Lebenssphäre)[61] of a corporation where the social concept of organizing the individual wills of their members *(Prinzip sozialrechtlicher Willensorganisation)*[62] matters more than shareholder investment interests.[63] Moreover, the *Reichsgericht* would not have subscribed to the proposition of Illinois and Massachusetts courts that shareholders may unite to make their power felt.[64] In spite of the judicial verdicts the issue lingered on whether the legal regime for a corporation did not, in fact, consist of both, corporative rules and shareholder agreements fleshing them out.[65]

3.3 **Post-War acceptance: voting agreements and close corporations**

3.3.1 *Bundesgerichtshof*

The *Bundesgerichtshof*, the post-war German Federal Supreme Court, began to move away from the *Reichsgericht* doctrine when it addressed the particular problems of voting agreements in close corporations (*GmbHs*). The *Bundesgerichtshof* ruling of 29 May 1967 authorizes the specific enforcement of shareholder voting agreements.[66] The court expressly recognizes that shareholder agreements may constitute a breach of the articles of incorporation (*Satzung*). Nonetheless, shareholder agreements initiated without observing the established procedures for an amendment of the *Satzung* are deemed to be lawful as long as they do not change the organizational structure of the close corporation.[67] Subsequent holdings have confirmed this approach.[68] From the

---

[61] *Supra* n. 45.

[62] *Supra* n. 46.

[63] Cf. *Exadaktilos* v. *Cinnaminson Realty Co.*, 400 A 2d 554, 561 (N.J.Super.L., 1979); *Balvik* v. *Sylvester*, 411 N.W. 2d 383, 386 (N.D., 1987); and Moll, "Shareholder Oppression in Close Corporations: The Unanswered Question of Perspective", 53 *Vanderbilt L.Rev.* (2000) 749, 793 et seq., on the investment interests of shareholders in a close corporation. From an agency theory point of view: Fama, "Agency Problems and the Theory of the Firm", 88 *J. Pol. Econ.* (1980) 288. German law tends to resolve this conflict by alluding to "membership" aspects (*Mitgliedschaft*) of being a shareholder, see: K. Schmidt, *Gesellschaftsrecht*, 3rd ed. (1997) 556 et seq., and Lutter, "Theorie der Mitgliedschaft – Prolegomena zu einem Allgemeinen Teil des Korporationsrechts", 180 *AcP* (1980), 84, 88 et seq.

[64] Cf. *Brightman* v. *Bates*, 55 N.E. 809, 810 (Mass., 1900); *Venner* v. *Chicago City Ry.*, 101 N.E. 949, 953 (Ill., 1913).

[65] See Noack's analysis, *supra* n. 51, 75; and Hoffmann-Becking, *supra* n. 51, 445.

[66] Bundesgerichtshof (BGH) 29 May 1967, *BGHZ* 48, 163, 172 et seq.; and BGH 20 January 1983, *NJW* [1983] 1910, 1911; 27 October 1986, *ZIP* [1987] 293, 295.

[67] BGH 7 June 1993, *BGHZ* 123, 15, 19, and Priester, "Satzungsänderungen und Satzungsdurchbrechung", 151 *ZHR* [1987] 40, 52 et seq.; Habersack, "Unwirksamkeit 'zustandsbegründender' Durchbrechungen der GmbH-Satzung sowie darauf gerichteter schuldrechtlicher Nebenabreden", *ZGR* [1994] 354, 363 et seq.

[68] See cases cited *supra* n. 66, 67.

perspective of US state corporation laws the *Bundesgerichtshof* cases are halfway between § 7.31 MBCA and § 7.32 MBCA. In validating voting agreements the *Bundesgerichtshof* honours shareholders' attempts to unite to make their power felt[69] and to pursue particular investment strategies. Under German law a shareholder voting agreement may operate as a control agreement. As the law on close corporations (*GmbH-Gesetz*) does not disallow shareholder instructions to the director of a close corporation a voting agreement may lawfully cover matters within the directors' realm.[70] It is for this reason that the *Bundesgerichtshof* insists on an all-shareholders' voting agreement. The court is cautious on liability issues. This may be due to the fact that German law is far from being clear on whether the equivalent of partnership law should be applied to close corporations where the shareholders "take over".[71]

3.3.2 *Whither shareholder agreements?*

It is doubtful whether present German case law may be read as to condone shareholder agreements as a device for optimizing a close corporation through private incentive and renegotiation mechanisms.[72] Legal writing promises a spirited debate on any such attempt.[73] Courts are likely to be ill-prepared to apply capital market standards once a shareholder agreement and a close corporation break apart.[74] Moreover, a major obstacle to incorporating extensive

---

[69] Cf. *Venner* v. *Chicago City Ry.*, 101 N.E. 949, 953 (Ill., 1913).

[70] § 37 GmbH-Gesetz; for a detailed commentary on this section: Lutter/ Hommelhoff, *supra* n. 49, § 37 Rn. 1 et seq.

[71] Fischer's proposal, "Das Recht der OHG als ergänzende Rechtsquelle zum GmbH-Gesetz", *GmbHR* [1953] 131, 132 et seq., to supplement the law on close corporations by partnership rules has not been taken up. Cf. K. Schmidt, *Gesellschaftsrecht*, *supra* n. 63, 983 et seq.

[72] Cf. Westermann, "Das Verhältnis von Satzung und Nebenordnungen in der Kapitalgesellschaft", *Hachenburg-Gedächtnisvorlesung* (1994) 42 et seq., and Zöllner's cautious analysis in: Henze/ Timm/ Zimmermann, *supra* n. 51, 104. See generally on side-agreements ensuring the realization of corporate strategies: Bamberg/ Coenenberg, *Betriebswirtschaftliche Entscheidungslehre*, 9th ed. (1996) 183; Ramakrishnan/ Thakor, "Cooperation versus Competition in Agency", 7 *J.L.Econ. & Org.* (1991) 248, 249 et seq.; and Easterbrook/ Fischel, *supra* n. 15, 16 et seq. on the corporate contract.

[73] See: Winter, "Organisationsrechtliche Sanktionen bei Verletzungen schuldrechtlicher Gesellschaftervereinbarungen?", 154 *ZHR* [1990] 259, 261 et seq.; Ulmer, "Verletzung schuldrechtlicher Nebenverträge als Anfechtungsgrund im GmbH-Recht", *NJW* [1987] 1849, 1850 et seq.; Lutter/ Hommelhoff, *supra* n. 49, § 3 Rn. 47; Hoffmann-Becking, *supra* n. 51, 450.

[74] German legal doctrine refuses to apply corporation law rules for listed corporations to close corporations: Martens, in: Lutter/ Ulmer/ Zöllner (eds.), *Festschrift 100 Jahre GmbH-Gesetz* (1992), 607, 615; Grunewald, "Die Auslegung von Gesellschaftsverträgen und Satzungen", *ZGR* [1995] 68, 81 et seq.; Zöllner/ Noack, "Die Geltendmachung von Beschlußmängeln im GmbH-Recht", *ZGR* [1989] 525, 541 et seq.; Zöllner, in: Henze/ Timm/ Westermann, *supra* n. 51, 89, 100 et seq.

private contracting into close corporations appears to be the enshrined principle that a corporation is "wholly separate and distinct" from its shareholders.[75] But then, the question is whether this is an adequate description of close corporations where shareholders contract for partnership-like arrangements in the absence of capital market influences.[76]

4. Market mechanisms v. shareholder agreements and close corporations?

Close corporations are special.[77] There is no market for shares in the close corporation and, unlike partnerships, a dissolution is not readily available.[78] Minority shareholders may be trapped in a freeze-out situation engineered by the majority without any perspective of reclaiming the capital. In authorizing stockholder agreements the courts (and, to a lesser extent, the US states' legislatures) have accepted the "personalization" of close corporations.[79] Shareholder agreements have to be construed in accordance with the law of contract rules on interpretation[80] and internally, partnership law may be applicable to close

---

[75] Compare the language in: *Jackson* v. *Hooper*, 75 A. 568, 571 (N.J.Err. & App., 1910), with Ulmer, *supra* n. 73, *NJW* [1987] 1849, 1853, and Winter, *supra* n. 73, 154 *ZHR* [1990] 259, 270 et seq.

[76] Cf. Zöllner, in: Henze/ Timm/ Westermann, *supra* n. 51, 110; Mestmäcker, *Organisationen in spontanen Ordnungen* (1992) 23; and Becker's proposition, in: *Verwaltungskontrolle durch Gesellschafterrechte* (1997) 4 et seq., 780 et seq., to compensate shareholders for the absence of an efficient control through capital market mechanisms by extending their right to challenge acts of the corporation in court.

[77] *Donahue* v. *Rodd Electrotype Co.*, 328 N.E. 2d 505, 515 (Mass., 1975); *Meiselman* v. *Meiselman*, 307 S.E. 551, 557 et seq. (N.C. 1983); Easterbrook/ Fischel, *supra* n. 15, 228 et seq.; F. Hodge O'Neal, "Close Corporations: Existing Legislation and Recommended Reform", 33 *Bus. Law.* (1978) 873, 884 et seq.; K. Schmidt, *Gesellschaftsrecht*, *supra* n. 63, 996 et seq.

[78] Every US state has a dissolution statute now to address issues of shareholder deadlocks or oppression of the majority: Cox/ Hazen/ O'Neal, *Corporations* Vol. II (2000), §§ 14.12, 14.14, cf. *Meiselman* v. *Meiselman*, 295 S.E. 2d 249, 253 (F2) (N.C. App.,1982); *Royals* v. *Piedmont Electric Repair Company*, 529 S.E. 2d 515, 517 et seq. (N.C. App., 2000).

[79] Courts have given up their hostility to close corporations as secret partnership agreements: *Bostwick* v. *Chapman*, 24 A. 32, 35 et seq. (Conn.Super., 1890); *Benintendi* v. *Kenton Hotel, Inc.*, 60 N.E. 829, 831 (N.Y., 1945); and recognize that a close corporation may be lawfully organized as a partnership: *Arditi* v. *Dubitzky*, 354 F. 2d 483, 486 et seq. (2nd Cir., 1965); *Donahue* v. *Rodd Electrotype Co. of New England*, 328 N.E. 2d 505, 592 et seq. (Mass., 1975); *Blount* v. *Taft*, 246 S.E. 2d 763, 771 et seq. (N.C., 1978); *Meiselman* v. *Meiselman*, 307 S.E. 2d 551, 557 et seq. (N.C., 1983).

[80] *Sanders Corporation* v. *Haves*, 541 S.W. 2d 262, 264 (Tex.Civ.App. Dallas, 1976); *Blount* v. *Taft*, 246 S.E. 2d 763, 771 et seq. (N.C. 1978); *Cooper* v. *Gottlieb*, 2000 WL 1277593 (S.D.N.Y., 2000).

corporations.[81] Under some circumstances, the action of all the shareholders of a close corporation binds the corporation.[82]

In the US, the analogy between close corporations and partnerships should not be understood as to ratify any shareholder scheme purporting to "optimize" a corporation where capital market influences are hardly felt. The courts step in to clarify the relationship between statutes and common law rules on fiduciary duties owed to minority shareholders.[83] It is common ground that the directors and the majority of a close corporation owe a fiduciary duty not to wipe out a minority shareholder's investment.[84] And yet, there are two schools of thought to ascertain when the minority in a close corporation is so oppressed that it may ask for court protection. Arguably, a fiduciary duty has been breached when the directors or the majority do not live up to the expectations of the minority.[85] But this interpretation ignores the capital market-related function of an investment into a close corporation.[86] Many U.S. courts have adopted an institutionalist approach that ensures the priority of a capital market perspective over an ad-hoc case law for close corporations:[87] The business judgement rule should be just as

---

[81] See cases cited *supra* n. 79, and state laws referred to *supra* n. 39.

[82] *Philadelphia Life Insurance Co.* v. *Crosland*, 234 F. 2d 780, 783 (4th Cir., 1956) (sole shareholder of corporation); *Snyder* v. *Freeman*, 266 S.E. 2d 593, 597 et seq. (N.C. 1980) (all shareholders of close corporation).

[83] *Donahue* v. *Rodd Electrotype Co. of New England*, 328 N.E. 2d 505, 515 et seq. (Mass., 1975); *Ritchie* v. *McGrath*, 571 P. 2d 17 (Kan.App., 1977); *Lerner* v. *Lerner Corp.*, 750 A. 2d 709, 720 et seq. (Md.App., 2000), cert.den. 757 A. 2d.810 (Md., 2000); Garza, *supra* n. 29, 619 et seq.

[84] Cox/ Hazen/ O'Neal, *supra* n. 78, § 14.16 (Fiduciary Duties in the Close Corporation).

[85] *Meiselman* v. *Meiselman*, 307 S.E. 2d 551, 563 et seq. (N.C., 1983); Peeples, *supra* n. 30, 501 et seq.

[86] See criticism in: *Kiriakides* v. *Atlas Food Systems & Services*, 541 S.E. 2d 257, 265 et seq. (S.C., 2001); *Lerner* v. *Lerner Corp.*, 750 A. 2d 709, 721 et seq. (Md.App., 2000), cert.den. 757 A. 2d 810 (Md., 2000). Cf. Moll, "Shareholder Oppression in close corporations: The Unanswered Question of Perspective", 53 *Vanderbilt L.Rev.* (2000) 749.

[87] Easterbrook/ Fischel, *supra* n. 15, 247 et seq.; cf. *Nixon* v. *Blackwell*, 626 A. 2d 1366, 1379 et seq. (Del., 1993) describing shareholder contracting as part of the normal bargaining process on the capital market: "... The tools of good corporate practice are designed to give a purchasing minority shareholder the opportunity to bargain for protection before parting with consideration. It would do violence to normal corporate practice and our corporation law to fashion an ad hoc ruling which would result in a court imposed stockholder buy-out for which the parties had not contracted." A Delaware court will not remedy a bad business judgement of a minority shareholder: *Sontrol Holding Co.* v. *Marceau Investissements*, 607 A. 2d 1177 (Del., 1992).

applicable to close corporations as to corporations with publicly traded stock.[88] This approach appears to make sense from the perspective of a capital market-minded director and the majority of a close corporation. It is, however, doubtful whether this would fully respect the initial investment decision of a minority shareholder.[89] Instead, courts should be invited to pay more attention to the interests of a rational investor buying stock in close corporations. In doing so, a hypothetical investment market for close corporations should be (re)constructed.[90] A finding for a breach of a fiduciary duty could be made when the directors or the majority of a close corporation disregard the rules of the (hypothetical) investment market.[91]

If one is serious about (re)constructing hypothetical investment bargains one can dispense with the requirement that all shareholders be a party to a shareholder agreement.[92] If the majority would frustrate the investment interests of non-participating shareholders the common law rules on fiduciary duties provide adequate protection. In turn, minority shareholders could invoke the terms of a majority control agreement if this were to prevent the majority from behaving in an oppressive way. German law is at odds with this concept. The *Bundesgerichtshof* cases on shareholder agreements[93] can be interpreted as an attempt to reconcile an institutionalist approach with the investments interests of the shareholders of a close corporation. It is unclear though, whether the institutionalist reasoning of the court holding focuses on capital market aspects or on the "sphere of corporative life" (*körperschaftliche Lebenssphäre*) of the close corporation. It is submitted that a market-oriented understanding of a *GmbH* would do greater justice to the investment interests of the shareholders. There is no reason why "hypothetical investment bargains"[94] should not also be incorporated into German legal analysis. Incidentally, the requirement that

---

[88] *Exadaktilos* v. *Cinnaminson Realty Co., Inc.*, 400 A. 2d 554, 559 et seq. (N.J.Super.L., 1979); *Delahoussaye* v. *Newhard*, 785 S.W. 2d 609, 612 (Mo.App.E.D. 1990); Peeples, *supra* n. 30; see generally on judicial control of board power and discretion: Green, "Reasonable Expectations" Define Board Power to Liquidate a Solvent Close Corporation in Bankruptcy", 41 *Drake L.Rev.* (1992) 421, 437 et seq.; Kaplan/ Young, "Corporate 'Eminent Domain': Stock Redemption and Reverse Stock Splits", 57 *UMKC L.Rev.* (1988) 67, 75 et seq.

[89] Moll, *supra* n. 86, 772 et seq.

[90] Moll, ibid., 794 et seq.

[91] Courts favoring the fairness test base their findings on various factors which – tacitly – include the hypothetical investment market: cf. *Nixon* v. *Blackwell*, 626 A 2d 1366, 1379 et seq. (Del., 1993); *Kiriakides* v. *Atlas Food Systems & Services, Inc.*, 541 S.E. 2d 257, 265 et seq. (S.C., 2001); *Lerner* v. *Lerner Corporation*, 750 A. 2d 709, 722 et seq. (Md.App., 2000) cert. den. 757 A. 2d 810 (Md., 2000); *Barter* v. *Diodardo*, 2001 WL 337352 (Pa.Super., 2001)

[92] See N.C.Gen.Stat. § 55-7-31(c); cf. Zöllner, in: Henze/ Timm/ Westermann, *supra* n. 51, 104.

[93] *Supra* n. 66, 67

[94] *Supra* n. 90.

control agreements have to be all-shareholder agreements could be dispensed with. Nor should minority shareholders face too many difficulties in challenging majority agreements before a German court if they establish a breach of a duty of loyalty (*Treuepflicht*).[95]

The expectations of the capital market and of the creditors of a close corporation dictate that the shareholders' freedom of contract has its limits. The U.S. state corporation laws that accept shareholder control agreements shift liability from the directors to the shareholders "taking over".[96] Moreover, the general rules on piercing the corporate veil remain unaffected.[97] Under German law the issue is unsettled. Apart from the intricacies of the law on corporate groups (*Konzernrecht*) German courts have shown little enthusiasm of piercing the veil of a close corporation.[98] It is a mere speculation whether the shareholders of a close corporation who agree to observe partnership rules among themselves could also be held liable under partnership law by third parties.[99]

---

[95] Cf. Zöllner, in: Henze/ Timm/ Westermann, *supra* n. 51, 104; Odersky, "Stimmbindungen im Pool und 'Unterpool'", in: *Festschrift Marcus Lutter* (2000), 557, 568 et seq.

[96] *Supra* n. 41

[97] Ribstein, *supra* n. 11, 129.

[98] See: K. Schmidt, *supra* n. 63, 224 et seq., 1220 et seq.

[99] Codified German law has not adopted the liability rules of many US state corporation laws which hold the parties to shareholder control agreement directly liable, but disallow the application of partnership liability law, *supra* n. 42. For special liability rules in corporate groups see: K. Schmidt, *supra* n. 63, 1220 et seq.

Ambivalences in the Fixing of Broadcasting Fees in Germany

Peter Lerche*

1. Introduction: relation to European Law

In a recent article in EBOR, Ernst-Joachim Mestmäcker remarks: "In a good drama we expect to be surprised in the third act by the revelation of hidden conflicts as well as the identity of the play's true hero."[1]

This literary insight, slightly modified, can be used in the depiction of certain internal conflicts which characterize the German legal rules on the financing of public broadcasting (both radio and television).

The declaration in the protocol on Article 92 [now Article 87] EC Treaty adopted at the Amsterdam Governmental Conference on 17 June 1997, made it clear that the German practice of funding public broadcasting from licence fees is, within certain limits, compatible with Community law.[2] So the EU did not let

---

* Professor of Law (emer.), Munich University. The translation was made by Karen Sokoll, LL.M.

[1] Mestmäcker, "The EC Commission's Modernization of Competition Policy", 1 *EBOR* (2000) 401, 403.

[2] For a summary, see A. Hesse, *Rundfunkrecht*, 2nd ed. (Munich: Vahlen 1999) 313 et seq.

Talia Einhorn, ed., Spontaneous Order, Organization and the Law – Liber Amicorum Ernst-Joachim Mestmäcker © 2003 T.M.C.Asser Press, *The Hague, The Netherlands*

an "Iron Curtain" fall to prevent from the outset the making of a play about the law of fee-financing on the national stage.

Indeed, much seems to speak for the assumption that the decision to finance public broadcasting by fees is closely related to the requirement of due respect for member states' national identity (new: Article 6 (3) Treaty on European Union). This source of funding makes public broadcasters, to a reasonable degree, independent of viewer ratings, thereby enabling them to carry out their cultural function in a particular way. In its decision on the European television directive, the German Federal Constitutional Court expressly stressed that broadcasting is "at any rate also a cultural phenomenon".[3]

However, the mere fact that broadcasting is a cultural commodity does not shift the legal responsibility away from the European Community, insofar as the EC actually has such a responsibility based on legal provisions.[4] Nonetheless, when considering the resulting issues of interpretation it must be borne in mind that the legal framework for broadcasting is of vital importance in the way a nation views itself, therefore coming close to the question of its contents which is protected by the requirement of due respect for the national identity. All the same, this should not be pushed too far. In particular, it should be taken into account that there are apparently already substantial variations among the member states as to the practical significance of the concept of national identity. Regardless of one's opinion on this matter, there is room for our play in the discussion on the law on broadcasting fees. It unfolds into the following three acts.

2. THE THREE ACTS OF FEE-FIXING

The play's text was delivered by the Constitutional Court's decision on 22 February 1994.[5] However, this text is not free of peculiarities. The decision primarily focuses on depoliticizing, as much as possible, the procedure for fixing broadcasting fees. In other words, it attempts to ensure by procedural safeguards that the freedom of broadcasting is not endangered by the state misusing fee-fixing to influence programming or for objectives of media policy. Accordingly, it may be admissible to fix the licence fee by means of an interstate treaty between Germany's states (the *Länder*) but, as far as the amount is concerned, three "acts" must be performed.

---

[3] *Entscheidungen des Bundesverfassungsgerichts* (*BVerfGE*) 92, 203, 238.

[4] Mestmäcker, "In welcher Weise empfiehlt es sich, die Ordnung des Rundfunks und sein Verhältnis zu anderen Medien – auch unter dem Gesichtspunkt der Harmonisierung – zu regeln?", *Verhandlungen des 56. Deutschen Juristentages*, Vol. 2 (Munich: Beck 1986) 9, 27.

[5] *BVerfGE* 90, 60.

In the first act, the play commences with the public broadcasters' autonomous programming decisions. They have the authority to declare their own financial requirements.

The second act comprises the external control of these declarations. It is a review as to whether the broadcasters keep within the legally defined function of broadcasting and have determined correctly and according to the principles of a cost-efficient economy the financial requirements derived from it. As a legal tool for this external control the court recommended a commission of experts. In establishing it, the legislature was able partly to resurrect a former body, the *Kommission zur Ermittlung des Finanzbedarfs* (*KEF*) (Commission on Financial Requirements). However, the *KEF* had to be altered with respect to details of organization and procedure. This was done in order in particular to legally ensure their independence while trying to achieve "freedom of policy issues".[6] It is obvious that here the court construed the notion of policy narrowly – almost as if dealing with a performance of Goethe's *Faust* ("*Ein garstig Lied! Pfui! Ein politisch Lied*"). By the way, Herder – as is of course known to MESTMÄCKER – also began a poem entitled "Coalition" with the exclamation: "*Politisch Lied, ein böses, böses Lied!*". Apparently the Constitutional Court had these lines in mind when talking of required freedom of policy issues.

The third act leads to the actual fee decision based on the reviewed declarations (see second act) of the public broadcasters (first act). The court permits this state decision to be adopted by an interstate treaty between the German states to which their respective parliaments consent. However, consistently the court does not allow the parliaments to change the treaty's content for programming-related or media policy purposes, but essentially only in the case where the fee decision would otherwise lead to an unreasonably high financial burden on the audiences.[7] Only to this extent may a state parliament take the role of *deus ex machina*. Apart from that, it must uphold the result of *KEF*'s findings.

3. AMBIVALENCES IN FIXING THE LEVEL OF THE FEES

Hidden conflicts can already be tracked down in the following relations:

The public broadcasters have the authority to take their programming decisions autonomously. Nonetheless, they must keep within the constitutional general legal limitations. These limitations are, according to the abovementioned ruling, rooted in the public broadcasters' task in the dual broadcasting system to offer programming that, on the one hand, remains in

---

6 *BVerfGE* 90, 60, 103: *politikfrei.*

7 *BVerfGE* 90, 60, 104.

accordance with the traditional function of broadcasting and, on the other, can keep up with the competition from private broadcasters.[8]

Therefore, according to the court, public broadcasters have no constitutional right to realize programming which is "not necessary" for this task.[9] However, the decision overlooks the fact that public broadcasters may very well be given other tasks and in turn exceed the classical broadcasting function. In this case, the legislature would have also to provide for its funding.

More importantly, the ruling even places the funding under the general limitation that only what is "necessary" (*erforderlich*) for the respective function may be financed. The term "necessary" is construed narrowly, meaning the same as "required" (*geboten*).[10] Consistently with earlier case law,[11] the latter is delimited from what is only "adequate for the function" (*funktionsadäquat*).

Consequently, the foregoing remarks on the third act mean that, on the one hand, in the case of the above-mentioned exceptional circumstances (i.e. an unreasonable burden for the audiences) the fee could be less than the amount which is required for the function (*funktionsgeboten*) while, on the other hand, the fee must never exceed the required amount, not even if the tasks to be financed are regarded as adequate for the function. Not even the *KEF*, the star of the second act, is allowed to grant more to the broadcasters.[12]

This result seems somewhat bewildering. Possibly not even the "required" amount may be allowed to be financed. This harshness can probably be moderated only by generally construing narrowly the decisive criterion (unreasonable burden). However, it is precisely this that entails further curtailing the creative power of the states' parliaments who make their stage appearance in the third act. They become mere tools for repairs, even though an issue which is vital for the general public[13] is at stake. This is the prize of the intended "depoliticization". At the same time, too much importance is attached to the rather obscure distinction between what is required for the function (*Funktionsgebotenes*) and what is adequate for the function (*Funktionsadäquates*) – a distinction which is at any rate open to interpretation. One encounters great difficulties when trying to stick to this differentiation, in particular where the law sets forth the public broadcasters' tasks rather broadly and vaguely.

---

[8] Ibid., 92.

[9] Ibid., 92.

[10] Ibid., 92.

[11] *BVerfGE* 74, 297, 342; 87, 181, 202 et seq.

[12] *BVerfGE* 90, 60, 102 et seq.

[13] For details see Badura, "Gewährleistung der Freiheit des Rundfunks, 'Funktion' des Rundfunks und 'öffentliche Aufgabe' der Rundfunkveranstalter", in: *Festschrift Knöpfle* (Munich: Beck 1996) 1, 5 et seq. Badura speaks in a more general way of the "ambivalence of broadcasting regulation", ibid., 5.

Basically, this lack of clarity can only be removed by a decision from the regulator for which no rational criteria exist.

4. Ambivalences in the parliaments' position

It is understandable that in the states' parliaments this allocation of a mere supporting role does not provoke much enthusiasm.

Generally, parliaments are in a weak position where interstate treaties are concerned. As a rule, they can only respond with either "yes" or "no". In our case their position is further weakened because here – as follows from the foregoing – they are generally obliged to vote for the tabled fee-fixing, with the rare exception that an "unreasonable burden" is placed upon the broadcasting audiences. (Another question is whether this exception – should it really be considered – would be sufficiently taken into account in the submitted text of the interstate treaty.)

It is, therefore, not surprising that efforts have been made to strengthen indirectly the parliaments' position by imposing regular duties on the public broadcasters. These duties include reporting their economic and financial situation, the situation of the companies in which they participate and intended structural decisions. A commission of representatives of all states shall supervise these reports jointly with other parties concerned.[14]

However desirable this gain in transparency may be, one thing cannot be denied. It would hardly be compatible with the afore-mentioned Constitutional Court's demand for "depoliticization" if in this way a supervisory practice were to develop which, after all, would revitalize the state's position by the backdoor. In any event, influence deriving from media policy interests is not admissible. However, the term media policy is obscure enough to allow for a certain scope of action – which brings us to yet another ambivalence.

5. Ambivalences in the procedure under the interstate treaty on broadcasting

When looking into the details of the procedure stipulated by the court and actual practice one finds even more uncertainties caused by the Constitutional Court's case law.

---

[14] See particularly the preamble of the Saxonian statute concerning the "Fünfter Rundfunkänderungsstaatsvertrag". Hereto see the report in *Evangelischer Pressedienst (epd medien)*, No. 100, 16. 12. 2000, 17.

5.1 Legal requirement for justification

As previously mentioned, the definite fee-fixing (third act) can differ from the *KEF*'s establishment of the broadcasters' financial requirements, even if only in exceptional circumstances (unreasonable burden). According to the court's ruling, the parliaments must then give a demonstrable explanation for the modification.[15]

This should not create any problems if the text of the treaty, as laid before the parliaments, already includes the intended change. In such case the justification requirement can be met, for example, by stating the reasons in the preamble.[16] But how does one proceed if the relevant version of the interstate treaty does not entail the modification and, for this very reason, a few (or several) parliaments do not want to assent to the treaty? Suppose, for instance, that the parliaments of less prosperous (e.g. East German) states consider the audiences in their respective state to be unreasonably burdened.

This almost occurred when the broadcasting fees were raised most recently and was averted only with great difficulty.

In such a case, how should the demonstrable explanation be indicated? Usually, the request to assent to an interstate treaty is rejected without a voting majority. The individual motives which, in the course of the parliamentary procedure, will have prompted such negative result may well be of a greatly varied nature. Moreover, they could hardly be documented merely by taking the minutes of the parliamentary debates – even these records would not unambiguously reveal the individual reasons that actually resulted in the decision of the respective members of parliament, i.e. the "legislature".

Therefore, the ruling raises questions in this regard as well.

5.2 On the actual procedural practice

Problems created by the present procedural practice under the Interstate Treaty are of a much more fundamental significance.

5.2.1 *Legal framework*

First, it is necessary to take a short look at the regulatory framework provided by the media-relevant interstate treaties.

According to the present procedure, the amount of the broadcasting fee is fixed by the *Rundfunkfinanzierungsstaatsvertrag*. This treaty is part of the

---

[15] *BVerfGE* 90, 60, 104.

[16] Section 7 (2) clause 3 Rundfunkfinanzierungsstaatsvertrag is, in contrast, unclear.

comprehensive *Staatsvertrag über den Rundfunk im vereinten Deutschland* (Interstate Treaty on Broadcasting in Unified Germany, hereinafter – "General Treaty"), Article 5. Other provisions regulating the fees, for instance, a possible fee exemption, can be found in the *Rundfunkgebührenstaatsvertrag* which is also part of the General Treaty (Article 4). Apart from this, the General Treaty contains a network of numerous other broadcasting regulations. These are summarized in further articles, particularly in Article 1, which deals with the provisions of the *Rundfunkstaatsvertrag* (Interstate Treaty on Broadcasting – a misleadingly wide expression). The latter treaty entails above all the crucial rules designed to prevent the emergence of a predominance of public opinion in nationwide private television. These provisions form the legal basis for the *Kommission zur Ermittlung der Konzentration im Medienbereich* (Commission on Concentration in the Media – *KEK*)[17] of which MESTMÄCKER is chairman.

Furthermore, there are other media-relevant interstate treaties and statutes outside this regulatory complex.

5.2.2 *Problematic procedural issues of the fee revision*

In order to determine anew the amount of the broadcasting fees, at the very least a modification of the relevant provision in the *Rundfunkfinanzierungsstaatsvertrag* is required. However, as seen in the example of the most recent procedure, the amendment does not confine itself to this specific, fee-related change. Rather, it is woven into an extensive amended version of the General Treaty,[18] which revises numerous other provisions of the General Treaty – above all, those of the *Rundfunkstaatsvertrag*. It also contains alterations to other media-related provisions.[19]

In practice this means that because the state parliaments' decision applies to the amended version of the interstate treaty <u>as a whole</u>, parliaments must extend their assent to <u>all</u> individual changes if they want to avoid the rejection of the amended version.

Furthermore, this means that as a rule, parliaments will thus be <u>forced</u> to assent to all single alterations because, according to the Constitutional Court's case law regarding the third act of our play, they are generally (i.e. apart from the above-mentioned narrow exceptions) obliged to follow the *KEF*'s findings. So, if the tabled amendment corresponds with the *KEF*'s decision, in general parliament has to assent to this specific change. Moreover, if this as usual forms part of a comprehensive amended version of the interstate treaty and the latter

---

[17] Particularly Sections 26 et seq. Rundfunkstaatsvertrag.

[18] "Fünfter Staatsvertrag zur Änderung rundfunkrechtlicher Staatsverträge".

[19] Article 7.

can only be accepted as a whole, it follows that the obligation to assent also applies to all other components of the treaty.

As parliament can generally only assent to all changes thus interlinked, parliament's weakness also concerns all other modifications entailed in the amended version of the interstate treaty, thereby eating its way through the whole reform material.

This state of affairs can raise doubts with regard to the separation of powers[20] and the parliamentary principle. Parliaments are also forced to assent to amendments to which they would not have agreed without this special obligation, therefore accepting the fact that because of their rejection the whole new treaty would have failed. Now they are barred from this possibility. It is true that this situation may become relevant only in the event of rare combinations of political factors. Still, precisely these cases are important because they show the significance of the parliamentary principle. Parliament must not be rendered impotent.

From a political standpoint, one could point out the fact that the essential regulations of each amended version of the interstate treaty use to be politically balanced. But this can hardly hold true for the issue of fee-fixing, precisely because it is, as a rule, already decided by the *KEF* (second act). Insofar as parliaments are able exceptionally to modify this decision, as described above, this has nothing to do with political balance.

Therefore, only one single argument may refute the assumption that the present procedure of the third act is unconstitutional: each parliament has the right to insist on taking the determination of fees out of the amended version of the interstate treaty and dealing with it in a separate treaty. After all, this possibility remains with the parliaments and in turn potentially secures their decisive influence in a way that can be considered to be sufficient.

5.3 **Recommendation**

But should one let it get as far as that? Should one not rather forestall such a possible worsening of the situation which could, above all, cause serious delays?

---

[20] For more general Swiss, Austrian, German and European law perspectives on the separation of powers, see the recent articles in Isensee (ed.), *Gewaltenteilung heute, Ossenbühl-Symposium* (Heidelberg: Müller 2000). For more general issues arising when interstate treaties are dealt with as packages loaded with different contents, see the as yet unpublished speech by Merten, "Gesetzgebung im demokratischen Rechtsstaat", *Korinek-Symposium* (Wien 23.11.2000). For amendments of the German Basic Law passed as a package in the course of German reunification, see *BVerfGE* 82, 316, 320 et seq.; 84, 90, 118 et seq.

In my view, the states' governments would be well advised to provide for an independent procedure for fee-fixing by making an independent Treaty. Each of the individual partial treaties (i.e. Articles) of the General Treaty has already been subject to specific regulation; especially their respective rules on terms of validity and termination have varied considerably. It would adopt this approach and, admittedly, go beyond it if the fee-fixing were to be left to an independent procedure. As a result, to this extent, no more constitutional concerns could arise.

At the same time, in conclusion it turns out that "the play's true hero" is – constitutional law.

Competition as a Basic Element of the Social Market Economy

Wernhard Möschel*

My article is structured into seven theses:

1. Competition as a value in itself

Competition is a value in itself. It is not directed towards specific objectives.

Market economy can be fitted into the categories of the theory of decision-making.[1] Decision-makers are individuals, not a collective entity like the state. The objects of decision-making are arbitrary and therefore necessarily unknown. Legally speaking, the participants are making use of their personal autonomy. The procedure of decision-making is the contract, the voluntary reaching of an agreement with another party. The order achieved through such a process cannot be directed towards specific objectives. The methodological reason for this is: freedom would be abolished if one attempted to define its content in advance. Market organisation through competition is the spontaneous order that results when people coordinate their actions by way of mutual adjustment in transmitting and receiving information. Only statements about the general structures of such a system (pattern predictions) are possible. Such a

---

* Professor of Law, University of Tuebingen, former chairman of the German Monopolies Commission.

[1] See also W. Möschel, *Rechtsordnung zwischen Plan und Markt* (Tübingen: Mohr 1975) p. 5.

Talia Einhorn, ed., Spontaneous Order, Organization and the Law – Liber Amicorum Ernst-Joachim Mestmäcker © 2003 T.M.C.ASSER PRESS, *The Hague, The Netherlands*

systemt results in mutual advantages for the individuals involved, and in economic overall advantages, as a generic term for growth, inducement and unfolding of technological progress and efficient allocation. This general social task that is achieved by the exercise of individual freedom remains recognisable, even though it may be difficult to discern in the individual case. This approach blends into a philosophical tradition stretching from Thomas Hobbes via Kant to John Rawls. If the idea were put in terms of an economic model, it would correspond to Pareto efficiency. It is an approach to law and justice based on contractual theory, as opposed to utilitarian philosophies and pure welfare-economics. Part of the latter is welfare-maximisation in the sense of the well-known Kaldor-Hicks-criterion: individual rights may be infringed if this leads to an increase of overall welfare. The opinion presented in this paper draws on ordoliberal theory, which is predominant in Germany. Internationally, ordoliberal theory is viewed as a teutonic exaggeration. Competition is perceived as being one means of achieving welfare goals. It thus becomes disposable and may be used interchangeably with other means. As former EC Competition Commissioner Karel van Miert noted: "The enforcement of competition principles is not an end in itself. Rather, competition policy is an instrument contributing to the achievement of fundamental objectives of the European Community."[2] Thus, industrial policy, foreign trade, welfare and state aid also come into play.

This first thesis is neither true nor false. It is based upon a decision in favour of certain values, but can claim the merits of systemic logic or conformity of order.

2. Constituting regulations

Organisation through competition requires constituting regulations.

Organisation through competition is only feasible if certain issues are regulated. Usually, this is the task of the "protective state". Well-defined property rights, a rule of law enabling the enforcement of individual rights, and not least a stable currency, are issues requiring regulation. Legal norms protecting competition from restraints or endangerment also belong here. The actors on the market depart from the legitimating foundation of their individual rights if the effects of their free actions destroy the necessary preconditions for the exercise of those rights. Viewed from this vantage point, a law against the restraints of competition is an extension of civil law by different means. This

---

[2] Karel van Miert, "Die Wettbewerbspolitik der neuen Kommission", *Competition Policy Newsletter*, vol. 1, no. 5 (1995) p. 1.

holds true for anti-competitive agreements, such as contracts to the detriment of third parties, and abuses of a dominant position depriving others of their freedom of trade. It also holds true for mergers that enable the participants to avoid the pressures of competition.

Special sectors of the economy may also require constituting regulations. Usually, organisation through competition requires no more than the clearing away of obstacles. After that, free competition unfolds, without any predictable results in specific cases. In exceptional circumstances, actively shaping interventions may be necessary to allow market forces to emerge. Examples are the industries of energy, which depend on the network infrastructure, and the telecommunications and health sectors. In telecommunications, for example, as long as no competition between different systems for accessing the end-user over the last mile is possible, a regulated "free access" to the monopolist's network may be called for. This necessity wanes as alternative modes of access, such as wireless local loop, power lines, and broadband-cable, become available. The possibilities of actively intervening are also influenced by technological developments. To extend the example of telecommunications, number-portability or call-by-call billing would be unthinkable without the current advances in computer technology. Modern telephone switch-systems are high-performance computers.

3. NO SUFFICIENTLY DEVELOPED THEORY

There is no sufficiently developed theory to determine a restraint of competition. To a great extent, such a determination is based on experience. It frequently involves questions of measure and degree that make a balancing of interests inevitable.

To be of any use in practice, a theory of competition needs to be sufficiently realistic and workable. None of the many existing approaches offers that. By and large, this holds true for concepts of perfect competition, the many different workability-doctrines, systemic approaches, and the concept of freedom of competition. The Austrian school (van Mieses, von Hayek, Hoppmann, Israel Kirzner) stands for the latter, but doubts exist about the criteria's operability. To a large extent one has to rely on knowledge gained by experience. Its importance, however, should not be underestimated: cartels for price, territories or quotas and economically motivated agreements for a collective boycott may in principle be prohibited per se. However, other types of cooperation among competitors, such as specialisation and rationalisation, are ambivalent in competition policy. They necessitate a difficult balancing of interests. This holds true even more for the individual behaviour of single enterprises. America Online (AOL), for example, has a market share of 80% in the US market for instant messaging (real-time communication between computers). It neither opens its standard for competitors, nor joins in the development of a common standard. AOL argues that by this strategy it is protecting its customers against hackers and spamming (i.e. unsolicited advertising). The question now becomes whether such behaviour is a restraint of competition, or whether it must be accepted in a market economy. Whoever is called upon to answer such questions can only attempt to make the lesser mistake.

4. Consequential effects of a rule of law regime

If competition is subjected to a rule of law, this entails a large number of consequential effects which cannot be avoided.

By now, legal criteria are generally used to control cartels and manifestations of an abuse of a dominant position. This is not equally the case in the area of merger control. Decisions in this area are often of a political nature, as can be observed, e.g., in Great Britain or France. And then, there are many intermediate forms. For example, independent commissions may be established to draft recommendations. However, experience has shown that the protection of competition is neglected if it is subject to a discretionary political decision. Franz Böhm named what is probably the most decisive reason: competition is without a lobby. If one decides on a rule of law for this reason, a large number of consequential effects arise.[3] A rule of law always requires the selection and attribution of importance to particular circumstances among the endless variety of interdependent economic interactions. Furthermore, only such elements can be distilled into legal norms that allow both general abstract evaluation and the determination of an infringement of the norm in the individual case. Another effect is that – due to the complexity of the subject-matter – difficulties of proving the facts are a primary concern when formulating the factual preconditions for a norm. Conflicts between the plausibility of a specific legal rule from the vantage point of competition policy, on the one hand, and the requirements of the possibility of judicial review, practicability and efficiency, on the other, cannot be avoided. Because of the limited insights that competition policy is able to offer to date, legal criteria for evaluation will frequently be unrefined and often resort will have to be had to approximate judgements and probabilities. Blanket clauses play a vital role in this context. Further limitations result from the particular type of enforcement proceedings that are applied. For example, administrative proceedings with subsequent control through the court cannot be compared with adversary civil proceedings. Criminal proceedings have the greatest limitations.

---

[3] W. Möschel, *Recht der Wettbewerbsbeschränkungen* (Köln: Heymanns 1983) paras. 70, 79.

In total, however, the preferable institutional arrangement remains a rule of law.

5. The current proposal for a reform of Community competition rules

The current proposals for a reform of Community competition law should be regarded critically.

The EU Commission presented its White Paper on Modernisation of the Rules Implementing Articles 81 and 82 of the EC Treaty on 12 May 1999.[4] A draft regulation became known in October 2000.[5] The proposals made by the Commission are quite complex, but in essence consist of the following: the current system of prohibition with the possibility of an administrative exemption will be converted into a directly applicable system of exemptions. Article 81 Sections 1 and 3 of the Treaty will be read as an integrated, directly applicable unity. In this way, the Commission hopes to combat restraints of competition more effectively. For competition policy, however, such a change is extremely risky. A system of directly applicable exemptions is clearly inferior to a system with prior notification:

- The cartel authorities do not receive any information;
- It leads to a complete lack of transparency for interested third parties, competitors, suppliers and customers, including consumers;
- Self-assessment by the enterprises and their respective attorneys cannot warrant the *public* interest in the protection of competition. There are three reasons for this. First, enterprises often lack the necessary data concerning the market. It is simply asking too much of them to apply Article 81 (3) of the Treaty themselves. It can hardly be described as a happy institutional arrangement, if potential sinners are invited to exonerate themselves. Second, by contrast, a notification system has many advantages. Such a system gives the cartel office the opportunity to work actively towards an arrangement that is consistent with competition principles before horizontal agreements take effect. This exercises discipline on the parties to a cartel. They will prefer to conclude contracts that conform with competition law, so as to be granted an exemption. Similarly, it reduces the incentive to change from a permitted cooperation to a prohibited one, since the enterprises are aware that the

---

[4] *OJ* [1999] C 132/1-33; see also W. Möschel, "Systemwechsel im Europäischen Wettbewerbsrecht?", *JZ* [2000] 61.

[5] Brussels, 27.9.2000 *COM* (2000) 582 final. 2000/0243 (CNS).

competition authority "knows". Third, moreover, notifications give the opportunity to grant exemptions in well-measured doses; they lead to a concentration of exemption decisions in specialised agencies which possess the appropriate experience and expertise.

These are not mere assertions. These statements are proven to be true by extensive experience, derived both from reviewing history and from comparing different legal cultures.[6]

It is an illusion to expect – as the Commission does – that enterprises will use civil suits to take action against restraints of competition of which they are a victim. Those courses of action are already available. They are rarely used in practice. In civil proceedings, the burden of establishing the facts rests on the parties; no action to acquire factual information is taken by the court itself. The prior decision of a competition authority is lacking. The difficulties encountered in discharging the burden of proof and the associated risks regarding costs are too great for an individual plaintiff. That is the reason why a specialised agency is given prime responsibility for fighting restraints of competition, in contrast to so-called unfair trade practices which are enforced by private individuals. It is correct that in US antitrust law, civil suits are a central tool in fighting restraints of competition. However, this requires a variety of supporting rules which do not exist in Europe, and which the EU does not have the jurisdiction to introduce.

- Civil enforcement requires a pre-trial discovery procedure. Thus, the private attorney would become a kind of public prosecutor.
- Contingency fees create an incentive for legal enforcement. They are, to a large extent, considered contrary to public policy in Europe.
- Treble damages provide an additional incentive. However, American decisions which include punitive damages are generally not recognised in Europe. In Europe punitive damages are deemed to violate public policy.
- The disadvantages of American antitrust enforcement should not be forgotten. The legal uncertainties are high. According to a well-known saying, the spirit of Senator Sherman sits on the board of every American corporation. But this only advances the lawyers' financial interests. Moreover, civil procedures can be used in the USA as an instrument for intimidation (another restraint of competition). A defendant who is wrongfully taken to court is left with his or her own costs, notably in the form of

[6] See Monopolkommission, *Sondergutachten 28, Kartellpolitische Wende in der Europäischen Union?* (Baden-Baden: Nomos 1999) paras. 23 et seq.

tremendous lawyers' fees. This all but forces the parties to reach an agreement.

It is utterly unexpected to see the draft propose that restraints of competition that may affect trade between Member States are *solely* to be judged according to Community law. The consequence is that national laws will become almost obsolete in light of the wide interpretation of the interstate trade clause in Article 81 of the Treaty. The Member States' regulations would in consequence be relevant only for restraints of competition of a local or regional kind. But even in these cases a differing treatment will not be politically explicable in the long run. One cannot treat small firms more strictly than big ones. In consequence, competition between the different legal systems, a contest for the better solution, will no longer be possible. The counter-argument of a level playing-field (that identical conditions for competition everywhere are preferable) is somehow naïve. It pretends that we know the best solution, which should then ideally be applied world-wide, or at least within the European Community. This is thinking by results. Yet, there is absolutely no indication that in competition law (of all topics) the process of learning has ended.

6. Cooperation between competitors – a new paradigm?

It is a risky tendency in competition policy to regard cooperation between competitors favourably rather than critically.

The Commission presented a Communication on the Application of Article 81 (3) of the Treaty to Horizontal Cooperation Agreements in the spring of 2000.[7] A similar, though more cautious approach is taken by the USA, FTC and the Department of Justice in their new "Antitrust Guidelines for Collaborations among Competitors", published in April 2000.[8] The German Federal Antitrust Authority (*Bundeskartellamt*) is examining whether the attitude towards cooperation between competitors needs to be re-evaluated.[9] Common to all three approaches is a break with the famous statement Adam Smith made in 1776. According to him, people of the same trade seldom meet together, even for merriment and diversion, but the conversation ends in a conspiracy against the public, or in some contrivance to raise prices. Instead, according to these new approaches, such cooperations should initially be viewed favourably. One

---

[7] Communication on the Application of Article 81 (3) of the Treaty to Horizontal Cooperation Agreements, *OJ* [2000] C 118/14.

[8] *Antitrust Report* (April 2000) pp. 16-42.

[9] See A. Scheidgen/ M. König, "Kooperationen zwischen Wettbewerbern – Ist eine Neubewertung erforderlich?", *WuW* [2000] 1205.

should move away from a rather legalistic understanding of competition as rivalry to a more economic one, using a result-oriented analysis. The prohibition of cartels should be limited to enterprises with a certain market-power.

This marks a clear departure from the understanding of an organisation through competition as expressed in thesis one. The difference may be clarified by an example. Two bakers agree on an arrangement about the price for buns. The new approach (as described with scepticism above) first inquires about the influence of that behaviour on the factual and locally relevant market, and makes a verdict depend on the outcome of that query. Under the more traditional view, the fact that the bakers made an arrangement about the price suffices in itself. The arrangement is sufficient indication for an effect on the market, as otherwise they would not have entered into the arrangement. If both were mistaken in their assessment of the situation, there would still be no reason for the legal system to revise its negative verdict.

The main reason given for this revision of the attitude towards cooperation between competitors is the change that has occurred in economic conditions. Globalisation and the development of innovative growing markets in context with the Internet are pointed to explain the change. This is supposed to have made competition fiercer. In the face of such dynamic economic change, cooperation is supposed to have become sensible. In my assessment the abovementioned developments are rather ambivalent. True, there has been a dramatic increase in the intensity of competition in some areas. Something similar, of course, also holds true for the potential for strategic behaviour restraining competition. One may clarify the point using an Internet-shopping platform (B2B-platform) as an example: initially there are no anti-trust concerns about electronic Internet-platforms used to organise the market for an industry, such as the purchase of parts for the automobile industry. In fact, they offer a potential for huge cost-savings. However, the conditions for a prohibited cartel are met if such a platform either replaces a price cartel by establishing an exchange of information among competitors or if it leads to purchasing power by bundling demand. Exercising control of behaviour to the detriment of dominant enterprises would be justified if uninvolved third parties were discriminated against.

7. No inclusion of populist goals

It is not advisable to burden anti-trust law with ideas that lie beyond the concept of competition.

In the context of the present wave of transborder mega-mergers, the suggestion to examine and (if necessary) prohibit mergers has been revived because of the inherent risks other than those associated with competitive reasons. It is said that the process of political opinion-forming and decision-making could be influenced unduly by accumulated economic power. Decision-making with far-reaching effects would become more centralized, diminishing the error-reducing effect of decision-making by a large number of entities. Furthermore, the individual would now find itself at the mercy of an individual's discretionary power, rather than subject to anonymous market forces. Looking at the enterprise-level, the amassing of key decisions in headquarters allegedly leads to alienation, to the deprivation of political communities of human resources on the management level, and to disregard of local or regional concerns while making political decisions.

Such a view of the problem is as old as it is important. One only has to remember the political argument between Jefferson and Hamilton, fathers of the American Constitution. Or the concept of a horizontal separation of powers between the state and groups in the society to avoid enabling one side to make itself master and the other servant. This is one of the core principles of the ordoliberal theory of an economic constitution. One should also remember draft legislation before the US Congress and the Carter administration in the latter half of the 1970s, when bigness as such, mere size, cap and spin off-solutions were key words.

I am not in favour of reviving those ideas in relation to mega-mergers. A merger control guided by competitive aspects can indirectly play a role in the fight against excessive economic power. With a view to the above-mentioned aims of socio-political policy, it has the same effect as a preventive measure against an emerging risk. Most signs point to the impossibility of sufficiently understanding economic power without referring to many other factors. These encompass anything from trade unions to churches, media and foreign-trade contexts. What seems certain to me is that the potential danger of economic power in relation to these socio-political aims can no longer be grasped in general and abstract rules. It is a legitimate question whether or not handing such issues to political decision-makers is a worse solution. The subjection of competition policy (including merger control) to a strict rule of law is one of the great achievements of the past decades. It should not be put at risk.

influenced unduly by accumulated economic power. Decision-making with far-reaching effects would become more centralized, diminishing the error- [illegible] Furthermore, [illegible] enterprise level, the centralising of key decisions in headquarters [illegible] leads [illegible]

[illegible]

Economic Power: a Productive Concept for the Law?

Knut Wolfgang Nörr*

1. The term 'power': notions, distinctions and formulae

Anyone approaching the phenomenon of power sets out by searching for definitions or rather formulae so as to somehow make the phenomenon tangible and graspable. In more recent publications, and by the way not only those of the German speaking community, it is Max Weber who is most frequently quoted as defining power as the chance for imposing one's own will even against opposition. At the same time, he described the term 'power' as sociologically amorphous, i.e. without form or structure. This characterisation left many unsatisfied, and so people have been looking for statements that could provide the term with a certain 'form' after all.

To begin with, we must distinguish between power as ability, at rest, so to speak, and the realisation of power. In the first case, we also speak about power in a fundamental and absolute sense, about power as an ability, a possession, a

---

* Prof. Dr. Dres. h.c., University of Tübingen. The article was translated from German by Debora Rebsch, M.A.

*Talia Einhorn, ed., Spontaneous Order, Organization and the Law –
Liber Amicorum Ernst-Joachim Mestmäcker © 2003 T.M.C.Asser Press, The Hague, The Netherlands*

trait, an attribute.[1] One example would be the power a landowner has with respect to the monopoly inherent in the piece of land belonging to him. When taking a closer look, power *in habitu* (as it can also be called according to a medieval distinction) presupposes a measure of probability, for it is hardly sensible to deal with this kind of power if its realisation lies beyond all probability. Such a realisation, or power *in actu* (according to the same distinction), presupposes a relationship to one or several persons who experience the realisation. Power then, is a relational term. This interpretation of the term particularly suggests itself to jurists who are used to thinking in terms of bilateral relationships – claims or rights of action – due to the dyadic or bipolar nature of legal argumentation (*aktionenrechtliches Denken* in a broader sense). When talking about the realisation of power, one is primarily concerned with the actual execution of power in one form or another; yet, power is also realised when a person exposed to it reacts in anticipation (a situation which then causes particular problems).

Moving on to look at the formulae attempting to express power *in actu,* we will often find that they contain a quantitative aspect.[2] (In the following, we shall use M as a short form for the more powerful person and N for the not-so-powerful.) Define power as the difference between M's possibility to exert influence and N's possibility to oppose. Or, define power as the difference between the advantage N could acquire, and the disadvantage he could suffer, from M. Or, power is defined by the costs M has to bear in order to realise power and the costs N has to bear when opposing.[3] In these cases, M's advantage does not have to correspond to N's disadvantage, neither do the costs on both sides have to be the same; in this respect we are not talking about a zero-sum game.[4] It is questionable whether one can talk about realisation of power if M is kicking

---

[1] Power as *Dispositionsbegriff* in Carnap's sense see K. Holm, 21 *Kölner Zeitschrift für Soziologie und Sozialpsychologie* (1969) 269.

[2] See also the overviews with further references, as there were, for example, R. A. Dahl, in: 12 *International Encylopedia of the Social Sciences* (1968) 405; N. Luhmann, "Klassische Theorie der Macht : Kritik ihrer Prämissen", 16 *Zeitschrift für Politik* (1969) 149; K. Lichtblau, in: 5 *Historisches Wörterbuch der Philosophie* (1980) 604; Karl Sandner, *Prozesse der Macht: zur Entstehung, Stabilisierung und Veränderung der Macht von Akteuren in Unternehmen* (Berlin: Springer 1990); W. Kersting, "Drei Theorien der Macht", 13 *Analyse & Kritik* (1991) 134; R. Kühn, in: Gerhard Göhler u.a., *Institution – Macht – Repräsentation: wofür politische Institutionen stehen und wie sie wirken* (Baden-Baden: Nomos 1997) 181; Peter Imbusch (ed.), *Macht und Herrschaft: sozialwissenschaftliche Konzeptionen und Theorien* (Opladen: Leske & Budrich 1998). From older writings: Richard Dolberg, *Theorie der Macht: die Macht als soziale Grundtatsache und als Elementarbegriff der Wirtschaftswissenschaften* (Wien: Peyer 1934).

[3] On the aspect of costs see especially J.C. Harsanyi, 7 *Behavioral Science* (1962) 67, 81.

[4] M's 'costs' might be much higher than N's: The delinquent threatens to bring a charge against his little aid; a reward tends to be disproportionately high.

at open doors, i.e. when N is behaving in conformity to power anyway.[5] This question touches upon the delimitation between 'power' and 'influence' on which, however, there exists no agreement (for our purpose, there is no need to further pursue this point). Or does power always presuppose alternatives and options among which N has any freedom of choice? Further, if – as is often the case – N is not completely powerless, but can realise power of his own against M: how do the reciprocal power relations interrelate? This can lead to negotiations, situations which theories of games and bargaining then deal with. The mutual power relations are, as a rule, of a different kind. They depend upon certain aspects (*aspektspezifisch* as one might say). Can they still be quantified by means of a common denominator and then added up so that the result indicates a surplus on the one side or – in a borderline case – no surplus at all? The issue of reciprocity would, of course, have to incorporate the notorious concept of countervailing power, its formation and exertion; notorious for the power-sum game, as it were, at the expense it entails for third parties.

Formulae (whether expressed verbally or by making use of matrices) can accompany us along part of the road that we have to tread. Then, however, reality in its manifold appearances wishes to speak; the jurist at least cannot prevent it. This reality is filled to the brim with power relations. The ubiquity of power caused Bertrand Russell, for example, to talk about power – in analogy to energy in physics – as "the fundamental concept in social science".[6] In general system theory, e.g. Talcott Parsons or Niklas Luhmann,[7] power is developed as a medium of communication similar to money.[8] Apart from such macro-concepts, as one might call them, others try to approach reality with typologies in order to at least somehow get control of the nearly infinite variety of appearances on which positions of power can be established. Others again compile the critical aspects that have to be considered in the treatment of the issue of power; long lists are thus being created, yet so far, no one has been able to provide analogous lists of solutions.

---

[5] If 'anyway' is based on the realisation of power of a third party (M_2), the reciprocal reference from M_1 to M_2 or vice versa cannot of course be to N's disadvantage.

[6] However, as far as I can tell, Russell was not the first. Rather, this analogy can already be found in Dolberg's preface, *supra* n. 2.

[7] N. Luhmann, Macht, 2nd ed. (Stuttgart: Enke 1988).

[8] Cf. Francesca Rigotti, *Die Macht und ihre Metaphern* (Frankfurt: Campus 1994) p. 183.

2. ALTERNATIVES OF THE NOT-SO-POWERFUL AND A THREEFOLD DISTINCTION

Of the distinctions made for the world of N we choose the threefold one of his spheres or fields, namely the sphere of values and goals that are related to his actions, then the circumstances and conditions surrounding his actions, and finally his actions themselves (subsequently, 'actions' will also include omissions). A premise for this distinction is the assumption that alternatives exist for the actions of N, i.e. that he is not confined to a single set of values or surroundings, or a single course of action from the outset or inevitably. If there is no alternative, we are dealing with existence as such (a newborn baby does not have the choice of not having been born), or with an act of pure violence (if there is no chance to resist the action). Alternatives do not presuppose that they are perceived by N, nor even that N is capable of perceiving them. A prime example of this, in the sphere of setting values and goals, is of course the power which the parent or guardian has over the child which is 'immature', i.e. not yet capable of perceiving alternatives. Realisation of power that is perceivable, yet is not perceived can, for example, be found in the field of tempting propaganda (in the business world also known as advertising). In a more extensive sense, one could here talk about examples of the power of information. Such power is not only expressed in the transfer of information, but also in its falsification and deliberate omission; in other words, information is 'filtered' by M. The theorem of the so-called *non-decision* is closely related to this phenomenon.[9] Information that reaches M through N or a third party is swallowed by M so to speak; it then does not constitute a factor that could change M's realisation of power in N's favour.

In our threefold distinction, this power of information can of course also affect the surroundings of the actions of N. The surroundings determine the content and limits of what N can actually achieve, thus influencing the minimum and maximum scope of his alternatives. In this context it is important to remember that a person's status, regardless of how one defines this term, is determined either by nature or his social context and that his actions will often be oriented to this status, yet also limited by it; social status, however, is also formed by power relations.[10] Which power 'basis' a person's status depends on, will often elude detailed analysis.

---

[9] In the sense of the papers by Bachrach/ Baratz in the *American Political Science Review* (1962) and (1963).

[10] Depending on the quality of this orientation we might also be in the sphere of setting values and goals.

Where actions based on circumstances are dependant on 'economic factors' or the state of the market, they become completely anonymous. Anonymous here means that M can no longer be located or that the number of Ms is so large that the individual's contribution can no longer be measured; then we can also neglect that N for his part, as a particle of this market is also a particle of the anonymity.

Therefore, N's actions are determined by his set of values and goals, his status, and a lot of other circumstances of his surroundings, and all of these factors are in turn influenced by outside powers. When N faces a choice of alternatives, M can influence this choice if he somehow causes changes in the sphere of N's values or in the circumstances surrounding N. Yet he can also influence N's actions without such changes, by persuading N to decide against the alternative he has already chosen or might be about to choose and convincing him to choose a second-rate alternative.[11] This is the field of threats and promises, and this is what we think of most of the time when we talk about the power that people use against each other. When talking about threats and promises we are touching upon the field of means or instruments which power makes use of for its realisation. Of course, they are not the only means – just consider misinformation in the form of lies or deception – but by far the most popular among them. Naturally, all these means can also be used in the sphere of values and goals (this means that the following as a rule can be transposed to this sphere, too). Promise and threat also work if N has not yet come to a decision, i.e. has either not discovered the alternatives or is treating them all as being equal. Promise and threat do not work if N – for different reasons – has already made exactly the decision which M wanted him to make; i.e. when M attempts to kick at the aforementioned open doors.[12] In this case we might be moving into the field of attempted realisation of power. For the law, the category of 'attempt' is an important one, whereas it hardly appears in social and economic studies.

We must distinguish a further constellation from this one, namely the decision N has already made because he either wants to forestall a threat and its enforcement (the 'punishment') or expects a promise to be made and kept (the 'reward'). These are instances of anticipated realisation of power.[13] If N is mistaken in his anticipation, this mistake may concern M's possibility of

[11] Substitutes – as far as they cause N higher costs (in the sense of perceived disadvantages) – must also be classified as second-rate. The same is true for the alternative of withdrawing (*exit*).

[12] Threats also function in the sense of causality (yet not that of intention) if N out of sheer defiance decides to take the exact opposite action, even though it might not be the alternative he would have normally chosen.

[13] Even merely watching a third party being exposed to the realisation of power can cause anticipation in N. If we were to play with quantifications, then we could work out the sum total of M's power from the willingness of people to anticipate and the frequency of anticipation.

realising power, or M's intention of doing so.[14] In the first case there is no relation of power whatsoever between M and N,[15] so that only the second case needs to be looked at more closely.

3. The problem of causality

This case, however, leads us to a fundamental dilemma contained in all discussions about power. For while the mistaken anticipation of an intention excludes the intentionality, it does not exclude the causality of M's power for the actions of N. Now, questions related to intentionality are generally neither very relevant nor very difficult for all disciplines concerning themselves with the phenomenon of power.[16] Questions of causality, however, are very much so. If, for example, a company can no longer keep up with its competitors, where do we look for the causalities? In the 'power of the consumers'? In the competitors' advantages? In the weaknesses of our own company, and in which weaknesses? Or, let us take the simple example of delegation from organisation theory (in which analysis of power and power relations is probably most advanced). Delegation in a hierarchical structure, i.e. from top to bottom, implies power realisation from bottom to top, for example by means of filtering the information that is passed on to higher levels. Or let us take a look at the general image of a private or public employer and the power he has over the employee: if you were to pursue causalities here, you would interpret the voluntary choice of a certain kind of training as being the voluntary choice of an alternative that necessarily merges into dependence on such employers as offer adequate possibilities for employment. Of course, such observations are trivial, as is the objection that – in the end of the day – employment, including training, facilitates a person's existence. For if we continue, we will arrive at the end or rather at the beginning at the statement that power represents a fundamental part of the *conditio humana,* which as such is not at our disposal. At the very best, one might be able to determine a sequences of causalities,[17] but do they run in a straight line or do

---

[14] The prototype of a power relation renouncing its realisation is the *dissimulatio* in canon law.

[15] Unless it was M who caused N's mistake.

[16] A short catalogue of intentional power exertion is contained in the so-called 'Wucherparagraph' (clause on profiteering) contained in the German Civil Code (§138 para. 2): 'A legal transaction is particularly void when a person takes advantage of the distressed situation, inexperience, lack of judgmental ability, or grave weakness of will of another to obtain the grant, or promise, of pecuniary advantages for himself or a third party that are obviously disproportionate to the performances given in return.'

[17] Admittedly, their visibility is reduced with temporal distance. They become hazy or fray out so to speak.

they rotate, are they transitive on return to any given starting point? More frequently we find ourselves facing an inextricable bundle of causalities that can no longer be temporally structured and which are very close to non-linear contexts. Yet, when talk about causality begins to waver, what certainty can talk about power claim?

In this case, only radical incisions can be of assistance. Either one applies normative measures which enable us to look at a few units or maybe only one, but set aside all others. This is how the law deals with the problem of causality, attempting to somehow cope with it more or less correctly[18] (and this is also how it will have to deal with the problem of economic power). Or else we allow causality in the context of the power-problem to be merged into other concepts, as has already been illustrated by the example of general system theory – power as a medium of communication.[19] Also, the terms structural power or structural force could deal with the complexity of causalities.[20]

4. FOUNDATIONS OF POWER AND ITS MEANS OF REALISATION

The problem of causality has already led us from N's world to that of M and thereby to the questions about the foundations of power and the means of realising it. If one attempts to gain an overview over possible foundations of power, one finds the abundance of life itself, so to speak. To compile a catalogue of those hardly seems sensible.

However, maybe one could make a distinction between the advantage of assets (*Ausstattungsvorsprung*), on the one hand, and its 'interest yield', on the other (in the literal and metaphorical sense). Your assets would be the physical and mental credits you possess on entering life, as well as a good education to promote and supplement these talents; in general, being embedded in advantageous conditions regarding time and place. Apart from personal talents, material belongings too are part of your assets, i.e. the wealth accumulated by inheritance and donations. Such a headstart in assets might be considered as the fountain of any musing about those rifts in human interrelations that are formulated as the problem of justice. According to experience, the imbalance of assets

---

[18] Does it even make sense to talk about causality, when the number of people N has risen into anonymity, but every person N has a disadvantage that is immeasurably small? However, even this situation might have to be considered in a normative manner.

[19] We would have to deal with the question of causality separately for each concept of power, the discursive or communicative one, the co-operative or participative one, etc.

[20] Yet the terms are not restricted to this; for example, institutions in the sense of systems of rules can form another link. Sometimes, though, a certain idleness in analysis seems to have played a role (not to mention political connotations).

form the driving force – possibly even being a logical condition – of any development of civilisation, so that, as such, they are not at our disposal. However, the consequences deriving from the imbalance of assets are not simply accepted. These then are the topics of justice, e.g. equal opportunities in further education, redistribution of property by means of taxation of inheritance or donations, etc. Especially, we need to ensure that individual imbalance of assets does not turn into a systematic-functional one (e.g. a polity of professional estates, a state of philosophers, expertocracy, plutocracy); out of this worry, the concept of democracy was born.

Other questions of justice are brought up by the 'interest' in assets, 'making the most of them'; for since the amount of yield not only depends on the assets themselves but also on all kinds of different conditions in the surroundings in which 'gaining interest' takes place, we are faced with the problem of how much these factors are to be given a share of the profit gained.[21]

With assets and interest we have by far not mentioned all the foundations of power.[22] We have already dealt with information as an element of power. A further source of power are e.g. 'attributions' on the part of N or a number of Ns; it is on these that the position of power is based by virtue of authority, prestige, emotional ties, 'identifications'. Of course, institutions also bestow power; and power is bestowed and secured by the law. Yet, power is also contained in the 'weak', as far as he enters coalitions, as is the case with public opinion or in collectives.[23] Naturally, power can increase when factors of the same or different kinds of power merge with each other. Here we would be entering the field of business, or more generally speaking that of organisations. When speaking of the 'increase' in power, an aspect of quantification of power positions is implied, a topic not unpopular in social and political studies. Yet little can be deduced from this, even if the problem of comparative power measurement could be solved (which is quite unlikely, given the analogy of the problem of measuring values in the concepts and thoughts of Utilitarianism).

The need to quantify also occurs when considering the costs – in the broadest sense[24] – of power acquisition, power preservation and power realisation. The

---

[21] Do we also have a problem of justice when no yield was achieved, even though one might have done so? What rate of overcoming lethargy does justice demand?

[22] As an example for a mirror image we might mention the power of the help- and asset-less, where compassion plays a role.

[23] For the sake of completeness, or rather repetition, we should point out that every N can turn into M when he is caught in a sequence of causalities. Also, when people speak of practical constraints that require the exertion of power – whereby M is merely an instrument or an execution officer – we have to do with the complexity of problems surrounding causality.

[24] An example is that 'it costs me a great effort', e.g. due to ethical or moral considerations. 'Rules of prudence' (*Klugheitsregeln*) that M abides by are also costs on his part.

statement that repeated execution erodes power as long as the opposition of N increases (Gossen's first law of power, so to speak), also has a quantifying quality.[25] Execution of power, however, can also bankrupt N, it more or less clears the position N had occupied; without an object, however, power (in its relative meaning) turns against itself.[26] Thus, you could say that every power relation is not a one-sided, but rather a two-sided, interdependent relationship. A completely different constellation from that of 'clearing' needs to be distinguished on the level of value and goal expectations, namely when M's power is converted into a learning process for N, and N internalises the values M has set; here, M's power does not come to an end, but is more or less 'preserved' (*aufgehoben*) within N's set of values.[27]

Power realisation of the latter kind is regularly based on the effective use of conviction, probably the most effective instrument which, however, is not given to everyone in power. Persuasion is related to conviction. Other instruments, such as threat, promise and deception have already been mentioned. 'Soft' forms of power realisation are, for example, distancing and admonishment, acceptance and praise.[28] These also belong to M's actions, whereas in other cases his mere position suffices, something which we have already come across in the context of anticipated power realisation; here power works without employing further instruments.

5. The interaction of power and law

For the social sciences, law is only one factor among many when it comes to the classification of the foundations and means of power; there is no kind of qualitative emphasis. The kinds of competence conceded by law and constitution, which can themselves be distinguished according to the limits of their discretionary scope, therefore also belong to the foundations of power.[29] Means of

[25] The phenomenon of the power of small steps or creeping power needs to be distinguished here; normative questions that are similar to the above mentioned minimal disadvantage of many Ns, could present themselves here.

[26] Naturally, the extinction of one power relation can lead to the strengthening of others as is illustrated by the company that has managed to get rid of all of its competitors and now abuses the power of its monopoly towards its customers and suppliers.

[27] Creating 'consensus' is a similar phenomenon of 'preserving' power.

[28] We could also classify actions that prepare the decision of whether or not to make use of more 'forceful' means, e.g. the inspection or hearing, as being 'soft'.

[29] According to some authors, we can no longer talk about a power relation once N has internalised the norms of the law into his sphere of values and goals, since – no matter what – N will choose that action that M seems to be causing in accordance with the law. We could then say, that abiding to the law allows no alternatives.

power are the formal procedures that the state keeps at its disposal for the execution of legal transactions, administrative acts, etc. by means of providing for trials and enforcements before (by virtue of its monopoly) it uses force against N in M's favour. If power is based on the law or makes use of the law for its realisation, we can sociologically also speak about *Herrschaft*. However, similarly to the above-mentioned exact differentiation between power and influence, so the precise (and controversial) distinction between the terms power and *Herrschaft* is of no further importance for our purpose.

The law itself cannot be satisfied with thus being placed at ground level, so to speak. According to its self-understanding, law must take the uppermost place among the formations securing the solidarity of human relationships in their smallest and largest dimensions. Power realisations do not stabilise a social or political unit *per se*, but only when they are combined with a set of values and norms. Such a set could have religious-ritualistic or religious-doctrinal roots, but also ethical-moral or cultural-conventional or whatever ones: historically, the normativity of the law has proven to be the most efficient form of stabilising human relationships[30] (the stabilisation of causalities and finalities according to some, or the stabilisation of structures according to others). Just like all sets of norms, law also determines its relation to power, since it is the law that produces definitions. It determines the preconditions, the content and the limitations of power *in habitu* and *in actu*. It secures the acquisition of power, the preservation of power and the execution of power, or it is disinterested in them, or it prohibits and penalises them. In the first instance, power is legalised, in the second it is tolerated (the province of the discretionary and the informal), in the third, finally, it is negated. Were we to move subject and object, then power would constitute the law and simultaneously obey it:[31] a state of balance and of a constitutional order. Or, power negates the law: a state of rebellion and revolution. In the relationship between law and power, we can talk about the perfect law (*ius perfectum*) when law employs the strength of enforcement to break power, as opposed to imperfect law (*ius imperfectum*), when power submits to the law without the law having the possibility of (lawful) enforcement.[32] Here,

---

[30] In our context we can leave aside the simultaneously emerging question about the positivity or transpositivity of the law.

[31] Many disciplines try to deal with the question of how, historically, we are to imagine the evolution of law; the most naive approach seems to be the ethnological-comparative one. The philosophers have tried to make a theoretical virtue out of a historical necessity: this is how the theory of social contract evolved.

[32] Examples: conviction of the state as a defendant by a court; or disputes of governmental organs before the constitutional court.

power has internalised the law in the sense mentioned above,[33] and accepts the authority of the law without further ado.

6. "Power or Economic Law": the position of the legal system

Differently from social sciences, economic science – where it even bothers to analyse the phenomenon of power – tends to include the aspect of law from the very beginning, and occasionally even equates the two terms more or less. (Here, we are talking about power as a general concept, not yet about economic power or other attributive expressions of power.) This peculiarity has its own history. The underlying theory concept is a specific one, namely that which considers it sensible to ask whether human actions are determined by and cannot even avoid following theory, or whether action is possible in opposition to theory, whether action can disturb, and even destroy theory. In the German speaking community, this question was rephrased as the formula 'Power *or* Economic Law?' in the famous presentation by Eugen v. Böhm-Bawerk. The question was basically answered in the first sense, but the formula was later significantly changed to 'Power *and* Economic Law?'[34] Under constellations of power, Böhm-Bawerk (according to general understanding) emphasised the influence that the state, on the one hand, and monopoly-like organisations, on the other, have on the economic situation. However, the state's influences primarily assume the form of laws or administrative measures based on the law; and monopoly-like organisations – Böhm-Bawerk had trade associations and trade unions in mind – were tolerated and even legalised by the legal system in Austria and Germany at the time.[35] Whenever law is included so intensively in the discussion, the question automatically arises how the law itself views the opposition or juxtaposition of 'power' and 'Economic Law'. The observation that no legal system has ever limited itself to economic concepts, or has accepted or been able to accept definitions from this perspective, is a mere triviality here. We are much rather concerned with two specific details of the discussion. For one, the temporal aspect: Böhm-Bawerk stated that, in the long run, power (the law) would abide by the economic law of equilibrium. This

---

[33] See *supra* n. 29.

[34] Hans K. Schneider/ Ch. Watrin (eds.), *Macht und ökonomisches Gesetz* (Schr. d. Vereins f. Sozialpolitik N.F. 74. Berlin: Duncker & Humblot 1972). Among older publication see Richard Dolberg, *Theorie der Macht*, *supra* n. 2, with further references.

[35] Remember the *Reichskaligesetz* of 1910. The courts had legalised monopolies and cartels by setting only immorality (*Sittenwidrigkeit*) as a limit to their activity (§§ 138, 826 BGB). For further information cf. Nörr, *Die Leiden des Privatrechts* (Tübingen: Mohr 1994) ch. 1.

prophecy, be it correct or not, is not very helpful for the legal system, since *per theoriam* it cannot create the great balance;[36] in addition it must, of course, *hic et nunc* deal with imbalances (be they of an economic or other nature) and make decisions regardless of entelechies.[37] Secondly, from the view of distribution theory – property vs. labour – a clear line is drawn between the functional and the personal aspect, and the limiting of power (the law) by 'Economic Law' is only maintained with regards to the former. Of course, the functional approach is not new to the law, yet, according to its self-understanding, it is itself only a product of the law (power). The distinction between functional and personal would then have to be transferred to within the law, so to speak.

7. Economic power equated with market power

The connection of the concept of power with 'Economic Law' was introduced as being a peculiarity of the German speaking community. Yet, it is not alone in this respect; a second peculiarity – we are now entering the terminological field of 'economic power' – results from the fact that one used to primarily concern oneself with certain extremes within the economic power structures, namely with monopolies and cartels. The origins lie before and within the Weimar period. From the very beginning, the question of economic power with regard to monopolies and cartels was directed at the state and its legal system.[38] Once again, the law was expected to provide definitions, legalise or tolerate or negate the power structures. Most favoured legalisation, very few – negation; yet, from those few the historically powerful movement of Ordoliberalism arose.[39] The Weimar approach and its continuation in the Federal Republic of Germany had the terminological consequence that economic power was and is closely connected to the notion of competition and market, for which reason economic power is being viewed as a falsifying factor for competition, and competition as

---

[36] Were the law to be resolved in economic theory's – pulsating – states of equilibrium, then nothing would stop legal terminology, methodology and theory from vanishing away.

[37] So, for example, if the smallest job supply was faced with a very large demand, one could literally pay employees a pittance far below the minimal living income, as long as those starved to death are replaceable, i.e. as long as the balance has not been achieved. Thus, strictly speaking in terms of economics, it is only in the long term that paying a pittance cannot be maintained. But law, of course, must concern itself equally with short-term matters.

[38] If the focus is set on the jeopardising of the state and its economic order, then 'economic power' has frequently been replaced by 'private power' (private here being completely pejorative).

[39] Where some ordoliberals, as is also the case with other theories by the way, consider law as being a frame condition, thus being expelled to the edges of the 'data', the jurist does not feel concerned any longer, and he moves on as he is destined to.

an economic instrument of negating power. Economic power then is terminologically resolved in market power.[40] Due to this viewpoint, the fact was nearly lost that even in a system of free competition, economic power can develop and be active. Thus if economic power as such could be measured in the abstract, one would have to raise the heretical question of whether it would not be able to develop better within a system of free competition than in an economy full of monopolies and cartels. Of economic liberalism, one can generally state that it has no objections to power as long as it is based on an advantage of assets (in the sense outlined above) and abides by the conditions of market and competitive economy. Be that as it may, limiting the term of economic power, and equating it with market power,[41] had its good sides. It was even extremely advantageous, since it enabled legal regulation (by means of the Act against restraints of competition) and the formation of a method, and development of corresponding dogmatics (by means of interpreting that Act).

8. Composition of the term of economic power

The result of our considerations is that 'power' is composed of causality and a further component. The latter we could, in the briefest formula possible, describe as negative 'alternativity'. What we mean by this is that it is M who determines which alternatives N can even choose from and furthermore, which of the existing alternatives is chosen by N. What is then understood by 'economic power', naturally depends on our understanding of the attribute 'economic'. If generally the aspect of scarcity is taken as a criterion here, then we are talking about states and actions that attempt to cope with the effects of the dictates of scarcity in the most rational manner possible. Power combined with the prefix economic can simultaneously mean power with another prefixed attribute, as in the case of political power ('political' understood as participating in the formation – or attempted formation – of a certain polity's conditions). The prototype of this double attribution is represented by the widely discussed power of associations. Just consider their influence on legislation. Corporate power could therefore be described as a combination of economic and political power. But in this respect it is not alone, governmental economic policy is also political and economic realisation of power in one (to just mention this example).

---

[40] We could also do without this term from the viewpoint of competitorial terminologies; cf. Erich Hoppmann, *Marktmacht und Wettbewerb* (Tübingen: Mohr 1977).

[41] For other suggestions made after 1945 on making the term 'economic power' usable, cf. (cursorily) Nörr, *Die Republik der Wirtschaft* (Tübingen: Mohr 1999) ch. 8.

9. From general to specific, or, the task of the law

Economic power can, therefore, be equated to causality plus negative alternativity under the dictates of scarcity. Were the legal system inclined to face a formula with such a high degree of generality on an equally general level, it would soon throw in the towel. Were it to split up the formula, it could at least provide a normative definition for causality in general expressions,[42] but no more for the other parts. Were it to focus on the whole contained in the formula, a general prohibition is just as inconceivable as a permission with a generally reserved right of control or a permission *per se.*

In principle, the law systems of continental Europe distinguish between private and public law, so that the question arises if economic power is to be controlled by means of rights to private action or by means of measures taken by the authorities. Yet this question is no longer at the most general level, but one of second degree generality, because it calls for distinctions to be made. If an M and an N are facing each other and if the balance of alternatives is obviously to N's disadvantage, then the law will tend towards a right to civil action. However, if M is faced with an anonymous number of Ns and if the negative balance for each N is minute, yet the sum of all negative balances in favour of M is quite considerable, then the instruments of public law have to take over[43] (in a primary or subsidiary or a competitive manner). The situation may be similar if M realises his power in smallest steps, 'creepingly', as it were. The reversed quantitative ratio also raises the private versus public issue, i.e. when it is the addition or summation of a number of power realisations (linear or progressive, merely causal or also intentional) which cause a negative balance for N.

Even at this 'second-degree' level of generality, the law can raise questions, yet not give answers; it will first distinguish between legal fields (environmental law would be an example for the constellation just mentioned), yet will not stop at that but rather move along the way from the general to the specific and only stop when it reaches the point at which it can and wants to set up legal control. This point results from a number of different factors, e.g. historical development, or the context of purpose, or the demands for predictability and legal certainty, and others. The specific point also determines whether the law attempts to control power already *in habitu* or only *in actu.* The search for the ideal point for legal regulation comes up at each step on the way from the general to the specific. And just to pick a few more from the bundle of questions presenting themselves: is the assessment of alternatives and, based on that, of

---

[42] This would break up and segment the way in which both sides, M and N, are embedded in chains of precedent and subsequent power relations – the cascades of power, so to speak.

[43] Actions of social organisations (*Verbandsklagen*) could be included here.

negative balance, made from N's subjective point of view, or do we need to apply an objective-normative scale?[44] Does the normative situation change if N stands in a power relation to M in more than one respect (problem of diversification on part of M)?[45] Is M expected to minimise N's negative balance, even if that increases his own costs? Specific legal questions occur when N has voluntarily entered a power relation, which he basically accepts.[46] And where there are contracts that, due to the dictates of scarcity, entail a power realisation against a third party, i.e. constitute, as it were, a conspiracy against it, there the legal system also cannot provide ready-made solutions.[47]

More examples of such hesitation on the part of the law with regards to the general, the as yet undeciphered, could easily be found. (By the way, even if the doctrines of contemporary institutional economics should at some point – through dogmatics – enter our legal system, it would not change this state of 'apathy' in the slightest.) The phenomenon that any legal control[48] depends on specific circumstances continues to be observable when certain units of economic life are looked at, such as the 'power of the banks' so often conjured. Not only would the legal system immediately distinguish between legal fields – company law, competition law, control of banks as a part of public economic law, etc. – but also start looking for ideal points of regulation in each of these fields. In the eyes of the legal system, to confine economic power as a term denoting a whole to the power of the banks as a term denoting a part would thus only appear to mean a decrease in generality. The same could be said about other sub-units, such as the power of entrepreneurs and managers or the power of interest groups and trade unions: everywhere, the law must first analyse, segment, localise, in order to be able to fulfil its task.[49]

---

[44] In the latter case, the character of 'well-understood interest' of N appears, which in extreme cases leads to his enforced happiness .

[45] From this, one has to distinguish the situation in which a diversifying 'carrier of power', e.g. an enterprise, takes on the role of M regarding one product, but that of N regarding another (towards suppliers, customers, competitors).

[46] An example with remuneration: an employer's right of direction; an example without remuneration: majorising the minority in company law (no remuneration on entering, but possibly when leaving).

[47] If we briefly take a look at the instruments of power realisation, a 'classic' device is the threat. It is tolerated or legalised by the law unless the threat contravenes it. This means that, in its details, law needs to be examined point by point to check whether a given threat is illegal or not (the law only deals with *unlawful* threats, § 123 BGB, § 240 StGB).

[48] Of course, all factors contributing to the formation of law are included, particularly the courts and not only legislation.

[49] As an example cf. Eric Homburger, *Recht und private Wirtschaftsmacht* (Zürich: Schulthess 1993).

10. Conclusion

Thus, we come to the conclusion that the term of economic power in its generality may have an appellative or evocative effect on the law, but that it is in no way able to shape and develop the law. The law *in toto* has nothing normative to accompany or oppose the term, it can only ever react *particulatim*. It must, so to speak, first step down from the higher echelons and examine the locks of all doors of existence before the fitting keys are made. When it finds a place at which it can begin to come in, to legalise or penalise a piece, a particle of economic power, then the term itself has already retreated, the generality of causality and alternativity, as well as the generality created by the dictates of scarcity, has paled in perspective and can only with difficulty be discerned in the distance far away.

Basic Issues of a Reform of the German Law Relating to Foundations

Dieter Reuter[*]

[*] Prof. Dr.iur., Institut für Wirtschafts- und Steuerrecht, Kiel.

Talia Einhorn, ed., Spontaneous Order, Organization and the Law – Liber Amicorum Ernst-Joachim Mestmäcker © 2003 T.M.C.ASSER PRESS, *The Hague, The Netherlands*

1. The development

1.1 The time before the entry into force of the BGB (German Civil Code)

As a socially effective idea the foundation is ancient. Entities similar to foundations existed already in the time of the Greek-Roman antiquity.[1] Nevertheless, the foundation as a specific legal instrument in the European legal systems is a legacy of the Christian age. Until the beginning of the Enlightenment, it was essentially the legal form of expression of the benevolence of the rich concerned with the salvation of their souls. The *pia causa* was an essential feature of an admissible foundation.[2] The Enlightenment brought about the secularisation of foundations without, however, also combining this with an end to the requirement that a foundation be legitimised by a pious purpose in the wider sense of the word. The Prussian General Civil Law of 1794, for example, only allowed "benevolent foundations" which were legally equivalent to the so-called paupers' institutions. Family foundations for the benefit of a family were not regarded as true foundations, but as a species of the so-called community family rights with a fluid transition to functionally comparable family estates in fee-tail.[3] It was only in the 19th century that the bases were created for today's practice in the law relating to foundations. This was done generally by means of a separation between the civil law as the legal constitution of society arising out of popular sentiment and, on the other hand, public law as the entirety of the state-made rules governing the relationship between citizens and the state.[4] Henceforth, the task of civil law was considered to be to transform the traditional law into suitable rules for community life and conflicts.[5] The task of public law was to intervene in the free play of social forces for ethical, economic or political reasons.[6] On the other hand, in the view of civil law, the question of the ethical, economic and political limits of social freedom was no longer important.[7] Interest was no longer focused on the objects of social conduct, but

---

[1] Staudinger (-Rawert), BGB, 13th ed. (Berlin: Sellier/ de Gruyter 1995) Vorbem. zu §§ 80 et seq. note 29.

[2] Schulze, "Historischer Hintergrund des Stiftungsrechts", in: Hauer/Goerdeler/Kreuser/ Frhr. von Pölnitz-Egloffstein (ed.), *Deutsches Stiftungswesen 1977-1988* (Bonn: Wissenschaft und Praxis 1989) 29, 43.

[3] ÂLR II 4 §§ 21 – 46. See Frommhold, "Die Familienstiftung", 117 *AcP* (1919) 87, 110 et seq.; Staudinger (-Rawert), *supra* n. 1, note 127.

[4] Hattenhauer, *Europäische Rechtsgeschiche* (Heidelberg: Müller 1992) 510.

[5] M. Weber, *Rechtssoziologie*, 2nd ed. (Neuwied: Luchterhand 1967) p. 205.

[6] Cf. Reuter, "Freiheitsethik und Privatrecht", in: *Marktwirtschaft und Rechtsordnung – Festschrift für E. Hoppmann* (Baden-Baden: Nomos 1994) 349, 350.

[7] Windscheid, "Leipziger Rektoratsrede of 31 October 1884", in: *Gesammelte Reden und*

on the legal forms in which it took place.[8] In the second half of the 19th century, the separation between private and public law was combined with a constitutional change which more and more reduced the significance of public law as a regulator of social conduct: the responsibility of the state for the national well-being was replaced by confidence in the ability of society to regulate itself. It was consistent with this that, among other things, the state gave up the requirement that associations obtain a state permit and submit to supervision by the state.[9] The law relating to foundations was one of the few areas in which public law retained its functions as a regulator of social conduct. Friedrich Carl v. Savigny, the most renowned German jurist ever, warned against a foundation of Saint Simonists for the purpose of disseminating subversive pamphlets and against the "rich testator" who "creates a foundation giving alms as a misconceived form of benevolence, disrupting and weakening the beneficial effects of the public paupers' institutions".[10] The authors of the Civil Code confirmed that the creation of a foundation went far beyond the limits otherwise set by the rules defining private autonomy. It was therefore considered that it was up to the public law of the individual federal states to decide under what preconditions foundations could be created and how freely they could act.[11]

1.2 The development since the entry into force of the BGB

Since that time, the German law relating to foundations has been a *compositum mixtum* of uniform national private law rules for the form of a foundation and particular public law rules relating to public permits and the supervision of foundations.[12] Their legal status remained unchanged also substantively until the mid-'fifties of the 20th century, characterised by distrustful administrative control over each foundation. This status was found and confirmed by the legislator at the turn of the 20th century. The revolutionary changes after the First World War left the law relating to foundations totally unaffected although in the meantime the Swiss Civil Code had created a model for a liberal foundation system.[13] On the one hand, foundations played no role in the social perceptions of democratic socialism, the major force behind social developments after the

---

Abhandlungen (Leipzig: Duncker & Humblot 1904) 100, 112.

[8] Schulze, *supra* n. 2, 29, 44 et seq.

[9] Cf. Staudinger(-Weick), *supra* n. 1, Einl. vor §§ 21 et seq. notes 59 et seq.

[10] Friedrich Carl von Savigny, *System des heutigen Römischen Rechts II* (Berlin: Veit 1840) 278.

[11] Motive I p. 321; Protokolle I (Berlin/ Leipzig: Guttentag 1888) 588.

[12] For the status today, see Staudinger (-Rawert), *supra* n. 1, notes 56 et seq.

[13] Art. 80 et seq. ZGB. Summary by Pavel, "Schweiz", in: Neuhoff/ Pavel (eds.), *Stiftungen in Europa – eine vergleichende Übersicht* (Baden-Baden: Nomos 1971) 61 et seq.

First World War. On the other hand, they had been decimated to such an extent by the war and the following inflation that they were hardly recognised anymore as a socially relevant factor. National socialism continued the work of destruction.[14] It is no doubt due only to the relatively short duration of its rule that it did not completely suffocate private foundations altogether, as the East German regime did in § 9 EGZGB of 1976.[15]

Since the second half of the 'fifties, the climate has gradually changed. The state bureaucracy no longer takes a suspicious view of foundations, but is in principle favourably disposed. The old laws of the federal states requiring them to be distrustful have been replaced throughout the entire country by state foundation laws which are ideologically indifferent.[16] The law basically provides a framework filled out by the competent authorities at their discretion. Today major foundation projects with a charitable purpose generally receive a permit, in most cases after negotiations in which the tax authorities are involved.[17] The supervisory authorities for foundations no longer behave like wardens, but more or less like partners of the foundations. The heavy hand of the authoritarian state has given way to persuasive dirigism by means of administrative and financial policy which, depending on the degree of correspondence with the ideas of the public administration as to what is useful, and also on the ability to mobilise political connections, accommodates the wishes of the founders and of the foundation organs.[18]

The result of this is rank growth. According to the conclusions of an empirical study in the year 1990, the granting of a permit for a foundation is regarded as an administrative act on the basis of a decision to be taken without discretion by 8 authorities handling such permits, whereas the other authorities believe they have discretionary power.[19] The minimum level of assets required by the authorities differs greatly. In some cases, it depends "on considerations of reverence, humane aspects, and political pressure".[20] Some authorities complain about political wheeling and dealing in the time leading up to the

---

[14] Cf. Liermann, *Handbuch des Stiftungsrechts* (Tübingen: Mohr 1963) 285 et seq.; Rawert (-Ajsensztijn) "Das Stiftungsrecht im Nationalsozialismus", in: v. Campenhausen/Kronke/Werner (eds.), *Stiftungen in Deutschland und Europa* (Düsseldorf: IDW 1998) 157 et seq.

[15] See for this v. Campenhausen, "Alte Stiftungen in den neuen Ländern", in: *Stiftungen in Deutschland und Europa*, ibid., 183 et seq.

[16] This also applies to Bavaria as a result of the most recent reform. Not yet so, Reuter, "Konzessions- oder Normativsystem für Stiftungen?" in: Hönn/Konzen/Kreutz (eds.), *Festschrift für Alfons Kraft* (Neuwied: Luchterhand 1998) 493, 495.

[17] Härtl, *Ist das Stiftungsrecht reformbedürftig?* (Baden-Baden: Nomos 1990) 163 et seq.

[18] Härtl, ibid., 163, 167.

[19] Härtl, ibid., 119.

[20] Härtl, ibid., 114 et seq.

creation of foundations.[21] In principle, family foundations are granted permits everywhere. Only in Bavaria and in the administrative district of Tübingen they are considered to be outdated. In Bavaria exceptions are made for so-called significant founders.[22] The tax exemption for charitable purposes requires the foundation, pursuant to §§ 55 et seq. of the Tax Code, to pursue exclusively the charitable purpose. The tax authorities insist on this in that business-holding foundations are not charitable if their charter obliges them not only to pursue the charitable purpose, but also to maintain and further develop "their" business. On the other hand, the charitable nature of the foundation is recognised if the charter prohibits the foundation – with practically the same effect – from changing to other assets and thereby turns the maintenance and further development of the business into a matter of survival.[23] The tax authorities go even further: in cases like Bosch, Bertelsmann and Hertie, they have even allowed the foundation assets tied up in the business to be managed not by the organs of the foundation, but by bodies which are committed exclusively to the interests of the business. On the one hand, the foundation holds practically all the shares in the limited liability company which runs the business, while, on the other, these shares do not grant any voting rights so that the organs of the foundation cannot enforce the interest of the foundation in achieving an income, neither by exerting pressure on the management of the business nor by means of an economically sensible sale. The entire voting right is concentrated in a minimal share in the limited liability company, and this share is held by a non-charitable foundation, by another limited liability company or by a limited partnership for the purpose of preserving and continuing the business.[24] The result is reflected in the published foundation directories. As the distributions to the charitable foundation depend on the extent to which the bodies concerned with preserving and continuing the business consider the use of the income of the business not to be indispensable for the business, the yield achieved by the foundations is generally far below the yield achieved from other comparable assets.[25]

---

[21] Härtl, ibid., 121.

[22] Härtl, ibid., 152 et seq.

[23] In more detail: MünchKomm (-Reuter), BGB, 4rd ed. (München: Beck 2001) Vor § 80 note 47.

[24] For the Bosch model, see Kronke, *Stiftungstypus und Unternehmensträgerstiftung* (1988) 271 et seq.; for an earlier and basically similar construction, see Reuter, "Privatrechtliche Schranken der Perpetuierung von Unternehmen", in: *Wirtschaftsrecht und Wirtschaftspolitik* (Frankfurt a.M. 1973) vol. 32, pp. 232 et seq.

[25] In more detail Reuter, *supra* n. 16, 493, 506 et seq. See also Herrmann "Funktioniert die Unternehmenskontrolle durch Stiftungen? Eine empirische Untersuchung der Performance stiftungsgetragener Unternehmen", *ZfbF* [1997] 499, 513.

2. THE NEED FOR A REFORM

2.1 The object of the reform: independence of foundations from the government

One would think that this evidently deplorable state of affairs in the actual practice concerning foundations and their tax treatment would set reform efforts in motion. In actual fact, this situation is the main reason why the efforts made during almost 40 years to free foundations from official permits and administrative supervision and instead to integrate the legal provisions dealing with them into the civil law have not made any progress. This is a deplorable state of affairs which exists in the satisfaction of interests not depending on equal and fair treatment, but on the ability to mobilise political connections, will naturally include influential defenders and thus opponents of change.[26]

In reality, the integration of foundations into the civil law, the legal constitution of a liberal society, is a task of eminent social significance and topicality. A liberal society needs not only an economy that is independent of the state, but also institutions independent of the state to handle and solve community tasks "which are not fulfilled, or only inadequately fulfilled by a market economy controlled by scarcity-induced prices and profit motives".[27] On the one hand, these desires contrast with a social development characterised by a continuously decreasing ability to perform on the part of the institutions – families, churches – which traditionally relieve the government. This is due to the fact that the commitment of individuals to their families and churches and thus their willingness to contribute to this ability to perform is continuously declining. On the other hand, this is the very reason why the potentials for direct individual initiatives to further the general welfare, which exist in addition to the long-flourishing social involvement in benevolent associations,[28] are growing. For many, it is a meaningful alternative today to use their savings, not for an inheritance within an alienated family, but rather to combat a social injustice perceived by them through a foundation in memory of its founder. This applies also and especially to persons who were professionally successful and are

---

[26] The Federal Association of German Foundations has especially become their speaker. See Hauer, "Von der Arbeitsgemeinschaft zum Bundesverband", in: *Stiftungen in Deutschland und Europa*, *supra* n. 14, 61, 71.

[27] Mestmäcker, "Soll das Stiftungsrecht bundesgesetzlich vereinheitlicht und reformiert werden, ggf. mit welchen Grundzügen?", *Verhandlungen des 44. Deutschen Juristentages II* (Tübingen: Mohr 1964) G3, 14.

[28] See Th. Nipperdey, *Deutsche Geschichte 1866-1918 I* (München: Beck 1990) 168 et seq.

therefore able to make especially valuable contributions of this kind, both in terms of their asset value and spiritually.[29]

2.2 Relevance of the founder's idea of general welfare

This requires legal rules for foundations that allow the creation and activities of foundations regardless of whether or not they are opportune from the government's point of view. In the light of a liberal constitution of the state as set out in the Basic Law, the creation of foundations must today, contrary to the ideas of the authors of the Civil Code,[30] be recognised as a privately autonomous act, just like the creation of an association. The Federal Administrative Court indirectly supports this point of view by recognising foundations once created as holders of basic constitutional rights.[31] A legal entity can be a holder of basic constitutional rights only if it is a medium for the exercise of such rights by natural persons.[32] If the founder did not act as a privately autonomous citizen when setting up the foundation, the foundation could not be the holder of basic constitutional rights. However, this approach did not prevent the Federal Administrative Court in the case of the Schönhuber Foundation from approving North Rhine-Westphalia's refusal to grant a permit to the foundation on the ground that it would endanger the general welfare, as the purpose of the foundation was to disseminate the political ideas of the Republican Party, which are said to disregard human dignity, to discriminate on the grounds of race, language, national origin, and faith, and to violate democratic principles.[33] If this is read with Saint Simonists instead of the Republican Party, it sounds almost originally like Friedrich Carl von Savigny in 1840. Surely nothing can be said against the denial of legal recognition of foundations which endanger the general welfare. On the contrary: if the point is to further private contributions to perform community tasks, the prohibition of endangering the general welfare is a matter of course. It is, however, a violation of the founder's rights within a system of private autonomy to identify an inconsistency between the majority view of what constitutes political correctness with a danger to the general

---

[29] Traditional reservations against the privatisation of the "a more fair and just distribution of wealth" still exist among the political left. See Fink, "Bessere Rahmenbedingungen für Stiftungen?", in: Deutsche Stiftungen, *Mitteilungen des Bundesverbandes deutscher Stiftungen* (Bonn 1999/ issue 2) 7, 8.

[30] The Parliamentary Commission was expressly opposed to an equal treatment, cf. Mugdan I, pp. 961 et seq. For the earlier parallel treatment of foundations and associations, see Th. Schiller, "Stiftungen im gesellschaftlichen Prozeß" (Baden-Baden: Nomos 1969) 34 et seq.

[31] *BVerwGE* 40, 347, 348.

[32] *BVerfGE* 21, 362, 369; 61, 82, 101.

[33] BVerwG, *NJW* (1998) 2545.

welfare. In comparison, associations cannot be denied state recognition simply because the public authorities believe they endanger the general welfare, but only if they actually do so by unlawful conduct.[34] It is precisely because the historical legislator regarded the creation of associations, as opposed to the creation of foundations, as a use of private autonomy, that associations are neither subject to political control when they are established nor subject to a requirement that they serve the general welfare in order to continue to enjoy state recognition.[35] In the case of the Schönhuber Foundation, the Federal Administrative Court ruled that the freedom to set up foundations could not be treated in the same way as the freedom to create associations because the activities of a foundation, as opposed to the activities of an association, take place with the special involvement and co-responsibility of the public administration. The court stated that the public authorities supervising foundations could not be expected to induce the organs of a foundation to pursue goals which may be inconsistent with the interests of the state and the constitution.[36] But if the freedom of foundation in the sense of the founder's freedom to set up foundations on the basis of his own idea of general welfare is incompatible with the co-responsibility of political institutions for the foundation's activities, the constitutional protection of the freedom of foundations ensures that it is not this freedom, but the involvement of the political institutions which must step back. Unless state supervision is to be eliminated altogether, responsibility for such supervision must be assigned to institutions which, like the institutions under the German *ex parte* Jurisdiction Act, are not politically dependent and answerable. How the case of the Schönhuber Foundation should be solved on the basis of a law which rests on the idea that the founder is autonomous is shown by the example of Switzerland. In spite of "some droll or otherwise politically hardly desirable foundations", the principle that the founder's idea of general welfare should be relevant has been resolutely upheld by the law for over 90 years,[37] the success of this being that the small country of Switzerland has about as many charitable institutions as its big neighbour Germany.[38]

---

[34] See § 43 (1) BGB and MünchKomm (-Reuter), *supra* n. 23, note 2.

[35] For this see MünchKomm (-Reuter), *supra* n. 23, § 87 note 4.

[36] BVerwG, *NJW* (1998) 2545, 2547 replied to the republicans' complaint that their equal chances in relation to other parties were violated by expressly pointing out the possibility to establish a registered association (!)

[37] Riemer, "Das deutsche Stiftungsrecht aus der Sicht des schweizerischen", in: *Stiftungen in Deutschland und Europa*, *supra* n. 14, 349, 356.

[38] For the figures for Switzerland, see Riemer, "Das deutsche Stiftungsrecht aus der Sicht des schweizerischen", in: *Stiftungen in Deutschland und Europa*, *supra* n. 14, 349; for Germany see Mecking, ibid., 107, 119.

2.3 Integration of foundation law into the general civil law

However, by recognising the creation and activity of a foundation as an exercise of private autonomous rights, the need for reforms in the law relating to foundations has not yet been fully addressed. Over and about that, the integration of foundations into the civil law, which corresponds with an end to individual administrative control by the authorities responsible for foundations, requires legal provisions to fit the foundations smoothly into the system of civil law. Compared to the second half of the 19th century, the civil law perspective has changed. Reality soon showed that the free play of social forces can bring about the expected positive results only if the rules are not also brought about by the free play of social forces, but by a legislator committed to ethical, political and economic goals.[39] The legislator at the end of the 19th century, including the parliament, which enacted the Civil Code was not at all satisfied with codifying a traditional law, but attempted in a visionary manner to define conditions for ethically, politically and economically acceptable further development of society.[40] Today, the responsibility of the state for just and fair social conditions is a constitutional requirement derived from the principle of a social state.[41] In particular, legal entities are subject to so-called normative conditions that "incorporate them and their life into the general legal order, ensure certainty and reliability in legal transactions . . . and take account of the legitimate interests of third parties or of the general public".[42] These normative conditions must be observed also if the creation and activities of foundations no longer depend on a permit granted by the public authorities or are no longer controlled by the public authorities.

Conditions which are regarded as indispensable to give other legal entities certainty and reliability in their legal transactions cannot be regarded as dispensable in the case of a foundation, as this would constitute a contradictory evaluation.[43] And above all, the foundation must not be turned in a counter-productive manner into a legal form by the choice of which the protective provisions existing with respect to other legal entities in the interest of third parties and the general public can be circumvented.[44]

---

[39] Basic reflections in Franz Böhm, *Wettbewerb und Monopolkampf* (Berlin: Heymanns 1933) 322 et seq.

[40] See Staudinger (-Coing), *supra* n. 1, Einl. zum BGB, notes 59 et seq.

[41] *BVerfGE* 22, 180, 204.

[42] BVerfG, *NJW* (1979) 699, 706.

[43] Crezelius/Rawert, "Stiftungsrecht – quo vadis?", *ZIP* [1999] 337, 343.

[44] Ibid., 345.

3. The involvement of the state in the creation and activities of foundations

3.1 Free creation of foundations?

The end of the individual control of foundations by the public authorities and the integration of the law relating to foundations into the civil law, is generally discussed as a problem of the transition from a licence system to the normative system: The involvement of the state in the creation of foundations is not to be eliminated, but transformed into a constituent implementation of a right on the basis of a preceding examination of the statutory requirements to be satisfied for the creation of a foundation (effectiveness of the foundation charter, minimum contents of the charter, etc.).[45] Originally, the draft reform proposal made by the Free Democratic Party went one step further. According to this, the foundation was the only legal entity under civil law not to need any state involvement to be created; the notarization of the charter was to be sufficient.[46] The creation of a legal entity as an independent participant in legal transactions makes it necessary, however, to provide special guarantees for certainty and reliability in legal transactions. The partners must be able to trust that they will not suddenly be left without a debtor simply because the legal act whereby the debtor was created is void or has been challenged by the parties. Consequently, it is necessary to have an institution that examines the validity of the creation of the foundation as well as compliance with the statutory minimum requirements before the permit is granted to the foundation to participate in legal transactions, and thereby prevent the parties after the permit is granted from claiming that the creation of the foundation was void.[47] This is not changed in any way by the fact that the courts and legal authors now also recognise so-called communities of joint owners with a name of their own and a domicile as bearers of rights and duties.[48] Even for the joint community of owners which most closely resembles a legal entity, namely the non-registered association, the individuals acting for the association are personally liable, which takes account of the fact that the legal existence of the association is inadequately secured in the absence of an examination and determination by a state institution.[49] In any event, in the case

[45] *Verhandlungen des 44. Deutschen Juristentages*, vol. I (Tübingen: Mohr 1962), part 5 (Opinion Ballerstedt and Salzwedel); vol. II (Tübingen: Mohr 1964) G 3 et seq. (speech Mestmäcker) and G 89 (Thesen); most recently K. Schmidt, *supra* n. 14, 229 et seq.; Reuter, *supra* n. 16, 493 et seq.

[46] *BT-Drucks.* 14/336 of 29 January 1999, § 80.

[47] See K. Schmidt, *Gesellschaftsrecht*, 3rd ed. (Köln: Heymann 1997) 148 et seq.

[48] See Grunewald, Gesellschaftsrecht, 3rd ed. (Tübingen: Mohr 1999) notes 101 et seq.

[49] MünchKomm (-Reuter), *supra* n. 23, § 54 note 33.

of a foundation, the issue is not the legal independence of an association of persons which can have a natural existence separate and apart from the individuals involved.[50] Instead, the point is the legal independence of assets which, regardless of the nature of their actual management, can always be a separate legal personality as well as being the non-independent special assets of another natural person or legal entity. It is thus not in the nature of things that a foundation should be a (limited) legal personality, regardless of a state review and determination of its suitability independently to take part in legal transactions. It is not by coincidence that Otto von Gierke, the most determined supporter of the free creation of legal entities in the 19th century, was not in favour of an analogous free creation of foundations.[51]

If the constituent state involvement in the creation of a legal entity in the form of a foundation is eliminated, the point of reference for crucially important legal consequences of the creation of a legal entity is eliminated too, although this would not be justified by the special nature of the foundation. Notarization is not an adequate substitute for a state admissibility examination. Not only does the law nowhere provide for any possibility to heal the nullity or challengeability by means of a notarization. What is more, the courts do not even trust the clauses drafted by the notaries themselves properly to weigh the interests involved. It is for this reason that the courts submit such clauses to judicial review as to whether they unduly benefit one party at the expense of the other.[52] As the courts must to the greatest extent possible avoid contradictory evaluations in the law, it is quite conceivable that the courts will deny the foundation the advantages of a legal personality such as the exclusion of personal liability on the part of the persons acting for it, and protection against retroactive nullity and legal challenge.[53] Again: the law relating to legal entities under civil law is not an uncoordinated co-existence of arbitrary legal forms, but a system based on uniform evaluations (and designed to have mutually supplementary effects between its component parts instead of neutralising effects). Good legislation takes this into account.

---

[50] For the significance of Gierke's theory of the real association personality for the doctrine of the company on an inadequate contractual basis, see Flume, *Die Personengesellschaft* (Berlin: Springer 1977) 17.

[51] *Deutsches Privatrecht I, 1895 – 1917* (München/Leipzig: Duncker & Humblot) 650.

[52] *BGHZ* 108, 164 et seq.; criticised by Medicus, *Zur gerichtlichen Inhaltskontrolle notarieller Verträge* (München: Beck 1989) 12 et seq.

[53] Crezelius/Rawert, *supra* n. 43, 343.

3.2 Licence or normative system?

3.2.1 *The arguments for maintaining the licence system*

There are renowned authors who dispute that the end of individual control of foundations by the administration and the integration of the law relating to foundations into civil law requires a transition from the licence system to the normative system under the rule of modern administrative law. According to this opinion, the binding force of normative conditions, which is the essence of the end of the individual control of foundations by the public authorities in favour of their integration into civil law, is to be separated from the question of whether it technically takes place without any constituent involvement by the state (earlier proposal of the Free Democratic Party), through a permit granted by the authorities (status quo), or through an entry in a register kept by the court. The choice between alternatives 2 and 3 is said to have to be made in favour of the *status quo* as long as the normative conditions do not have the clarity which could justify doing without the relatively greater flexibility and the advisory effect of an administrative permit procedure and instead installing a strictly formalised implementation procedure in the nature of a procedure to register with a public register.[54]

3.2.2 *Criticism*

The criticism to be sounded against this is that the content of the task is not at all irrelevant for the answer to the question through which procedure and before which institution it should be fulfilled. The continuing competence of the administrative authorities for state involvement is incompatible with the right to set up foundations contingent upon the fulfilment of certain normative conditions, especially if the normative conditions allow for latitude in evaluation. It is these latitudes of evaluation which are the entry gates for administrative opportunism within the framework of a bound administration. The judgement in the case of the Schönhuber Foundation not only shows that the right to set up a foundation provided the general welfare is not endangered, allows a practice which differs in no way from the traditional practice of granting permits for foundations at the discretion of a public authority.[55] It is all the more important

---

[54] K. Schmidt, "Konzessionssystem und Stiftungsrecht" in: *Stiftungen in Deutschland und Europa*, *supra* n. 14, 229, 233 et seq., 242; Flume, *Die juristische Person* (Berlin: Springer 1983) 134 et seq.

[55] BVerwG, *NJW* (1998) 2545, 2547 expressly states that the danger to the general welfare need not have reached the level where the purpose of the foundation is not allowed, as otherwise the recommended solution, i.e. to set up an association, could not be considered because of the in-

Maintaining a system of supervision of foundations by public authorities is, on the contrary, problematic because it essentially creates the same frictions between the task itself and the organisation for fulfilling the task as does the continuation of the (technical) licence system: the task is to implement rights. The use of a foundation for public purposes beyond the extent required by law and the charter is, as the Federal Administrative Court has confirmed,[67] as much prohibited as is a waiver of rights for reasons of political opportunism. The performance of the task shall nevertheless be entrusted to an institution within the realm of politics which cannot be expected to consider the assistance by foundations in its administrative activities to be inconvenient even if the law and the charter do not cover such conduct. Considering that any misconduct on the part of the foundation organs can be combated by legal means only through the supervisory authorities, and misconduct on the part of the supervisory authorities only by the organs of the foundation,[68] the danger of an arrangement to the disadvantage of the foundation cannot be denied altogether. A "good relationship", as it exists in the opinion of the Federal Association of German Foundations between the executive committees of many foundations and the supervisory authorities, is therefore a reason for concern rather than, as the Federal Association believes,[69] an argument for maintaining the system of administrative competence.

4. THE NORMATIVE CONDITIONS UNDER THE LAW RELATING TO FOUNDATIONS

4.1 Subsumable normative conditions as a precondition for the right to create a foundation

It is necessary for subsumable normative conditions to be formulated not only for the registration system, but also for a legal right to have the intended foundation recognised. Without this the licence system is inevitable; likewise and inversely the requirement of proper and appropriate organization makes the registration system necessary if subsumable normative conditions are available.[70] The authors of the German Civil Code still denied the possibility of

---

67 *BVerwGE* 40, 347, 352.

68 See Blydt/ Hansen, *Die Rechtsstellung der Destinatäre der rechtsfähigen Stiftung Bürgerlichen Rechts* (Frankfurt am Main: Lang 1998) 159 et seq.

69 v. Campenhausen, *Tonbandprotokoll der Sachverständigenanhörung der F.D.P.-Fraktion of 22 March 1999*, p. 106.

70 K. Schmidt, "Konzessionssystem und Stiftungsrecht", in: v. Campenhausen/Kronke/ Werner (eds.), *Stiftungen in Deutschland und Europa*, *supra* n. 14, 229, 237.

subsumable normative conditions for the creation of foundations on the basis of the outdated ground, however, that the state should keep control over the development of foundations because of their alleged subversive tendencies.[71]

4.2 Requirements for a foundation as a legal entity

Today there are two issues: first the foundation deed (among living persons or *mortis causa*) must satisfy the general requirements as to the creation of a legal entity. It is therefore necessary to provide a foundation substrate in the form of assets dedicated to a particular purpose in an amount sufficient for this purpose, to give this substrate an identity of its own (name, domicile), and to create an organization whereby it can act (appointment and dismissal of the members of its institutions).[72] There is much to support the arguments that one of the neuralgic points of the current licensing practice, namely the requirement of assets suitable for the purpose of the foundation,[73] should be relaxed by limiting the registry judge's power to the right and the duty to reject an application for registration on the ground of evidently inadequate assets. In this respect there is scope for evaluation, which, because of the nature of the matter, cannot be narrowed down to a subsumable fact before the limits of a manifest inadequacy have been reached. The same solution has been found for the registration of undercapitalised corporations.[74] Certainly, as experience in Switzerland has shown,[75] the consequence of this can be that foundations will increasingly have to be dissolved soon after they are created because it is impossible for them to achieve their purposes. In Switzerland it has therefore been considered whether an administrative preliminary examination should precede the registration. However, in the final analysis this thought was dropped because it was agreed that the intended benefit could not outweigh the threat that this would constitute to the idea of a foundation.[76] To be distinguished from the requirement of sufficient assets for the foundation is the question whether, before allowing an independent foundation to be set up, thereby creating what might be called a seriosity threshold, a minimum capital required by law should be introduced, similar to the minimum capital required for a limited liability company and a stock corporation. That this should be done is suggested not only by the model in company law, but also because the workload upon the courts through

---

[71] Mugdan I p. 961 (Report by the Reichstag Commission, Berlin).

[72] Basics in John, *Die organisierte Rechtsperson* (Berlin: Duncker & Humblot 1977) 74 et seq.

[73] Härtl, *supra* n. 17, p. 114 et seq.

[74] K. Schmidt, *supra* n. 47, p. 522.

[75] Riemer, *supra* n. 14, 356.

[76] Riemer, ibid., 356 at the end.

registration and supervisory tasks can otherwise easily become disproportionate.[77] As for the minimum assets threshold, the model of limited liability company law suggests a valuation of DM 50,000.[78]

4.3 **Immanent limits of the founder's autonomy**

4.3.1 *No profit-oriented foundation*

Secondly, the specific preconditions for creating a foundation must be determined. Even the fact that the founder's subjective concept of general welfare is relevant does not allow him to identify his own private benefit with the general welfare in principle. It is almost unanimously agreed that the foundation must involve a transfer of assets; therefore, the so-called foundation for the founder is not admissible.[79] Otherwise, it would be possible to evade one's creditors by creating assets without liability. If the founder contributes his assets to a foundation, his creditors can no longer seize these assets, subject to the German Voidability Act and the provisions in the Insolvency Act providing for the voidability of legal transactions. The foundation is not liable for the founder's debts; the founder holds no foundation shares which his creditors could seize. It is evident that such consequences are inconsistent with the provisions of private law dealing with liability. This verdict naturally concerns also family foundations which differ from a foundation for the founder only in that the founder creates assets without liability not for himself, but for members of his family.[80] Nevertheless, most argue *de lege lata* that such a foundation can be granted a permit and *de lege ferenda* that it can be registered.[81] Those who take this point of view are also not distracted by the fact that, in the 19th century, a family foundation was regarded as a modified form of the family estate in fee-tail, which has been prohibited since the Weimar Reich Constitution[82] and is therefore regarded as prohibited in Austria and Switzerland as is the family estate in fee-tail itself.[83] The draft reform presented by the parliamentary group of Bündnis 90/Die Grünen at least takes account of such concerns regarding family

---

[77] K. Schmidt, *supra* n. 14, 240 et seq.

[78] More rigid K. Schmidt, ibid., 229, 241: DM 100,000.

[79] Soergel (-Neuhoff), BGB, Vor § 80 note 8; Staudinger (-Rawert), *supra* n. 1, note 9; Leisner, "Staat und Stiftung", in: *Deutsches Stiftungswesen 1966-1976* (Bonn: Wissenschaft und Praxis 1977) 85, 122.

[80] Reuter, *supra* n. 16, 493, 501 et seq.

[81] Soergel (-Neuhoff), *supra* n. 78, notes 57 et seq.; Flume, *supra* n. 54, 133 FN 145; Interministerielle Arbeitsgruppe Stiftungsrecht, *Deutsches Stiftungswesen 1966-1976*, *supra* n. 79, 361, 392 et seq.

[82] See references in Schulze, *supra* n. 2, 29, 41 et seq.

[83] Crezelius/Rawert, *supra* n. 43, 345 with FN 92.

foundations by limiting their duration to 30 years, subject to a unanimous resolution by all beneficiaries and reversioners to continue the foundation beyond that period. The draft is a response to the fact that inheritance law allows the testator to commit his estate for a period of no more than 30 years.[84] However, it still does not adequately address the inconsistency between a family foundation and the rules of civil law regarding liability.

4.3.2 *No foundation as an end in itself*

As a starting point, there is agreement by and large that the main purpose of the foundation must not be limited to the administration of the foundation assets. A foundation as an end in itself is ruled out because only the natural person himself, but not the legal entity, can be an end in itself.[85] However, already the extent of this notion is highly controversial. Some believe that it is not relevant to a business-holding foundation, as the preservation of a business is always also in the interests of third parties (employees) and of the general public. At least, where, as in the case of Zeiss, the preservation of the company is officially designated by the charter of the association as a means to further a special social culture or to perform a task of social policy ("to give the people in the city of X work and food"), this is said to help to overcome the inadmissibility of the foundation as an end in itself.[86] It is even the dominant opinion that a foundation that is committed to investing its assets in a particular company can have a charitable purpose (e.g. support of sciences),[87] although the preservation and further development of the business thereby becomes an existential issue and thus the primary interest of the foundation. The "charitable purpose" in this case is in fact a *falsa demonstratio*, as it does no more than indicate what is to be done with the proceeds which are indispensable for the preservation and further development of the company.

Essentially, the (open or disguised) business-holding foundation as an end in itself is the legal realisation of the "business as such", which has kept the imagination of lawyers and economists busy since Walter Rathenau first formulated the thought in his publication "Of Stock Corporations".[88] For this reason the reservations which have always been entertained against business as such are

---

[84] Following Staudinger (-Rawert), *supra* n. 1, notes 132 et seq.

[85] Staudinger (-Rawert), *supra* n. 1, note 88; Soergel (-Neuhoff), *supra* n. 82, note 70; MünchKomm (-Reuter), *supra* n. 23, note 7.

[86] Kersten, "Stiftung und Handelsgesellschaft – Ein Beitrag zur Unternehmensstiftung und ihren Erscheinungsformen", in: *Festschrift für den 45. Deutschen Juristentag* (Karlsruhe: Müller 1964) 123, 130; Kronke, *supra* n. 24, 225 et seq.

[87] Soergel (-Neuhoff), *supra* n. 78, note 71; K. Schmidt, *supra* n. 47, 183 et seq.

[88] Wiedemann, *Gesellschaftsrecht I* (München: Beck 1980) 301 with further references.

directed also against foundations whose purpose is a business. To begin with, the corporate interest which the individuals acting for the foundation are to be committed to cannot be defined, but must be found in a process whereby the particular interests integrated in the business are reconciled.[89] The problem of how this reconciliation process must be organised in order to achieve the relatively best possible decision has not been solved; there is good reason to doubt that it can be solved at all.[90] In the final analysis, there is little to do other than recognise as the realisation of the corporate interests, what the management of business says it is. The consequence of this is a practically limitless rule by management.[91] From the point of view of the law relating to foundations, this is especially worrying because state supervision, which not least of all is designed to determine any responsibility for damage to the foundation, thereby becomes ineffective. The same applies to dual constructions such as Bertelsmann. In the case of a dual construction, supervision fails to reach those actually responsible for developing the assets of the foundation, not only because of the absence of sufficient legal ties, but also because they are not organs of the foundation at all.[92] Secondly, the "business as such" conflicts with mandatory law. In particular, the interests of the employees, surely the most important partial element of the interests of the company, cannot be internalised to the necessary extent, as employees have mandatory rights which they can exercise, regardless of whether they are consistent with the interests of the company. Where these rights are set out in collective agreements, they cannot be waived by the employees without the consent of the parties to the collective agreement, as the cases of Viessmann and Burda show.[93] To summarise: a business-holding foundation as an end in itself cannot be integrated into the German civil law system.

---

[89] Laske, "Unternehmensinteresse und Mitbestimmung", *ZGR* [1979] 173 et seq.; Teubner, "Unternehmensinteresse – das gesellschaftliche Interesse des Unternehmens 'an sich'?", 149 *ZHR* (1985) 470, 479 et seq.; Reuter, "Der Einfluß der Mitbestimmung auf das Gesellschafts- und Arbeitsrecht", 179 *AcP* (1979) 509, 516 et seq.

[90] See the attempt made with respect to the foundation whose object is a company itself by Kronke, "Stiftung, Kapital- und Personengesellschaften – Gestaltungsprobleme bei mittelbaren Unternehmensträgerstiftungen", *ZGR* [1996] 18, 33 et seq.

[91] Mestmäcker, *Verwaltung, Konzerngewalt und Rechte der Aktionäre* (Karlsruhe: Müller 1958) 14; Wiedemann, *supra* n. 87, 322.

[92] See also Kronke, *supra* n. 24, 272; Reuter, *Privatrechtliche Standpunkte der Perpetuierung von Unternehmen* (Frankfurt a.M.: Athenäum 1973) 94 et seq.

[93] BAG, *NZA* [1999] 887; see also Kübler, *Gesellschaftsrecht*, 5th ed. (Heidelberg: Müller 1989) 166.

4.3.3 *Limits of the economic activities of foundations*

To be distinguished from the issue of the admissibility of a business-holding foundation as an end in itself is the question whether and to what extent the foundation is allowed to engage in economic activities as a means of pursuing a non-commercial purpose, in particular whether a business may be conducted by the foundation. An answer to this question is to make this contingent, as in the case of an association with a non-profit purpose, upon whether the economic activity remains a side activity.[94] In fact, this is quite practicable provided the economic activity is an (exchangeable) source of financing. Insisting that the foundation should devote itself primarily to achieving the non-commercial purpose prevents the transition from the service of the business for the foundation to the service of the foundation for the business.[95] It is not necessary that the economic activities be spun off to a legally independent subsidiary. The widespread assumption that creditors of the company would thereby be better protected[96] fails to appreciate the effect of the tying up of capital by company law. This compensates for the limitation of the shareholder's liability by at least partially enforcing a connection between the economic fate of the company assets and the shareholders' assets.[97] Compared to the unlimited liability of the operator of the business, it is certainly more unfavourable for the creditors of the business.[98] This is true also if the business is operated by a foundation (or a non-profitable association). If at all, the spin-off can be necessary to protect the foundation. But that is more a question of the risks in each individual case, which must be answered by the executive committee of the foundation at its due discretion. Only the participation in a partnership as its personally liable partner must be generally prohibited for the foundation as it involves the risk that the existence of the foundation will be endangered, not by its own decisions controlled by the supervisory authorities, but through decisions taken by other partners.[99]

More difficult to define are the limits for the economic activities of foundations where these do not serve to maintain a source of financing, but to achieve

---

[94] Following Mestmäcker, *supra* n. 27, G3, 19 et seq. MünchKomm (-Reuter), *supra* n. 23, Vor § 80 note 7; Staudinger (-Rawert), *supra* n. 1, Vor § 80 note 29; disagreeing: Seifert/v. Campenhausen-Hof, *Handbuch des Stiftungsrechts*, 2nd ed. (München: Beck 1998) note 56 with references.

[95] More detail in MünchKomm (-Reuter), *supra* n. 23, Vor § 80 notes 46 et seq.

[96] Representative BGH, *NJW* (1983) 569, 571.

[97] More detail in MünchKomm (-Reuter), *supra* n. 23, § 21, 22 note 11.

[98] See already K. Schmidt, "Der bürgerlich-rechtliche Verein mit wirtschaftlicher Tätigkeit", 182 *AcP* (1982) 1, 29.

[99] More detail in MünchKomm (-Reuter), *supra* n. 23, Vor § 80 note 49 at the end.

its objects, e.g. in the case of hospitals or nursing homes operated by charitable foundations (or charitable associations). Such cases have long not been a problem for the simple reason that it was considered until very recently that operating nursing homes and the like commercially was excluded. But circumstances have changed. It is now a matter of course that nursing homes offer nursing services in a profit-oriented market where non-profit organisations such as foundations and associations compete with profit-oriented organisations, especially as the social state ensures that the need for adequate prices will not narrow down the circle of beneficiaries contrary to the charter of the association. Some authors of publications on foundations have derived an argument from this for the general admissibility of foundations as operators of businesses. But this overlooks, on the one hand, that the problem is not limited to foundations, but also concerns non-profit associations, which can under no circumstances operate a business, as § 22 BGB makes clear. On the other hand and especially, it is not quite clear that the main commercial activity of a foundation or an association in the form of the operation of a nursing home, hospital or opera should naturally be admissible only because these business objects used to be – abstractly and/or concretely – the domain of non-commercial main activities. Where the change of legal form to a stock corporation or limited liability company cannot reasonably be expected due to special circumstances, an exceptional permit for the association as an economic association is possible pursuant to § 22 BGB.[100] The same procedure is possible for foundations.

5. Independence of Foundations and Foundation Tax Law of the State

In the discussion on the future of foundations and foundation law, it is taken as a matter of course that the independence of foundations from the state reaches limits under tax law. It is said that the state may be denied the right to make its admissibility contingent upon the usefulness in its view of a foundation, but not the tax privileges of foundations.[101] This thesis is logical if the tax advantages enjoyed by the founder and the foundation are grounded upon the effects of the

---

[100] MünchKomm (-Reuter), *supra* n. 23, § 21, 22 notes 54 et seq.

[101] Walz, in Walz: Wagner/Walz, *Zweckerfüllung gemeinnütziger Stiftungen durch zeitnahe Mittelverwendung und Vermögenserhaltung* (Baden-Baden: Nomos 1997) 99 ("Gesamtsicht" maßgebend).

foundation activities in relieving the public authorities.[102] But this is not the only possible approach. It is also possible to consider the fact that the founder reduces his economic power by providing assets to the charitable foundation and that the foundation can simply not become subject to the Income Tax Act because of its obligation to distribute its proceeds to the beneficiaries. This is all the more true because it is not *per se* excluded that the proceeds will be taxable for the beneficiaries.[103] In any case, the reduction of the ability to pay taxes is the approach which fits better into the tax system. Under German law, the privilege is the founder's right to claim the equipment of the foundation as an item of special expense, whereas the effects of the foundation activities in relieving the state from its tasks suggests the solution put into effect in Great Britain, for example, namely that the tax paid by the founder on the acquisition of the assets transferred to the foundation is refunded to the foundation (!).[104] But if one assumes that the tax relief for the founder and the foundation reacts to a reduced or missing ability to perform economically, this tax relief can in principle also be granted for objectively altruistic establishments and activities of foundations. The further precondition of objective charitability is not necessary so that the admissibility of the foundation under civil law and the recognition of the foundation under the tax law go hand in hand. It is true that the current starting point in Germany, i.e. the foundation's effect in relieving the state from its tasks, also dominates the tax law relating to foundations in the other European states. However, the opposing concept does have models: ERNST-JOACHIM MESTMÄCKER already pointed out in 1962, in his speech to the 44th German Jurists Convention, that in the USA it is not necessary in order to assume a charitable purpose (which involves privileges both under civil law and tax law) to examine "whether the object of the foundation is positively in the public interest", but is limited essentially to "excluding unlawful and manifestly abusive objects".[105] Anyone who reads this almost 40 year old speech in its entirety and compares it with the above considerations will see to what extent ERNST-JOACHIM MESTMÄCKER served as a teacher in the true sense of the word also on the law relating to foundations. The 75th birthday of the honoured teacher is once again an occasion for the student gratefully to remember him.

---

[102] With criticism Flämig, "Die Deformation des gemeinnützigen Stiftungswesens durch das Steuerrecht", in: *Deutsches Stiftungswesen 1977-1988*, *supra* n. 2, 165, 168 et seq., who also demands tax privileges for activities serving the general welfare in a manner deviating from the government's point of view.

[103] Cf. MünchKomm (-Reuter), *supra* n. 23, Vor § 80 note 109.

[104] Hill, "England und Wales", in: *Stiftungen in Europa*, *supra* n. 13, 219, 242.

[105] Mestmäcker, *supra* n. 27, G3, 15.

Syndicate Agreements in Hungarian Company Law

Tamás Sárközy*

1. Introduction

As a result of the specific directions taken by development in Hungary (the economic reform after the year 1968 – gulaschcommunism, soft-dictatorship, pseudo rule of law) various elements of company law appeared in Hungary already in the 1960s. A particular company law came into existence within the state enterprises and the cooperatives (civil law partnerships, joint enterprises, associations – their unified regulation is to be found in law decree 4 of 1978), and the Hungarian Civil Code of 1959 maintained in force several of the commercial company forms regulated by the Commercial Code from before the Second World War. Therefore as of 1972, when the partnership of Western enterprises in Hungarian companies became possible, the Kft.-s (limited liability company) and the Rt.-s (company limited by shares) also appeared but sparsely in the Hungarian economy.

In the field of small-scale industry citizens had the possibility to found unlimited partnerships as early as 1958. The land in Hungary was not nationalized, and even though the peasantry was forced into agricultural cooperatives, as members of the cooperative they were allowed the right of disposition over a relatively large household farming plot. The independence within the cooperative was also much more apparent than, for example, in the Soviet Union. At the beginning of the 1980s the foundation of so-called small enterprises became a right of citizens, which mainly operated in the form of lease, but also company forms like small cooperatives and economic working communities were established, which in turn meant a relatively large corpus of joint citizen private

* Professor of law, Budapest University of Economics and Business Administration.

Talia Einhorn, ed., Spontaneous Order, Organization and the Law – Liber Amicorum Ernst-Joachim Mestmäcker © 2003 T.M.C.ASSER PRESS, *The Hague, The Netherlands*

property (as of 1980 a single Hungarian entirely private economic working community – the form that is compatible with the German *offene Handelsgesellschaft* – was entitled to have 30 employees, which would have been impossible in other socialist countries).

The relatively fast-developing market institutions in Hungary resulted in the adopting of the Act on Business Organisations (Act VI of 1988) two years prior to the political change of regime. Pursuant to said Act foreign and domestic natural persons and legal entities were granted the right to establish unlimited partnerships, limited partnerships, limited liability companies and companies limited by shares. Going by the Hungarian traditions from before 1945 the structure of the 1988 Act followed the principles of German company law, and also included modern tendencies, such as the law of concerns. On the basis of the 1988 Act numerous private companies were established in Hungary (by 2000 the number of private limited partnerships and limited liability companies exceeded one hundred thousand); on the other hand, the majority of state enterprises were transformed into companies limited by shares, then on the basis of Act XXXIX of 1995 they transferred the shares into private property pursuant to specific privatization contracts. *In Hungary institutional privatization* – in second place among the socialist countries, where Germany was the first – *had come to an end by 2000*, and the proportion of national wealth represented by private property reached 85%. More than 50% of the Western capital instreaming into Eastern-Western Europe was invested in Hungary, with approximately three-thirds of the 200 largest companies operating with a foreign partner.

In the course of the *legal harmonization procedure* necessary for Hungary's joining the European Union the Hungarian legislation relating to companies and company registration had been modernized, the company law directives of the European Union had been taken into consideration, and the law regarding company groups had also been re-regulated (Acts CXLIV and CXLV of 1997). On the basis of this company law practice seems to have stabilized in Hungary. Within this framework contractual institutions related to company law, such as merger and division agreements, management contracts (agreements concluded for company management), and the syndicate agreement constituting the subject of the present essay also appeared in Hungarian law.

2. Classification of the Syndicate Agreement

In compliance with international practice the syndicate agreement in Hungarian law is not regulated as a contract named by either the Act on Business Organisations or the Civil Code. Given its nature the syndicate agreement may have greatly differing content, therefore it might be best classified as a specific *heterogeneous innominate type of contract.*

Certain cases of the syndicate agreement, for example, as occasional or permanent consortia might even be classified *as agreements establishing a civil law partnership* (section 568 of the Civil Code). In other cases the syndicate agreement may be deemed as a *preliminary agreement* under section 208 of the Civil Code aimed at the subsequent conclusion of articles of association, under which the parties undertake to conclude articles of association (or in case of a company limited by shares to adopt the deed of foundation or statutes of the Company) at a later point in time. In general, however, the syndicate agreement is not simply a special preliminary agreement, which is terminated by the conclusion of the articles of association, but practically as a *framework agreement* it remains in force for the entire life of the company, and in a given case it might exist constitutionally parallel to the Company (for example, syndicate meetings might be held). Alternatively, although in general syndicate agreements are concluded prior to the articles of association for the Company, the parties can conclude the syndicate agreement simultaneously with or even after the conclusion of the articles of association.

The syndicate agreement is a civil law contract (pertaining to the rights of property), that is, it is essentially more than a simple ethical type of gentleman's agreement or a one-sided declaration of intent. On the other hand, the syndicate agreement – although it generally contains provisions regarding the articles of association and the operation of the company – *is an agreement independent from the articles of association for the Company*. In Hungary the Act on Business Organisations shall not be applied to the syndicate agreement. Even though the syndicate agreement is also an organised type of obligation aimed at cooperation, the parties in many cases may establish their own independent organization similar to that of the company's (for example, the syndicate meeting to be convened regularly every year generally prior to the general meeting of the company.). The syndicate agreement has to be evaluated pursuant to the general rules relating to contracts of the Civil Code as an independent agreement that cannot be categorized under a named type of contract.

Therefore, the provisions relating to the articles of associations establishing companies (unlimited partnerships, limited partnerships, limited liability companies), such as qualified form of document, obligation of notification towards the court of registration, do not have to be applied. The syndicate agreement can by no means be deemed as the precompany of the company to be established – the 1997 Hungarian Act on Business Organisations adopted the institution of the German *Vorgesellschaft* (sections 15-16) for the timeframe between the conclusion of the articles of association and the incorporation of the company. As noted above, it is not at all necessary to conclude the syndicate agreement prior to the conclusion of the articles of association (adoption of the deed of foundation or the statues in case of a company limited by shares) – although in practice this happens in the majority of cases. The syndicate agreement can by all means be concluded after the incorporation of the company in the trade registry. Although the parties of the articles of association and the syndicate agreement are generally the same, this is also not a necessity. In the case of companies limited by shares it is quite frequent that only a few majority shareholders take part in the syndicate agreement, the minority shareholders do not participate. There is nothing to hinder the participation of a legal entity in the syndicate agreement who is not a member of the company. A person/ legal entity becoming a member of the company shall not automatically become a party to the syndicate agreement; the new member must declare its joining the syndicate agreement and this declaration must be accepted by the parties of the syndicate agreement, since another party entering the agreement means the modification of the syndicate agreement (change in the parties – increase in the number of the parties).

The effect of the syndicate agreement in general corresponds to the term (life) of the company, but the syndicate agreement, unless otherwise set out by the parties, shall not cease to exist automatically with the cancellation from the trade registry of the company with regard to which the syndicate agreement was entered into. There is also nothing to hinder the maintenance of the effect of the syndicate agreement after the termination of the company; for example, the parties may use the agreement to settle the issues still pending after the termination of the company – in a given case to control a provision related to prohibition of competition pursuant to which the parties to the syndicate agreement undertake not to establish with other partners for a given term of time a company pursuing a similar basic activity as the terminated company.

3. The aim of the syndicate agreement

No obligatory form has to be applied to the syndicate agreement in Hungarian law. Therefore, in principle, it can be concluded also verbally or by implied behaviour. It is a different issue that in general the written form is applied. The syndicate agreement does not have to be submitted to the court of registration, its content is not public, it is the private business secret of the parties.

The syndicate agreement in Hungarian law practice is typically associated with companies limited by shares, although due to the great popularity of limited liability companies in Hungary (similar to the German GmbH), they are quite frequent in the case of limited liability companies as well. In the case of companies uniting persons (unlimited partnerships and limited partnerships) syndicate agreements occur only as an extreme exception.

Pursuant to Hungarian practice (which basically corresponds to the international trend) parties conclude syndicate agreements basically for three reasons:

a) To settle the terms of their *cooperation* during the period lasting until the execution of the articles of association, which in the case of larger companies may take several months, or even years (for example, an agreement on the order pursuant to which the preliminary evaluation by the auditor of the contributions in kind should take place);

b) By utilization of the almost entirely dispositive regulation of the syndicate agreement (which aligns to the Civil Code) *to mitigate* the strictness of the basically compulsory provisions of the Act on Business Organisations (see paragraph 1 of section 9 of the 1997 Act on Business Organisations). These are, in particular, the so-called voting agreements determining, for example, how they shall vote on the composition of the board of directors and the supervisory board, the utilization of the after tax profits etc. With respect to companies being founded with the participation of foreign partners it is particularly important that pursuant to the basic principles of the conflict of laws the articles of association (in the case of a company limited by shares the deed of foundation or the statutes) shall be governed by the law of the country of the seat of the company. On the other hand, in the syndicate agreement, foreign substantive law can also be stipulated as the applicable law;

c) In the syndicate agreement the parties may settle elements of the company's operation that they do not want to disclose to the public. These issues may need to be settled by the parties in an agreement, but at the same time they cannot be provided for in the articles of association, because – due to the publicity of the trade registry – these would also consequently become public (with the result that the company could suffer disadvantages, for example, in respect of competition).

4. The Conflict of Content between the Articles of Association and the Syndicate Agreement

Since pursuant to what has been set forth above the articles of association and the syndicate agreement can be mutually narrower and wider than the other in content, the content of the two agreements could be in conflict. Such conflict could result in the voidness of both the articles of association and the syndicate agreement. Furthermore, the syndicate agreement might also violate the mandatory rules of the Act on Business Organisations.

With respect to any conflict between the Act on Business Organisations and the syndicate agreement, Hungarian legal practice generally considers the provisions of the syndicate agreement *effective* if they are aimed at the specific application of the mandatory rules of the Act on Business Organisations to the company. Thus, the provisions of the syndicate agreement regarding the voting rights of the members of the organs of the company will not be considered void. For example, in the syndicate agreement of a limited liability company that consists of three members the parties may agree that at the members' meeting all three of them shall be entitled to appoint a managing director and shall vote in such a way that all three of them shall be elected by the members' meeting, or the parties shall agree that in the event of an intention of either of the parties to sell its business shares in the company neither of them shall exercise its right to preemption as a member with regard to the business shares intended to be sold.

On the other hand, the Hungarian court practice considers as *being void* the provisions of the syndicate agreement that explicitly violate the mandatory provisions of the Act on Business Organisations. For example, where the members of a limited liability company agree that they shall hold one members' meeting annually and the balance sheet shall also be approved by way of voting in writing (the Hungarian Act on Business Organisations obliges limited liability companies to hold one annual members' meeting and the balance sheet can only be approved at the members' meeting).

According to the majority opinion – which also corresponds to mine – the fact that the provisions of the syndicate agreement are in conflict with the provisions of the articles of association *does not affect the content of either of the agreements* since these are independent agreements. According to the minority opinion the provisions of the articles of association concluded after the syndicate agreement shall – if in conflict with the provisions of the syndicate agreement – automatically modify the respective parts of the syndicate agreement.

It is obvious from the above that the violation of the syndicate agreement cannot have direct company law consequences, and only the civil law consequences of the violation of the syndicate agreement can be applied. That is why the parties attempt to incorporate as many guarantees into the agreement as possible. Therefore, where, for example, in the case of a limited liability company the majority owner undertakes to vote for the persons suggested by the minority owners to be members of the supervisory board but not so act at the members' meeting of the limited liability company, the resolution of the members' meeting shall be effective, and the party that had suffered a disadvantage as a result of the violation of the syndicate agreement will only have contractual claims against the party violating the agreement.

* * *

The syndicate agreement will increasingly become a part of the very extensive Hungarian company law, mainly because foreign investors choose this type of agreement in order to secure their company foundations. As a result of the syndicate stipulations suggested by foreigners more and more business knowhow will be incorporated into Hungarian company law and this will most probably assist the Hungarian Act on Business Organisations as well as Hungarian company law practice to become "eurocompatible" by the time the Hungarian Republic joins the European Union.

Kant and Private International Law

Kurt Siehr*

1. PRAELUDIUM HAMBURGENSE

Hamburg may not be known as a city of art, science and culture. It is a port and a place of business and commerce. The cultural treasures of Hamburg do not originate from princely collections. They were bought by the city of Hamburg or were donated by citizens. One of these important testamentary bequests is exhibited in the Hamburger Kunsthalle: the marble bust of Immanuel Kant by Carl Friedrich Hagemann (1773-1806), a pupil of Johann Gottfried Schadow (1764-1850).[1] This bust, which is said to be the most impressive portrait of the philosopher of Königsberg, was commissioned by Jonas Ludwig von Heß (1756-1823), a student of the Albertus University of Königsberg, author of historical and scientific works and admirer of Immanuel Kant. Since that time many authorities and followers of Kant have been domiciled in Hamburg. To one of the present advocates of Kant's legal philosophy – Professor ERNST-JOACHIM MESTMÄCKER – these lines are dedicated.

---

* Professor of Law, University of Zürich.

[1] Joist Grolle, *Kant in Hamburg. Der Philosoph und sein Bildnis* (Hamburg: Hamburger Kunsthalle 1995).

Talia Einhorn, ed., Spontaneous Order, Organization and the Law – Liber Amicorum Ernst-Joachim Mestmäcker © 2003 *T.M.C.ASSER PRESS, The Hague, The Netherlands*

2. Law and philosophy

2.1 Private international law in the 18th century

Modern private international law is a product of the late 19th century, shaped by scholars such as Friedrich Carl v. Savigny (1799-1861), Joseph Story (1779-1845), Andrés Bello (1781-1865), Pasquale Stanislao Mancini (1817-1888) and Tobias Michael Carel Asser (1838-1913), codified in the Codice civile of 1865, the EGBGB of 1896 and in Hague Conventions, and applied in a growing number of cases. Private international law was still uncodified during the 18th century. Heinrich v. Cocceji (1644-1719) and Johann Nikolaus Hert (1651-1710), the *Duumviri illustres*,[2] were the main German authorities in this field. Hert's *Dissertatio de collisio legum* of 1688 seems to be the first monograph exclusively devoted to conflict of laws.[3] This book had been published in three editions by 1737.[4]

In Prussia, Samuel v. Cocceji (1679-1755), the son of Heinrich v. Cocceji, drafted a *Corpus iuris Fridericianum* which never entered into force.[5] It was finally the efforts of Johann Heinrich Casimir, Graf von Carmer (1721-1801) and of Carl Gottlieb Svarez (1746-1798) that led to the codification of Prussian law in the *Allgemeines Landrecht für die Preußischen Staaten* of 1794.[6] This codification also applied in Königsberg where Immanuel Kant (1724-1804) taught and wrote his books.

2.2 Kant's categorical imperative

In 1785 Kant published his *Grundlegung der Metaphysik der Sitten* and formulated the categorical (unconditional) imperative: "Handle nur nach derjenigen Maxime, durch die du zugleich wollen kannst, daß sie ein allgemeines Gesetz werde." ["You should act according to that maxim which you would like to be

---

[2] Günter Herrmann, *Johann Nikolaus Hert und die deutsche Statutenlehre* (Berlin: de Gruyter 1963) at p. 158; cf. also Max Gutzwiller, *Geschichte des Internationalprivatrechts* (Basel/ Stuttgart: Helbing & Lichtenhahn 1977) at pp. 191-200 (Cocceji) and at pp. 201-209 (Hert).

[3] Herrmann, *supra* n. 2, 160; cf. the translated new edition of "De collisio legum dissertatio" in: Christian v. Bar/ Peter Dopffel, *Deutsches Internationales Privatrecht im 16. und 17. Jahrhundert II* (Tübingen: Mohr 2001) at pp. 588 et seq.

[4] Herrmann, *supra* n. 2, at p. 174.

[5] Hans Hattenhauer in: *Allgemeines Landrecht für die Preußischen Staaten von 1794. Textausgabe* (Frankfurt a.M., Berlin: Metzner 1970) 11, at pp. 12 et seq.

[6] Hattenhauer, *supra* n. 5, at pp. 13 et seq.

fixed as a general statutory rule"].[7] Twelve years later Kant drew some conclusions in his *Die Mataphysik der Sitten* and added: "Das Recht ist also der Inbegriff der Bedingungen, unter denen die Willkür des einen mit der Willkür des anderen nach einem allgemeinen Gesetze der Freiheit zusammen vereinigt werden kann."[8] ["Hence the law epitomizes the conditions on which the freedom of a person can be combined with the freedom of another person according to a general rule of liberty".]

Kant did not discuss problems of conflict of laws. But this is not necessary. His categorical imperative should be followed everywhere. Sadly enough this is not done. "The spirit indeed is willing, but the flesh is weak." Modern legislatures are worse than Jesus' disciples who fell asleep. They intentionally enact provisions violating the categorical imperative.

3. Problems of private international law

The term "private international law" was coined by Joseph Story in 1834[9] and since then was used in Continental European countries as "internationales Privatrecht",[10] "internationaal privaatrecht",[11] "droit international privé",[12] "derecho internacional privado"[13] and "diritto internazionale privato".[14] Today,

---

[7] Kant, *Grundlegung zur Metaphysik der Sitten* (Riga: Hartknoch 1785) 52 = Kant, *Werke in sechs Bänden* (W. Weischedel [ed.]), IV (Darmstadt: Wissenschaftliche Buchgesellschaft 1956) 51.

[8] Kant, *Die Metaphysik der Sitten. Erster Theil: metaphysische Anfangsgründe der Rechtslehre* (Königsberg: Nicolovius 1797) 33 = Kant, *supra* n. 7, at p. 337.

[9] Joseph Story, *Commentaries on the Conflict of Laws* (Boston: Billiard, Gray & Co. 1834) § 9, at p. 9: "This branch of public law [conflict of the laws] may be fitly denominated private international law, since it is chiefly seen and felt in its application to the common business of private persons, and rarely rises to the dignity of national negotiations, or national controversies." John Westlake, *A Treatise on Private International Law or The Conflict of Laws* (London: Maxwell 1858) at p. 1.

[10] Wilhelm Schaeffner, *Entwicklung des internationalen Privatrechts* (Frankfurt am Main: Sauerländer 1841) at p. 3.

[11] T.M.C. Asser, *Schets van het internationaal privaatrecht* (Haarlem: Bohn 1880) at pp. 1 et seq.

[12] Jean-Jacques Gaspard Foelix, *Traité de droit international privé ou du conflit des lois de différentes nations en matière de droit privé* (Paris: Joubert 1843) at p. 2; François Laurent, *Droit civil international I* (Bruxelles/Paris: Bruyland/Marescq 1880) at pp. 9 et seq.

[13] Manuel Torres Campos, *Principios de derecho internacional privado ó de derecho extraterritorial de Europa y America en sus relaciones con el derecho civil de España* (Madrid 1881).

[14] Niccola Rocco, *Dell'uso e autorità delle leggi del Regno delle Due Sicilie ossia Trattato di diritto civile internazionale*, 2nd ed. (Palermo: Garofalo 1843); Pietro Fiorentino, *Saggio di un esame critico dei codici italiani sulle disposizioni generali premesse al Codice civile e specialmente su quelle che riguardano il diritto internazionale privato* (Messina: Tipografia del Commercia 1869) at pp. 113 et seq.

several principles of private international law are taken for granted, at least in Europe:

- There is no international "private law" with the exception of some rules of substantive law that have been unified or harmonized by international instruments.
- There are at least as many legal systems as there are national states.
- The basic function of private international law is to
  - fix national jurisdiction;
  - determine the applicable law;
  - coordinate international legal assistance, especially the recognition and enforcement of foreign judgments.
- Private international law does not directly decide a dispute. It designates the law by reference to which the dispute should be resolved.
- This very formal reference (*Verweisung*) has to designate the law of the State with which the case has the closest connection.
- Such a reference does not distinguish between different types of legal systems. Every system is treated equally.
- If the result found according to the applicable foreign law violates the public policy of the forum State, the result will be adjusted and corrected.

4. Violations of the categorical imperative in private international law

4.1 Special treatment of citizens of the forum state

Personal matters of natural persons (e.g., capacity, marriage, divorce, child–parent relationships, succession) may be governed by the law of the person's domicile, habitual residence or by the person's *lex patriae*. If the *lex patriae* governs and the respective person is a national of more than one State, the "effective" nationality has to be determined and the law of the "effective" nationality governs.[15] The efficacy of a *lex patriae* is determined according to the person's closest connection with one of the *leges patriae*. Article 5 (1) sent. 1 EGBGB reads: "... the law of that of these States applies with which the person is closest connected, especially by his habitual residence or by the course of his life". This is a correct general rule which should be valid for domestic and foreign double nationals. Yet, many States do not read Kant and deviate from

[15] Austrian IPR-Gesetz of 1978 § 9 (1) sent. 3; German EGBGB Article 5 (1) sent. 1; Italian Legge D.I.P. of 1995 Article 19 (2) sent. 1; Swiss IPRG of 1987 Article 23 (2).

general conflict of laws' principles and make an exception for domestic *Mehrstaater*: the nationality of the forum State prevails irrespective of any efficacy.[16] Apparently some "practical" deliberations (ease of applying the law), or strange ideas of public international law (protection of domestic citizens), are stronger than a just and undiscriminating categorical imperative. Such a deviation may even create unconstitutional results. For example, a German couple lives in Italy. The wife is also an Italian national. The couple is most closely connected with Italy. German courts, however, will apply German law because they share a common German nationality (EGBGB Articles 14 (1) No. 1; 5 (1) sent. 2). However, because the wife's German nationality is not "effective" the spouses' law of common habitual residence should apply as it would if the spouses were both French but the wife was also Italian. The spouses are treated unequally and this should be corrected by a restrictive interpretation of Article 5 (1) sent. 2 EGBGB.[17]

4.2 ***Renvoi* and the homeward trend**

Whoever had classes in conflicts law may recall the lesson when the law professor entered the classroom cool, calm and collected, hardly dared to say good morning, but mysteriously whispered, "Today, I shall try to explain to you the problem of *renvoi*". Dean William L. Prosser (1898-1971)[18] may have had his undergraduate studies in mind when he confessed: "The realm of the conflict of laws is a dismal swamp, filled with quaking quagmires, and inhabited by learned but eccentric professors who theorize about mysterious matters in a strange and incomprehensible jargon. The ordinary court, or lawyer, is quite lost when engulfed and entangled in it."[19] One of these "mysterious matters" is the problem of *renvoi* labeled as a "vicious circle",[20] "Trojan

---

[16] Austrian IPR-Gesetz of 1978 § 9 (1) sent. 2; German EGBGB of 1986 Article 5 (1) sent. 2; Italian legge D.I.P. of 1995 Article 19 (2) sent. 2.

[17] Siehr in: *Münchener Kommentar zum BGB*, vol. X, 3rd ed. (Munich 1998) Article 14 EGBGB, marginal note 22.

[18] In 1948-1961 *William L. Prosser* was Dean of the Law School of the University of California at Berkeley. He wrote the "Handbook of the Law of Torts", 4th ed. (St. Paul, Minn.: West 1971) and edited the collection "The Judicial Humorist" (Boston: Little, Brown & Co. 1952, reprint Littleton: Rothman 1989).

[19] William L. Prosser, "Interstate Publications", 51 *Mich.L.Rev.* (1952/53) 959, 971 = id., *Selected Topics on the Law of Torts* (Ann Arbor: University of Michigan Press 1953) 70, 89 = Culp (ed.), *Selected Readings on Conflict of Laws* (St. Paul, Minn.: West 1956) 585, 591.

[20] John Westlake, *A Treatise on Private International Law*, 5th ed. (London: Sweet & Maxwell 1912) 31.

Horse",[21] or "ping pong game".[22] Similar characterizations exist in other languages.[23] The problem may be briefly described as one of a common lack of primary interest of the *fora* concerned. Forum A refers to the law of forum B but this law also declines to have any primary interest and refers back to the law of forum A. Such a courteous "After you!" may lead to a deadlock and urges a solution.

The categorical imperative disqualifies such an attitude. Some solutions must be given and there are some. Either abstain from any *renvoi*[24] or accept only a *renvoi* to your own substantive law.[25] If international harmony cannot be achieved, every legislator should refrain from betraying basic principles by preferring a homeward trend to the general goal of applying the law of the closest connection. Such a betrayal can, however, be found in some legislations.[26]

4.3 The law governing companies

In international company law two basic principles are used to determine the law which governs companies: the principle of incorporation and the principle of the seat of central administration. According to the principle of incorporation, as applied in the Netherlands, Switzerland and the United States, the incorporators may choose the *lex corporationis* by deciding in which State to incorporate. They may then establish their headquarters somewhere else. Being afraid that such liberalism may encourage incorporators to evade mandatory domestic law rules, some legislators preferred to fix the *lex corporationis* more objectively at the factual seat of the company's central administration. The *Centros* decision of the Court of Justice of the European Communities[27] vividly highlights the problems arising from applying these two opposing principles. Recently Italy codified Italian private international law. The law governing companies is determined in Article 25 (1). In general, the law of the State of incorporation applies. However, if the seat of administration or if the principal activity of the

---

[21] Arthur Taylor von Mehren/ Donald Theodore Trautman, *The Law of Multistate Problems* (Boston/ Toronto: Little, Brown & Co. 1965) at p. 513.

[22] John Delatre Falconbridge, "Partial Renvoi and Total Renvoi", in: id., *Essays on the Conflict of Laws*, 2nd ed. (Totonto, Canada: Law Book Co. 1954) 170, 187.

[23] Cf. Kurt Siehr, "Renvoi: A Necessary Evil or is it Possible to Abolish it by Statute?" in: Ian Flechter/Loukas Mistelis/Marise Cremona (eds.), Foundations and Perspectives of International Trade Law (London: Sweet & Maxwell 2001) at p. 204.

[24] Cf., e.g., Article 32 of the Greek Civil Code.

[25] Cf., Article 18 (1) of the Portuguese Código civil.

[26] Cf., e.g., § 5 (2) Austrian Statute on Private International Law; Article 4 (1) sent. 2 EGBGB.

[27] Case C-212/97 (*Centros Ltd.* v. *Erhvervs- og Selskabsstyrelsen*), [1999] *ECR* I-1459, and Behrens, "International Company Law in View of the *Centros* Case", 1 *EBOR* (2000) 125.

enterprise is located in Italy, Italian law governs. Such a general reference to the *lex fori* may be qualified as a concealed *ordre public*, and, as such, it is an emergency clause which does not violate the Kantian categorical imperative. Here prevails the exception: "necessity knows no law". But is it really necessary to make such an exception? I can imagine that it would have sufficed to require strict observation of some local mandatory rules.

4.4 Indirect jurisdiction

One of the major improvements of modern international legal assistance is the recognition and enforcement of foreign judgments. Multilateral conventions and EC regulations make sure that law suits in foreign countries furnish executory titles – unless they do not meet the requirements of the recognizing State.[28] One of these is the requirement that the jurisdiction of the foreign court conform to the standards of the recognizing State.[29] The categorical imperative applies to these standards: you should not deny foreign jurisdiction in those circumstances in which you would assume jurisdiction of the domestic courts. You should even be more liberal and recognize a datum created abroad even if a domestic court would not have assumed jurisdiction. Indirect jurisdiction of foreign courts for recognition purposes (*in favorem recognitionis*) should be broader than direct jurisdiction for proceedings in domestic courts. This principle is violated when foreign decisions are not recognized simply because they have been given against a person domiciled in the recognizing State.[30]

4.5 Reciprocity

People may be indifferent or egoistic but they should never be arrogant and impertinent. Unfortunately they are and courts are even directed by statutory authority to behave in this way in matters of international civil procedure. Many states decline to recognize and enforce foreign judgments if the foreign state of origin does not recognize and enforce the decisions of the requested State, or, in other words, if the foreign State does not grant reciprocity (*Gegenseitigkeit, reciprocité, reciprocità*).[31] The effect of such a requirement may be that a

---

[28] Cf., e.g. EU Regulation 44/2001 of 22 December 2000 on Jurisdiction and Recognition and Enforcement of Judgments in Civil and Commercial Matters, *OJ(EC)* [2001] L 12/1.

[29] Cf., e.g., § 328 (1) No. 1 German Code of Civil Procedure.

[30] Cf. Articles 65 (2) (a), 149 (2) (a), (c), (e) and (f) Swiss IPRG of 1987.

[31] Cf. § 328 (1) No. 5 German Code of Civil Procedure; Article 167 (1) (c) Romanian Statutes on Private International Law; Article 166 (1) Swiss IPRG of 1987. Cf. already Foelix, *supra* n. 12, at pp. 376 et seq.

foreign State is "kindly" invited to do more than the domestic State is willing to do: If you recognize first, I shall follow suit!

"Die 'Gegenseitigkeit' ist eine große Gemeinheit."[32] ["Reciprocity is a dirty trick".] The requirement of reciprocity violates the categorical imperative because one does not act unconditionally but impolitely asks the other party for a kind of advance performance. This is not only an unreasonable demand. It is also an unfair taking of hostages. Private parties are taken as hostages because the states failed to stipulate treaties providing for reciprocal recognition and enforcement of judgments.

The precondition of "reciprocity" should be abolished. It is a remnant of bygone ages when the application of foreign law and the recognition of foreign judgments were held to be generous sacrifices of national sovereignty or a matter of comity of nations.[33] In private international law, however, law is applied because private parties rely on fair treatment of their matters.

5. Conclusion

Immanuel Kant never left his native city of Königsberg. He was not only a master of philosophy but also a "Genie der Pedanterie und Pünktlichkeit." ["Genius of pedantry and punctuality."][34] He hated any disturbance of his daily way of life, abhorred any noise and complained: "Diejenigen, welche zu den häuslichen Andachtsübungen auch das Singen geistlicher Lieder empfohlen haben, bedachten nicht, daß sie dem Publikum durch eine solche l ä r m e n d e (eben dadurch gemeiniglich pharisäische) Andacht eine große Beschwerde auflegen, indem sie die Nachbarschaft entweder mit zu singen oder Ihr Gedankengeschäft niederzulegen nötigen." ["Those who have recommended the singing of religious songs in addition to domestic worship did not realize that they caused hardship to the public by imposing such a noisy (and thereby commonly self-righteous) devotion and forced the neighbors either to join singing or stop thinking."][35] Therefore, I shall stop lamenting about some

---

[32] Friedrich Nietzsche, "Aus dem Nachlaß der Achtzigerjahre", in: id., *Werke III* (K. Schlechta [ed.]) (Darmstadt: Wissenschaftliche Buchgesellschaft 1966) 415, 670.

[33] J.M.B. Scholtens, Het begrip comitas in het inernationaal privaatrecht van de hollandse juristenschool der Zeventiende eeuw (Utrecht/ Nijmegen: Dekker & van de Vegt 1949) at pp. 11 et seq.; Alan Watson, *Josep Story and the Comity of Errors* (Athens/ London: University of Georgia Press 1992) at pp. 18 et seq.

[34] Wilhelm Weischedel, "Kant und die Pünktlichkeit des Denkens", in: id., 34 *große Philosophen in Alltag und Denken. Die philosophische Hintertreppe*, 16th ed. (Munich: Nymphenburger 1990) at p. 213.

[35] Immanuel Kant, Die Kritik der Urteilskraft, 2nd ed. (Berlin: Lagarde 1793) at p. 223 = Kant, *Werke*, *supra* n. 7, vol. V, at p. 434.

deficiencies of private international law and hope that in the future scholars, legislators and courts live up to another Kantian imperative of Enlightenment: Sapere aude! [Dare to be wise!][36]

[36] Immanuel Kant, *Beantwortung der Frage: Was ist Aufklärung* (1783), in: Kant, *Werke*, *supra* n. 7, vol. VI, at p. 53: "Habe Mut, dich deines eigenen Verstandes zu bedienen!"

Polish Competition Law in the 1990s – on the Way to Higher Effectiveness and Deeper Conformity with EC Competition Rules

Tadeusz Skoczny*

1. Introduction

The last 10 years of the 20th century can surely be perceived as one of the most important decades of Polish history. Following the political decisions taken by the Poles in 1980 (the establishment of 'Solidarity') and 1989 (the Round Table, and semi-free election), on 29 December 1989 – by amendment of the old Constitution 1952 – Poland rejected the political and economic system introduced after World War II. By breaking free from the totalitarian socialist state, Poland pronounced its support for a democratic state of law that fulfils principles of social justice. By rejecting the centrally-planned state economy it chose market-oriented economy based on freedom of economic activity and ownership guarantee. Finally, by breaking free from the Soviet block it insisted on its return to a European community based on values of democracy, rule of law, national identity and peaceful cooperation of independent states.

It is obvious that such radical change to the political and economic system could not happen over night. With the Constitution Amendment Act of 1989, the implementation of a transformation programme had only begun. From that moment however, three main transition objectives have been implemented:

---

* Professor of law, Holder of the Jean Monnet Chair on European Economic Law at the Warsaw University Faculty of Management.

Talia Einhorn, ed., Spontaneous Order, Organization and the Law –
Liber Amicorum Ernst-Joachim Mestmäcker © 2003 T.M.C.Asser press, The Hague, The Netherlands

a) the establishment of the legal and institutional foundations of a democratic system (free elections, a system of state authorities, self-governmental authorities based on division and balance of powers, and a pluralistic party system) protecting human and citizen rights;
b) the creation of the legal basis for a market economy within the economy transition programme, called also the 'Balcerowicz Plan' (giving of freedom of contract its proper role and re-enacting of commercial law), as well as the establishment of many institutions guaranteeing a proper functioning of market mechanism (e.g. an independent National Bank and a stock exchange);
c) the action taken to achieve Polish participation in the process of European integration – as early as 1991 the Europe Agreement was signed; in 1994 an application for EU membership was submitted; in 1998 the formal accession negotiations commenced.

Even though none of these objectives has been implemented in its entirety, it is clear that the Polish system transformation[1] has been a great success. The new Constitution of 1997[2] can be seen as the final proof of that success.

Whereas the political system changes saw pluralism replace monism, the transformation of the economic system saw market competition replace state planning. The role of market competition was recognised from the very beginning of the transition process.[3] Apart from trade liberalisation, policies playing an essential role in the process included the restructuring and privatisation of state-owned enterprises, the policy of competition development (demonopolisation policy) and protection (antitrust policy) have played an essential role in this process.[4]

---

[1] See Mestmäcker, "Systemtransformation im Spiegel der Rechtstheorie", in: Drobing/ Hopt/ Kötz/ Mestmäcker, *Systemtransformation in Mittel- und Osteuropa und ihre Folgen für Banken, Börsen und Kreditsicherheiten* (Tübingen: Mohr Siebeck 1998) 89 et seq.

[2] Constitution of the Republic of Poland of 2 April 1997 (*Journal of Laws* No. 78, item 48). It has replaced the so-called Small Constitution – Act of 17 October 1992 on reciprocal relations between legislative and executive powers in the Republic of Poland as well as on territorial self-government (*Journal of Laws* No. 84, items 426 with later amendments) as well as certain provisions of the "old" Constitution of 1952 which remained in force under the above-mentioned Small Constitution.

[3] See Competition policy in an economy undergoing a transition period: an address by Anna Fornalczyk, President of Polish Antimonopoly Office, at the Conference on the Promotion and Protection of Competition – the Polish experience, 12 April 1992.

[4] See B. Slay, "Industrial Demonopolization and Antitrust Policy in Hungary and Poland", paper presented at the Panel on Industrial Organization in the Post-Communist Transition at the 24th National Convention of the American Association for the Advancement of Slavic Studies, 19-22 November 1992, Phoenix, Arizona; A. Fornalczyk, "Competition Law and Policy in Po-

In view of its importance, legislation promoting free and fair competition of equal market competitor was enacted. As early as the beginning of the 1990s, the new Antimonopoly Act was passed,[5] antimonopoly enforcement authorities were created,[6] and a special governmental programme promoting the development of competition was implemented.[7] Shortly thereafter, the Unfair Competition Act was introduced.[8] The end of the decade saw the enacting of the State Aids Act,[9] as well as many consumer-protecting acts. The President of the Office for Competition and Consumer Protection (OCCP) was given discretionary powers by all of these acts.

At the same time, success in regional integration was made the essential aim of governmental policy. This attempt soon culminated in the Europe Agreement, establishing an association between Poland, the European Communities and their Member States,[10] and in the Free Trade Agreement between Poland and the EFTA States.[11] The Central European Free Trade Agreement (CEFTA) was also concluded.[12] All of the agreements contained competition

---

land in 1990-1995", in: *Harmonisation of the Polish Competition Legislation with Competition Rules of the European Communities. Summary and Recommendation* (T. Skoczny [ed.]) (Warsaw: OCCP 1997) 37; J. Fingleton/ E. Fox/ D. Neven/ P. Seabright (eds.), *Competition Policy and the Transformation of Central Europe* (CEPR 1996) 174.

[5] The Act of 24 February 1990 on Counteracting Monopolistic Practices (*Journal of Laws* No. 14, item 89) was amended several times afterwards; the last consolidated version of this Act was published in the *Journal of Laws* (1999) No. 52 item 547 (later: Antimonopoly Act of 1990); see in detail T. Skoczny, "Poland: Chapter 3 – Competition law", in: S. Breidenbach/ Ch. Campbell (eds.) *Business Transactions in Eastern Europe*, vol. 2 (Lexis Publishing 1977) § 2.

[6] The Antimonopoly Office (AMO), with branch offices (nine at present), was created by the Act on Counteracting Monopolistic Practices of 1990. In 1996, its name was changed to the Office for Competition and Consumer Protection (OCCP). The Antimonopoly Court (AMC) was created by the Minister of Justice's Regulation of the of 13 April 1990 (*Journal of Laws* No. 27, item 157).

[7] See "The Government Programme for the Development of Competition in 1991-1993", approved by the Council of Ministers on 19 May 1991, published in English in: *Bulletin. Antimonopoly Office of Poland* (Warsaw, Year I, 1994, Number 0) p. 11.

[8] See Law on Combating Unfair Competition of 16 April 1993 (*Journal of Laws* No. 47, item 211). See in detail T. Skoczny, "Poland: Chapter 3 – Competition law", *supra* n. 5, § 3.

[9] See Law on conditions of admissibility and monitoring of state aids for undertakings (*Journal of Laws* No. 60, item 704).

[10] Europe Agreement Establishing an Association between the Republic of Poland, of the One Part, and the European Communities and Their Member States, on the Other Part, signed on 16 December 1991 (effective on 1 February 1994). See Decision of the Council and the Commission of 13 December 1993 on the conclusion of this Agreement (*OJ* [1993] L 348/1).

[11] See Free Trade Agreement between the EFTA States and Poland signed on 10 December 1992 (effective on 15 November 1993).

[12] See Central European Free Trade Agreement concluded by the Czech Republic, the Republic of Hungary, the Republic of Poland and the Slovak Republic, signed on 21 December 1992 (effective on 1 March 1993).

rules reflecting the competition rules of the European Communities and regulating the trade between the contracting parties.[13]

There is no doubt that Poland has, from the outset, sought to become a member of the European Union.[14] This had already been ascertained in the Preamble to the Europe Agreement: "*paying constant attention to the fact that Poland's final goal is membership in the Communities and Association, in the opinion of the Parts, helps Poland to reach for this goal*". For this reason, among others, the Parties "*recognised that the approximation of Poland's existing and future legislation to that of the Community is the essential precondition for Poland's economic integration with the Communities*". Poland, however, made a unilateral commitment "*to endeavour to the best of its ability to conform its future legislation to that of the Community*", among others with respect to "*competition rules*".[15]

Finally, it is already clear that Poland, like other candidate countries,[16] will have to accept and implement in its entirety the *acquis communautaire* in the area of "competition policy". Nevertheless, since this *acquis* consists primarily of norms and acts applying directly, those will apply from the moment of accession. From the point of view of accession, the emphasis of the adjustment obligations is on approximating rather than accepting the law.[17]

The dynamic development of the Polish competition (antimonopoly) law in the 1990s should be examined in the light of two main factors. Firstly, the political and practical necessity to establish and maintain a level playing field for competition as an essential element of successful economic transformation must be taken account of. Secondly, the political and legal requirement to adjust to the *acquis communautaire* Polish rules relating to the development and protection in the field of competition must be emphasised.

---

[13] See E. Szymanska, "Competition Rules in International Agreements Entered into Poland in the 1990s and the Principles of Enforcement thereof", in: *Harmonisation of the Polish Competition Legislation with Competition Rules of the European Communities*, *supra* n. 4, 109 et seq.

[14] The formal application was submitted on 8 April 1994.

[15] See Articles 68 and 69 of the Europe Agreement, *supra* n. 10.

[16] Regarding the comparison of the competititon law in the books and in practice, see in more detail: R. Pittman, *Some critical provisions in the Antimonopoly Laws of Central and Eastern Europe* (US Department of Justice, Antitrust Division, Economic Analysis Group Discussion Paper, 20 September 1991); T. Skoczny, *Competition Legislation in Post-Socialist Countries. CSFR, Hungary, Poland, Russia* (Warsaw: Friedrich Ebert Stiftung Warsaw Office 1992) 7 et seq.; Fingleton/ Fox/ Neven/ Seabright, *supra* n. 4, 70 et seq.; T. Skoczny, "The adaptation of law and economy to the principle of non-discrimination on grounds of nationality, in particular in areas of freedom of establishment, free movement of service and free movement of capital", in: J. Swierkocki (ed.) *Accession Negotiations – Selected Results. Interim Report* (Lodz: Conference Papers, European Institute in Lodz 2000) 181 et seq., 187 et seq.

[17] Similar Fingleton/ Fox/ Neven/ Seabright, *supra* n. 4, 179.

The new[18] Antimonopoly Act of 1990 created the legal basis and institutions aimed mainly at "ensuring the development of competition"[19] to the benefit of the competition mechanism rather than advancing the interests of the competitors themselves. It was amended many times[20] in order to broaden the substantive and subjective[21] scope[22] of its application as well as to approximate its provisions to the EC "competition rules relating to undertakings". Similar effects have been achieved through broad and intensive application of this Act; especially the AMC (Antimonopoly Court) judges have proven over and again that they understand the role played by competition in the transformation of Polish economy. Therefore, it can be said that the judges are not only familiar with these standards but also that they accept them.[23]

However, at some point it was necessary to face the fact that the possibilities of improving the existing legislation have been exhausted. Therefore, after 10 years of improvements via amendments and judicial interpretation, the Antimonopoly Act 1990 was replaced by a new Competition and Consumer Protection Act 2000, which entered in force on 1 April 2001.[24]

Let us present in detail the developments and the present stage of Polish competition legislation and its enforcement. Substantive rules countering the three anti-competitive strategies of undertakings (abuse of dominant position,

---

[18] Since competition law is useful only under market economy conditions, the attempt to create legal grounds for competition development and protection (Act of 28 January 1987 on counteracting monopolistic practices in national economy, *Journal of Laws* No. 3, item 18) in the framework of the so-called economic reform of the late 1980s, was left without significant effects. See L. Wiszniewska, "Das polnische Antimonopolgesetz von 1987", *GRUR Int.* [1988] H. 5, p. 395; E. Piontek, "Polish Antimonopoly Law", 12 (3) *World Competition* (1989) 41.

[19] See U. Schulze, "Der rechtliche Rahmen der Wettbewerbspolitik und Privatisierung in Polen, Wirtschaft und Wettbewerb", *Wirtschaft und Wettbewerb* [1991] H. 1, p. 23; W.K. Sievers/ A. Spark, "Competition Law and Policy in Poland", 2 *ECLR* [1993] 77. See also lately published: A. Fornalczyk, "Company Groups and Development of Competition in Poland", 2 *EBOR* (2001); Ch. Harding/M. Kepinski, "The Polish Law Against Monopolistic Practices", *ECLR* (2001) 22(5), 181 et seq.

[20] The most important were the Antimonopoly Amendments Acts of 1995 and of 1998.

[21] Thanks to the Antimonopoly Amendment Act of 1995, the original Act covers also the "public undertakings" as defined under Art. 86 EC Treaty.

[22] The extra-territorial application of Polish competition legislation has been provided from the outset (see Art. 1 of the Antimonopoly Act of 1990 and Art. 1 of the Competititon and Consumer Protection Act of 2000).

[23] See T. Skoczny, *Polish Antimonopoly Case Law* (Warsaw: ELIPSA 1995) 203; See I. Wiszniewska, "Approximation of the Polish Competition Law to European standards", *Revue Internationale de la concurrence/ International Review of Competition Law* 193 3.2000, p. 28; S. Gronowski, "The responsibility of the judiciary in the implementation of competition policy" in: <http://www.oecd.org/daf/clp/Roundtables/JUG11.HTM>.

[24] Act of 15 December 2000 on competition and consumers protection (*Journal of Laws* 2000, No. 122, item 1319).

competition restricting agreements, excessive concentration) will be described, as well as main features of the procedural system, the sanctions and institutions created for their enforcement.

2. Prohibiting abuse of dominant position

It was not a coincidence that Polish competition law was named 'antimonopoly law', since it was neither trusts nor cartels that posed the greatest threat to competition in the beginning of the 1990s. The post-socialist Polish economy was so highly monopolised and concentrated,[25] that the Antimonopoly Act of 1990 placed the heaviest emphasis on prohibiting individual firms abusing their market power or even their contractual supremacy.[26]

It needs to be emphasised that the original legislative concept of counteracting individual "monopolistic practices" was quite different from the *acquis communautaire*;[27] some of those differences were corrected through case law and amendments of the Antimonopoly Act of 1990, the remaining were eliminated through the new Competition and Consumer Protection Act of 2000.

Firstly, the Antimonopoly Act of 1990 treated differently practices of undertakings having a "monopolistic" position and those having a "dominant" positions. It defined them *ex lege* as undertakings "not encountering competition" (Article 2 point 6) and undertakings "not encountering significant competition", respectively, on a national or local market. According to the legal presumption an undertaking is deemed to hold a dominant position "if its market share exceeds 40%" (Article 2 point 7). Such differentiation was introduced because the legislator decided to absolutely prohibit only practices of undertakings holding monopolistic positions (especially excessive pricing). On the other hand, it subjected the prohibition of the abuse of a dominant position to the legal rule of reason (Article 6). However, subsequent application of this rule by the adjudicating authorities was very rare in practice. Practically, the enforcement of the

---

[25] See M. Tadeusiak, "Competititon and Consumers Protection on Monopolised markets in the Light of Antimonopoly Decisions in 1990-1995", in: *Harmonisation of the Polish Competition Legislation with Competition Rules of the European Communities*, *supra* n. 4, 75 et seq.

[26] Over 80 % of all administrative decisions of the President of the AMO/ OCCP, as well as the judgements of the AMC, issued between 1990 and 2000, related to individual monopolistic practices. See T. Skoczny, *Polish Antimonopoly Case law*, *supra* n. 23, pp. 104 et seq.; some tables with most relevant information for 1990-1995 are provided by Fingleton/ Fox/ Neven/ Seabright, *supra* n. 4, pp. 107 et seq.

[27] For more details see T. Skoczny, "Harminization of the Polish Antimonopoly Law with the EC Competittion Rules", in: *Harmonisation of the Polish Competition Legislation with Competition Rules of the European Communities*, *supra* n. 4, 103 et seq.

rules relating to dominant position abuse in Poland did not significantly differ from *acquis communautaire* based on Article 82 of the EC Treaty.

Secondly, the Act prohibited not only the abuse of monopolistic and dominant position (Articles 5 and 7), but also certain "monopolistic practices" (imposing onerous contract terms or tie-in obligations (Article 4 (1), points 1 and 2)) of any single undertaking. However, according to the case law, the Antimonopoly Act "*does not apply these provisions irrespective of the position occupied by the given entity in a given market*".[28] Consequently, the former provisions, too, were used for prohibiting dominant and monopolistic firms (especially to natural monopolists) following certain practices. On the other hand, orders to terminate practices had not been issued to entities which had not a "*qualified market position*".[29] Thus here, too, case law adjusted Polish antimonopoly law to European standards before legislative action was taken in that direction. The Antimonopoly Amendment Act of 1995 eliminated these provisions. The amended provisions were taken over by the Competition and Consumer Protection Act of 2000. Imposing onerous contracts, tie-in obligations and some other individual practices are prohibited now only if they constitute an abuse of a dominant position (see a non-exclusive list similar to Article 82 EC Treaty).

The original concepts and the practical experience concerning counteracting individual monopolistic behaviour shows that they exceeded the classical objective of competition law, namely to protect the mechanism of "effective competition". Among the legally prohibited practices – in theory and in practice – exploiting practices have taken the lead. The enforcement authorities were acting in the interests of consumers (not seldom – individual ones) rather than competitors; the anti-competitive practices were rarely the subject of antimonopoly proceedings. This tendency was strengthened by the institutional changes taken in the mid-1990s. One could say the Polish system was – at least in practice – closer to the old French concept of counteracting *concurrence defusse* than to the German concept of protecting *funktionsfähigen Wettbewerb*, which has become the basis for the competition rules of the EC Treaty.[30]

This phenomenon finds its confirmation in the fact that most antimonopoly cases handled by Polish enforcement authorities in the 1990s related to abuse of market power or contractual supremacy by undertakings holding a natural (mostly – network) or a statutory monopolistic position. These authorities found illegal, dozens of times, the exploiting practices of energy distributing

---

[28] See the AMC judgement of 10 May 1993 (XVII Amr 6/93).

[29] See the AMC judgement of 26 September 1990 (XV Amr 1/90).

[30] Compare R.H. Folson (ed.), *European Competition Law in a Nutshell* (St. Paul, Minn.: West 1992).

firms (e.g. abusing their position against investors by imposing unfair conditions for accessing their networks) or of Polish Telecom (e.g. abusing its position against mobile operators by setting fees for accessing its telephone network). Yet, their findings were illegally deprived of their legal force due to the fact that the President of AMO/OCCP was until recently also the actual regulator in these areas.[31] The situation has already changed, or is going to change, since new regulatory authorities are currently being established to bear the responsibility for maintaining the balance between the interests of firms and their clients (including consumers) as well for development of competition.

The new Competition and Consumer Protection Act of 2000 changed few but very important elements of the old legislation, consequently adjusting Polish law entirely to the *acquis communautaire*.

Most importantly, the new Act departed from the relativity of the prohibition of dominant position abuses; as in Article 82 EC Treaty, it is now a general prohibition which does not allow for exemptions on the basis of a rule of reason. Also new is the prohibition of the abuse of dominant position by groups of undertakings, which will allow to effectively control the state and the development of competition on oligopolistic markets. The Act also eliminated the distinction between monopolistic and dominant position; in theory and in practice, it was difficult to justify the maintenance of this distinction. Therefore, the Act relates only to a dominant position, the definition of which however has been changed. According to the new Article 4 point 9, dominant position means a position "which allows [the undertaking] to prevent effective competition on the relevant market thus enabling [the undertaking] to act to a significant degree independently from its competitors, contracting parties and consumers". It is easy to notice that this definition is based on the *United Brands* and *Hoffmann La-Roche* standards. It must nevertheless be emphasised that such understanding of dominance was introduced by the AMC already in 1993; it considered dominance as the capacity to act "*to a large extent independently of the competitors and clients, thus also the consumers*".[32] Thanks to the AMC's judgements also the relevant product and geographical markets are defined on the basis of the criteria of "*close commodity substitutability*" and "*homogenous competition conditions*".[33]

---

[31] Similar Fingleton/ Fox/ Neven/ Seabright, *supra* n. 4, 178.

[32] The judgement of the Antimonopoly Court of 8 November 1993 (XVII Amr 39/93).

[33] See the AMC judgements of 8.10.1993 (XVII Amr 29/93) of 8 November 1993 (XVII Amr 27/93) and of 2.02.1999 (Ama 76/98). Both cases are presented in more detail in: Skoczny T., "Poland", in: W. Rowley/ D. Baker, *International Mergers – the Antitrust Process*, 3rd ed. (London: Sweet & Maxwell 2000) 487 et seq.

3. Prohibition of competition restricting agreements

As above-mentioned, the structure of the Polish economy had been highly concentrated and monopolised. Moreover, the trade distribution networks were very much underdeveloped. Due to both of these reasons, the provisions of the Antimonopoly Act of 1990 aimed at counteracting collective "monopolistic practices" (agreements) could hardly find application. In 1990-2000 there were only a few proceedings concerning horizontal restrictive agreements (cartels). This was the case also regarding patent and know-how licensing agreements. Only distribution agreements were investigated by the authorities quite often.[34]

The original concept of counteracting "monopolistic agreements" in Poland was significantly different from Article 81 EC Treaty.[35] First of all, it did not contain a general prohibition of competition restricting agreements. On the one hand, certain agreements (contracts and understandings between entrepreneurs or resolutions of group of undertakings) – listed in Article 4 (2) of the Antimonopoly Act of 1990 exhaustively or by way of example (after the Amendment Act of 1995) – were deemed (tautologically!) as "contrary to this Act" (Article 2 point 3). These were especially price and other typical cartels (agreements between competitors). From a formal point of view, also agreements of minor importance could be deemed as "contrary to this Act".

Nevertheless, all the illegal agreements could be justified on the grounds of the legal rule of reason (Article 6) if they were necessary for the undertaking and did not result in significant restraint of competition. Such individual exemptions could take place only after *ex post* control proceedings.

On the other hand, specialisation agreements and agreements on joint sales or purchases, detrimental to the interests of other undertakings or consumers, were not "contrary to this Act". Yet their implementation could be prohibited by the enforcement authority if such agreements led to a significant restraint of competition or infringed consumer interests without bringing any economic benefits (Article 9 of the Antimonopoly Act of 1990). Such a decision could only be issued after *ex post* control proceedings.

Neither notifications nor *ex ante* controls nor group exemptions were foreseen under this legislative concept.

In any event, the enforcement approach of Polish adjudicating authorities to "monopolistic agreements" was definitely critical and corresponding to

---

[34] See T. Skoczny, *Polish Antimonopoly Case Law*, *supra* n. 23, 72 et seq. There have been almost 40 AMC judgements on vertical restraints so far.

[35] For further details see T. Skoczny, "Harminization of the Polish Antimonopoly Law with the EC Competittion Rules", in: *Harmonisation of the Polish Competition Legislation with Competition Rules of the European Communities*, *supra* n. 4, 104 et seq.

international standards. Especially regarding cartels, in particular price cartels, the administrative decisions which ordered the cessation of such practices were usually upheld by the AMC. Such was the case of the sugar cartel, a phenomenon which occurred in Poland but is also known in the competition law of the EC.[36] The Polish law has remained harmonious with EC law also when considering indirect evidence as discharging the burden of proof regarding a cartel taking the form of a concerted practice.[37] Polish case law displays a particularly critical view of the issue of vertical restraints, especially exclusivity and franchising (which is even more critical than that taken with respect to other competition rules).[38] One could say that this approach was too critical (interventionist) since Polish law – as a national law – does not contain European integration as an objective.[39] However, counteracting the exclusivity clauses which restrict access to markets monopolised by entities having a "*qualified market position*" conforms to international standards.[40]

The same could be said with respect to the treatment of licensing agreements.[41]

The legislator was therefore faced with the uneasy task of creating such a new system that would counteract agreements restricting competition and be adjusted to the *acquis communautaire*, yet at the same time not over-restricting the development of distribution networks.

It seams that the model chosen is not only adjusted to the Community concept, but also anticipates its future evolution.

The Competition and Consumer Protection Act of 2000 generally prohibits agreements which have as their object or effect the prevention, restriction or distortion of competition on the relevant market (Article 5 (1)), unless those are of minor importance (Article 6), or are exempted under a regulation of the Council of Ministers. The prohibited agreements are null and void (Article 5 (2)).

The Act also allows for a finding an individual agreement not infringing Article 5 if it meets the conditions for group exemption but is not covered by such an exemption (Article 11 (2)). These conditions are literary the same as in

---

[36] See: the judgement of the Antimonopoly Court of 1 March 1993 (XVII Amr 37/92).

[37] Ibid.

[38] See AMC judgements of 21 July 1992 (XVII AMR 12/92) and of 6 December 1992 (XVII Amr 35/93).

[39] See Wiszniewska, "Approximation of the Polish Competition Law to European standards", *supra* n. 23, 33.

[40] See the judgements of the Antimonopoly Court of 6 December 1990 (XV Amr 5/90) and 21 July 1992 (XVII Amr 12/92).

[41] See Wiszniewska, "Approximation of the Polish Competition Law to European standards", *supra* n. 23, 34.

Article 81 (3) of the EC Treaty. This means that the primacy of the *ex post* control of individual agreements restricting competition has been kept; the previous intention to introduce a notification (*ex ante* control) system has been dropped. Hence, the radical change of the system of implementation of Articles 81 and 82 of the EC Treaty – lately proposed by the Commission – has been anticipated.[42]

Therefore, it can be said that the new Polish system is entirely harmonised with the EC competition rules. It is also to be hoped that it will allow the differentiated – more economically than formally – treatment of horizontal and vertical restraints of competition. It should be so in particular in the case of vertical distribution agreements (covering exclusivity, franchising or selective distribution),[43] which lead to the restraint of competition among the distributors of the same brand product (intra-brand competition), yet most often promote the increase of competition among the competitors of such brand products (inter-brand competition). Also, although less often, certain agreements between competitors enhance co-operation between undertakings which is beneficial for the economy and the consumers rather than in restraint of competition.

4. Preventive control of concentrations

The primary goal of competition legislation in the countries undergoing economic transformation is promotion of the development of competition. The huge degree of concentration of Polish economy in the beginning of the 1990s, and hence the lack of real threat from competition through concentration processes, caused the Antimonopoly Act of 1990 to put much emphasis on demonopolisation. It also established the legal grounds for prohibiting and controlling mergers and acquisitions.[44]

The Act gave the AMO the power to order division or liquidation of undertakings which have a dominant position on a market if they permanently restrain competition or the conditions for its emergence (Article 12 (1)). Thanks to many such decisions, some local markets (e.g. those related to the processing of and trade in agricultural or wood products) have been successfully

[42] Proposal for a Council Regulation on the implementation of the rules on competition laid down in Article 81 and 82 EC Treaty and on the Amendment of Regulations (EEC) 1017/68, 2988/74, 4056/86 and 3975/87. See Document 500PC0582 <http://europe.eu.int/eur-lex/en/com/dat/2000/en_500PC0582.html>.

[43] Similar Fingleton/ Fox/ Neven/ Seabright, *supra* n. 4, 180.

[44] See A. Cylwik, "The Role of the Antimonopoly Office in Structural Economic Transformation", in: *Harmonisation of the Polish Competition Legislation with Competition Rules of the European Communities*, *supra* n. 4, 51 et seq.

demonopolised. On the other hand, demonopolistion powers "to limit economic activity of an undertaking" simply "holding a dominant position on a market" (Article 12 (4)) could not be applied due to the danger of violating a constitutional rule of law.

The above-mentioned divisions or liquidations of dominant undertakings; the breaking-up of State-owned undertakings by the State; trade liberalisation; and the developing privatisation, increasingly with foreign participation, have given Polish economy a more varied and differentiated structure.

The original scheme regarding mergers and acquisitions of sole or joint control was not effective enough. It included *ex post* control, which prohibited property, capital and personal mergers or acquisitions which were deemed "monopolistic practices" (Article 4 (1) points 3 and 4). Preventive, *ex ante*, control only existed for mergers (amalgamations) of organisational character (Article 11).[45] By the Antimonopoly Amendment Act of 1995, this scheme was replaced by a broad unitary system of preventive control of anti-competitive mergers and acquisitions.[46] This system was based on the concept provided in the EC Merger Regulation 4064/89.[47] However, concentration transactions subject to this control were not defined according to Article 1 of the EC Merger Regulation, but listed in line with the German Cartel Act 1957.[48]

Too low turnover thresholds of the concentration transactions needed to be notified (2 and 5 millions EUR) resulted in thousands of notifications reaching the AMO/OCCP in the following years. In almost all of these cases, after having them processed, the authority issued an administrative "no objection" clearance letter. Even after increasing these thresholds to 25 million EUR by the Antimonopoly Amendment Act of 1998, only few serious merger cases took place in the late 1990s. Only three prohibitions were issued; two of them were annulled by the AMO.[49] In one case the AMO annulled the decision of the OCCP President and decided that a re-examination was appropriate.[50] The OCCP President, after re-examination re-issued a prohibition, which has

---

[45] For a more detailed presentation see T. Skoczny, "Poland", in: W. Rowley/ D. Baker (eds.), *International Mergers – the Antitrust Process*, 2nd ed. (London: Sweet & Maxwell 1996) 1209, as well as the Supplement to the 2nd Edition (1998), at p. 307.

[46] For a more detailed presentation see T. Skoczny, "Poland", in: Rowley/ Baker (eds.), *International Mergers – the Antitrust Process*, 3rd ed., *supra* n. 33, p. 48-3.

[47] Council Regulation (EEC) 4064/89 of 21 December 1989 on the control of concentrations between undertakings (*OJ* [1989] L 395/1) with amendments introduced by Council Regulation (EC) 1310/97 (*OJ* [1997] L 180/1).

[48] See § 35 of the Gesetz gegen Wettbewerbsbeschränkungen (GWB). Bekanntmachung der Neufassung vom 26. August 1998 (*BGBl.* I, 2546).

[49] See the detailed analysis of these three cases in: T. Skoczny, "Poland", in: Rowley/ Baker, *supra* n. 33, p. 48-13.

[50] See the AMC judgement of 2.2.1999 (XVII Ama 76/98).

recently been confirmed by the AMC.[51] Therewith, a planned strengthening of a dominant position on a local market of bulk concrete and concrete mortar was frustrated.

The new Competition and Consumer Protection Act of 2000 furthered the approximation of the Polish law of merger control to the EC Merger Regulation.

First of all, it adopted the Community mode of defining concentration transactions that must be notified. As in Article 2 (1)-(3) of the Merger Regulation 4064/89, mergers, (sole) acquisition of controls and joint ventures are subject to control by the OCCP President. Regarding joint ventures, the Act does not distinguish between "concentrative" (or "playing all the functions of an undertaking") and "cooperative" ones; application problems are surely to be expected.

It must be stressed that the Competition and Consumer Protection Act of 2000 went beyond the scope of preventive, *ex ante* control of "concentrations" as defined in Article 2 (1)-(3) of the EC Merger Regulation. Even transactions which do not lead to "acquiring control" over other entrepreneur(s), including acquisitions of minority block of shares, have to be notified.

On the other hand, it is to be emphasised that the Act increased the turnover thresholds once again (to 50 million EUR) and excluded from the notification procedure concentrations of minor importance. This will eliminate unnecessary control proceedings.

It is also very important that the new scheme adopted precisely the "double" evaluation test provided in Article 3 (3) of the Merger Regulation 4064/89. The former provision, providing that the President of the OCCP "*may*" prohibit a given merger or "*may*" renounce the issue of such a prohibition notwithstanding its leading to the gaining or maintenance of a dominant position on the market (without formulation of any legal prerequisites for its application), raised doubts regarding its compatibility with the constitutional principle of rule of law. On the other hand, the new evaluation test surely creates a significant challenge for an OCCP having limited resources and experience. Given the conditions of a transforming and emerging economy, it will not be easy to provide an economic analysis evidencing that an intended merger will "significantly restrict competition on the market" in the future.

Merger Guidelines, using tests applied in more developed merger control systems, would have created the necessary measure of legal certainty and transparency.

---

[51] Not yet published.

5. Procedures, sanctions, institutions

Substantive law provisions are important, but do not in themselves suffice to ensure effective enforcement of statutory prohibitions of restrictive practices and abuse of dominant position, as well as preventive control of concentrations. Unfortunately, the provisions concerning procedural rules and fines were rather few in the original Antimonopoly Act of 1990. These were improved by later amendments but lagged far behind European standards. This situation was radically changed by the Competition and Consumer Protection Act of 2000.

The new Act comprises 2/3 of procedural provisions. Included are many which are *lex specialis* to the general Administrative Procedure Code. The most important ones entrust the OCCP President with very extensive powers in administrative proceedings necessary for providing effective investigations in antitrust cases (e.g. to require information, order witnesses to give testimony, hear experts, and provide control). Some of these powers go even beyond the powers of the EC Commission or those of national authorities. For instance, the OCCP may be authorised by the AMC not only to search the premises of firms (Articles 58-60), but also to ask the AMC for permission to search the living quarters of the firms' managers (by functionaries of State Police with the participation of OCCP officials).[52] Unfortunately, these possibilities are not limited to the formal antimonopoly proceedings as defined in Article 42 (1) (after the statement of objections has been submitted to the "accused" party). Thus, it may be expected that the AMC will hinder using (misusing!) these powers in so-called "explanatory proceedings" initiated by the OCCP President *ex officio* in order to make a preliminary assessment of antimonopoly infringements, an assessment of infringement of consumer interests or carry out market research (Article 43). Given this exception, the new Act provides in general for proper protection of the rights and interests of the undertakings subject to administrative proceedings before the OCCP President.

According to the new Competition and Consumer Protection Act of 2000, the OCCP President is also empowered to impose fines for infringements of statutory prohibitions (Article 101 (2) point 1), for failing to comply with obligations provided in merger control provisions, including an obligation to notify an intended concentration (Article 101 (1) point 1) and for other breaches of statutory and administrative obligations. He or she may also impose periodic penalty payments for any kind of delays in implementation of statutory and

---

[52] The Commission will eventually get this power under the new Regulation implementing Articles 81 and 82 that will replace Regulation 17/62. See Document 500PC0582 <http://europe.eu.int/eur-lex/en/com/dat/2000/en_500PC0582.html>.

administrative obligations (Article 102). In any case, the quantity of these fines and penalty payments should be higher.

Unfortunately, the new Competition and Consumer Protection Act of 2000 has not changed the Polish institutional enforcement concept. The increased scale of application of competition law, and the growing complexity and political relevance of cases being brought before the OCCP, make it necessary to work out a new institutional formula for the OCCP, providing for more uniform enforcement policy and for higher independence and quality of its activity. In any case, we should look for solutions enabling the separation of investigative from ruling powers of the OCCP President.[53] A possible solution could be found by way of establishing within the OCCP an independent "council" or "board" for competition (as in Spain or Hungary) or special "adjudicating boards" (based on the German example) having adjudicative powers, composed of persons having the most experience with such cases and of competition rules practitioners. The provisions of the Civil Procedure Code should then be applied to the proceedings before such institutions.

One could also say that the present system of enforcement institutions in Poland does not fulfil all the standards of the rule of law, since there is in practice only one antimonopoly instance, comprising both the administrative authority (i.e., the OCCP President, acting as a first-line adjudicator) and the court (the AMC as a second-line adjudicator). The change of the internal structure and division of the investigative and ruling powers within the OCCP, as well as the creating of the Appeal Antimonopoly Court would complete the reform of the Polish enforcement system.

6. Conclusions

If the purpose of this contribution has been achieved, the reader will surely agree with its author that in the 10 years of development of Polish competition law it is possible to notice a consistent attempt to achieve two objectives in parallel:

---

[53] Also recommended by Fingleton/ Fox/ Neven/ Seabright, *supra* n. 4, 177, 179, as well as by the International League of Competition law by resolution of the Saint-Malo Congress, published in: *Revue Internationale de la Concurrence/ International Review of Competition Law*, 193 3.2000, p. 16-18. See also the International Report concerning question 2: "Should the national or supranational authorities responsible for the application of competition law be totally independent from political power both from the beginning of the investigation and at the time of the decision? If the answer is affirmative, how should that independence be guaranteed?", as well the Polish National Report concerning this question prepared by T. Skoczny (not yet published).

a) permanent adjustment of the legislation and its enforcement principles to the requirements of developing and protecting competition in a constantly evolving and differentiating economy; and
b) their gradually adjustment to EC competition rules.

As shown above Polish competition law began by providing the basis for structural demonopolisation and the counteracting of abuses of monopolistic and dominant position, mainly by State-own enterprises, often being natural (network) monopolies. The new Competition and Consumer Protecting Act of 2000 will surely provide it with the basis for finding and prohibiting horizontal agreements restricting competition (especially so-called “hard core cartels”). Additionally, unnecessary barriers to cooperation agreements (especially of SMEs) and agreements creating distribution networks, that support rather than limit inter-brand competition, have been removed. It is very likely that in Poland, too, an increasing number of concentrations, posing a great challenge for the OCCP, will take place during the newly started decade.

One can say that it is not only the substantive provisions of the new Competition and Consumer Act of 2000 that satisfy the requirements of the economy in the present as well as the foreseeable future. The Polish enforcement system, too, seems to be quite well-prepared for the protection of competition against agreements which seek to restrain it, and against abuses of dominant position and excessive concentration. This holds true even if some improvement in the procedural and institutional framework is advisable. In order to ensure effective investigations, it is necessary to provide the OCCP President with the power to issue interim orders. The respect of fundamental rights and economic interests of firms makes it necessary to restrict the use of some investigative powers of the OCCP President to the formal administrative provisions, and not allow their being used, for instance, for sectoral inquiries. Protecting the rights and interests of firms would also be served by the establishment of a second (appellate) instance of judicial jurisdiction. This would strengthen the balance between the effectiveness of antimonopoly investigative proceedings, on the one hand, and the legality of intervention in rights and interests of undertakings, on the other.

Even if the Polish administrative enforcement authority will remain a single-man organ, combining investigative and ruling powers, it can still provide for protection of “effective competition”, due to the strengthening of its independence under the new Competition and Consumer Protection Act of 2000 (the President will be nominated for a 5-year terms).

Finally, as was demonstrated above, Polish competition legislation and enforcement is, by and large, adjusted to EC competition rules relating to undertakings.[54] This means that Poland not only "approximated" its legislation to the competition rules of the *acquis communautaire*, but that it is also well-prepared and equipped to apply the primary and secondary competition legislation of the Community from the first date of joining it. This is of extreme importance since the future system of implementation of Article 81 and 82 should be more decentralised.[55]

For the time being, there is no doubt that Polish competition law, shares the following characteristics with EC competition law:

- It is directed against the same three anti-competitive strategies of undertakings: agreements restricting competition (Article 5), abuse of market position (Articles 8) and excessive concentration (Articles 12);
- It is based in certain cases on the principle of prohibition – relative in case of agreements restricting competition (Article 5-7) and absolute in case of abuse of market position (Article 8), and in other cases on the principle of preventive control – in the case of concentrations (Article 12-16);
- It is likely to be applied in the same way – effectively and legally – as the OCCP President has almost the same (sometimes even stronger) investigative powers (Articles 44-100) and may impose the same kinds of fines and periodic penalty payments (Articles 100-106) as the European Commission and the competition authorities of the EC Member States; the OCCP has already today a large degree of adjudicative independence (Article 24), and its decisions are subject to the control of an independent court – AMC (Article 78).

---

[54] See T. Skoczny, "Harmonisation of the Polish Antimonopoly Law with the EC Competition Rules", in: *Harmonisation of the Polish Competition Legislation with Competition Rules of the European Communities*, *supra* n. 4, 96; similar in T. Skoczny, "Hamonization of the competition law of the EC associated countries seeking for EU membership with the EC competititon rules: example Poland", Paper for Fourth ECSA-World Congress <www.ecsanet.org/conferences/skoczny.htm>.

[55] See E.-J. Mestmäcker, "The EC Commissions's Modernization of Competition Policy: A Challange to the Community's Constitutional Order", 1 *EBOR* (2000) 401.

Finally, as was demonstrated above, Polish competition legislation and enforcement is, by and large, adjusted to EC competition rules relating to under-takings. [illegible]

[illegible]

The Public Spirit of the Corporation

Christine Windbichler*

1. Dr. Faust's Stradivari

Imagine yourself sitting in the Berlin Philharmonic Hall, listening to a concert given by the Berlin Philharmonic Orchestra. On the stage-bill is the Second Piano Concerto by Johannes Brahms. I especially like this concerto because it comes as a nice double pack: Hidden in the third movement is a wonderful cello concert. Therefore, you can be sure that this important cello-solo will be played by Dr. Faust, the first solo-cellist of the Berlin Philharmonic, on an original

* Professor of Law, Dr. iur. LL.M. (Berkeley), Humboldt University Berlin.
I dedicate this paper to Joachim Mestmäcker on the occasion of his 75th birthday. For helpful comments on earlier versions I thank the interdisciplinary working group "*Gemeinwohl und Gemeinsinn*" (chair: Herfried Münkler) of the Berlin-Brandenburg Academy of Science, and colleagues from the University of California, Berkeley, and Cornell Schools of Law, especially Richard M. Buxbaum and Melvin A. Eisenberg at Berkeley.

Stradivari from 1798. Dr. Faust discovered this extraordinary instrument on one of the many tours of the Orchestra. His enthusiasm, however, was immediately dampened as he realized that neither he personally, nor the Orchestra, nor the Association of the Friends of the Orchestra, could afford to buy it. But then, Dr. Faust recalled a recent conversation with Hilmar Kopper, at that time CEO of Deutsche Bank AG. The Deutsche Bank, a public stock corporation, showed public spirit and financed the cello.[1]

Now, where is the problem? Perhaps JOCHEN MESTMÄCKER doesn't like Brahms or cello music. But, given his long standing interest in and powerful contributions to understanding the delicate interplay of private initiative and government intervention, he may find the following remarks entertaining. Private initiative is not limited to individuals; the "corporate citizen" as well constitutes an important part of the private sector. My example raises questions familiar to corporation lawyers from various jurisdictions: A bank is a bank and not a dealer in antique musical instruments. Can a CEO make this kind of decision by himself according to his personal preferences? The workforce would probably prefer the money to go to a certain soccer team. What did the workers' representatives on the supervisory board think about it, what the customers paying charges for their checking accounts? Under a German perspective, financing of cultural events and institutions still is predominantly a responsibility of the government and should be under democratic control. The extension of corporate power into the realm of cultural life is seen with some reservations.[2]

2. SOME CLASSICAL CASES AND CURRENT DISCUSSIONS

2.1 *Evans* v. *Brunner, Mond & Company*[3]

In this older English case, the directors of a chemical manufacturing corporation had passed a resolution to distribute £100,000 to universities for the furtherance of scientific research without further restrictions. A shareholder challenged the resolution, arguing that the money might be used for scientific education in astronomy or some other branch not useful to the chemical trade and that, besides, the benefit if any was too remote; in fact, even competitors might get the benefit. At the time of the gift, scientists and chemists in particular

---

[1] I am grateful to Dr. Georg Faust for personal communications in this matter.

[2] The problems of contributions to political parties and campaign funding will not be discussed in this paper.

[3] Ch. 359, 90 L.J. Ch.Div. 294 (1921) after Lattin, *The Law of Corporations*, 2nd ed. (Mineola, NY: Foundation 1971) p. 210.

were in short supply. The court applied the rule that the contribution must be one that can fairly be regarded as incidental or conducive to the purposes for which the company was formed. This rule was construed rather generously. The court found that persons trained in other sciences would be useful in the chemical branch as well by virtue of their knowledge of scientific methods and procedures. While the donor corporation might not acquire any of the sponsored scientists, it had the opportunity of acquiring them and given the shortage of scientifically trained people this was the best way to relieve the shortage.

2.2 *A.P. Smith Manufacturing Company* v. *Barlow*[4]

In this case, a gift of $1500 to the trustees of Princeton University was challenged as a waste of corporate assets since it resulted in no direct economic benefit of the corporation. The court used an interesting analogy between individuals and legal persons: "When the wealth of the nation was primarily in the hands of individuals they discharged their responsibilities as citizens by donating freely for charitable purposes. With the transfer of most of the wealth to corporate hands and the imposition of heavy burdens of individual taxation, they have been unable to keep pace with increased philanthropic needs. They have therefore, with justification, turned to corporations to assume the modern obligations of good citizenship in the same manner as humans do." So there is room for a public spirit of corporations, but how much and who decides on the recipient? In the case at hand, the gift was seen appropriate as in furtherance of the free enterprise system on which the corporation's success was dependent. Moreover, "there was no showing that the gift in question was made to a *pet charity* in furtherance of personal rather than corporate ends."

Nowadays, in the US state legislation, the Model Business Corporation Act, the ALI Principles on corporate governance, and state courts generally recognize the corporate power to make donations. Still controversial are the limits to such generosity. To varying degrees, additional tests apply as to some connection of the gift to the corporation's business and as to the amount being reasonable in relation to the business' size and earnings. Reference is also made to the treatment of such gifts under tax law.

---

[4] N.J. 145, 98 A.2d 581, 39 A.L.R.2d 1179 (1953), appeal dismissed, 346 US 861, 74 S.Ct. 107, 98 L.Ed. 373; see also discussion in Cox/Hazen/O'Neal, *Corporations* (New York: Aspen Law & Business 1997) p. 64; Jennings and Buxbaum, *Corporations, Cases and Materials*, 5th ed. (St. Paul, Minn.: West 1979) p. 124; O'Kelley and Thompson, *Corporations and Other Business Associations, Cases and Materials*, 3rd ed. (New York: Aspen Law & Business 1999) pp. 269-270.

2.3 *Dodge* v. *Ford Motor Co.*[5]

This case is usually quoted in support of the theory that corporations should be run exclusively in the interest of shareholders.[6] Henry Ford owned 58 % of the company's stock, the Dodge brothers held 10 %. The company yielded large profits and paid generous dividends. Mr. Ford, the dominant force in the business, pursued a plan to cut dividends; the selling price of the cars should be reduced, the capacity of the plant should be increased. "My ambition", said Mr. Ford, "is to employ still more men, to spread the benefits of this industrial system to the greatest possible number, to help them build up their lives and their homes. To do this we are putting the greatest share of our profits back in the business." The Dodge brothers challenged this plan and contended that the apparent immediate effect will be to diminish the value of shares and the returns to shareholders. The court agreed with the plaintiffs. "There should be no confusion (of which there is evidence) of the duties which Mr. Ford conceives that he and the stockholders owe to the general public and the duties which in law he and his co-directors owe to the protesting minority stockholders. A business corporation is organized and carried on primarily for the profit of the stockholders. The powers of directors are to be exercised for that end. The discretion of directors is to be exercised in the choice of means to attain that end and does not extend to a change in the end itself, to the reduction of profits or to the non-distribution of profits among stockholders in order to devote them to other purposes."

An older English case may be quoted as well as a more recent Alabama case in the same line of argument. Lord Bowen argued 1883 that "Charity has no business to sit at boards of directors qua charity". A railroad company wanted to offer, after its winding up, its unemployed workers severance pay.[7] The Alabama Supreme Court held in 1963 that gifts to the widows of former corporate officers were an invalid waste of corporate assets.[8] These cases show

---

[5] N.W. 668 (Mich. 1919).

[6] See e.g. Margaret M. Blair, *Ownership and Control: Rethinking Corporate Governance,* (Brookings Institution 1995) p. 202, reprinted in: Clarkson [ed.], *The Corporation and its Stakeholders. Classic and Contemporary Readings*, (Toronto: University of Toronto Press, 1998) p. 47, 51: point . . . made crystal clear; E. Merrick Dodd Jr., "For Whom Are Corporate Managers Trustees?", 45 *Harv.L.Rev.* (1932) 1145, reprinted in: Clarkson [ed.], ibid., pp. 31, 43 n. 3: a vigorous assertion of this view; O'Kelley/Thompson, *supra* n. 4, p. 267: a classic example of shareholder litigation seeking to change or obtain redress for corporate policies that are intended to bestow significant benefit on non-shareholder constituencies.

[7] Wiethölter, *Interessen und Organisation der Aktiengesellschaft im amerikanischen und deutschen Recht* (Karlsruhe: Müller 1961) p. 5.

[8] *Adams* v. *Smith*, 153 So.2d 221 (Ala. 1963).

that benefits for employees and their families fall, in some people's view, within the scope of donations or charity.

2.4 An example from a recent German discussion: slave labor claims

We all know of the intricate problem of compensation for forced and slave labor during Nazi Germany. Such compensation is now being arranged by a foundation funded partly by German businesses, partly by the German Government, i.e., tax money. A German lawyer named Philipp argued in an article that contributions of German stock corporations to the foundation were illegal under current stock corporation law, void, even unconstitutional.[9] No payments were owed in terms of actually existing claims and, therefore, expenditures towards the foundation were detrimental to the rights and interests of the current shareholders. The moral aspect – ethical responsibility for misdeeds in the past –, so goes the argument advances, applies only to individuals, not to legal persons. Threats of boycott in foreign markets (i.e. the US) against businesses unwilling to join the foundation were illegal, even criminal actions.

The legal position just described certainly is an extreme exception. The general opinion among corporate lawyers is that the managing board is entitled to contribute to the Foundation "Remembrance, Responsibility and the Future".[10] This is especially important as the call to join the foundation covers all German businesses including those that were founded only after the war. The author's contention that no payments are owed is true at least for those new enterprises. However, there is involuntary irony in the Philipp's philippic. He complains that the treatment of the World War II forced labor issue shows a blatant attempt of the US to exert hegemony over European and German private law. The German legal tradition, however, is much more open to a civic spirit of legal persons, expressed by contributions for non-business causes, than the American line of argument in *Dodge* v. *Ford* or the so called finance model that calls for management of the corporation exclusively in the interest of shareholders, or even the more moderate view that requires at least some distant benefit of donations for the corporation. This needs further elaboration (4.2.2).

---

9 Philipp, "Darf der Vorstand zahlen? Die Zwangsarbeiter und das Aktienrecht", *AG* (2000) 62.

10 Mertens, "Der Vorstand darf zahlen", *AG* (2000) 157.

3. Legal issues

All the given examples have something in common. They share the premise that the corporation is to be run for the profit of its shareholders according to its stated business purpose. Nobody denies that. The controversies arise around additional or competing corporate goals and other constituencies' than the shareholders' interests.

In corporate law, three sets of issues can be distinguished. First, we have the more technical question as to whether the corporation has the power to show "public spirit". Second, we have the corporate governance problem of the decision making process and its control. Last but not least come the substantive issues as to which goals and interests are legitimately forged into the spirit of the corporation.

3.1 Ultra vires acts and the powers of the corporation

The limits of the powers of a corporation based on common law, its charter, or its articles of incorporation are well discussed and lost much of their original impact. Generous interpretation of implied powers and the application of agency law, with apparent authority to fall back on, enlarged the scope of authorized business. Therefore, cases based on *ultra vires* will be extremely rare nowadays. The emphasis shifted to the business judgment rule and whether directors acted reasonably in what they believed advanced the corporation's best interest.

The German legal tradition from early on followed a different concept. Legal persons incorporated according to private law enjoy full legal capacity.[11] Limitations of authority of managing directors are of interest only within the internal relationship between the director and the corporation but not towards third parties. The notion of unlimited representative power is well established in commercial law. It facilitates commercial transactions in an environment of complicated organizations.

As a result, we can assume that the cello mentioned in the introduction can stay where it is and serve its wonderful purpose. Even *Philipp*, the outspoken advocate of strict profit maximization, has to resort to collusion in order to make void contributions to the Foundation "Remembrance, Responsibility and the Future". His argument goes: if the Foundation is aware (i.e., read his article) that contributions are illegal under German law, acceptance of gifts amounts to

---

[11] For discussion whether the concept of legal entity includes constitutional rights under the First and Fourteenth Amendments see Buxbaum and Hopt, *Legal Harmonization and the Business Enterprise. Corporate and Capital Market Law Harmonization Policy in Europe and the U.S.A.* (Berlin: de Gruyter 1988) pp. 155 et seq.; for the respective dispute in German law see commentaries on Art. 19 GG.

intentional collaboration with the management to the detriment of the corporation, one of the very few exceptions to the unrestricted representative power of managing directors.

The ultra-vires problem taken care of by modeling the legal person in analogy to the individual, there still is the question of the decision-making process within the corporation and the foundation as well as the legitimization of a "public spirit".

3.2 The decision making process and its control

The impact of a business purpose statement in the articles of incorporation and the scope of the management's decision-making powers are closely related. The perspective taken depends to a large extent on the legal culture and environment. German lawyers love abstract discussions. They fill books and articles with reasoned definitions of the "*Unternehmensinteresse*", i.e. the interest of the enterprise as an abstract concept, and whether or not there is a difference between the interest of the enterprise or the corporation and the interest of it's shareholders, and what the interest of "the shareholders" might be given the diversity of the shareholder population.[12] A scholar coming from the common law tradition, I assume, would not bother so much about definitions but would rather ask who is empowered to decide which interests will guide the decisions. The limits to such powers then will be discussed in terms of fiduciary duties and to what extent the business judgment rule protects the management. Despite the differences in focus, the decision-making process is an important issue in the international corporate governance discussion. Here, we find the shareholders' and other constituencies' interests addressed as well as which decisions should go to the shareholders' meeting.[13]

Coming back to my cello-example, the decision-making issues are whether the CEO needed a resolution of the managing board or the approval of the supervisory board or even of the shareholders' meeting, and whether it made a difference whether the articles of incorporation of the Deutsche Bank or some other internal rules say something about business purpose and gifts.

Interestingly enough, all cases and examples deal with decisions made by the management or the board of directors. That the shareholders' meeting could be

---

[12] Peter O. Mülbert, "Shareholder Value aus rechtlicher Sicht", *ZGR* (1997) 129, 142 with further references.

[13] See, e.g., OECD Principles of Corporate Governance, <http://www.oecd.org/daf/governance/principles.htm> [last visited 31 August 2001]; German Panel on Corporate Governance, Code of Best Practice, <http://www.corgov.de> [last visited 31 August 2001]; DVFA Deutsche Vereinigung für Finanzanalyse und Asset Management e.V., Corporate Governance Scorecard©, <http://www.dvfa.de/pdf/scorecard.pdf> [last visited 31 August 2001].

involved is mentioned only as a possibility.[14] No case or example actually gave jurisdiction to the shareholders' meeting. Practically speaking, this is very sensible. Shareholders' meetings are expensive, usually held only once a year, and burdened with many technicalities. Whoever once attended the Annual General Meeting of a large corporation (I take my students every year to such an event, and they are always shocked) will be well aware of the limits of this device as a decision-making body. Not only practically but legally as well we are dealing with decisions within the powers of the board of directors. The board is certainly free to submit issues to the shareholders; in our cases, though, it will rarely do so. The division of powers within the corporation seems to be rather similar in all the jurisdictions mentioned.

3.3 Which interests are to be served?

Whoever has the power to decide upon corporate activities he, she, or it will be bound by some substantive criteria. Usually, these are defined negatively as the issue turns up whenever a transgression is alleged. The furtherance of a "pet charity" by the chairman of the board as it was mentioned in *A.P. Smith* would constitute such a transgression. However, is it enough to meet the criterion "pet charity" when the CEO of the Deutsche Bank happens to like cello music or old instruments? Probably not. As positive tests whether contributions are within the powers of the management are mentioned in the examples: Tax law, quantitative criteria, i.e. the relation of the amount donated to capital or earnings, secondary benefits for the corporation like positive publicity, etc. Still, this leaves plenty of interests mentioned in *Dodge* v. *Ford* and other cases – the workforce, consumers, education, art, sports, etc. – that may or may not be served by more or less inspired corporate officers. As this is one of the topics of the ongoing corporate governance debate – shortly, the shareholder v. stakeholder debate – I will present a short comparative overview over some aspects of German and American law.

4. Shareholder value, codetermination, and public interest in a comparative perspective

4.1 Internal and external governance

There is one feature common to all jurisdictions although rarely presented with prominence. That is the distinction between internal and external governance.

---

[14] *A.P. Smith Mfg. Co.* v. *Barlow*, *supra* n. 4.

External governance of the corporation involves, e.g., tax law, regulations of the industry, consumer protection laws, restrictive contract law concerning standard terms, labor and employment law. External governance is everything that regulates the behavior of a legal person as well as of an individual conducting a business with respect to third parties. Internal governance comprises all the rules that govern the internal decision-making processes within the corporation, be they procedural or substantive, based on contract (articles of incorporation), regulation, or default rules.

To illustrate the distinction just made, I would like to go back to the old English case where the board wanted to offer severance pay to laid off workers. As of 1883, such payments were purely voluntary; they were labeled as "charity" and discussed under the heading whether the directors of a corporation were allowed to use corporate funds for charitable contributions - a question of internal governance. Under current German law, severance payments accompanying plant closings are mandatory – "*Sozialplan*" according to § 112 *Betriebsverfassungsgesetz*, in other jurisdictions such plans are agreed upon in collective bargaining. In all cases, based on contract with third parties, collective agreement, or statute, we are dealing with external governance. The management has to take such costs into account when calculating whether the closing of a plant makes economic sense or not. This is not a question of "charity" anymore. Whether a bank is willing to finance a cello is the result of an internal decision making process and, therefore, only subject to internal governance rules.

As an aside I may add that, in German legal analysis, benefits or other payments not included in employees' individual contract or owed on the basis of a collective agreement are still considered "wages" or "salary" in a broad sense. That is, such payments are not gifts but compensation for work done within a long term, relational and necessarily incomplete contract. The underlying theory is quite different from the doctrine of "employment at will".[15] As already pointed out, there are many faces of labor and employment law – completely independent from corporate law – in the comparatist's world. Therefore, discussions based on employment at will look path-dependent to me.

More homogenous is another aspect of external governance by regulation. General laws apply to all corporations (and businesses conducted in various forms). At least within the respective jurisdiction, such laws have a so-called cartel effect, i.e. competition in the specifically regulated area is excluded. Internal governance, however, shapes the standing of the corporation in the market where it faces other corporations with their outcomes of their internal

---

[15] Katherine Van Wezel Stone, "Policing Employment Contracts Within the Nexus-of-Contracts Firm", 43 *U. of Toronto L.J.* 353 (1993).

decision-making process.[16] In this respect, human resources management can be a source of competitive advantage. This line of argument comes easily to someone used to thinking in categories of competition and the market process. In academic circles, however, fields of interest are often painstakingly kept separate. The company law professor does not venture into labor law or antitrust. It takes someone like JOCHEN MESTMÄCKER to overcome such limitations. He would take up the discussion and navigate into deeper waters of social philosophy. I rely on his generosity and understanding for the topicality of this paper.

Many interests – I don't want to go into the question of the definition of "stakeholders" in this context – are protected by external governance, be it contractual or by regulation. Therefore, it would be a big mistake to surmise that stakeholders' interests are neglected if they are not included in the scope of the substantive criteria of management decisions.[17] When it comes to shareholders, we see another picture.[18] Aside from their position defined by corporation law (which is "regulation", too, as far as mandatory provisions are concerned), there is very little in terms of external governance. We could think of capital markets law. However, there, the shareholder is protected as an investor in general. She should be well and fairly informed in order to follow the "Wall Street rule", i.e. buy, sell, or hold her stock. But this has little or no relation to the internal functioning of the corporation. Seen from the internal governance side, shareholders have, e.g., voting rights. Also important are articles of incorporation, by-laws, and mandatory or default corporation law provisions. These are the rules to

---

[16] Eisenberg strikes a similar note applying the prisoner's dilemma: Melvin A. Eisenberg, "Corporate Conduct That Does Not Maximize Shareholder Gain: Legal Conduct, Ethical Conduct, the Penumbra Effect, Reciprocity, the Prisoner's Dilemma, Sheep's Clothing, Social Conduct, and Disclosure", 28 *Stetson L.Rev.* (1998) 1, 10 et seq. See also Sadowski/Junkes/Lindenthal, "Labour Co-Determination and Corporate Governance in Germany: The Economic Impact of Marginal and Symbolic Rights", in: Schwalbach [ed.], *Corporate Governance* (Berlin: Springer 2001) p. 146; Schuler/Turnheim/Jackson, "Human Resource Management: Past, Present, Future", in: Blanpain/Engels [eds.], *Comparative Labour Law and Industrial Relations in Industrial Market Economies*, 6th ed. (The Hague: Kluwer 1998) 181, at p. 207.

[17] Clark, *Corporate Law* (Boston: Little, Brown 1986) pp. 17 et seq., 678: many obligations to non-shareholders.

[18] This is well discussed especially in the economic literature; shareholders are considered recipients of the residual, and this serves as a premium for the risk they assume. Cheffins, *Company Law: Theory, Structure, and Operation* (Oxford: Clarendon 1997) p. 54; for a critical assessment see also Jonathan R. Macey, "An Economic Analysis of the Various Rationale for Making Shareholders the Exclusive Beneficiaries of Corporate Duties", 21 *Stetson L.Rev.* 23 (1991).

which the shareholders subjected their investment.[19] From a German point of view, I would add the "membership" component: the stock corporation is a variation of the "*Verein*", the basic form of association in a separate legal entity where members have administrative rights and privileges as to the pursuit of the purposes of the association. The creation of the separate legal entity is undoubtedly based on some kind of "contract" or private ordering; the nature of such "contracts", however, is organizational and distinct from other kinds of market exchanges. Rights emanating from the organizational or membership side of the corporation are found on the internal side of governance and show that shareholders are dependent on internal than on external governance to a much larger extent than other stakeholders.

There is another approach to analyze the firm (sometimes seen as the equivalent of the corporation, sometimes not), the nexus-of-contract theory. It didn't take hold in the courts' jurisprudence, and only to a limited extent in the legal literature. It is popular, however, among business and law-and-economics scholars and serves several valuable purposes. As a lawyer, though, I don't like to talk about "nexus of contracts" without a caveat: the concept of what constitutes "contract" is not the same in law and in economics.[20] And even in law, the concept of "contract" varies from country to country according to varying legal traditions.[21] So, this kind of economic analysis transplanted into legal reasoning very quickly hits fatal snags.[22] If you define the corporation according to Jensen and Meckling as a cluster of contracts, "*the private corporation or firm is simply one form of legal fiction which serves as a nexus for contracting relationships and which is also characterized by the existence of divisible residual claims on the assets and cash flows of the organization which can generally be sold*

---

[19] A similar line of argument provides Macey, ibid., at pp. 36-39: shareholders as residual claimants face severe contracting problems with respect to defining the nature and the extent of obligations owed to them by officers and directors of the corporation whereas other constituencies, at least theoretically, have less contracting problems. They are further protected through gap-filling by courts in context with pre-existing contracts. The local communities should resort to the political process.

[20] Melvin A. Eisenberg, "The Conception that the corporation is a Nexus of Contracts, and the Dual Nature of the Firm", 24 *J.Corp.L.* (1999) 819, 822 et seq.

[21] The above-mentioned construction of employment contracts as "employment at will" (i.e. a series of discrete transactions) or long-term, relational and incomplete contracts gives a taste of such differences.

[22] Windbichler, Vor § 15 in: *Großkommentar zum AktG* (Hopt and Wiedemann [eds.]), 4th ed. (Berlin: de Gruyter 1999) note 19; Cheffins, *supra* n. 18, pp. 31 et seq.

without permission of the other contracting individuals".[23] Clark, one of the early critics of this theory, comments: "*This extreme contractualist viewpoint is almost perverse.*"[24] I don't want to discuss this controversy in detail but single out some aspects. I think that an undiscriminating efficiency analysis according to agency-theory – that is what many contractualists do – gives short shrift to the inside-outside perspective germane to legal analysis of legal entities. And, as already mentioned, a lawyer will find it difficult to deal with an highly abstract definition of "contract" that glosses over our (continental) differentiation between contract and organization, if not the concept of the legal person in general.[25] These legal perceptions – or constructions, if you like that better – are more or less well established, according to the legal system at hand,[26] and useful. And they are not foreign to economic thinking. The distinction between contract and organization reflects the distinction between market and hierarchy.[27] Moreover, they offer a better understanding of the mechanisms of regulation, default laws, and actual contracts.

The "nexus-of-contract" approach is intriguing for another reason, though. Given the strong emphasis of American law on the role of directors as trustees for the shareholders, the "nexus-of-contract"-theory allows the extension of fiduciary duties to other constituencies.[28] The effect is an increase of managers' discretion in decision-making. Therefore, the argumentative role of the appeal to the "common weal" or "public spirit" is just the opposite in law as is its role in political theory. There, it usually describes constraints of decision-making power. Another powerful incentive to engage in a nexus-of-contract analysis is the conundrum of the doctrine of employment at will.[29]

---

[23] Michael Jensen and William Meckling, "The Theory of the Firm: Managerial Behavior, Agency Costs and Ownership Structure", 3 *J.Fin.Econ.* (1976) 305, reprinted in: Putterman and Kroszner [eds.], *The Economic Nature of the Firm*, 2nd ed. (Cambridge: Cambridge University Press 1997) p. 315; see also Easterbrook and Fischel, *The Economic Structure of Corporate Law* (Cambridge, Mass.: Harvard University Press 1991) pp. 40 et seq.

[24] Clark, *supra* n. 17, p. 60; see also Melvin A. Eisenberg, *supra* n. 20, 819.

[25] Eisenberg, *supra* n. 20, criticizes that the nexus-of-contract theory fails to explain where the "nexus" begins and where ordinary contractual relationships with the corporations start.

[26] The concept of organizational contracts is known in the common law tradition as well as in the code law traditions; the extent to which it is emphasized and analyzed varies, however. Law and economics scholars seem to have an inclination for exchange-type contracts and only gradually engage in organizational perspectives.

[27] Ronald Coase, "The Nature of the Firm", 4 *Economica* (1937) 386, reprinted in: Putterman and Kroszner [eds.], *The Economic Nature of the Firm*, 2nd ed. (Cambridge: Cambridge University Press 1997) p. 89; Williamson, *The Economic Institutions of Capitalism: Firms, Markets, and Relational Contracting* (New York: The Free Press 1985).

[28] Eisenberg, *supra* n. 20, p. 833.

[29] See, e.g., Stone, *supra* n. 15; Margaret M. Blair and Lynn Stout, "A Team Production Theory of Corporate Law", 85 *Virginia L.Rev.* (1999) 101.

Other theories to the same effect, that is freeing the management from its obligation to further only shareholders' interests, tried to avoid the shortcomings of the nexus-of-contract-theory. I don't want to engage in a detailed discussion of these well-written about endeavors.[30] Some of them I will mention in the context of coping with the separation of ownership and control, and some of them you will recognize in earlier European ideas. Especially intriguing is the similarity between social responsibility and team-production[31] arguments and the German discussion in the 1920s and later in the 1960s and 1970s that included many constituencies but led to the current workers' co-determination model.

4.2 Separation of ownership and control

All the theoretical concepts I mentioned have in common that the interests of the shareholders have to be considered; there is no controversy about that. The controversy begins with the role of other constituencies. To raise the question whether management should consider interests other than the shareholders' is possible only in the light of separation of ownership and control. The fact of this separation is undisputed. Dysfunctional AGMs of large corporations with a population of many small shareholders rendered managements quite independent. This is all too familiar. However, the historical context and the factual developments that brought about the analysis of the separation of ownership and control vary considerably from country to country. I hope that the following comparative aspects will take away a little bit the *déja-vu* sensation.

4.2.1 *The American approach*

I will make this very short. Starting with the predominant role of the board to manage the corporation,[32] a logical reaction to the separation of ownership and control was the imposition of fiduciary duties to the benefit of shareholders. As the law of trust, the ultimate source of fiduciary duties is germane to the Anglo-American legal system, this approach is path-dependent, and so are the attempts to extend fiduciary duties to other constituencies, even if construed in a contractual environment.[33] The ways to increase management's discretion beyond straight profit maximization were shown above in the sample cases. The business purpose was generously construed to include concepts like corporate

---

[30] See e.g. the collection Clarkson [ed.], *supra* n. 6.

[31] Blair/Stout, *supra* n. 29; Sadowski/Junkes/Lindenthal, *supra* n. 16, p. 146.

[32] Lattin, *supra* n. 3, p. 239.

[33] Cf. Eric. L. Talley, "Fiduciary Duties and Industrial Developments", *U.C. Davis L.Rev.* (2001) (forthcoming).

identity, corporate citizenship, and investment in human resources, and everything and everybody is now enchanted by the spell of the "long-term perspective".

The more recent shareholder-value discussion was ignited by spectacular, highly leveraged take-over cases that generated huge profits for some managers, investment bankers, and lawyers to the detriment of the shareholders. I think that the contention that shareholders enriched themselves to the detriment of employees, small suppliers, communities, consumers, etc. cannot be generalized and is untrue in many instances, especially when shareholders were hurt by economically unsound financing. Multi-constituency arguments and even statutes can be traced to defense mechanisms of endangered managers.[34] Whether a take-over is hostile or friendly is an issue of perspective, usually the perspective of the incumbent management and therefore not beyond doubt. "Other constituency statutes" should not be overrated. Many authors do not consider them a genuine shift in the definition of fiduciary duties.[35] Moreover, the states that enacted them do not seem to be the major incorporation venues (Indiana, Iowa, and Pennsylvania as opposed to Delaware).

4.2.2 *The German approach*

I would like to spend a little more time on the German legal development. The emphasis in legal analysis from the 19th century on imparted much more on the phenomenon of the legal entity. Early in the 20th century, the dysfunctionality of the shareholders' meeting was evident. At best, it ratified management's decisions. The reaction was the introduction of a constitution-like system of checks and balances between shareholders' meeting, supervisory board and managing board (in the two-tier system). This organizational solution included further separation of management from the shareholders. The business, firm, or enterprise undertaken by the corporation became a major subject of interest and legal research. At the same time, that is during the 1920s, the term "*Aktienanstalt*" (difficult to translate, probably "business institution") emerged, and Walter Rathenau wrote his essay on the "enterprise in and of itself" ("*Das*

---

[34] Cox/Hazen/O'Neal, *supra* n. 4, pp. 69 et seq.; O'Kelley/Thompson, *supra* n. 4, p. 266; cf. also *Revlon, Inc.* v. *MacAndrews & Forbes Holdings, Inc.*, Del. Supr., 506 A.2d 173 (1986).

[35] O'Kelley/Thompson, *supra* n. 4, p. 267; for a comparative view of the older German discussion of a multi-constituency representing board see Vagts, "Reforming the 'Modern' Corporation: Perspectives from the German", 80 *Harv.L.Rev.* (1966) 23, partly reprinted in Jennings/Buxbaum, *supra* n. 4, p. 164.

Unternehmen an sich").[36] A pluralistic approach came almost naturally with this perception of the phenomenon of the large public corporation, and the idea of shareholder supremacy faded more and more. The then new corporate governance ideas were transformed into law by an amendment to the commercial code that took out the stock corporation law of the code and created a separate statute, the *Aktiengesetz* of 1937, especially its famous § 70 subsec. 1. As the year indicates, this development coincided with National-Socialist ideology covering more and more areas of political, cultural, and economic life. This coincidence, however, led to misunderstandings pertaining to the structure of the German stock corporation law.[37]

The law provided that the managing board shall manage the corporation on its own authority with respect to the best interest of the enterprise and the workforce, and the common weal of the people and the country (. . . *wie das Wohl des Betriebs und seiner Gefolgschaft und der gemeine Nutzen von Volk und Reich es fordern*). The wording was in the style of the times, certainly, but the major substantive statement was the mandatory division of power between management and shareholders' meeting. The shareholders' meeting was not the supreme instance anymore; its remaining powers, however, were mandatory by law and could not be taken away by articles of incorporation, the management, or shareholders' resolutions. The current provision on the managing board, § 76 subsec. 1 *Aktiengesetz* 1965, does not contain the express pluralistic description of goals anymore. It simply states that the managing board shall manage the corporation on its own authority. Jurisprudence and legal scholars concur in general that this includes the power to take multiple constituencies' interests

---

[36] Laux, *Die Lehre vom Unternehmen an sich. Walther Rathenau und die aktienrechtliche Diskussion in der Weimarer Republik*, (Berlin: Duncker & Humblot 1998) pp. 59 et seq., Riechers, *Das >Unternehmen an sich<. Die Entwicklung eines Begriffes in der Aktienrechtsdiskussion des 20. Jahrhunderts* (Tübingen: Mohr Siebeck 1990); Wiedemann, *Gesellschaftsrecht, Band I: Grundlagen*, (München: Beck 1980) pp. 301 et seq. – The notion of the large corporation as an institution of public interest moves corporation law away from private law and closer to public law, an approach now taken by some "progressive" American scholars; see, e.g., Kent Greenfield, "Using Behavioral Economics to Show the Power and Efficiency of Corporate Law as Regulatory Tool", *U.C. Davis L.Rev.* (2001) (forthcoming). Again, the definitions of public law and private law may vary considerably between legal systems. In civil law jurisdictions, public law refers to the involvement of government in relation to the citizen; private law may very well be shaped according to public policy as, for instance, forced by EU Directives on consumer contracts.

[37] For instance, it is said that the new law incorporated the « Führer-principle » by giving the chairman of the managing board a tie-breaking vote. Compared with other stock corporation laws, this rule seems only mildly hierarchical. The position of the president-directeur-général (PDG) in French law has always been much stronger. Until 1965 in Germany and, with slight changes, until now in Austria, the 1937 statute was/is in force and does not present exceptional governance problems.

into account.[38] Further reaching theories claiming an obligation of the management to pursue such pluralistic goals didn't take hold either academically or practically.[39] Especially the problems of who should monitor a management owing multiple-constituency duties and which remedies should be available to whom were never resolved.

Given the German historical context it is not surprising to find workers' representatives on supervisory boards, first without voting rights but with the right to participate and speak according to the *Betriebsrätegesetz* of 1920.[40] This statute about *Betriebsverfassung* (statutory framework for employees' rights in enterprises) was a generalization of rules promulgated to entice special industries into extraordinary war efforts (*Gesetz über den vaterländischen Hilfsdienst* 1916).[41] After the Second World War, the Allied Forces in the western part of occupied Germany fell back on the - rather modern – 1920s model of co-determination. On the board level, the co-determination law for the coal and steel industry set a prominent example for an even farther reaching concept. It provides for an equal number of workers' and shareholders' representatives on the supervisory board plus on neutral person co-opted by both groups. This law was enacted in 1951 and was supposed to assist in the pacification of potentially war relevant industries.[42] However, the procedural involvement of workers representatives on the supervisory board doesn't change the substantive powers and responsibilities of management.[43] Nowadays, it's mainly of symbolic value.[44] But note the historical irony in

---

[38] Hueck, *Gesellschaftsrecht*, 19th ed. (München: Beck 1991) § 23, VII; Hüffer, *Aktiengesetz*, 4th ed. (München: Beck 1999) § 76 note 12.

[39] A prominent advocate of the mandatory pluralist approach – based on Art. 14 of the German constitution – is Schmidt-Leithoff, *Die Verantwortung der Unternehmensleitung* (Tübingen: Mohr Siebeck 1989) pp. 155 et seq., pp. 214 et seq; for a discussion why marginal or symbolic rights are not meaningless cf. Sadowski/Junkes/Lindenthal, *supra* n. 16.

[40] As the term Betriebs*verfassung* (constitution) suggests, this body of law was considered at the outset as public law. The discussion about its legal character has been settled much later (1970s); now, *Betriebsverfassung* is firmly grounded in private law. Cf. Reichold, *Betriebsverfassung als Sozialprivatrecht. Historisch-dogmatische Grundlagen von 1848 bis zur Gegenwart* (München: Beck 1995).

[41] Reichold, *supra* n. 40, pp. 185 et seq.

[42] Mertens, in: Zöllner [ed.], *Kölner Kommentar zum Aktiengesetz*, Vol. 2, 2nd. ed. (Köln: Heymanns 1996) Anh. § 117 C MontanMitbestG note 2.

[43] Hueck, *supra* n. 38, § 24, II, 1 c); Hüffer, *supra* n. 38, § 116 notes 2, 7; Kraft/Kreutz, *Gesellschaftsrecht*, 11th ed. (Neuwied: Luchterhand 2000). Practically, however, the institutional setting ensures the inclusion of employees' interests in the decision-making process.

[44] Christine Windbichler and Gregor Bachmann, "Corporate Governance und Mitbestimmung als 'wirtschaftsrechtlicher ordre public'", in: *Festschrift für Gerold Bezzenberger*, (Westermann/Mock [eds.]) (Berlin: de Gruyter 2000), p. 797. For an overview over theoretical frameworks regarding human resources management see Schuler/Turnheim/Jackson, *supra* n. 16, p. 181 at pp. 199–205. Empirical research stayed rather inconclusive, cf. Gerum, *Mitbestimmung und Corporate Governance* (Gütersloh: Bertelsmann Stiftung 1998) with further references.

the fact that a governance model established to further a war effort was later used to democratize heavy industry in the name of peace-keeping. Be that as it may, the historical development, together with a different understanding of the employment contract, account for path-dependency in the specific field of labor relations.

There's another interesting structural detail. According to the co-determination law for the coal and steel industry, the workers' representatives are elected by the shareholders' meeting upon binding proposals by the works councils. This shows how deeply entrenched in corporate law models the way of thinking was in 1950. Who else but the shareholders' meeting could possibly elect board members, even if it is bound by another body's decision. The fact that later co-determination laws, starting with the *Betriebsverfassungsgesetz* 1952, provide for either direct elections or, according to the size of the corporation, elections by electors indicates a significant change from pure corporation law to enterprise or enterprise-constitution law. This German background to the pluralistic approach, together with the financing traditions – bank loans, banks as stockholders, retained profits and lean dividends –, led to sleepy stock markets and a low percentage of the general population that owned stock. Shareholders were almost forgotten. If they were thought of at all, they were considered stupid and impertinent. Stupid because they gave money to a corporation, and impertinent because they expected dividends.

The scenario changed dramatically with the opening-up of capital markets, first within the EU, then worldwide. Financial globalization brought the shareholders back into focus. Starting roughly with the 1990s, the term "shareholder value" attracted more and more attention. The international corporate governance debate as well as the American discussion and European developments focus on shareholder value vs. other constituencies or stakeholder value. The incentives to do so, however, differ considerably. In Germany, the shareholder virtually had to be reinvented.[45] Especially business administration scholars' endeavors in this direction lead to overreactions and the promotion of rigid profit-maximizing standards.[46]

---

[45] This is the course of the German Governments commission on Corporate Governance; a summary of its report is available on <http://www.bundesregierung.de/dokumente/Artikel/ix_48101_1400.htm> [last visited 31 August 2001].

[46] See e.g. Theodor Siegel, Peter Bareis and Dieter Rückle, "Stille Reserven und aktienrechtliche Informationspflichten", *ZIP* (1999) 2077.

5. Conclusion

To draw a conclusion: In a worldwide comparison including the OECD Principles of Corporate governance[47], or the DVFA Corporate Governance Scorecard©,[48] or the German Panel on Corporate Governance's suggested best practices[49], we find the common trait of "enlightened shareholder value", or, "TQM" (total quality management). The term "enlightened shareholder value" is used, for instance, by The Company Steering Group of the British Department of Trade.[50] Eisenberg speaks of "enlightened corporate self-interest".[51] The construction of the current sections of the German corporation law (§§ 76, 93 *Aktiengesetz*) pertaining to the powers and duties of the managing board is very similar to the American fiduciary duties of directors in the light of other constituency statutes and the more generous jurisprudence. An obligation to act with "social responsibility" beyond compliance with the law, however, is harder to find, especially when it comes to full-fledged control mechanisms and actionable positions.[52]

An exclusive philosophy that the board of directors' one and only duty is to maximize profits is common only among those authors who write against this position. At least in law, no one really argues strongly for such an attitude. This may be different in finance and business administration.[53] When it comes to other constituencies' interests, first and foremost the Principles, Guidelines,

---

[47] *Supra* n. 13, Section III. The role of stakeholders in corporate governance: The corporate governance framework should recognise the rights of stakeholders as established by law and encourage active co-operation between corporations and stakeholders in creating wealth, jobs, and the sustainability of financially sound enterprises.

[48] *Supra* n. 13.

[49] *Supra* n. 13.

[50] "Modern Company Law for a Competitive Economy" <http://www.dti.gov.uk/cld/final report> [last visited 31 August 2001].

[51] Eisenberg, *supra* n. 16, especially pp. 5 et seq. for the "ethical-conduct principle".

[52] A major argument against the empowerment of management to include non-shareholder interests in the business perspective is that, by this empowerment, management is protected against control. There will always be a respectable interest management can claim to have protected when a decision is challenged by shareholders. Vice versa, if substantive claims could be made as to other constituencies' interests, they would be hopelessly tangled with conflicting but equally valuable interests. Remedies are sought in disclosure and more subtle reputational sanctions; see, e.g., Cynthia Williams, "Corporate Social Responsibility in an Era of Economic Globalization", *U.C. Davis L.Rev.* (2001) (forthcoming).

[53] Cf. *supra* n. 46; there are voices, however, that advocate management induced forms of workers' participation, e.g. Sadowski/Junkes/Lindenthal, *supra* n. 16; Schuler/Turnheim/Jackson, *supra* n. 16, at p. 207 (there is no "one-best-way approach"); see also Biagi, "Forms of Employee Representational Participation", in: (Blanpain/Engels [eds.]), *Comparative Labour Law and Industrial Relations in Industrial Market Economies*, *supra* n. 16, 341, at pp. 379-381.

and Best Practices, and whatever soft law may be around, call for compliance with the existing laws, i.e. compliance with what I called external governance. An argument in favor of regulation needs to pay specific attention to the legal positioning of such regulation; an imposition of fiduciary duties, e.g. owed to consumers, would be regulation of the internal decision making process, whereas laws calling for information of consumers, warranties, or liability would be external governance. Moreover, a civic spirit that manifests itself in donations and contributions and the general policy of the corporation is well received everywhere and by no means illegal from a corporate law perspective. Tax law bears witness to that. Taxation belongs to what I called external governance but gives incentives for the internal decision-making process. Benefits for the workforce are not given as charity but as an investment in human capital.

This substantive notion does not include the path-dependent procedures via co-determination, extension of management discretion or fiduciary duties. Executives of union-managed pension-funds have to deliver conflict of interest-prone duties: investing money profitably for their clients and, at the same time, staying loyal to union goals. They resort to the magic formula of "long-term goals", the point in the infinite distance where parallels intersect. In this last area – relations to the workforce – however, my convergence-model does not apply to the same extent. Here, we find a distinct "path-dependency", that is approaches and attitudes follow different paths according to legal culture and historical development. When looking at other jurisdictions' conflict resolution tools, path-dependent and functional analysis is required. An analysis of German co-determination will show that its function on the enterprise level is, to a large extent, external governance.[54] Both, establishedment-level and board-level co-determination, shall ensure compliance with protective regulation.[55]

Certainly, there will always be cases and applications that rise controversy about whether and to what extent management can invoke non-shareholders' interests. One example from the European legal development is the never ending discussion of the management's rights, privileges, and duties when facing a so-called hostile takeover. How "neutral" are managers supposed to

---

[54] The works council (*Betriebsrat*) enters into collective agreements with the employer, i.e. the corporation represented by management. This collective contract can, therefore, not be a constituting element of the corporation that is a party to the contract. If not the corporation but the "firm" is considered as the phenomenon constituted by a nexus of contracts, we leave legal analysis and find ourselves in the realm of economics or sociology where the term "contract" obviously does not have the same meaning as in law. Cf. Eisenberg, *supra* n. 20. Internal governance is called upon when management is obliged by law to inform the *Betriebsrat* and discuss decisions in advance. For this kind of co-determination, procedural in its nature, only procedural remedies are available whereas in the field of substantive mandatory co-determination (§ 87 *Betriebsverfassungsgesetz*) a tie-breaking arbitration process is provided (*Einigungsstelle*).

[55] See especially § 80 I 1 *Betriebsverfassungsgesetz*.

be? The history of the 13th EU Directive on take-over bids is full of this controversy.

I don't want to take up this very specific topic but come back to some of my sample cases. First, the German example of the Foundation "Remembrance, Responsibility and the Future". Can a legal person have moral sentiments and take ethical responsibility? What about those businesses that were founded only after World War II? Or merged with foreign corporations (DaimlerChrysler, Aventis [Hoechst/RhônePoulenc]? It should be noted that the Foundation is funded by the whole of the German business sector, not only corporations subject to potential claims. Giving money to this special initiative constitutes an act to improve the business climate, an act of corporate citizenship, of public spirit. This is acceptable as long as the overriding goal to make profits is not given up, the contributions keep within reasonable proportion to the businesses size and earnings, and the corporation is not morphed into a non-profit organization.[56] I happen to infer from a personal conversation that DaimlerChrysler pays its share out of the marketing budget.

Last but not least *Dodge* v. *Ford*. Henry Ford's attitude is sometimes interpreted as ahead of its time. profit sharing may nowadays be a sound business strategy to increase the good will of the company and benefit long-term perspectives.[57] However, I find another bit of information quite interesting. The judge in Dodge warned in strong words that the corporation is to be run in the best interest of its shareholders, and that there is no room for personal generosity. Judicial review of management decisions should not interfere with a certain leeway business judgment needs, though. "*The judges are not business experts. It is recognized that plans must often be made for a long future, for expected competition, for a continuing as well as an immediately profitable venture. The experience of the Ford Motor Company is evidence of capable management of its affairs.*" The mentioning of future competition was especially delicate in the case at hand. The brothers Dodge were planning, as they later did, to set up their own business of manufacturing cars. The profits from their investment in Ford was contributing to their capital. Decreasing dividends meant lack of funds for the new enterprise. Lower car prices would have made the market entry more difficult; they would have had to meet the lowered Ford prices. Why did Henry Ford take refuge to the eleemosynary disguise? Saying openly that his business purpose was to fend off future competition from the Dodge brothers would have been a clear-cut violation of Sec. 1 Sherman Act. This probably explains why the attempted "public spirit" was not discussed as

---

56 Mertens, *supra* n. 10, p. 158.

57 Lattin, *supra* n. 3, pp. 211 et seq.

to its merits for the reputation of the corporation, furtherance of long-term goals, legitimacy of large and profitable corporations etc.

Again, the comparative, intra-, and interdisciplinary approach that I always associate with JOCHEN MESTMÄCKER's work brings about the larger picture. This permits me a more personal observation. One of my capital expenditures as a student was the acquisition of MESTMÄCKER's "*Europäisches Wettbewerbs-recht*"; it still produces dividends.

The public corporation is without any doubt entitled to ventilate a public spirit. Shareholders cannot object to that. The limits for expenditures made for such civility vary from case to case and jurisdiction to jurisdiction but are not at variance in principle. This convergence in dogmatic structure ends where significant path-dependency is encountered; the practical outcomes, however, may still be in confluence. But when explaining and justifying outcomes we always need to pay proper attention to the dynamic interchanges of internal and external governance. And there should be no confusion of contract with "contract". Here, I would like to borrow from a famous line by Gertrude Stein: A contract is not a contract is not a contract. So we can sit back leisurely and listen to Dr. Faust's Stradivari, or is it Deutsche Bank in a cello-case for sheep's clothing?[58]

---

[58] Eisenberg, *supra* n. 16, p. 14.

to its merits for the reputation of the corporation; furtherance of long-term goals; legitimacy of large and profitable corporations, &c.

[illegible]

Annex

Principles for European Integration – Roads to a European Civil Society

Foreword

The following papers were presented at the academic symposium "Principles for European Integration – Roads to a European Civil Society", held on October 6, 2001, at the Max-Planck-Institute for Foreign Private and Private International Law, Hamburg, to celebrate the 75th birthday of its emeritus director *Ernst-Joachim Mestmäcker.*

The symposium takes up a theme that is central to *Ernst-Joachim Mestmäcker*'s work. Academically and *in praxi* he has shaped and accompanied the process of European integration from the very beginning, reflecting upon the legal order for a civil society in which people can live together peacefully and freely.

Building on the Kantian idea of strong individual rights, he underscored and developed their importance for the process of European integration, thereby redefining the limits of state power as well as framing the outer boundaries of individual freedom, especially in the field of competition law. Drawing on philosophy as well as on economic theory to identify the principles behind legal problems, *Ernst-Joachim Mestmäcker* has crossed the established boundaries between academic disciplines and has thus set new standards in dealing with European law.

The contributions to the symposium reflect the theme of European integration in different aspects and demonstrate how topical his work is – they all join *Ernst-Joachim Mestmäcker* in the quest for foundations and rules for a further evolvement of a European civil society's order.

By initiating this symposium, we – *Ernst-Joachim Mestmäcker*'s current research assistants – wished to create a forum to honour his groundbreaking academic work. Having had the privilege of working with him, we also wanted to honour a person who continues to impress us with the density and depth of his thoughts and with the integrity in living his liberal convictions.

Hamburg, April 2002

Dr. Heike Schweitzer *Dr. Jan Christoffer Tolkmitt*

Talia Einhorn, ed., Spontaneous Order, Organization and the Law –
Liber Amicorum Ernst-Joachim Mestmäcker © *2003* T.M.C.ASSER PRESS, *The Hague, The Netherlands*

European Political Integration, Comparative Law and Private Enforcement of Competition Law

Walter van Gerven*

In an article published in 1971,[1] I attempted to demonstrate – drawing doctrinal support from an article by Professor Biedenkopf in the *Festschrift für Franz Böhm* (1965)[2] – that more complete understanding of private law would have allowed judges to better incorporate into their legal reasoning the values inherent in *equality* between economic operators and *solidarity* with weaker market participants. This, in turn, would have enabled them to attain in their case law a better balance between those values and *freedom*, which was too narrowly understood as an exclusive right of the stronger economic operators. I know that, with this theme, I am trespassing on the intellectual premises of *Professor Mestmäcker* who in his early work defended this proposition and reiterated it as recently as 1991 in an article concerning the transition of the East-European countries to a market economy where he stated

> "In diesen höchst ernüchternden Erfahrungen sieht man vielfach den Beleg dafür, daß man die Möglichkeiten der Marktwirtschaft überschätzt habe . . . Näheres Zusehen zeigt jedoch, daß wir es eher mit einer Unterschätzung der Marktwirtschaft zu tun haben . . . Es geht ebenso um die Institutionen, die sich in der Gesellschaft auf

* Professor of Law, Leuven University, former Advocate General at the European Court of Justice.

[1] W. van Gerven, "Schets van een Belgisch Economisch Grondslagenrecht", *SEW, Tijdschrift voor Europees en Economisch Recht* (1971) 404, at p. 412.

[2] With a reference also to an article by Meyer-Cording in *Festschrift für H. C. Nipperdey* (München 1965).

Talia Einhorn, ed., Spontaneous Order, Organization and the Law – Liber Amicorum Ernst-Joachim Mestmäcker © 2003 T.M.C.ASSER PRESS, The Hague, The Netherlands

der Grundlage des bürgerlichen Rechts im Zusammenhang mit einer rechtsstaatslichen Verwaltung herausgebildet haben".[3]

In other words, private law institutions and the basic values inherent therein must be seen in context with, and as part and parcel of, the foundations of basic "rechtsstaatsliches Denken und Handeln".[4] That applies also to the EU Member States' behaviour at the supranational level.

In what follows, I would like to address the three themes referred to in the title of this celebration speech in honour of *Professor Mestmäcker*, who in his writings has dealt with those themes in a much more thorough way than I would be able to do myself.

1. European political and legal integration: from "Wirtschafts-verfassungsrecht" towards "Verfassungsrecht tout court"

In the beginning of the era of European economic integration the constitutional debate turned on the issue of "Plan- v. Marktwirtschaft" (planned economy vs. market economy) and, accordingly, on the two basic approaches to economic integration. The first approach involved integration by intervention, i.e., from above – an approach represented in the Rome Treaty (as the EEC Treaty was then called) by the "common policies" (mainly the Common Agricultural Policy).[5] The second, opposing approach involved integration by competition, i.e., from below. According to the latter, the market system is a self-organizing

---

[3] "These most disillusioning experiences provide ample proof that the opportunities offered by the market economy have been overestimated . . . On closer look, however, it becomes clear that we are dealing here not with overestimation but rather with underestimation . . . This is also the case regarding the institutions that have developed in society on the basis of civil law and an administration operating under the rule of law" – E.J. Mestmäcker, "Die Wiederkehr der bürgerlichen Gesellschaft und ihres Rechts", *Rechtshistorisches Journal* (1991) 171, also published in E.J. Mestmäcker, *Recht in der offenen Gesellschaft. Hamburger Beiträge zum deutschen, europäischen und internationalen Wirtschafts- und Medienrecht* (Nomos 1993) 60, at p. 66.

[4] "Constitutional thinking and acting", as stated by Judge, now again Professor Kapteyn, in a speech at the University of Amsterdam on 19 September 2001.

[5] In a doctoral thesis submitted at the University of Leuven (unpublished), G. Wils has documented the passive attitude of the ECJ; the Court, by adopting a much too deferential attitude has not been conducive enough in defending the free market concept against overprotective regulations. See further my address, "Toward a coherent constitutional system within the European Union", held on the occasion of a symposium in honour of U. Everling at Bonn University in 1995, later published in: *Die Verfassung der Europäischen Union* (Bonner Europa Symposium, Zentrum für Europäisches Wirtschaftrecht 1995) 9-62, at p. 47.

system which competition law must protect against anti-competitive behaviour.[6] It would be presumptuous to underline the constitutional importance of competition law in the presence of *Professor Mestmäcker* who, in the same article referred to above, pointed out with a reference to Walter Eucken's theory of "Interpendenz von Ordnungen" that

> "das Privateigentum an Produktionsmittlen zu den Voraussetzungen der Machtbalance zwischen Staat und Gesellschaft gehört. Die Bindung der Unternehmen an das öffentliche Interesse ist die Aufgabe des Wettbewerbs auf den Märkten und ergänzend die der Gesetzgebung, die den Wettbewerb vor Beschränkungen durch die Unternehmen schützen soll."[7]

Allow me, nevertheless, to briefly recall the history of European political integration. At the level of, first, the sectoral European *Coal and Steel* Community and, shortly thereafter, the broader European *Economic* Community, the mix of *Markt- und Planwirtschaft* led to a "functional" political integration driven in the 1950s by

> "a belief that European integration would best be furthered by focusing on discrete economic sectors which could be managed efficiently and technocratically by supranational institutions, away from the fray of politics",

and evolving in the 1960s into a view of integration seen as

> "a process based on spill-over from one initially non-controversial, technical sector to other sectors of possibly greater political salience, involving a gradual reduction in the power of national government and a commensurate increase in the ability of the Community to deal with sensitive, politically charged issues".[8]

---

[6] See further M.E. Streit and W. Mussler, "The Economic Constitution of the European Community – 'From Rome to Maastricht'", in: *Constitutional Dimensions of European Economic Integration* (F. Snyder [ed.]) (Kluwer Law International 1996) 109, at pp. 118-119.

[7] " . . . that private ownership of the means of production is one of the prerequisites of [a healthy] balance of powers between state and society. The task of compelling enterprises to act in the public interest is assigned to market competition and, by extension, to the legislature, who should protect competition from restraints created by the enterprises", Mestmäcker, *supra* n. 3, at p. 71.

[8] The first quotation is taken from P. Craig and G. De Búrca, *EU Law*, 2nd ed. (Oxford University Press 1998) p. 5; the second is taken from an excerpt reproduced ibid., p. 5, of J. Lodge, *The European Community and the Challenge of the Future* (Pinter 1993), "Introduction", xix.

As pointed out by P. Craig and De Búrca,[9] from whose book the foregoing quotations are drawn, this functional approach was in turn challenged in the 1970s by intergovernmentalism. During this phase, the supranational EC institutions appeared to lose initiative and influence to the individual Member States (cf., the so-called Luxembourg veto). Consequently, the Member States were regarded, more than the EC institutions, as the key actors in the integration process. The renewed dynamism in the 1980s and the deepening of the integration process with the signature on 17 February 1986 of the Single European Act, followed by the Intergovernmental Conferences of the early 1990s that led to the Maastricht Treaty, generated "counterclaims of a *neo-federalist* revival".[10] This dialectical evolution led more recently to the debate concerning the supranational/intergovernmental dichotomy underpinning the integration debate, resulting in emphasis being placed on a system of multi-level governance (combining the supranational approach of the first pillar with the intergovernmental approach of the second and the third pillars of the European Union). This multi-level governance paradigm focuses on the role played by a wide range of actors and institutions, national and supranational, public and private, in the law and policy-making within the Union.[11]

Needless to say, this political evolution went hand in hand with, and was made possible by, the increased economic integration. From the very outset, the Community abandoned the concepts of a free trade area and a customs union in favour of a common market, which allows not only the free movement of goods but also of factors of production (labour, capital and enterprises) and evolving gradually into a truly monetary and economic union.[12] It is not my intention to examine here whether, and how, this growing economic integration went hand in hand with, and was shaped by, the above-mentioned stages of political integration, and *vice versa*. Obviously, there must have been some relationship between the petroleum crises in the 1970s, and the upsurge of the nation-state paradigm, just as the economic growth in the 1990s, and the opportunities it offered, was clearly responsible, together with the unification of Germany, for the deepening and the enlargement of the European Union.[13]

---

[9] Ibid., at pp. 5-6.

[10] Ibid., at p. 6.

[11] Ibid. On the European multi-governance system see, in particular, C. Joerges, "Interactive Adjudication in the Europeanisation Process? A demanding perspective and a modest example", *European Review of Private Law* (2000) 1-16, and previous publications by Joerges referred to ibid., note 2.

[12] P.J.G. Kapteyn and P. VerLoren van Themaat, *Introduction to the Law of the European Communities*, 3rd ed. (edited by L.W. Gormley) (Kluwer 1998) at p. 780.

[13] For a chronological overview of political integration as brought about by European summit meetings from the 1960s until the end of the 1990s, see H. Reichenbach *et al.*, *Integration: Wanderung über europäische Gipfel* (Baden-Baden: Nomos 1999).

Equally fascinating, however, and more related to my own field of interest, is the interaction between political and legal integration. Certainly in the early years of the Community, political integration was strengthened by the creative attitude adopted by the ECJ towards political (more than economic[14]) integration in its case law, a fact that has occasionally subjected the Court to severe criticism of its judicial activism. I do not share this criticism, insofar as the creative role displayed by the ECJ in its case law (starting with the early judgments in *Costa/Enel* and *Van Gend en Loos*) relates primarily, if not exclusively, to the development of judicial remedies intended to ensure the protection by national courts of subjective rights that individuals derive from Community law (so-called Community rights).[15] By developing the doctrine of direct effect, the ECJ made it possible for individuals to have their Community rights enforced by national courts against Member States, and, in some instances, also against other individuals (as in the case of Article 141 [ex 119] EC on equal pay for male and female workers[16]). This doctrine may actually be regarded as a starting point for the constitutionalisation of the Community Treaties; provisions of an international agreement, i.e., a contract between states, are interpreted – provided that they are sufficiently precise and unconditional – as having general binding force not only between the Contracting States, but also in favour of and, eventually, against third parties.[17] It has also dramatically improved the direct access of individuals to the Member States' courts and their indirect access, through the preliminary ruling procedure, to the ECJ, unlike their limited access to judicial relief from the Community court(s) under Articles 230 and 232 [ex 173 and 175, respectively] EC.

A further step towards constitutionalisation was taken when the ECJ, with the "encouragement" of national constitutional courts and, in particular the *Bundesverfassungsgericht*, was induced to upgrade the judicial protection of citizens even further by accepting that not only the economic freedoms provided for in the Treaty but also classic human rights and fundamental

---

[14] G. Wils, *supra* n. 5, described in detail the ECJ's reluctance to interfere with policy decisions of the Council or Commission.

[15] In other matters, where regulations or directives must be interpreted, the ECJ takes a much more cautious attitude resorting to orthodox methods of interpretation. See W. van Gerven, "Community and national legislators, regulators, judges, academics and practitioners: living together apart?" in: *Law Making, Law Finding, and Law Shaping* (B.S. Markesinis [ed.]) (Oxford University Press 1997) 13, at pp. 28-32. For a recent example of such a cautious approach, see the *Dietzinger* case, Case 45/96, [1998] *ECR* I-1199, and comments on this case by C. Joerges, *supra* n. 11.

[16] Case 43/75 *Defrenne II*, [1976] *ECR* 455.

[17] See W. van Gerven, "The horizontal Effect of Directive Provisions revisited: the Reality of Catchwords" in: *Institutional Dynamics of European Integration, Essays in honour of Henry G. Schermers* (D.Curtin & T.Heukels [eds.]) (Nijhoff 1994) 335, at pp. 337-339.

freedoms form an integral part of the general principles of Community law.[18] It follows that "measures are not acceptable in the Community which are incompatible with observance of the human rights thus recognized and guaranteed. . . ".[19] Of course, the direct access of individuals to the Community courts remains limited because of the restrictive interpretation which those courts attach to the terms "of direct and individual concern" in Article 231 [ex 174] EC. However, this lack of judicial protection before the Community courts is to some extent corrected by the ability of the Member States' courts to grant relief in national proceedings, eventually after having addressed a preliminary question to the ECJ (as was illustrated by the proceedings before the German administrative courts in the so-called "banana saga").[20]

The emphasis which the ECJ put on protection of Community rights, both in its case law on direct effect (not only of Treaty provisions but, later on, also of secondary legislation, including directives, at least as against public authorities) and in its case law on the protection of human rights and fundamental freedoms, has resulted in a growing awareness of "subjective rights" and in a transformation, as Norbert Reich puts it, of the group of persons protected by the present European Union from "market to Union citizens". Indeed, due to the increased attention of EC law, following the Single European Act and the Treaties of Maastricht and Amsterdam, to the social aspects of Community policies, and to education, science and culture, as well as the special status granted to the protection of consumers and the environment, ever larger groups of individuals who were initially seen as market participants came to be regarded as citizens of the Union. This was mainly due to secondary law, primarily directives, which made larger numbers of private persons beneficiaries of Community rights within ever more diverse areas of Community law.[21]

It is difficult to deny that the growing legal integration which has permitted the ECJ to refer to the (then) EEC Treaty as the "constitutional charter" of the Community,[22] has stimulated and underpinned political integration to the point that, by the Treaty of Maastricht, a Part Two on "Citizenship of the Union" was added to the EC Treaty, which states in Article 8 [now 17] that "every person

---

[18] For the first time in Case 29/69 *Stauder* [1969] *ECR* 419, at p. 425 and solemnly confirmed in Case 11/70 *Internationale Handelsgesellschaft*, [1970] *ECR* 1125, at p. 1134.

[19] Case C-299/95 *Kremzow*, [1997] *ECR* I-2629, at p. I-2645.

[20] For an extensive discussion on the role of the ECJ regarding the protection of human rights, see B. De Witte, "The Past and Future Role of the European Court of Justice in the Protection of Human Rights", in: *The EU and Human Rights* (P. Alston [ed.]) (Oxford University Press 1999) 859, at p. 876 (the "banana saga").

[21] See N. Reich, *Bürgerrechte in der Europäischen Union* (Baden-Baden: Nomos 1999) at pp. 45 and 49.

[22] Case 294/83 *Les Verts* [1986] *ECR* 1339, at 1365.

holding the nationality of a Member State shall be a citizen of the Union" (para. 1) and "shall enjoy the rights conferred by this Treaty and shall be subject to the rights imposed thereby" (para. 2). In Articles 18-21 [ex 8a-d] the general right to move and reside freely is guaranteed to every citizen and a number of specific political rights are granted: the right to vote and stand as a candidate at municipal elections, the right to diplomatic protection and the right to petition the European Parliament.[23] Moreover, Article 13 [ex 6a] provides the legal basis for the Community institutions to take appropriate action to combat discrimination "based on sex, racial or ethnic origin, religion or belief, disability, age or sexual orientation". Regarding the protection of human rights, Article 6 [ex F] TEU has confirmed the ECJ's case law by declaring the respect for human rights and fundamental freedoms, along with liberty, democracy and the rule of law, to be principles on which the Union is founded. The culminating point in that area was the proclamation in Nice on 7 December 2000 of the Charter of Fundamental Rights of the European Union which contains a (non-binding) list of rights, ordered under six headings: dignity, freedoms, equality, solidarity, citizens' rights, and justice, which go far beyond the fundamental rights recognized so far by the ECJ.[24]

The emphasis in legal and political integration has thus gradually shifted from "Wirtschaftsverfassungsrecht" to "Verfassungsrecht *tout court*", an evolution which became even more conspicuous in the proclamation of Laken of 15 December 2001 on the future of the European Union, which outlined the path towards a European Constitution and proposed a Convention to prepare the debate on the future of the Union. All this should not prevent us from having an equally important and, in the immediate future, more practical debate on the reform of the European institutions, the transparency of their functioning and the simplification and efficiency of the decision making process.[25] This debate, which should be brought to conclusion before the accession of new Member

---

[23] For a reference in the Court's case law to the provisions on Citizen rights, see Case C-85/96 *Martinez Sala* [1998] *ECR* I-2691, I-2725-2726; and the comment of S. O'Leary, "Putting flesh on the bones of European Union citizenship", *European Law Review* (1999) 68-79.

[24] For an overview, see K. Lenaerts and E. De Smijter, "A 'Bill of Rights' for the European Union", *Common Market Law Review* (2001) 273-300. See also F. Jacobs, "Human Rights in the European Union: the Role of the Court of Justice", *European Law Review* (2001) 331-341. For the first reference in a judicial document to one of the new rights in the Charter, namely, Art. 31 (2) on the workers' right to limitation of working hours, see the Opinion of Advocate General Tizzano in case C-173/99, *Broadcasting, Entertainment, Cinematographic and Theatre Union (BECTU)* [2001] *ECR* I-4881.

[25] On this subject, see *inter alia* D. Curtin, "Citizens' fundamental Right of Access to EU Information: an evolving digital *Passepartout*?" *Common Market Law Review* (2000) 7-41, analysing the case law of the Community courts and commenting on Art. 255 [ex 191a], para. 2 EC, as inserted by the Treaty of Amsterdam on the right of access to documents.

States, received a strong impetus from the resignation of the Santer Commission, [26] and the resulting outcry for good governance, and led to the publication of the Commission's White Paper on European Governance.[27] The democratic deficit of the Union, and, even more importantly, the absence of a European public opinion focusing on pan-European issues, as reflected in truly European political parties and press-media, render it necessary to have codes of conduct prescribing good governance behaviour, to organize (individual and collective) political responsibility and accountability of all those in power, whether in the European Commission, the Council or the European Parliament. Such codes on standards in public life may help to alleviate the lack of democratic legitimacy at the European level and to compensate for the arrogance of power of bureaucratic institutions.

2. Comparative law and codification of private law

In *Bulmer* v. *Bollinger*,[28] Lord Denning made his famous statement that Community law is "like an incoming tide. It flows into the estuaries and up to the rivers" (referring, in the first place, to the river Thames). Later, in an extra-judicial statement, he added that "European law is like a tidal wave bringing down our sea walls and flowing inland over our fields and houses – to the dismay of all".[29] Though exaggerated, Lord Denning's statements are not incorrect. In substance he refers, implicitly, to the phenomenon that

[26] The Committee of Independent Experts has issued two reports: *Allegations regarding Fraud, Mismanagement and Nepotism in the European Commission* (15 March 1999) and *Reform of the Commission* (10 September 1999). Chapter 7 of the second report, "Integrity, Responsibility and Accountability in European and Administrative Life", was particularly critical. Regarding these reports, see "The [First] Report of the Committee of Independent Experts: An Ill Wind", Editorial Comment, *Common Market Law Review* (1999) 269-272, and W. van Gerven, "Ethical and Political Responsibility", Guest Editorial, *Common Market Law Review* (2000) 1-6; see also W. van Gerven (who was a member of the Committee), "Managing the European Union: For Better or for Worse", in: *The Clifford Chance Millenium Lectures. The Coming Together of the Common Law and the Civil Law* (B.S. Markesinis [ed.]) (Oxford: Hart 2000) 91-104.

[27] *COM* (2001) 428 (final). For a short comment, see A. Arnull, "Editorial", *European Law Review* (2001) 411-412. For a broader perspective, see also D. Curtin, "The European Commission in Search of Accountability: From Chamber of Secrets to Good Governance", in: *Principles of Proper Conduct for Supranational, State and Private Actors in the European Union: Towards a ius Commune. Essays in honour of Walter van Gerven* (J. Wouters and J. Stuyck [eds.]) (Intersentia 2001) 5-19.

[28] [1974] *Ch.* 401.

[29] Quoted by D. Anderson, "Shifting the Grundnorm (and other tales)" in: *Liber Amicorum in honour of Lord Slynn of Hadley*, Vol. I: Judicial Review in the European Community (D. O'Keeffe [ed.]) (Kluwer Law International 2000) at p. 344.

Community law, whether through legislative acts or judicial interpretation of Treaty provisions, not only harmonises the national laws of the Member States in a specific area (the "cohesive" and bright side of harmonisation) but also "de-harmonises" the national law in each of the Member States (the disruptive and dark side of harmonisation).[30] The reason for this dual effect is the principle of "attribution of specific competences", laid down in Article 5, para. 1, and Article 7 (1), para. 2, EC, according to which the Community legislature and the Community courts have jurisdiction *only* in those limited areas of the law, mainly relating to "transborder" issues, which have been conferred upon them by the Treaty. Even then, where those competences are not exclusive, they are subject to the principle of subsidiarity laid down in Article 5, para. 2, EC. Consequently, Community legislative acts and Community case law frequently "cut through" pre-existing national law by affecting the latter only to the extent that it relates to matters for which jurisdiction has been transferred to the Community and leaving it intact for all other matters.[31] The most adequate method to maintain homogeneity in such a situation would be for the national legislatures and courts to make the national rules dealing with "purely national" matters conform as much as possible with the Community, or national, rules dealing with "Community" matters. However, any decision to do so must be taken, eventually, by the institutions of the Member States, which are *not* bound to do so by virtue of any Community law obligation (not even the duty of cooperation under Article 10 EC).[32]

The reason for raising this matter under the heading of comparative law is because both the cohesive and the disruptive effect of European Community harmonisation (or any other supra- or international harmonisation) demonstrate that comparative law has now become of *strategic* importance for both the enhancing of harmonisation measures and the limiting of resulting disparities. Previously, before harmonisation was imposed, comparative law was of a *persuasive* nature mainly, if not only (i.e. persuading legislators, courts, academics etc. that a foreign law solution may be better than the one offered by their own law).[33] In the words of Zweigert/Kötz: "Damit stellen sich auch der

---

[30] See further W. van Gerven, "A common law for Europe: the future meeting the past?", *European Review of Private Law* (2001) 3, at pp. 4-6, and, more recently, "Codifying European private law? Yes, if. . .! ", *European Law Review* (2002) 156-176.

[31] See further, the examples in the first article by van Gerven, *supra* n. 30, at pp. 6-8.

[32] Some national legislatures (in Belgium, the Netherlands and the United Kingdom) have taken the initiative of enacting national anti-trust rules for purely national situations which conform with the Community competition law rules and have requested their courts to interpret the former in accordance with the interpretation attached by the Community courts to the latter.

[33] See W. van Gerven, "Comparative Law in a Texture of Communitarization of National Laws and Europeanization of Community Law", in: *Liber Amicorum in honour of Lord Slynn of Hadley*, *supra* n. 29, 433, at pp. 435-440.

Rechtsvergleichung neue Aufgaben. Sie sollte nicht nur in der Absicht betrieben werden, Vorschläge zur Fortbildung eines bestimmten nationalen Rechts zu entwicklen . . . Es sollte ihr auch darum gehen, über die nationalen Rechtsordnungen hinauszugelangen, auf vergleichender Grundlage ein eigenes gemeineuropäisches System zu entwickelen und für bestimmte Gebiete. ... zu zeigen , ob es in Europa allgemein akzeptierte Regeln gibt, welches diese Regeln sind und ob ihre Entwicklung in Europa auf konvergierende oder auch divergierenden Linien verlauft".[34]

Thus conceived, comparative law searching for a common substratum of concepts and principles on which Community law can be built, also contributes, to borrow on the words used by *Professor Mestmäcker*, to strenghten "the democratic legitimacy of European law".[35]

To summarize, the reasons which require Community courts and the Community legislature to follow a comparative law approach in finding "general principles common to the laws of the Member States" (as stated in Article 288, para. 2, EC regarding the non-contractual liability of Community institutions), are: (i) a political reason – "if the [European] Court wishes to pursue its creative function in developing Community law, it must look systematically for common ground in the legal systems of the Member States on which it can build its edifice"; (ii) a purely legal reason – ". . . to strenghten within each legal system and between the legal systems of the European Union, those elements which preserve homogeneity in the face of growing divergencies. . . "; (iii) an economic reason – "for economic operators to be able to function adquately within a single market, legal disparities must be kept to a minimum. . . "; and (iv) a cultural reason (as prescribed by Art. 151, para. 1, EC) – to "contribute to the flowering of the cultures of the Member States, while respecting their national and regional diversity and at the same time bringing the common cutural heritage to the fore".[36] Building Community law on common ground, with the help of comparative law research, is, at the end of the day, a matter of democratic legitimacy, in that it applies a bottom-up approach,

---

[34] "This presents comparative law with a challenge. No longer can it confine itself to making proposals for the reform of national law . . . Comparative law should go beyond national systems and provide a comparative basis on which to develop a system of law for all Europe; it can do this by taking particular areas . . . and showing what rules are generally accepted throughout Europe and whether they are developing on convergent or divergent lines", K. Zweigert und H. Kötz, *Einführung in die Rechtsvergleichung*, 3rd ed. (Mohr 1996) at pp. 28-29 (in English: *Introduction to Comparative Law* (translated by Tony Weir), 3rd ed. (Clarendon 1998) at pp. 29-30).

[35] E.J. Mestmäcker, "Can there be a European law?" (a question which Mestmäcker answers in the affirmative), *European Review* (1994) 1, at p. 7.

[36] The quotes under (i), (ii) and (iii) are taken from W. van Gerven, "Taking Article 215 [now 288] EC Treaty seriously", in: *New Directions in European Public Law* (J. Beatson and T. Tridimas [eds.]) (Hart 1998) 35, at pp. 46-47.

in searching for the roots of the Member States' legal systems, and for the underlying value judgments and policy decisions, and in doing so brings Community law in the Member States "closer to the citizens".

Turning now to the subject of *codification of private law*, the search for common roots must provide the context for the present discussion concerning the feasibility and desirability of European codification of parts of private law. Those are: the law of contract, tort, unjust enrichment and fiduciary relations (*cum amico*, i.e. agency, as well as *cum creditore*, i.e. credit securities law). This discussion has been put on the political agenda by the recent publication of a European Commission Communication on European Private Law.[37] Without dwelling too long on this subject, which I have discussed on other occasions,[38] I need only say that comprehensive codification should not be excluded in areas of private law such as those mentioned above. Indeed, in these areas there is already much convergence. Where important differences still exist, they are of a manageable nature. Moreover, in these areas many academic efforts have already been undertaken to highlight similarities and to reduce differences within acceptable limits. That is particularly true for the law of contracts and, to a lesser extent, for the law of torts (thanks to European Directives relating mainly to consumer contracts and to case law of the European courts in the area of tort liability). However, with the ECJ's *Tobacco*-judgment of 5 November 2000,[39] in which the Court annulled, at the request of the German government, Directive 98/43/EC relating to the advertisement and sponsorship of tobacco products for lack of competence, it became clear that Article 95 [ex 100a] EC does not offer a *general* legal basis to undertake comprehensive legislation, which goes beyond the scope of consumer law (and competition law, see *infra*).[40] In its judgment, the Court indicated indeed that Article 95 does not give the Community institutions a *general* power to regulate the internal market, but that it can only serve as a legal basis for those *specific* measures which were intended to *improve* the conditions for its establishment and functioning.

---

[37] Communication from the Commission to the Council and the European Parliament of 11 July 2001, *COM* (2001) 398 (final); now published in *OJ* [2000] C 255/1. For a comment, see D. Staudenmayer, "Die Mitteilung der Kommission zum Europaischen Vertragsrecht", *EuZW* (16/2001) 485-489.

[38] See the articles by W. van Gerven, *supra* n. 30, especially the second one.

[39] Case C-376/98 *Germany v. Parliament and Council*, [2000] *ECR* I-8419, para. 84 (see also para. 107). In other words, a real and concrete risk of obstacles or distortions must be proven in each case.

[40] In the same sense, see S. Leible, "Die Mitteilung der Kommission zum Europaischen Vertragsrecht – Startschuss fur Europäisches Vertragsgesetzbuch?" *EWS* (10/2001) 471, at p. 479. But see J. Basedow, "A common contract law for the Common Market", *Common Market Law Review* (1996) 1169-1195, who presents a different view in an article written before the *Tobacco* judgment.

According to the Court, "a mere finding of disparities between national rules and of an abstract risk of obstacles to the exercise of fundamental freedoms or of distortions of competition liable to result therefrom" is insufficient.[41] This would only be different if a specific measure of harmonisation, or unification, is aimed at effectively improving the establishment or functioning of the internal market (or contributes effectively to the elimination of significant distortions of competition) either with regard to present impediments or to future obstacles to trade if such are likely to emerge.[42]

Article 95 EC would certainly offer the easiest way of harmonising large parts of private law since it allows the adoption of either regulations or directives by qualified majority in the Council and by absolute majority in the European Parliament (as provided for in the co-decision procedure (Art. 251 EC referred to in Art. 95). However, even if Article 95 could provide sufficient legal basis (*quod non*), one may still wonder whether it is appropriate to use this procedure, which enables a group of Member States to impose comprehensive codification on Member States which do not have a tradition of codification, but could be outvoted under the co-decision procedure.[43] That would, of course, be different if these Member States were to agree, at a future intergovernmental conference (IGC), to amend the EC Treaty (as was done in the Amsterdam Treay (Art. 65 EC) for conflict of law rules.[44] Another option would be to allow some Member States to go ahead, by making use of the provisions on enhanced cooperation, a possibility facilitated by the Nice Treaty.[45] Indeed, the decision

[41] For an early comment, see "Taking (the limits of) competences seriously", Editorial Comment, *Common Market Law Review* (2000) 1301-1305.

[42] Para. 95 and 96 of the judgment. In a later judgment of 9 October 2001 in case C-377/98 *Netherlands* v. *Parliament and Council* [2001] *ECR* I-7079, the Court was of the opinion that this was the case with regard to Directive 98/44/EC relating to the legal protection of biotechnological inventions, which aimed to "promote research and development in the field of genetic engineering in the European Community". In this case, the Court found that the approximation of national laws pursued by the Directive was essential for achieving the Directive's stated purpose.

[43] The countries which have no codification tradition are obviously the common law countries, but also, to some extent, the Nordic countries. This is even more likely to be the case if the Code becomes very comprehensive in content and scope. See L. Sevón, "Statutory Lawmaking: a Nordic Perspective"in: *Towards Universal Law: trends in national, European and International lawmaking* (Nils Jareborg [ed.]) (Uppsala: Iustus 1995) 179-191. The qualified majority procedure would allow to outvote the UK, Ireland, Denmark, Sweden and Finland.

[44] See further J. Basedow, "The Communitarization of the Conflict of Laws under the Treaty of Amsterdam", *Common Market Law Review* (2000) 687-708, who exposes the inconveniences of international agreements as an instrument of unification.

[45] On the modifications contained in the Treaty of Nice concerning the weighing of votes under the qualified majority procedure and concerning the conditions for enhanced cooperation, see K.St.C. Bradley, "Institutional Design in the Treaty of Nice", *Common Market Law Review* (2001) 1095, at pp. 1109 and 1113.

taken at the time of the Laken proclamation (15 December 2001) to make use of the "Convention" instrument, as was already done for the preparation of the EU Charter of Fundamental Rights, may make future Treaty amendments easier to prepare and adopt.

The foregoing does not mean, however, that academic efforts to make codification possible should not be undertaken any further, quite the contrary. As a matter of fact, this could be done in two stages[46]: first, by consolidating the existing *acquis communautaire* in the area of consumer law not only by eliminating inconsistencies but eventually also by turning directives, and their implementing national laws, into regulations, an endeavor for which there seems to be a legal basis in Community law.[47] Secondly, by preparing the groundwork for an even more comprehensive codification – if the need therefor is really felt[48] – which, pending agreement on a broader legal basis, must be achieved by way of an international agreement.

Codification by means of an international agreement naturally requires more time. However, as explained above, codification by means of the qualified majority procedure would require an amendment of the EC Treaty. In both cases, national parliaments of all Member States will have to be involved. In a matter as important as comprehensive codification, this may be seen as an advantage from the perspective of democratic legitimacy. In the words of *Professor Mestmäcker*: "Conflicts and, at the very least, strains are inevitable where democracies transfer law-making powers to international institutions that are far removed from the political process in the member States. If continuous and effective political control of law-making is desired, there are strong arguments for the control of Community institutions by the democratically elected institutions of the Member States, particularly by national parliaments."[49]

This is also in line with Declarations 13 and 14 added by the Maastricht Treaty which encourage, even for matters coming within the jurisdiction of the EU, the involvement of national parliaments.

---

[46] See further W. van Gerven, "Codifying European private law? Yes, if. . . !", *supra* n. 30.

[47] See Art. 153 EC which, although referring in para. (3) to Article 95 EC (including para. 3, thereof), does not appear to limit (in para. 1) the objective of protecting the interests of consumers to transborder aspects only. But see W.-H. Roth, "Europäischer Verbraucherschutz und BGB", *JZ* (10/2001) 475, at pp. 477-479; also "Europeanization of Private Law – Part 2", Editorial Comments, *Common Market Law Review* (1998) 1013-1018.

[48] If the effort is worth the candle or, in terms of transaction costs, if the input justifies the output.

[49] Mestmäcker, *supra* n. 35, at p. 8. The instrument of an international agreement would require that new Member States also adhere to the agreement. This may be regarded as an inconvenience (cf. J. Basedow, *supra* n. 40, at p. 688), but may also be regarded as an advantage: it would be unfortunate if a civil code, especially if it encompasses various parts of civil law, would be seen by the candidate states as another example of Fortress Europe.

The codification of important parts of national civil laws may be time-consuming (it took more than four decades to draft the Dutch Code which, however, covers all areas of private law including, e.g., consumer and company laws). This time should be used well by preparing legal materials, such as textbooks, casebooks and sourcebooks, that will allow judges, practitioners, academics and students to prepare themselves for the new legislation. Indeed, in the words of the Vice-President of the Dutch *Hoge Raad* responsible for the enactment of the Dutch Code in the final stage,[50] new codification at the national level and, *a fortiori*, at the European level, requires "the re-education of judges, lawyers and other practitioners, of a kind that must not be underestimated. . . ", and, in the words of Helmut Coing,[51] new *curricula* for law schools "where the basic courses present the national law in the context of those legal ideas which are present in the legislation of different nations, that is, against the background of the principles and institutions which the European nations have in common". To bring that formidable task to a successful conclusion, legal materials are absolutely necessary to enable those whose duty it is to apply the new law to do their job properly rather than work in a legal vacuum.[52]

3. Private enforcement of competition law

Private enforcement of Community law is a subject almost as old as Community law itself, as it relates to the protection of Community rights of individuals vis-à-vis public authorities, whether Community or national, before national courts. This issue was indeed the very essence of the famous 1963 judgment, already mentioned, in *Van Gend en Loos* where individuals were given the *ius standi* to sue Member States before national courts for breaches of directly applicable Community law provisions, and thus be able to participate directly in the private enforcement of Community law.[53] Consequently, as known all too well to be recalled here in more than the briefest of terms, the direct effect doctrine and the accompanying general remedy of setting aside national measures inconsistent with Community law, has been gradually

---

[50] W. Snijders, "The Organisation of the Drafting of a European Civil Code: a Walk in imaginary Gardens", *European Review of Private law* (1997) 483, at p. 485.

[51] As quoted by H. Kötz, "Comparative Legal Research and its Function in the Developments of harmonized Law. The European Perspective", in: *Towards Universal Law*, supra n. 43, 21, at p. 29.

[52] See further van Gerven, *supra* n. 30.

[53] See also van Gerven, *supra* n. 17, and the text accompanying the footnote, where I argue that this case law constitutes the starting point of the constitutionalisation of Community law.

expanded and supplemented by making available more specific remedies, such as restitution, interim relief and compensation, although these have to be mainly intended to provide a remedy against the illicit conduct of Member States and their public authorities. ECJ judgments like *Simmenthal* and *Fantask* (restitution), *Factortame I* and *Zuckerfabrik Süderdithmarschen* (interim relief) and *Francovich* and *Brasserie du Pêcheur* (compensation) are familiar examples.[54]

In addition to those specific remedies for enforcing Community law against public authorities, there is also the remedy of nullity in the area of competition law, expressly provided for in Article 81 [ex 85], para. 2 EC, regarding which the ECJ stated (as it has also said of Art. 82 [ex 86] EC) that it "produce[s] direct effects in relations between individuals and create[s] rights for the individuals concerned which the national courts must safeguard".[55] Until recently, however, it was not clear whether the horizontal direct effect that the Court attached to Articles 81 and 82 EC and the concomitant "absolute" effect of the nullity sanction ("an agreement which is null and void by virtue of this [Article 85, now 81] provision has no effect as between contracting parties and cannot be set up against third parties"[56]) also resulted, *mutatis mutandis*, in the availability of other remedies, not expressly provided for in the Treaty, in the first place the remedy of *compensation* in horizontal relations, that is *between individual parties*. That such is the case was made clear by the ECJ in a judgment of 20 September 2001 in *Courage/Crehan*.[57]

In that judgment, referring to *Van Gend en Loos*, *Costa/ ENEL* but also to *Francovich*, the Court stated that rights of individuals "arise not only where they are expressly granted by the Treaty but also by virtue of obligations which the Treaty imposes in a clearly defined manner . . . on individuals" (para. 19). It went on to state that, "[a]s regards the possibility of seeking compensation for loss caused by a contract or by conduct liable to restrict or distort competition . . . (para. 25) . . . (t)he full effectiveness of Article [81] of the Treaty and, in particular, the practical effect of the prohibition laid down in Article [81] (1) would be put at risk if it were not open to any individual to claim damages for loss caused to him by a contract or by conduct liable to restrict or distort competition" (para. 26). Consequently, it would appear that the Court has now fully endorsed the proposition that, by virtue of Community law itself (and therefore not only when the applicable national law entertains such a claim), *individuals* who have breached provisions which, like Articles 81 (1) and 82, are directly

---

[54] For an overview, see W. van Gerven, "Of Rights, Remedies and Procedures", 37 *Common Market Law Review* (2000) 501, at pp. 509-521.

[55] Case 127/73 *BRT and SABAM* [1974] *ECR* 51, para. 16.

[56] Case 22/71 *Béguelin* [1971] *ECR* 949, para. 29.

[57] Case C-453/99, [2001] *ECR* I-6297.

applicable also horizontally, may be held liable, in contract and/or in tort (the language of the judgment covers both), towards other individuals who have sustained damage as a result of the infringement.[58]

The *Courage/Crehan* judgment assumes special importance in the context of the pending so-called "modernization" proposals which the EC Commission wishes the Council to adopt regarding the implementation of Article 81 EC, a subject which has been dealt with exhaustively and critically by *Professor Mestmäcker* at the fifth annual EC Competition Law and Policy Workshop organized by Professors Amato and Ehlermann at the Robert Schuman Centre of the European University Institute (EUI) in Florence.[59] According to those proposals, it is up to the national competition authorities *and* the national courts to apply not only the provisions of Articles 81 (1) and (2) and 82, but also the provisions of Article 81 (3) which the Commission in its proposals now regards as directly applicable as well. Obviously, even if one is prepared to go along with the proposals which seem to have reached a point of no return, it must be recognized that many deficiencies still need to be addressed, both with regard to administrative enforcement (by a network of national competition authorities) and with regard to private enforcement (before civil and commercial courts). If these deficiencies are not addressed, the new rules may not become a valid substitute for the central enforcement by the Commission services of the competition law now in force under Regulation no. 17.[60] I will not discuss these problems here,[61] except to say that, in my opinion, (i) it is arguable that there is a legal basis in the Treaty for the new system of implementation (provided that the ECJ "overrules" its position in its first competition judgment – *De Geus* v. *Bosch*; (ii) bearing in mind that law-making and decision-making in important matters will remain in the hands of the Commission, the proposed reform does

---

[58] In my Opinion, as Advocate General, in *Banks*, Case C-128/92 [1994] *ECR* I-1209, para. 36-45, I had already advocated that position.

[59] E.J. Mestmäcker, "The Modernization of EC Antitrust Policy: Constitutional Challenge or Administrative Convenience?" in: *European Competition Law Annual 2000*: *The Modernization of EC Antitrust Policy* (C.D. Ehlermann and I.Atanasu [eds.]) (Hart 2001) 223-258. See also E.J. Mestmäcker, "The EC Commission's Modernization of Competition Policy: a Challenge to the Community's Constitutional Order", *European Business Organization Law Review* (2000) 401-444.

[60] On these deficiencies, see J. Basedow, "Who will protect Competition in Europe? From central enforcement to authority networks and private litigation", *European Business Organisation Law Review*, *Liber Amicorum E.J. Mestmäcker* (2001) 443-468.

[61] See my report, "Substantive Remedies for the Private Enforcement of EC Antitrust Rules before National Courts", also presented at the EUI workshop in Florence, however in 2001. The report exists in mimeographed form and will be published in Robert Schuman Centre's *European Competition Law Annual 2001* (forthcoming).

not appear to constitute an inadmissible transfer of enforcement competences from the Commission to the private sector (or, in the words of *Professor Mestmäcker*, does not amount to an unconstitutional change in the "Macht-balance zwischen Staat und Gesellschaft"[62]; and (iii) with the assistance of the Community and national authorities, the national civil and commercial courts may be able to deal with the issues inherent in the application of Article 81 (3) EC.[63] Having said all this, doubts remain whether the objectives of simplification and concentration on important issues pursued by the proposals were not attainable under the present implementing rules, nor whether loss of legal certainty incurred by abolishing the notification requirement for cartel agreements, is not too high a price to pay, bearing in mind that national authorities, and especially national courts which are already overburdened with work, will need additional human and financial resources, as well as new legal instruments, to perform their new task. This may not present a huge problem to an efficient national enforcement body like the German *Kartellamt*, but it certainly creates problems in some of the other Member States, not to mention the candidate countries.

Finally, I shall focus briefly on private enforcement. Private enforcement of competition rules is a concept that has many supporters, but which does not always work out very well in practice. In Community law, for example, apart from nullity claims between contracting parties, not many compensation claims have been brought by third parties before national courts.[64] The reasons therefor are manifold but a major factor is certainly the fact that the outcome of the litigation for the plaintiff is uncertain, to say the least, even in Member States like France and Belgium, where substantive tort law makes it easy for plaintiffs to bring actions in tort. The major problem is that plaintiffs who are third parties to the restrictive agreement or practice, will not be in a position to prove the existence of an infringement,[65] without the help of a public prosecutor or a cartel authority. It is even more difficult to establish causation and the existence and

---

[62] "Balance of power between state and society". See the quotation in the text accompanying n. 7 *supra*.

[63] But see R. Wesseling, "The draft regulation modernising the competition rules: the Commission is married to one idea", *European Law Review* (2001) 357-378.

[64] Basedow, *supra* n. 60, at p. 461.

[65] That will be even more difficult under the proposed new Regulation where it will be for the parties involved to prove an exemption under Article 81 (3). See now, to the contrary, the ECJ's judgment in joined cases 56 & 56/64 *Consten and Grundig* v. *Commission*, [1966] *ECR* 429, where the Court held, at p. 501, that "the Commission may not confine itself to requiring from undertakings proof of the fulfillment of the requirements for the grant of the exemption [under Article 85 EC] but must, as a matter of good administration, play its part, using the means available to it, in ascertaining the relevant facts and circumstances" (translation taken from [1966] *CMLR* 418).

amount of damages. That will not change by the mere fact that the ECJ has now stated in *Courage/Crehan* that "the existence of such a right [of an individual plaintiff] strenghtens the working of the Community competition rules and discourages agreements or practices, which are frequently covert, which are liable to restrict or distort competition. From that point of view, actions for damages before the national courts can make a significant contribution to the maintenance of effective competition in the Community" (para. 27).

Although it is now up to the ECJ to flesh out the conditions for contractual or tort liability that arises as a result of breaches of competition rules, it is not certain, judging from past experience (in the areas of State liability and product liability), that the Court will be offered many opportunities to clarify the applicable rules in preliminary ruling procedures. Even if the opportunity does present itself, it is not at all certain that the Community Court would want to go too deeply into substantive and, more importantly, remedial or procedural aspects of compensation claims.[66] Rather than leave these delicate questions to the ECJ, it would be for the Commission to prepare a second draft regulation for the Council on the basis of Article 83 EC dealing with the substantive and procedural aspects of private enforcement. Such a regulation should set out the conditions for the remedies of nullity, restitution, compensation, restitutionary and/or exemplary damages, interim relief and, eventually, protection of diffuse (consumer) interests, as well as the procedural and evidential rules to make them operational.[67] In the absence of such a regulation that makes available a variety of remedies with the same, or at least a sufficiently uniform, scope and content in all Member States and, in the absence of additional resources and expertise at the national level, the national courts will have to cope with legal issues which they have neither the time nor the human resources to analyse, nor adequate legal instruments to resolve. Assigning new tasks to the courts, without providing them with the means to perform those tasks, as the Commission proposes to do, does not comply with standards of good governance.

4. Conclusion

It is tempting to look for a link between the three themes addressed in this paper: political and legal integration, strategic importance of comparative law, and

---

[66] On the procedural law aspects of private enforcement, see the report of A.G. Jacobs at the EC Competition Law and Policy Workshop of 1-2 June 2001. For a judgment of the ECJ dealing with the applicability of a one-year time-limit set by national law for the bringing of claims for compensation under the principle of State liability, see C-261/95 *Palmisani*, [1997] *ECR* I-4025, para. 23-40.

[67] Attached to my report, referred to *supra* n. 61, is a proposed draft for such a regulation.

enforcement of Community competition rules through private law remedies. In the context of this symposium in honor of *Professor Mestmäcker*, it is not difficult to find that link: democratic legitimacy, good governance and respect for the values inherent in civil society, as expressed in the basic principles of a Rechtsstaat. In other words, taking principles, institutions and rights seriously. This, no doubt, has also been the essence of *Professor Mestmäcker*'s work. Thank you all for allowing me to participate in the celebration of the life and work of a very special person.

On the Direct Effect of the WTO Agreements

Claus Dieter Ehlermann*

My contribution to the panel discussion is devoted to the controversial question of the place of the WTO Agreements in the constitutional system of the European Community.

In ERNST-JOACHIM MESTMÄCKER's discussion of European civil society, the rules of the EC Treaty play a central part. Particularly important are the fundamental freedoms and competition policy. Together with the two fundamental constitutional principles of direct effect and primacy they guarantee the internal market. They form the foundation of the principle of the open market economy with free competition which governs the political economy of the EC.

Endowed with direct effect and primacy, the fundamental freedoms primarily guide the legislation and administration of the EC Member States. They also – at least in principle – guide the legislation and administration of the EC. It is therefore correct to count them among the constitutional principles of the EC. The EC's constitutional order thus contains, as we know, more guarantees of the free economic activity of the citizens and enterprises within the Community than do the constitutions of the EC Member States.

However strong the guarantees of economic freedom within the Community are, the constitutional guarantees relating to the Community as a world-trading partner are weak. To be sure, the EC is extremely active externally: it has concluded an impressive number of bilateral and multilateral association, cooperation and free-trade agreements, it is a member of international organizations, and it is a founding member of the WTO. All these agreements are binding on the Community institutions and on Member States (Art. 300 (7) EC). Free trade and association agreements can be invoked by citizens and enterprises before the courts; their provisions are capable of producing direct effect. (I am using the term "direct effect" as shorthand for the capacity to invoke a provision before the courts).

Things are different for the old GATT and the WTO Agreement that replaced it. According to the case law of the Court of Justice, the old GATT was, by its nature and structure, unable to produce any kind of direct effect. Accordingly, its individual provisions did not have to be examined as to whether they were

---

* Prof. Dr. Dr. h.c., Senior Counsel, Wilmer, Cutler & Pickering, Brussels.
I am indebted to Lothar Ehring and Nicolas Lockhart who have accompanied my reflections by stimulating and critical discussions.

suitable to produce that effect. This case law relating to the GATT seemed to contradict the Court's favourable approach towards international law in the area of association and free-trade agreements, and was therefore overwhelmingly criticized. Its opponents hoped that the WTO new dispute settlement system would compel the Court to reverse its negative general attitude, so that the question of the direct effect of individual WTO provisions would become relevant in the future.

As we know, however, the Court has maintained its fundamental rejection of direct effect in its case law concerning the WTO agreements. In its view, the new agreements are equally fundamentally unsuitable for bringing about direct effect. Accordingly, the question of the direct effect of individual provisions continues to be of no relevance. The decisive factor for the fundamental rejection of direct effect is no longer the nature and structure of the WTO, which has changed significantly through the new dispute settlement procedure. Instead, it is the lack of reciprocity in the recognition of direct effect of the WTO agreements between the EU and its most important trade partners. The Court's fundamental denial of direct effect affects all plaintiffs: neither private persons nor Member States can invoke the WTO agreements. Not surprisingly, the Court's position regarding the direct effect of the WTO agreements has been criticized even more harshly than that regarding the old GATT. The Court of Justice has ultimately been reproached for acting on political rather than legal grounds.

Undoubtedly, the constitutional guarantees of European civil society would have been strengthened significantly had the Court of Justice modified its case law concerning the GATT in light of the new WTO dispute settlement procedure, by affirming that the WTO agreements are, in principle, suitable for producing direct effect. From the viewpoint of the promoters of the European civil society, the fundamental denial of direct effect of the WTO agreements is indeed to be regretted very deeply.

However, is the Court's recent case law as scandalous as the majority of academic critics thinks? I shall present my opinion on this matter by means of the following theses.

1. General international law does not prescribe, as a matter of principle, whether international agreements must have direct internal effect.
2. Individual international agreements, however, can make a choice in this matter. They can either require or exclude direct effect, or leave the choice to each Contracting Party.
3. Like the old GATT, the WTO agreements do not determine the question of direct effect. Switzerland's proposal to expressly require direct effect was rejected during the Uruguay Round. The ECJ justified the "neutrality" of the WTO agreements (in relation to direct effect) by referring to the options explicitly given by the dispute settlement system to all WTO Members

"condemned" because of a WTO violation. The Court's critics may well be right in their assessment of the extent and nature of the flexibility allowed to Members. However, they overlook a number of provisions that the Court did not cite, but which nonetheless confirm its conclusion that the WTO Agreement is "neutral" as regards direct effect. An international agreement that requires direct effect would not state:

"Before bringing a case, a Member shall exercise its judgment as to whether action under these procedures would be fruitful. The aim of the dispute settlement mechanism is to secure a positive solution to the dispute. A solution mutually acceptable to the parties to a dispute and consistent with the covered agreements is clearly to be preferred" (Art. 3 (7) of the Dispute Settlement Understanding).

4. The debate on the pros and cons of direct effect has so far taken place almost exclusively from the internal perspective of the Community. In my opinion, this view is too narrow. The discussion should include the effects that the recognition of direct effect would produce on the WTO as an international organization, on its functioning and on the likely conduct of its Member States.
5. At first sight, the (unilateral) recognition of direct effect by one Contracting Party is to be welcomed by all other Parties. As EC experience shows, direct effect greatly increases the effectiveness of an international norm, because private persons can use domestic courts to enforce the norm's provisions. Shouldn't the international organization and its members be interested in this efficiency gain, that apparently costs them (the organization and the members) nothing?
6. The initial impression is deceptive: the (unilateral) recognition of direct effect by no means leads to a "win-win" situation.
7. It is obvious and has long been recognized that the (unilateral) recognition of direct effect raises the threshold for consent to future agreements. It is naïve to believe that the degree of domestic effectiveness of an agreement has no effects on the process for assent to new agreements under the national constitution. In other words, the conclusion of new agreements will be made more difficult.
8. The treaty partners of the Member State that (unilaterally) recognizes direct effect might initially rejoice at the fact that private persons have taken over the "dirty work" of enforcing the agreements through the dispute settlement bodies of the international organization (in this case, the WTO). But their joy will not last long. The Member State whose courts grant direct effect will become an aggressive partner in the context of dispute settlement between States, if it wishes to uphold the balance of rights and duties that flow from the agreement among the treaty partners. This shift in the balance results from the fact that the state that recognizes direct effect exposes itself domestically to private actions against violations of the agreements, while

there are no comparable court actions in the partner countries. A state that is keen to maintain the balance of rights and obligations will be compelled by economic and political considerations to defend the interests of its exporters and investors before the dispute settlement bodies of the international organization. It will enforce rights before these dispute settlement bodies that it would either not have defended at all in "judicial" form, or at any rate not at that moment in time, if the agreements at issue had no direct effect in its domestic jurisdiction.

9. It is obvious that recognizing the direct effect of international agreements results in a shift of power between constitutional institutions: the position of the government and the parliament is weakened, and that of the courts strengthened. Supporters of direct effect and promoters of civil society favour such an effect because they want to discipline the omnipotence and arbitrariness of government and parliament. Were the shift in weight confined to the domestic level, I could conclude on this point. But power will also shift at the level of the international organization, because the probable increase in the number of complex actions before the international dispute settlement bodies will lead to an increase in status of these bodies at the expense of the organization's political bodies. This increase will also occur if the dispute settlement bodies do not periodically review the conduct of the international organization's political bodies (as the ECJ does in the EC). There would be no objection against such an increase if organization's political bodies were capable of making political decisions in a fashion similar to governments and parliaments or EC institutions. In the WTO, however, this is unfortunately not the case. In fact, the WTO is already characterized by a troubling imbalance between dispute settlement procedures and political process. To put it provocatively, the WTO's most powerful organ is the so-called Appellate Body, not the collectivity of the Member States in their various political functions, which traditionally decides only by consensus. Consensus among over 145 Member States is a rarity compared to decision by three members of the Appellate Body, who rule not only on the import of bananas but also on the use of growth hormones, or of asbestos. I am convinced that even the existing imbalance between political and (quasi-)jurisdictional bodies is dangerous, since it threatens the present system of dispute settlement in the long run. Accordingly, I warn against any step that will heighten the already existing imbalance further in favour of the (quasi-)jurisdictional bodies for dispute settlement. Instead, it is the process of political decision-making that ought to be strengthened.

BACK TO THE ECJ AND TO EC LAW

As we know, EC Law does not expressly regulate to what extent international agreements concluded by the EC have direct effect, and what rank they occupy in the hierarchy of community norms. The prevailing opinion is that these matters are regulated with binding force by Article 300 (7) EC Treaty, according to which "[a]greements concluded pursuant to this Article . . . are binding on the Community bodies and on the Member States".

I do not believe that Article 300 (7) EC Treaty dictates to the Court of Justice its findings on direct effect and the primacy of international agreements of the Community. Rather, the outcome is the result of legal policy considerations by the Court. In this context, it is good to recall that the provisions of the association and free-trade agreements that were to be interpreted by the Court had been copied from corresponding provisions in the EC Treaty; that the Court of Justice had just acknowledged the direct effect and primacy of the EC Treaty provisions over the laws of Member-States; that, at that time, direct effect and primacy were not – as they are today – an uncontroversial *acquis* of EC law; and that the Court of Justice wished to avoid the reproach of inconsistency, i.e. of measuring with different scales. In my view, this explains the striking parallelism between the direct effect of EC Treaty provisions, on the one hand, and corresponding provisions of EC association and free-trade agreements, on the other. It also explains the classification in the hierarchy of EC law of international treaties concluded by the EC, namely, recognition of their primacy over secondary EC law and any kind of national law of the Member States. Legal policy considerations – not the EC Treaty – mandated the rejection of the reciprocity argument put forward by the Commission in the *Polydor* case. Legal policy considerations – not binding rules of the Treaty – were also behind the refusal to grant the political organs of the Community a role in recognizing or rejecting direct effect.

Against this background, it is not surprising that the EC law justification of the Court's case law on the legal effect of the WTO agreements (in contrast to the interpretation of these agreements in international law) is not convincing.

On one point, I consider this case law simply wrong and untenable, indeed dangerous. I share the view of all those who accuse the Court of *deni de justice* vis-à-vis the Member States. In my opinion, considerations of (constitutional) EC law require that Member States involved in annulment actions before the ECJ should be able to invoke the (justiciable) provisions of the WTO agreements. In contrast to a number of authors, I do not believe that Member States and private persons have to be treated equally in relation to the invocability of the provisions of international treaties. The denial of justice to Member States as plaintiffs contrasts the admission of invocation of the GATT or WTO agreements in breach-of-treaty procedures brought by the Commission against Member States as defendants before the Court of Justice; while the latter is justified, the former is unjustified. Moreover, the denial of legal protection before the Court of Justice might induce Member States to insist on the political enforcement of their legal views, i.e. by means of unanimous voting in the Council. Is this desirable from the perspective of legal policy?

By contrast, I regard the denial of the direct effect of WTO agreements with respect to private persons as correct in principle, although I would justify it differently.

The overwhelming majority of authors defends the position that the direct effect of international agreements can only be determined on the basis of the EC Treaty and the agreement in question. Therefore, the decision on direct effect is a matter reserved exclusively for the Court of Justice. The opinions of the political bodies assenting to the agreement, namely the Council and – exceptionally – also the European Parliament, are regarded as irrelevant. In light of the development of the Court's case law on the direct effect of international agreements concluded by the EC, this seems about right: the majority view corresponds to the position taken by the Court of Justice on the question of the criteria and the institutional distribution of roles when deciding the direct effect of directives.

I have no doubt that the Court of Justice thought the same for a long time. Whether it still does today is doubtful, because its case law concerning the situations in which it allows private persons to invoke WTO law is not fully compatible with the thesis of the irrelevance of the Council's opinion. The Court of Justice's decisions *in re Nakajima* (reviewing the legality of provisions in the Council's anti-dumping regulation according to the WTO anti-dumping agreement) and *in re Fediol* (reviewing a decision by the Commission according to the standards of the EC's international obligations (i.e. also the whole of WTO law) show that the Court does attach importance to the Council's view. In its fundamental decision on the lack of direct effect of the WTO agreements, the Court mentions the Council's position, but without according it decisive importance.

Recent studies on the domestic role of international norms show that the recognition of direct effect requires a subtle balancing of a number of contradictory considerations. The development of the Court's case law, initially with regard to the GATT and, more recently, with regard to the WTO agreements, shows that "all or nothing" solutions can be unsatisfactory, indeed even wrong. A more nuanced procedure is necesary. The thesis that the required distinctions can be derived from the EC Treaty alone is not credible. In my view, it would be more appropriate to attach greater – perhaps even decisive – importance to the intention of the EC's treaty-making bodies. Thus, individual agreements such as the TRIPS agreement, could produce direct effect, while other agreements like the GATT and the GATS would continue to be denied direct effect. Similarly, direct effect could be granted to parts of agreements. The enforceability of international treaty provisions in the EC, and in European civil society, would thus benefit more than it does from insistence on traditional positions. As already mentioned, these positions were the result of equating direct effect of internal Community norms with the norms of international treaties. This sort of equal treatment is neither required nor desirable given the present stage of EC law.

In the debate on the direct effect of the WTO agreements, the Court's critics should not lose sight of two considerations:

The first consideration is of a structural nature, and is due to the combination of direct effect and the primacy of international treaty provisions in EC law over any sort of domestic secondary law. This combination gives an extraordinarily strong position to agreements concluded by the EC. But, at the same time, it poses a potential hindrance: the political organs of the EU will include it in their considerations regarding their position on future agreements. The conclusion of new agreements will not be facilitated but hampered.

The second consideration is a conjunctural one. The controversies concerning the direct effect first of the GATT and later of the WTO agreements were sparked off by the organization of the banana market. One had better also bear in mind the hormone dispute which the EC lost in Geneva. Nevertheless, the EC did not withdraw its hormone ban. Something similar may also happen in the area of genetically modified organisms. Are the critics of the Court's case law on direct effect of the WTO agreements prepared to abandon the room for manoeuvre that the enforcement system of the WTO clearly leaves to parliaments and governments of WTO members? I do not think so, and I believe that proponents of European civil society would agree with me.

European Political Integration, Comparative Law and Private Enforcement of Competition Rules

Dieter Wolf*

I assume that I have been invited to this panel as one of the first outspoken critics of the Commission's White Book and its proposals concerning the so-called "modernized application" of Articles 81 and 82 EC Treaty, while serving as the President of the Federal Cartel Authority. Subsequently, in order to avoid disturbing my successor, I have deliberately remained silent on the subject, but not because my opinions on the matter have substantially changed. However, I do not intend to break this silence today: Time has passed and the majority in favor of the Commission's proposals is as substantial as it is impressive. Being a practical person, I have come to accept this reality. In my opinion, it is now important to make the best of this new regulation, in order to achieve maximum protection of fair competition. Therefore, my criticism is aimed towards the future and avoids attacking what has become a reality. Please be so kind as to interpret my contribution and the criticism contained therein in this sense.

Nevertheless, I cannot avoid deviating once from my stated intent: The doubts expressed by our Jubilar *Prof. Mestmäcker* on the compatibility of the Commission's proposals with the competition rules of the EC Treaty – the primary law of the Union – have never been properly addressed in the scientific or political discussion, although they are well substantiated and are formulated, at least in my opinion, in an extraordinarily convincing manner. Even Prof. van Gerven has (again) excluded from his discussion the question of whether a directly applicable exemption is compatible with Article 81 EC Treaty and, instead, opted for the laconic remark that "it is arguable". However, what I have heard from German judges who adjudicate such matters, is far from laconic. They suggest that the first decision to be given on the new law will be a preliminary question concerning this very question with which they will confront the ECJ. Therefore, let us wait and see what the future holds.

Let us now return to the main question: how to make the best of the given situation? Prof. van Gerven is right when he says that the key element of the successful implementation of the Commission's proposals will be "private enforcement before the national courts". Cooperation between the national competition authorities and the Commission is an equally tempting point of

---

* Dr. h.c., former President of the German Cartel Authority. Dr. Katerina Elmaliah, attorney at law in Switzerland and Tel-Aviv, Israel, translated the German original.

discussion, but this would clearly go beyond the time allocated to this contribution.

Prof. van Gerven is also right in pointing out that, under existing law, the cooperation between the Commission and the National Courts has been relatively rare, notwithstanding the fact that it has always been extensively possible, as stated also in a special "Notice" issued by the Commission in 1993. If I understand him correctly, Prof. van Gerven shares my doubts that effective "private enforcement before national courts" can be achieved without the incorporation of specific incentives in supplementary EC Law. He has even presented a draft directive to that effect. I also agree with his contention that the reasons for the reluctance of private parties (in particular in continental Europe) to defend their competitive position in court are mostly of cultural nature: a more skeptical attitude towards litigation, perhaps a less-developed culture of competition (although on this point I would beg to differ), combined with the absence in the civil law of the Member States of institutions such as "class actions", "contingency fee arrangements", "treble damages" and "discovery procedures". Surely, Prof. van Gerven assures us that he is not contemplating the "transplantation" of the US legal atmosphere in Europe. Milder incentives would suffice for achieving the goal. Nonetheless, it is hard to ignore that his suggestions are, in essence, modeled on the American institutions. Such proposals can only be supported if we regard these common law institutions as being of exemplary nature. Whether such legal institutions are also desirable from a legal policy perspective should, at the very least, be critically examined in accordance with the maxim *quod est demonstrandum*. The mere fact that these institutions increase readiness to litigate (which is achieved anyway by favoring the plaintiff's side in the American law regarding trial expenses) and thus, incidentally, also serve the legal profession well, is not a good enough reason. This also calls for considering the ensuing intended promotion of establishing law firms specializing in such proceedings. Could such "promotion" mean that we should no longer leave this matter to be taken care of by the market alone?

Even assuming that it would be desirable to adopt the American approach with respect to Articles 81 and 82 EC Treaty, I am doubtful that this would be compatible with Article 93 EC Treaty. This concerns not only the relationship between EC Competition Law and the respective Member States' secondary competition law which is based upon it. I can hardly imagine a special law of damages which is limited to competition law only. Neither is this the case in the US legal system. The adoption of the US approach would therefore, in my opinion, involve a general harmonization of the entire torts law of the Member States to include "collective claims mechanisms" (which, at the end of the day, would mean the introduction of "class actions"), pre-trial discovery procedures (however "inexpensive" they may be), and payments beyond provable suffered damages, such as "exemplary" or "punitive damages", *inter alia* to "protect diffuse interests". Mr. van Greven remains silent on this point. However, it is hardly possible to favor parties damaged by a competition offence over other parties damaged, for example, as a result of environmental torts.

It is my understanding that the EC Competition rules are generally based on the coexistence of EC competition law and the competition laws of the Member States, and that Article 83 para. 2 lit. (e) EC Treaty empowers the Council, to determine the relationship between these two regulatory systems. Such a determination cannot subject all national competition rules to an overall primacy of Community competition law, since that would prevent any "relationship" between these two different levels of law (this is the problem of Art. 3 of the draft Regulation, criticized by *Mestmäcker*, which stipulates that when an agreement or practice is capable of affecting trade between Member States, Community competition law applies exclusively). Much less still, Article 3 empowers to shape the legislation of Member States outside the competition law as, for instance, the entire civil torts law. This would be a matter of harmonisation in the sense of Articles 94 and 96, for which – like the EU Commission – I do not see a Community-wide consensus in the foreseeable future.

Personally, I can envisage injured parties being allowed to include their claims for damages in proceedings under Articles 81 and 82 EC Treaty taking place before national competition authorities, in a manner similar to the German law institution of *Adhäsionsklage* in criminal proceedings. Although not unproblematic, such a solution might be covered by Article 83 EC Treaty.

However, in my opinion, this may not be equally true with respect to Basedow's suggestion, as adopted by van Gerven, to lighten the burden of proof for private claimants of damages. Personally, I wish whole-heartedly that the courts would increasingly assume *prima facie*, in Article 81 or 82 cases, the existence of fault or negligence on the part of the defendant as well as the existence of a causal link between the offence and the damages sought, and thereby *de facto* place the burden of proof on the defendants. Nevertheless, the question remains whether the suggested direct exemption of Article 81 para. 3 EC Treaty will not instead have the effect of increasing the litigation risks of the claimant considerably as compared with the situation at present. After all, the time-consuming court proceedings are not clear-cut cases of hard-core cartels but gray-area cases. In such cases, the defendant will – naturally with legal advice, perhaps also with the support of expert opinions – claim that, in spite of its detailed and conscientious examination of the facts, it erred with respect to the exemption, thereby preventing the *prima facie* evidence against him from being presented in the first place.

In conclusion, the chances of creating incentives for parties suffering damages from competition offences to bring private claims are not very promising. I agree with Prof. van Gerven that the second round of legislative measures that he suggests may already be introduced, if only for reasons of efficiency with regard to the first package of legislative measures, i.e. the implementation of the proposals contained in the White Paper. However, this will remain a long-term project at best, considering, *inter alia*, that the interests of enterprises, governments and the Commission in that second package of legislative measures differ fundamentally from their interests in the first.

Institutional Competition in an "Ever Closer Union"

Wolfgang Schön*

It is an honour for me to find myself among the speakers contributing to the academic symposium celebrating the 75th birthday of Professor MESTMÄCKER. I stress this point especially because I am the only person on the panel who is not a specialist in competition law, the field in which you have received acclaim on an international scale. Nevertheless, I assume that your far-reaching scientific interest extends to a subject which has brought the concept of "competition" to many other areas of legal and economic writing. I refer to the idea of "institutional competition", which makes us think of the allocation of regulatory power between public institutions, e.g. townships, states and supranational bodies. A famous example of this idea of institutional competition is provided by the way in which the Member States and the institutions of the European Union interact and by the question which legislative competence should be retained at the level of the Member States and which should be allocated to the level of the European Union. In this context, the idea of competition meets with the concept of "subsidiarity", which is now enshrined in Article 5 para. 2 of the EC Treaty.

In the European Union, the classical legal-economic concept of its legal order was described by the notion of an "ever closer union", in which harmonisation would eventually lead to a common legal system in many if not all areas of law. The economic gains resulting from harmonisation have always been identified as the reduction of transaction costs (transparency of the legal setting) and the creation of a "level playing-field" in Europe, in which economic agents make their decisions based on economic and technical factors, not on the basis of the legal disparities between the Member States. The promoters of institutional competition are skeptical regarding the economic merits of such a level playing-field, because they fear the cartelisation of Member States under the umbrella of the European Union, and they stress the danger that the harmonisation of laws may not provide the best solution to a regulatory problem. In their opinion, it would be better to let Member States seek their own solutions and then see which concept proves to be the best. The adoption of that concept by the other Member States, would eventually lead to spontaneous harmonisation.

The point I wish to make in this context is that institutional competition does

* Professor of Law, Director of Max Planck Institute for Intellectual Property, Competition and Tax Law, Munich.

Talia Einhorn, ed., Spontaneous Order, Organization and the Law –
Liber Amicorum Ernst-Joachim Mestmäcker © *2003* T.M.C.ASSER PRESS, *The Hague, The Netherlands*

not take place in a uniform setting, but that there are different "marketplaces" in which the Member States act. I would like illustrate this point by considering three different fields of legal work: company law, accounting law and taxation law.

In company law, the rules for institutional competition differ fundamentally depending on whether private international law follows the "incorporation theory" or the "real seat theory". Under the "incorporation theory", the company is governed by the rules of the country in which it is incorporated regardless of whether the bulk of its economic activities are carried out in that country. Under the "real seat theory", the company is governed by the rules of the country where the effective management of the company takes place. In other words, if the founders of a company want to make use of a specific company law, they must move the centre of the economic activities of the company to that state. This means that they have to consider the legal and economic setting of each country as a whole and decide which country offers the most favourable "package". Under the incorporation theory, on the other hand, the founders of a company are in the position to choose a legal order for their company without submitting to the whole legal system of that country. This leads to a "pick and choose" situation that fuels the legal competition between Member States with unprecedented speed.

In accounting law, we have to bear in mind that the economic and legal functions of accounting have their own particular qualities as well. Proper accounting should generate adequate information on the capital market, leaving investors to decide in which enterprise to invest. The comparability of company information and the homogeinity of accounting rules are of utmost importance to the "preparers" and "users" of company accounts. This leads to "network externalities", i.e. a situation in which the international harmonisation of accounting rules provides in itself for a higher quality of the legal setting, by enabling investors to compare the information they receive from capital-seeking enterprises from different countries and to allocate their capital resources to the company that will generate the highest return. It is therefore natural that accounting rules tend to be harmonised at an international level, not just at the level of the European Union but also throughout the industrialised world. In the near future, "International Accounting Standards" will govern the accounting practice of firms in most countries.

Another specific marketplace emerges in relation to taxation law. In this field, the legislator performs a double function. On the one hand, tax law has a regulatory aspect, affecting the economic decisions of individuals and enterprises, especially when it comes to the choice between investing in domestic or foreign-based companies. On the other hand, taxation supplies the state with the funds it needs to perform its duties. The level of taxation in a country is decisive for the level of public goods which can be provided by the state, ranging from law and order to education, social security and cultural goods. Therefore, a government has to bear in mind both aspects of taxation: the regulatory and the fiscal aspect. In practice this has led to governments trying to attract as much investment as possible without losing too much of the tax revenues. One technique used in this context is known as "ring-fencing", i.e. the granting of tax benefits only to foreign investors, excluding the ordinary domestic taypayer from the tax-saving schemes. Another feature of tax competition is that states try to focus on highly-mobile production factors such as financial capital or highly qualified employees. The institutions of the EC and the OECD have for some years scrutinized these developments and tried to distinguish between "fair" and "unfair" tax competition, in order to set up rules for "fair" behaviour in international institutional competition.

This leads us to the common question underlying these three (and all other) examples of institutional competition: do we need a meta-system of rules to govern the competition between the Member States of the European Union, and is there a need for a "cartel law" or a law on monopolies in the market for regulation? Economic and legal thinking still have not yet a long way to go before they can answer these questions. The most I can do here is to present these questions to you. It takes a man like *Ernst-Joachim Mestmäcker* to answer them.

government has to bear in mind both aspects of taxation: the regulatory and the fiscal aspect. In practice this has led to governments trying to attract as much [illegible]

Imposed Liberty and its Limits – The EC Treaty as an Economic Constitution for the Member States

Christoph Engel*

Good constitutions are short and obscure. The original version of the EC treaty seems quite clearly to have been designed in accordance with this view. Not even the preparatory materials have been published. Many of the provisions that later turned out to be the most powerful seemed inoffensive on first reading. The decisive steps were procedural: the introduction of an independent Commission, and a Court with almost unlimited jurisdiction. From Karl Popper we know: Institutions are like fortresses; they must be wisely designed and appropriately manned.[1] In the EC they were handled in this manner, and during the decisive period, ERNST-JOACHIM MESTMÄCKER was one of the prominent figures to see to this task with respect to European antitrust policy. For more than a decade, no antitrust decision was issued by the Commission that did not bear his imprint. Like-minded officials in other Directorate Generals and in the Court forged powerful tools from the fundamental freedoms and the provisions on state aid. It took a while before outsiders realized what had happened, namely, that some scanty provisions of the EC treaty had been transformed into a coherent constitution for the economy. MESTMÄCKER himself wrote a number of programmatic articles on the subject: "Economic Order and State Constitution"

---

* Director, Max Planck Project Group "Common Goods: Law, Politics and Economics", Bonn. I am grateful to Talia Einhorn. Had she not coaxed me into it, I would never have written this text down. Thanks are also due to Darrell Arnold for his painstaking efforts to make me sound like an Englishman.

[1] Karl Popper, *Das Elend des Historizismus* (Tübingen: Mohr 1987).

of 1975 paved the way;[2] "*Ordnungspolitik* for Europe" of 1987[3] ensued; the views culminated in "The Return of Civil Society and its Law" of 1991.[4] This is an attractive program (as shall be discussed in section 1 below). But it meets with serious criticism too (section 2). An appropriate solution consists of the division of labour between Europe and the Member States (section 3).

1. The programme

A shorthand version of the normative programme reads thus: Civil society, the *Bürgerliche Gesellschaft*, is beneficial for all, and should return, fostered and secured. European Community law contains a constitution for the economy, whose main task consists of safeguarding civil society. This makes Europe the stronghold of the fight to save the Member States' civil society.

Civil society is a society of liberty. Its economy is reigned by sovereign consumers. Economic planning is decentralized. Individual economic plans are co-ordinated in the marketplace. The proper task of government is to provide the institutions necessary for a "society of private law", namely, private law and antitrust law – the latter preventing the market from self-destruction.

This is a long-term strategy. Public-choice theory helps clarify why it has attained so little credit in the Member States. Politicians have a much better chance of winning the next election when they go for short-term effects.[5] They pump small amounts of money into the economy. They protect national industries from global competition. They allow interest groups to organize effectively. The long-term growth of the economy is sacrificed for short-term distributional gains, or simply for a quiet life now.

It is much easier for the EC to combat this type of slack than for Member States' institutions to do so, because both the European Commission and the European Court of Justice are powerful organs, not directly controlled by the electorate.[6] The EC Treaty turns out to be a ruse of reason. Its fundamental

---

[2] Ernst Joachim Mestmäcker, "Wirtschaftsordnung und Staatsverfassung", *FS Franz Böhm zum 80. Geburtstag* (E. Sauermann and E. J. Mestmäcker [eds.]) (Tübingen: Mohr 1975) 383ff.

[3] Ernst Joachim Mestmäcker, "Auf dem Weg zu einer Ordnungspolitik in Europa", *FS von der Groeben zu seinem 80. Geburtstag* (E. J. Mestmäcker [ed.]) (Baden-Baden: Nomos 1987) 9-49.

[4] Ernst Joachim Mestmäcker, "Die Wiederkehr der bürgerlichen Gesellschaft und ihres Rechts", 10 *Rechtshistorisches Journal* (1991) 177-192.

[5] See only James M. Buchanan and Gordon Tullock, *The Calculus of Consent. Logical Foundations of Constitutional Democracy* (Ann Arbor: University of Michigan Press 1962).

[6] Programmatic Giandomenico Majone, "Nonmajoritarian Institutions and the Limits of Democratic Governance. A Political Transaction-Cost Approach", 157 *Journal of Institutional and Theoretical Economics* (2001) 57-78.

freedoms, antitrust rules and institutions for the supervision of state aid were all meant to combat protectionism and protect the common market. But they have also a beneficial side-effect within the Members States. Even if the States have not succeeded in setting up a proper economic constitution internally, one is imposed on them from the outside. The Member States come under a regime of imposed liberty.

This is a good thing on three counts. Economists, when they argue normatively, tend to be utilitarians.[7] Thomas Jefferson engrained one of the best-known and most succinct utilitarian phrases into the American Declaration of Independence: the right to "the pursuit of happiness".[8] In the realm of economics, the greatest happiness consists in economic growth. The normative goal, to use another famous formula, is to make the cake bigger so that everyone can get a larger piece.

Civil society, based on private and antitrust law, is also a society of individual liberty. Economic decisions are not centrally ordained, but individually chosen. Giving individuals economic freedom is also the best way to secure their independence from the dictatorial will of others. Power and responsibility become linked. Whoever wants to exercise power over other people has to pay for it and must forgo alternative, more profitable ways of using his funds. The German Ordoliberals have always stressed this point.[9]

Finally, the institutions of a private law society also have a beneficial side-effect on democratic government. The democratically elected parliament is legally free to make decisions within the confines of the constitution. But politically, parliamentary autonomy is always precarious. Individuals and organized groups always try to impose their wills on members of parliament and on political parties. A market economy is not a vaccination against this disease, but of all the economic orders it is the least dangerous for democracy, since competition permanently endangers and often actually erodes economic power. Antitrust law is thus also a means for safeguarding parliamentary autonomy. This point has also been made repeatedly by Ordoliberals.[10]

---

[7] The founding father of utilitarianism is Jeremy Bentham, see Jeremy Bentham, *The Principles of Morals and Legislation* (Buffalo, NY: Prometheus Books 1988).

[8] The Declaration of Independence of July 4, 1766, reads: "We hold these truths to be self-evident, that all men are created equal, that they are endowed by their Creator with certain unalienable Rights, that among these are Life, Liberty, and the *pursuit of Happiness*. That to secure these rights, Governments are instituted among Men, deriving their just powers from the consent of the governed" (emphasis added).

[9] See only Walter Eucken, *Die Grundlagen der Nationalökonomie* (Berlin, New York: Springer 1965).

[10] See only Franz Böhm, *Wirtschaftsordnung und Staatsverfassung* (Tübingen: J.C.B. Mohr 1950).

2. QUALIFICATIONS

Single-mindedness can be a good thing, if the one goal on which all efforts are concentrated is a worthy one. Ordoliberals are convinced that this is the case. So far, history seems to be on their side. Since the foundation of the European Economic Community in 1957, the Member States have experienced decades of economic growth, individual freedom, self-fulfilment and peace. After the fall of the iron curtain, Central European countries were only too willing to follow suit. But, although they introduced the institutions of a private law society almost overnight, most of them are still nowhere nearly as successful as their Western counterparts. There are certainly many reasons for this partial failure,[11] but it does not seem far-fetched to take this experience as evidence that a market economy must be embedded in a much richer set of formal and informal institutions.[12] These additional institutions have to address at least three concerns, which will be discussed in the following sections: Market failures (section 2.1), the relativity of normative starting points (section 2.2), and the difficulty to sustain a market economy without a policy of redistribution (section 2.3). The European Community is well-prepared to meet the first challenge. It goes some way in responding to the second concern. But it has little to offer in response to the third concern.

2.1 **Market failure**

Welfare economics has long investigated the many reasons why markets fail. Externalities, natural monopolies, information asymmetries and prohibitive transaction costs are among the most prominent ones.[13] European Community law has not ignored the problem, and the Community itself has limited jurisdiction to legislate in these areas.[14] If the Community lacks jurisdiction, or has not exercised it, a complex system of rules and exceptions ensures that Member States are able to address the problem, while still remaining under European supervision. Fundamental freedoms have their explicit and implicit limitations. Antitrust rules have appropriate loopholes. The control over state aids exercised

---

[11] From the rich literature see only Jens Bastian, *The Political Economy of Transition in Central and Eastern Europe. The Light(s) at the End of the Tunnel* (Aldershot, U.K.: Ashgate 1998).

[12] More on the embeddedness of markets from Marc Granovetter, "Economic Action and Social Structure. The Problem of Embeddedness", 91 *American Journal of Sociology* (1985) 481-510.

[13] Comprehensive Michael Fritsch, Thomas Wein *et al.*, *Marktversagen und Wirtschaftspolitik. Mikroökonomische Grundlagen staatlichen Handelns* (München: Vahlen 1999).

[14] The basic provisions are Art. 94 and 95 EC Treaty (ex Art. 100 and 100a ECT).

by the Commission gives the Member States sufficient freedom to correct market failures.

2.2 Fundamental normative relativity

The Ordoliberal programme has three normative roots: utilitarianism, liberalism and democracy. It is hard to find institutions serving that many purposes at once. But there are, nonetheless, competing normative starting points, competing models of man and competing models of nature.[15] Fairness concepts rank among the most prominent. They define happiness in relative, not absolute, terms. Those who adhere to these concepts value a fair chance for everybody, maybe even equality, more than overall welfare.[16] There is no theoretical basis on which one of these starting points could supersede the other.[17]

European Community law is much less prepared for this challenge. It is true that, with each revision, more and more provisions have been introduced into the Treaty to balance the original market orientation. A high level of employment in areas enjoying social protection, the equality of men and women, economic and social cohesion, and solidarity now rank among the Community's explicit goals.[18] The Community has its own health, cultural and consumer protection policy.[19] Under the heading of subsidiarity, the Member States are given more and more leeway in treating what they consider to be a public service.[20] These represent substantial inroads into the original Ordoliberal programme. Yet, to date, the Community lacks a proper institutional framework for balancing competing, but incompatible, normative conceptions. This is not surprising because, despite all the reforms, the Community remains an issue-specific polity. Unlike a sovereign state, its jurisdiction is strictly limited to the issues the Member States have conferred upon it.

---

[15] Programmatic M. Thompson, Richard Ellis *et al.*, *Cultural theory* (Boulder, Colo.: Westview 1990).

[16] Fairness concepts are pretty divergent. From the rich literature see K.G. Binmore, *Game Theory and the Social Contract* (Cambridge, Mass.: MIT Press 1994); John Rawls, *A Theory of Justice* (Cambridge, Mass.: Belknap Press of Harvard Univeristy Press 1999).

[17] For the consequences of this insight see Christoph Engel, "Offene Gemeinwohldefinitionen", 32 *Rechtstheorie* (2001) 23-52.

[18] Art. 2 EC Treaty.

[19] Art. 3 p, q, t EC Treaty.

[20] Art. 86 II, 16 EC Treaty, see also Commission Communication on Public Services, *OJ* [2001] C 17/4; *COM* (2001) 598/5 of 17 October 2001.

2.3 Distribution

The third concern is the most serious. European economic policy is not based on a distribution policy, although, admittedly, it has some distributional elements. The Common Agricultural Policy is basically a redistribution machanism, and "cohesion" in Europe means regional redistribution. The European Community spends more than three quarters of its budget on these two policies. But the Community budget is negligible, compared to the budgets of the Member States.[21] More importantly, Community redistribution is confined to the abovementioned sectors. Admittedly, there is also a section of the EC treaty on social policy. It even includes plans to set up a European social fund.[22] But this does not mean that true European solidarity aims at social justice across Europe.[23]

Most Ordoliberals will intuitively think that this is not a weakness, but rather one of the strengths of the European Community. They have seen too much naked rent-seeking clothed in terms of distributional justice.[24] They may even recall Jean-Jacques Rousseau's *volonté générale* degenerating into *volonté de tous.*[25] Those who do not believe in utilitarian or liberal values will not be concerned by this criticism. But this will only lead to a conceptual impasse in the form of incompatible normative starting points. On closer examination, however, even utilitarians and liberals must admit that some degree of redistribution is inevitable. Even a civil society governed by private and antitrust law cannot do without it. There are four reasons for this.

First of all, individuals are not born under a true veil of ignorance or uncertainty.[26] In the US, a dishwasher can become a millionaire. But very few dishwashers actually do, and even fewer millionaires become dishwashers later in life. Parents and education remain good predictors for economic status. Everybody can seize the opportunities provided by private and antitrust law, but some do start from a much better position. In conformity with this perspective, a

---

[21] For the details see Der Wissenschaftliche Beirat beim Bundesministerium für Wirtschaft: *Neuordnung des Finanzierungssystems der Europäischen Gemeinschaft: Gutachten vom Februar 1998 bis Juli 2000* (Stuttgart 2000) 2005-2041.

[22] Comprehensive Maximilian Fuchs, *Kommentar zum Europäischen Sozialrecht* (Baden-Baden: Nomos 2000).

[23] This is the prime concern of Fritz Wilhelm Scharpf, *Regieren in Europa. Effektiv und Demokratisch?* (Frankfurt: Campus 1999).

[24] Classic on this Geoffrey Brennan and James M. Buchanan, *The Reason of Rules. Constitutional Political Economy* (Cambridge, New York: Cambridge University Press 1985).

[25] Jean-Jacques Rousseau, *Du contrat social; ou, Principes du droit politique* (1763).

[26] Rawls is immune against this criticism. He employs the veil of ignorance as a normative construct, not as an assumption about the facts; Buchanan and Tullock; Brennan and Buchanan seem more vulnerable, since they insist on the application to real people.

policy of redistribution offers compensation to those with less favourable opportunities in exchange for their acceptance of rules that allow the rich to become even richer.

Secondly, the institutions of private and antitrust law not only distribute opportunities in an asymmetric manner; not so rarely, they even inflict distributional losses on chance victims. This is pervasive for what welfare economists call pecuniary externalities. Usually, proponents hasten to add that these externalities are normatively irrelevant.[27] Indeed, introducing a general policy to compensate for pecuniary externalities would be tantamount to abolishing the market economy, since competition in static markets is both a positive and a negative sanction at the same time. If the market share goes to a competitor, it is lost for the original provider. If his offer is below his long-term average costs, his firm will lose money. Actually, competition is often even harsher. A successful substitute can ruin a whole industry. Hard-nosed utilitarians will not have much sympathy for the loser. But it is not always the loser's fault, and those who depend on him are even less at fault.

While all this is well known to economists, many are not aware that it is not so rare for the institutions of private law and antitrust law to inflict even technical externalities on outsiders. One example is legal personality. In principle, torts are a legal tool for internalising potential externalities. The tortfeasor has to offer compensation to the victim for appropriations outside the market place. But if the tortfeasor goes bankrupt, this legal obligation does not help the victim. Now the very purpose of legal personality is to limit liability. Put bluntly, the legal order accepts occasional uncompensated torts because it has an interest in the potential for growth inherent in the option to run a business under a regime of limited liability. The many restrictions inherent in tort law provide another example. Some damages are never compensated for, like the opportunity cost of time. The standard of proof for others is so high that victims rarely win their case. Complex causal relations between an action and the violation of a protected good are a case in point. In such situations, jurisprudence is not content with mere causality. It requires that a social or professional rule be violated.[28] From a utilitarian perspective, these restrictions make sense, because liability, even for the least likely damage, might easily have a chilling effect on economic activities. Instead, those who become chance victims of pecuniary or technical externalities, which are justified by the institutions of a

---

[27] Cf. Fritsch, Wein *et al.*, *supra* n. 13, 75.

[28] The technical term of German tort law is *Verkehrssicherungspflicht*, illustrative Ulrich Foerste, "Deliktische Haftung", *Produkthaftungshandbuch* (F. G. v. Westphalen [ed.]) (München: Beck 1997) 1-977.

private law society, must receive compensation through a general policy of redistribution.

Thirdly, a society of private law faces specific risks unknown to other societies. The first has been well studied by Ordoliberals: it is even the hallmark of their school. They have always recognised the possibility of markets destroying themselves. This is precisely why they have called for a strong state, able to impose antitrust rules on egoistic market players.[29] But even the Ordoliberal state is not a dictatorship. It is bound by the rule of law. And not so rarely, this means that there is an implementation deficit.[30]

Similarly, those responsible for institutional design have not been unaware of the systemic risk inherent in market economies.[31] Inflation and deflation, bankruptcy cascades and speculative bubbles all hit outsiders, too. There are powerful institutions to contain these risks: central banks and agencies for banking supervision and capital markets supervision. But none of these institutions can have more than a best-efforts policy. If an organization's best efforts prove insufficient, a general social network, i.e. redistribution, must be used.

Fourthly, there is rarely just one institution to correct an instance of market failure. Typically, the institutional options are characterised by significantly different distribution effects. If they are clever, rent-seekers go for these options, rather than for pure redistribution based on majority decisions. That way, distributional gains are concealed and thus less open to public scrutiny. More importantly even, it would often be irrational for those who lose on the distribution side to oppose the institution once it has been implemented, since, even considering the distributional loss, they would often still be worse off without the institution. This is the case if the unchecked public bad hits them even harder than the distributional loss.[32] *Ex ante*, there is not much to be done about this problem. Virtually all institutions that aim at correcting market failures have distribution effects. And the available institutional options differ in many other ways: How reliably do they correct the market failure? How great is the transaction cost involved? How well are the rule of law and democratic control preserved? How cognitively sophisticated is an institution? How well is it prepared for its own

---

[29] For a comprehensive view of one of the most prominent current partisans of the Ordoliberal school see Wernhard Möschel, "The Proper Scope of Government Viewed from an Ordoliberal Perspective. The Example of Competition Policy", 157 *Journal of Institutional and Theoretical Economics* (2001) 3-13.

[30] Illustrative Christoph Engel, *Verhandelter Netzzugang* (Baden-Baden: Nomos 2002).

[31] Comprehensive Martin Hellwig, "Systemische Risiken im Finanzsektor", *Finanzmärkte im Spannungsfeld von Globalisierung, Regulierung und Geldpolitik* (D. Duwendag [ed.]) (Berlin: Duncker & Humblot 1997) 123-150.

[32] This is the basic point of Jack Knight, *Institutions and Social Conflict* (Cambridge, England/ New York, NY: Cambridge University Press 1992).

evolution?[33] But if a certain degree of rent-seeking is included in the costs of running a market economy, some general policy of redistribution must exist to compensate those who have no opportunity to play this game.

3. A DIVISION OF LABOUR BETWEEN THE EUROPEAN COMMUNITY AND THE MEMBER STATES

All this might read like an outright rejection of the Ordoliberal approach, but that would be a gross misinterpretation. Civil society, as safeguarded by the institutions of private law and antitrust law, is indeed highly precarious. Market economy and majority rule are not easily wed. In principle, the balance might be struck inside Member States. Institutions like the former *Bundesbank* and the *Bundeskartellamt* take some steps in this direction. A constitutional court as powerful as the *Bundesverfassungsgericht* is, in principle, well-prepared to impose liberty on political actors and majorities who are too narrowly focused on short-term gains. But, in practice, the *Bundesverfassungsgericht* does not have a particularly strong record on protecting economic freedoms. Most of the Member States of the European Community do not even have a similarly powerful constitutional court. It therefore makes a lot of sense to entrust the protection of the Ordoliberal ideals to an outside actor. When designing or, in our case, developing these outside institutions, however, one should keep in mind that optimisation, not maximisation, is the goal. Civil society is not a proper model for society as a whole. It is one important and beneficial concept for living together that must be properly balanced with competing, equally legitimate views. It must also be embedded in an adequate policy of redistribution.

When carrying out this optimisation exercise, one should consider the interplay between the Community and the Member States. The Member States are in a better position to balance civil society concerns with different normative views, as only the Member States are true democracies to date. The Member States are also better placed to design and implement a social safety network and other elements of redistribution, because so far there is no true European *demos*. Solidarity is basically still a national affair. This approach has two important ramifications: (i) The European Community must give the Member States sufficient leeway to perform their complementary tasks, and (ii) it might not be so wise to integrate more and more competing goals and tasks into the European Community. What has been a healthy division of labour might otherwise turn into a fuzzy multiplication of regulatory authorities.

---

[33] Illustrative for institutions solving waste management problems Christoph Engel, *Abfallrecht und Abfallpolitik* (Baden-Baden: Nomos 2002).

List of Publications Ernst-Joachim Mestmäcker

I Books

1. Verbandsstatistiken als Mittel zur Förderung und Beschränkung des Wettbewerbs in den USA und Deutschland; 1952 (Diss.).
2. Verwaltung, Konzerngewalt und Rechte der Aktionäre. Eine rechtsvergleichende Untersuchung nach deutschem Aktienrecht und dem Recht der *corporations* in den Vereinigten Staaten; 1958.
3. Die Vermittlung von europäischem und nationalem Recht im System unverfälschten Wettbewerbs; 1969.
4. Europäisches Wettbewerbsrecht, C. H. Beck, München 1974;
   (New edition in preparation, expected 2002)
5. Die sichtbare Hand des Rechts. Über das Verhältnis von Rechtsordnung und Wirtschaftssystem;
   Nomos, Baden-Baden 1978 (collection of essays).
6. Recht und ökonomisches Gesetz. Über die Grenzen von Staat, Gesellschaft und Privatautonomie;
   Nomos, Wirtschaftsrecht und Wirtschaftspolitik Band 50, Baden-Baden 1978; 2. Aufl. 1984 (collection of essays).
7. Medienkonzentration und Meinungsvielfalt. Eine vergleichende wirtschaftsrechtliche Untersuchung im Auftrage des Bundesministers des Inneren;
   Nomos, Wirtschaftsrecht und Wirtschaftspolitik Band 54, Baden-Baden 1978.
8. Europäische Kartellpolitik auf dem Stahlmarkt. Zum Rechtsschutz stahlverbrauchender Unternehmen in der Montanunion;
   Nomos, Wirtschaftsrecht und Wirtschaftspolitik Band 72, Baden-Baden 1983.
9. Der verwaltete Wettbewerb. Eine vergleichende Untersuchung über den Schutz von Freiheit und Lauterkeit im Wettbewerbsrecht;
   Mohr (Siebeck), Wirtschaftswissenschaftliche und wirtschaftsrechtliche Untersuchungen (Walter Eucken Institut Freiburg i. Br.) Band 19, Tübingen 1984.
10. Recht in der offenen Gesellschaft. Hamburger Beiträge zum deutschen, europäischen und internationalen Wirtschafts- und Medienrecht;
    Nomos, Wirtschaftsrecht und Wirtschaftspolitik Band 125, Baden-Baden 1993 (collection of essays).
11. Aufgaben des Rechts in marktwirtschaftlichen Ordnungen;
    translated into Japanese by Prof. Masaru Hayakawa, Kyoto 1997.

Talia Einhorn, ed., Spontaneous Order, Organization and the Law – Liber Amicorum Ernst-Joachim Mestmäcker © 2003 T.M.C.ASSER PRESS, *The Hague, The Netherlands*

II Shorter publications

1. Das marktbeherrschende Unternehmen im Recht der Wettbewerbsbeschränkungen; Mohr (Siebeck), Tübingen 1958.
2. Sind urheberrechtliche Verwertungsgesellschaften Kartelle?; Vahlen, Berlin/Frankfurt a.M. 1960.
3. Über Mitbestimmung und Vermögensverteilung; Mohr (Siebeck), Vorträge und Aufsätze des Walter Eucken Instituts Freiburg Band 43, Tübingen 1974.
4. Vereinbarkeit von Preisregelungen auf dem Arzneimittelmarkt mit dem Recht der Europäischen Wirtschaftsgemeinschaft; Nomos, Schriftenreihe Europäische Wirtschaft Band 97, Baden-Baden 1979.
5. Regelbildung und Rechtsschutz in marktwirtschaftlichen Ordnungen; Mohr (Siebeck), Vorträge und Aufsätze des Walter Eucken Instituts Freiburg Band 100,Tübingen 1985.
6. Organisationen in spontanen Ordnungen. Friedrich A. von Hayek-Vorlesung 1991; Hrsg: Albert-Ludwigs-Universität Freiburg im Breisgau, Walter Eucken Institut Freiburg im Breisgau, Haufe, Freiburg 1992.
7. Die Wirtschaftsverfassung in der Europäischen Union. Referat im Rahmen der Vortragsreihe „Das Weißbuch der Kommission und die Realität des Binnenmarktes – Erfolge und Mißerfolge“, Bonn, 8. Februar 1993; Rheinische Friedrich-Wilhelms-Universität Bonn, Zentrum für Europäisches Wirtschaftsrecht, Vorträge und Berichte Nr. 28.
8. Bausteine zu einer Wirtschaftsverfassung – Franz Böhm in Jena [Referat in Jena am 14. Juni 1995 im Rahmen der] Vortragsreihe „Lectiones Jenenses“; Schriftenreihe des Max-Planck-Instituts zur Erforschung von Wirtschaftssystemen Heft 4, Jena 1996.
9. Wandlungen in der Verfaßtheit der Europäischen Gemeinschaft; Bielefelder Universitätsgespräche und Vorträge Heft 8 (2000).

III Co-Author und Editor

1. Ziele und Methoden der europäischen Integration. Bericht über eine Arbeitsgemeinschaft im Zentrum für interdisziplinäre Forschung der Universität Bielefeld (Hrsg. zus. mit H. von der Groeben); Nomos, Wirtschaftsrecht und Wirtschaftspolitik Band 31, Baden-Baden 1972; 2. Aufl. 1974 unter dem Titel: Verfassung oder Technokratie für Europa?, Fischer Athenäum Taschenbücher.

2. Normenzwecke und Systemfunktionen im Recht der Wettbewerbsbeschränkungen; (gemeinsam mit E. Hoppmann);
Mohr (Siebeck), Vorträge und Aufsätze des Walter Eucken Instituts Freiburg Band 50;Tübingen 1974.

3. Kommentar zum deutschen Urheberrecht (Co-Autor und Hrsg. zus mit E. Schulze);
Loseblattsammlung, Metzner, Frankfurt a.M. 1974 ff. bzw. Luchterhand, Neuwied.

4. Kommunikation ohne Monopole. Über Legitimation und Grenzen des Fernmeldemonopols (Hrsg.)
Ein Symposium des Max-Planck-Instituts für ausländisches und internationales Privatrecht, Hamburg, Nomos, Wirtschaftsrecht und Wirtschaftspolitik Band 67, Baden-Baden 1980.

5. Franz Böhm. Freiheit und Ordnung in der Marktwirtschaft (Hrsg.);
Nomos, Wirtschaftsrecht und Wirtschaftspolitik Band 60, Baden-Baden 1980 (Sammlung).

6. Eine Ordnungspolitik für Europa. Festschrift für Hans von der Groeben zum 80. Geburtstag (Hrsg. zus. mit H. Möller und H.-P. Schwarz);
Nomos, Baden-Baden 1987.

7. Rechtsstaat und Menschenwürde. Festschrift für Werner Maihofer zum 70. Geburtstag (Hrsg. zus. mit A. Kaufmann und H. F. Zacher);
Klostermann, Frankfurt a.M. 1988.

8. Offene Rundfunkordnung: Prinzipien für den Wettbewerb im grenzüberschreitenden Rundfunk (Hrsg.);
Verlag Bertelsmann Stiftung, Gütersloh 1988.

9. Wettbewerb in der Weiterbildung an Hochschulen. Die Anwendung des Wettbewerbsrechts auf das Angebot wissenschaftlicher Weiterbildung durch die staatlichen Hochschulen. Rechtsgutachten (zus. mit W. Veelken);
Hrsg.: Bundesminister für Bildung und Wissenschaft, Reihe Bildung – Wissenschaft – Aktuell Nr. 2/90, Bonn 1990.

10. Rules for Free International Trade in Services. Symposium in Tel Aviv (Hrsg. zus. mit D. Friedmann);
Nomos, Wirtschaftsrecht und Wirtschaftspolitik Band 107, Baden-Baden 1990.

11. Selbstkontrolle und Persönlichkeitsschutz in den Medien. Ein Symposium der Bertelsmann Stiftung am 27. März 1990 in Gütersloh (Hrsg.);
Verlag Bertelsmann Stiftung, Gütersloh 1990.

12. Der Einfluß des europäischen Gemeinschaftsrechts auf die deutsche Rundfunkordnung (zus. mit Chr. Engel, K. Gabriel-Bräutigam u. M. Hoffmann) Nomos, Wirtschaftsrecht der internationalen Telekommunikation Band 15, Baden-Baden 1990.

13. Die Gaswirtschaft im Binnenmarkt. Beiträge zur gemeinschaftsrechtlichen und ordnungspolitische Diskussion von Marktordnungen, Common Carriage und Preistransparenz (zus. mit H. Gröner u. J. Basedow);
Nomos, Wirtschaftsrecht und Wirtschaftsrecht und Wirtschaftspolitik Band 109, Baden-Baden 1990.

14. Selbstkontrolle und Persönlichkeitsschutz in den Medien. Ein Symposium der Bertelsmann Stiftung am 27. März 1990 in Gütersloh (Hrsg. unter Mitarb. von M. Schmidt und M. Spilker);
Verlag Bertelsmann Stiftung, Gütersloh 1990.

15. Das Gesellschaftsrecht der Konzerne im internationalen Vergleich. Ein Symposium des Max-Planck-Instituts für ausländisches und internationales Privatrecht, Hamburg (Hrsg. zus. mit P. Behrens);
Nomos, Wirtschaftsrecht und Wirtschaftspolitik, Band 110, Baden-Baden 1991.

16. Das Embargo gegen Irak und Kuwait. Entschädigungsansprüche gegen die Europäische Gemeinschaft und gegen die Bundesrepublik Deutschland. Rechtsgutachten (zus. mit Chr. Engel);
Nomos, Wirtschaftsrecht und Wirtschaftspolitik Band 117, Baden-Baden 1991.

17. Natural Gas in the Internal Market. A Review of Energy Policy (Hrsg.);
Graham & Trotman, International Energy and Resources Law and Policy Series, London 1993.

18. Wanderer zwischen Musik, Politik und Recht. Festschrift für Reinhold Kreile zu seinem 65. Geburtstag (Hrsg. zus. mit J. Becker/P. Lerche);
Nomos, Baden-Baden 1994.

19. Kommunikation ohne Monopole II. Ein Symposium über Ordnungsprinzipien im Wirtschaftsrecht der Telekommunikation und der elektronischen Medien (Hrsg.);
Nomos, Wirtschaftsrecht der internationalen Telekommunikation Band 23, Baden-Baden 1995.

20. Multimediadienste. Struktur und staatliche Aufgaben nach deutschem und europäischem Recht, (auf der Grundlage eines Rechtsgutachtens für das BMWi) (zus. mit M. Bullinger);
Nomos, Wirtschaftsrecht der internationalen Telekommunikation Band 30, Baden-Baden 1997.

21. EG Wettbewerbsrecht, Kommentar (Hrsg. zus. mit U. Immenga);
2 Bände, Verlag C.H. Beck, München 1997.

22. Systemtransformation in Mittel- und Osteuropa und ihre Folgen für Banken, Börsen und Kreditsicherheiten (Hrsg. zus. mit U. Drobnig, K. H. Hopt, H. Kötz);
Mohr Siebeck, Tübingen 1998.

23. Netzwettbewerb, Netzzugang und „Roaming" im Mobilfunk. Eine Untersuchung nach TKG, GWB und dem Recht der EG (zus. mit H. Schweitzer);
Wirtschaftsrecht der internationalen Telekommunikation Band 38, Nomos, Baden-Baden 1999.

24. GWB – Gesetz gegen Wettbewerbsbeschränkungen, Kommentar (Hrsg. zus. mit Immenga);
Beck, München 1981, 2. Aufl. 1992; 3. Aufl. 2001.

25. Aufbruch nach Europa. 75 Jahre Max-Planck-Institut für ausländisches und internationales Privatrecht (Hrsg. zus. mit J. Basedow/U. Drobnig/R. Ellger/K.J. Hopt/H. Kötz/ R. Kulms);
Mohr (Siebeck), Tübingen 2001.

IV Articles in Law Journals, Festschriften, Collections of Essays and Encyclopedias

1. Preis- und Produktionsregelungen im Rahmen von Rationalisierungskartellen?
in: JZ 1953, S. 329 ff.

2. Ausschließlichkeitsverträge, Kopplungsverträge und offene Märkte,
in: JZ 1954, S. 162 ff.

3. Offene Preise, Diskriminierungen und Wettbewerbsbeschränkungen in der Montanunion,
in: WuW 1955, S. 155 ff.

4. Der Böhm-Entwurf eines Gesetzes gegen Wettbewerbsbeschränkungen,
in: WuW 1955, S. 285 ff.

5. Der Bericht der englischen Monopolkommission,
in: ORDO Band VIII (1956), S. 266 ff.;

6. Diskriminierungen, Dirigismus und Wettbewerb,
in: WuW 1957, S. 21 ff.; S. 92 ff.

7. Dekartellierung und Wettbewerb in der Rechtsprechung der deutschen Gerichte,
in: ORDO Band IX (1957), S. 100 ff.

8. Artikel zu den folgenden Stichwörtern im Staatslexikon der Görres-Gesellschaft (1958):
Diskriminierungen von Einzelunternehmen
Europäische Gemeinschaft für Kohle und Stahl
Kartelle
Konzerne
Wettbewerbsbeschränkungen.

9. Eingriffserwerb und Rechtsverletzung in der ungerechtfertigten Bereicherung, in: JZ 1958, S. 521 ff.

10. Die Unternehmenskonzentration im ausländischen Recht, in: Die Konzentration in der Wirtschaft, Schriften des Vereins für die Socialpolitik N.F. Bd. 20/II, 1960, S. 989 ff.

11. Zur Auslegung des Verbots von Tarifdiskriminierungen im Recht der Europäischen Gemeinschaft für Kohle und Stahl, in: Annales Universitatis Saraviensis Bd. VII (1959), S. 203 ff.

12. Das Verbot von Preisdikriminierungen im Recht der Europäischen Gemeinschaft für Kohle und Stahl, in: Kartelle und Monopole im modernen Recht, Bd. I, 1961, S. 309 ff.

13. Zur aktienrechtlichen Stellung der Verwaltung bei Kapitalerhöhungen, in: BB 1961, S. 945 ff.

14. Das Rabattkartell im Gesetz gegen Wettbewerbsbeschränkungen, in: ORDO Bd. XIII (1962), S. 233 ff.

15. Soll das Stiftungsrecht bundesgesetzlich vereinheitlicht und reformiert werden? Ggf. mit welchen Grundzügen? in: Verhandlungen des 44. Deutschen Juristentages Bd. II, 1964.

16. Wirtschaft und Verfassung, in: D(tm)V 1964, S. 606 ff.

17. Das Verhältnis der Wirtschaftswissenschaft zur Rechtswissenschaft im Aktienrecht, in: Verhandlungen auf der Arbeitstagung der Vereins für Socialpolitik, 1963 = JuS 1963, S. 417 ff.

18. Über die normative Kraft privatrechtlicher Verträge, in: JZ 1964, S. 441 ff.

19. Offene Märkte im System unverfälschten Wettbewerbs in der EWG, in: Wirtschaftsordnung und Rechtsordnung. Festschrift zum 70. Geburtstag von Franz Böhm, 1965, S. 345 ff.

20. Competition Law in the EEC, in: World Unfair Competition, Vol. I, 1965, S. 38 ff.

21. The Relation of the Law of Unfair Competition to the Law on Restraint of Competition in Germany, Reprint from: Unfair Competition, edited by the British Institute of International and Comparative Law, London 1966.

22. Zur Beurteilung von Unternehmenszusammenschlüssen nach Art. 86 EWG-Vertrag, in: Probleme des europäischen Rechts. Festschrift für Walter Hallstein, 1966, S. 322 ff.

23. State Trading Monopolies in the EEC, in: 20 Vanderbilt Law Review 321 (1967).

24. Zur Systematik des Rechts der verbundenen Unternehmen im neuen Aktienrecht, in: Das Unternehmen in der Rechtsordnung – Festschrift für Heinrich Kronstein, 1967.
25. Über das Verhältnis des Rechts der Wettbewerbsbeschränkungen zum Privatrecht, in: AcP 1968, S. 235 ff.
26. Verpflichtet § 22 die Kartellbehörde, marktbeherrschenden Unternehmen ein Verhalten aufzuerlegen, als ob Wettbewerb bestünde? in: Betrieb 1968, S. 1800 ff.
27. Die Wettbewerbsregeln des EWG-Vertrages im nationalen Recht – Eine Kritik der Zweischrankentheorie, in: Wettbewerb als Aufgabe. Nach zehn Jahren Gesetz gegen Wettbewerbsbeschränkungen, 1968, S. 567 ff.
28. Rechtliche Aspekte des Stiftungswesens, in: Wissenschaft und Wirtschaft 1969, S. 11 ff.
29. Parallele Geltung von Verbotsnormen des deutschen und europäischen Rechts der Wettbewerbsbeschränkungen, in: BB 1968, S. 1297 ff.
30. Verfaßte Freiheit in einer neuen Universität, in: Was wird aus der Universität? Standpunkte zur Hochschulreform, 1969, S. 101 ff.
31. Die Abgrenzung von öffentlich-rechtlichem und privatrechtlichem Handeln im Wettbewerbsrecht, in: NJW 1969, S. 1 ff.
32. Pressefreiheit im Lichte des Wettbewerbsrechts, in: Juristen-Jahrbuch Bd. 10, 1969/70, S. 102 ff. = Pressefreiheit, Entwurf eines Gesetzes zum Schutze freier Meinungsbildung und Dokumentation des Arbeitskreises Pressefreiheit, 1970, 127 ff.
33. Der Mißbrauch marktbeherrschender Stellungen im deutschen, italienischen und europäischen Recht, in: Veröffentlichungen des Vereins für den Gedankenaustausch deutscher und italienischer Juristen e.V., 1970, Heft 5, S. 1 ff.
34. Wettbewerbs- und Strukturpolitik. Zur Reform des Gesetzes gegen Wettbewerbsbeschränkungen, in: Tagungsprotokoll Nr. 34 der Aktionsgemeinschaft Soziale Marktwirtschaft, 1970, S. 26 ff.
35. Das Stiftungswesen in Deutschland (gemeinsam mit D. Reuter), in: Schriftenreihe zum Stiftungswesen Bd. 5, 1971; English version in: Trusts and Foundations in Europe, 1972, S. 95 ff.; French version in: Les Fondations en Europe, 1973.

36. Die Beurteilung von Unternehmenskonzentrationen nach den Wettbewerbsregeln des EWG-Vertrages,
in: Die Konzentration in der Wirtschaft, Schriften des Vereins für Socialpolitik, N.F. Bd. 20/I, 2. Aufl. 1971, S. 733 ff;
English version in: Journal of World Trade Law 1972, S. 615 ff, 1973, S. 36 ff..

37. Warum das Kartellverbot nicht am Privatrecht scheitert. Zur funktionalen Interpretation von Normzwecken,
in: WuW 1971, S. 835 ff. (Festschrift für Eberhard Günther).

38. On the Multinational Corporation,
in: Antitrust Law Journal 1971, S. 986 ff.

39. Das Ende der Schutzrechtsgrenzen im Gemeinsamen Markt. Zum Grammophon-Urteil des Europäischen Gerichtshofes,
in: Schulze, Rechtsprechung zur Urheberrecht EuGH Nr. 1.

40. Probleme des Staatshandels im internationalen wie im europäischen Wirtschaftsrecht,
in: WiR Heft 1/1972.

41. Macht – Recht – Wirtschaftsverfassung. Vortrag, gehalten auf der Hundertjahrfeier des Vereins für Socialpolitik in Bonn am 5.9.1972,
in: Verhandlungen auf der Tagung des Vereins für Socialpolitik in Bonn 1972, Macht und ökonomisches Gesetz, Erster Halbband, 1973, S. 183 ff.
= ZHR 137 (1973), S. 97 ff;
English revised version in: German Economic Review Vol. 11, Nr. 3, 1973, S. 177 ff. = Law and State Vol. 10, 1974, S. 117 ff.

42. Das Prinzip der *rule of reason* und ähnliche Ausnahmemechanismen im Recht der Wettbewerbsbeschränkungen,
in: Kartell- und Monopolrecht, Cartel and Antitrust Law, Gottlieb Duttweiler Institute, 1973, S. 231 ff.

43. Wettbewerbspolitik in der Industriegesellschaft,
in: ZgesStaatsw 1973 = Liberal 1972, S. 610 ff.

44. Competition Policy in Germany,
in: Hearings, U.S. Senate, Antitrust Subcommittee, 2.10.1973; Bulletin de l'I.I.C.C. 1975, No. 3, S. 7 ff.

45. Durch Mitbestimmung zum neuen Laissez-faire,
teilw. abgedruckt in: FAZ vom 9.3.1974 unter dem Titel: Durch Mitbestimmung zum Nachtwächterstaat;
sowie in: Mitbestimmung – Wirtschaftsordnung – Grundgesetz. Protokoll der Wissenschaftlichen Konferenz des DGB vom 1.-3. Oktober 1975 in Frankfurt a.M., hrsg. von Heinz Oskar Vetter, Frankfurt a.M. 1976, S. 370 ff.

46. Zur gesellschaftsrechtlich organisierten Berufsfreiheit,
in: Festschrift für Harry Westermann zum 65. Geburtstag, 1974, S. 411 ff.

47. Den Markt zum Lehen,
in: Wirtschaftsordnung und Staatsverfassung. Festschrift für Franz Böhm zum 80. Geburtstag, 1975, S. 3 ff.

48. Wirtschaftsordnung und Staatsverfassung.
in: Wirtschaftsordnung und Staatsverfassung. Festschrift für Franz Böhm zum 80. Geburtstag, 1975, S. 383 ff.

49. Funktionen und bisherige Tätigkeit der Monopolkommission,
in: Schwerpunkte des Kartellrechts 1974/75, 1976, FIW-Schriftenreihe Heft 73, S. 43 ff.;
revised English version in: The German Economic Review, Vol. 14, 1976, S. 173 ff.

50. Wettbewerbsordnung und Betrieb,
in: Handwörterbuch der Betriebswirtschaft, 4. völlig neu gestaltete Auflage 1976, S. 4444 ff.

51. Multinationale Unternehmen im nationalen und internationalen Wirtschaftsrecht,
in: Sozialwissenschaftliche Studien für das Schweizerische Institut für Auslandsforschung Bd. 4 (NF), Recht und Macht in Politik und Wirtschaft, 1976, S. 109 ff.

52. Copyright in Community Law,
in: Journal of World Trade Law, Special supplement of Vol. 10, 1976.

53. An den Grenzen der Wettbewerbspolitik,
in: Wettbewerb im Wandel. Eberhard Günther zum 65. Geburtstag, 1976, S. 57 ff.

54. Selbstliebe und soziale Gerechtigkeit bei Adam Smith,
in: Festschrift für Konrad Duden zum 70. Geburtstag, 1977, S. 319 ff.

55. Die sichtbare Hand des Rechts,
in: Freiheit und Sachzwang. Beiträge zu Ehren Helmut Schelskys, 1977, S. 294 ff.

56. Franz Böhm in memoriam,
in: ZgS Bd. 133 (1977), S. 573 f.

57. Mißbrauch der Nachfragemacht und Möglichkeiten ihrer kartellrechtlichen Kontrolle,
in: Schwerpunkte des Kartellrechts 1976/1977, 1978, FIW-Schriftenreihe Heft 81, S. 15 ff.

58. Über die Rolle der Politik in der Marktwirtschaft. Dargestellt anhand eines unveröffentlichten Briefes von Franz Böhm,
in: ORDO Bd. 29 (1978), S. 3 ff.

59. Strukturwandel und Verfassung der Medien,
in: BDZV-Schriftenreihe Heft 14, 1979, S. 5 ff.

60. Grenzen der Gesellschaftspolitik in einer marktwirtschaftlichen Ordnung. Festvortrag anläßlich des 125jährigen Jubiläums der IHK Münster am 7. September 1979,
hrsg. von der IHK Münster 1.10.1979.

61. Die Rolle des Wettbewerbs im liberalen Gemeinwesen,
in: Liberalismus – nach wie vor. Grundgedanken und Zukunftsfragen, 1979, S. 103-121.

62. Über Selbständigkeit und Solidarität in der Marktwirtschaft,
in: Ludwig-Ehrhard-Preis für Wirtschaftspublizistik, hrsg. von der Ludwig-Erhard-Stiftung, Bonn 1980, S. 36 ff.

63. Fernmeldemonopol und Nachfragemacht. Wirtschaftsrechtliche und ordnungspolitische Probleme der hoheitlichen und unternehmerischen Funktionen der DBP,
in: ders. (Hrsg.), Kommunikation ohne Monopole. Über Legitimation und Grenzen des Fernmeldemonopols. Ein Symposium des Max-Planck-Instituts für ausländisches und internationales Privatrecht, Hamburg. Nomos, Wirtschaftsrecht und Wirtschaftspolitik Band 67, 1980, S. 161-199.

64. Freiheit und Ordnung in der Marktwirtschaft,
in: Franz Böhm, Beiträge zu Leben und Wirken. Forschungsbericht 8 der Konrad-Adenauer-Stiftung, 1980, S. 37-52.

65. Die nationale Preispolitik im Rahmen von Art. 30 EWGV,
in: Theorie und Politik der internationalen Wirtschaftsbeziehungen. Hans Möller zum 65. Geburtstag, 1980, S. 339-348.

66. Competition Policy and Antitrust. Some Comparative Observations.
in: Competition Policy: German and American Experience. A Symposium. ZgS 136 (1980), 387-407.

67. Mehrheitsglück und Minderheitsherrschaft. Zu Jeremy Benthams Kritik der Menschenrechte.
in: Wirtschaftspolitische Chronik (Institut für Wirtschaftspolitik an der Universität zu Köln), Heft 3, 1980, S. 179-192 ;
= Öffentliche Meinung und sozialer Wandel. Für Elisabeth Noelle-Neumann, 1982, S. 316-327.

68. Die Gewährleistung gerechter Wettbewerbsbedingungen in den Freihandelsabkommen der EG.
in: Festschrift für Konrad Zweigert zum 70. Geburtstag, 1981, S. 681-701.

69. Vom Bürgerkrieg als Utopie,
in: ORDO Bd. 32 (1981), S. 103-107.

70. Die Prävention in der Fusionskontrolle,
in: Europäisches Rechtsdenken in Geschichte und Gegenwart. Festschrift für Helmut Coing zum 70. Geburtstag, Hrsg. Norbert Horn, 1982, Bd. II, S. 373-394.

71. Providing Fair Conditions of Competition Under the Free Trade Agreements of the European Community,
in: Revista de Assuntos Europeos 1982, S. 39-61.

72. Stellungnahme zum Sondergutachten 11 der Monopolkommission "Wettbewerbsprobleme bei der Einführung von privatem Hörfunk und Fernsehen" (Nomos Verlag, Baden-Baden 1981),
in: WuW 1982, S. 273-275.

73. Die Anwendbarkeit des Gesetzes gegen Wettbewerbsbeschränkungen auf Zusammenschlüsse zu Rundfunkunternehmen. Festschrift für Eugen Ulmer zum 80. Geburtstag,
in: GRUR Int. 1983, S. 553-560.

74. Auf der Suche nach einer neuen Medienordnung,
in: Kooperativer Föderalismus – ein Modell für die Medienpolitik? Veröffentlichung der Stiftung für Kommunikationsforschung, 1983, S. 15-23.

75. Socialist Elements as Limits to Economic Growth – A Comment,
in: ORDO Bd. 34 (1983), S. 13-15.

76. Rechtsgrundlagen der Verträge über die Errichtung großer Industrieanlagen und Anlagen zur Rohstoffgewinnung auf Kompensationsbasis in den Beziehungen zwischen der Bundesrepublik Deutschland und der Sowjetunion.
in: Deutsches und sowjetisches Wirtschaftsrecht II.
Studien zum ausländischen und internationalen Wirtschaftsrecht Band 9, Mohr (Siebeck), Tübingen 1983, S. 207-226.

77. Comment on the papers by Robert W. Crandall and C. Christian v. Weizsäcker,
in: New Opportunities for Entrepreneurship, Symposium 1983 (hrsg. v. Herbert Giersch), Mohr (Siebeck) Tübingen 1984, S. 129-131.

78. Der selbstverwaltete Wettbewerb,
in: BAG-Nachrichten, 24. Jahrg., Nr. 7/8, 1984.

79. Freier oder selbstverwalteter Wettbewerb? Ein Gespräch über Konflikte zwischen Wettbewerbspolitik und Mittelstandsschutz,
in: Standpunkte 1, Veröffentlichung der Ludwig-Erhard-Stiftung, 1984, S. 1-47.

80. Pressefreiheit im Lichte des Wettbewerbsrechts,
in: Pressefreiheit, hrsg. von Jürgen Wilke, Wissenschaftliche Buchgesellschaft, Darmstadt 1984, S. 435-458.

81. Rechtsfragen einer Ordnung der Weltwirtschaft,
in: Einigkeit und Recht und Freiheit. Festschrift für Carl Carstens zum 70. Geburtstag, 1984, S. 417-427.

82. The Applicability of the ECSC-Cartel Prohibition (Article 65) During a "Manifest Crisis",
in: Michigan Law Review, Vol. 82, 1984, S. 1399-1414.

83. Die Vereinbarkeit der Leerkassettenabgabe und der Geräteabgabe (§ 53 Abs. 5 UrhG) mit dem europäischen Gemeinschaftsrecht,
in: GRUR Int. 1985, S. 13-19.

84. Performing Rights Organisations in the Common Market: Comparative Observations, in: International Business Lawyer, February 1985, S. 71-75.

85. The Impact of Deregulation on Trade in Services Agreements and on Telecommunications Monopolies in Europe,
in: Speakers' Papers, World Telecommunication Forum, organized by the ITU (April 18-19, 1985 in Washington), S. 307-323.

86. Rechtsfragen einer Ordnung der Weltwirtschaft,
in: Internationales Privatrecht, Internationales Wirtschaftsrecht (Referate eines Symposiums der Alexander von Humboldt-Stiftung vom 26.-30.9.1983 in Ludwigsburg), Heymann 1985, S. 25-36.

87. Schelskys Theorien der Institutionen und des Rechts,
in: Recht und Institution – Helmut Schelsky-Gedächtnis-Symposium Münster 1985. Münsterische Beiträge zur Rechtswissenschaft Band 15, Duncker & Humblot 1985, S. 19-31.

88. Zur Erinnerung an Franz Böhm aus Anlaß des 90. Geburtstages,
in: Recht und Gesittung einer freien Gesellschaft. Zur Erinnerung an Franz Böhm. Standpunkte 2, Veröffentlichung der Ludwig-Erhard-Stiftung, 1986, S. 49-52.

89. Meinungsfreiheit und Medienwettbewerb,
in: ZUM 2/1986, S. 63-68.

90. The Influence of Political and Legal Conditions on the Development of Media
In: Medientrends (Congressdokumente). Eine Zusammenfassung von Beiträgen und Referaten vom Intermedia Congress Hamburg 1985. Hamburg 1986, S. 124-135.

91. The Impact of Deregulation on Trade in Services Agreements and on Telecommunications Monopolies in Europe,
in: Telecommunication Journal, Vol. 53, No. XI, 1986, S. 639-645.

92. Wettbewerbsprobleme in Rundfunksektor (Auszüge aus dem Referat auf dem 56. Deutschen Juristentag, Berlin 1986, Abteilung Rundfunkrecht),
in: Medienspiegel, Jg. 10, Nr. 37, 1986, S. II-IV.

93. Wer weiß schon, was dem Bürger frommt (Teilveröffentlichung des Referates auf dem 56. Deutschen Juristentag),
in: DIE ZEIT vom 12.9.1986.

94. Zur Fusionskontrolle in der Wettbewerbspolitik,
in: AG 7/1986, S. 181-185.

95. La Mano Visible del Derecho: Derecho y Economía en Adam Smith
in: Estudios Públicos, Nr. 23, 1986, S. 59-88; translation of "Die sichtbare Hand des Rechts" in: Recht und ökonomisches Gesetz, 2. Aufl. 1984, S. 104-135 (translated into Spanish by Prof. Enrique Barros).

96. Regelbildung und Rechtsschutz in marktwirtschaftlichen Ordnungen (translated into Japanese by Prof. Masaru Hayakawa). in: Sandai Law Review, Vol. XX, Nr. 1, 1986, S. 77-103.

97. In welcher Weise empfiehlt es sich, die Ordnung des Rundfunks und sein Verhältnis zu anderen Medien – auch unter dem Gesichtspunkt der Harmonisierung – zu regeln? in: Verhandlungen des 56. Deutschen Juristentages, Berlin 1986, Band II (Sitzungsberichte), Teil O, C.H. Beck, München 1986, S. 9-37.

98. Auf dem Wege zu einer Ordnungspolitik für Europa, in: ders. (Hrsg.), Eine Ordnungspolitik für Europa. Festschrift für Hans von der Groeben zum 80. Geburtstag, 1987, S. 9-49.

99. Verwalteter Wettbewerb contra Verbraucherinteressen, in: Dynamisch den Verbraucherwünschen entgegen (Jahrestagung des Bundesverbandes der Selbstbedienungswarenhäuser e.V. am 24.3.1987 in Düsseldorf), Frankfurt/M. 1987, S. 11-22.

100. Wettbewerb in der Verteilungsgesellschaft, in: Frankfurter Allgemeine Zeitung vom 11.4.1987.

101. Competing Goals of National Telecommunications Policies, in: Id. (ed.), The Law and Economics of Transborder Telecommunications. A Symposium, Nomos, Wirtschaftsrecht der internationalen Telekommunikation, Band 1, Baden-Baden 1987, S. 13-29.

102. Towards a New Regime for International Telecommunications, in: Speakers' Papers, World Telecommunications Forum, Organized by the ITU (21.-23. Oktober 1987 in Genf), Part 3: Legal Symposium, S. 229-233.

103. Elektronische Medien in der europäischen Wirtschafts- und Kulturgemeinschaft, in: ders. (Hrsg.), Rechtsstaat und Menschenwürde. Festschrift für Werner Maihofer zum 70. Geburtstag, 1988, S. 269-282.

104. Staatliche Souveränität und offene Märkte, Konflikte bei der extraterritorialen Anwendung von Wirtschaftsrecht, in: RabelsZ 52 (1988) 205-251 (Extraterritoriale Anwendung von Wirtschaftsrecht).

105. Wege zur Rundfunkfreiheit in Europa, in: ders., Offene Rundfunkordnung: Prinzipien für den Wettbewerb im grenzüberschreitenden Rundfunk, Verlag Bertelsmann Stiftung, Gütersloh 1988,S. 9-43.

106. Staat und Unternehmen im europäischen Gemeinschaftsrecht. Zur Bedeutung von Art. 90 EWGV, in: RabelsZ 52 (1988) 526-582 (Ulrich Drobnig zum 60. Geburtstag).

107. Fusionskontrolle im Gemeinsamen Markt zwischen Wettbewerbspolitik und Industriepolitik,
in: Europarecht, Heft 4/1988, S. 349-377
Translation: Merger Control in the Common Market: Between Competition Policy and Industrial Policy,
in: 1988 Annual Proceedings of the Fordham Corporate Law Institute, North American and Common Market Antitrust and Trade Laws, B. Hawk (ed.), Matthew Bender, New York 1989, S. 20-1 – 20-34.

108. Zur Anwendung von Kartellaufsicht und Fachaufsicht auf urheberrechtliche Verwertungsgesellschaften und ihre Mitglieder,
in: Festschrift für Rudolf Lukes zum 65. Geburtstag, 1989, S. 445-460.

109. Der Kampf ums Recht in der offenen Gesellschaft,
in: Feier zur Verleihung des Ernst Hellmut Vits-Preises, 2. Dezember 1988. Hrsg. Gesellschaft zur Förderung der Westfälischen Wilhelms-Universität zu Münster, o.O., o.J. [Münster 1989], S. 13-27;
abgedr. ferner in: Rechtstheorie 20 (1989) S. 273-288.

110. Zur Urhebervergütung für Tonträger im europäischen Gemeinschaftsrecht,
in: Urheberrechtliche Probleme der Gegenwart, Festschrift für Ernst Reichardt zum 70. Geburtstag, 1990, S. 141-167.

111. Marktzugang und Monopolmißbrauch auf deregulierten Märkten,
in: Festschrift für Ernst Steindorff zum 70. Geburtstag am 13. März 1990, 1990, S. 1045-1064.

112. Wirtschaftsrecht,
in: RabelsZ 54 (1990) 409-430.

113. Rundfunkfreiheit im Bundesstaat und in Europa,
in: Privatfunk in Hamburg – Zulassung, Programme, Perspektiven, Hamburgische Anstalt für neue Medien, Hamburg, 2. Aufl. 1990, S. 77-79.

114. Free Trade in Services: Regional and Global Perspectives,
in: Rules for Free International Trade in Services, Symposium in Tel Aviv, D. Friedmann/E.-J. Mestmäcker (Editors), Nomos, Wirtschaftsrecht und Wirtschaftspolitik, Band 107, Baden-Baden 1990, S. 9-23.

115. Vorwort zu : Walter Eucken, Grundsätze der Wirtschaftspolitik,
Hrsg.: W. Eucken/K. P. Hensel, Mohr (Siebeck), 6. Aufl. Tübingen 1990, S. V-XVI (UTB 1572).

116. Erdgas im europäischen Binnenmarkt,
in: E.-J. Mestmäcker/H. Gröner/J. Basedow, Die Gaswirtschaft im Binnenmarkt. Beiträge zur gemeinschaftsrechtlichen und ordnungspolitischen Diskussion von Marktordnungen, Common Carriage und Preistransparenz,
Nomos, Wirtschaftsrecht und Wirtschaftspolitik Band 109, Baden-Baden 1990, S. 7-98;
English translation: Natural Gas in the European Internal Market: A Comparative Analysis of Common Carriage and Price Transparency:
Michigan Journal of International Law Vol. 11 No. 3 (Spring 1990) 691-767.

117. Durchleitungspflichten auf dem Binnenmarkt für Erdgas,
in: J. F. Baur (Hrsg.), Leitungsgebundene Energie und der Gemeinsame Markt. Eine Analyse der Vorschläge der Kommission der EG, Nomos, Veröffentlichungen des Instituts für Energierecht an der Universität zu Köln Band 61, Baden-Baden 1990, S. 39-52.

118. Die Kraft des Freiburger Imperativs: Vom Sozialismus zum Kapitalismus: Wirtschaftsysteme im Übergang. Die Aktualität der Euckenschen Ordnungstheorie für die deutsche Einigung;
in: F.U. Fack/F.K. Fromme, G. Nonnenmacher Hrsg.), Das deutsche Modell, Freiheitlicher Rechtsstaat und Soziale Marktwirtschaft; Wirtschaftsverlag Langen Müller Herbig, München 1990, S. 187-196.

119. Zwischen freiem und verwaltetem Wettbewerb – Möglichkeiten und Grenzen der Wettbewerbspolitik,
in: Neue Zürcher Zeitung Nr. 226 vom 29./30.9.1990, S. 91.

120. Urheberrechte und Verwertungsgesellschaften im Europäischen Gemeinschaftsrecht (Neubearb.),
in: Mestmäcker/Schulze, Kommentar zum deutschen Urheberrecht, Bd. I, Teil III: IntR, 6. Abschnitt: Europäische Abkommen,
Metzner, Frankfurt a.M., 6. Lfg. Juli 1990 (Loseblattausg.) 120 S.

121. Demokratie, Rechtsstaat, Marktwirtschaft,
in: Zeitschrift für Wirtschaftsrecht Bd. 39 Heft 3 (1990), S. 289-294.

122. Einführung in die Tagungsthematik,
in: ders. (Hrsg.), Selbstkontrolle und Persönlichkeitsschutz in den Medien, Ein Symposium der Bertelsmann Stiftung am 27. März 1990 in Gütersloh, Verlag Bertelsmann Stiftung, Gütersloh 1990; S. 9-13;
Schlußbetrachtung und Zusammenfassung: ebd. S. 107-111.

123. Zur Rechtsstellung urheberrechtlicher Verwertungsgesellschaften im europäischen Wettbewerbsrecht,
in: Beiträge zum Handels- und Wirtschaftsrecht, Festschrift für Fritz Rittner zum 70. Geburtstag, Beck, München 1991, S. 391-404.

124. Die Wiederkehr der bürgerlichen Gesellschaft und ihres Rechts,
in: Rechtshistorisches Journal Bd. 10 (1991) 177-192 = Jahrbuch der Max-Planck-Gesellschaft 1991, 24-36
gekürzte Fassung abgedruckt in: DIE ZEIT Nr. 32 vom 2.8.1991.

125. „Widersprüchlich, verwirrend und gefährlich" – Wettbewerbsregeln oder Industriepolitik: Nicht nur in diesem Punkt verstößt der Vertrag von Maastricht gegen bewährte Grundsätze des Vertrages von Rom;
in: FAZ vom 10.10.1992.

126. Zur Anwendbarkeit der Wettbewerbsregeln auf die Mitgliedstaaten und die Europäischen Gemeinschaften,
in: Europarecht – Energierecht – Wirtschaftsrecht. Festschrift für Bodo Börner zum 70. Geburtstag, Heymann, Köln usw. 1992, S. 277-288.

127. The New Germany in the New Europe,
in: William James Adams (ed.), Singular Europe. Economy and Policy of the European Community after 1992, University of Michigan Press, Ann Arbor, Mich. 1992, p. 43-53.

128. Energy Policy for Natural Gas in the Internal Market – An Overview,
in: Mestmäcker (ed.), Natural Gas in the Internal Market. A Review of Energy Policy, Graham & Trotman, International Energy and Resources Law and Policy Series, London 1993, p. 1-17.

129. Zur kartellrechtlichen und medienrechtlichen Beurteilung eines gesellschaftsrechtlichen Wettbewerbsverbots zwischen Fernsehunternehmen – Eine Besprechung des Urteils des Landgerichts Hamburg in Sachen RTLplus/UFA/VOX vom 6.10.1992,
in: ZUM 5/1993, S. 201-213.

130. Schutz der ausübenden Künstler und EWG-Diskriminierungsverbot,
in: GRUR Int. 1993, S. 532-536.

131. Gemeinschaftsrechtliche Schranken für die Begründung und Ausübung besonderer oder ausschließlicher Rechte nach Art. 90 Abs. 1 EWG-Vertrag,
in: Europarecht, Kartellrecht, Wirtschaftsrecht. Festschrift für Arved Deringer, Nomos, Baden-Baden 1993, S. 79-94.

132. Diritto dell'economia,
in: Enciclopedia delle Science Sociali, Rom, Vol. 3, 1993, 90-98.

133. Aufklärung durch Recht,
in: H. F. Fulda/R.-P. Horstmann (Hrsg.), Vernunftbegriffe in der Moderne. Stuttgarter Hegel-Kongreß 1993, Klett-Cotta, Stuttgart 1994, S. 55-72;
abgedr. auch in: Marktwirtschaft und Rechtsordnung. Festschrift zum 70. Geburtstag von Prof.Dr. Erich Hoppmann, Nomos, Baden-Baden 1994, Wirtschaftsrecht und Wirtschaftspolitik Band 133, S. 311-327.

134. Can there be a European law?,
in: European Review, Vol. 2, No. 1, 1-13 (1994).

135. Zur Wirtschaftsverfassung in der Europäischen Union,
in: Ordnung und Freiheit, Festgabe für Hans Willgerodt zum 70. Geburtstag, Gustav Fischer Verlag, Stuttgart, Jena, New York 1994, S. 263-292.

136. Von der Wirtschaftsgemeinschaft zur Wirtschafts- und Währungsunion,
in: P. Hommelhoff/P. Kirchhof (Hrsg.), Der Staatenverbund der Europäischen Union. Beiträge und Diskussionen des Symposions am 21./22. Januar 1994 in Heidelberg, C.F. Müller, Heidelberg 1994, S. 113-130 (MTM, Bd. 65).

137. Über das Verhältnis der europäischen Wirtschaftsordnung zu den Mitgliedstaaten,
in: G. Seiffert (Hrsg.), Vereinigtes Europa und nationale Vielfalt – ein Gegensatz? Referate gehalten auf dem Symposium der Joachim Jungius-Gesellschaft der Wissenschaften Hamburg am 29./30. Oktober 1993, Vandenhoeck & Ruprecht, Veröff. der Joachim Jungius-Ges. Wiss. Hamburg Band 77, Göttingen 1994, S. 149-169.

138. On the Legitimacy of European Law,
in: RabelsZ 58 (1994) 615-636.

139. Rechtsstellung und Marktstellung der Inhaber gewerblichen und kommerziellen Eigentums im europäischen Gemeinschaftsrecht. Zum Verhältnis von Art. 36 und Art. 86 EGV;
in: Wanderer zwischen Musik, Politik und Recht: Festschrift für Reinhold Kreile zu seinem 65. Geburtstag, Nomos, Baden-Baden 1994, S. 419-428.

140. Über den Einfluß von Ökonomie und Technik auf Recht und Organisation der Telekommunikation und der elektronischen Medien,
in: ders. (Hrsg.), Kommunikation ohne Monopole II. Ein Symposium über Ordnungsprinzipien im Wirtschaftsrecht der Telekommunikation und der elektronischen Medien, Nomos, Wirtschaftsrecht der internationalen Telekommunikation Band 23, Baden-Baden 1995, S. 13-177.

141. Zum Begriff des Mißbrauchs in Art. 86 des Vertrages über die Europäische Gemeinschaft,
in: Unternehmen, Recht und Wirtschaftsordnung, Festschrift für Peter Raisch zum 70. Geburtstag, Heymann, Köln usw. 1995, S. 441-467.

142. Wettbewerbsrecht und Wettbewerbspolitik in der Europäischen Union,
in: Europa zwischen Ordnungswettbewerb und Harmonisierung. Europäische Ordnungspolitik im Zeichen der Subsidiarität, Hrsg. von Lüder Gerken, Springer, Berlin 1995, S. 191-211.

143. Wirtschaftsordnung und Geschichtsgesetz.
in: Wirtschaftsordnung als Aufgabe. Zum 100. Geburtstag von Franz Böhm. Symposion der Ludwig-Erhard-Stiftung Nr. 34 [Hrsg. von der] Ludwig-Erhard-Stiftung. Sinus, Krefeld 1995, S. 111-136;
abgedr. ferner in: ORDO Band 46 (1995) 9-25.

144. Anmerkung zu: BGH, Beschluß v. 21.2.1995 – KVR 4/94 (OLG Stuttgart) [Mißbrauchsaufsicht über Versorgungsunternehmen],
in: JZ 1995, 965-967.

145. Die koordinierte Sperre im deutschen und europäischen Recht der öffentlichen Aufträge (gemeinsam mit Eckhard Bremer);
in: BB 1995, Beilage 19 (zu Heft 50).

146. Das Privatrecht vor den Herausforderungen der wirtschaftlichen Macht. Zugleich eine Besprechung des Buches von Knut W. Nörr „Die Leiden des Privatrechts. Die Kartelle in Deutschland von der Holzstoffkartellentscheidung zum Gesetz gegen Wettbewerbsbeschränkungen",
in: RabelsZ 60 (1996) 58-71 (Hein Kötz zum 60. Geburtstag).

147. Die Rückforderung staatlicher Beihilfen nach europäischem und deutschem Recht am Beispiel staatlich verbürgter Kredite (zus. mit K. J. Hopt).
in: Teil I Wertpapiermitteilungen 50, 753-761, und
in: Teil II Wertpapiermitteilungen 50, 801-810 (1996).

148. Die Rolle des Wettbewerbs als Entdeckungsverfahren für technologische Schlüsselprodukte.
in: Bundeskartellamt, Wettbewerbs- und Industriepolitik in West und Ost: Vorfahrt für den Markt? Berlin 1996, S. 46-60.

149. Alte Monopole und neue Märkte in der Telekommunikation. Zur Entscheidung der EG-Kommission v. 9.11.1994 „Media Service GmbH".
in: J. Kruse/O.G. Mayer (Hrsg.), Aktuelle Probleme der Wettbewerbs- und Wirtschaftspolitik, Erhard Kantzenbach zum 65. Geburtstag, 1996, S. 167-176.

150. Risse im Europäischen Contrat Social,
in: Hanns Martin Schleyer-Preis 1996/1997 S. 53-65;
auch unter dem Titel „Risse im Europäischen Gesellschaftsvertrag"
in: FAZ v. 4.10.1997.

151. Konstituierung und Sicherung der Wettbewerbsordnung
in: Soziale Marktwirtschaft als historische Weichenstellung. Eine Festschrift zum 100. Geburtstag von Ludwig Erhard, ST-Verlag 1997, S. 51-62.

152. Systemtransformationen im Spiegel der Rechtstheorie.
in: Systemtransformation in Mittel- und Osteuropa und ihre Folgen für Banken, Börsen und Kreditsicherheiten. (Hrsg. zus. mit U. Drobnig, K. H. Hopt, H. Kötz)
Mohr Siebeck, Tübingen 1998, S. 89-106.

153. Beschäftigungspolitik als neue Aufgabe der Europäischen Union
in: J. Basedow, K.J.Hopt/H. Kötz (Hrsg.), Festschrift für Ulrich Drobnig zum 70. Geburtstag, Mohr (Siebeck), Tübingen 1998, S. 81-96.

154. Entgeltregulierung, Marktbeherrschung und Wettbewerb im Mobilfunk,
in: Multimedia und Recht (Beilage) 8/1998, 20 S. (1998).

155. Übermittlung und Inhalt von Medienleistungen – Wege zur Konvergenz von Regelungsmustern.
in: R. H. Weber (Hrsg.), Symposium Schluep. Querbezüge zwischen Kommunikations- und Wettbewerbsrecht, Schulthess Polygraphsicher Verlag, Zürich 1998, S. 7-18.

156. Daseinsvorsorge und Universaldienste im europäischen Kontext. Ein Beitrag zur Funktion von Art. 90 Abs. 2 EGV.
in: F. Ruland/B. v. Maydell/H.-J. Papier (Hrsg.), Verfassung, Theorie und Praxis des Sozialstaates. Festschrift für Hans F. Zacher zum 70. Geburtstag, C.F. Müller, Heidelberg 1998, S. 635-651.

157. Geistiges Eigentum und Kultur im Spannungsfeld von nationaler Regelungskompetenz und europäischem Wirtschafts- und Wettbewerbsrecht aus Sicht der Verwertungsgesellschaften.
in: Jürgen Schwarze, Jürgen Becker Hrsg.), Geistiges Eigentum und Kultur im Spannungsfeld von nationaler Regelungskompetenz und europäischem Wirtschafts- und Wettbewerbsrecht, Nomos, Baden-Baden 1998, 53-74.

158. The Role of Competition in a Liberal Society.
In: P. Koslowski (Ed.), The Social Market Economy, Theory and Ethics of the Economic Order, Springer Verlag, Heidelberg, New York 1998, 329-350.

159. Regulierende Mißbrauchsaufsicht.
in: B. Großfeldt, R. Sack, Th. M. J. Möllers, J. Drexl, A. Heinemann (Hrsg.), Festschrift für Wolfgang Fikentscher zum 70. Geburtstag. Mohr Siebeck, Tübingen 1998, 557-573.

160. Die rechtliche Stellung öffentlicher Unternehmen und staatlicher Monopole im deutschen und EG-Recht.
in: Antimonopolrechte und Marktwirtschaft. Veröffentlichung der Chinesischen Akademie für Sozialwissenschaften, Beijing 1998 (in Chinesisch).

161. Soziale Marktwirtschaft und Europäisierung des Rechts.
in: K. W. Nörr and J. Starbatty (Hrsg.), Soll und Haben – 50 Jahre Soziale Marktwirtschaft. Marktwirtschaftliche Reformpolitik, Schriftenreihe der Aktionsgemeinschaft Soziale Marktwirtschaft Band 3, Lucius & Lucius, Stuttgart 1999, 129-152.

162. Kants Rechtsprinzip als Grundlage der europäischen Einigung.
in: G. Landwehr (Hrsg.), Freiheit, Gleichheit, Selbständigkeit. Zur Aktualität der Rechtsphilosophie Kants für die Gerechtigkeit in der modernen Gesellschaft. Veröff. Joachim Jungius-Ges. Wiss. Hamburg Band 87, Vandenhoeck & Ruprecht, Göttingen 1999, 61-72.

163. Ein Systemwechsel im europäischen Kartellrecht. Handelsblatt 160, 47 (1999).

164. Grenzen staatlicher Monopole im EG-Vertrag.
in: Erfahrungen mit der Privatisierung von Monopolunternehmen, Referate des XXXII. FIW-Symposions, Schriftenreihe des Forschungsinstituts für Wirtschaftsverfassung und Wettbewerb (FIW) Band 179, Carl Heymanns, Köln, Berlin, Bonn, München 1999, 71-82.

165. Wie lohnt der Staat die gute Tat? Zur Reform des Stiftungsrechts. FAZ 292, 52 (1999).

166. Versuch einer kartellpolitischen Wende in der EU. Zum Weißbuch der Kommission über die Modernisierung der Vorschriften zur Anwendung der Artt. 85 und 86 EGV a.F. (Artt. 81 und 82 EGV n.F.),
in: Europäische Zeitschrift für Wirtschaftsrecht (EuZW) 17, 523-529 (1999).

167. Marktversagen und Staatsversagen in der Europäischen Union.
in: St. Grundmann (Hrsg.), Systembildung und Systemlücken in Kerngebieten des Europäischen Privatrechts: Gesellschafts-, Arbeits- und Schuldvertragsrecht. J.C.B. Mohr (Paul Siebeck), Tübingen 2000, 53-65.

168. Veranstalterrechte als Fernsehrechte.
in: K. P. Berger, W. F. Ebke, S. Elsing, B. Großfeld, G. Kühne (Hrsg.) Festschrift für Otto Sandrock zum 70. Geburtstag., Verlag Recht und Wirtschaft, Heidelberg 2000, 689-700.

169. Die Vergabe von Fernsehrechten an internationalen Wettbewerbsspielen deutscher Lizenzligavereine.
in: K. Vieweg (Hrsg.), Vermarktungsrechte im Sport, Beiträge zum Sportrecht Bd. 6, Duncker & Humblot, Berlin 2000, 53-94.

170. Begrenzt abschreckend. Kommentar, WuW 7/8, 683 (2000).

171. The E.C. Commission's Modernization of Competition Policy: A Challenge to the Community's Constitutional Order. In: European Business Organization Law Review Vol. I, 401-444 (2000).

172. The Modernization of EC Antitrust Policy: Constitutional Challenge or Administrative Convenience?
in: E.-D. Ehlermann/I. Atanasiu (Eds.) European Competition Law Annual 2000, The Modernisation of EC Antitrust Policy, Hart Publishing, Oxford 2001, p. 223-240.

173. Unternehmenskonzentrationen und Urheberrechte in der alten und „neuen“ Musikindustrie,
in: Zeitschrift für Urheber- und Medienrecht (ZUM) 3/2001, Nomos Verlagsgesellschaft Baden-Baden 2001, S. 185-272.

174. Die Wirtschaftsverfassung der EG zwischen Wettbewerb und Intervention,
in: Th. Bruha/J. J. Hesse/C. Nowak (Hrsg.), Welche Verfassung für Europa? Erstes interdisziplinäres „Schwarzkopf-Kolloquium“ zur Verfassungsdebatte in der Europäischen Union, Schriftenreihe des Europa-Kollegs Hamburg zur Integrationsforschung Bd. 33, Nomos Verlagsgesellschaft Baden-Baden 2001, S.163-189.

175. Medienkonzentration im Internet,
in: Aufbruch nach Europa. 75 Jahre Max-Planck-Institut für ausländisches und internationales Privatrecht (Hrsg. J. Basedow/U. Drobnig/R. Ellger/K.J. Hopt/H. Kötz/R. Kulms/E.-J. Mestmäcker), Mohr (Siebeck), Tübingen 2001.

176. Gedanken zur deutschen Vereinigung und der europäischen Osterweiterung,
in: Hrsg.: Aktionsgemeinschaft Soziale Marktwirtschaft, ASM-Bulletin Nr. 2/2001, Tübingen 2001 (in print).

177. Europäisches Wettbewerbsrecht im Zeichen der Globalisierung.
in: Beitrag zu einem Symposium des Europa-Instituts Freiburg am 6./7. Juli 2001 in Freiburg i. Br., Symposiumsband (Hrsg.: J. Schwarze), Nomos, Schriftenreihe Europäisches Recht, Politik und Wirtschaft, Baden-Baden (in print).